DS
706
H8

Hu

China: its people, its
society, its culture

SURVEY OF WORLD CULTURES

CHINA

its people   its society   its culture

Chang-tu Hu

IN COLLABORATION WITH

Samuel C. Chu

Leslie L. Clark

Jung-pang Lo

Yuan-li Wu

Editor

Hsiao Hsia

HRAF PRESS *New Haven*

LIBRARY OF CONGRESS CATALOG NUMBER: 60–7382

© COPYRIGHT 1960

HUMAN RELATIONS AREA FILES, INC.

NEW HAVEN, CONN.

ALL RIGHTS RESERVED

MANUFACTURED IN THE UNITED STATES OF AMERICA BY
UNITED PRINTING SERVICES, INC.

PROBABLY AT NO TIME IN HISTORY have thoughtful men everywhere been so conscious of the need to know about the different peoples of the world. Such knowledge is not in itself a formula for human understanding but it is an indispensable first step. The Survey of World Cultures, of which *China* is the sixth in the series, is one of several means by which the Human Relations Area Files seeks to promote and facilitate the comparative study of human behavior and a greater understanding of cultures other than our own.

These surveys, though augmented by original research, are primarily a collation and synthesis of the best and most authoritative materials, published and unpublished, on the societies selected. For many of these societies excellent specialized studies exist, but the materials are often so widely scattered as to be virtually unavailable to all except the most determined scholar. It was to meet the need for a comprehensive readable volume, bringing together all those aspects of a country and culture usually studied separately, that these books were undertaken.

The present series is based in part on background studies prepared for limited distribution. Under the direction of the Human Relations Area Files an interdisciplinary team with area competence was assembled for each study. The enterprise involved, in all, contributions from several hundred scholars resident at some twenty universities.

The original studies have been extensively revised: materials have been added and the body of the work rewritten, edited, and adapted to a new format. Owing to special requirements imposed on the program, footnotes and citations customary in works of this nature were omitted. Both lack of funds and dispersal of the original teams of scholars have unfortunately made it impossible to supply this critical apparatus. However there are cited in the editor's note and in the bibliography at the end of each volume the most important materials on which each study is based.

One result of the process of collecting and selecting information from many, often widely scattered, sources has been to reveal new relationships, making explicit in these surveys much which had remained implicit in previous separate studies. Gaps in existing knowledge have become apparent. The series should, then, raise a number of general questions, at the same time offering certain factual answers and providing guidance for further research. That there will also result increased understanding of the seemingly endless and diverse ways in which men approach the experience of living with one another is the wish of all who have participated in making this series.

EDITOR'S NOTE

THE PUBLICATION OF THIS STUDY has been made possible by the devoted work of a great many individuals over a period of years and to thank each separately would be a formidable task. The acknowledgements here are necessarily limited.

The authors were free to draw upon and acknowledge their indebtedness to monographs prepared under contract for HRAF in 1955-1956 at two universities: *A General Handbook of China* (three volumes), *A Regional Handbook on Northwest China* (two volumes), *A Regional Handbook on Northeast China,* and *A Regional Handbook on the Inner Mongolia Autonomous Region,* compiled by the Far Eastern and Russian Institute of the University of Washington; and *North China* (two volumes), *Central South China* (two volumes), *East China* (two volumes,), and *Southwest China* (two volumes), prepared by the staff of the China Project at Stanford University.

Special thanks are due Professor Hellmut Wilhelm, general editor of the monographs prepared at the University of Washington, and Professor George E. Taylor, Director, Far Eastern and

Russian Institute, for their advice and permission to use these monographs, particularly *A General Handbook of China,* upon which this study is based.

Certain sections of the chapters, "Geography and Population," "Ethnic Minorities," "Languages," "Theory and Structure of Government," "Education," "Values and Patterns of Living," and "National Attitudes," are taken from the Stanford monographs and the authors are grateful to Professor Shau Wing Chan, Director of the China Project, for permission to use this material.

Permission to use selections from an unpublished bibliography originally prepared for *A General Handbook of China,* cited above, was extended by the Far Eastern and Russian Institute, University of Washington, and their cooperation is deeply appreciated.

Two chapters were written especially for the present volume: the chapter, "Foreign Relations," by Howard L. Boorman, Director, Research Project on Men and Politics in Modern China, Columbia University; and the chapter, "Science and Technology," by Robert H. G. Lee, Research Assistant, HRAF. We thank both for their important contributions.

To Kenneth Scott Latourette, Sterling Professor of Missions and Oriental History, Emeritus, Yale University, who graciously read an early draft and made valuable comments; and to Francis L. K. Hsu, Professor of Anthropology, Northwestern University, who also read parts of the book, particularly the sociological chapters, we are most grateful.

Thomas Fitzsimmons, editor of previous volumes in this series, provided valuable editorial guidance in the early stages of manuscript revision. Adrienne Suddard deserves a special word of thanks for her assistance in the final editing.

A number of publishers have graciously given us permission to reproduce their copyrighted maps, plates, and statistical material, as cited in the text, and we wish to thank the following: William Sloane Associates, Inc.; McGraw-Hill Book Company, Inc.; Bookman Associates, Inc.; John Wiley and Sons, Inc.; the Center for Japanese Studies, University of Michigan, and the University of Michigan Press; and the Institute of Far Eastern Languages, Yale University.

In preparing this volume a number of arbitrary editorial decisions had to be made and the reader's attention is directed especially to the following:

(1) In the chapter, "Historical Setting," the dates given in parentheses for each emperor refer to his birth and death rather than his reign so as to be uniform with the dates given for the other historical figures.

(2) Geographic names are spelled according to the United States Board on Geographic Names: Gazetteer No. 22, *China* (two volumes, 1956) except where the gazetteer recognizes conventional Anglicized spellings.

(3) The transliteration of Chinese words and proper names is based on the Wade-Giles system as used in Mathews' *Chinese-English Dictionary* (Revised American Edition, 1952) except where another Anglicized spelling has become conventional. Exceptions are also made in the romanization of Chinese names for ethnic minorities.

(4) Other names of ethnic groups follow in general the form given in the *Outline of World Cultures* by Professor George P. Murdock (Revised Edition, 1958).

(5) A multiplicity of exchange rates in effect at various times since 1949 in China has led us to convert the old JMP (Jen-min-pi, People's Currency) into new JMP and to adopt a uniform rate of 2.46 new JMP for US $1.00 wherever the text calls for a simple American dollar equivalent.

(6) Because of the vastness of the literature on China, entries in the bibliography are confined for the most part to English-language materials, with the exception of a few Chinese sources used in the tables and plates.

Although gratefully acknowledging the contributions of many others to the China study, the authors and editor assume sole responsibility for whatever shortcomings it may have.

Hsiao Hsia

New Haven, Connecticut
October 1959

THE HUMAN RELATIONS AREA FILES

THE HUMAN RELATIONS AREA FILES is a nonprofit research corporation affiliated with Yale University and sponsored and supported by its seventeen member universities. HRAF was established in 1949 "to collect, organize, and distribute information of significance to the natural and social sciences and the humanities." It has concentrated upon furthering a fresh approach to the study of societies, culture, and social behavior.

The Files themselves contain carefully selected sources analyzed according to G. P. Murdock's *Outline of Cultural Materials*. Located at each of the member universities, they are a new kind of reference library in which basic information about nearly two hundred peoples can be consulted with ease and speed. Preparation of the present study was facilitated by the use of the following Files: China, North China, Central China, East China, Southwest China, South China, Manchuria, Mongolia, Inner Mongolia, Sinkiang, and Tibet.

MEMBER UNIVERSITIES

University of Chicago
University of Colorado
Cornell University
Harvard University
University of Hawaii
Indiana University
State University of Iowa
University of Michigan

University of North Carolina
University of Oklahoma
University of Pennsylvania
Princeton University
University of Southern California
Southern Illinois University
University of Utah
University of Washington

Yale University

CONTENTS

Contents (*continued*)

LIST OF MAPS

LIST OF PLATES

LIST OF TABLES

List of Tables (*continued*)

CHINA

THE CULTURE AND THE SOCIETY

FROM THE VIEWPOINT OF WORLD HISTORY, the most significant event since World War II may well be the emergence on the China mainland of a dynamic, aggressive, and totalitarian government controlling the largest single sector of the world's population—the six hundred and fifty million Chinese. The growing status of this new regime stems from the fact that it is in a position not only to direct the course of this oldest of living civilizations in its adaptation to the modern world but also to exert a dominant influence on the future of Asia and the world.

In sharp contrast with its position in recent decades, when it was unable to maintain order and unity within or to defend itself against aggression from without, China has now become a nation that possesses the largest standing army in the world, supported by modern technology and employing modern organizational techniques. The new regime, strong enough to impose its will on the Chinese population, has also become a threat to its Asian neighbors. This dramatic metamorphosis of a prostrate and humiliated nation into a strong, aggressive state not only has altered the balance of power in Asia but also assumes primary importance in the strategic thinking of the world.

China's recent transformation under Communism is, however, but one of the many upheavals the country has undergone in the last hundred years. Looking back over China's long history, the geographic and environmental factors in the development of its civilization assume much significance. The Chinese world view was conditioned by the fact that this civilization developed in relative isolation from other civilizations of comparable level. For millennia, the Chinese possessed the only major civilization of eastern Asia and the complexity and richness of China's cultural forms and patterns of living made it the natural center of the world not only from the Chinese view but also in the eyes of its neighbors. Thus, it was not surprising for the Chinese to regard themselves as the only custodians of civilization and their country the hub of the world. Prior to the nineteenth century, there was no historical experience that would have led them to modify the concept of China as the repository of a superior culture and way of life to which all mankind aspired. This view has been called culturocentric, lacking as it did a strong sense either of ethnic or national identity. It was also influenced by China's traditional ignorance of the outside world and its concern with the problem of defending the country along its northern and western borders against the perennial threat of invasion by the restless nomadic peoples of Central Asia—fierce tribal warriors looked down upon as "barbarians" by the Chinese. On the other hand, the long sea coast did not assume importance as a doorway to the outside world or as a spur to the growth of commerce as did proximity to the sea in the ancient civilizations of the Mediterranean. As a result, this land-oriented civilization, almost entirely preoccupied with an agrarian mode of life, found its values in stability, conservatism, and continuity.

The philosophic heritage of China, notably the Confucian tradition, can be seen both as a product of these environmental influences and as an idealization and perpetuation of the world view stemming from them. Although Confucianism was but one school of thought that developed during the remarkable age of Chinese philosophy between the sixth and third centuries B.C., it can truly be called the dominant element in Chinese intellectual life throughout most of the two-thousand-year span of Chinese history, providing a stable ideology for the empire and a satisfying philosophy for the individual.

Chinese society, permeated by a philosophical outlook that was humanistic, secular, rational, practical in tone, and conservative in spirit, was an open society without a hereditary privileged class. The leadership role in the society and the administrative functions of the government were assumed by an elite recruited through a civil service examination in which excellence in Confucian scholarship was the criterion. These examinations, which in theory and generally in practice were open to everyone, had stimulated considerable social mobility. Success in the examinations could bring a man, even of humble origin, legally privileged status, social prestige, access to a career in officialdom, and the means of acquiring wealth.

1. *The Culture and the Society*

The scholar-official class thus formed is usually designated the gentry—although analogous to the gentry of Europe only in that it constituted an elite. In China it was not land or birth as in Europe but education which created the gentry as a class. This single standard resulted in a remarkable uniformity in ideological outlook, which essentially was Confucian, as anyone anxious to rise in Chinese society had to first devote long years to the mastery of the Confucian classics. A similar economic status marked the gentry since economic opportunities were generally limited and the only practical avenue to status and wealth lay in government service. The state also found a consistently dependable political leadership in the gentry class. While in office, the gentry staffed the entire state bureaucracy and, upon retirement, assumed informal but important responsibility in local affairs.

Central to an understanding of the society, however, is an appreciation of the important role of the extended family, the basic social and economic unit on which the entire value system of the Confucian order was based. The family was the microcosm of the society at large and the authority of the family head was analogous to the larger authority of the emperor in the state. Confucian morality clearly stipulated that the virtue of *hsiao* (filial piety, that is, family duty) took precedence over the conflicting demands of the state, but the state promoted this virtue largely because family solidarity built upon filial submission was regarded as the cornerstone of social order and the instrument of state control over the people.

The family-based and gentry-led society of China in the later imperial period had developed political institutions peculiarly suited to the perpetuation of its central features. The Chinese emperor headed a state system which had become increasingly authoritarian. He ruled through an apparatus of government control in which he could on occasion assume the role of an absolute despot, but he remained dependent upon the services of a bureaucracy indoctrinated in Confucian humanism.

The essential nature and pattern of government were seldom questioned and its evolution into something fundamentally different in character was therefore beyond the realm of possibility so far as the Chinese were concerned. Only the internal weakness of a dynasty after long periods of stability and prosperity, sometimes a century or more, would precipitate a change in administration. A strong new dynasty would then succeed the old, beginning anew what historians refer to as the dynastic cycle in Chinese history, but little affecting the basic form and structure of government.

The political and social order of traditional China lacked, however, sufficient resilience to withstand intact the challenge of the West in the nineteenth century. On the eve of the arrival in China of the dynamic forces of the West in search of colonial empires and fields for economic expansion, China's last imperial dynasty—the Manchu or Ch'ing—had about run the full course of its cycle. In the disastrous century following the Anglo-Chinese War (1839-42) a series of crises arose from both external pressures and internal troubles and demonstrated to the world the inability of the Chinese political system, and indeed of its underlying ideology as well, to provide satisfactory solutions to new problems of an unprecedented nature. The government's ineffectiveness in dealing with this threatening situation resulted in the loss of territory and various sovereign rights. Although China remained an independent empire, the unrelenting pressures from the competing western powers forced it to cede extraterritorial concessions and many other rights and to acquiesce in the country's division into spheres of influence. The Chinese became alarmed about the threat to their national integrity and painfully aware of their country's humiliating international position.

The attempt of the western powers to force China to surrender aspects of its sovereignty was obviously designed to facilitate economic penetration. The concession cities became great commercial centers where economic interests incompatible with traditional Chinese values and disruptive of traditional economy were allowed to develop. Chinese economy began to undergo transformation as the West's grip tightened. This was accomplished through the employment of western commercial and industrial techniques such as modern banking and marketing systems, the displacement of rural handicraft by factory-made industrial goods, and the preferential legal status and the guarantees of monopolistic interests secured by the western powers for their nationals. An important concomitant development was the emergence of a new Chinese industrial and financier group in the treaty ports and the power this group achieved through its increasing ability to link its interests with those of the bureaucracy.

The influences emanating from the foreign concessions were not all economic; in the realm of ideas, these windows on the non-Chinese world often served to widen horizons and to provoke disillusioned reappraisals of the old order on the part of a growing group of disaffected intellectuals. But before the struggle between western-oriented liberals and traditional conservatives had reached its climax, the imperial period ended and the old civilization collapsed. China faced the modern world with both the society and the economy undergoing fundamental transformation, while its leaders sought an effective solution to the problems of national existence. In their indefatigable search for new and viable ideas and government models, inspirations were drawn from such diverse sources as the Meiji restoration and the subsequent modernization of Japan, the German federation established by Bismarck, the democratic government of the United States, and most significant of all the Bolshevik experiment in Russia.

It was in this uncertain and confused atmosphere that the Nationalist party of Sun Yat-sen and his political heir, Chiang Kai-shek, attempted to establish a new order. Sun Yat-sen died in 1925 before it was achieved, but in 1927 Chiang Kai-shek became the leader of a newly constituted national government that fulfilled with some success the aspirations of the Chinese people. But from the historical viewpoint, this success had resolved only a few of the fundamental problems. The failure of the Nationalist government may be attributed to a combination of circumstances, such as the relentless pressure from a strongly militaristic Japan, the continued presence of foreign influence, the inability of the government to deal decisively and effectively with its own social and economic problems, and the persistent opposition of the Communist party operating both as an armed movement from its own territorial bases and as a subversive underground. By the end of World War II, these circumstances led to an intensified crisis out of which emerged the present Communist state.

Nominally, the new political order accepts nothing from China's past; it is a totalitarian one-party state that assumes the responsibility for ordering every aspect of the lives of its people. Although presented to the Chinese people and to the world as a people's democracy formed by a coalition of the so-called democratic and progressive parties, it is in fact a dictatorship that maintains total and rigid control of all sources of power, chief of which are the armed forces, the state administration, and the police. It has forged the world's largest Communist party—over ten million members—into an instrument for political control that extends to all levels of society. This new regime has no precedent in Chinese history.

However, comparisons between the new Communist state and

the old empire have often been drawn and an analysis of them should be illuminating. The basic features of Chinese society under Communism are highly reminiscent of China's imperial past, and the resemblance between the present regime and some of the earlier dynasties is in certain respects quite striking. Indeed, the top leadership of the Chinese Communist party, as represented by its Central Committee and headed by Mao Tse-tung, wields as much or more power and is as autocratic in its behavior as its imperial predecessors. The ideology of Communism which has replaced Confucianism admits even less deviation and tolerates no rivalry. Where mastery of the Confucian classics and passage of examinations once constituted the major avenue of social advancement, today power and prestige result from personal identification with the party and adherence to its ideology.

The element of continuity must not, however, be overemphasized for Communism is both dynamic and militant, and the coercive forces under its control, by virtue of modern technology, far exceed those commanded by China's past rulers. Nor are the Communist leaders subject to the moral restraints of Confucianism which, however subtly, guided rulers in the past.

The Marxian view of history stresses contradiction and struggle, and the dialectic dynamics of progress. Traditional Chinese thought, on the other hand, denied progress and exalted harmony as the positive element in the proper functioning of the cosmos. Instead of stressing class conflict, it advocated an ideally cooperative society; it sought to regain a golden age in the past instead of viewing the historical process as one driven by the conflict between antithetical forces within itself to inevitable progress toward a golden age of the future. No two views of the world and of man's place in it could be further apart.

In spite of its somewhat tenuous resemblance to traditional Chinese society in political totalitarianism, ideological rigidity, and social regimentation, Communist rule constitutes a more fundamental break with the past, as revealed by the changes it has wrought in many aspects of Chinese life. In the old family-centered society, age demanded respect and submission of youth; women lacked equality with men; and the family was recognized as the natural unit of authority and responsibility, of social organization and economic activity, of education and religious observance. The new social ideals and the large-scale experiments in creating a Communist society deny all these traditions, denouncing them as "remnants of a degrading feudal past." New social values have been found which reflect clearly this change of attitude and behavior. "Love matches" replace family-arranged marriage; obedience to the state replaces obedience to family authority; devotion to the welfare of society, to be achieved through personal sacrifice, replaces devotion to the immediate good of the family and honor to the ancestors who represent the family's link with the past. The breakdown of the traditional family and the denial of the values represented and preserved by it have isolated the individual in his dealings with the impersonal machinery of the state, which operates without regard to his basic personal needs. While human relationship has become increasingly calculating and callous, as evidenced by the violence of the so-called land reform and the anti-counterrevolutionary campaigns, state control over the people, especially in rural areas, has been greatly facilitated by the introduction of the commune system.

No more striking instance of transformed social values can be found than that which now attaches to the role of the military. Despised in the past as parasitical, destructive, and worthless, the military career is now regarded as exemplary and honorable.

Such transformation of values is also reflected in the ideals of personal motivation which the new regime urges on its followers: whereas formerly one strove for the family and for oneself, with a strong sense of local ties and an awareness of the credit which any personal achievement would bring to one's locality, the individual now is urged to strive for the state and for social progress, to give up his dialect and local loyalty, and to seek personal fame through identification with the national cause by becoming, for instance, an army veteran, a "labor hero," or a "red and expert" cadre. Whereas the old Confucian morality recognized a disparity between the claims of personal cultivation and public service, it was individualistic at least to the extent that it left the ultimate decision to a man's conscience, and stressed the role of his self-perfected character as a guide in such decision. In the new society, self-cultivation is no longer a central concept, and no contradiction is permitted to exist between a man's family responsibility and the demands on him of state and society. Individual conscience is now superseded by social conscience as defined by the state's interests, and the purpose of education is no longer personal cultivation but the acquisition of the skills of science and technology, the application of which will advance society and strengthen the state.

While it may be difficult to determine to what extent the Chinese Communists have achieved their goal in conditioning human spirit, significant success is evident in the social and economic transformation of the country. The structure of Chinese economy in the past was based on intensive agriculture, supported by handicraft industry and commerce. Agriculture plays no less an important role today, but its methods are being completely altered and reorganized, first through the cooperative farm and now through the commune, which functions as the production unit of a large area and employs all available manpower as a hired labor force both in farming and in subsidiary production and construction activities. Although at the present stage the transformation of society and economy subsequent to the establishment of the communes is almost too vast to be comprehended and certainly cannot have been achieved in as short a time as claimed by the Communists, it is clear that the over-all aim of the communalization movement is to rid the new society of all ties and appurtenances of the past and to effect radical changes on every aspect of Chinese life. The issue, however, is not so much the intent as the capability to achieve such a goal, which still remains uncertain.

In the forced, accelerated industrialization of the country, a corollary to the total reconstitution of society and economy, impressive gains have been achieved through the exploitation of the agrarian sector and the rapid expansion of heavy industry at the expense of the consumer goods industry which serves the people. There is also evidence that planning has at times lost touch with reality and that the old pattern of economic relationships and the demands of the old agrarian economy still persist.

Industrialization and rural communalization, while changing the basic structure of Chinese economy, have created at the same time new areas of tension. In this unprecedented social transformation, there are many signs of danger or, to use Mao Tse-tung's phrase, "new contradictions," some of which were also present in traditional China. The sectarian and divisive forces within Chinese society are still strong and the tendency toward overcentralization in administration and planning cannot but result in sharper and more acute conflict between the central and regional powers.

The Communist insistence upon strict adherence to the party line in all forms of human activity, from political behavior and religious attitudes to artistic expression, is tantamount to a total denial of individual initiative and creates a conflict between orthodoxy and liberal thought. Conflict also exists between the people and the Communist bureaucracy, which far exceeds in size any of its imperial predecessors. Its administrative procedures have proved cumbersome and inefficient despite modern communications and transportation. The tendency of the bureaucracy to perpetuate itself and to protect its own interests at the expense of the population has created a potentially explosive antagonism among the people.

The prospects for the future of this new regime must ultimately depend on the extent to which it can make its artificially imposed new values assume as much meaning and significance as those it has attempted to displace, and on the extent to which it can fulfill the promises it holds out to the people. On the one hand, it should be recognized that the regime does satisfy many of the long frustrated national aspirations of the Chinese people and that it has been skillful in making these satisfactions outweigh the resentments stemming from many of its domestic policies. On the other hand, the Chinese Communists face difficulties of immense scope. Production, however feverishly pursued, lags behind population increase. Delayed fulfillment of the many promises which have won for the government some measures of popular support must eventually weaken its leadership and make the cost of repressive control ever higher. The initial momentum of a revolutionizing regime now ten years in power must be in part artificially maintained by inventing fresh tensions and crises, a process in which returns tend to diminish.

In spite of what has often been said and predicted, a careful, objective appraisal of current events and future trends does not seem to produce evidence to suggest that the present regime will be easily displaced or deflected from its goals. It has exploited the force of nationalism rather shrewdly and ruthlessly, and although professedly internationalist and socialist, it has in fact drawn more strength from carefully fostered nationalism than has any former regime. This is but one example of a great tactical flexibility, overlaying what no doubt is an equally great ideological rigidity. It may be said that the Communists court danger in fostering the growth of a sentiment that is in ultimate conflict with their ideological orientation, but they have profited from it to date. The regime has been thorough and effective in channeling the resources and energies of the entire population to its will. Its ways and means appear to be wholly adequate for dealing with the opposition that must still be latent in many sections of Chinese society. Any opposition that appeared, however, has been eliminated, neutralized, and often transformed, through indoctrination techniques, into positive support. Not the least of the regime's achievements is its proven ability to manipulate the minds and feelings of the masses into accepting its dictates and impositions.

The new Chinese society is still in a state of flux with a vast conglomeration of opposite forces all at work at the same time— forces that are internal as well as external, old as well as new. But whatever the course toward which the present regime forcibly leads the Chinese nation, an equilibrium must be attained between national aspirations and their fulfillment, between promises and performance, between satisfaction of the larger needs of state and society and the equally pertinent needs of the individual. The first decade under the Communist regime has been an uninter- rupted march of revolutionary events, each a step toward the socialist goal; the second may prove to be decisive indeed in that it will determine the character and direction of Chinese society for a long time to come.

HISTORICAL SETTING

BECAUSE IT IS THE STORY of the world's oldest contemporary civilization and the record of the world's most populous nation, China's history is long and intricate. Like the history of any other nation, it contains the dynamic as well as the static, the progressive as well as the stereotyped. The wax and wane of power and the fusion and fission of empire have been periodic phenomena in Chinese history. But superimposed on the pattern of recurring "cycles of Cathay" were more crucial changes—such as the shift of economic centers from north to south, sudden spurts in population growth, the rude and turbulent encounter with the West— that left a permanent mark upon the vast complex that is China today.

The Chinese people are extraordinarily conscious of their history. They love to read and retell the past, which to many is a mirror reflecting the present. In contrast to weakness and decrepitude in modern times, China has known strength and vitality; in contrast to misrule, a monarchy comparatively more enlightened than many of its contemporaries; in contrast to intermittent chaos and division, long periods of peace and unity.

Prehistory and Antiquity

Like other peoples the Chinese possess a body of folklore concerning the creation of the world and the origin of their nation, but they have neither dignified their myths into a cult nor claimed divine descent as a chosen people. Their mythology begins with P'an Ku, the creator, who was followed by a succession of mythical figures and semidivine beings from whom men learned the rudiments of civilization. Then came a train of legendary rulers beginning with Huang Ti (the Yellow Emperor), who was supposedly the progenitor of the Chinese people. Among his successors the best known are the model emperors, Yao and Shun, whose reigns are regarded as the golden age; they are reputed to have governed wisely and well and to have chosen the ablest and most virtuous men, rather than their own sons, to succeed them. As Yao chose Shun, so Shun chose Yü, a man who had rendered meritorious service to the people during China's Great Flood. Yü, however, left his throne to his son, thus originating the system of hereditary succession. He founded Hsia, the first known Chinese dynasty. The last king of the Hsia, a tyrant, was overthrown by an uprising of the people led by a noble named T'ang, who founded the Shang dynasty; here began the principle of the people's right to depose a ruler.

Whether these rulers actually existed or were created by Confucius and his contemporaries to justify their political theories, whether they are primitive race heroes or tribal chieftains from the murky beginnings of Chinese history, are unanswered questions. What early Chinese history does indicate is that the people of Han-Chinese stock had reached a high level of culture and had established themselves in the region of the Yellow River at a very early date. While it may be farfetched to trace a connection between them and the hominids (Peking Man) who roamed North China millions of years ago, archaeological evidence shows that the culture of China goes back at least as far as the transitional chalcolithic stage, when bronze tools were being substituted for stone and the people were making pottery, tilling land, and domesticating animals. Scholars place this stage in China at somewhere between 2200 and 1700 B.C.

The discovery of thousands of inscribed bones and tortoise shells, used for divination, has enabled historians to be on fairly firm ground with regard to the Shang dynasty, which lasted from about the sixteenth to the eleventh century B.C. It is known that the Shang people had a system of writing and used bronze wares and that their society was based on agriculture and hunting; their political system was aristocratic and they employed well-organized armies. The dynasty ended when its last ruler was denounced as oppressive and overthrown by Wu, chief of a vigorous people from the west, who founded the dynasty of Chou (circa eleventh century to 256 B.C.).

The early Chou rulers established their capital in the Wei River valley near the great bend of the Yellow River, where successive dynasties also had their capitals. The small royal realm and the cluster of Chinese states around it, occupying the region that today includes Shensi, Shansi, and Honan, comprised the "Middle Kingdom." Around it was a ring of semibarbarian states that were gradually Sinicized; farther off were the "barbarians." Chinese culture spread and many of the barbarians, especially those in the region of the Yangtze and those on the eastern seaboard, were assimilated. Others, particularly those of the inhospitable steppes and deserts of the north and west, hardier and more warlike, resisted the Chinese and pushed into the Middle Kingdom whenever there was any recession of Chinese power. In 771 B.C., under the threat of barbarian invasion, the Chou court was obliged to abandon the Wei River valley and move its capital eastward to the present province of Honan.

This movement of the capital from west to east was a recurring phenomenon in the history of China and to a degree was indicative of the rise and fall of Chinese power. A strong and vigorous ruler would expand the empire to the west and north, moving the capital farther inland; a change in the relative strength of the barbarian forces, endangering the capital, would bring withdrawal again toward the east.

The political system during the Chou period, known as *fengchien*, was somewhat similar to the feudalism of medieval Europe, with power and influence vested in an aristocracy. The Chou king was the liege lord to whom the feudal barons pledged their fealty, but as his power declined they gradually asserted their independence and fought among themselves for territorial aggrandizement. From 722 to 481 B.C.—called the period of "Spring and Autumn" from a historical chronicle of the same name— there was still some recognition of the titulary authority of the Chou king. From 481 B.C. until the final collapse of Chou power in 256 B.C.—known as the period of the Warring States—internal warfare of increasing frequency and intensity reduced the multitude of rival states to seven major contenders for power which assumed a position of equality with the powerless Chou court.

The feudal lords devoted themselves to building strong, prosperous states, determined not only to survive but to triumph over their rival neighbors. They carried out administrative, military and fiscal reorganizations in order to mobilize manpower and resources for war; introduced government monopolies and developed agriculture, commerce, and industry to enrich the state; regimented the people by stern laws and trained and encouraged them in military pursuits. They employed statecraft to weaken their adversaries and armed might to overwhelm them. The use of force to achieve political ends has been called the "way of the hegemon," *pa-tao,* and was condemned by later Confucian scholars, who exalted rule by virtuous example and moral suasion, calling it the "kingly way," *wang-tao.*

These centuries of civil strife were accompanied by fundamental economic and social changes. While wars and the extinction of states, political turmoil, and economic distress reduced many members of the aristocracy to the level of commoners, forcing their scions to accept employment in the courts of the major states, the spread of education and the development of domestic and interstate commerce, stimulated by the introduction of coinage, elevated the social position of the plebian classes and particularly that of the merchants. Iron came into general use, replacing bronze and making possible not only the forging of deadlier weapons but also the manufacture of tools for farming and industry.

Perhaps the most remarkable development was in the realm of philosophy. The chaos of the times filled men with a desire for peace and order; a growing awareness of the ephemeral nature of worldly changes led to contemplation of extramundane questions; expanding geographic horizons brought ideas from the outside. The revolt against the existing social and political order was paralleled by a revolt against established patterns of thought.

So many thinkers arose that there were, figuratively, a hundred schools of philosophy. Some taught methods of war, others diplomacy; some dabbled in dialectics, others in metaphysics and the occult sciences; some preached pacifism and universal love, others, notably the Taoists, remonstrated against government and urged men to hark back to the simplicity and primitiveness of the past. But the philosophic system that had the most lasting effect on the minds of the Chinese was the one known as Confucianism, founded by Confucius (K'ung Ch'iu, *circa* 551-479 B.C.). Confucius was a reformer who sought to teach men the virtues of kindliness and benevolence, tolerance and devotion; he strove to achieve social and political harmony in this world by instructing men in the principles of social intercourse, by stressing the remolding of men's minds through education, and by working out a theory of government based upon popular support and administered by men of moral rectitude. His ideals were further developed by his disciple Mencius (Meng K'o, *circa* 372-289 B.C.), best known for his theory of the innate goodness of human nature. Mencius was also the exponent of "humane government," mainly concerned with the improvement of the people's welfare.

Another Confucian follower, Hsün Tzu (Hsün Ch'ing, third century B.C.), made a radical modification of Mencius' humanistic ideas. Hsün Tzu started off on the premise that man, being born evil, required moral restraints to bind and correct him. Preaching a gospel that social harmony could be achieved if everyone were content in his station in life, he insisted upon a rigid differentiation between superior and inferior. To him the state was a glorified organization for regulating the wants of the people.

Two of Hsün Tzu's disciples, Han Fei (d. 233 B.C.) and Li Ssu (d. 208 B.C.), brought these ideas to full flower in the doctrine of Legalism, which stressed the rule of the law, government of the people by rewards and punishments, exaltation of the state, efficiency and power, restriction of the liberties of the people at home, and the use of Machiavellian diplomacy and armed force abroad. The statecraft of Li Ssu was, in fact, of great importance to the growth of the Ch'in state, which, benefiting also from legalistic and military reforms, became strong enough to defeat its rivals and by 221 B.C. was master of all China.

Imperial China

The triumph of the Ch'in state under the First Emperor (Shih Huang-ti, 259-210 B.C., personal name Ying Cheng) united the Chinese empire for the first time under a strong central government. The former feudal states were reorganized as provinces administered by officials appointed by the central government and a number of measures were taken to safeguard and strengthen the empire against both internal and external dangers.

The right to private land ownership, a privilege guarded as a source of power by the former feudal lords, was extended to the people and agriculture and commerce were encouraged. Standardization throughout the empire was effected in such matters as forms of writing, codes of law, coinage, and even the axle length of vehicles. To silence criticism of imperial rule, scholars unsympathetic to the regime were put to death and books deemed detrimental to it were burned. The population was redistributed wherever too great concentration of wealth might occur and all weapons were confiscated. To protect the country from barbarian invasions, the Great Wall was extended and, as Ch'in armies pushed into new areas, settlers and political offenders were sent out to open up the virgin lands, especially in South China.

The tremendous levies of manpower and resources required by these activities caused hardship and resentment among the people, which led to revolts upon the death of the First Emperor. Civil war and dissension at the court finally brought the Ch'in dynasty to an end less than twenty years after its triumph.

By 202 B.C. a petty official named Liu Pang (Emperor Kao-tsu of Han, 247-195 B.C.) was able to gain control of the empire. Under the dynasty of Han (206 B.C.-220 A.D.) which he founded, most of the political machinery of the Ch'in was retained though some of the harsher aspects were modified or abolished. The capital was located at Ch'ang-an (now Sian) in the Wei River valley, and Confucian scholars, who had been out of favor during the Ch'in period, were brought back into high offices. The recruitment of civilian bureaucracy through examination and the inculcation of ethics through education were introduced into the machinery of the state.

Han was a period of such military renown that to this day Chinese still proudly call themselves "sons of Han" (hence the name Han-Chinese). During the long reign of Emperor Wu (Wu-ti, 156-87 B.C., personal name Liu Ch'e) Chinese armies invaded and annexed parts of Annam and Korea, pushed back the Huns (Hsiung-nu) in the north, and extended Chinese influence westward to Ferghana and Bactria in Central Asia. After a temporary eclipse of Chinese power during the interregnum of Wang Mang (33 B.C-23 A.D.), the Chinese again marched to the west, as far as the Caspian Sea. At one time, they emerged victorious from a brief encounter with the Roman Legionaries.

Occasionally when the Han court found its military power unequal to a situation, it would resort to such diplomatic maneuvers as "pitting barbarians against barbarians" or buying peace with valuable gifts of Chinese goods. The weakness stemmed partly from interference in the government by relatives of the imperial consorts and by palace attendants, and partly from social and economic problems. At the beginning of the dynasty lighter taxes afforded the people a breathing spell after the destructive civil war. But with the increasing extravagance of the court and the rising cost of foreign campaigns, the requirements of the state mounted, while its revenue was slashed by currency depreciation, instability of prices, and the increase in area of tax-free land owned by patrician families. The attempt made by the government to regulate prices in 110 B.C. met with strong protests from the Confucian officials and others determined to protect their privileges. At the beginning of the Christian era, Wang Mang, who had usurped the throne, tried to curb the power of the rich aristocratic families and of the merchants by instituting what have been termed socialistic measures for the nationalization and equalization of land, stabilization of prices, and the formation of governmentoperated monopolies of salt and iron. These measures only worsened the lot of the people, however, and popular uprisings brought an end to Wang Mang's reign. When a scion of the House of Liu restored the Han dynasty the capital was moved to Loyang in Honan and the empire enjoyed a brief period of power, but eventually the combination of palace intrigues, weak emperors, internal unrest, and external pressure brought the dynasty to an end in 220 A.D.

The collapse of Han was followed by three and a half centuries of division and disorder. The empire was first divided into the Three Kingdoms. This period is remembered by the Chinese for its romances of chivalry and stratagems, valor and adventures. For a brief time the Chin dynasty (265-420) that followed achieved a semblance of unity, but it was too weak to hold back the tide of barbarian advance and in 317 the Chin court was driven to seek refuge in the south, below the Yangtze River, where it established its capital at the present city of Nanking. The southward drive of the barbarian invaders was halted by a Chinese victory in the historic battle of the Fei River in 383. In South China a succession of four native dynasties managed to preserve Chinese culture and develop the resources of the region, but North China came under the domination of barbarian chieftains. Confucianism declined and, with increased contacts abroad, foreign philosophic and religious theories such as Buddhism gained credence, acquired Chinese complexion, and merged into Chinese life and culture.

Finally in 589 the empire was once more united under the short-lived dynasty of Sui (589-618). Once more the capital was moved back to Ch'ang-an and Lo-yang; once more the government undertook large-scale construction works, the most important of which was a canal system to transport supplies from the fertile central-east to the political and strategic centers in the north; once more Chinese forces sallied forth in campaigns against neighboring states. Sui armies held in check the newly risen power of the Turks; a Sui fleet invaded Liu-ch'iu (Ryukyu); and amphibious units struck at Korea in the northeast and at Annam in the south.

The people, chafing under crushing taxes, revolted again and in the turmoil one of the nobles, Li Shih-min, later known as Emperor T'ai-tsung (597-649), overthrew the Sui dynasty to found the T'ang.

The T'ang period (618-906) witnessed a flowering of Chinese culture, due partly to stimuli received from abroad and partly to the renewed vigor of the Chinese people. Civil service examinations for the selection of officials and the bureaucratic machinery were perfected; the T'ang government and T'ang code of laws became models for neighboring states. It was the golden age of literature and art. The patriotic sentiments of Tu Fu's (712-770) lines, the lyric magic of Li Po's (circa 701-762) verses, and the stylistic purity of Han Yü's (768-824) essays stir readers to this day. Painting reached a new height, as did sculpture, which bore traces of the Hellenic influences entering China in the wake of Buddhism. Block printing was invented and one of the world's earliest extant books, a Buddhist sutra, was printed in 868. Foreigners came from afar to receive the polish of Chinese education and their presence enhanced the cosmopolitan atmosphere of the T'ang capital, Ch'ang-an. In the tolerant climate of early T'ang, foreign missionaries came to propagate their faiths—Mazdaism, Manichaeism, and Nestorian Christianity—while Moslem merchants and soldiers of fortune introduced Islam. Colonies of foreign merchants sprang up in Chinese ports. The Chinese did not hesitate to employ foreigners in their government, to use foreign imported goods in daily life, and to adopt new ideas and technology.

Through their military prowess the early T'ang rulers built up a larger empire than that of the Han. In the west they defeated the Turks and established a protectorate over Turkestan; in the east they vanquished the land and sea forces of the Japanese and the Paekche Kingdom of Korea. A Chinese-led army even penetrated into India.

By the middle of the eighth century, however, T'ang power had ebbed. Turkestan was lost to the surging might of Islam and a part of southwestern China fell to the Thai Kingdom of Nanchao. Uigurs and Tibetans sacked the T'ang capital. Although the authority of the T'ang court was temporarily restored its days were numbered. Eunuchs and favorites gained dominance at court while military satraps asserted their independence in the provinces. Misrule and economic exploitation drove the people to revolt and the insurgents under Huang Ch'ao rampaged through the empire.

Political weakness and dissension made it possible for northern invaders to pour in, bringing the T'ang dynasty to an end in 906.

The period following the fall of T'ang was known as that of the Five Dynasties, from the five short dynasties that ruled North China. South China was divided into ten minor states. Although the Sung dynasty (960-1279) was able to reunite most of the empire, unification was not complete. The Khitan state of Liao and the Tangut state of Hsia held large areas in the north and northwest; throughout the Sung period the Chinese were occupied with the wars against them, and later against the Jurchen state of Chin (1115-1234). In 1127, with the occupation of North China by the Jurchens, the Sung court was constrained to transfer its capital to Hangchow, a move which signalized the abandonment of interior provinces in favor of coastal regions as the seat of government; it also had to pay tribute to the Chin court and to acknowledge a position of inferiority.

The Sung period marked the commencement of modernity in China, not only in government and social organization but also in the cultural and economic life of the people. Determined to prevent the emergence of too powerful military governors, which in the past had led to the fall of T'ang and the disintegration of the Five Dynasties, the first Sung emperor, himself a general elected by his men, assumed absolute powers, subordinating the military to civil control and concentrating all authority in the imperial court.

This centralization of governing powers added to the importance and prestige of the imperial court, but, given the poor communications and transportation of the period, soon proved a source of weakness in the political organization. A contemporary writer commented, for example, that the transfer of a single soldier or the levy of tax on a single item by local authorities required approval at the court. The inherent inefficiency of the government was compounded by the court policy of encouraging officials and scholars to voice their views on all matters of state, the consequence being that every issue was subject to prolonged discussion.

To increase government efficiency, promote prosperity, and build a strong army were the accepted objectives, but controversy over the method of accomplishing these objectives divided the court between the reformers led by Wang An-shih (1021-86), who had the support of the emperor, and the conservative officials.

Wang An-shih was at first successful in pushing through a series of measures whose specific goals were: changes in the examination system to stress practical studies, a beginning toward economic planning and state monopolies, equalization of the tax burden and a system for loans to farmers, abolition of the corvée, stabilization of commodity prices, and conscription and the streamlining of the army. The measures failed to achieve the desired results, to some extent for lack of able administrators. The still powerful conservative gentry, whose determined opposition had also contributed to the failure of the reform program, pressed the advantage and gradually gained ascendancy over the more progressive officials at the court.

One result of the political and economic changes of the Sung period was greater social mobility. The power of the old patrician families was gone while the development of printing, the extension of educational opportunity, and the growth of a money economy had all contributed to the emergence of a new class of wealthy and influential businessmen, who increasingly took part in the conduct of public affairs. Whereas land and public office had traditionally been the almost exclusive avenues to social status and power, industry and commerce opened up another source of wealth and influence and the sons of wealthy businessmen joined the ranks of the elite gentry class in ever greater numbers. At the same time some members of the existing gentry, going back for precedent to the Chou period when there had been no stigma against trade, turned to business themselves.

In the economic field the demands of war obliged the government to seek new sources of revenue and it embarked upon business enterprises and set up state monopolies. Governmental encouragement of maritime commerce and the introduction of the mariner's compass spurred the development of shipping and navigation techniques to such an extent that the Chinese were able to wrest from the Arabs the maritime commerce of the Orient.

As in the feudal period the vicissitudes and political impotence of the government in the face of barbarian encroachment placed a premium on the achievement of peace and order. Some Confucian thinkers, among them Wang An-shih, believed the solution lay in institutional reform and in utilitarianism. Other Confucian thinkers, by blending Buddhist metaphysics with fresh interpretations of Confucian ideas, worked out a new cosmic order and a system of moral philosophy which emphasized the acquisition of knowledge as a means of cultivation for the individual and which stressed the clear demarcation of superior and inferior status as the key to social and political relations. These ideas, synthesized and publicized by Chu Hsi (1130-1200), became known as Neo-Confucianism and although they diverged in many ways from the teachings of Confucius were subsequently regarded as orthodox Confucianism. As such they dominated the minds of the Chinese down to the nineteenth century.

Sung China's cultural advances provided little protection, however, from harassment by the warlike nomadic peoples to the north. Already weakened by its protracted defensive action against Khitan and Jurchen attacks, China faced a new threat from the Mongols. Fresh from victories over North China, Korea, and the Moslem kingdoms of Central Asia and two penetrations into Europe, the Mongol invaders, under the leadership of Kublai Khan (1214-94), began their drive against the Sung. After successfully defeating the Chinese army and fleet in the south, they established the Yüan dynasty (1260-1368), the first non-Chinese regime to control all China.

Mobilizing the resources of China and adopting many of the Chinese facilities, such as paper money and state monopolies, to obtain funds for their war chest, and utilizing Chinese manpower and technology, the Mongols continued their drive to the east and south launching expeditions against Japan, Annam, and Java. Internally the Mongols turned their attention to public works, such as completion of the Grand Canal. While a large number of foreigners entered China and took service under the Mongols the Chinese people were exploited and discriminated against by nationality laws designed to bolster Mongol rule.

As in the Sung period China had suffered humiliations as a nation so under the Yüan the Chinese endured humiliations as a people, and these factors combined to stir up not only a surge of national consciousness but also an antiforeign feeling. Rebellions, which broke out in the Yangtze region, cut off the Mongol government from its source of supplies; the Yüan court was split by dissension, and in 1368 the Mongol rulers were ousted from China by Chu Yüan-chang (1328-99), a peasant leader who had fought his way to power.

A man of humble origin, Chu Yüan-chang (Emperor Hung-wu), founder of the Ming dynasty (1368-1644), was conscious of the needs of his people. Having restored the traditional form of government he instituted strict laws to check official excesses. To give the people a respite from the years of war he maintained a policy of noninterference in the affairs of neighboring states. To turn the attention of the people to farming, regarded as the foundation of China's economic structure, he favored agriculture at the expense of industry and commerce.

But the first Ming emperor was also concerned with consolidating his rule and furthering his type of absolutism. He abolished the office of prime minister, personally taking over the government, and arrested and executed hundreds of gentry-scholars on charges of treason. His action set a precedent for later emperors who often entrusted affairs of state to their own attendants, untutored eunuchs, rather than to the trained bureaucrats.

The zenith of Ming power was reached during the reign of the third emperor, Yung-lo (1360-1424, personal name Chu Ti). Chinese armies reconquered Annam and kept back the Mongols; the Chinese fleet, under Cheng Ho (1371-1435) and other commanders, ranged the China Sea and the Indian Ocean, cruising as far as the east coast of Africa. The nations of maritime Asia sent envoys to pay homage to the Chinese emperor, and the tribute which they sent, along with the gifts China gave in return, reached a volume large enough to constitute international trade.

China's ascendancy over East Asia was transient. As in previous dynasties the aggressive vigor of the early part of the Ming dynasty gave way to languor and lessening of strength. The bureaucracy became conservative; the emperor was weak and a prey to the eunuchs. Economic and social problems mounted, drawing the attention of the people inward, while the recrudescence of Mongol power forced the nation to face the land frontier and turn its back to the sea. The forays of European adventurers and Japanese pirates on the southeastern coast were but minor annoyances compared to the deadlier threat from the north. Costly and long-drawn-out wars against the Mongols, the newly risen Manchus, and a Japanese invasion of Korea drained the resources of the empire and, combined with maladministration and economic distress, drove the people to rebellion. Rebel armies captured the capital, Peking, in 1644 and put an end to the Ming dynasty. Taking advantage of this power vacuum the Manchus, with the help of Chinese collaborators, pierced Chinese defenses and made themselves masters of North China.

Ming adherents resisted the Manchus for many years in South China, and it was not until the last Ming pretender had been made prisoner, the Ming stronghold on Taiwan held by Cheng Ch'eng-kung (Koxinga, 1623-62) and his descendants captured, and the rebellion in South China quelled that in 1683 all China came under the rule of the Manchus, founders of the Ch'ing dynasty (1644-1911).

The consolidation and expansion of Ch'ing power were primarily the work of two emperors: K'ang-hsi (1654-1722) and his grandson, Ch'ien-lung (1711-99). Under them the bureaucratic system of government, based on the Ming model, was further elaborated. The vigor of these early emperors was directed at the improvement of economic conditions, and under them the empire enjoyed almost 150 years of internal peace and prosperity. Once more China was strong enough to extend its power abroad. Chinese armies drove back the Mongols and reasserted Chinese dominance over Mongolia and Turkestan. Russian expansion in the far north was checked, and by the treaty of Nerchinsk (1689) Russia was blocked from access to the Pacific. The opening of the southwestern provinces was followed by the invasion of Tibet, Nepal, Bhutan, and Annam. Nations on the periphery of China paid tribute and acknowledged Chinese overlordship. Belief in China's strength and superiority persisted into the nineteenth century, long after China ceased to be a great power and had begun to show signs of weakness and decay.

Modern China

The manifestations of decline were everywhere as China entered the nineteenth century. The Ch'ing dynasty had passed the vigor of its prime: its army of Manchu bannermen was degenerating into a rabble, its recent emperors had been effete, and its government was graft-ridden and inept.

The stagnation to which the Ch'ing dynasty had been reduced could perhaps be traced to a number of factors. As a racial minority ruling over a large and populous nation the Manchus found in the Neo-Confucianism of the Sung school a useful instrument of government. Because it preached the right of the superior to rule and the duty of the inferior to obey and be content with their lot, it became the orthodox philosophy used by the Manchu rulers to prevent sedition and threats to their power and to maintain peace and order. The Neo-Confucian concept of China's cultural superiority and centrality tended to encourage ethnocentrism and disdain toward outside peoples and foreign ideas. The civil service examinations, which had already become corrupted under the Ming, became more rigid and formalized under the Ch'ing: the memorizing of Confucian classics and the writing of stylized essays, *pa-ku*, were emphasized at the expense of the spirit of Confucianism or the study of the practical affairs of the state. As the examination system constituted the royal road to social prestige, power, and wealth, the new emphasis had the effect of paralyzing intellectual growth and intensifying conservatism. To discourage independent thinking the government carried out a literary inquisition, in which books were proscribed and scholars arrested; at the same time it sought to engross and dull the minds of other scholars by engaging them in the compilation of literary and philosophical compendiums.

Another factor debilitating the Chinese empire was economic pressure due to a phenomenal increase of population during the Ch'ing period. Toward the end of the seventeenth century the population had grown from approximately 70 million to more than 100 million; by the beginning of the nineteenth century it was around 300 million; fifty years later it passed the 400 million mark (for current population figures, see Chapter 3). With this rise the average per capita landholding dwindled from two acres to less than half an acre. The situation, aggravated by maldistribution and maladministration, was unrelieved by commerce and industry, which the Ch'ing government disapproved of and made no effort to develop. Unemployment created discontent among the people and banditry was rife.

Discontent was, however, not confined to the common people. Scholars, too proud to serve an alien master and seeking to liberate the Chinese mind from the shackles of Neo-Confucianism, went back to the Confucianism of the Han and pre-Han periods; the antimonarchial tone of their political writings stirred the nationalistic spirit of the people and provided an ideological basis for the movement against the Manchus.

Rebellions finally broke out early in the nineteenth century on the island of Taiwan; brigandage in the provinces matched in ferocity the piratical depredations on the coast. Secret societies such as the White Lotus Sect in the north and the Hung Society in the south gained ground, and embattled farmers, driven by social iniquities to take up arms, formed organizations animated by nationalism and religious ideologies. By the middle of the century, anti-Manchu movements reached a flood tide in the insurrections of the Moslems in the northwest and the southwest, the Niens in the north, and, most formidable of all, the T'ai-p'ings (1851-64) in the south.

The T'ai-p'ings, a popular group led by a Christianized Chinese, Hung Hsiu-ch'üan (1813-64), at first carried out drastic social reforms, winning such wide support that at one time they were almost able to overthrow the Manchus; gradually, however, the leaders lost their reforming zeal and their rule degenerated into one of terror. In disgust many of the gentry as well as the peasantry turned from the T'ai-p'ings to support Tseng Kuo-fan (1811-72), a Confucian scholar who had rallied to the government's cause. Tseng and his colleagues fought not only in defense of the Manchu rule, but also for the preservation of the traditional culture of China; they built up an effective army which succeeded in crushing the T'ai-p'ings.

Torn and exhausted by civil commotion and economic affliction China also suffered blows from the outside. The West was growing in strength and vigor. Having conquered much of the world and subjugated millions, proud of their progress in government and science, the men of Europe looked down upon China as backward and decadent. The Chinese, in turn, arrogantly regarded them as ignorant barbarians, rebuffed their diplomatic overtures, spurned their desires for trade, and isolated them in a single port, Canton. The Chinese considered these foreigners uninvited guests whose unreasonable demands and importing of opium to drug the people constituted abuse of Chinese hospitality.

In 1839 when the Chinese government adopted severe measures to ban the import of opium and confiscated the narcotics brought in by British merchants, the British government retaliated with a punitive expedition against southern China. Unprepared for war the Chinese were defeated and in the Treaty of Nanking (1842) acquiesced to British demands. They were forced not only to cede the island of Hong Kong and legalize the opium traffic, but also to grant diplomatic equality and commercial privileges to British subjects. The privileges granted to the British and later (1844) to the Americans by the "most-favored-nation clause" were shared by other nations through the conclusion of separate agreements. When the Chinese balked at the infringements of sovereignty imposed by these treaties, an allied British and French force, on the pretext of protecting their nationals in the interior, attacked to extract additional concessions. In 1860 they seized Peking and set fire to the Summer Palace. The pattern by which foreign powers kept China subjugated had been set:

each time the Chinese stirred to resist foreign pressure, their inevitable defeat by overwhelming military force was used by the foreigners to demand more concessions.

The resultant treaties gave the Europeans a privileged position in China and a stranglehold upon its economic life. In the treaty ports, some of them far inland, the foreigners established concessions administered by their own officials. Chinese laws and the authority of the Chinese government stopped at the borders of the concessions; the jurisdiction of the foreign consuls was exercised not only over their own nationals, but, through the mixed courts, over the Chinese residents also.

The influence of the Europeans was felt throughout the Chinese empire. They administered China's maritime customs and the postal system, and set the schedule of tariffs on the import of their own goods into China. They had the right to establish factories, open mines, operate shipping in coastal and inland waters, and construct railways to funnel commerce through ports under their control. Their warships, patrolling the rivers and coasts, served to ensure the execution of the one-sided provisions that the Chinese called "unequal treaties."

To the existing debilitation and impoverishment of the country had been added the demoralizing exploitation of foreigners. China gradually was deprived of the military means of defense; the intense development and concentration of wealth in the coastal treaty ports proceeded at the expense of the economic development of the hinterlands; foreign rule and the sway of foreign customs in the coastal cities undermined the structure of Chinese society.

As China's weakness grew, so did the ambitions of the foreign powers. Russia penetrated into Manchuria, Mongolia, and Chinese Turkestan. One by one the peripheral states that had once acknowledged the suzerainty of China came under the domination of foreign powers. France, victorious in a war with China in 1883, made Annam its protectorate; Great Britain extinguished China's limited suzerainty over Burma; Japan, newly emerged from its century-long seclusion, annexed the Liu-ch'iu Islands and, by defeating the Chinese in Korea (1894-95), gained control of that peninsula as well as of Taiwan.

The defeat by Japan stripped China of its remaining prestige and foreign nations negotiated the division of the vast empire into spheres of influence. Only greed and disagreement among the European nations saved China from dismemberment. Finally a proposal of the United States for an "open door" policy providing equal access into China was accepted by other foreign powers.

The military, political, and economic blows battering China were matched by the slower but more disintegrating impact of western ideas and institutions. China plunged from its pedestal of self-styled superiority to so low an estate that it was not even master of its own house, and the momentum of the fall shook the very foundation of its civilization.

While the Manchu government was impotent and most of the people too occupied with the immediate problems of survival to ward off the dangers that threatened their civilization, some Chinese refused to accept their impending fate without a struggle. As early as the Opium War members of the scholar-official class had attempted to acquire western guns and warships in order to resist the westerners. Toward the end of the century men such as Li Hung-chang (1823-1901) and Chang Chih-tung (1837-1909) went a step further, building arsenals, dockyards, factories, and modern means of communications in order to establish an industrial base for the creation of military strength; they also dispatched diplomats and students to Europe and America to familiarize themselves with western knowledge.

Whereas Japan's rise to power had been a forceful demonstration to the Chinese of what an oriental nation could accomplish by modernization, it was the translation of western books into Chinese that opened the eyes of China's intellectuals. Many of the more foward-looking officials and scholars became convinced that western thought and institutions were as necessary to the strengthening of China as western military and industrial technology, and in their minds the problem was to find ways and means to graft western ideas onto the base of Chinese culture. In 1898, a group of scholars, led by K'ang Yu-wei (1858-1927) and Liang Ch'i-ch'ao (1873-1929), who had protested strongly against the signing of the treaty with Japan in 1895, gained the support of the emperor and immediately launched a series of measures aimed at basic social and institutional reforms. The objectives were increased efficiency by reorganization of the government machinery, education of more and better administrators by changes in the examination system and the establishment of modern schools, strengthening of the armed forces by modernization of equipment, and the encouragement of commerce and industry through construction of railways and factories. But the measures were blocked by the extreme conservative and reactionary elements in power.

By 1900 conditions in the country had become so bad that the pent-up emotions of the Chinese broke out in a paroxysm of fury and violence. The I-ho T'uan, an organization supported by the Manchu court and led by secret societies known to the West as the Boxers, rampaged over North China with the avowed intention of ousting the foreigners. In the end it was defeated by an allied expeditionary force that relieved the beleaguered Legation Quarters in Peking. Additional terms were imposed, including the right to station foreign troops in China and to raze Chinese fortifications.

Fearful of the rising temper of the people the Ch'ing government was belatedly constrained to carry out certain reforms, but the gesture was futile. Many Chinese were convinced that the only solution lay in outright revolution and the establishment of a new order. The leader of the revolutionaries was Sun Yat-sen (Sun Wen, 1866-1925) who in 1905 organized the T'ung-meng Hui (Brotherhood Society), later renamed the Kuomintang (Nationalist party). The efforts of the revolutionaries to overthrow the Ch'ing government were favored and accelerated by rampant anti-Manchu riots, and the chance explosion of a bomb at Wuch'ang on October 10, 1911 touched off a relatively bloodless revolution that swept away a monarchial system more than two thousand years old, installed a republic, and ushered in two decades of disorder and misrule. Yüan Shih-k'ai (1859-1916), sent by the Ch'ing government to negotiate with the revolutionary leaders, concluded a settlement providing for the abdication of the last Ch'ing monarch, the five-year-old P'u-yi (Emperor Hsüan-t'ung, 1906——), and the establishment of the Republic of China (1912) with himself as president.

The Republican Period
The first years of the republic saw futile attempts to set up a parliamentary form of government. The revolutionaries were inexperienced and the conservatives paid only lip service to the cause of democracy. The situation was complicated by the dictatorial ambition of Yüan Shih-k'ai, who, instead of making any effort to check the economic imperialism of the western powers and the encroachment of Japan, plotted to exalt himself as emperor. During World War I, the activities of Japan were directed less against its enemies, Germany and Austria, than against its neigh-

bor, China. Japan had violated China's sovereignty and neutrality by fighting Russia on Chinese soil in the war of 1904-05.
It now seized Tsingtao, which the Germans had previously taken,
and extended its control over the other parts of the Shantung
province. Going a step further, the Japanese issued an ultimatum,
the so-called Twenty-one Demands, intended to subordinate the
whole of China. May 9, 1915—the day China was forced to accept
a toned-down version of these demands—has since been observed
as a national day of humiliation.

China entered the war in 1917, hoping to recover its lost
province. The denial of that hope at the Versailles Peace Conference in 1919 created a storm of protest: there were student
demonstrations in Peking, and these together with the intellectual
and literary activities that followed have been jointly called the
May Fourth Movement, a high-water mark in the effort to
modernize and rejuvenate China. (Shantung was restored to
China by the Washington Conference of 1922.)

But with the death of Yüan Shih-k'ai and the further weakening
of central government, the nation disintegrated into a number
of local regimes ruled by military governors or warlords who
waged civil war for aggrandizement while the phantom government at Peking clung to its claims of legitimacy. A faction of the
defunct parliament, mostly southern revolutionists led by Sun
Yat-sen, moved to Canton to form a separatist government.

Ignored by the western democracies to whom he had appealed
for succor and support, Sun Yat-sen in 1922 accepted offers of
assistance and guidance from the newly created Soviet government in Russia. Soviet advisers, the most prominent of whom was
Michael Borodin, came to help reorganize and consolidate the
Nationalist party and to train its troops. Members of the Communist
party of China, which had been formed just a year before, joined
the Nationalist party as individuals; later, the Communist party
grew and gained strength until it was able to influence the policies
of the Nationalist party.

During this time—while his lieutenant Chiang Kai-shek (Chiang
Chung-cheng, 1887——) supervised the Whampoa Military Academy, which became the cradle of the Nationalist army—Sun Yat-
sen wrote the *Principles of National Reconstruction* and expounded
his political philosophy, the Three People's Principles, which became the gospel of the Nationalist party. Briefly, the principles
are: (1) nationalism, to achieve political unity so as to resist
imperialism; (2) democracy, to establish a centralized govern-

ment on a popular base; and (3) people's livelihood, to elevate the living standard and the welfare of the people. These aims were to be achieved in three consecutive stages: military operations to unify the nation; political tutelage to train the people in representative government; and finally democracy. Sun Yat-sen died in 1925 before his plan could be realized.

The first stage of military operations began in 1926 with the launching of the Northern Expedition by the Nationalist army. In 1928, with the defeat of some of the warlords and the voluntary submission of others, the nation was brought under the domination of the Nationalists, led by Chiang Kai-shek. Meanwhile, the Chinese Communists overreached themselves in their attempts to seize power and in 1927 were purged from the Nationalist party; later they withdrew to Kiangsi to build a new base and rally their forces.

Having united the country, the Nationalists established their capital at Nanking. Following the ideas of Sun Yat-sen, they organized a government which sought to harmonize western political institutions with Chinese traditions; to the western divisions of executive, judicial, and legislative functions of government were added control and examination functions corresponding to those exercised by the censorate and civil service examination system of the past. Power was vested in the party, which was to act as a guardian of the people and exercise authority in their name during the period of political tutelage—a role the party was reluctant to relinquish.

In the diplomatic field, tariff autonomy was achieved, some of the alienated territories were recovered, and some foreign nations were persuaded to surrender their extraterritorial rights. Foreigners consented to concede many of their special privileges because a semblance of order had been restored in the country. The Nationalist government acted energetically to modernize the legal and penal systems, stabilize prices, amortize debts, reform the banking and currency systems, build railways and highways, promote public health, legislate against traffic in narcotics, and augment industrial and agricultural production.

Great strides were made in education. In 1912, there were only four universities with 500 students; in 1937 there were 108 universities with 43,000 students. Most remarkable was the progress made in adult education by what was known as the "mass education movement," in the promotion of a new literary style based upon the vernacular, the new scientific approach to the study of

China's past, and the reinterpretation of China's cultural heritage. Concomitant with these movements was a program to popularize the national language and overcome dialectal variations. The spread of various media of mass communications, greater availability of radio and motion pictures, and improvement of transportation contributed to a developing sense of unity.

Japan moved to halt Chinese progress. On September 18, 1931, in what came to be known as the Mukden Incident, Japanese troops invaded Manchuria and established there a puppet state—Manchoukuo—under P'u-yi, the last Manchu emperor; on January 28, 1932 Japanese forces landed in Shanghai in an attempt to compel China's acquiescence to Japan's seizure of Manchuria. The League of Nations, to which the Chinese appealed for help, refrained from imposing effective sanctions on Japan.

With Manchuria as a base, the Japanese began to push over the Great Wall into North China. Failing to bring about the secession of the northern provinces, Japan was able to force Nationalist agreement to the creation of a so-called autonomous regime in North China to exploit Chinese resources and markets and by smuggling and selling narcotics sought to weaken the moral fabric and economic strength of the Chinese people. While the Nationalist government struggled with difficulty to restrain its people until the nation could be prepared to wage a modern war effectively, anti-Japanese demonstrations and boycotts increased, enraging the extremists in Japan.

The Nationalist government was harassed throughout this period by dissident elements and internal enemies, all of whom demanded an immediate showdown with Japan. The Communists were the major internal threat. Having established a Soviet government in Kiangsi they had switched from a policy aimed at organizing the urban workers and had concentrated on mobilizing the rural population. By 1932 they controlled millions of people in the rural areas and mountainous regions of China Proper. The Nationalists had launched six campaigns against the Communists and in 1935 they succeeded in dislodging them from their stronghold in Kiangsi. The main force of the Red Army broke through the Nationalist cordon and fled by a circuitous route through the wilderness of Southwest China (in a trek now celebrated as the Long March) to the northwest province of Shensi, where they established a new Soviet government at Yenan.

At this time Soviet Russia, preparing for an inevitable struggle with Japan and Germany, shifted its policy toward the western democracies from hostility to friendship; the Chinese Communists, following suit, proclaimed a united front of all Chinese factions against the common enemy, Japan. At this point a fortuitous event played into their hands. The Nationalist troops stationed at the nearby city of Sian were those who had been ousted from Manchuria by the Japanese. They had become susceptible to Communist inducements. In December 1936, led by their commander Chang Hsüeh-liang (1898——), they kidnapped Chiang Kai-shek and forced him to agree to a policy of armed resistance against Japan. This, in effect, began a war that was to exhaust Nationalist China and to give the Chinese Communists time to rebuild and develop their strength.

The first clash between Chinese and Japanese troops occurred on July 7, 1937 outside Peiping (name of Peking during the Nationalist period, 1928-49) at Marco Polo Bridge. At first the Chinese responded with fervor to the national crisis. All factions submerged their differences; Nationalist and Communist troops fought side by side against the common foe. Despite local successes, however, the Chinese could not stop the Japanese advance; the government was forced to move from Nanking to Chungking, which became the wartime capital of China. The Japanese occupied the coastal region and China lost 95 percent of its industry; despite the industrial development of the interior provinces its capacity for war was considerably reduced.

By 1940 the war had reached a stalemate. Manchuria, North China, the coastal regions, and the rich Yangtze valley of central China were under Japanese occupation and administered by puppet regimes. Pushing southward the Japanese occupied Indochina, severing the Nationalists' main supply line; following the bombing of Pearl Harbor, they seized Burma to cut off China's last line of communication with the outside world. The outbreak of World War II made China a partner of powerful democratic nations, but by then China was geographically isolated.

The war years severely strained the Chinese economy. Production failed to keep pace with demand and the resultant scarcity of consumer goods together with the over-issue of currency fed a spiraling inflation. The government was forced to increase its levies on the people and, as popular discontent and war-weariness grew, to adopt repressive measures. Corruption and incompetence were becoming common among government officials and there was general awareness that the army was too large, poorly equipped, and inadequately officered. When minority parties demanded a greater voice in the affairs of state, the Nationalists countered with the argument that political tutelage was still required.

The most articulate critics of the Nationalist government and the strongest contenders for control of China were the Chinese Communists. After a brief period of collaboration, antagonism between the Nationalists and the Communists flared up anew during the war and they fought each other as well as the Japanese. Animosity between them had grown so bitter by the end of the war as to make reconciliation impossible.

Nationalist China emerged from the war nominally a great power, but actually a nation economically prostrate and politically divided. The Nationalist government was unable to cope with the problems of reconstruction and of rehabilitating the formerly Japanese-occupied areas. The economy, sapped by military demands, sabotaged by the Communists, undermined by speculations and hoarding, deteriorated despite assistance from the United States. Famine came and millions were rendered homeless by floods. The value of the Chinese dollar dropped out of sight and officials were driven to accept graft.

The situation was further aggravated by the Yalta Pact—concluded between the United States and Soviet Russia without China's cognizance—which brought Russian troops into Manchuria against the Japanese and consequently enabled the Rusians to dismantle and take away the industrial equipment of that region. China signed an agreement with Soviet Russia in which Russia pledged to recognize and support the Nationalist government, to respect China's sovereignty in Manchuria and Sinkiang, and to establish Dairen as a free port; China pledged to hold a plebiscite to determine the status of Outer Mongolia. The agreement, declared effective for thirty years, was immediately violated by Russia, which held onto Dairen and stayed in Manchuria long enough to enable the Chinese Communists to move in and arm themselves with the equipment surrendered by the withdrawing Japanese army. The plebiscite in Outer Mongolia legalized the alienation of that region from Chinese control.

The Nationalists had attached great importance to the recovery of Manchuria, hoping to utilize its resources and industry to rebuild their shattered economy. They found it converted, with Russian connivance, into a strong base of operations for the Chinese Communists, who became so powerful that they were able to challenge the Nationalists on the field and to treat with contumacy the United States' mediation efforts.

The attempt by the United States to reconcile the two major factions in China was a continuation of its wartime policy. Through the influence and personal prestige of General George C. Marshall, a *rapprochement* was almost achieved in 1946, only to prove illusory; neither side dared be the first to lay down its arms for fear of treachery, and in the end the American intermediaries withdrew, convinced of the hopelessness of the task. The Nationalists intensified their efforts to stamp out the Communist rebellion and put an end to the separatist government. The Communists, who had continued their aggrandizement during the truce talks, worked to expand the territories under their control.

The discontent of the people grew as their plight worsened. Instead of the peace they had longed for they found themselves caught in a civil war as widespread and destructive as the struggle against Japan. To placate those clamoring for political reorganization the Nationalist government initiated reforms to broaden the popular base of its structure and promulgated a new constitution to mark the inauguration of democracy and the end of political tutelage. The Communists, who earlier had been the most vociferous in their demands for participation in the government, spurned the invitation to join. But political reform came too late to arrest the government's disintegration, and its fiscal policy accelerated its collapse. In 1948, in a last-ditch attempt to check the plunge of its finances, it ordered the surrender of all silver, gold, and foreign notes held by the people in exchange for a new currency. The scheme failed, the people were dissatisfied and resentful, and many of the students and intellectuals openly espoused the cause of the Communists.

Given this context of discontent and political and economic chaos that followed the popular rejection of the Nationalist government, the Communists were able to assume the role of a crusading force. They called their army the People's Liberation Army and their propaganda proclaimed the deliverance of a subject people. In the fall of 1948 they began their drive southward, at the same time expanding their control in North China; early in 1949 Peking and Tientsin fell; in the summer they moved into Nanking and Shanghai. By the end of the year all mainland China was under Communist domination and the Nationalist government had withdrawn to Taiwan.

The Communist Regime

From their new seat of government in Peking the Communists extended their control over the whole country, dividing it into six large military and administrative regions. Land redistribution was carried out on a nationwide basis, and energetic measures were adopted to arrest inflation. All opposition was suppressed and the people were enrolled in tightly controlled organizations. Non-Communist intellectuals were subjected to a series of thought-reform movements designed to convert them to the official ideology which had been imposed upon every form of expression. An expedition, sent out to Tibet in 1950, brought that semi-independent region once more under effective Chinese control. By then Communist China had won recognition from most of the countries that recognize it today. The United States, however, was "waiting for the dust to settle" as the Nationalist government prepared for its last stand on Taiwan.

The outbreak of the Korean War (1950-53) brought about a radical change in the Far Eastern international situation. The United States sent its Seventh Fleet to patrol the Taiwan Strait, thus extending its unequivocal protection to the Nationalist regime. The entrance of the Chinese Communist army into the Korean conflict alienated world opinion and prevented its government from being admitted into the United Nations. Domestically, the Communists intensified their campaign against "counterrevolutionaries and reactionaries." In rural areas, large numbers of landlords and rich peasants were deprived of their properties, sent to labor camps, or executed. In the urban centers, merchants and industrialists were harassed by government regulations and by the Three-Anti and Five-Anti campaigns which were ostensibly aimed against corruption, tax evasion, and other forms of economic crimes. By the time of the Korean truce in 1953, the Communists had decided that the process of consolidation was over and that China was ready for a major political reorganization and the introduction of five-year plans.

In conjunction with the proposed First National People's Congress under the new constitution to be promulgated in 1954, the first modern national census was taken in 1953, claiming a Chinese population of 600 million, far in excess of previous estimates. The census was also a necessary step toward the inauguration of a planned economy embodied in the First Five Year Plan (1953-57). The major political reorganization preceding the adoption of the constitution was the abolition of the large regional administrations, thus making possible more centralized control of the Peking government over the provinces. The 1954 National People's Congress elected Mao Tse-tung (1893——) the first chairman of the People's Republic of China and Chou En-lai (1898——) became prime minister.

The Korean truce diverted Communist attention from the northwestern Pacific to Southeast Asia. Chinese military assistance turned the tide of battle in Indochina in favor of Ho Chi Minh, the Communist Vietminh leader. Their military position deteriorating rapidly, the French agreed to the Geneva Conference of 1954 which both ended the Indochina conflict and heralded the entrance of Communist China into world diplomacy. A year later, Communist China participated in the Bandung Conference of twenty-nine Asian-African countries, from which Nationalist China was excluded. A period of active contacts with these nations ensued, resulting in increasing diplomatic, cultural, and economic ties. Meanwhile, the Taiwan Strait had become the focus of military tension. Here Communist aggressiveness was confronted by determined resistance on the part of Chiang Kai-shek and his American ally. Since then the Communists have kept up the military pressure by intermittent bombardments of the Nationalist-held offshore islands of Quemoy and Matsu.

In order to fulfill its First Five Year Plan, the Peking regime initiated a series of collectivization movements which affected the entire social and economic structure of the Chinese mainland. The process of agricultural collectivization, accelerated since 1953, was completed three years later. Nationalization of industrial facilities proceeded at the same time and by 1956 the transformation of private commercial and industrial enterprises into state-owned or joint state-private enterprises had gained such momentum that private enterprises in China had practically been eliminated.

Events in Communist China in 1957 were influenced by upheavals elsewhere in the Communist bloc. Khrushchev's denunciation of Stalin in the Soviet Twentieth Party Congress was followed in China by a period of relative liberalization dubbed the "Blooming and Contending" movement (from the slogan "Let a hundred flowers bloom and a hundred schools of thought contend") when criticisms against party and government functionaries were allowed to be heard. However, in the wake of the Hungarian Revolution, the implications of which were fully understood by Chinese party leaders, an anti-rightist campaign was launched and attained full fury in 1957, its victims coming from every sphere of life. Ideological control over students and intellectuals was deliberately strengthened.

With the beginning of the Second Five Year Plan (1958-62) the Peking government decided to accelerate agricultural and industrial growth. This decision was implemented by the organization of communes which made possible the more efficient utilization of China's greatest asset—rural manpower. But the rapid changeover disorganized the country's distribution system and caused commodity shortages in the cities amidst claims of unprecedented production increases. Being more susceptible to centralized control, the communes subject the people to an even greater degree of government regimentation.

The communalization movement has been condemned by western public opinion and is looked upon as a dubious experiment even by Communist critics. Its inauguration damaged rather than enhanced Communist China's international prestige. In 1959 the Tibetan rebellion and the subsequent flight of the Dalai Lama to India exposed the inadequacy of China's nationality policy and aroused the suspicion of its Asian neighbors. Ten years after its establishment, it has not yet been able to gain admittance into the United Nations or eliminate the challenge of the Nationalist government on Taiwan. Nevertheless, it has wrought indelible changes on the land. China's huge natural resources are being tapped systematically, its industrial and military potentials are expanding rapidly, and its influence is being felt in international affairs.

It is not possible to forecast the future of the Chinese Communist regime although historians tend to claim for China a clear historical pattern which points to a certain sequence of changes. Out of disorder and division has come a strong, ruthless dynasty to unify the nation by arms, enforce peace, and reassert the military domination of China beyond its frontiers. After a relatively short interval the strong dynasty is overthrown, succeeded by one longer in duration and more moderate in character. Gradually this government loses power; the empire is again divided into a number of semi-independent states at war with one another; the people suffer privation and misery—until another strong dynasty reunites the empire to begin another cycle.

This configuration of China's historical progress, the alternation of strength and weakness, unity and division, internal peace and foreign invasions, is presented graphically in the accompanying chart of three thousand years of China's past.

A CHART OF CHINESE HISTORY

Legend (POLITICAL STRUCTURE):
- □ STRONG UNITY CENTRALIZATION
- ⊞ WEAK UNITY DECENTRALIZATION
- ▓ DIVISION

CENTURY	EXTERNAL RELATIONS	DYNASTIES (NON-CHINESE ITALICIZED)	POLITICAL STRUCTURE	INTERNAL DEVELOPMENTS
B.C. 1000-	Chinese Expansion	W. CHOU	FEUDALISM	
900-				
800-	Barbarian Invasions			
700-		E. CHOU		Rise of philosophic schools / Confucius and Confucianism / Taoism, Mohism, Legalism
600-				
500-				
400-		WARRING STATES		Coinage
300-				
200-	Chinese Expansion / Caravan Trade	CH'IN		Great Walls built / Peasant revolts
100-	Introduction of Buddhism	W. HAN		Establishment of bureaucracy / Confucianism as a state cult / Reforms of Wang Mang 8-23 A.D.
A.D 1-	Chinese Expansion			
100-		E. HAN		Peasant revolts (Yellow Turbans, etc.)
200-		THREE KINGDOMS		Beginning of the decline of the NW and growth of the SE
300-	Barbarian Invasions	W. CHIN / *BARBARIAN STATES* / E. CHIN		
400-	Beginning of Maritime Commerce	*WEI* / FOUR CHINESE DYNASTIES		Buddhism flourished
500-		*BARBARIAN STATES*		
600-	Chinese Expansion	SUI		Canal to Ch'ang-an

Timeline chart — Chinese dynasties and historical events

Date	Foreign/Western Contact	Dynasty	MONARCHY AND BUREAUCRACY
700	Foreign Religions / Foreign Invasions	TANG	Government and Civil Service examination system perfected
800			Golden Age of art and literature / Rebellion of An Lu-shan / Invention of Printing
900	Foreign Invasions	FIVE DYNASTIES / 10 STATES	Peasant revolts (Huang Ch'ao, etc.)
1000		LIAO / N. SUNG	Widespread use of paper money
1100	Foreign Ideas and Maritime Commerce	CHIN / N. SUNG	Reforms of Wang An-shih 1069-85
1200		S. SUNG	Capital transferred to coast / Neo-Confucianism, Chu Hsi
1300	Chinese Expansion	YUAN	Canal to Peking / Peasant revolts
1400	Naval Expeditions	MING	
1500	Foreign Invasions	MING	
1600	Europeans Came by Sea	MING	Peasant revolts
1700	Chinese Expansion	CH'ING	
1800	War with the West	CH'ING	T'ai-p'ing Rebellion, 1851-64 / Modernization and Reform
1900	Cultural Impact of the West / Two World Wars Soviet Influence	REPUBLIC	Revolution of 1911 / Nationalist government
		PEOPLE'S REPUBLIC	Communist government

3

GEOGRAPHY AND POPULATION

AN AREA OF FOUR MILLION SQUARE MILES and a population of well over six hundred fifty million people make China one of the largest and most populous countries in the world today. It compares favorably with the other Pacific nations in natural resources and geographical location. Though possessing an extensive coast line with many good harbors on the eastern seaboard, China developed as a land power rather than as a sea power, the fertile plains of North China being the historic center of Chinese expansion and influence.

Besides a certain resemblance in size and contour (see Outline Map of China Superimposed on the United States), China and the United States, lying largely in the same latitudes (25° N. to 45° N.), share a comparable, continental-type climate and vegetation. There is, however, a marked difference in topography. Whereas the United States, bounded by two oceans, tends toward an equal development of east and west, China expands from the loess highland and the central plains eastward and southward to the sea. In the northwest, China has a vast hinterland of deserts and plateaus screened off from Soviet Central Asia by high mountain ranges. The borders between southwestern China and India and Burma are as yet undelimited.

A majority of Chinese cities are found in the central, eastern, and southeastern areas favored by a temperate climate and gentle terrain. The west, though known to abound in natural resources, has remained only partially explored because of its adverse terrain and climate. Improved transportation and communications will doubtless change this development pattern. Exploration, irrigation, and reclamation projects in the northwest and southwest have been incorporated in the Communist government's five-year plans and the industrialization of Manchuria is fast transforming it into an area comparable to the northern New Jersey-New York complex.

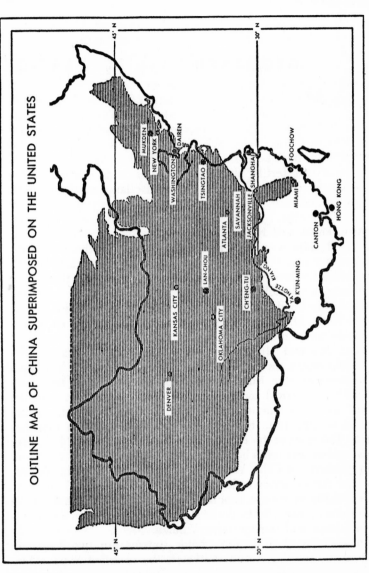

OUTLINE MAP OF CHINA SUPERIMPOSED ON THE UNITED STATES

Winfield, Gerald F., *China: The Land and the People* (New York: William Sloane Associates, 1948), p. 20.

Physical Setting

Extending over 2,500 miles from its Pacific coast to the Pamir plateau in Central Asia, China exhibits great variety in topographical relief. Surrounding the plateau of Tibet in the southwest are mountains the loftiest of which rise over 25,000 feet while some depressions in the Turfan basin in Sinkiang are 141 feet below sea level. The Mongolian plateau, the world's widest, stretches for a distance of over 2,000 miles. The desolate high plateaus in Tibet and Tsinghai (Kokonor), enclosed by mountain ranges, contrast with such rich lowlands as the Red Basin of Szechwan and the lake basins along the middle and lower Yangtze valley. Great fertile plains, particularly in the coastal delta area of the great rivers, are located amidst large masses of hills and uplands.

Mountains, Rivers, and Harbors

From the Pamirs, a central mountain knot of all the mountains of Asia, four major limbs of the Central Asia ramparts extend toward China. The Altai, T'ien Shan, Kunlun, and Himalayan mountain systems each consist of several parallel chains and form the chief watersheds of all the principal rivers in China. Their passes afford natural land routes between China and its neighbors in Mongolia and Central Asia.

The Altai and Himalayan systems form the natural boundaries of China in the northwest and southwest; the T'ien Shan divides Sinkiang; the Kunlun system branches all over the country, forming the backbone or skeleton of its topography. Running eastward from the Pamirs, the Kunlun system divides the Tarim basin of Sinkiang from the high plateaus of Tibet, then branches off into three separate chains: (1) the Altin Tagh–Nan Shan ranges in the north, which divide the inland drainage of the Mongolian plateau from the Yellow River; (2) the Tsinling–Ta-pieh ranges in the center, which form the major watershed between the Yellow River and the Yangtze; and (3) the Thanglha Ri range in the south, which meets the eastern end of the Himalayan system in Sikang and northwestern Yunnan.

In addition to these four major systems are two mountain groups in the northeast and southeast, the so-called Sinic mountains, which seem to have no direct relation to any of the major systems in the west. In between the mountains of the northern group are valley plains, such as the Chiao valley plain between

T'ai Shan and Lao Shan in the peninsula of Shantung; and the Sungari-Liao plain surrounded by Hsing-an Ling (Khingan), Ch'ang-pai Shan, and the Jehol hills in Manchuria. The southern ranges, the Nan Ling, form a major geographical divide between the lower Yangtze and the various short independent streams which flow separately into the southwestern China Sea.

Since the general topography of China orientates toward the east, all the great rivers flow eastward to the Pacific. In the northeast, the Amur (Hei-lung Chiang) drains a great part of the Manchurian basin as it winds along its 2,500-mile course. Though navigation is limited to small steamers and native craft, these can go as far as the confluence of its two upper reaches and even beyond during the flood season. Other Manchurian rivers include the Liao Ho, the chief river in southern Manchuria, as well as the Tumen and the Yalu, which form the boundary between China and Korea. Carrying very little ordinary shipping, the importance of the Yalu lies primarily in hydroelectric power development and in its timber traffic.

The main river of North China, and the second largest in the country, is the Yellow River (Huang Ho), which acquires its characteristic yellowish muddy color from the tributary rivers of the loess plateau of Kansu. From Kansu it winds 2,980 miles through the northern provinces eastward to Shantung where it empties into the Gulf of Chihli (Po Hai). The Yellow River valley includes an area of 600,000 square miles. Abundant silt and an almost unvarying water level limit its transportation capacity, creating as well a control problem. To keep the flow channeled, the Chinese have been continuously building up its embankments with the result that the present river bed is 16 feet or more above the general level of the surrounding plain, held to its course by man-made levees. Along its lower course, the Yellow River floods regularly, particularly in late summer and early autumn, and no important towns have grown up along its banks.

Central China is drained mainly by the Yangtze and its numerous tributaries. The Yangtze (Ch'ang Chiang) is by far the largest river in China. From sources only 50 miles (as the crow flies) from those of the Yellow River, it travels 3,237 miles, draining over 700,000 square miles. From the confluence of its two headwaters in the upland of southern Tsinghai, it flows southward to western Szechwan as the Chin-sha Chiang; then, beyond the great bend in northwestern Yunnan it turns sharply to the east and traverses the whole length of Central China to the East China Sea.

The Yangtze can be divided into three parts: a torrential upper course that includes many rapids and falls; a middle course of 960 miles, on parts of which (such as the Yangtze gorges) navigation is limited to junks and river steamers of no more than 200 tons; and a lower course of 1,062 miles navigable by both coastal and ocean-going vessels. On its way to the sea, the Yangtze is divided by the Ch'ung-ming Island into two channels. The southern channel, known as Wu-sung, has a deeper entrance closer to Shanghai, from which ocean-going vessels can sail up to Hankow, 630 miles inland.

In Central China, the Huai Ho and the Fu-ch'un Chiang are next to the Yangtze in importance. The Fu-ch'un Chiang is one of the main rivers along the Chekiang coast. The Huai, the largest river between the Yangtze and the Yellow, is unique in that it is the only long river without a natural outlet, and consequently it frequently floods.

Important rivers that drain the southeastern coastal regions are the Min Chiang and the Chu Chiang (Pearl River). The Min is navigable over most of its course although upstream navigation is rather difficult in the flood season. The Pearl, the chief river in Kwangtung and Kwangsi, is the fourth largest river in China and its valley covers a drainage area of 150,000 square miles. The Pearl is a general name for a network of three waterways, which meet south of Canton to form a big estuary consisting of many channels separated by a number of islets. The main eastern channel, Hu Men (Boca Tigris), enters the sea near Hong Kong, while the main western channel flows close to Macao.

Farther southwest are two independent rivers, the Mekong (Lan-ts'ang Chiang) and the Red River (Yüan Chiang), of which only the upper courses are in Chinese territory. Both flow southward through a large part of Indochina before entering the sea, but are unnavigable in China.

Pacific drainage accounts for 50 percent of China's total drainage area; inland drainage, 39 percent; and the Indian Ocean and the Arctic, the remaining 6 and 5 percents respectively. Today, with Outer Mongolia and Tannu Tuva independent, none of the Arctic drainage except a small portion of the upper Irtysh (one of the upper reaches of the Ob River) via the Zaisan Nor is in China Proper. Fairly long stretches of the upper reaches of the principal rivers of the Indian Ocean drainage are in China, but these rivers enter the sea through other nations' territories. The Salween (Nu Chiang), the Irrawaddy, and the Tsangpo (Ya-lu-ts'ang-pu) all have their sources in the mountainous regions of Tibet and western Szechwan. The Tsangpo flows eastward from its Himalayan home to drain southern Tibet, then bends abruptly south to India, where under the name of Brahmaputra it merges with the Ganges to empty into the Bay of Bengal. The upper courses of both the Salween and Irrawaddy drain a large portion of western Yunnan before they reach the sea by way of Burma.

Inland drainage covers a number of upland basins in the vast dry interior of North and Northwest China. Due to meager rainfall and difficult terrain, the inland rivers are as a whole rather small and lack outlets to the sea. They generally flow into lakes or die in the desert, most of them entirely inside China. The Tarim, the longest inland river in the country, consists of numerous streams coming down from the mountains in southern Sinkiang.

While the inland rivers are valuable for irrigation in the dry interior of northern and northwestern China, their water supply from the snow-clad mountains is rather limited. On the other hand, the upper courses of the Red River, Mekong, Salween, and Irrawaddy provide potential sources for the development of waterpower in the plateaus of Southwest China. There are too many torrents and rapids, especially in the summer monsoon season, to make navigation possible. No transportation is available along their courses except on some parts of the upper Red River, the upper Irrawaddy, and the east-west stretch of the Tsangpo, where small native craft are sometimes seen. At 12,000 feet the Tsangpo or upper Brahmaputra is the highest navigable river in the world.

The coast line of China extends from the mouth of the Yalu River in the northeast to the mouth of the Pei-lun River in the south. It forms a great arc with the peninsulas of Liaotung and Shantung in the north and that of Luichow in the south protruding respectively into the Yellow Sea and the South China Sea. The coast is separated from the Pacific Ocean by a chain of islands and archipelagos, such as Liu-ch'iu, Taiwan, Pescadores (P'eng-hu), Hainan, and the Pratas (Tung-sha), Paracel (Hsi-sha), and Spratly (Nan-sha) groups, which not only gives China a continuous series of partially enclosed coastal seas like the Gulf of Chihli, the Yellow Sea, the East China Sea, and the South China Sea, but also forms the two great gulfs of Liaotung in the north and Tonkin in the south.

The general configuration of the coast line comes to a length of 2,500 miles. If the minor inlets are included, the distance amounts to nearly 7,000 miles. Of this total, some 3,000 miles are sandy and the rest, rocky. The sandy coast is characterized by wide, relatively flat beaches on a shore line of long straight stretches coupled with sweeping curves. The adjoining country is often low and flat with marshes or lakes. Shoals and generally shallow water are usual along these sandy coastal areas although good natural harbors, as at Shanghai, can be found at the mouths of the larger rivers. In contrast, the rocky parts of the coast of China are often highly indented. Fairly deep seas broken by numerous islands and islets are characteristic of these coastal areas. Such conditions create many good natural harbors but the characteristics of the hinterlands, hilly to mountainous, limit the exploitation of these coastal features. Thus no port of importance has been developed except at or near the mouth of a large river, as at Canton. The big port planned for South China is to be situated at Huang-pu (Whampoa) on the estuary of the Pearl River.

Other ports of importance are An-tung at the mouth of the Yalu River, Port Arthur (Lü-shun), and Dairen (Ta-lien) on the Liaotung Peninsula. Port Arthur is the leading naval base and Dairen the chief commercial port of Manchuria. There are also three developed ports along the Shantung coast; Chefoo (Yen-t'ai) on the north; Wei-hai-wei, not far from the tip of the peninsula; and Tsingtao, lying on its southernmost part at the entrance to the bay. Farther south, numerous good harbors can be found all along the coast. Some of the moderately developed ports are Yin-hsien (Ningpo), Foochow, Amoy, Swatow, and Chan-chiang.

Climate

Although most of China lies inside the temperate belt, it has an extreme continental climate with a summer temperature (especially in Central and South China) higher than that of the tropics and a winter cold which in the far north is more severe than in the frigid zone. In winter the temperature decreases rapidly from south to north, ranging from an average of 60° F. south of the Nan Ling range to about 40° F. along the middle and lower Yangtze valley, to just below freezing or about 30° F. in the North China plain and southern Manchuria, and to well below freezing at about 0° F. and −17° F. in central and northern Manchuria respectively. In summer the temperature is more nearly uniform over the whole country, with a July mean of 80° F., but northern China has much cooler nights and a shorter hot period than southern China.

Rainfall is essentially seasonal, most of it occurring in the summer. The amount of precipitation decreases from south to north, with an annual average of 60-80 inches in the Pearl River valley and the hilly land along the southeastern coast, 40-60 inches in the Yangtze valley, about 25 inches over the North China plain, and less than 10 inches in the interior. To the northeast, in the Manchurian basin, the rainfall varies from about 30 inches in southeastern areas to less than 10 inches in the Barga district and the eastern Gobi.

Most of the late summer rain along the southeastern coast is due to typhoon influence. Typhoons bring some cooling, a temporary relief from the prolonged summer heat, but also cause damage to crops and to a considerable degree determine the type planted. The crops grown along the southeastern coast of China are therefore predominantly low standing—peanuts and sweet potatoes are common—in preference to higher standing crops that would be more easily damaged by typhoons.

Soils

The soils of China can be classified into three main groups: nonacid or sweet soil in the north, acid soil in the south, and neutral soil in the central area. The leaching effect of the nonacid soil is weakened by flat topography, low annual rainfall, and limited irrigation whereas the acid soil of the south is subjected to leaching by hilly terrain and abundant rainfall. For climatic reasons more crops are raised in the southern regions where the soil is poor than in the northern areas where the soil is rich. The nonacid soil region represents the wheat area, and the acid soil region, the rice area.

The transitional belt of neutral, slightly acid soil includes western Hupeh, southern Shantung, the Yangtze delta, and northern Szechwan. The deltaic plains, both north and south, such as the lower Yangtze valley plain and the Pearl River delta, are all only slightly leached, contain a fair percentage of calcium and other soluble minerals, and are quite fertile.

Broadly speaking, the productivity of the land in China corresponds to the distribution of the population. The populous areas are the valley plains of the winter wheat and millet area (the loess plateau of Northwest China), the winter wheat and kaoliang

area (the North China plain and Shantung highland), the Szechwan rice-growing area (Red Basin), the rice and wheat area (the
lower Yangtze valley plain), and the double-cropping rice area
of the Pearl River delta. The Yangtze delta and the Red Basin of
Szechwan, which have slightly leached and weak acid soils, are
the most densely populated areas.

Political Divisions

Politically, China is divided for administrative purposes into a
number of provinces and autonomous regions (see the map, Political Divisions, 1959). The eighteen provinces of China Proper
south of the Great Wall were the core of Chinese political influence, which later extended to the border regions of Manchuria,
Mongolia, Sinkiang, and Tibet. Together they constitute what is
generally known as Greater China.

At present there are seventeen provinces in China Proper. In
the north are the four provinces of Hopeh, Honan, Shansi, and
Shantung. In the northwest are the two border provinces of Shensi
and Kansu. In Central China are the four provinces of Anhwei,
Kiangsi, Hupeh, and Hunan; to the east, the two provinces of
Kiangsu and Chekiang. In the southwest interior are the three
provinces of Szechwan, Yunnan, and Kweichow. In South China
are the two coastal provinces of Fukien and Kwangtung; Kwangsi,
formerly a province, has been made into an autonomous region of
the Chuang people.

Some of the outlying regions of Greater China have become
provinces, while others have more recently been made into autonomous regions. In Manchuria are the three provinces of Liaoning,
Kirin, and Heilungkiang. At the western end of Kansu is Sinkiang,
also known as Chinese Turkestan; formerly a province, it is now
an autonomous region of the predominant Uigur population.
Southwest of Kansu is the province of Tsinghai, formerly a part of
Inner Tibet with a large Tibetan population. Sikang, formerly a
province carved out from Szechwan and Tibet, has lost its provincial
status and been incorporated into Szechwan. Preparations are
being made to incorporate Tibet as an autonomous region. The
Autonomous Region of Inner Mongolia consists of Chahar and
Suiyuan, parts of Jehol and Kansu, and the western part of Manchuria. Ningsia is now an autonomous region of the Hui people.
Outer Mongolia, formerly a Chinese dependency, has become
the Mongolian People's Republic. On the other hand, Taiwan (the

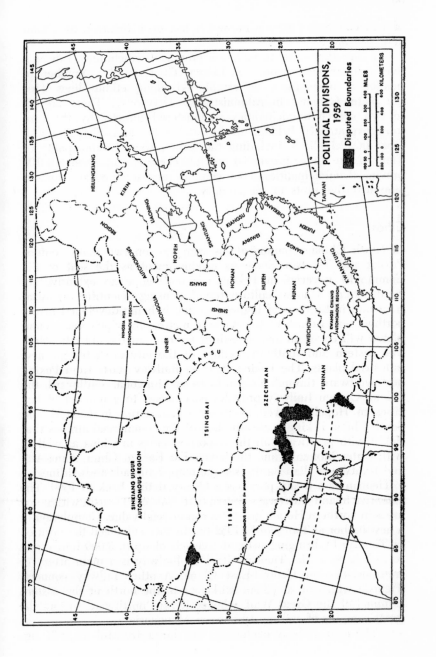

POLITICAL DIVISIONS, 1959

Disputed Boundaries

official Chinese name for Formosa) has been included as a Chinese province.

Today there are twenty-two provinces (including Taiwan), five autonomous regions (including Tibet), and a number of smaller autonomous areas established along ethnic lines (see the plate, Changes in Administrative Divisions). There are also two special municipalities administered directly by the central government; Peking, the capital city, and Shanghai. All other municipalities, including the former special municipality of Tientsin, are under provincial control. There are an estimated 100 provincial municipalities, 2,000 counties, and some 80 autonomous administrative units in the country.

Cities

In North China communications converge on two main centers, Peking and Tientsin. Since its establishment as the seat of the Communist government Peking has undergone an extensive reconstruction. A new "culture town" housing scientific organizations and institutions of higher learning is being developed in the northwestern suburb of this historic metropolis which when completed will cover an area one-third larger than the old city itself. The eastern and southern sections of the city are sites for new industrial plants. The Peking–Pao-t'ou Railway starts from Peking northwestward through Kalgan to Inner Mongolia. Southward, the Peking–Canton Railway provides easy access to a number of key cities in Hopeh as well as to important cities in Central and South China. Peking is also the hub of the commercial airlines that link it with practically all the important cities in China as well as with Outer Mongolia and the Soviet Far East at Chita, Alma-Ata, and Irkutsk via Ulan Bator (see the map, Railroads and Airlines).

Tientsin as a treaty port has a history dating back to 1860. The extensive inland waterways system that connects Tientsin with many areas in northern Hopeh gives it a commercial value. Completion of a new harbor at T'ang-ku in 1952 has further enhanced the position of Tientsin by bringing sea-going vessels of up to 3,000 tons direct to its wharves. The Tientsin–P'u-k'ou Railway is a main artery of transportation in Central-East China. Another railway connects Tientsin with Lin-yü (Shan-hai-kuan) to the north at the eastern terminal of the Great Wall, whence it runs northward to join the great complex of railway systems in Manchuria.

The main railway centers of Manchuria are Mukden, Ch'ang-

CHANGES IN ADMINISTRATIVE DIVISIONS

During the 1930's   1959

The Original Eighteen Provinces

ANHWEI	KIANGSU
CHEKIANG	KWANGSI[a]
FUKIEN	KWANGTUNG
HONAN	KWEICHOW
HOPEH	SHANSI
HUNAN	SHANTUNG
HUPEH	SHENSI
KANSU	SZECHWAN
KIANGSI	YUNNAN

Manchuria

LIAONING	LIAONING
KIRIN	KIRIN
HEILUNGKIANG	HEILUNGKIANG

Inner Mongolia

CHAHAR	INNER MONGOLIA
JEHOL	AUTONOMOUS REGION
SUIYUAN	
NINGSIA	NINGSIA HUI
	AUTONOMOUS REGION

Outer Mongolia

(*Under nominal Chinese suzerainty*)	(*Mongolian (People's Republic*)

Tibet

TSINGHAI	TSINGHAI
SIKANG	(*Incorporated into Szechwan province*)
TIBET (*under nominal Chinese suzerainty*)	TIBET AUTONOMOUS REGION (*preparatory stage*)

Chinese Turkestan

SINKIANG	SINKIANG UIGUR AUTONOMOUS REGION

Taiwan

(*Japanese*)	TAIWAN (*province*)

[a] In 1958 Kwangsi was reorganized into the Kwangsi Chuang Autonomous Region, with the exception of a small area in the south which was incorporated into Kwangtung province.

Adapted from Cressey, George Babcock, *Land of the 500 Million* (New York: McGraw-Hill, 1955), p. 36.

ch'un, and Harbin, respectively the capitals of Liaoning, Kirin, and Heilungkiang. From Harbin, two trunk lines run eastward and westward to Siberia, the first to Vladivostok and the second through Hailar to Chita on the Trans-Siberian Railway. In southern Manchuria, many new industrial sites have arisen, notably the coal- and iron-mining areas of Fu-shun and An-shan.

Lan-chou, the key communications junction of China's vast but only partially developed Northwest, has become the chief link between China and Soviet Central Asia just as Harbin is the chief link between China and Soviet Siberia. Lying on the southern bank of the Yellow River, it can be reached from the other parts of China by highway, railway, and airline. The latter is the Peking–Alma-Ata Line that stops at Sian and Lan-chou before the long westerly flight across the deserts and oases of Sinkiang by way of Urumchi to its Alma-Ata terminal. There are also highways stretching out from Lan-chou westward across the national boundary to Russia (see the map, Major Highways). The Pao-t'ou –Lan-chou Railway connects Lan-chou with Inner Mongolia, the Hsi-ning–Lan-chou Railway links Lan-chou with Tsinghai, and the railway from Lan-chou to Urumchi in Sinkiang is now under construction.

In East China, Shanghai is by far the largest city. It is also the second largest in East Asia and ranks with New York, London, and Tokyo as a great commercial port. Since the Communist occupation it has lost some of its importance due to the shift of political power from Nanking to Peking and the decline of the foreign investments and influence that once made Shanghai the financial citadel of the nation. Nevertheless, Shanghai still remains the major commercial port and industrial city of East China. As the center of the country's light industry, particularly the textile industry, and increasingly of heavy industry, Shanghai has undergone much reorganization, and its northwest section is being developed into an industrial "city within a city." In foreign trade, Shanghai, situated at the mouth of the Yangtze, occupies an advantageous position in the flow of manufactured goods and agricultural products from China to the outside world and vice versa. There are three main routes inland from Shanghai: the Shanghai-Nanking Railway, the Shanghai-Hangchow Railway, and the Yangtze River. Farther inland from Nanking the river route extends west to Hankow and the rail lines extend north via P'u-k'ou to Tientsin and southwest to Wu-hu in Anhwei. From

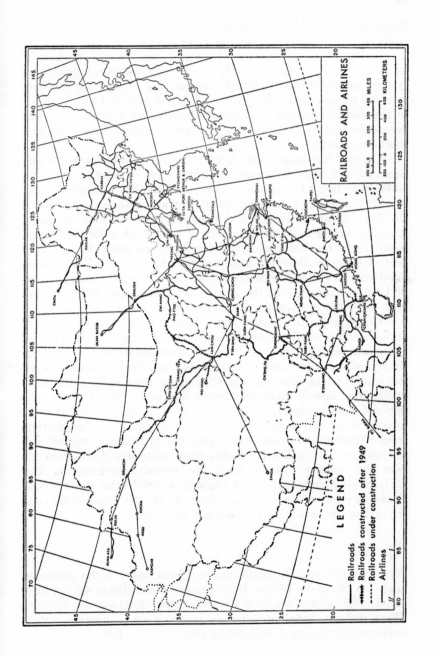

RAILROADS AND AIRLINES

LEGEND

— Railroads
━┿━┿━ Railroads constructed after 1949
┅┅┅ Railroads under construction
─── Airlines

Hangchow the Chekiang-Kiangsi Railway links the important cities in these two provinces to those of Central China.

The triple city of Hankow, Han-yang, and Wu-ch'ang—known as Wu-han—constitutes the hub of rail and water transportation systems in the heart of China. To the east and west of the Wu-han area ply steamers over the confluence of the Han and the Yangtze; to the north and south runs the Peking-Canton Railway that cuts across the entire length of the country to join Peking with the southern regions.

Canton, the largest and most populous southern city, is the financial and trade center of the hinterlands of South China. In addition to being the southern terminal of the Peking-Canton Railway, it is also the converging point of water transportation along the Pearl River. South of the city runs the Canton-Kowloon Railway that brings it to the doorsteps of the British colony of Hong Kong. Since the last century Canton has been the chief southern port of entry as Shanghai has been the chief port in East China. Western ideas as well as western goods first entered China by way of Canton and some of the earliest diplomatic and military contacts with the European powers took place here.

Chungking, the largest trade port in Szechwan, is located at the conflux of the Yangtze and the Chia-ling. Before the development of modern land and air transportation, the Yangtze River and its tributaries were the only practical trade routes in the southwestern interior, and Chungking from early times controlled the inland trade of eastern Szechwan. As a temporary national capital during World War II, Chungking expanded in area to three and a half times its original size and in population from 400,000 to over 1,000,000 as government agencies, educational institutions, and industrial plants were relocated there from all over the country. Today, with the recent completion of the Ch'eng-tu–Chungking Railway forming a link to the western half of the province, Chungking continues to be the commercial center of Szechwan and its neighboring provinces.

Population

Well over 650 million people live in China today if the estimates made on the basis of the 1953 census—a population of approximately 583 million and a 2 percent annual increase—are correct. These millions form an immense reservoir of manpower vitally important to the rapid industrialization of China but also generate

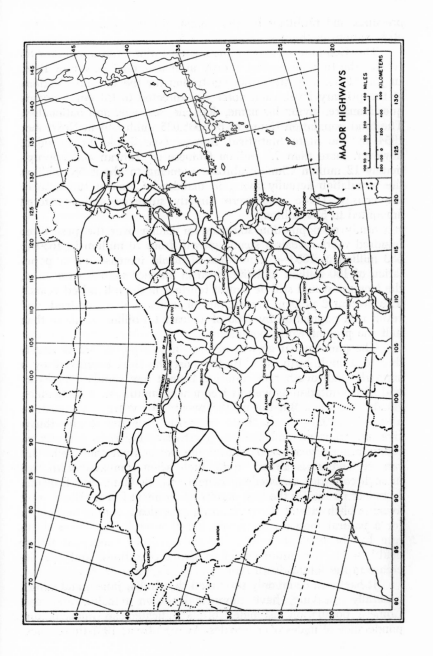

MAJOR HIGHWAYS

pressures and problems for the Communist regime as well as the other nations of the world.

The Communists began their preparations for a nationwide census, the first since 1909, shortly after assuming power in 1949. In June 1953, as part of the registration for the general elections at the primary level, each voter was directed to fill out a census questionnaire, giving his name, domicile, sex, age, and nationality. The total population figure of 601,938,035 published in November 1954 by the State Statistical Bureau (see Table 1) included, however, more than 7.5 million Chinese on Taiwan and approximately 12 million Chinese abroad, reducing to about 583 million the population actually living in mainland China at the time of the census. Those who were directly surveyed and registered amounted to 574 million.

Study of population statistics for China over the past three hundred years reveals a steady growth from 70 million in 1650 to 583 million in 1953—a more than eightfold increase. (If a population of 150 million in 1650, given in another source, were used, the increase would still be almost fourfold in three hundred years.) The present 2 percent annual rate of increase, if maintained, will result in a population by 2000 of at least 1.5 billion, or more than half the present world population.

The phenomenal growth of the Chinese population is largely due to a high birth rate. In the past this was countered by a similarly high death rate resulting from a low standard of living and poor sanitation as well as frequent calamities such as famines, floods, and wars. But during the twenty-two years of the Nationalist rule (1927-49) the birth rate was estimated to be thirty-five per thousand and the death rate twenty-five per thousand, representing a yearly net gain of ten persons per thousand. This rate of increase is already quite high when compared with that in such countries as Sweden, Switzerland, Belgium, and England. In one of its studies the Communist government has set the present average birth rate at thirty-seven and the death rate at seventeen, for a natural increase of twenty per thousand. The lower death rate has been attributed to the government's successful public health work, the improvement in living conditions, and the decrease in the infant death rate.

It has been commonly presumed that India, Japan, and China, generally speaking, have more males than females, and past Chinese population estimates often indicated an unusual preponderance of males over females. As recently as 1927 the Chinese government, in a population report of twelve provinces, showed the sex ratio to be 124 : 100. Previous investigations revealed an even greater excess of males. This may be due in part to the traditionally low position of women in society, which used to lead to the abandonment of baby girls, but may also reflect the tendency not to report females, especially young ones, in past years. The nearly equal sex ratio of recent years is therefore one indication of the new social status enjoyed by women. The 1953 census, covering a directly registered population of 574 million, reports 297,553,518 males and 276,652,422 females, a sex ratio of 107 : 100, much lower than any previous ratio. It agrees, however, with the normal distribution of sexes among many other peoples and there seems to be little doubt of its validity.

Of the 574 million Chinese, 338,400,000 persons belonged to the age group of eighteen and over, constituting 59 percent of the total registered population. Of this group 1,850,000 persons were eighty to ninety-nine years old; 3,384 had reached the age of one hundred or more, the oldest recorded age being one hundred fifty-five (sex not given). On the other hand, 235,200,000 persons belonged to the age group of seventeen and under, constituting 41 percent of the total registered population. Of this group 89,500,000 were children up to four years of age, 63,100,000 were between five and nine, and 82,600,000 were from nine to seventeen. With forty-one persons out of every one hundred in the seventeen-and-under group, the source of China's manpower in the next few decades will be very large indeed.

The life expectancy of the Chinese has never been very high. Judging from the results of recent sample studies, the life expectancy of the present-day Chinese at birth is 31.9 for males and 34.2 for females; at the age of 20 the figures are 35.6 and 39.3 respectively; at 40 they are 23.5 and 25.6; at 60 they are 11.5 and 12.1. Compared with other Asian nations, life expectancy in China is slightly higher than in India, but less than in Japan.

A comparison of the age compositions of the populations in China and in the United States reveals a general similarity in age distribution for the group between five and fifty-four, and life expectancy figures within this group seem to be much the same in both countries. There are important differences, however, in the four or under and fifty-five or over categories. A higher Chinese birth rate, even though offset to a certain extent by a higher infant mortality rate, results in a much higher proportion of infants four years old or younger in the Chinese population. The United

States population, on the other hand, reflects a longer life expectancy at fifty-five and over in a higher precentage of people in this age group.

Migrations

In an agricultural country with poor transportation facilities population mobility is reduced to a minimum. In addition the Chinese have an attachment to their ancestral homesteads and family traditions that makes them almost immobile. In past centuries only civil wars, foreign invasions, and natural calamities sent large groups wandering from one part of the country to another in search of food, shelter, and relief. Sometimes economic inducement and the lure of official promotion prompted the young and able-bodied to seek their fortunes away from home, but on the whole the percentage of such voluntary migrations was rather small and often such migrants eventually returned to their native villages.

Three major population movements took place in the twentieth century prior to 1949. First, there was a rural to urban movement which had been in progress for several decades and which became intensified as a result of the growth of treaty ports such as Shanghai, Tientsin, Hankow, and Canton into modern cities. With the steady inflow of foreign capital, the establishment of factories and schools, the concentration of banking and other financial institutions, the facilities of modern communications systems, as well as the protection that foreign concessions provided for their inhabitants during the time of China's numerous civil wars, these port cities grew rapidly in size and population, fed by a continuous stream of migrants from the villages.

Then there was a migration from the thickly settled agricultural communities in North China to the frontier regions of Manchuria, Inner Mongolia, and Sinkiang, a movement that had started in the late nineteenth century. As soon as restrictions on migration were removed in the last years of the Manchu government, large groups of hard-pressed Chinese peasants from the northern provinces of Shantung, Honan, and Hopeh flocked to Manchuria to cultivate its fertile soil and to settle down as agricultural colonists. As a result large cities began to grow in Manchuria during the early years of the Republic. The Japanese invasion and occupation of Manchuria (1931-45) put a temporary halt to this migration, but it was resumed after the war, though on a smaller scale and for different motives. Migrants from the interior also ventured to the vast but sparsely populated northern frontier, comprising the steppes of Chahar and the irrigated fields of Kuei-sui, Ho-t'ao, and Ningsia along the Yellow River bend, and extending as far west as the oasis of the Kansu corridor, the upland pastures of Tsinghai, and the Tarim basin. Here pioneer Chinese farmers and traders penetrated into regions of the nomadic peoples.

The loss of the coastal provinces and urban centers to the Japanese during the war (1937-45) effected a third large-scale exodus of the Chinese population, this time to the southwest hinterlands. Most of the wartime refugees were well-to-do people and wage earners of all types and ages. No reliable statistical data are available on the total number of persons who were involved in this migration, though there must have been at least three and a half million people from the twenty-four large cities under Japanese occupation. In addition, about another eleven million workers from all parts of the country emigrated from their native lands. By and large these immigrants were drawn from the urban areas of the country and their contribution to the cultural, economic, and industrial development of the southwest interior was immense and lasting even after their rehabilitation at the end of the war.

Since the establishment of the Communist government in 1949, the nature of the migration movement has changed in the following directions: (1) A systematic effort is being made by the government to relocate the population and to reverse the rural-urban trend by encouraging the unproductive city dwellers to return to the countryside. (2) There is a definite government policy to colonize the frontier regions of Greater China and to use the colonizers in large-scale construction work and industrial projects. (3) Because of this policy, the migration movement is mainly government-sponsored, and there have been voluntary as well as involuntary migrations; in addition to economic inducements, the government uses mass persuasion, patriotic appeals, and, not infrequently, pressure or force. (4) The composition of the migratory groups has undergone a radical change from a hitherto overwhelmingly rural population to the present combination of farm hands, industrial workers, and demobilized soldiers. This is particularly true of the migrants to Manchuria and Kansu.

According to scattered reports in the press, not only have farmers moved from Shantung to Manchuria as in the early decades of the present century, but urban workers from the coast, such as engineers, managerial personnel, and factory workers, both skilled and unskilled, also have been transferred through special government efforts to the frontier regions in Manchuria, Kansu, and Sinkiang. This population movement has been continuing at an accelerated pace.

Along with the labor force, students have been recruited to act as technicians, organizers, and activists in these industrial enterprises. Young college graduates, both men and women, are encouraged to apply for jobs in undeveloped areas though the work assignments and destinations are entirely in the hands of government authorities. While many young people with a patriotic drive or thirst for adventure may have voluntarily asked to be sent to some distant region, it is quite probable that there have been also those who, because of fear of being ostracized and branded as bourgeois comfort seekers, felt compelled to take the job assigned them.

Another source of manpower in the development of the frontier regions is army colonization and forced labor camps. As repeated press reports indicate, the army has been tilling the virgin land on a fairly large scale for some years in Sinkiang and Heilungkiang. The regulations concerning forced labor published in 1954 and the comments of public security officials do not conceal the fact that similar reclamation work is being undertaken on the vast wastelands of the Northwest by forced labor, probably under the direction of the army.

In addition to directing these internal population movements, the Communist government has also been active in an effort to facilitate the homeward journey of the overseas Chinese, particularly those who are well-established and influential in their own communities. These people are important in the Communist propaganda efforts to win the loyalty of the Chinese abroad from the Nationalist government on Taiwan. Among those responding to the call of the "Fatherland" or lured by offers of government positions have been some rich financiers like "rubber king" Ch'en Chia-keng (Tan Ka-kee) from Singapore, but most are intellectuals, engineers, and technicians whose training in foreign countries assures their useful employment in the industrial development of the country. A sizable number of young men and women have returned to China for advanced education, while many small businessmen came back after promises of financial rewards. In spite of complaints by those who found the Communist way of life unsatisfactory and have since left the mainland, propaganda for such migration has been widespread among Chinese communities in Southeast Asian countries, particularly in Singapore, Thailand, Indonesia, and the Philippines.

There also has been a counter movement of external migration of Chinese intellectuals from the mainland to foreign countries. A large exodus took place at the time of the Communist victory in 1949, when an estimated two million civilians and 700,-000 military personnel evacuated to Taiwan with the Nationalist government. Another large group sought refuge in Hong Kong, while a small number, mostly intellectuals and former government officials, managed to come to the United States. This voluntary exile of western-trained intellectuals, while insignificant numerically, has caused a shortage of trained personnel for the first few years in China's educational and technical fields which the present regime in Peking has been trying to remedy.

Population Problems

The most serious problem confronting the Chinese Communist government today is overpopulation in both the big cities and the thickly settled farming areas of the North China plain and the Yangtze delta. Based on total area, the average population density of China, 160 persons per square mile, would hardly indicate overcrowding. The picture becomes different, however, if the much more meaningful figure (for an essentially agricultural country) of population per square mile of cultivated land is used. The density of the North China plain, in these terms, is from 800 to 1,200; of the Yangtze delta, where overpopulation is critical, as much as three times the densities recorded for the North China plain. The fundamental cause of this overcrowding of agricultural areas, a scarcity of cultivated land, is apparent in the figure for China as a whole: 1500 persons per square mile of cultivated land or about 0.4 acre per person.

In the big cities population has increased rapidly in recent years in spite of the efforts of the government to return the unemployed and others to the villages. An analysis of the report of the State Statistical Bureau indicates that from 1949 to June 1953, the total urban population increased by 35 percent, with the result that the population in some cities like Shanghai, Peking, Tientsin, and Mukden had grown to 6.2 million, 2.8 million, 2.7 million, and 2.3 million respectively. Other cities with more than one million population are Canton, Nanking, Harbin, Lü-ta (Port Arthur and Dairen), Wu-han, and Chungking. According to more recent information, in Shanghai alone, for example, the population increased to seven million by 1957. In the meantime, other industrial centers, especially in Manchuria, have sprung up and their populations have doubled in the same period. With the industrialization program going at full speed during the two five-year plans, the trend toward an increase in the number and size of industrial centers will continue unabated. The crucial problem is to feed this growing urban population.

To be sure, China has not yet reached the ultimate stage of overpopulation since its arable lands have not all been brought under the plough, nor have all its natural resources been developed. In the past, however, the farm land per capita was so extremely small that the average yield in normal years was barely sufficient for a meager living for the tillers, with no surplus left over for the frequent bad years. The recent increases in food production, provided that the year is good, may be sufficient to meet the demands of the population and even leave a surplus for export. Nevertheless, living conditions have not noticeably improved and the problem remains serious as long as the people's livelihood is dependent mainly upon an agricultural economy that can barely support the total population.

The Communist government's efforts to meet this problem, by moving people from overcrowded cities to less densely settled farming areas, have met considerable difficulties. In 1952, for instance, 130,000 city workers were sent back to the villages, but the registration of unemployed city workers revealed a sudden influx the same year of poor farmers to the cities. Ultimately, the Ministry of Internal Affairs had to forbid the peasants to go to the cities to seek employment, but later reports showed that nothing was able to stop effectively the steady movement of the people from the village to the city and vice versa. In Manchuria, a similar flow of peasants to the cities led to a conference of government officials in Mukden in early 1955 to discuss the situation, and special party cadres were organized to persuade and escort the peasants back to their villages. These measures were apparently far from effective. In January 1958 new regulations were adopted by the government to control population movement, especially the infiltration of peasants into the cities.

External migration to foreign lands has been considered a possible partial solution to the population problem. During the past century economic pressures forced many Chinese from the coastal regions of Kwangtung and Fukien to seek their fortunes abroad, particularly in Southeast Asia, where they engaged in trade and farming, often building up large, prosperous communities of Chinese settlers. Many of the areas to which the Chinese traditionally emigrated are now closed to them, however, and the overseas Chinese in Southeast Asia who retain a dual citizenship and continue to be loyal to their homeland have considerable difficulty with the governments of these countries.

Essentially, the solution of China's population problem must be sought within the country itself but outlets for internal colonization in the frontier regions of the northeast, northwest, and southwest are also limited. In the recent past Manchuria had received immigrants from North China, averaging one million a year. At this rate it too will begin to feel the pressure of population. In the dry interior of Northwest China openings for reclamation and colonization depend in a large measure upon irrigation projects not yet realized. Although the climate of the southwestern hinterland is much more favorable for plant growth, there is a shortage of arable land due to the mountainous topography.

In recent years the Communist government has encouraged birth control. The question of planned parenthood was discussed in newspapers as well as in government councils, and high government officials—such as the Minister of Public Health—publicly advocated its promotion. Side by side with other Communist drives, a birth control campaign was launched in 1957 with exhibitions of methods and equipment and free distribution of birth control literature; clinics were reported to have been crowded with people seeking advice. The movement was, however, largely restricted to urban areas with the industrial worker as its main target. In the countryside, among the more conservative farming population, such antitraditional measures were not readily accepted. Resistance against birth control grew not only among the people but also among influential Communist groups. In 1958, probably because of ideological considerations, the Communist regime reversed its policy and, instead of stepping up mass persuasion and education concerning birth control, openly condemned those who subscribed to the Malthusian theory, and claimed that, under socialism, population increase would provide the nation with greater manpower and therefore should not be checked. Whatever the official attitude, there can be little doubt that the population problem in China remains crucial and that none of the Communist measures to relieve the population pressure in China have so far proved to be successful.

ETHNIC MINORITIES

THE CHINESE COMMUNISTS use the term "minority nationalities" to designate ethnic minorities within the People's Republic of China. A minority nationality is defined as a community of common origin, bound together by a common language, a continuous area of residence, and a sense of group identity in economic and social matters as well as in standards of behavior and other distinctive traits. Physiological elements are considered secondary although marked physical differences exist between the various nationalities in China.

In the past the Han-Chinese attitude toward the non-Han ethnic groups was that of the bearers of a high civilization toward primitive tribal peoples. Steeped in age-old prejudice, the Han-Chinese had formed misconceptions based largely upon incorrect and improbable tales rather than on their own observations and personal contact.

In recent years, however, a significant change has taken place in the Chinese attitude toward the minority peoples. During the Nationalist administration a minimal effort was made to allay the traditional Han-Chinese prejudice toward these groups, to discourage categorization of them as "barbarians" and "aborigines," as well as to assimilate them into the national norm.

While also trying to minimize group divergences, the Chinese Communists have recognized that at the present stage the millions of minority peoples can achieve social and cultural progress only in their own accustomed patterns and habits of living. Present efforts are therefore concentrated on bringing the leaders of the ethnic groups into closer association with the government and on training the minority youths in Chinese schools and universities to undertake the task of social and economic transformation among their own people. In economic, cultural, political, educational, and public health activities, the Communist government endeavors to diminish the differences among the groups without trying actually to absorb them into Han-Chinese culture. The goal of Communist nationalities policy is to remove the factors that had for centuries caused them to defy the central government and, through better communications and direct contact, to bring them under effective control. The government has, however, shown by its recent suppression of the Tibetans that it will not tolerate more than a mild degree of resistance among these groups.

Classification and Distribution

There are probably few areas in the world where so many ethnic groups have lived together for so many centuries as in China. These groups, distributed over a wide area both in the hinterlands and the border regions, have undergone a complicated historical process of migration, assimilation, and transformation. Moreover, designations for these people have changed from time to time, making it difficult sometimes to trace the origin of particular groups or to keep track of their movements from one region to another.

The minority nationalities, constituting about 6 percent of China's 650 million population, are concentrated mainly in seven border regions: (1) Manchuria; (2) Inner Mongolia; (3) Sinkiang, Tsinghai, and Kansu; (4) Tibet; (5) Szechwan, Yunnan, and Kweichow; (6) Kwangtung and Kwangsi; and (7) Taiwan (see the map, Minority Nationality Areas). Ten of the non-Han ethnic groups have a population from one million to over six million (see the plate, Larger Minority Nationalities in China). Among them, the Koreans in Manchuria are immigrants from Korea; the Manchus, who were of Tungus origin, have become completely Sinicized; and the Hui, descendants of Turkic-Uigur soldiers and merchants who moved to China more than a thousand years ago, have lost much of their racial identity through intermarriage with the Han-Chinese. Aside from these, the more important and distinctive non-Han ethnic groups in China are the Mongols, the Uigurs, the Tibetans, the Miao-Yao, the Chuang, the Yi, and the Puyi.

The Mongols constitute the major ethnic groups on the Mongolian steppes and are divisible into three groups: the Eastern

Mongols, the largest group in Inner Mongolia, related to the Khalka of Outer Mongolia; the Western Mongols, or Oirat; and the Northern Mongols, or Buryat. Small numbers of Mongols are found in Sinkiang, Manchuria, and Kansu. Other ethnic groups in Inner Mongolia include the Daur, Orochon, Yakut, Solon, and Tungusic immigrants from Manchuria. All are relatively unimportant numerically.

The Uigurs (New Uigurs, or Eastern Turks) live mainly in the southern part of Sinkiang and generally call themselves after the names of their adopted cities. Other groups in Northwest China include the Hui, Kazak, Kirghiz, Monguor, Tadjik, Tatar, and Uzbek.

The Tibetans are distributed principally in Tibet and in the Chamdo region of Szechwan; some are found in Tsinghai and Kansu, where their neighbors include the Monguor, Salar, and Turki.

The Miao and Yao, though not closely related, are often classified together. They constitute one of the most important groups in South and Southwest China. The Miao are distributed widely over the mountainous areas of Kweichow and Yunnan in the west to Hunan, Kwangtung, and Kwangsi in the central south. The Kwangtung group, located on Hainan Island, is descended from Miao soldiers brought there centuries ago by the Chinese government to quell the rebellious Li. The Miao are subdivided into such groups as the Red, Black, Blue, White, and Flowery Miao. The Yao inhabit the mountainous regions of Kwangtung and Kwangsi.

The Chuang, numbering over six and one half million, constitute the largest of the ethnic minorities in China. This Thai-speaking group is located principally on the plains and in the valleys of western Kwangsi.

The Yi (Lolo) are located principally in the Liang Shan area on the borders of Szechwan and Yunnan.

The Puyi (Chungchia) are distributed in low marshy areas around Kuei-yang and in southwestern Kweichow province.

Many of these minority nationalities are indigenous groups that settled in their homes in ancient times; others moved to their present locality only in recent centuries. Although their migratory routes were different, they seem to have followed a general southward movement from the deserts and plateaus of the north to the Yellow River plains, or from the central south and southwest regions toward the tropics. While northern groups like the Mongols, Manchus, and Tungus have repeatedly pressed southward and have just as often been pushed back to their original abode by the Han-Chinese, southern groups such as the Thai and Miao penetrated beyond the Chinese national boundary into Burma, Indochina, and Thailand.

Languages

The non-Han languages of the minority peoples in China may be divided regionally into four major groups: Sino-Tibetan (south-west), Turkic (northwest), Mongol (north), and Tungus (north-east). The Mon-Khmer is the only linguistic group in Southwest China that does not belong to the Sino-Tibetan family. The latter includes, besides the Chinese, the following three groups: Kam-Thai, Miao-Yao, and Tibeto-Burman (see the plate, Languages of China in Chapter 5).

The Thai language, used by approximately nine million people, is closely related to Chinese. It is spoken by different ethnic groups in Kwangsi, Yunnan, and Kweichow with the result that there are a number of Thai dialects. These can be classified into two large groups: Northern Thai, which includes some of the Chuang dialects spoken in a great part of Kwangsi; and Southern Thai, dialects spoken mainly outside China.

In China, most of the Thai dialects have no scripts of their own. The only exceptions are a few dialects in Yunnan, which employ either the Shan alphabet, taken from Burmese, or an alphabet closely related to the one used by the speakers of the Southern Thai dialects. Both types of alphabet were originally derived from Hindu sources.

The ancient Thai language had four tones analogous to the four tones in the Chinese language. Each of these four tones was further divided into two groups according to whether the initial consonant was originally voiced or voiceless. Modern Thai dialects possess eight or more tones as a result of vowel development.

In one important respect, the Thai language differs from Chinese: adjectives in Thai, as in French, are generally placed after the substantives they modify.

Closely related to Thai and often classified together with it is a group of dialects known as Sui-Kam-Mak. Though sharing a common origin with Thai, the primitive Sui-Kam-Mak must have been separated from Thai very early and developed special features.

MINORITY NATIONALITY AREAS

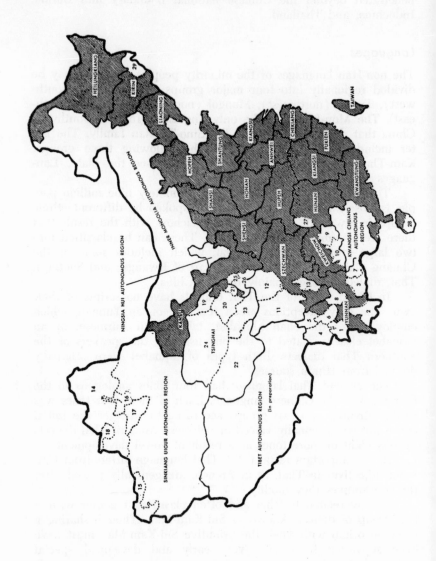

NATIONALITY AUTONOMOUS DISTRICTS (CHOU)

YUNNAN

1. Te-hung (Thai and Chingpo)
2. Hsi-shuang-pa-na (Thai)
3. Hung-ho (Hani and Yi)
4. Nu-chiang (Lisu)
5. Ti-ch'ing (Tibetan)
6. Ta-li (Pai)
7. Wen-shan (Chuang and Miao)
8. Ch'u-hsiung (Yi)

KWEICHOW

9. Southeastern Kweichow (Miao and Tung)
10. Southern Kweichow (Puyi and Miao)

SZECHWAN

11. Kan-tzu (Tibetan)
12. A-pa (Tibetan)
13. Liang-shan (Yi)

SINKIANG UIGUR AUTONOMOUS REGION

14. I-li (Kazak)
15. K'e-tzu-le-su (Khalka)
16. Ch'ang-chi (Hui)

TSINGHAI

17. Pa-yin-kuo-leng (Mongol)
18. Po-erh-ta-la (Mongol)

TSINGHAI

19. Hai-pei (Tibetan)
20. Hai-nan (Tibetan)
21. Huang-nan (Tibetan)
22. Yü-shu (Tibetan)
23. Kuo-lo (Tibetan)
24. Hai-hsi (Mongol, Tibetan, and Kazak)

KANSU

25. Lin-hsia (Hui)
26. Southern Kansu (Tibetan)

HUNAN

27. Western Hunan (Tuchia and Miao)

KWANGTUNG

28. Hainan (Li and Miao)

KIRIN

29. Yen-pien (Korean)

Peking Review, Vol. II, No. 21, May 26, 1959, p. 9.

LARGER MINORITY NATIONALITIES IN CHINA

Nationalities	Population	Distribution	Occupation	Language	Religion
Lisu	310,000	Northwestern Yunnan	Agriculture; animal husbandry and hunting	Lisu	Christianity and polytheism
Li	360,000	Hainan Island	Agriculture	No written language	Polytheism
Thai (Paiyi)	470,000	Southwestern and southern Yunnan	Agriculture	Thai	Buddhism
Hani	480,000	Southeastern Yunnan	Agriculture	No written language	Polytheism
Kazak	500,000	Northern part of Sinkiang Uigur Autonomous Region	Animal husbandry; some agriculture	Kazak	Islam
Pai (Minchia)	560,000	Ta-li and Chien-ch'uan hsien of Yunnan	Agriculture	No written language; some Chinese	Polytheism, some Christianity
Yao	660,000	Kwangsi, Hunan, Kwangtung, and Yunnan	Agriculture; some forestry	No written language	Polytheism
Tung	710,000	Area where Kweichow, Hunan, and Kwangsi meet	Agriculture; some forestry	No written language	Polytheism
Korean	1,120,000	Yen-pien area in Kirin	Agriculture	Korean	Buddhism, some Christianity
Puyi (Chungchia)	1,240,000	P'an-chiang valley in southwestern Kweichow	Agriculture	No written language	Polytheism
Mongol	1,460,000	Inner Mongolia Autonomous Region, Kansu, Liaoning, Kirin, and Heilungkiang	Agriculture; animal husbandry	Mongolian	Lamaism
Manchu	2,410,000	Liaoning, Kirin, Heilungkiang, Inner Mongolia and Peking	More or less similar to occupations of the Han people	Chinese (Manchu language no longer used)	Similar to religions of the Han people

Miao	2,510,000	Southeastern Kweichow and western Hunan	Agriculture	Miao	Polytheism
Tibetan	2,770,000	Tibet and western Szechwan	Agriculture; animal husbandry	Tibetan	Lamaism
Yi (Lolo)	3,250,000	Great and Little Liang-shan areas between Szechwan and Yunnan	Agriculture	Newly created Yi language	Polytheism
Hui	3,550,000	Ningsia Hui Autonomous Region and numerous places throughout China	Agriculture; some small business	Chinese	Islam
Uigur	3,640,000	Sinkiang Uigur Autonomous Region	Agriculture; some handicraft and commerce	Uigur	Islam
Chuang	6,610,000	Kwangsi Chuang Autonomous Region	Agriculture	No written language	Polytheism

Adapted from "Wu-kuo yu na-hsieh shao-shu min-tsu (What are some of the minority nationalities in our country)," *Shih-shih shou-tse* (Current Events Handbook), No. 17, 1956.

The language of the aboriginal Li people on the island of Hainan has not been adequately studied. It has been observed that the Li dialect is related to the Thai dialects, but the degree of relationship is in doubt.

The Miao-Yao language is spoken by more than three million people of the many primitive groups in mountainous areas throughout Southwest China. Formerly it was believed that Miao belonged to the Mon-Khmer branch of the Austroasiatic language family and that Yao was related to Thai. But recent studies have established the close relationship between Miao and Yao, as well as their position in the Sino-Tibetan family. Miao, for instance, resembles Chinese in that it is largely monosyllabic and has a number of tones.

A great number of dialects in southwestern China belong to the Tibeto-Burman group, spoken by at least three million people. Unlike other Sino-Tibetan languages, these dialects use the word order of subject-object-verb. Moreover, the tonal system is not as complicated as the others. Presumably, there were originally many consonant clusters both at the beginning and the end of the words. The qualities and combinations of these clusters may have contributed to the tonal development of these dialects.

The Tibeto-Burman languages can be divided into two major subgroups, the Tibetan and the Lolo-Moso. Tibetan is spoken in Tibet proper as well as in northwestern Yunnan by the Trung and Nung and in western Szechwan by the Jarung and Chiang. The earliest record in Tibetan language dates back to the ninth century when the Tibetan alphabet was first derived from the Hindu alphabet. A large amount of Tibetan literature, mainly Buddhistic, has been preserved.

In southern and western Szechwan, and throughout Yunnan and Kweichow, there are tribes like the Yi, Nahsi (Moso), Lisu, and others which speak somewhat similar dialects. This group usually has five or six tones. The Yi people have their own syllabic writing, used largely in religious texts. The Nahsi possess two systems of writing, one pictorial and the other syllabic, employed mainly by the priests. Several alphabetic systems for the Lisu dialect have been devised by westerners who have worked among the Lisu people in the Yunnan-Burma border. The language of the Minchia people who live in western Yunnan may possibly belong to this group. It shows a strong Chinese influence in vocabulary and probably in word order.

The Turkic, Mongolian, and Tungus peoples in the Altai Mountain region all speak languages which may be grouped together as Altaic. Although their relationship has not been definitely established, they have several features in common. For instance, unlike the Sino-Tibetan, these languages have inflectional elements but no tones.

The speakers of the Altaic languages are spread over a very wide area in Asia Minor, Central Asia, and Siberia, while only small groups of them are found in China. Turkic languages are spoken by some four million Kazak, Kirghiz, and Uigurs in Sinkiang as well as in scattered districts in Mongolia and Kansu. The Uigurs have their own script; the other groups use Arabic alphabets. The Mongolian languages are spoken by one and a half million Mongols in the Inner Mongolia Autonomous Region and by other Mongols outside China in the People's Republic of Mongolia and in Siberia. The Mongols use a writing system which they adopted from the Uigurs. The Tungus languages are spoken by two and a half million Manchus, Goldi, and others in northern Manchuria. The written language of the Manchus was derived from the Mongolian but today most of the Manchus have been completely Sinicized and, except for small groups in Kirin and Heilungkiang, no longer speak or write their own language.

Only very small groups of tribal people like the Wa, Puman, and Palaung (less than 100,000) along the Yunnan-Burma border speak the Mon-Khmer languages of the Austroasiatic family. Negligible in a general language map of China, the existence of the Mon-Khmer group serves to stress the fact that in the border regions are many minority groups who speak various languages, many of which have linguistic affiliations with peoples outside the political boundaries of China.

Cultural Features

Culturally the minority groups show considerable local variation. In the recent past some groups still retained elements of an aboriginal society, some reached the level of slave or feudal society, while others were so completely assimilated by the Han-Chinese that little trace of their original culture was discernible. Contemporary changes have further increased the complexity of the social and cultural nature of the minority peoples. But because information about these changes is scattered and inadequate for systematic presentation, the cultural patterns of the seven major ethnic groups described below relate only to the pre-Communist period.

The Mongols

Inner Mongolia, where most of the Mongols are found, is largely an elevated plateau surrounded by hills and valleys. Here the typical Mongol is either a nomadic pastoralist or, where soil conditions permit, a sedentary farmer. The relatively flat grassland of the plateau is especially suited to cattle raising but because of low and variable precipitation the pastoralist must be a nomad, wandering from place to place to find suitable pasturage for his horses, cattle, and sheep. These nomads live mostly in the western and southwestern parts of the region. In the spring they take their belongings and herds to good pasturage areas, divide the herds for grazing, and set up camp. Due to customary use families come to have a recognized right to certain pasture areas, but within these areas horses, cattle, or sheep are allowed to wander quite freely. As few as two herdsmen may be in charge of herds of as many as five hundred animals. During the long, severe winter of Inner Mongolia the herdsmen set up their tents on protected mountain slopes, and the animals are left to forage for themselves through the ice and snow.

The nomads' diet is based largely on animal products such as milk, cheese, mutton, and beef. Yurts—collapsible, portable felt-covered tents—serve as homes as well as store houses and even sometimes school rooms.

Sedentary Mongols, who considerably outnumber the nomads, live mostly in the southeastern part of Inner Mongolia. Strongly influenced by Chinese farmers who have infiltrated the area, they practice agriculture, following the Chinese pattern, and some live in Chinese-style mud houses grouped into villages or in clay yurt-like structures.

A third group, semisedentary Mongols, herd cattle as their dominant economic activity but engage in agriculture as a subsidiary occupation. They plant millet, kaoliang, and wheat in the spring, casting the seed over barely cultivated soil, and then give no more attention to the fields until harvest time.

The typical Mongol household is a patrilocal extended family, including elder parents, their married sons and wives, and their unmarried children. The extended family is the primary social and economic unit in Mongol society. Generally each nuclear family (husband, wife, and children) occupies a separate tent. Authority in the family rests with the father, but the mother directs the activities of the household.

No traces of a former clan organization remain, but a lineage system still functions to regulate marriage: people of the same lineage have the same surname and marry outside the lineage. The lineage is not a residence group, however, and a village or camp community may have representatives from several lineages. Aside from the two seasonal shifts annually made by entire nomad communities in the course of tending flocks and herds, individual families exhibit considerable mobility in moving from one community to another at any time during the year.

Personal relations within the family are close, but kinship ties outside the immediate family tend to be loose. Since kinship is not a cohesive force in the larger society there must be other social mechanisms for achieving integration. The visiting pattern is one of these. The country is crisscrossed by numerous well-defined routes, and visiting is very popular. In this arid plateau the scarce wells and water holes serve as important centers for social intercourse. Caravans and herdsmen gather in large numbers from time to time for religious observances and social activities. Social unity is also fostered by the custom of mutual aid and cooperative work projects, common in both pastoral and agricultural activities.

The Mongols are followers of Tibet Lamaism, and prior to the establishment of Communist rule, the lamas were a powerful and privileged class in Mongolian society. Lamas functioned in many sectors of daily life, and the monasteries were important social and economic centers.

There are a number of annual festivals, each retaining certain elements of pre-Buddhist religion; the most important, however, is the New Year celebration in the spring. While these festivals involve a good deal of religious ceremonial, they are primarily social gatherings and the occasion for large-scale economic activity.

The Uigurs

Sinkiang, enclosed on the north, south, and west by great mountain masses and on the east by a barren plateau, is largely desert, and the home of the Uigurs. The southern two-thirds of this area is the Tarim basin, one of the driest deserts in the world. The presence of oases makes agriculture possible, however, and this is the habitat of the sedentary farming Uigurs. The oases in the north consist of fringes of land in which rainfall-farming prevails. Farms, ranging from one to eight acres, surround each oasis, utilization of land depending on its proximity to the center of the oasis. Toward the center, cultivation of garden crops is intensive with use of night soil; outward from the center, the use of fertilizer decreases and hardier crops such as potatoes, millet, and kaoliang are grown. North of the T'ien Shan range winter wheat is an important crop and cotton is grown as a cash crop. Silkworms are raised south of the T'ien Shan.

The family group, living together under one roof, is the basic producing unit in this agricultural society and often includes married children. Despite pressure on the limited landholdings, such large families are considered desirable because the water available to a family depends upon the quantity of labor supplied in the cooperative irrigation enterprises. Families living in a single community are bound together not by kinship ties but by economic necessity. Irrigation agriculture, upon which the community depends for its existence, is based upon communal labor.

Islamic attitudes toward the family prevail among the Uigurs. The family is considered a basic aspect of human civilization, and marrying and raising a family a religious obligation. A family man is respected and esteemed; it is a disgrace for a woman not to have children.

Polygyny is permitted according to Islamic law, but the few who can afford two or more wives keep them in separate parts of town or even in different towns. The status of Uigur women is not as low as in some Moslem communities, and wives generally do not tolerate rivals.

Wealth gained through efficient irrigation and farming practices is the basis of Uigur class structure and the "landed gentry" holding title to fifty or more acres are at the top of the social and political structure. The small peasantry make up about two-thirds of the society. Though numerically small, the clergy and the merchants are an integral part of Uigur society, the merchants having become politically important.

Being Moslems of the Sunni sect, the Uigurs maintain ties with the rest of the Moslem world and feel themselves to be members of a world Moslem community. They are not, however, strict in their observance of ritual practices. Few persons among them perform the daily ablutions or regularly say the prescribed prayers. Few women wear the veil and many habitually go about unescorted. Dietary habits of Islam are followed to a certain extent, but alcoholic beverages are consumed freely.

Islam as practiced by the Uigurs retains much of the Uigur folk religion. Their Moslem shrines, found everywhere, betray in their names association with the older ancestral cult. The shrines are associated with the curing of disease and with childbirth, and many of the pilgrims are women. A strong belief in ghosts is evident and witchdoctors are among the chief medical practitioners. Elements of pagan festivals color the present-day Moslem celebrations. Diseases are attributed both to good and evil spirits, the latter identified with the Moslem jinns.

In addition to various mosque officials, there are two classes of Moslem clergy: the judges and priests, who perform judicial functions in addition to religious ones; and the mullahs. Any adult male who can read and write and who wears a turban is included among the mullahs.

The Tibetans

Two basic subsistence patterns, depending upon geographical environment, prevail among the Tibetans: one nomadic, the other sedentary. The nomadic herders occupy the northern plateau region, where they pasture their sheep and yaks for the greater part of the year, descending into the Brahmaputra valley for only the coldest months. Herds of a thousand sheep and two hundred yaks are not uncommon. From late spring until winter the herds are moved to successively higher pastures, the short growing season for each successive pasture necessitating such frequent shifts. Maximum cooperation is required to keep the herds together and to re-establish camp circles after each move.

Winter is a time for trading, for repairing equipment, for weaving yak hair cloth, and so on, as well as the occasion for intensified social life.

The farmers, comprising a great majority of the Tibetan population, work mostly as tenants on monastery lands or on the lands of nobles and other large landholders. The poor, sandy soils along the streams in the south and southeast of the country are fertilized mainly with human and animal excreta. Crop rotation and fallowing are known but are not systematically carried out. Rain often comes too late to be effective and irrigation practices are not efficient. The principal crop is barley, but turnips, potatoes, wheat, and millet are also grown, and peas are raised as fodder for horses. Some beef and dairy cattle are raised as sidelines, but they are generally poor and yields of milk and butter are small. These products, however, are much valued.

Other occupations among the Tibetans include those generally carried on by townspeople such as commerce, trade, handicraft, and government employment.

Several forms of marriage exist. Property and the problems of preserving it, preventing its division, and increasing it appear to be the factors determining the form chosen in any particular case. Variations include monogamy, fraternal polyandry, and polygyny. Although polyandry, in which one woman cohabits with several men, usually brothers, has attracted the most attention from the outside world, monogamy is the most common form of marriage in Tibet. In polygynous marriages the additional wives occupy separate tents.

The economic function of the Tibetan family is fundamental to its existence and contributes to its stability. Individual opportunities for sons are rare, and the frequency of migration and the need for close cooperation to exploit the scarce resources all act as cohesive factors. Sons desiring greater opportunities may, however, attach themselves to some nomad group.

Larger social groupings among the sedentary Tibetans differ from those of the nomadic Tibetans. The basic form of communal organization of the nomads is the encampment, or tent-circle, comprising a group of from five to eighty households, who band together for cooperation and protection. Within the encampment the households may represent related families. There is considerable mobility on the part of households from one encampment to another.

The sedentary community may be composed of a similar number of families living together, but in closely adjacent houses. Village organization is more rigid and there is a formally elected village headman, with a council of elders. Groups of villages may be organized into larger units, sometimes under the authority of a monastery. The village is a tight-knit organization, economically and politically. The Tibetans insist upon simultaneous group action, for example at planting or harvesting.

The noble class, whose members live largely in the cities, comprises the large landowners in Tibet. Included in the nobility are descendants of the families of former Dalai Lamas, descendants of those who have performed meritorious political or military service, and descendants of early monarchs.

The formal or state religion of the Tibetans is Lamaism, an

adaptation of Buddhism. Such concepts of Buddhism as karma, nirvana, transmigration, and reincarnation are thus basic to Lamaism. It is divided into two sects: the Red and the Yellow. The prevailing cult in Tibet is the Yellow Sect, of which the Dalai Lama is the *de facto* head. The Dalai Lama, whose residence was in Lhasa until he fled the Communist forces, was formerly also the political leader of Tibet. The Panchen Lama, who resided at Shigatse, has been elevated by the Communist government to the position vacated by the Dalai Lama. There has long been some rivalry between the two, and the followers of the Panchen Lama claimed that his spiritual powers rival those of the Dalai Lama. Both are reincarnations of their predecessors. When either dies the priesthood must determine in which newly born child he has been reincarnated. The reincarnation can occur anywhere, often in a peasant family, but such a family automatically becomes a member of the noble class.

The basis of Lamaism is the monastery system. Monasteries are found throughout Tibet, many of them housing upwards of five thousand monks, or lama priests. The priesthood has been estimated to comprise up to 20 or 25 percent of the total population of Tibet, which represents a huge drain on the available manpower. The monasteries often have colleges associated with them and serve both as centers of learning and as repositories of Buddhist literature.

Present-day Lamaism embraces elements of a much older religion, the Bon or Bon-pa. This was a shamanistic religion involving belief in nature spirits, evil spirits, practices of propitiation, and magic. Elements of this religion are still practiced among tribesmen more remote from the influence of formal Lamaism. Among these people, as well as among more orthodox Lamaists, illness is attributed to evil spirits and must be cured by magical means. Lamas sometimes cure illness by chanting sutras or ritualistic incantations. Divination or fortune telling is popular and takes numerous forms.

The Miao-Yao

Widely scattered in a variety of environments, the Miao and Yao exhibit considerable regional cultural variation. Certain cultural characteristics, however, are general throughout the area. The people are mainly agriculturists and their agricultural techniques and tools, as well as many items of material culture, have been influenced by centuries of contact with the Han-Chinese.

In Kweichow, where the Miao are most numerous, there is a scarcity of arable land and what there is must be used intensively. The higher mountain slopes are cultivated by age-old slash-and-burn methods. Such crops as corn, millet, barley, kaoliang, and beans are grown, but because double cropping is practiced the soil becomes depleted in about four years. Wet rice is grown on the scarce level land as well as on terraces along river banks and on lower mountain slopes. The higher terraces are laboriously cut into the sides of mountains and depend upon rainfall and subsoil seepage. Lower fields are irrigated by an elaborate system of bamboo pipes and steam-powered water mills. The total harvest in good years is barely adequate for subsistence while in bad years the people face starvation.

Cash crops include tea and tung oil seeds (which are sold to Chinese mills), tobacco, sugar cane, and indigo. Fishing is economically important and fish are caught by hook and line, nets, traps, and by poisoning streams. Some cows, horses, pigs, sheep, ducks, and chickens are raised.

Handicrafts include a variety of objects of bamboo—mats, hats, baskets, boxes, and fish traps. Women weave cloth and men have become silversmiths, blacksmiths, and carpenters. Surplus craft articles are sold. Farming, however, occupies by far the largest number of people.

Traces of former clan organization are said to remain among the Yao, but the Miao have no kin groupings larger than the family. Among these peoples, as throughout much of Southwest China, the nuclear family, consisting of husband and wife and their unmarried children, is the primary social unit. Perhaps due to scarcity of land, extended families are not formed and the nuclear family is the usual household unit. This family owns its fields, house, animals, and furnishings, and both men and women perform agricultural labor in the fields.

The predominant form of marriage is monogamy although concubines may be kept in separate household establishments. The Miao-Yao favor cross-cousin marriage, though among those Miao who have had intimate contact with the Han-Chinese there is a tendency to avoid marriage between families bearing the same surname. Children marry by the seventeenth or eighteenth year. Considerable sexual license is permitted young unmarried people: some Miao villages have youth houses in which young people can meet to sing and to establish liaisons.

Settlements are generally found on mountain slopes and along streams, usually far enough off main transportation routes to be inaccessible and highly defensible. Villages are surrounded by mud or stone walls. The houses, strewn irregularly along zigzag streets and alleys, have three or four rooms separated by pillars rather than walls and include stalls for domestic animals as well as storage rooms for grains.

The Miao have two parallel religious systems, which they distinguish as the native and the "guest" (Chinese) religions. Each has its own sphere, its own priesthood, its own ritual, and there is no conflict involved in practicing elements of both religions.

A belief in supernatural beings pervades Miao life. All are referred to generically as ghosts, whether they be ancestral spirits or nature spirits. Extraordinary phenomena are attributed to the workings of the spirit world.

Of the numerous ghosts in the Miao religion, at least forty are the objects of special ritual observances. The rituals and ceremonies, over half of which are of Chinese derivation, are quite elaborate in many cases, involving a large body of paraphernalia and a long succession of precise activities including animal sacrifice. Some of these rituals are performed at routine intervals for general purposes, others only when something particular is sought. Thus spirits may be propitiated as a cure for disease, for safe childbirth, to prevent disaster, and so on. Elements of religion and magic are inextricably interwoven in most rituals.

Nearly every Miao village has one or more shrines to an earth god. Special rituals are performed there twice annually, and this earth spirit is propitiated frequently for protection against wild animals.

The soul is believed to leave the body during sleep. Sickness is caused when a man's soul is enticed away by a spirit. At death souls ascend to the skies, where some become evil spirits.

The Chuang

No systematic ethnographic study of the Chuang is available, material on their culture being fragmentary. They have become thoroughly assimilated to the Han-Chinese and are not easily distinguishable from them. In some of their customs, however, they more closely resemble the neighboring Miao groups.

The Chuang are largely sedentary agriculturists like their Chinese neighbors and have adopted many Chinese farming practices, particularly wet rice agriculture on irrigated fields. The water buffalo is used in plowing but is more important to the Chuang as a measure of wealth than as a means of production. Chuang settlements are generally situated near water and their dwellings are elevated on piles or stilts.

A clan organization regulates marriage although clan exogamy is not as rigid as among the Han-Chinese. Marriage is arranged with the services of a middleman and is usually performed at festival times. The bride remains with her parents until a child is born, and only then goes to live with her husband. Polygyny was quite common in the past.

Little has been recorded of religious beliefs and practices. There is a spring festival characterized by fertility rites, sexual license, and dancing and singing. Magicians are prominent and a form of sorcery using doll images is practiced. Cremation as a means of disposal of the corpse has apparently become secondary to earth burial in a coffin.

The Yi

The typical social organization of the Yi or Lolo in Szechwan has been marked by strict class division. The dominant class is the Black Lolo, whose members own all property and are in political control of the villages. The lower class, which does the household work and performs all agricultural labor, has two divisions: White Lolo and Han-Chinese slaves. Both are regarded as property by the Black Lolo and can be bought and sold. The White Lolo can improve their status in time by renting land from their Black Lolo masters. When economic independence has been attained, they become known as civilian slaves. There is no mobility between the Black Lolo and the lower classes, but barriers between White Lolo and Chinese slaves are less rigid and the latter may acquire status as White Lolo after having been assimilated into the group. This kind of organization, however, has been undergoing radical changes since the penetration of Chinese Communist influences into the Lolo region in the last ten years.

The clans in Lolo society are patrilineal, each made up of members claiming descent from a common ancestor. Clan organizations tend to be fairly large, each having several main and auxiliary branches. Members of a clan live together in a village; larger clans occupy a number of adjacent villages. The villages are highly cohesive, being tied together by bonds of kinship as well as physical proximity and the need for defense. As there is no formal system of succession to village leadership such as by age or inheritance, a man becomes leader through a process of common consent and on the basis of personal characteristics. Wealth is a factor, but successful military leadership and desirable personal qualities such as tact are more important.

There has been a good deal of feuding between clans, often for motives of blood revenge, but sometimes also for theft and pillage. Counterbalancing this state of constant feuding, however, is frequent visiting between members of different clans. Such visits are occasions for payment of indemnities to settle feuds, for gift giving, and for marriage arrangements—practices that serve to integrate the larger society.

The basic unit of Lolo society is the nuclear family, which is also the landowning group. Marriage is regulated by both class and clan. The clan is exogamous, the preferred partner being a cross cousin, but classes are rigidly endogamous. Polygamy is rare although village leaders attempt to contract several marriages so as to extend their political influence through their wives' families. Wives in such arrangements are of equal status.

The main economic activity of the Lolo is agriculture and the major crop, in terms of volume produced, is corn. Seed is planted in small holes in fairly well tended fields. After harvest the corn is dried and stored in a room in the house and the stalks are dried for fuel. Following the corn harvest, wheat and beans are planted; these in turn are harvested just before it is again time to cultivate the land for corn. This is all dry farming dependent upon the fairly scarce rainfall. Buckwheat, the second important crop, is cultivated by slash-and-burn methods. After sowing, the fields are unattended until harvest. Double cropping soon exhausts the soil and the field must be abandoned for several years. Some potatoes, oats, and vegetables are grown, and rice, a relatively minor crop, is cultivated on irrigated fields.

Agricultural land is owned by the clan but allotted to individual families who treat it as private property, passing it on to heirs. Pasture and forest land is communally owned and used.

Sheep and goat herding, though economically less important than agriculture, are looked upon as suitable occupations by the Black Lolo, who tend their own herds. Wool is cut three times annually, the woven cloth being used in the characteristic long overcoats of the Lolo. Shearing time is a big social occasion when several clans may bring their herds together.

Dwellings are mud or stone-walled structures, enclosed within a mud outer wall, and animals, including horses and oxen, are penned within this household compound. Building a house is a cooperative venture involving the whole clan.

The basis of Lolo religion is a well-developed animism. The world is peopled with spirits, both good and bad: every mountain, tree, stream, and so on, has its spirit. Evil spirits are very numerous and all have their own names and special functions. Sickness and misfortune are attributed to the influence of such spirits.

The chief religious specialist is the Pimu, a man who combines the functions of priest and sorcerer. This is a hereditary position, the necessary ritual and paraphernalia being passed down from father to son, or from maternal uncle to nephew. Magic pervades all aspects of Lolo life, and the Pimu has the techniques for controlling magic. He performs cures by exorcising the evil spirits that cause sickness, and he brings rain by propitiating the mountain spirits who control rain. A second specialist, the Simu, acquires his power by recovering from serious illness, at which time a spirit attaches itself to him, giving him supernatural powers as a curing specialist.

A fundamental concept among the Lolo is that of destiny—of good and bad luck controlled by the spirit world. Divination is therefore a necessary procedure for foreseeing the future through magical practices. Warfare is never undertaken without first resorting to divination. Consistent with this belief in good and bad luck, all Lolo wear amulets which have the power to protect the individual in hunting and warfare.

Many ceremonies and festivals are conducted annually. The "farewell parties" to ghosts are repeated several times during the lunar year, their purpose being to rid the family of harmful spirits, thereby ensuring family welfare.

The Puyi

Although called by different names such as Tujen, Tuchia, and Chungchia in various parts of Kweichow, the Puyi form a homogeneous group and are not divided into tribes like the Miao. A close similarity between Puyi and Han-Chinese cultures has resulted in the Puyi being readily assimilated into Chinese communities. In villages where the Puyi and the Chinese live together, the two groups are not easily distinguishable. Puyi men and women dress like the Chinese, though among older women the tribal costume of a tight-fitting jacket and a long skirt is still common. The Puyi were originally a Thai-speaking people, but today many of them can speak, read, and write Chinese. They are not despised by the Chinese as are the Miao. As a minority group, the Puyi of Kweichow actually do not pose any problem for the Chinese administration.

Most Puyi are peasants; only a few settle in towns and cities to engage in trade. Puyi women do more work in the fields than Han-Chinese women, and their social position is even lower than that of their Chinese counterparts. The Puyi, who usually own the land they cultivate and are well-to-do, would be much more likely than other ethnic groups in Southwest China to resist collectivism in agriculture.

The religious beliefs and practices of the Puyi are more or less similar to those of their Han-Chinese neighbors in Kweichow. They believe in a plurality of gods and spirits common in Chinese folk religion, but some Puyi are also Buddhists like the other Thai groups in southwestern China. Since the beginning of the twentieth century, western missionary influences have penetrated into the interior and a number of Puyi peasants and traders have embraced Christianity. In this respect it is worthwhile to observe that among the major ethnic groups in China, only the Puyi and the Miao have been exposed to this foreign religion.

Relations with Han-Chinese

Relations of the ethnic minorities with the dominant Han-Chinese have not been without strain and tension. The history of the frequent conflicts and wars between the Chinese and various tribal groups on the country's borders discloses in fact certain recurrent patterns. The ethnic groups of the south and southwest, such as the Miao, Yao, Chuang, and Yi, mostly agriculturists, would rebel whenever the local Chinese government became weak or oppressive, only to be reconquered by superior Chinese forces after a few years of resistance. The numerous campaigns undertaken by the government to quell these uprisings resulted in further penetration of Chinese influence into the remote mountainous regions and valleys, once the strongholds of these groups. To govern them more efficiently, the Chinese government adopted a policy of ruling the natives through native chieftains; this *t'u-ssu* (native official) system, first introduced as early as the third century A.D., was eminently successful in later centuries. The Han-Chinese were also successful in building up and training an army of one tribal group to be used in fighting against another whenever expedient.

Sometimes native officials were assigned Han-Chinese assistants to protect the interests of the Han-Chinese population in the area, but these officials also came under the supervision of the provincial authority, to whom they had to pay taxes and for whom they had to provide soldiers in case of war. The *t'u-ssu* system, most fully developed and organized during the Ming dynasty (1368-1644), was not abolished until the twentieth century, when the territories of these minority groups were put under direct government administration. Among some groups like the Tibetans and Yi, the power of the tribal chieftains never was broken and their continued rule was the cause of local disturbances in the republican period (1912-49). The Thai chieftains in southwestern Yunnan at the Burma border also continued to function up to recent times, serving as buffers in border conflicts.

The pattern of conflict in the north and northeast, somewhat different from the south's, was also on a larger scale. The mainly nomadic and more warlike groups along China's vast northern frontier at times grew strong enough to seize large parts of Chinese territory and twice succeeded in conquering the whole country and establishing their own rule. In the thirteenth and fourteenth centuries, the Mongols established a vast Asian empire with its seat of government in modern Peking. The Manchus were the masters of China for almost three hundred years until their power was broken in 1911. After World War II the Mongols in Outer Mongolia, backed by the Soviet Union, obtained official Chinese recognition of their independence and brought the nominal Chinese suzerainty there to an end.

As a corollary to these contacts over the centuries a great number of individuals from the minority groups, attracted to the more advanced Chinese civilization, were assimilated to the Chinese people. Chinese colonization of the frontiers also resulted in a preponderance of Han-Chinese in some minority regions, especially in Manchuria, where they constitute 95 percent of its population; the Manchus, on the other hand, have almost completely lost their group identity. This is a typical example of the gradual spread and penetration of Chinese cultural and political influences into the border regions and the absorption of the minority people through intermarriage and acculturation. Other minority groups in Manchuria, like the Mongols and Tungus, have also been absorbed by the Han-Chinese, and only the Koreans there present problems different from the others. For one thing, the Koreans in Manchuria are more steeped in western civilization and more productive than the Chinese. Furthermore, unlike the more modernized Russians who even in their own settlements at Harbin are outnumbered by the Chinese, and unlike the Japanese who have never considered Manchuria their permanent home, the Koreans settle mostly in areas where they outnumber the Chinese and where they persist in preserving their cultural traditions without even learning the Chinese language. The establishment by the Communist government of the Yen-pien Korean Autonomous District in Manchuria is evidence of the ethnic integrity of the Koreans and a matter of some international significance.

In Inner Mongolia also, the Han-Chinese outnumber the Mongols and other ethnic groups. It has been estimated that there is a total Chinese population of five million, most of them in southeastern Mongolia, compared to about one million Mongols. The Mongols vary in culture and degree of Sinification. The sedentary groups, as mentioned before, have adopted much of the Chinese way of life. The most Sinified groups are found in the southeastern area and among the Tumet of the former Suiyuan province, which the Chinese have colonized. On the whole, neither the Mongols nor the smaller Tungusic groups, most of them nomads, seem to have had much conflict with either the agricultural and urban-oriented Han-Chinese communities or the Chinese administration in these regions. The establishment by the Communist regime of the Inner Mongolia Autonomous Region aims to reduce what tension might have existed in the past.

Relationships between the Han-Chinese and the minority nationalities in the west and northwest, however, have been tense. There has been a definite racial antagonism between the Han-Chinese and the other ethnic groups in these areas. An old and deep animosity exists between the Turkic people and the Chinese due partly to the greater efficiency and industriousness of the Chinese, who have managed to displace the Turkic people in much of their agricultural work. The Kazak, a proud and freedom-loving people, dislike any political supervision and are known to have avoided tax collectors by crossing the national borders to Soviet Russia. Successive Hui uprisings were put down at the cost of much bloodshed. The Salar, who have a reputation for being fanatical Moslems, participated in all the Hui uprisings of recent centuries.

The question of Tibetan independence presented a serious problem to the Chinese. Tibet had won a quasi-independent status from the weakened Chinese government at the beginning of the twentieth century and did not surrender this status until after its penetration in 1950 by Communist forces. An agreement was reached between the Peking government and the Lhasa authority for the autonomy of Tibet and the organization of a preparatory committee for the Autonomous Region of Tibet with the Dalai Lama as chairman; nevertheless, friction and antagonism developed between Chinese and Tibetans. The lack of cooperation from local authorities forced the Communists to postpone the proposed land reform. By 1958 uprisings of the Khamba tribes broke out with the tacit support of the Lhasa officials; these led to the rebellion in Lhasa itself, the subsequent flight of the Dalai Lama to India in March 1959, and his public denunciation of the Chinese occupation. After having suppressed the rebellion, the Communists abolished the local government and handed its functions and powers to the preparatory committee, elevating the Panchen Lama to acting chairmanship. In July 1959 a resolution by the preparatory committee called for the abolition of serfdom and the reduction of land rents. Thus Tibet which has been most resistant to Chinese influences is being compelled to overhaul its centuries-old social and political structure.

Communist Nationalities Policy

Anticipating these and other difficulties, the Chinese Communist regime had introduced earlier a number of measures designed to ameliorate the relationship between the central government and the minority peoples. Large-scale migration of Han-Chinese to these regions was encouraged to hasten the process of assimilation; schools were erected in almost all villages, towns, and cities to propagate a sense of national consciousness; an intensive development of natural resources was initiated to raise the local standard of living; and regional autonomy was offered to induce cooperation from the minority groups.

Chinese Communist leaders and writers have claimed "gigantic achievements" in their administration of the minority nationalities. Theoretically, there is no single Chinese nation, but a multinational Chinese state, a fraternal cooperative of Han-Chinese and minorities, each holding equal rights. The basic policy is the promotion of regional autonomy through the establishment of autonomous areas, varying from the large autonomous regions (*ch'ü*) to smaller autonomous districts (*chou*), counties (*hsien*), and townships (*hsiang*). But "equality for the minority nationalities" and the "unity of all nationalities" must take place within the context of the Communist transformation of agriculture, handicrafts, commerce, and industry. To attain this final objective, the minority peoples are compelled to undergo a rapid transition to the intermediate stage of socialism.

Political Administration

In 1959 there were more than eighty national autonomous areas in China, excluding smaller units below the county level. The two most important are the Inner Mongolia Autonomous Region and the Sinkiang Uigur Autonomous Region, both containing large territories and situated in a strategic position on the Sino-Russian border. Other large minority areas are the Ningsia Hui Autonomous Region and the Kwangsi Chuang Autonomous Region; the Tibet Autonomous Region remains in a preparatory stage. It is planned that altogether more than twenty million people out of the total minority population of thirty-five million will be incorporated in autonomous regions covering approximately 60 percent of the total area of the country.

The autonomous areas are of four different types: (1) areas inhabited by one minority group only; (2) those inhabited by one dominant minority group, but including other smaller groups; (3) those inhabited by two or more minority groups of approximately the same size; and (4) those inhabited primarily by Han-Chinese, but including some minorities. In Southwest China, where the ethnic composition is extremely complex, most autonomous areas contain more than one minority group.

In the south and southwest the boundaries of certain autonomous areas coincide with the former domains of the native officials, who have either been given a seat in the new administration or liquidated, according to whether their attitude toward the national regime was friendly or not. Some areas—such as the Hsi-shuang-pa-na (Sip-song-pa-na) Thai Nationality Autonomous District in southern Yunnan and the Kwangsi Chuang Autonomous Region—are Thai agglomerations which could well form the base for the spread of the "Free Thai" movement in Laos and Vietnam. From this viewpoint, the autonomous areas along the Yunnan-Burma border and on Hainan Island assume special significance.

The autonomous areas are administered by a people's council composed of representatives of the respective minorities and the Han-Chinese. Special non-Han cadres are trained for work in the minority areas at the Central Academy of Nationalities in Peking, which has several thousand students from the various minority groups and which gives instructions in the languages, modern knowledge and technology, and political ideology. After a period of training these cadres are sent to the tribal areas as native leaders to work among the people for the numerous programs of the government. Both Communist party activists and the People's Army stationed along the border regions take an active part in these programs.

Economic Transformation

The changes in the economic lives of the minority peoples have been drastic and profound due mainly to the Communist policy of mobilizing all resources, including those of the ethnic minorities, for economic reconstruction. It is for this purpose that the Communist government has made efforts to improve the means of transportation, to promote trade and small industry, and, most important, to introduce land reform in the nationality autonomous areas.

To carry out the new program, land has been redistributed and mutual-aid teams and cooperatives for marketing and supplying have been organized according to the national pattern. Relief funds and credits in grain and seeds have been issued, suitable farm implements are distributed without charge, and nationality trading companies have been organized to facilitate the purchase of draft animals and articles of daily need. Slash-and-burn agriculture in the southwestern regions is prohibited and the farmers are urged to lay out terraced fields to raise crops in the mountainous areas.

Agricultural producers' cooperatives have been established in all the ethnic minority areas. In the north and northwest, producers' cooperatives have been organized for both the farming and nomadic populations. The Inner Mongolia Autonomous Region, for instance, had in 1956 some 11,000 agricultural producers' cooperatives. In the same region in February 1957 there were 543 animal husbandry producers' cooperatives with a total membership of 18,000 households. Credit cooperatives and mutual-aid teams were operative in Inner Mongolia as well as in Sinkiang, where by the end of 1956 the Communist regime had established 5,100 agricultural cooperatives and 629 animal husbandry cooperatives. By the end of 1958, however, most of these had been incorporated into the communes.

These measures were designed to promote agriculture and livestock production within the minority settlements, but quite often, particularly in the more thickly settled southwestern areas, farmers were forced to move into villages at some distance from their homes in order to till the lands assigned them. Despite promises made at the initial stage, landlords among the minority peoples were treated with the same harshness as the Chinese landlords: the same strict penalties were imposed or they were executed and their families left in a state of destitution. The situation was complicated by the fact that in the minority areas, with the exception of the Yi landlords who treated their tenants with cruelty, the relationship between landlords and tenants was not particularly strained.

The improvement of transportation facilities in minority areas has been another important aspect of Communist policy. In Yunnan, for example, where the long rainy season used to make travel difficult, new highways have been built and old ones are being kept in a state of good repair with the result that travel between K'un-ming, the provincial capital, and the southwestern parts of the province is practical most of the year. Goods are transported in great quantities before the beginning of the rainy season in July to ensure well-stocked markets during the summer. The upper Salween region in northwestern Yunnan has new postal roads open to traffic all the year round; a steel bridge was built across the Mekong; and a main road was constructed along parts of the Salween valley. The 1,300-mile-long Hsi-ning–Lhasa highway, which runs through the northeastern part of Tibet, intersects other highways radiating from Lan-chou in Kansu. In Sinkiang arterial highways are centered in Urumchi, which is connected with a number of oasis cities where the Han-Chinese and Uigurs intermingle. In Inner Mongolia the highway mileage increased from 300 in 1950 to 3,000 in 1955.

Trade with the minority peoples is promoted through special trade organizations which coordinate the purchase and marketing of native and special products such as cowhides, sheepskins, furs, dried bamboo shoots, brick tea, and various medicinal herbs.

In recent years the Communists have attempted to make full use of the natural resources and native products of the minority regions so as to incorporate them into the national economic system. While large-scale industrialization projects in the Northwest and Northeast are all government-sponsored projects run by Han-Chinese workers, the minority peoples in the southwestern regions are encouraged to set up their own small factories to supplement their income from agricultural and home industry products such as charcoal, cotton cloth, plaited mats, bamboo utensils, and others. A notable example is the composite factory in the Hsi-shuang-pa-na region of Yunnan at Ch'e-li, the district capital, which was set up to distill wine from glutinous rice and to press oil from cotton seeds and peanuts. A water tower and power plant were also built at Ch'e-li to service the city. Factories in other minority areas of Yunnan weave cloth, produce farm tools, and process tea. Workers from the cities have been summoned to instruct the people in operating these industrial units. Iron works that have been established in the autonomous region of the Lisu people along the upper Salween are said to belong to the minority peoples who operate them. It is also reported that Thai, Lahu, and Chingpo women who are skilled in handling improved looms have been elected "model workers." Other industrial enterprises run by the tribespeople are the iron and coal mines, saw mills, and farm implement plants of the Miao autonomous area in western Hunan. Power plants have been set up in the district capitals. Thus most of these minority regions have been undergoing a steady economic change that is bound to affect the life of the various peoples.

Social and Cultural Changes

The Communist government has taken a number of steps to raise the cultural level of the minority nationalities, initiating changes that will have far-reaching effects. To minimize in the interim the resentment of these minority peoples to the superiority implied in the traditional Han-Chinese attitude toward them, the Communists, like the Nationalists before them, banned the use of derogatory words. Place names containing words with insulting allusion to the tribal people—"dogs," "barbarians," and others—have been changed, sometimes to a name from the tribal language.

The Communist government aims to provide the minority nationalities with scripts of their own. The creation of a written language for the Chuang people has been announced. For the Yi people of Szechwan and Yunnan, a latinized script has been devised and textbooks for primary schools have been printed and used. The Communists have adopted, after "improvement," the scripts provided by foreign missionaries for the Miao, Chingpo, and Lisu. The Mongols, Manchus, and Tibetans all have their own scripts, in which much of their literature, both religious and secular, has been preserved. The Uigurs and Kazak use the Arabic alphabet, which is common in all parts of Sinkiang. There is the probability, however, that in several years Russian script will prevail among the Turkic peoples of Sinkiang and the Mongolian people of Inner Mongolia.

A sharp increase in educational activities among the ethnic minorities is evident in the growing number of elementary and secondary schools, as reported in the Communist press. In addition to the Central Academy of Nationalities at Peking, regional nationality cadres schools to train political workers among the ethnic groups have also been established in minority areas throughout the country.

The Communist government has made a concerted drive to increase the effectiveness of the media of mass communication. General education is promoted by the distribution among the literate populace of a large number of books, pamphlets, illustrated periodicals, and photographs. Film projectors, motion pictures, and radios have been sent to towns and rural centers in all areas for propaganda purposes. Most of the written and visual materials concern technical and agricultural improvements, working conditions in factories, and construction of dams and other public projects.

The government also has made important attempts to improve health and sanitary conditions. Health centers have been established and mobile medical teams sent out for vaccination against smallpox and for the treatment of trachoma, which is common in tribal areas. In malaria-afflicted regions in Yunnan and Kweichow, measures have been taken to prevent the spread of the disease among the people. Women are instructed in infant and maternity care. Efforts are made to persuade the people to abstain from superstitious practices in dealing with diseases. The establishment in certain minority areas of hospitals and sanitariums where free medical care is given to the patients has been reported.

Minority religious beliefs and customs are breaking down under the onslaught of new ideas and innovations introduced through the media of mass communication, but ancestor worship involving the sacrifice of domestic animals such as buffaloes and pigs is especially discouraged. The present regime has shown some tolerance, however, toward Islam and Lamaism. The Moslem leadership has helped promote Communist China's relationship with the Islamic world, and Lamaism has proved useful in winning the loyalties of the Lamaistic peoples of Tibet and Mongolia. In general, the government has shown a certain restraint in interfering with strictly religious practices and personalities, but whenever the influence of the Moslem imams and Tibetan lamas has run counter to Communist interests, the regime has not hesitated to initiate campaigns to denounce them for their "counter-revolutionary activities." Recently the government has intensified the campaign against the lamas in retaliation for their support of the Dalai Lama in the Tibetan revolution.

Through study of published materials and fresh field investigation where necessary, the Communist rulers have undertaken a re-evaluation of tribal beliefs, customs, and habits. Those elements deemed favorable to Communist policies will be retained and developed as national characteristics while others incompatible with these policies will be eventually eliminated through persuasion or force.

While giving the minority nationalities a semblance of self-rule, the government maintains a control more effective and efficient than that exercised by any previous regime. The minds of the people are impregnated with the new ideology, and public enthusiasm is stirred up for the common cause. Days of political significance are celebrated by mass meetings, processions, and parades accompanied by dancing teams and drummers. Broadly speaking, the Communist regime has displayed considerable caution in carrying out its nationalities policy, but its ultimate objective remains the total absorption of the minorities and the eradication of their identities. The larger groups such as the Mongols, Uigurs, and Tibetans will, however, try to frustrate this scheme and therein lies one source of future friction and conflict.

Indications exist that some of the minority peoples resent the strict control of their affairs under the guise of autonomy. Unused to the feverish speed and pressure in industrialization which run counter to their accustomed way of life, they instinctively resist some of the sociocultural changes imposed upon them. It is questionable whether the Communist government will succeed in eradicating the mutual animosity between the different ethnic groups and integrating them into a multinational Chinese state through the process of "socialist transformation." The recent uprising in Tibet, the purge of the so-called rightist Moslem and Uigur leaders in Kansu, Sinkiang, and Ningsia, as well as the Communist propaganda against "regional chauvinism" are indicative of the difficulties encountered by the Communist regime in the implementation of its nationalities policy.

LANGUAGES

THE CHINESE LANGUAGE in its various dialectal forms is spoken by a great majority of the six hundred fifty million people in China and Taiwan. In the course of its evolution the spoken language has undergone extensive and important modifications, some of which can still be traced from early records. Since the colloquial form was more flexible than the written and easily adaptable to changing circumstances, the transformations of time, geographical barriers, as well as the occasional infusion of foreign blood and culture left indelible marks on spoken Chinese, especially in pronunciation and modes of expression, with the result that a number of dialects have developed.

On the other hand, except for differences in the style of the script, the Chinese written language has changed very little since the beginning of the Christian era. Its continuity has been a significant factor in the uniformity and homogeneity of Chinese culture. But it is difficult to learn to read this language, which is nonalphabetic and consists of many thousands of ideographs with complicated strokes; therefore literacy in China has never been high and it is to combat illiteracy and its concomitant social problems that language reform has been advocated in recent decades.

Languages and Dialects

There is a multiplicity of languages and dialects in China. In addition to the many dialects of Chinese are the languages of the numerous minority nationalities in the border regions. Some of these languages are related to Chinese, which is the most important branch of the Sino-Tibetan language family, while others belong to other language families such as Altaic and Austroasiatic (for classification and distribution, see the plate, Languages of China). These speech communities intermingle and often overlap, some extending beyond national boundaries (see Chapter 4, Ethnic Minorities).

The Sino-Tibetan languages are spoken by a larger population than any other minority languages. Presumably they originated in the Pamirs and then branched out over the eastern half of the Asian continent from the Tibetan plateau eastward to the coastal regions of China, and from the Indochina peninsula northward to Sinkiang, Mongolia, and Manchuria.

Like most Sino-Tibetan languages, Chinese has a basically monosyllabic structure, which means that the basic constituents of Chinese words and phrases are single syllables. While most Chinese words consist of one syllable each, there are a number of polysyllabic words.

The Chinese language contains a system of tones: the relative pitch levels used in pronouncing the syllables. Chinese, Tibetan, Burmese, and Thai all have tones, and similar developments of the tonal systems in these languages have been traced. In ancient times, there were four tones in the Chinese language; these developed into eight tones, not all of which are present in modern dialects. Mandarin, the standard Chinese dialect, has four tones: two even tones, p'ing-sheng (the upper even, yin-p'ing, and lower even, yang-p'ing); one rising tone, shang-sheng; and one falling tone, ch'ü-sheng. For the sake of convenience, these are designated respectively by western scholars as the first, second, third, and fourth tones. In a language that abounds in homonyms, tones are essential in distinguishing words that sound the same but have different meaning. In Chinese, tense, number, and case are not distinguished by inflection as in some European languages.

Dialects

Mandarin, by a wide margin the most extensively used Chinese dialect, is followed in importance by Wu, Hsiang, Hui, Kan, Hakka, Min, Yüeh, and a number of more local dialects. Although derived from a common base, quite different pronunciation and linguistic structure from dialect to dialect make most of them mutually unintelligible.

Formerly the language of the officials, Mandarin spread from North China to the Central-East and Southwest and is today the mother tongue of some 380 million people in many parts of China. Three main groups of Mandarin dialects have been distinguished.

LANGUAGES OF CHINA

I. *Sino-Tibetan Family*

A. Chinese Branch—

1. Northern Mandarin: North China (China Proper to the north of the Ch'in Ling mountains, the Han River, and the Huai River), Manchuria, and Sinkiang.

2. Southwestern Mandarin: Szechwan, Kweichow, Yunnan, northern Kwangsi, western Hunan, most of Hupeh, and southern Shensi.

3. Southern Mandarin: Anhwei and Kiangsu north of the lower Yangtze.

4. Wu (Soochow) Dialect: Kiangsu, Chekiang, and eastern Kiangsi south of the lower Yangtze.

5. Hsiang Dialect: Hunan along the Hsiang, Yüan, and Tzu rivers.

6. Kan Dialect: Kiangsi around Lake P'o-yang.

7. Hakka Dialect: southern Kiangsi, northern Kwangtung, western Fukien, parts of Kwangsi, Hunan, Szechwan, and Taiwan (also settlements in Indochina, Thailand, Malaya, and Indonesia).

8. Yüeh (Cantonese) Dialect: Kwangtung and Kwangsi (also settlements in Indochina, Thailand, Burma, Malaya, and Indonesia).

9. Min Dialect: Fukien, Taiwan, Hainan, and northeastern Kwangtung.
   (a) Northern Min: Foochow.
   (b) Southern Min: Amoy and Swatow.

10. Minor dialects: southern Anhwei; southwestern Hunan; northeastern Kwangsi, etc.

LANGUAGES OF CHINA—*Cont.*

B. Kam-Thai Branch—

1. Sui-Kam-Mak: southeastern Kweichow; parts of northern Kwangsi.

2. Thai—
   - (a) Northern Thai—
     - Chuang: Kwangsi.
     - Chungchia, Manchia, Penti, etc.: southern Kweichow.
     - Sha and Tulao: southeastern Yunnan.
     - Li: Hainan.
   - (b) Southern Thai—
     - Shan [Paiyi]: Yunnan-Burma border.
     - Lu [Shui Paiyi]: southern Yunnan.
     - Thai Blanc, Nung, Tho, etc.: southwestern Kwangsi; southwestern Yunnan.

C. Miao-Yao Branch—

1. Miao: mountain regions in western Hunan; Kweichow; parts of northern Kwangsi; southern Szechwan; Yunnan (also Indochina and Thailand).

2. Yao: mountain regions in northwestern Kwangtung; southern Kweichow; parts of Kwangsi and Yunnan (also Indochina and Thailand).

D. Tibeto-Burman Branch—

1. Tibetan—
   - (a) Tibetan—
     - Western Tibetan (including Balti, Ladakhi, etc.).
     - Central Tibetan (including Lhasa).
     - Eastern Tibetan (including Sikang and Tsinghai).
   - (b) Hsifan—
     - Hsifan and Kutsung: Sikang; northwestern Szechwan; northwestern Yunnan.
     - Trung [Chiutzu] and Nung [Nutzu]: northwestern Yunnan.
   - (c) Jarung and Chiang: western Szechwan.
   - (d) Himalayan dialects.

2. Lolo-Moso—
   - (a) Lolo: Yunnan; northwestern Kweichow; southern Szechwan and Sikang (also Indochina and Thailand).
   - (b) Moso: Yunnan and Sikang along the Chin-sha Chiang.
   - (c) Minchia: around Ta-li in Yunnan.
   - (d) Woni, Lisu, Lahu, Aka, etc.: Yunnan-Burma border.

3. Kachin (Chingpo): northwestern Yunnan.

4. A-Chang, Maru, Lashi, etc.: Yunnan-Burma border.

II. *Altaic Family*

A. Turkic Branch—
1. Central Turkic: southern Sinkiang (Uigur), district of Ha-mi, and Kansu.
2. Western Turkic: northern Sinkiang, including Kazak, Kirghiz, etc.

B. Mongolian Branch—
1. Eastern or Southern Mongolian: Inner Mongolia, including Chahar, Suiyuan, Jehol, Ningsia, and parts of Manchuria.
2. Khalka: Outer Mongolia except western part.
3. Kalmuck: western Outer Mongolia and northern Sinkiang.
4. Buryat: parts of northern Mongolia and Heilungkiang (chiefly in Siberia).

C. Tungus Branch—
1. Southern Tungus (Manchu, Goldi, Daur, Solon, etc.): Kirin and Heilungkiang.
2. Northern Tungus (Maneghir, Birar, Samaghir, etc.): parts of Heilungkiang (mostly in Siberia).

III. *Austronesian Family*

Indonesian-Formosan Branch—

1. Atayal   4. Tsou   7. Puyuma
2. Saiset   5. Rukai   8. Ami
3. Bunun   6. Paiwan   9. Yami

IV. *Austroasiatic Family*

Mon-Khmer Branch—Wa-Palaung—
(a) Wa
(b) La
(c) Puman
(d) Palaung
Yunnan-Burma border

V. *Indo-European Family*

Iranic Branch—   Tadjik: southwestern Sinkiang.

Based on Tung, Tung-ho, *Languages of China* (Taipei: China Culture Publishing Foundation, 1953), pp. 3-14.

(1) Northern Mandarin, of which Peking Mandarin is the representative, is spoken in an area that encompasses the entire Yellow River basin and extends to Manchuria in the northeast and Sinkiang in the northwest. (2) Southwestern Mandarin, a fairly homogeneous group of dialects, occurs in a large part of China's southwestern hinterland, including the Szechwan Red Basin, the Yunnan-Kweichow plateau, and the central Yangtze plains. (3) Southern Mandarin, basically similar to the northern group, is spoken in the lower Yangtze valley from Hankow eastward to Nanking.

The Wu dialect, spoken by approximately thirty-five million people, had its origin in Soochow, one of the cultural centers of the imperial period. From there it spread to regions south of the lower Yangtze and gained great importance with the rise of Shanghai as a metropolitan center in East China. There are generally six to eight tones in the Wu dialect.

A group of minor dialects occurring south of the Yangtze valley consists of Hsiang, spoken by fifteen million people in central Hunan; Hui, spoken by three million people in southern Anhwei; and Kan, spoken by eight million people in northern Kiangsi. The Hsiang or Hunan group resembles to some extent Southwestern Mandarin. The number of tones varies from six to seven.

The Hakka dialect is found over an area extending on an east-west axis from Fukien to Kwangsi, including southern Kiangsi and northern Kwangtung, with offshoots in Taiwan and Hainan; it also spreads to the Chinese settlements in the Philippines, Indochina, Burma, Thailand, Malaya, and Sumatra. In China itself speakers of Hakka number approximately ten million.

There is a great resemblance between Hakka and Kan, and they are sometimes grouped together. In northern Kiangsi, the Hakka and the non-Hakka speech communities have intermingled to such an extent that it is difficult to ascertain whether the dialects they speak are Hakka, Kan, or a mixture of both. When the two dialects are not mixed they are distinguishable. Hakka differs from Kan mainly in tonal system and final consonants.

The Min or Fukien dialect can be divided into two groups: Northern Min and Southern Min. The former, spoken by six million people in northern Fukien, is represented by the Foochow dialect; the latter, spoken by fifteen million people, is represented by the Amoy dialect in southern Fukien and by the Swatow dialect in northeastern Kwangtung and on Hainan Island. The original Chinese population in Taiwan speaks the dialect of

Chang-chou (Lung-ch'i), a city some twenty miles from Amoy. In their variant forms, the Southern Min dialects have been taken by Chinese emigrants to Indonesia, Malaya, and the Philippines. The tonal system resembles that of the Wu and Hakka groups.

Yüeh or Cantonese is spoken by some forty million people in China and abroad. Its speakers include not only those in the provinces of Kwangtung and Kwangsi, but also many overseas Chinese in various parts of the world. For instance, the dialect of Chung-shan is popular among the Chinese people in Hawaii, and the dialects of T'ai-shan (Toishan), K'ai-p'ing (Hoiping), and others are used by Chinese residents in Chinatowns of the United States. Cantonese is also the dialect of a number of Chinese communities in Indochina, Thailand, Malaya, and Indonesia.

Written Language

The earliest written records of the Chinese people were the Shell and Bone inscriptions, *chia-ku-wen.* This form was superseded by the Seal Script, *chuan-shu,* and the Scribe Script, *li-shu.* With the use of the writing brush and paper in the early Christian era, Chinese writing gradually assumed its present form known as the Regular Script, *k'ai-shu.* In the evolution of the Chinese written language, there clearly has been a tendency toward the simplification of the written forms (see the plate, Evolution of Chinese Writing).

The structure of the Chinese characters is very complicated. They are divided into six main categories: pictographs, ideographs, compound ideographs, phonetic loan characters, phonetic compounds, and derivative characters. Among these, the pictographs and the simple ideographs are the basic forms from which the others are derived, but the phonetic compounds constitute the largest class of Chinese words, and many new forms are currently being coined.

The creation of new words and expressions is, however, characteristic mainly of vernacular Chinese, *pai-hua,* in contradistinction to literary Chinese, *wen-yen* or *wen-li,* based on the language of the Chinese classics and preserved by scholars in an inflexible and conservative style for the last twenty centuries. The literary language, which lends itself to a remarkably concise style through the omission of the particles ordinarily used in daily speech, has been the medium for many masterpieces of Chinese literature but differs so greatly in syntax and grammar from vernacular Chinese as almost to constitute a separate language. This disparity reduces any confusion between the two, and a Chinese scholar fluent in the classical language considers it quite natural to turn to his dialect for everyday purposes.

Pronunciation of literary Chinese depends upon the dialect of the reader: a Mandarin speaker will read the literary language with Mandarin pronunciations and a Wu speaker with Wu pronunciations. Sometimes, because of its terseness, literary Chinese cannot be fully understood when read aloud. Certain written characters have no colloquial rendering, and some colloquial words have no written equivalents. In the latter case, a character of the same meaning may be used as a substitute, or a "vulgar character" may be invented.

Despite its shortcomings, literary Chinese has exerted a tenacious influence on Chinese intellectuals, who are still able to read with ease the classical literature of ancient China as no other people can read their ancient language and literature. The ability to read and write in literary Chinese is the hallmark of a Chinese scholar of the old type just as the ability to use a foreign language is an asset to a modern Chinese scholar.

Language Reform

With the rise of nationalism in China, language has emerged as a significant political factor in the struggle toward "one state, one people, and one language." Just as the Chinese people are bound spiritually to their ancestors by a common literary style and cultural heritage, so they seek a greater unity among themselves through a common spoken language. This aim has spurred several attempts in recent decades to: (1) adopt Mandarin as a standard national language; (2) popularize the Chinese language among the minority nationalities; (3) simplify the written words; (4) compile lists of Basic Chinese to be used in textbooks for adult education; (5) eliminate illiteracy; and (6) alphabetize the Chinese language. The much heralded language reform of the Communist regime is but the latest of these attempts.

An attempt to establish a common spoken language was made as early as the beginning of the Chinese Republic more than forty years ago. In the late 1910's, the Chinese Renaissance movement led by Hu Shih created a demand for a vernacular literature based on the Mandarin dialect, because it is spoken by more than two-thirds of the population and would therefore be the most logical

EVOLUTION OF CHINESE WRITING

	servant	to fish	turtle	chicken	horse
SHELL AND BONE INSCRIPTION B.C. 1700–1400					
GREAT SEAL SCRIPT B.C. 776–250					
SMALL SEAL SCRIPT B.C. 250–A.D. 25					
SCRIBE SCRIPT A.D. 25–220					
REGULAR SCRIPT A.D. 380–present day					
CURRENT SIMPLIFIED FORMS					

Hsia, Tao-tai, *China's Language Reforms* (New Haven: Yale University, Institute of Far Eastern Languages, 1956), p. 106.

choice for the national language. Peking Mandarin was selected at that time as the standard form for writing and speaking. By the end of the 1920's Mandarin was being taught in schools throughout the country, making it possible for educated Chinese to converse with each other in Mandarin no matter what dialect had originally been their mother tongue.

Soon after the Communists came to power in 1949, a Committee for Chinese Language Reform was established to work toward the goal of a new written language based on the Latin alphabet. Before such a change can be introduced, uniform pronunciation must be adopted to minimize dialectal differences. In the spring of 1956, the campaign for promoting the use of Mandarin went into high gear following the committee's publication of a draft plan for the phoneticization of the Chinese language. In conjunction with the Ministry of Education the committee issued directives to all government agencies and mass organizations to push plans for the popularization of Mandarin. At the same time all the local branches of the committee launched a similar drive in provinces and cities to urge the non-Mandarin-speaking people to accept Mandarin as their "common speech," *p'u-t'ung-hua.*

The Communist government has encouraged the study of the Chinese language by the non-Han ethnic groups by adopting the Han [Chinese] Language Popularization Plan for the teaching of Chinese in elementary and secondary schools in the autonomous border districts. The diverse minority groups within China can obviously be welded more closely together through the use of a common language. "Popularization of the common speech," asserted a newspaper editorial in April 1956, "is an absolutely necessary step not only in the consolidation and development of the Chinese people politically, economically, and culturally, but also in strengthening the unity among the various brother nationalities in the country and in the promotion of our country's socialistic reconstruction."

Simplified Characters

A major problem in Chinese language reform is the simplification of the script. The radicals of some characters have a large number of strokes, and the compound forms are even more complicated. Several Chinese characters have as many as twenty or more strokes and much time must be consumed to write them out stroke by stroke. Of the devices evolved in the past to expedite the writing of Chinese characters, the most important are: (1)

SPECIMENS OF SIMPLIFIED CHINESE CHARACTERS
(The characters in brackets are the original complex forms.)

罢 (罷)	辟 (闢)	丰 (豐)	电 (電)
卜 (蔔)	朴 (樸)	妇 (婦)	垫 (墊)
备 (備)	扑 (撲)	复 (復複	独 (獨)
宝 (寶)	么 (麼)	覆)	夺 (奪)
报 (報)	迈 (邁)	达 (達)	对 (對)
办 (辦)	霉 (黴)	斗 (鬥)	断 (斷)
板 (闆)	蒙 (朦濛	担 (擔)	多 (夥)
帮 (幫)	懞)	胆 (膽)	东 (東)
别 (彆)	弥 (彌瀰)	当 (當噹)	劲 (勁)
标 (標)	蔑 (衊)	党 (黨)	态 (態)
表 (錶)	庙 (廟)	灯 (燈)	台 (臺檯
边 (邊)	面 (麵)	敌 (敵)	颱)
宾 (賓)	范 (範)	淀 (澱)	头 (頭)
补 (補)	奋 (奮)	点 (點)	体 (體)

Hsia, Tao-tai, *China's Language Reforms* (New Haven: Yale University, Institute of Far Eastern Languages, 1956), p. 23.

the use of a running hand or cursive style for quick writing; (2) the adoption of simpler variant forms for complicated words; (3) the substitution of simpler characters for complex ones having the same sound; and (4) the omission of redundant parts in a character.

Using these simplified forms, which have gained wide currency, as well as newly coined forms of their own, the Committee for Chinese Language Reform has prepared several lists of simplified characters which have been officially approved by the State Council and are being used in publications throughout the country (see the plate, Specimens of Simplified Chinese Characters). One list gives fifty-four simplified character-components, each of which appears in a large number of compound words. Adoption of these simplified components will entail the simplification of more than a thousand words. It is estimated that with the compilation and adoption of more lists, the total number of simplified words to be used would come to at least thirty-five hundred or about one half of the seven thousand commonly used words.

Lists of Basic Words

Another language reform measure, which had its origin in the mass education movement of the early 1920's, is the compilation of lists of basic Chinese words, somewhat like Basic English, to be used for adult education. Prior to the Communist period, several such lists, most of them based upon frequency of word occurrence, had been compiled for use in textbooks to provide the learner with a vocabulary large enough for basic needs in reading and writing. In 1952 the Communist government issued through the Ministry of Education its own list of commonly used characters. A striking feature of this list is the emphasis on words supposed to have common currency among farmers and workers.

Alphabetization

Another problem whose solution must be part of any effective language reform is to replace the system of Chinese characters with a phonetic alphabet. The tedious process of learning the written language character by character—an important factor in the low literacy rate—provides a compelling reason for the interest of educators and officials in the alphabetization of the Chinese language. Such scholarly tools as dictionaries, indexes, bibliographies, and catalogues, which have traditionally been arranged on the basis of a complex system of fundamental characters (radicals) or the number of strokes in each character, could be compiled more simply in an alphabetic order. In modern communications, too, Chinese characters have created special problems. Telegraphic messages must be sent in numerical codes; it has proved almost impossible to devise a workable typewriter; and the setting of Chinese printing types is vastly more complicated than typesetting in western languages.

These considerations have spurred many proposals for alphabetic systems, ranging from romanizations to kana-like symbols used by the Japanese, shorthand systems, and picture-scripts. The first such system was a set of thirty-nine phonetic symbols, *chu-yin tzu-mu*, officially promulgated in 1918 by the government and later incorporated in Chinese-language textbooks at the grade school level. The Nationalist government further encouraged its use in the 1930's. These phonetic symbols were not intended to replace Chinese characters but to be printed alongside the Chinese text as a phonetic guide to pronouncing Chinese words in the standard Mandarin dialect. The device proved to be rather cumbersome and did not gain wide support from readers and publishers. Its use was confined to school textbooks but even there it failed to achieve the desired aim.

There was also great interest in the romanization of the Chinese written language. Previously, long before the Chinese themselves had been aware of their language problem, Christian missionaries to China had used Roman letters to transcribe Chinese sounds as an aid to learning the spoken language. From these early attempts evolved the Wade-Giles system, named for Sir Thomas Wade and Herbert A. Giles, two English Sinologists, that has become the standard system of romanization used widely by Chinese language experts in the United States. In the mid-1920's scholars in China were eagerly discussing the possibility of evolving a romanized script not merely to help foreigners study Chinese but to take the place ultimately of the Chinese ideographic script. One of the romanized systems that attracted the attention of scholars is the Gwoyeu Romatzyh (National Language Romanization) made by Chao Yüan-jen (Y. R. Chao). But resistance has been strong against the adoption of a romanized script for the Chinese language, and with little popular support, the Gwoyeu Romatzyh has remained mostly a matter of academic interest.

About the same time, Soviet linguists, with the help of a group of Chinese students in Moscow, were formulating another system of romanized script known as Latinxua (latinized script).

The leading Chinese exponents were Ch'ü Ch'iu-pai, who was later executed by the Nationalists in 1935, and Wu Yü-chang, who is today chairman of the Committee for Chinese Language Reform in the Communist government. It is interesting to note here that these Moscow proponents of Latinxua, instead of using Cyrillic, the Russian alphabet, adopted a Latin script for the proposed new language. Beginning in 1931, textbooks and periodicals in Latinxua were published in Russia for the use of Chinese communities in the Soviet Far East. In China the first Latinxua books did not appear until 1934 and were soon banned by the Nationalist government as an instrument of Communist subversion. As a whole, little progress was made in the romanization of the Chinese language during the Nationalist regime.

Latinization, however, continued to receive Communist support in the regions under Communist control. In 1941 the Latinxua Association was founded at Yenan and popular literature written in Latinxua was published. Immediately after the establishment of the Communist government in 1949, the effort to introduce Latinxua was renewed with great intensity. At the National Conference on Language Reform held in Peking in October 1955, six alphabetic systems were presented for consideration: four of these used block-line letters derived from the Chinese ideographic script, one was a Cyrillic alphabet already adopted in the Inner Mongolia Autonomous Region, another was the Latin script. From these six, the Latin alphabet was chosen by the conference for further study, discussion, and experimental use. In December 1956 Peking announced that a committee of linguistic experts appointed by the Chinese Communist government had decided to adopt the twenty-six-letter Latin alphabet for the Chinese written language. Similar Latin scripts are being devised to transcribe the languages and dialects of China's minority nationalities.

As a part of the Latinization program, it is considered practical to write and print the Chinese words horizontally from left to right as in western writing instead of in vertical lines from right to left in the traditional manner. Such a practice is by no means new, having been adopted in pre-Communist days by many scientific and learned journals, but the Communist government first gave it official sanction. Since 1955 all important national publications and newspapers have started printing their texts in horizontal lines. Pens and pencils are also commonly used in place of the time-honored writing brush.

Another measure in conjunction with this program is the government directive regarding the use of standard punctuation marks in all official and private publications. There was no punctuation in Chinese literary writing until a set of marks was introduced during the late 1910's. The new system was copied from the West, the only difference being that a small circle was used instead of a period at the end of a sentence. Since then punctuation marks have been adopted in most Chinese publications and the Communist directive merely gave formal approval of their standardization.

A number of questions have been raised by those who have reservations about the Latinization program. It has been asked, for instance, if adoption of an alphabetic script will deny traditional literature to those who are unable to read the written characters. As it will be impossible to translate all the ancient texts into a romanized form, a large body of China's literary, historical, and philosophical writings will be unavailable to the people who use only the alphabetic script. It is difficult to imagine that the discontinuation of the use of Chinese characters would not constitute a serious loss in China's cultural heritage.

As a whole, Chinese Communist leaders have been persistent in their efforts to reform the Chinese language. They have followed Mao Tse-tung's dictum that the Chinese written language must be reformed in certain ways and have declared that unless the written Chinese characters are completely reformed, China's scientific and cultural progress will be hampered. But they are aware that the written language of a people cannot be changed by artificial means and that the evolution of any system of writing has to follow a natural course; they are also aware of the resistance which may develop to any drastic change in the language. Their present policy, therefore, is to give official sanction and encouragement to popular practices that have already been in current use. As of now, the twenty-six-letter Latin alphabet is used only as an aid to pronouncing the characters, but not as their replacement. The government has been proceeding rather cautiously in taking the final revolutionary step, the complete Latinization of the Chinese written language.

RELIGION

THE TWO MAJOR CULTURAL ELEMENTS discernible in the religious tradition of China up to modern times were the complex of varying but related local beliefs and practices of the common people and the three great literate traditions—Confucianism, Taoism, and Buddhism—of the educated classes. These apparently disparate elements were, however, often combined in the ceremonial worship of ancestors and the concomitant reverence for the family institution.

Foreign religious influences were minimal. Of the three literate traditions only Buddhism was borrowed, becoming thoroughly assimilated to Chinese culture after initial rejection by the scholars. Islam and Christianity, on the other hand, remained alien to most Chinese. Convinced that conflict existed between ancestor worship and the prescribed loyalty to the Islamic community, between veneration of the Chinese classics and veneration of the Koran, Chinese Moslems even after a thousand years on Chinese soil continued to isolate themselves, to varying degrees, in social communities of their own. Chinese Christians, too, by refusing to accept ancestor worship, drew opposition from the imperial government and Confucian scholars. Today, however, this refusal is no longer an important argument against Christianity.

It has only been in the last ten years that a foreign ideology has seriously threatened the continuity of the Chinese religious tradition. Professing religious tolerance, the Communists proceeded upon asuming power in 1949 to identify "religion" with "superstition" and to move toward the eventual eradication of all such beliefs in favor of dialectical materialism. To what extent the Communist regime has been, or will be, successful in substituting a monolithic political philosophy for the religious heritage of the Chinese people will be discussed after a brief examination of Chinese religions.

Ancestral Cult

The ancestral cult was the oldest and most pervasive of Chinese religions. Found in all classes of society and in all geographical areas, ancestor worship surpassed any other Chinese religious practice in social utility and was so interwoven into the very fabric of life as to be an integral part of the Chinese ethic.

The basis of ancestor worship was the assumption that the living can communicate directly with the dead and that the dead, though living in another realm, can influence and be influenced by events in this world. In anticipation of his role in the afterlife, a Chinese would make every effort to avoid a violent death or any form of death that would result in his entering the spirit world in mutilated form.

Among the many duties of a faithful descendant, the primary duty was veneration of his ancestors' spirits. Most homes had a small chapel or a shelf containing ancestral tablets, pieces of wood inscribed with the name, title, and sometimes birth and death dates, of an ancestor. The use of the wooden tablet as the spirit throne had kept such ancestral shrines generally free from idols. If there were ancestral portraits, they were valued as family heirlooms, not as religious objects. Ceremonies in which incense was burned and candles were lighted usually took place before the tablets on the first and fifteenth days of the month in the lunar calendar. On festivals, such as New Year's Day, and occasions such as a change of residence, official promotion, and the birth and death anniversaries of ancestors of the last three generations, a complete meal was offered. All offerings of food, rice, and wine were accompanied by kowtowing which the parents and children performed according to their seniority.

Most ceremonies and offerings to ancestral tablets took place in the home, but once every year, at the Ch'ing-ming festival in spring, the family graveyard was cleaned and repaired, and yellow paper currency was burned for the use of the departed. These two cult centers, the ancestral shrine and the grave mound, had been from earliest times the two physical centers of ancestor worship.

The personal nature of ancestor worship all but precluded the organization of the ancestral cult into groups larger than the family and at the same time made ancestor worship particularly resistant to changes in philosophic thought, such as the humanistic and rationalistic tendencies of the Neo-Confucian thinkers. Rejection was the ultimate fate of any idea—such as the Buddhist, Islamic, and Christian concepts of heaven—that could not be reconciled to this ritualized and personal relationship with ancestral spirits. The ritual had also become a social tradition to the extent that the social accretions would have survived the withdrawal of the religious purpose. It is difficult therefore to overestimate the universality or importance of the ancestral cult in traditional Chinese culture.

But having flourished with unabated vigor century after century—from before the fifth century B.C. and Confucius' time to the first decade of the twentieth century—the ancestral cult abruptly began to lose vitality. Less and less important in modern Chinese society, the historical patriarchal family system and the traditional beliefs about the afterlife, both fundamental to the existence of the cult, were being sacrificed to the demands of modern political and social theories. What had been a religious attitude toward ancestors had become in modern times little more than a sentimental tie.

Folk Religion

A curious mixture of sophisticated ideas and gross superstition derived from ancestor worship and the world of spirits as well as of the three literate traditions, folk religion varied widely from person to person and region to region.

Basic to the structure of folk religion was belief in a direct and reciprocal relationship between this world and the other world, as well as between various gods and spirits and human beings generally. Gods, ancestors, and other spirits shared a mutual dependence with human beings, bestowing aid in return for worship and honor.

The other world, a shadowy but real counterpart of life here on earth, was the home of both departed ancestors and a diverse pantheon of local deities—dragons, ghosts, demons, and animal spirits as well as deified heroes of Chinese history. Gods, men, and animals were jumbled together with no hard and fast rules for distinguishing them.

The reality of this other world in the Chinese peasant's mind led to very definite beliefs concerning death. The ghost of a person who had suffered a violent or unjust death, for example, found compensation in his next abode in increased force or good fortune. To be killed by a thunderbolt, on the other hand, was regarded a frightful disgrace, evidence that the person had been an unfilial son or a criminal.

An admixture of Buddhist ideas of judgment contributed to a further refinement of the concept of afterlife among many peasants. Death was understood as a summons by Yen-lo Wang (Yama Buddha), the king of Hades, who would send an emissary to call the soul to him. But before the person's soul departed on the long journey to the underworld, his ghost first appeared before the local god to receive a preliminary judgment. Final judgment was rendered when the ghost reached the underworld.

Chinese folk religion contained an important body of ideas concerning the soul. Some believed there were two souls in every human being: the *p'o*, or animating agent, which belonged to all living creatures, returned with the body to the earth at death; the *hun*, or rational soul, belonged only to man and at death ascended to heaven. The heart was the seat of the soul, but sometimes the soul had its residence in the breath. The latter belief gave breathing exercises important religious overtones. According to some, a person's name was a "handle" to the soul, and control over names through curses, charms, and other devices amounted to control over the person. There was a ceremony to recall the soul at death and there had developed taboos of ancestral and imperial names. Shadows were believed to be real parts of the soul and care was taken in the funeral ceremony to keep shadows out of the coffin and grave. Dreams too had spiritual qualities: they were means of communication with the spirit world.

The belief that spirits and souls might enter into or possess animate or inanimate objects was the basis for a well-developed animism. For most Chinese, the grave was treated as a fetish, hence the Chinese concern for fêng-shui (literally, "wind and water," that is, occult influences) when choosing a site for the family grave. Certain animals, especially the tiger, wolf, fox, crane, unicorn, phoenix, dragon, and tortoise, were considered fetish objects; so were flags, books, mirrors, pictures, and trees. But from ancient times, the most important spiritual media in many regions were human agents called *wu* or shamans.

The shaman was a person of singular physical and mental characteristics who, possessed himself by a spirit, was an expert in dealing with the spirit world. The services of a shaman were usually sought when affairs or persons were *in extremis*. The office of the shaman was hereditary, passing from father to son, and the greater the number of generations who had practiced shamanism, the more powerful the in-dwelling spirit in the present incumbent.

The educated Chinese despised and rejected shamans, necromancers, geomancers, fortunetellers, and sorcerers but the Chinese masses constantly sought supernatural aid in their lifelong struggles. Ancient religious practices flourished in spite of hostility and repression by the ruling class, most of whom were Confucian scholars. The shaman always remained a peasant and seldom betrayed the aims of the peasant society in which he enjoyed high prestige. His knowledge of the spirit world was supposed to be the best possible preparation for conduct of affairs in this world.

For the Chinese peasant there was no clear line between ancestral spirits and gods or between impersonal forces and men. All mysterious or unknown elements in the universe were interpreted in terms of another world peopled by personal gods. Thus blessings and fate were not the result of chance but the gifts of divinities who gave them to human beings as they chose. These divinities were organized into an enormous hierarchy akin to Chinese imperial society, with most gods holding a temporary office subject to promotion or demotion just like earthly functionaries. This pantheon included many deceased men who had been elevated to godly rank, and thus many gods had human ties and biographies. Buddhism introduced ethical considerations when the assignment of the deceased to divine posts was made to depend upon merits acquired in previous existences. Deity, just like public office, was a charge. The title did not vary, but the officeholders changed and succeeded one another. Some were degraded and returned to earth as men. The highest, however, never returned to earth and never died, but held office indefinitely, having attained immortality.

Peasant ideas about the upper level of the celestial hierarchy were not the same everywhere. Many peasants attributed supreme lordship to Shang-ti, the Emperor Above, or to T'ien, the Emperor of Heaven. The chief deity was also known as Yü-huang, the Jade Emperor. Whatever his name, the Supreme Being was omnipotent and omniscient. He saw and heard all; he decided everything according to his pleasure; he was just, aiding the good and punishing the wicked. He maintained a constant order and saw that the seasons rotated in an orderly fashion.

One of the most important gods was a household divinity, the kitchen god. Even well-educated persons revered this tutelary deity, who kept an account of all the good and bad deeds of the family during the year so that he could report to the Emperor of Heaven before the end of the year. As he left his niche in the family kitchen, his image was burned to provide his ascent to Heaven. In many homes incense was offered to the kitchen god on a number of occasions.

The worship of local deities had greater variations and underwent more modifications with the passage of time than the worship of household gods. Each village or town had its own shrine or temple dedicated to a tutelary god, *t'u-ti*, who had charge of the local census and to whom all deaths were reported.

Like the tutelary gods, the *ch'eng-huang* (gods of walls and moats) were the spirits of men of some local importance. They were appointed, promoted, and dismissed in the heavenly hierarchy just as were their confreres in this life. Their temples served the same purpose in the spiritual environment that magistrative courts serve in this world. The Chinese also worshiped *ts'ai-shen*, the god of wealth. The rural population as well as urban tradesmen and shopkeepers welcomed him on New Year's Eve. Among shopkeepers in certain localities, participation in the feast in his honor constituted an unwritten agreement by an employee to remain with the shop for another year.

In parts of rural China, the rain god was equivalent to a god of wealth. In areas where the absence of rain signified ruin for most people, the cult of the rain god was the most popular village cult. The rain god was represented by *lung-wang*, the dragon king. Rivers, mountains, sun, and moon were worshiped as divinities. Old rocks and old trees might also develop into supernatural spirits.

Not all spirits were benevolent. The world was also inhabited by such evil spirits as demons, monsters, and goblins. The commonest were *kuei*, the disembodied spirits of the dead. Certain animals had supernatural powers, especially foxes and snakes, which might assume charming forms to seduce young men and slowly devour their spiritual essence. Badgers and tigers were supernatural. The ghosts of people eaten by tigers tried to attract others as replacements so as to free themselves. Children were particularly exposed to evil spirits and thus had to wear amulets for special protection.

Almanacs were useful in that they told of auspicious or unlucky days. In the past the peasant's religious life, like his agricultural life, was integrated into a calendar, according to which he made his round of work and worship. Since he believed that pious works permitted escape from the underworld, he patronized Buddhist and Taoist shrines as deeds of penance. He made small contributions for the restoration of temples, the erection of statues, the copying of holy books; he gave alms, saved life by freeing captive fish and birds, and practiced vegetarianism in the Buddhist tradition. He even had recourse to faith in the devout repetition of the Buddha's name, as taught by Buddhist evangelists. He was deferential toward Buddhist and Moslem idiosyncrasies. He refused to burn candles made of sheep fat before Buddhist shrines and avoided the presentation of pork to Moslem believers. Modified by, and politely deferential to, the organized faiths, folk religion contains traditions as old as antiquity and has remained until very recently a potent force in the life of the Chinese peasant.

Literate Religious Traditions

The teachings of the Confucian school recorded in the Chinese classics, Taoist teachings drawn from Chinese religious and philosophical traditions and similarly preserved in the classical language, and Buddhist teachings composed mainly of Chinese translations from Sanskrit with commentaries by Chinese Buddhists comprise the three great literate traditions, sometimes referred to as "the three religions" of China. The term "religion" is, however, somewhat of a misnomer in this context as the literate traditions of China, though on occasion providing spiritual guidance and enlightenment, were philosophical systems rather than religious systems in the strict sense. "Churches," defined as organized bodies of believers with a uniform doctrine, failed to materialize.

Confucianism

The historically most important literate tradition of China is Confucianism, consisting of a body of philosophical and literary writings attributed to Confucius and his followers. Some scholars have gone so far as to state that Confucianism is the embodiment of the moral and religious aspects of Chinese civilization. Curiously enough, it has remained an intellectual tradition without formal organization.

Two different components of Confucianism must be noted: the earlier *Ju-chia* or Confucian school of philosophy, and the later *K'ung-chiao* or Confucian religion. The *Ju-chia* represented a political-philosophical tradition which was extremely important in imperial times. This was the element most directly connected with the person and teachings of Confucius. The *K'ung-chiao* represented state efforts to meet religious needs within the framework of the Confucian tradition.

For almost two thousand years the Confucian philosophy reigned supreme as official political ideology and dominant intellectual tradition. The Confucian emphasis on morality provided a rational basis for the conduct of affairs of government and the ordering of Chinese society and was so successful as a political philosophy that even a ruler who had developed a personal preference for Buddhism or Taoism would continue practical support of Confucian teachings. But an inherent religious neutrality made Confucianism too impersonal to fill the emotional needs of the people, who respected the Confucian scholar but turned elsewhere for spiritual consolation and guidance. Thus the intellectual triumph of Confucianism was attained only at the price of an even wider breach between the learned bureaucrat and the unlettered peasant.

Under the administration of the Confucian scholars, the imperial sacrifices, though containing some religious appeal, had become chiefly ceremonial, and the emperor was not in the slightest degree a high priest. The popularity of Buddhism, however, had so alarmed the literati that they tried to extend the archaic imperial cult into a public state cult, making a place for the sage Confucius and the local protective deities. This was the origin of the state cult of Confucius, or *K'ung-chiao*. Confucian temples were erected at his ancestral home, in the capital, and in all prefectural and county seats. He was canonized first as "Supreme Master," then as "King," "Perfect Sage," and "Highest Saint"; and his image was placed in the schools.

To the scholar class, Confucius was the symbol of ideological unity, and as such was also the center of the state cult. To the peasantry, he always represented the interests of the state and was never popular. He was venerated but not worshiped and, despite state support, *K'ung-chiao* never became a popular religion.

The modern period saw the collapse of Confucianism as a religious institution as identification of Confucian teaching with the Chinese empire created a determined opposition to Confucianism in all its forms. The civil service examinations based on Confucian classics were abolished in 1905. Sacrifices in the Confucian temple were discontinued in 1928. A number of abortive attempts to bolster Confucianism as a state cult merely discredited it further in the eyes of the Chinese intelligentsia. Some Nationalist leaders sought to accord more honors to Confucius, but studiously kept free from any religious involvement. Reduced to a philosophy, Confucianism survived only in the intellectual world, and even there it is in danger of being supplanted by new systems of thought from the West, in particular, the dialectical materialism of the Communists.

Taoism

Taoism, like Confucianism, was both a philosophy and a religion. The Taoist religion, which emerged several centuries after Taoist philosophy, was eclectic, borrowing many important religious features from its chief rival, Buddhism, and absorbing from folk religion a number of its practices and beliefs.

Traditionally, the organization of Taoist religion is said to have had its beginning in the first century after Christ. It was a kind of Taoism that some scholars suspect was based on Persian Mazdaism. This cult practiced confession of sin, cure of diseases, prayers to the spirits, and an elaborate angelology; it introduced a priesthood and a tight organization in order to compete with the Buddhists. Later, Persian influence on Taoism was forgotten, but the organization it had given the Taoist religion and the Taoist church remained for the rest of its history.

Taoism appealed to the mystical side of human nature, evoking responses more religious than philosophical. It asked for faith and in return promised blessings and immortality. Taoism grew into a warm personal religion and supplied a human need Confucianism had neglected. It finally became very difficult to draw a line between Taoism and folk religion, so closely were they linked. It might be said that whenever folk religion became literate, systematized, and intellectualized—thus losing its primitive character—it became Taoism.

The organization and ritual of Taoism were blatant imitations of Buddhism. Taoism introduced religious rules for monks and the laity; it founded monasteries and adopted a tight parish organization with hereditary patriarchs, presided over by the *T'ien-shih,* known to the West as the "Taoist Pope." Its clergy, called *tao-shih* (Taoist priests), were elected and ordained in ways very similar to those of the Buddhists and were of two classes: non-monastic *tao-shih,* who remained with their families while observing a religious rule; and regular *tao-shih,* who resided as groups in monasteries. Both types were bound to fast, recite liturgies, and conduct ceremonies as the occasion demanded. Unlike Buddhist monks, Taoist priests kept their family names as well as their hair. But a strong Buddhist influence could be found in the architecture of Taoist temples, called *kuan* and *kung,* as well as in Taoist ceremonies and music.

The Taoist pantheon, like the Buddhist, was large. In the divine hierarchy, headed by the Jade Emperor, all the ancient folk deities such as the kitchen god, guardian spirits, the god of wealth, and many others were assigned their respective places. The Taoist cult also embraced the rich reservoir of native superstitions: geomancy, divination, witchcraft, fortunetelling, astrology, communication with the dead, alchemy, and others.

The association of alchemy and Taoism began in very early times. A fourth-century Chinese treatise describes at length the manufacture of the drug of immortality and the transmutation of cinnabar and mercury into gold. The chemical knowledge that this treatise evidences is of considerable interest and importance. Both alchemy and medicine continued to be identified with Taoism throughout Chinese history and were therefore consistently despised by educated Confucians as superstitious practices.

Still another indication of the cosmopolitan quality of Taoism is to be found in its introduction of breathing controls, somewhat similar to Indian yoga practices, and a special diet designed to prolong life. This facet is still considered an area of proficiency for the Taoist practitioner.

The scientific and philosophic contributions of Taoism continue to interest scholars but the Taoist church had begun to decline in importance even before the end of the nineteenth century. The official end came when the last hereditary *T'ien-shih,* presiding over the Taoist headquarters in the Dragon and Tiger Mountain in Kiangsi, was dispossessed by the Nationalist government in 1927.

Buddhism

Buddhism, the third literate tradition of China, originated in the teachings of Gautama Buddha, an Indian prince who lived in the sixth century B.C. A Buddhist tradition developed and in the centuries that followed Buddhism was introduced to other countries, becoming a dominant influence throughout Asia.

Chinese Buddhism was mainly of the Mahayana school, so named to distinguish it from the earlier form of Buddhism known to the West as Hinayana. Whereas the Hinayanists taught that the historical Gautama was the only Buddha, a great teacher and not a divinity, and that no prayers, invocations, and offerings were to be made to him, the Mahayana Buddhists believed that Gautama was merely one of a series of incarnations, and that he listened to the prayers of mankind, responded to invocations, and delighted in offerings. In Chinese Buddhism, the Indian bodhisattva Avalokiteshvara, originally a male divinity, became the Goddess of Mercy, Kuan-yin; Amida Buddha (Amitabha), another bodhisattva, became the ruler of the western heaven. Hells and purgatories appeared in short order.

Buddhism was first introduced into China at least as early as the first century after Christ. Its chief appeal lay in its promise of salvation. Chinese Buddhists used Mahayana materials to create a Chinese version of Mahayana Buddhism. In popular Chinese Buddhist sects, nirvana was replaced by the western heaven; monasteries became havens of peace rather than schools of discipline. Buddhism became a worldly church contributing to the practice of a serene and kindly life. Buddhism, which exhibited religious restraints in early India, took the most profoundly religious forms in China.

In their Chinese guise, Buddhist gods were not distinguished from the Taoist gods who lived in palaces like emperors, were surrounded by officials, and held audience in courts. Buddhist images were worshiped and sacrifices were offered to them. Buddhist temples and ceremonies were replicas of the imperial palace and court ceremonies. Public officials demanded two things—loyalty and gifts—and these were also expected of Buddhist worshipers. Buddhist theology which loomed so large in the Indian environment seemed to lose much of its importance in the Buddhist world of the Chinese masses. Chinese Buddhism, though derived from Indian Buddhism, was quite different from the latter, and in a very real sense was Chinese rather than foreign.

In China, Buddhist sanghas (religious communities) developed clergy and masters of ceremony who attended to rituals rather than theology. These were less respected by the scholars but won the favor of the masses. Like Taoism, Chinese Buddhism organized great ceremonies of penitence and of the sacrifices for dead ancestors, festivals which gave to individuals the personal religious life they sought. In a small way, the sanghas also aided social mobility. The career of a monk had certain advantages over that of many a commoner because it provided educational opportunities which might open the way to fame and influence.

The influence of Buddhism in China was great. It encouraged

direct contact between China and India with Chinese monks undertaking pilgrimages to India and Indian Buddhist patriarchs and teachers taking up residence in China to spread the Buddhist gospel. The Buddhist Dhyana school, a meditative or institutional group, founded by the Indian monk Bodhidharma, grew into the prominent Ch'an contemplative school. It claims that all human beings contain the germ of Buddhahood, and that this state is to be realized by contemplation. Ch'an Buddhism so rejected theology and avoided written texts that it was denounced as heretical by the other schools. Through China this school was transmitted to Japan where under the name of Zen it became even more famous.

There were periods in which Buddhism was welcomed by both the ruling class and the masses of China, while at other times it suffered persecution at the hands of Taoist-inspired emperors or Confucian-oriented bureaucrats. At no time, however, did religious persecutions in China assume such proportions as to be comparable to persecutions in the West.

Chinese rulers made political use of Buddhism in their efforts to control the Mongol and Tibetan peoples who adhered to Lama-ism, a form of Mahayana Buddhism adulterated by native shaman-istic beliefs and elaborate ritualistic practices. Although Lamaism never made much impression upon the matter-of-fact settled pop-ulation of China Proper, the imperial government sedulously cul-tivated and fostered Lamaism with all its hierarchal organization as a potentially useful form of political and social control, especially in Tibet.

Buddhism suffered serious setbacks as modern ideas swept China. Bitter hostility from radical elements—freethinkers to mili-tant atheists—led to iconoclastic destruction. The government, faced with the mounting cost of external and internal wars, im-posed special taxes on religious properties or in some cases simply confiscated such properties. From 1929 to 1933 the Nationalist government severely regulated all Buddhist temples and clergy. Without popular support, many monasteries in rural areas reverted to local ownership and were converted to other uses. Only a shrunken clergy, disorganized and disheartened, remained in China.

Adversity seemed to renew, however, the inner strength of Buddhism. The sanghas produced in the twentieth century im-portant religious teachers such as Abbot Yin-kuang, an eloquent preacher; T'i-hsien, who taught a form of Buddhist pietism; and Ou-yang Ching-wu, who led a revival of the Idealist school. The

Abbot T'ai-hsü gave a new stimulus to Ch'an idealism. He represented China at the Asian Conference on Buddhism in Japan, instituted Chinese conferences on Buddhism, and sent Chinese students to study Buddhism in Thailand, Ceylon, and Tibet. He revived the Chinese Buddhist Society in 1939 in Chungking, and by 1947 the organization claimed four and a half million members. Intellectual revival also led to the founding of several Buddhist colleges and institutes. By 1937 there were forty-five active Buddhist seminaries. From 1920 to 1950 there was a large-scale reprinting of Buddhist texts.

Probably under the pressure of rival Christian mission activities the Buddhists developed youth organizations, founded hospitals and orphanages, and engaged in many types of social work. A Buddhist revival was certainly in progress just before the Communist conquest.

Foreign Religions

Many foreign religions such as Judaism, Nestorianism, Manichaeism, and Mazdaism at one time or another had a temporary foothold in China, but the only foreign religions that had weathered Chinese governmental opposition and gained a large following were Islam and Christianity.

Islam

Islam, one of the most important foreign religions, found a permanent place in China. (Buddhism lost its status as a foreign religion as a result of the relentless process of Sinicization that accompanied its spread as a popular faith.) But its unbending monotheistic insistence that there is but one God, Allah, and Mohammed is his prophet kept Islam from becoming widespread in China.

Chinese generally referred to Islam as "Hui-Hui chiao," which probably meant the religion of the Uigurs, a Turkic tribe settled mainly in Sinkiang. Islam was the faith of the Uigur, Arabian, Iranian, and other immigrants who had settled down in China and who came generally to exhibit little racial difference from their Han-Chinese compatriots. Almost one half of the Chinese Moslems spoke a Turkic language as their native dialect. The best pre-Communist sources estimated a total of ten to fifteen million Moslems in China; official Communist sources initially reported an aggregate of ten million. Though distributed in a number of

Chinese provinces, the most important traditional centers were in Yunnan, Kansu, Sinkiang, Ningsia, and Inner Mongolia, where they constituted a significant percentage of the total population.

The religious life of the Moslem community exhibited an almost puritanic simplicity. The lack of a strong centralized authority encouraged local autonomy. Imams (prayer leaders) and akhunds (mosque ministers) were elected by the local mosques and led the services every Friday and on special festivals. In the most important mosques, Arabic-speaking mullahs replaced the akhunds in ceremonial offices. These Moslem preachers lived on teaching pay, public donations, and fees for the slaughter of animals (a religious monopoly). Spokesmen for the Chinese Moslem community, with more prestige than authority, were appointed by the government throughout Chinese history in a generally successful attempt to keep the sect under Chinese political control, but such representatives were never considered religious officers.

The Islamic community never sought to identify itself with Chinese culture. Chinese Moslems for a long time regarded themselves as foreign tributaries, and as such recognized imperial political control. But they thought any idea that they would become completely Chinese as foolish as the idea that all Chinese would be converted to Islam. Like Moslems everywhere, Chinese Moslems had a predilection for Arabic and avoided the Chinese language in a religious context whenever possible. The standard Chinese version of the *Life of Mohammed* was not written until 1712, almost a thousand years after Islam's entrance into China. More recently there was a revival of interest in a Chinese translation of the Koran.

Moslem social customs were also preserved tenaciously, especially the marriage and burial rites. The bride and groom did not make the usual obeisance to heaven and earth and wedding certificates were written in Arabic. Burial took place in segregated Moslem graveyards. Arabic and Persian phrases were preserved, especially in polite salutations. Turbans were customary, and food laws were observed. Children were named from the Koran; boys were circumcised at seven and mated at fifteen. Sons could take Chinese wives, but daughters were never permitted to marry out of the faith. Shunning usury, divination, geomancy, and the stage, Moslems generally lived in secluded quarters, preferring military to civil posts although there had been Moslem viceroys and governors throughout Chinese history. They referred to their villages as "barracks" and "quarters."

Chinese Islam was one of the most isolated and provincial communities in the Islamic world. It very early lost its overland and overseas contact with the Arab centers. When a Chinese imperial ban on traveling abroad was lifted in the seventeenth century, some Chinese Moslems made the pilgrimage to Mecca and re-established contact with the outside. Chinese Moslem leaders noted the political consolidation that had taken place in the Islamic world, and judged their own earlier democratic traditions unorthodox. A series of evangelistic reformers, of whom Muhammed Amim (Ma Ming-hsin) has been the most important, campaigned for a return to orthodoxy. The "new doctrine" (*hsin chiao*) demanded a centralized, institutionalized, orthodox Moslem state, and introduced ritual differences to mark its changed political outlook from the "old doctrine."

Strife between followers of the old and new doctrines was the most important factor in the Moslem defeat in the nineteenth century revolts. The "new doctrine" sect wanted to found a separate Moslem state within Chinese territory in the tradition of Yakub Beg. The "old doctrine" Moslems surrendered to imperial Chinese troops and aided in restoring order among their own people. The new sectarians accused the "old teachers" of betraying their cause, but they were so divided that they recognized no common leadership. After 1911, a "new, new sect" arose that preached a liberalized Islam in terms of social custom, political theory, and religious faith. It gained adherents in the large coastal cities.

Chinese Moslem literature also displayed a new vitality in recent decades. Thirty to forty titles, including the Koran itself, were translated from Arabic and Persian into Chinese. Monthly magazines such as *Islamic Monthly*, *Crescent*, and *Light of Islam* were founded and flourished during the republican period (1912-49).

The same period opened the way to political and military power for many Moslems. Stimulated by the military-political successes of prominent Moslem leaders in the Nationalist government, several thousand Moslem students attended military academies. Under pressure of the Sino-Japanese War (1937-45), the Nationalist government encouraged the formation of the Chinese Islamic National Salvation Federation to support the government in its struggle. Japan sought political support from the All-China Moslem League established in areas under Japanese occupation.

Chinese government encouragement made it possible for Moslems to re-establish the pilgrimage to Mecca. From 1923 to 1934,

834 Chinese Moslems made the journey to Mecca. After a temporary suspension during the Sino-Japanese War, the hadj was continued and since then an average of 200 have made the pilgrimage each year. It may be said that in terms of religious vitality, political power, intellectual resilience, and international position, Chinese Islam advanced markedly in the forty years of the republican era.

Christianity

There is no generally accepted term for Christianity in Chinese. Catholicism and Protestantism, which were introduced separately, are called respectively "T'ien-chu chiao" (doctrine of the Heavenly Lord) and "Chi-tu chiao" (doctrine of Christ). Apart from a mutual recognition of such fundamental doctrines as baptism, both groups maintained an isolation as studied as that between two different religions.

Christianity first entered China in the T'ang dynasty in the form of Nestorianism, a sect of the Eastern Church. This soon disappeared after the religious persecution of 845, and except for a brief contact between the Mongol emperors and the papacy in Rome, Christianity was not reintroduced to China until the sixteenth century in the wake of European exploration of the Pacific regions.

At that time, the Jesuits, under the leadership of Matteo Ricci, established Catholic churches in Peking and other Chinese cities in the Yangtze valley. By means of their scientific knowledge, and especially their mathematical and astronomical skills, they displaced the Moslem officials who regulated the calendar, and received a stipend from the emperor for their services. Their diligent cultivation of the Chinese language and literature won them the good will of the Confucian scholars. Their success encouraged other religious bodies such as the Franciscans and Dominicans to follow them to China. But internal discord among these missionary groups started the so-called Rites Controversy which found the Chinese emperor and the Pope in irreconcilable opposition. The papal decision in 1742 forbidding Chinese Christians to observe ancestor worship and to participate in other Confucian rites was denounced by the emperor who ordered all Chinese Christians to conduct such worship as befitted loyal Chinese. This impasse meant the end of official favor for Catholic missions and the recurrence of local persecution, which had first started late in the sixteenth century. The French Revolution, the rise of secularism, and the suspension of the Jesuit order reduced European support and greatly weakened the religious foundation that had been so carefully laid over a period of two hundred years.

The modern phase of Christian missionary work began at the time of China's defeat by European powers in the mid-nineteenth century. In the treaties China concluded with the western nations, missionaries were guaranteed the right to live and travel in the interior, the protection of their own governments, and immunity from Chinese interference. Christian successes caused increasing apprehension among Chinese government officials. The double threat of Christian alliance with foreign imperialism and its theoretical contribution to native rebellions generated much anti-Christian sentiment among the tradition-bound Chinese, culminating in the Boxer Rebellion of 1900. In spite of hostility, Christian expansion among the Chinese people continued. At the beginning of the republican period there were an estimated one and a half million Catholics and one-third of a million Protestants in China.

Missionary efforts—both Catholic and Protestant—to teach western learning contributed to the ferment that gave birth to the revolution of 1911 and the establishment of the Chinese Republic. Westerners saw in the nascent republic the emergence of a new China built on western premises. Veteran missionaries played the role of public servant, sometimes for China and sometimes for western governments. Chinese Protestant and Catholic clergy took part in the organization of their own churches on a national basis. In spite of foreign wars and internal strife, mission work flourished during the republican period.

This was a time of dramatic growth in the Chinese Christian Church. The Confucian bureaucracy lost its position with the demise of the empire as western education became the prerequisite training for government work. As western education was made available through the efforts of missionary organizations, relations between church and state were friendly and the church flourished. Opposition to Christianity, however, did not die; it merely smoldered. Some Chinese champions of their own secularism, resenting the position of Christianity, tried to gain support for their humanism in the anti-Christian humanism of the West. Other Chinese nationalists turned to radicalism in an effort to find a counterbalance to Anglo-American influence. These found a congenial home in Chinese Communism. Even before the Communist conquest of China, its anti-Christian, antireligious propaganda had been a powerful influence. As a whole, however, missionary work expanded as foreign men and money poured into China.

In the post World War II period, over three million baptized Roman Catholics were reported in China. The Chinese Catholics received their first cardinal, the Most Reverend Thomas T'ien (T'ien Keng-hsin), Archbishop of Peiping, in December 1945, and by April 1946 a complete Chinese hierarchy had been established. Approximately half of the 5,442 priests, 1,304 brothers, and 6,456 sisters were native Chinese; while 1,214 senior seminarians and 4,143 junior seminarians ensured an increasing supply of native Chinese priests. A large international body, representing as many as thirty-six different nationalities and thirteen large orders (Jesuit, Dominican, Franciscan, Maryknoll, and others) laid foundations for the church in mission stations throughout the country. As a result of their efforts, Catholics were found all over China, but the largest concentrations were in Peking, Shanghai, Canton, and the lower Yangtze valley.

By 1948 the Catholic church was operating 776 primary schools and 155 middle schools with 220,000 students, and 3 universities. The medical work of 288 hospitals, 866 dispensaries, 320 orphanages, and 8 leper hospitals was coordinated through a Catholic Welfare Committee. Postwar publications failed to equal the number in 1935, when 115 periodicals (53 exclusively Chinese) and 26 printing establishments supplied Catholic literature. However, a Catholic daily, *I-shih pao,* gained wide circulation in a number of Chinese cities and a Catholic press service supplied information to independent papers.

During World War II, approximately 170 Protestant missionary societies from a dozen western countries maintained foreign missionaries in China. More than 2,000 Chinese ministers and 900 foreign missionaries maintained 12,000 separate places of worship in China. Religious training for Chinese ministers and catechists was given in 50 theological schools and 160 Bible schools.

Although Protestants generally left responsibility for the organization of the Chinese church to the Chinese, native Chinese also produced the same divisions and schisms as western Protestantism. Most of the million baptized Protestant Chinese in the postwar period belonged to thirteen Chinese Christian churches. The most important were: the Church of Christ in China (Presbyterian-Congregational), Methodist, Episcopal, Baptist, and Lutheran. From 1922 most of the larger denominations participated, on the basis of liberal theological tendencies, in the National Christian Council of China. Fundamentalist Protestants, however, persisted in non-cooperation.

Chinese Protestant Christians were mostly found in large cities and in the treaty ports along the coast, where foreign contacts were most numerous. One missionary society, the China Inland Mission, dedicated itself exclusively to evangelism of the interior. The middle class with western professional training, including educators, lawyers, doctors, scientists, and merchants, constituted the backbone of the membership of most major Protestant bodies. City workers, a by-product of China's rudimentary industrialization, sometimes found a place in fundamentalist Protestant chapels.

All through the modern period, Protestant missionary societies paid great attention to education. After World War II they maintained 13 Christian colleges and 2,301 Christian middle schools in 103 cities. There were at least a quarter of a million alumni of Christian schools in China.

Medical work, too, was greatly emphasized. In 1948, Protestant missions supported 216 hospitals, 23 leprosariums, 38 clinics, 5 medical schools, and 40 nursing schools. These ministered to 5 million outpatients and 60,000 inpatients per year. According to one reliable source, these education and medical services cost American church missions the largest part of its annual budget of 8 million American dollars. The Associated Board of Christian Colleges in China provided another 1.25 million American dollars annually.

Most Protestant churches sought to produce Christian literature through the Christian Literature Society in Shanghai. Two of its most important periodicals were *Happy Childhood* and the *Christian Farmer*. In 1947 it distributed 37 new publications and 147 reprints. Bible printing and distribution were also united ventures. In the same year the China Bible House sold 88,898 copies of the Bible and many times that number of portions of the Bible.

Another important cooperative venture was the National Christian Relief Council. During World War II this body cooperated with the Chinese Nationalist government in providing and distributing relief. In certain relief stations in the interior, separate Protestant churches made some effort at rural missions which contributed to the rural reconstruction movement.

Apart from the churches, the most important Protestant Christian organizations were undoubtedly the Young Men's Christian Association (YMCA) and the Young Women's Christian Association (YWCA). The YMCA, introduced to China for the Chinese in 1885, grew rapidly and came under complete Chinese control earlier than the churches. It was more liberal, possibly because its short history isolated it from contact with orthodox theologies. The YMCA served the Chinese labor battalion in World War I, conducted extensive literacy campaigns, promoted public health and athletic sports, and supported liberal social and political programs. In the twilight days of Nationalist China, the YMCA courted public support for the Communist cause and provided many of the Christian spokesmen for the Communist government in China.

State and Religion

Throughout China's history religious activity has to greater or lesser degree been subject to government control. In the imperial period, religious organizations and activities were always strictly limited by the state. Public and private morality was based on a combination of philosophical principles and secular mores rather than on any religion. Only after the government had decided that their beliefs and practices were conducive to morality and the welfare of the state would the adherents of any particular religion be granted a carefully defined sphere of activity. Anything beyond this sphere sanctioned by the state was *ipso facto* subversive and detrimental to public welfare, and the religion was promptly curbed or suppressed. In consequence the conditions were never present for the emergence of an independent and powerful church in China capable of influencing public morality or state policy.

With the slow collapse of the traditional order, the effectiveness of governmental control of religion diminished. In the late nineteenth and early twentieth centuries, as western powers gained more and more political concessions from a weakening China, they also demanded and obtained the "rights" of religious and missionary activity which no strong Chinese government would have granted. But the rise of nationalist sentiment in the past centuries brought with it hatred of foreigners and their religion—a hatred that exploded repeatedly in antiforeign, anti-Christian riots.

Meanwhile another trend was visible. Religious groups and a number of outstanding political leaders began to feel that China could not become a truly modern nation unless it was reformed from the moral base upwards. Religion had furthered the power and success of western nations. Would not a religion based on Confucianism, a revitalized Buddhism, or even Christianity help bring about the basic transformation that China so sorely needed?

This view was rejected by two overlapping groups which had decisive power in state and society after 1925. The first group consisted of intellectual leaders who were increasingly committed to some form of materialistic philosophy which considered all religions to be parasitic, corrosive, and nonprogressive. The second group consisted of Nationalist officials, many of whom derived their antireligious views from the intellectual leadership. Consciously or unconsciously, they reverted to the view that no strong self-respecting government should permit independent religious bodies to challenge the government's right to control all aspects of public or private life.

Religion in twentieth-century China was thus caught in the cross fire of negative sentiment and attack. To modernize or to become militant was to provoke state suppression, and the efforts of religious leaders to stem the rising tide of intellectual materialism failed. In the countryside, in spite of peasant persistence, the old folk religion continued to show signs of withering away. Religious Taoism and Confucianism were dying of spiritual anemia, while the Buddhist revival was ephemeral and Chinese Islam remained isolated. Christianity made some advances, but it was always tainted by its foreignness and by the fact that its missionaries came with the backing of western gunboats.

Religion under Communism

Communist policy toward religion is in many respects the culmination of these trends. The fact that there was in China not one unified church but a number of widely varied religious beliefs and practices made Chinese religions especially vulnerable to the determined assault of the Communists, whose policy, as stated before, is to eradicate all religious traditions among the people, substituting a monolithic Communist ideology. The Communist regime has adopted different methods and techniques to bring the various religious groups under its control. Because of the lack of organizational framework, Confucianism, Taoism, and Buddhism readily succumbed under this attack.

On the other hand, Islam and Christianity have a clearly defined laity, a well-organized church, and a strong political background in the rest of the world, and this partly explains the different treatment they have received at the hands of the Chinese Communists.

Popular Beliefs

Traditionally individuals worshiped as members of a family, seeking good fortune for the family as a group. Even though worship sometimes took place outside the home, wherever it was observed it was by and for the family. This was one of the factors that led to the Chinese Communist attack on the traditional patriarchal family system, which provided a social coherence that competed with Communist forms of social control. Naturally, the ancestral cult, the religious concomitant of the traditional family, was repudiated at the same time. The Communists poke fun and scoff at it, denouncing it as superstitious, antisocial, and unscientific. Some Marxist sociologists have stigmatized it as a fossil remnant of a tribal past. Ceremonial adjuncts of the cult are denounced for the additional reason that they demand expenditure of time and money.

The study groups organized among the peasants during land reform programs and in the winter slack season spend a part of their time ridiculing ancestor worship and folk religion. These are invariably depicted as ignorant superstitions, psychological crutches for a weak and cowardly people. When the peasant is sympathetic to the Communist movement, he accepts the Communist cadre's teachings as modern and scientific. But when the peasant views his new life as bondage, he remains obstinate and purposely inconspicuous in his old beliefs. The rigid organization of the rural communes, however, has reduced any noticeable peasant resistance to Communist indoctrination in religious matters.

Confucianism

As a religion, Confucianism has disappeared without a trace in Communist China. All local Confucian temples or shrines that remained were converted into schools, cultural centers, or storage depots. This was made easy by the fact that there were generally no priests or caretakers about the premises, and the local people were sympathetic to the idea that these temples should be put to practical use. Thus all the external appurtenances of the Confucian cult have disappeared. At the same time Confucianism as a system of philosophy finds it increasingly difficult to withstand the attack of modern ideologies.

Taoism

Like all the other religions, Taoism has suffered the same repressive measures with the same disastrous results. The only difference is that Taoism is internally so weak and internationally so insignificant that it has even less chance of revival in spite of the recent organization with official sanction of a Chinese Taoist Association.

Buddhism

Buddhism presented more of a problem to the Communist government, for there existed a group of people who were identified with the faith. In order to undermine organized Buddhism, local temples were deprived of their economic base of support by the confiscation of monastery lands during the land reform. At the same time local Communist officials were directed to put Buddhist buildings to public use. In rural areas they most frequently became government granaries for storage of grain; in towns and cities they often became workers' "cultural palaces." In conjunction with this confiscation, priests were forced to abandon their profession and enter "productive occupations." Some monks have opened restaurants specializing in Buddhist vegetarian dishes, while others have either worked on nearby farms and mills, or converted their temples into small factories to produce handmade articles.

By 1950 Chinese Buddhism had been stripped of its temples, income, and priesthood. A pamphlet published by a group of Chinese Buddhists in Taiwan reported that altogether there were less than a hundred Buddhist establishments in mainland China in 1954. This is a sharp decrease when compared to about 130,000 Buddhist establishments in 1947 and 268,494 such establishments in 1930. It was also estimated that out of a total number of 500,000 to 600,000 Buddhist clergy in 1931, only 2,500 remained in China by 1954, and among them half were Communist party agents. It would appear that the Buddhist clergy as a group has been eliminated and that its influence in society is nearing the vanishing point.

While the Chinese Communists have virtually exterminated Buddhism as a religion, they have not failed to exploit it for political purposes. In 1949 the People's Political Consultative Conference included two Buddhist representatives and five Christians.

In November 1952 a new Communist-inspired Chinese Buddhist Association was formed, ostensibly to participate in land reform, struggle against counterrevolutionaries, resist America and aid Korea, and recognize the Buddhist duty to conduct a new religion in the new society. It was, however, simply a cultural-front organization designed to serve the Communists as a propaganda organ. The Association was used as a propaganda device to allay the fears among the Buddhist countries of Southeast Asia that China was an enemy of Buddhism; it was also used to pacify and control Buddhist populations in Mongolia and Tibet. A Chinese delegation was sent by Peking to the Buddhist celebration in Burma in 1956-57.

Aside from these government-sponsored organizations and activities, Buddhist religion has a poor chance of survival in Communist China. There is little in the Buddhist doctrine to steel the believer against the blandishments of totalitarianism or the trend of the changing times. The willingness of some Buddhist leaders to openly embrace Communist doctrine has probably undermined what little will to resist there may have been.

Islam

Islam is the only religion in China which has held its own in spite of the Communist tactics of alternating encouragement and repression. This is because it has semiautonomous political control of certain geographical areas in Northwest China and is more important politically than religiously. The Communists have in general dealt with Islam as a minority nationality rather than as a religion. Presenting themselves as defenders of the Moslem minorities from Han-Chinese oppression, they promise equality in an attempt to integrate local Moslem leadership into their own framework of political and military control. The Communists have succeeded in finding collaborators in Chinese Islam. Akhund officers have joined the Communist army, and mullahs the local governments. Approximately fifty prominent Moslems serve as representatives in the governments of autonomous regions or as minority representatives in coalition governments.

In other respects the Chinese Communists have been less successful. Public dissatisfaction in the Northwest forced them to suspend a slaughter tax during three Moslem festivals in 1950. During the land reform movement, the Communists tried to deprive the mosques of their economic base by confiscating their landholdings just as they had confiscated Buddhist and Taoist temples. But the Moslem population would not tolerate this interference with their religious establishments and rose in armed revolt. The Communists blamed the bloodshed on "adventurist" tendencies among the cadres and amended the land reform laws to permit mosques to retain ownership of land. The Communist press, however, continued to admit cases of open rebellion. Such rebellions have not completely subsided.

In the cities Communist control has been more effective. Moslem schools have been established and made instruments for Communist indoctrination. Islam is taught in the Central Academy of Nationalities and the Chinese Moslem College in Peking. The latter reported more than a thousand students in 1951. A nationwide Chinese Islamic Association was organized in 1953 with Burhan, a Moslem leader, as chairman. The new organization is for "peace partisans and democrats of the Islamic faith."

The most important mission of the Islamic Association is to aid the expansion of Communism in the Islamic world, but its efforts have not been entirely successful. The Association has attempted to make the Arabic language an instrument of Communist propaganda by publishing in Arabic important documents and writings of Chinese Communist leaders. The illustrated publication, *Religious Life of Chinese Moslems,* has texts in Chinese, English, and Arabic.

Although its leadership is generally discredited by collaboration, Islam has not lost its lay support. Its chances for survival are also increased by the fact that the Communists are anxious to preserve at least a skeleton of Islam in China to win friendship in the Islamic world, especially in Southeast Asia and the Middle East.

Christianity

The Communists believe that Christianity has contributed to the resistance movement against Communism and may provide through missionary organizations a possible contact with anti-Communist activities abroad. So they have waged a determined campaign for the elimination of all foreign influences in Chinese Catholic and Protestant churches, and have met from the Catholic Church a bitter resistance not experienced in their drive against the other religions.

The Communist campaign to eliminate Protestant Christianity is marked with finesse and shrewdness. There is no overt, forceful repression; no Chinese is executed for being a Christian. The Communists do not intend to create martyrs and leave a root of faith in the hearts of the common people. They fabricate cases against Christians and charge them with criminal deeds or counterrevolutionary activities. In the same way, they do not liquidate religious organizations. Communists infiltrate and use these organizations to discredit and disparage Protestant doctrines. Communist collaborators subvert the Protestant leadership to serve Communist goals so that the organization disintegrates from inner contradiction.

During land reform, all rural churches were closed as part of a general order forbidding all public assemblies. In many cases the buildings were used in this interval for public functions, meetings, classes, storage, billeting, and so on. After land reform was completed, each individual congregation had to receive permission from police headquarters to resume its activities, but the permission was seldom granted. Thus Protestant Christianity in rural China was greatly weakened.

The first antireligious educational campaign began in mid-1950. The schools, under strict Communist control, launched a nationwide study movement which gave "scientific" answers to the problems of the origin and evolution of man and the world. "Men are descended from monkeys, and work, not God, is the agent of creation," the students were told. This study was of course a political tool to discredit religious teaching. The campaign was strongest in the Christian schools where students tended to be lukewarm to the Communist ideology. The immediate purpose was to replace Christian teaching with "scientific Marxism." Any Christian who argued against this disparagement of Christian doctrine was denounced as a reactionary. If he persisted he was jailed or simply disappeared.

The Communists denounce Christianity as an aspect of western imperialism in China. Any good it may have done is discounted on the grounds that its over-all purpose had been to serve imperialistic ends. In May 1950 Chou En-lai summoned the leaders of the National Christian Council from Shanghai to Peking. As a result of this meeting, a Protestant reform movement was forced on all Protestant churches in July 1950.

The chief organizer of the movement was Wu Yao-tsung, who had strong Communist support. He had come under the influence of liberal American theologians while a student at Union Theological Seminary in New York and, returning to China, became a YMCA secretary and a leader of the Chinese branch of the pacifist Fellowship of Reconciliation. Considered very "progressive" and interested in the social gospel, he bitterly opposed the Nationalists and was sympathetic to the Communists. The announced goal of his Protestant reform movement was threefold: self-government, self-propagation, and self-support of the Chinese Christian Church.

The real purpose of the movement was to drive out all foreign missionaries and to separate Chinese Protestant Christianity from its overseas contacts. Mission work in China was denounced as serving imperialist ends, the result of clever plotting by missionary imperialist agents.

By October 1950 the National Christian Council had acquiesced in the leadership of Wu Yao-tsung and published a Christian Manifesto to be read, studied, and signed by each individual Christian. This political document, which accepted Communist views on Christianity, agreed that Christianity had been an agent of western imperialism and promised that in the future Chinese Christians would support the Communist party and government in building a new China. By damning the church's past, the Communists hoped to discredit it in the eyes of its constituents, and by soliciting signatures the Communists hoped to bind people closer as collaborators with the Communist regime.

This Christian Manifesto caused great turmoil in the leadership of the Protestant churches. To argue openly against it brought the charge of counterrevolutionary activity and punishment by the state. Certain prominent Protestant leaders suffered imprisonment as a result of their refusal to sign. But other Chinese Protestant leaders chose collaboration and set their church organization at the service of Communist goals.

Overt Chinese participation in the Korean War led to a United States embargo on the remittance of funds to China. Protestant schools and institutions, churches, and personnel were at once deprived of their economic support. The Communist government used this as an occasion to place all Christian schools, hospitals, and other institutions under direct government control.

Assured of cooperation and obedience from the Protestant leadership, the Communists began extensive campaigns of re-education for all church members. Meetings were held to ridicule and denounce "feudal practices" as well as "foreign imperialism." Church groups condemned alleged American germ warfare and pledged to support the Korean War and aid in every way possible the destruction of "decadent reactionary America." The denunciation of the United States government and foreign missionaries was repeated continually to the public. Any Christian spokesman brave enough to champion his own organization against Communist attacks was quickly arrested or bullied into silence. There was no room for debate.

Theological seminaries were taken over by the state but were not closed. Teachers who would support the Communist program were retained; others were forced into retirement. Some seminaries, under Communist direction, began campaigns to discredit their own teachings so that gradually the young theologians would be made to transfer their loyalty from Christianity to Communism.

The Communist campaign to destroy the churches from within has made great headway among the Protestant churches. The Episcopal Church, for instance, in six years of Communist control, lost 40 percent of its membership (from 69,000 in 1949 to 42,000 in 1955). Only some Protestant fundamentalists have resisted Communist pressure and perversion. In the large cities, especially Shanghai and Peking, there are individual churches which have refused to take part in the Communist propaganda programs and still remain open. The regime resents their independence but has not yet resorted to force to destroy them.

The Communists employed the same techniques against the Catholics that were used against the Protestants—their usual combination of force and subversion to destroy from within—but have met with considerably less success.

Catholic institutions, unlike their Protestant counterparts, were less dependent upon funds from abroad. Their main support, like that of Moslem mosques, came from the land. The Communists, however, had eliminated their economic base by land confiscation during land reform. In some places churches were compelled to make financial payments to redress the "wrongs" they had done in the past. By 1951 Catholic churches, like the Protestant, had been reduced to dire poverty.

But the Communists had a much more difficult time in finding collaborators in the Catholic hierarchy. Small beginnings appeared in November 1950 when a Szechwanese Protestant convert to Catholicism called for a pro-Communist campaign to reform the church. In January 1951 another Szechwan diocese issued a "patriotic" manifesto calling for a break with the papacy and the establishment of an indigenous national Catholic church. These movements received sympathy from only a minority of the Catholic laity. Communists suspected that opposition was sparked by foreign priests and began public campaigns against them. Mission schools were pictured as centers of spying and sabotage activities for the United States Army. The Vatican was depicted as the tool of American imperialism, and the Catholic clergy as an organized spy network. These charges led to arrests and trials in Tientsin, Nanking, and Shanghai. Foreign priests were publicly dishonored, jailed, or expelled. Some of the laity were frightened, but others formed a hard core of resistance loyal to the Church.

The battle between "progressive" (pro-Communist) and orthodox Catholics reached a high point in 1951 when Monsignor Riberi, the papal nuncio, was dramatically expelled from China. A progressive Vicar General of the Archdiocese of Nanking, Li Wei-chiang, with Communist support took control of Catholic properties and affairs in the lower Yangtze valley as the head of the Central Catholic Bureau of Shanghai. An obscure bishop of Lu-an (Hopeh province) was installed as the head of the "Sino-Catholic" church in Peking, representing Communist interests among the Catholics in the capital. Most of the laity, however, refused to associate with the Communist collaborators, and the Communists were forced to repress the orthodox hierarchy by force to give the progressives an opportunity to achieve their aims.

By August 1954, 126 out of 143 dioceses had lost their superiors; 78 foreign bishops had been expelled; between 100 and 200 Chinese priests, 315 brothers, and 14 nuns had been executed or died in prison. Many more have simply disappeared. From 30 to 40 non-Chinese are known to have been killed. Of the 5,496 foreign religious leaders who were originally resident in China, less than 100 remained. The Communists were thus forced to destroy the hierarchy in their search for collaborators. At the same time they also goaded the Chinese Catholics to sever their ties with the Vatican and other western Catholic bodies in the so-called "Patriotic Catholic Church" movement. As a result of this some Chinese bishops were ordained without first obtaining the approval of the Vatican and were subsequently excommunicated.

The chief difference between the Catholic and Protestant churches in China is that in the Protestant churches there has been little articulate opposition to the new leadership that in every way follows the dictates of the Communist government, whereas within the Catholic Church an intense struggle has been going on since 1949. Although the progressives have not been able to obtain complete control, they have had some success in their efforts to organize a Chinese hierarchy free from Vatican influence. The continuing arrests of non-cooperating priests, however, is evidence that the Communists still lack satisfactory collaboration from the majority of the Catholics.

Prospect for Religion in China

Regardless of what scattered resistance to the Communist program may remain, the current status of religion in China reflects the triumph of materialist philosophy and the imposition of materialism as the intellectual orthodoxy. Communist policy is highly nationalistic and antiforeign and the government insists that all organizations of a religious nature cease receiving support from abroad and assert their distinctive Chinese character. The most effective apparatus of control and coercion China has ever known is being employed to carry forward the systematic undermining of all religious institutions in China.

The Chinese Constitution provides that "citizens of the People's Republic of China have freedom of religious belief." In practice, however, this means that people of various persuasions are allowed a limited and ever smaller area of belief and action by an authoritarian government which reserves the right to dictate religious practice as well as to control religious organization. The Communist promise to remake society is not an idyllic promise; the other side of the coin is their determination to destroy all remnants of the preceding regimes. What they propose to supplant they denounce as "feudal," "semicolonial," or "imperialist." On the grounds of antisuperstition, anti-imperialism, and antifeudalism, the Communist party and government have been moving steadily with only an occasional tactical retreat towards the liquidation of religion in China. With the further stabilization and growth in power of the Communist government, prospects are that formalized religion in China will continue to decline and wither away as an institution in the life of the Chinese people.

SOCIAL ORGANIZATION

THE CLASSLESS SOCIALIST SOCIETY envisioned by Karl Marx is the ultimate goal for the Chinese Communist planners. To effect the transition from capitalism to socialism requires firm leadership by the Communist party, but the political power now held in trust by the Communist state will revert to the people once socialism has been realized. Then, the people are told, the repressive measures taken by the state will become unnecessary and the administrative function will be transferred to the production process, the state having ceased to be.

The core of the problem for the Communists is the existence of private property—specifically, the control of the means of production by the capitalist class. In the final phase of the class struggle—between the capitalists and the proletariat—the revolution advances from the earlier redistribution among the people of the means of production to the eventual abolition of all private ownership of property and the merging of all classes in a true socialist society.

The Communist revolution in China has increased social mobility to the extent that the former supports of wealth and power have been eliminated together with the scholar-gentry and landlord classes. The shift to industrialization has led to the rise of a growing urban population. Considerable numbers of Communist party members have moved up from the lower ranks and there is room at present for some groups to climb the social scale. Thus a new social structure has been created, one which appears to have considerable stability as changes are largely controlled by the regime itself.

Traditional Social Structure

The positive and fundamentally idealistic social system developed by the Chinese from Confucian teachings remained basically unchanged for over two thousand years from about the beginning of the imperial period in the third century B.C. to the latter part of the nineteenth century. Chinese social philosophy was based on the belief that the perfect society, where all segments of the society lived harmoniously together, could be achieved if each member would recognize and accept his position in relation to other members, perform his social duties, and conduct his life according to a set of guiding principles for personal behavior. Emphasis in the Confucian ethic on the doctrine of the "golden mean" made the avoidance of any extreme a virtue. A ruler was expected to be tolerant, benevolent, and restrained in the exercise of his power; commoners were to be respectful, industrious, and obedient.

Although the necessity for a hierarchy of classes was recognized in the Confucian scheme of social structure, its authoritarian character was counterbalanced by the ideal of moral rectitude, which could be cultivated through education and the discipline provided by a firm knowledge of etiquette and music. The stress on ethics and on education, the major criterion in determining social status and an indispensable qualification for the task of governing others, gave the system a humanistic outlook and ensured some social mobility and no closed classes. The ruling class in traditional China was able, however, to make of this social system a powerful weapon for the perpetuation of its power.

To a considerable extent the continuity of the Chinese social order was assured by the traditional, predominantly agrarian, economic system: the small educated ruling class was amply taken care of by an overwhelming majority of the population who lived frugally and worked the land with a simple technology. This agrarian economy provided little incentive, however, for the development of commerce and manufacture, thereby precluding the emergence of a middle class in the modern sense. Successive changes in dynasties affected only the composition of the ruling class; the basic social structure remained intact.

The four factors that determined social status—moral character, political position, wealth, and education—also operated to separate the population into two broad strata, the rulers and the commoners. But of the four classes—namely scholars, farmers, artisans, and merchants—distinguished in traditional society below the nobility, only the scholars belonged to the ruling class.

In reality these class distinctions were by no means completely clear-cut. The three classes of commoners, although forming theoretically separate occupational groups, were often intermixed. In the villages and market towns, it was the usual thing for farming and handicraft manufacturing to be undertaken simultaneously by one group. In the cities, handicraft manufacturing was linked with buying and selling, and the distinction between an artisan family and a merchant family therefore blurred. There were professional merchants, but few artisans engaged solely in manufacturing.

The scholar class, unique in traditional Chinese society, was not in the strict sense an occupational group, although its members were mostly educated men who had passed the imperial examinations and had become government officials. As officials, the scholars attained a gentry status next only to the nobility. Upon retirement from public careers, many would retain their scholarly position by teaching and writing books; some would become gentleman farmers; others withdraw into religious solitude. Very few ever actually needed to earn a living.

In almost every period the scholar-gentry occupied the top of the class hierarchy and enjoyed numerous privileges denied others. But the scholar-gentry never constituted an exclusive privileged class: the lower classes were neither strictly nor permanently excluded from the scholar ranks because official status was attainable through government examinations. The only prerequisite, a combination of personal effort and the opportunity to be properly educated, made the imperial examinations an avenue to officialdom and social prestige open to all except a small segment of the population excluded by "occupational meanness."

Gentry status implied leadership for the community whether as a government official or as a landowner. It should be emphasized, however, that a member of the gentry was not necessarily a landlord, nor a landlord necessarily a member of the gentry: a landless gentry member could be very influential, while land ownership without gentry status carried little prestige.

The civic leadership of the gentry could range from the planning, direction, or even in some cases the financing of public welfare projects, such as an irrigation system or public granaries, to cooperation with local officials on relief programs or the establishment of public cemeteries and foundling homes. In addition the gentry contributed heavily to the establishment of schools, subsidies for students, and the construction and repair of examination halls. Although possessing no judicial authority, the local gentry were often asked to arbitrate or mediate disputes and the villagers looked to them for guidance according to traditional moral teachings. The organization and administration of any local defense program almost inevitably fell to the gentry. Finally, the gentry played a traditional political role. It was their duty to voice the opinions and sentiments of their communities on occasions such as drought, flood, serious failure of the main crop, heavy damage caused by war or local rebellion, or injustice done by incompetent government officials. The gentry in such cases would interpose on behalf of the people to secure a tax exemption or grant of relief grain, to obtain permission for those who wished to migrate to another part of the country, or to plead for the removal and punishment of undesirable officials.

On the other hand, powerful gentry members could evade payment of taxes or even divert some of the local revenues for their own use. The gentry themselves were exempt from labor conscription and sometimes would also arrange for a fee for the commoners to avoid conscription. The gentry's leadership in the management of local affairs gave them many opportunities for illegal economic gains, and there were always those who seized these opportunities for personal profit.

Although inferior to the gentry in social, political, and legal positions, commoners were not legally barred from higher status. Many members of the ruling class were of humble origin. Wealthy merchants could earn gentry status by purchasing "irregular" academic degrees and official titles. Even individuals in the mean occupations could advance socially although it might take several generations for a low-class family to gain recognition and prestige. The government could, and occasionally did, grant gentry rank for exceptional service in its behalf. Moreover, traditional political thought sanctioned rebellion against predatory governments, and the change of dynasties invariably resulted in the rise to eminence of persons of low social status.

During imperial times, certain special groups were outside the main groups of gentry and commoners. Members of the imperial clan were not officials and did not necessarily participate in the administration of the state, but they had a number of special privileges, of which the most important was the right to secure some of the best tax-free lands. The nobility not related to the imperial family formed a less privileged subgroup whose status tended to be higher under a Chinese than under a non-Chinese dynasty. In periods of dynastic decline members of the nobility or imperial clan often controlled the emperor or even usurped his power and by their monopoly of political power were able to amass great wealth.

At the other end of the social pyramid were the slaves, who were of two types: domestic and productive. The latter were used in farm work, handicrafts, mining, and several other trades. The institution of slavery, however, underwent many changes as dynasties changed, and at no time was it widespread enough to affect the basic economic structure of the country. Moreover, the number of slaves steadily decreased as time went on, and by the end of the nineteenth century, there existed only isolated cases of domestic slaveholding.

Although class distinctions were clear enough to minimize interclass social relationships, contact between classes did occur, primarily between adjacent classes or through the social groups and institutions that by their nature cut across class barriers. Most important among the latter was the clan. Social barriers, of course, existed within the clan as gentry families tended to dissociate themselves from nongentry families. But clan activities as a whole tended to lower these barriers. For example all children in the clan, from whatever social class, attended the same clan school. If a boy from a poor family showed promise, the clan leader might see to it that the boy was given further educational opportunities.

The clan used to have many social and economic functions, nearly all of which involved crossing class barriers. The institution of clan property, for example, was designed chiefly to give financial aid to the poor in the clan. Land was donated by well-to-do families, administered by leaders of the upper class and functionaries from the lower strata, and farmed for the benefit of needy clan members.

Similar in function was the provincial club of the national and provincial capitals as well as of important business centers throughout the country. It was an organization of people from the same province or district who came to the city to do business, to participate in imperial examinations, or to take government posts. Because they were alien to the city, they bound themselves together for mutual aid. All reputable natives of the home province or district were eligible for membership in the club.

Among the important functions of the club were: provision for suitable burial of the dead (a club invariably had its own cemetery, and graves, even coffins, would be provided free or at reduced rates for poorer members); relief work for members or for nonmembers from the same home province or district; mediation of disputes between members and local persons or officials; legal aid to members who needed it; provision of educational facilities for members' children and those of other compatriots in the community; and social and recreational activities, important to those who were aliens isolated from the local community.

The secret societies, which might consist of different social groups, were generally either political or religious in nature. Occasionally there were such fringe groups as professional beggars or homeless veterans. Religion and politics were not, however, mutually exclusive. Political organizations often employed religious ceremonies to strengthen and deepen their sense of solidarity, while religious organizations were sometimes used for political ends.

Religious societies were found primarily in the north, and political societies in the south. The northern societies existed sporadically, while the southern ones were relatively permanent. This difference was largely due to a difference in membership. Members of the northern societies were mostly poor peasants who had been forced by extremely harsh circumstances to organize themselves for mutual protection; but as soon as the immediate objective was reached they would disband completely. In the south, secret organizations, whose members were mostly townspeople, existed continuously; membership was for life. During periods of weak or corrupt government, they openly opposed the existing administration, while during periods of strong government they remained underground. A large majority of the overseas Chinese belonged to one or more of the southern secret societies.

Social Stratification in the Transitional Period

Toward the end of the nineteenth century, as China began a series of changes in response to the impact of western influences, the traditional class structure began to give way to a more complex stratification. The decline of the Confucian order and the abandonment of the imperial examination system, by removing the absolute criteria, resulted in a less sharp demarcation between the scholar-gentry and the commoners; new economic and social opportunities in the transitional period made possible the emergence of new social groups. The old gentry members, still regarding themselves as the leading class, had lost their monopoly on officeholding and positions of political power and became increasingly dissatisfied with existing political conditions.

Well-to-do landowners or absentee landlords constituted a small section of the rural population. Some of them were former gentry members who had lost their privileged social status, others were newcomers from a rich peasantry who through effort or chance had succeeded in rising above their own class. The group as a whole was linked with business families in small towns or cities. Usurers and pawnshop owners who had become influential in local economic life could also be considered members of this class.

Much of the power on provincial and national levels was seized by another group, the military. In the so-called warlord period (1910's-1920's), members of this group replaced civilian officials in administering the country. The warlords and their lieutenants came from very different social milieus: many had risen from army ranks; some came from the gentry; others from middle-class backgrounds in the treaty ports; and a few had been bandits. What they had in common was their military training, which was the basis of their official career. But most of them had no broad general education to qualify them for government administration.

Around foreign concessions or international settlements in treaty ports emerged a new Chinese middle class, which shared either directly or indirectly in the foreigners' exemption from Chinese government control. In contrast to the merchants and artisans in the interior, who were constantly under the thumb of the officials, the new business group was comparatively free from official interference. Its establishments in the treaty port area could not be arbitrarily taxed, and while inland trade depended on the tolerance of local administrators and was burdened by tariffs, urban trade suffered less from official exactions.

This middle class could be subdivided into two groups according to income and occupation. The storekeeper and retail trader, with the exception of the owners of big department stores, had a lower social status and living standard than industrialists, bankers, and the owners of large trading firms. In their attitudes and political views these groups were, however, not far apart. Knowing the advantages of western technology and leading a semi-western life in the treaty port concessions, they understood the strategic importance of China's modernization. But though living under foreign protection, they remained nationalistic and favored the restoration of Chinese sovereignty.

Of less political importance was the group of industrial workers in and around the modern cities. In the early years of the 1920's, labor unions in such cities as Shanghai and Canton had become comparatively strong and politically effective under a joint Nationalist-Communist leadership. But with the split between Nationalists and Communists in 1927 and the elimination of the Communist labor union leaders in Shanghai, the union movement ceased to be important. Later Communist attempts to infiltrate labor organizations were unsuccessful, and when in 1931 the Communists shifted their activities to rural areas, labor became less politically significant than any other group.

Continuing the tradition of a political elite were the western-trained intellectuals—students in particular—who formed a politically active group, quickly roused to protests, strikes, and demonstrations. In fact, political agitation and debate were a regular part of student activities. While asserting its political leadership, this group was divided on political programs. Hostile to tradition and under the influence of western thought, new intellectuals were confused and undecided as to the most desirable pattern of social and political institutions. A small number accepted Communist ideology; others joined the Nationalist party or cooperated with the Nationalist government. But for the most part the intellectual leaders remained critical of both Nationalist and Communist doctrines; and the relationship between the universities and the government became precarious whenever the latter attempted to suppress all antigovernment political views.

During the Nationalist period there emerged a new officialdom made up of military leaders, businessmen, and intellectuals in top positions in the government. Its rank and file were recruited from trainees in political institutes set up by the party. Nationalistic in outlook and antitraditional in attitude, most of them, however, paid only lip service to western concepts of democracy.

Thus, immediately before the Communist seizure of power there existed in China no leading social group which possessed the inner cohesion or performed the over-all functions of the scholar-gentry in the imperial period. The traditional gentry role had been divided among such groups as military leaders, party bureaucrats, western-educated intellectuals, and the few gentry members remaining in rural districts. The beginning of industrialization had created a new middle class of businessmen and industrialists as well as a new labor force in the cities. The largest group, however, was still the peasantry. In areas of population pressure and in areas affected by natural catastrophe, heavy taxation, and warlord exploitation, life was harsh for a majority of the peasants and their discontent and restlessness was an important factor in the success of the Communist revolution.

Social Structure in Communist China

Officially, the Communists divide Chinese society into five classes: landlords and compradors; national bourgeoisie; petty bourgeoisie; semiproletariat; and proletariat. These classes are differentiated on the basis of economic and political criteria. Economically, the population is divided into groups according to the extent of control they exercise over the means of production and the wealth of the society. Politically, the peasants and industrial workers can be more surely counted upon to support the "socialist revolution" than can the other classes who still retain the "bourgeois" way of thinking. These groups do not necessarily represent the present stratification of Communist China, but they are important in the policy-making functions of the regime.

According to the Communists, the landlords and compradors, along with warlords, bureaucrats, bureaucratic capitalists, and usurers, constituted the major group which formerly controlled political power, economic production, and wealth, manipulating them for its own profit at the expense of the other classes. This group, considered the enemy of the people because of its opposition to the revolution and its willingness to collaborate with foreign imperialists, was the first to be singled out for extinction as soon as the old social order was overthrown.

The national bourgeoisie comprised "all those capitalist relations which exist between town and country." This would include the rice retailer who operates a rice-husking mill in the country, the middleman between the farmer and the markets, and the owner of a factory or a service organization. The political behavior of this class was inconsistent, for while its members were determined in their opposition to foreign imperialism, they were undependable in a social revolution which sought to do away with the production relations beneficial to them.

Thus, in connection with the activities of the national bourgeoisie, the Communists made a careful distinction between three types of capitalist industries and consumer services: those dominated by foreign capital, those operating with special privileges through their "connections" with the bureaucracy, and those operated by Chinese capital and personnel without either foreign or bureaucratic protection. The first two types have been completely eliminated; the third still exists, mostly on a joint state-private basis.

The petty bourgeoisie consisted of rich and middle peasants, master handicraftsmen, traders, office clerks, petty intellectuals—primary and middle school teachers—and lower government functionaries. This group can also be divided according to economic status into those who have a slightly surplus wealth, those who are just self-supporting, and those whose standard of living is comparatively low.

Within the semiproletariat were five categories: tenant peasants, poor peasants, handicraftsmen, shop assistants, and peddlers. Again, further subdivisions into upper, middle and lower groups within the general class category were possible, based on whether or not a group was able to acquire a small yearly surplus of goods or services due. On the whole, this group was considered politically "unconscious" but susceptible to "proper indoctrination and manipulation."

The proletariat formed the last but most important group in Communist social planning. Comprised of men employed in all industries, including railways, mining, maritime transport, textiles, shipbuilding, and others, its importance lay not so much in numbers as in the political and social role assigned them by the state. The proletariat remained high in the social hierarchy because, according to the Communists, they are more "politically conscious" than any other class; they are skilled in political warfare and agitation of all types; and they are linked in their background with the peasantry. This group is augmented by a subgroup, for example coolies and farm laborers, who sell their labor for a living.

Mao Tse-tung pointed out the political significance of this analysis very clearly when he wrote that all those in league with imperialism were to be regarded as enemies. "The industrial proletariat is the leading force in our revolution," he continued. "All sections of the semiproletariat and the petty bourgeoisie are our closest friends. As to the vacillating middle class, its right wing may become our enemy and its left wing may become our friend, but we must be constantly on our guard toward the latter and not allow it to create confusion in our front."

This analysis was intended to show the actual and potential relations of each class to the Communist revolution. By defining the nature and characteristics of each sector of the population, the regime could make use of those groups which would help bring about Communist objectives and guard against others which would hinder the ultimate aim of destroying the "classes" and moving toward a "classless" society; in fact, each move taken in the process of destroying classes results in the further strengthening of party power. One example of this is the Communist effort to eliminate traditional sources of prestige, especially the public leadership and the accumulated wealth, power, and status of the gentry. In this process, antagonism between the classes is aroused and amplified in order to speed the socialist revolution, as in the case of the land reform program, in which cadres were trained to build up and heighten tension between landlord and tenant, and then to release the pent-up hatred in violent public trials and on-the-spot executions.

Less than ten years after the Communist take-over, landlords and compradors were completely eliminated from the social structure, and the party and its mass organizations held the reins of power and control. Major industries have become state property and the few private businesses allowed to survive are under joint state-private management. The peasants have been organized into communes, in which their movement is rigidly controlled. As a result, social stratification is now based on occupation, income, way of life, and, above all, adherence to party doctrine.

In both urban and rural areas, the new elite of Chinese society consists of Communist party members, numbering approximately ten million (as of October 1956). They have become firmly established in positions of importance and responsibility, constituting the new bureaucracy set up to build the future socialist society.

At the top of the new hierarchy are veteran Communist leaders who have worked together through long and hard struggles and who won their current high positions through unswerving loyalty to the party. The second level of the hierarchy includes those who have served the party for a number of years and are now the core of the state apparatus, responsible for the implementation of policies formulated by the top leadership. By virtue of some special skill or knowledge, a considerable number of non-Communist but politically reliable persons has been absorbed into this group. College students who joined the party before or during the Sino-Japanese War (1937–45) make up the majority of the third level of the hierarchy, which also includes a number of other sympathetic intellectuals. A fourth level of the hierarchy contains loyal but sometimes unlettered Communist followers who now function as active cadres in county, *hsien,* and district, *ch'ü,* governments. Although lowest in the new hierarchy, the cadres have the most direct influence on the populace and form the basic elements in the Communist movement.

A cadre, *kan-pu,* is a Communist agent or activist entrusted with the task of carrying out party policies on all levels. Some of them are regular party members while others are recruited from the local peasantry for their willingness to cooperate with the new regime. They usually remain in their native villages and continue to farm; they are seldom promoted to higher positions requiring them to leave the village. Few have any formal education. Those especially active and cooperative may eventually become party members and are then placed in some position of authority over the villagers. It may be said that these men form the auxiliaries of the party machinery and the mainstay of the village government.

Industrial workers constitute the group most favored by the Communist elite, but their gains are few and far between. While they are provided with such fringe benefits as welfare funds, hospitalization and other medical care, and educational and recreational facilities, their working hours remain long and their wages low. In the Communist view, the greatest gain the worker has made does not lie in material rewards, but in the moral satisfaction of being able to contribute directly to the government effort of achieving a greater good for all the people.

The number of women workers has increased significantly since the Communists came into power. Women are encouraged, through equal recognition with male workers and praise for their accomplishments, to work in factories. Many are loyal to the regime for the opportunities and benefits provided them by the state.

For the individual peasant, his gain under the Communist regime is small and the collectivization and commune programs run counter to his traditional desire for land. So in order to weld the peasants into an effective ally in the Communist revolution, the government has to rely on a proliferation of mass organizations, some with overlapping personnel, to engage in a constant propaganda campaign to enlist the peasants' support and to help exercise the function of "self-policing" in the rural districts. An attempt is being made to mold the peasants in the communes into a new way of life.

Among the bourgeoisie, the so-called "old intellectuals," comprising scholars, writers, and professors, are in a rather precarious position in the Communist regime. Their status differs more widely than that of any other social group, their acceptance or rejection by the regime being dependent on their political trustworthiness and the degree to which their services can be used profitably by the state. Even in the technical schools, political learning and indoctrination are considered far more important than the teaching of technology and science. Outstandingly competent scholars with technical training have been subject to intensive "thought reform" after which they are given good positions so that their knowledge and experience can be fully exploited for the benefit of the new society. Intellectuals who are unsympathetic to the government and who do not have useful technical skills have been either persecuted or left alone to scramble for a living.

The "national capitalists," on the other hand, have been gradually eliminated as a class. After an initial period during which these capitalists were encouraged to continue their business operations by promises of full protection of property and special interests, the government proceeded to socialize their businesses one by one, making the former owners salaried managerial personnel in the resulting state-owned enterprises.

Social Mobility

The degree of rigidity of the Chinese Communist social structure is hard to determine. Generally speaking, the Communists try to tighten their control on key positions in organizations and institutions so that opportunities for advancement to the new elite are limited. Nevertheless it is still possible to move up the social scale on the basis of merit and service to the party and government. The emergence of comparatively obscure party workers in the upper echelons of the hierarchy proves that the Communist structure is flexible enough to admit a certain number of new people. Long-range plans also call for the building up of a strong group from among the younger generation. Furthermore, party channels are not the exclusive routes upward; scientists and engineers who are "politically disinterested" may advance on their merits alone without party membership.

Social mobility is to be expected in a Communist society, where economic factors operate jointly with political factors. Vulnerability increases as one goes up in the hierarchy; one is constantly balancing the "safety" of one's position against the "rewards" one will get in moving upward. As usually employed, the purge clears away opposition to those in the top hierarchy and stems deviation from the party line, but it may also serve as a partial release of accumulated tensions that build up within a totalitarian framework by providing scapegoats for inefficiency and repression. In addition, purges clear away certain strata of the hierarchy, thereby making room for new members. It is characteristic of Communist governments to purge certain personnel from the organization but to leave the organization itself relatively untouched; in this way, personnel may shift on all strata except at the policy-making top. It should be noted, however, that to date purges of local cadres and officials at regional levels have been mostly limited to the elimination of the "old social elements" rather than to that of the "revolutionaries" themselves.

The distribution by social class of party membership is no indication of the degree of mobility at that level. The great majority of party members are peasants but a peasant party member, although his political connection might be assumed to improve his chances for social advancement, is by the nature of his work rarely able to develop into a true "activist": his workday is too full and his free hours too few. His importance to the regime lies in his numbers as the need for a highly sensitive network of loyal party members to control the peasant masses makes the concentration of party membership among the agricultural population a political necessity.

Conformity

One of the most important tasks for the new rulers of China is to induce conformity in belief, attitude, and action among all social groups. As agents of such conformity, the mass organizations are critical in the operation of the regime. They are intended to replace the provincial clubs and other associations considered too local in outlook and too specialized in purpose to be useful in a socialist society.

The classification of persons according to political reliability rather than social status is one of the underlying principles governing the activities of Communist-sponsored mass organizations. These organizations help to disseminate Communist ideology; they instruct and guide the membership in proper behavior and action. Participation, whether voluntary or compulsory, serves to separate the individual from his family and absorb his time and energy outside the family circle. In short, the weakening of family loyalty forces the individual to look toward the mass organizations for his goals and his rewards. Since the individual relies on mass organizations for political advancement, which is the prerequisite for economic and social betterment, these organizations are most important in determining his place in the new order. The regime thus exercises the power to control the career expectancies of the members of mass organizations, rewarding those who work for the party leadership and punishing with ostracism or more severe measures those who rebel against it.

These organizations are directed and controlled by the party. Most officers are party activists, receiving operational orders from the authorities in Peking. The over-all content of these orders includes the promotion of class struggle, the definition of all social and economic activities in Marxist terms, and the supervision of the life of each member either by the cadres themselves or by group-elected leaders.

The Communists have always identified their program with the magic symbol of "the people": their revolution was the people's revolution; the regime is "the People's Republic"; the government is "the People's Government"; the army is "the People's Liberation Army." Even today the promotion of the people's welfare is still a powerful and compelling slogan. But in practice the drive toward goals considered correct by the party elite is pursued with no provision for the expression of public sentiment, and "the people" are left with no alternative but to do what is demanded of them. Communist social control is so pervasive that conformity is the sole means of survival.

Present Trends

On the whole, class distinctions in the current social structure are not as marked as those of prerevolutionary China. The very great divergencies in wealth and power between rich landlords, officials, and capitalists on the one hand and poor peasants on the other have been somewhat reduced by compressing both ends of the social pyramid. Particularly in the present stage of consolidation and expansion of the party, opportunities exist for upward mobility from the lower ranks and the channels are still relatively free from such potential barriers as hereditary prerogatives.

However, differential rewards to the different classes continue to exist. The limited amount of consumer goods and services that are available is reserved for those with special privilege. Perhaps the most noticeable change from prerevolutionary days is that the spoils of success are distributed with more regard to merit than to political favor: the extent, rather than the type, of differential rewards has changed.

The major efforts of the regime will probably continue to be directed toward the correct handling of contradictions among the various groups without significantly altering the class structure. Thus the dissatisfaction of the peasants and the unwillingness of some local segments to be communalized are countered by strengthening party control over rural groups. Rural directors of state farms and communes are drawn from local sources to reduce antagonism toward "outsiders." A continual emphasis on the dignity of the workingman characterizes campaigns launched against cadres who flaunt their authority over others, both on farm and in factory. Such campaigns also serve to arouse the social consciousness of the workers and to make them content with their present status.

Some increase in mobility through increased education is to be expected. With the raising of their cultural level, many cadres of peasant or industrial worker background will be moving upward in the party hierarchy. However, since little material reward can be offered either peasants or workers for some time to come, an increase in competition for the few material advantages as well as for the nonmaterial rewards of power, control, and prestige enjoyed by the upper hierarchy will make some curbing of this upward movement necessary. In the meantime some start has been made by building up the social status of the industrial working class and by increasing party activity in rural areas. But it will take considerable ingenuity to handle the workers and peasants as they gradually come to realize that their nominally favored position in the new order means no more than all hard work and very little reward. The present campaign for the establishment of the communes and the recasting of school curriculums to include manual labor with the objective of eventually eliminating the dis-

tinction between urban and rural life may be considered as one of
the means the government has chosen to reduce the potential contradictions among the various social classes. This, however, is a
long-range program and does not by itself remove the differences
between top-ranking groups and the masses.

8

FAMILY

As THE PRINCIPAL FOCUS of economic, social, and religious activities in traditional China, the family was closely bound to the social and economic order by relations of mutual support, extended through larger kin groups such as clans and through kinship usages beyond clan membership. The central importance of the family institution in the traditional order has made the family the logical first target of reformers throughout the modern era. Both the Nationalists and the Communists initiated legal changes and propaganda efforts aimed at its transformation.

To fully understand the significance of family reform, however, it is necessary to consider the organization and functions of the traditional family structure, as well as the effects of westernization, industrialization, urbanization, and especially the changing character of social and economic life under the Communists. Thus a firm basis will be provided for understanding current attitudes toward, and predicting future changes within, family organization.

Traditional Family

The family, one of the most fundamental social groups in any society, played a particularly important role in traditional China where the whole social structure reflected the kinship organization. Chinese society was composed of families rather than of individuals. The concept of a country or nation was expressed by the term *kuo-chia*, which means, literally, "nation-family." The emperor was regarded as the head of the nation-family, and his subjects owed him respect and obedience in the same way that members of an individual family recognized the authority of the family head.

The family rather than the state provided the individual with economic and social security and education. It was the family which supervised his moral and political behavior. The state, in turn, dealt not with individuals but with family heads, the family head bearing responsibility for the support, education, and even the behavior of the members of his family. If a person committed an offense against society or against the state, the head of his family might be held to account for the crime. Any or several members of a family might be punished for a crime if the guilty individual could not be apprehended. The individual was held accountable to his family; the family was responsible for its individual members. In this sense the family was the minimal unit of social identity.

According to Confucian theory, well-regulated families ensured the well-being of the state. The pattern of subordination to authority, instilled within the family, was extended to the emperor and the ruling hierarchy. Thus did the state make use of the behavior and attitudes inculcated within the kinship group to establish cohesiveness in the larger nonkin grouping. There were of course occasions on which loyalty to the family conflicted with loyalty to the state. The pressure to secure posts for one's relatives made nepotism and inefficiency in the official bureaucracy a real problem, especially in periods when the government was weak. It should be realized, however, that nepotism functioned to buttress and extend the welfare of the family, a heavily stressed value, and can therefore be regarded as a natural outcome of this emphasis even though its consequences were inimical to an efficient and honest administration. The idea that an individual's life was not his own to dispose of but must be preserved to perpetuate the family line and to observe the rites for the ancestors appeared to compete with ideas of patriotism and a hero's death, but Confucian ethics did exalt the person who died in the service of the emperor or the state.

Until fairly recently, the large family or extended family, one which included close relatives other than a man, his wife (or wives), and their offspring, was thought to be typical of Chinese society. Recent studies have shown, however, that it was not characteristic of all social classes, although it does seem to have been the ideal of all.

The Nuclear Family

The nuclear, conjugal, or small family has been the characteristic family type for the majority of Chinese over a period of centuries.

The nuclear family includes a man, his wife, and their unmarried offspring, thus comprising two generations. It is the minimal social unit of procreation and was often also the primary unit of production, consumption, education, and recreation.

Ordinarily the nuclear family lived in a separate dwelling, and in such cases the nuclear family and the household were identical. In rural areas the pattern was for each peasant family to inhabit its own small house of one or two rooms. In the towns, storekeepers and artisans usually lived in their shops or in buildings adjoining them.

But even poor and middle-class nuclear families often had living with them dependent relatives or unrelated hired laborers. In these cases the nuclear family and the household were not identical. This was also true when an extended family was divided but continued to live under one roof. Individual nuclear families cooked, ate, and managed their finances separately, but remained physically together within one large household.

Descent had been strictly patrilineal in China for many centuries. There is some evidence that matrilineal descent may have existed in prehistoric times, and some of the minority nationalities living within China's borders today are not entirely patrilineal, but for the vast majority of Chinese, the father's family and the male line of descent were the foci of kinship interest. Sons were desired intensely to carry on the male line, and the family name and property were handed down from father to son. Residence was patrilocal: daughters left their own homes and families to live with their husbands. The head of the household was always a male unless no adult male survived. The Chinese family was also patronymic and patriarchal, and all members of the family were related to one another through a father or husband.

The most important relationship was that between father and son. The father in traditional China held, at least in theory, the power of life and death over his offspring, and it was a son's duty to revere and support his parents. Mourning and worship after the death of his parents were integral parts of a son's role. A father, on the other hand, was obliged to support his son and provide a wife for him. At his death, the property of a father went automatically to his male heir. In a sense, father and son were identified in that a son's economic and social position was largely defined by that of his father. A son was regarded by outsiders as the heir to his father's prestige and property (or lack of them) even during the lifetime of his father. The father-son relationship was one of authority-submission. A son never attained equal adult status with his father during the father's lifetime. The gap between generations was never bridged regardless of the age or maturity of the son.

The husband-wife relationship was less reciprocal than that of father and son. Although a son was subordinate to his father, he eventually inherited not only his father's wealth and prestige but also his authority. A wife, conversely, had to submit to her husband as long as he lived and, after his death, to the authority of his family or her son, at least theoretically. Although a husband might beat his wife, she could never strike him. He owed her support, of course, and if he treated her too badly she might return to her parents' home. This was not ordinarily feasible, however, as her family might be unable or unwilling to care for her and might attempt to send her back again. In the last extreme she might commit suicide, which brought disgrace upon not only her own family but also her husband's.

The relationship between a mother and her son had a special significance because in large measure a wife's status depended upon her producing a male offspring. A wife's first duty, the reason for her introduction into the family, was to produce sons to continue the male line and her position in her husband's family was unenviable before this duty had been fulfilled. But the birth of her first son, which insured the continuity of her husband's family, immediately made her position more secure. A woman naturally felt much warmth for this son whose arrival had improved her status. Her authority over him was less than his father's, especially after infancy, but she sometimes interceded for him with his father and often was responsible for choosing his wife.

The relationship between father and daughter was less formally defined. A girl was not ordinarily supposed to be much involved with her father. She was really but a temporary member of the family as she left it at marriage for her husband's family and, especially if her new home was some distance from the old, her contacts with her own family tended to be infrequent.

Mother and daughter had a closer relationship. The principle of sex segregation insured that they had more contact with each other than did father and daughter. Before marriage a girl always remained with her mother and was trained in household tasks while a boy came under the tutelage of his father or a teacher, depending upon the family circumstances.

The older brother to younger brother relationship was similar to that between father and son. An older brother had authority over and might discipline the younger, while the younger brother had to defer to the older. This was especially true after their father's death. Brothers were supposed to live in harmony and much emphasis was placed upon the idea that they were from a common source.

As a result of the sex segregation practiced in higher levels of the society, brothers and sisters did not associate closely. The principle of male dominance meant that when authority was in question a brother was dominant over his sister. After marriage, the girl, living in another household, might see her brother only very rarely.

The relationship between sisters was extremely unformalized—probably another reflection of the temporary nature of a girl's residence with her parental family. If sisters married into distant households they might seldom meet after marriage.

Age, generation, and sex were the dominant influences on behavior in interpersonal relationships. Relative age determined precedence even in the case of siblings born only a year apart: the younger had always to defer to the elder. Only difference in generation could alter the rule regarding relative age. For example, even if a boy were in actual age older than an uncle, the uncle would take precedence because he belonged to the generation of the boy's parents. The age principle was also modified by the question of sex. Women were subordinate to men under most circumstances. A widowed mother of a young son might be considered the head of her family, but once the son was grown any transactions made by the mother would be invalid unless her son approved.

As in many societies, these principles of age, generation, and sex, as well as the patterned interpersonal relationships, represented cultural norms that might not hold in a particular case. Individuals varied in their approximation to the norms and might deviate considerably from the patterns described. Factors such as relative size and strength, intelligence, and aggressiveness of brothers might well alter the conventional brother relationship. The existence of deep affection between man and wife, or the union of an unaggressive man with a shrewish wife, could reverse the stereotyped husband-wife pattern. The warmth of the relationship between father and son was sometimes affected by the number and age of the sons. A father might be less strictly authoritarian, for example, with an only son born to him in his later years than with several sons. In some cases father and daughter achieved a close relationship, so close that the daughter might be educated as a son or even married matrilocally to keep her from having to leave the parental home. And, of course, in describing types of relationships it is impossible to assess the degree of warmth or intensity which may have characterized any particular situation.

All the family property, including the house itself, was controlled by the male head of the family. All income earned by family members was likewise controlled by the family head, who dispensed it according to his judgment. This control was, however, not absolute. For example, a father could not sell the family property under his control without the consent of his grown sons. Even if he attempted to do so against their wishes he would find no buyers.

The families of peasants, artisans, and small merchants were units of production. In peasant families, the men and boys usually cultivated their own homesteads or rented land, while the women and girls performed the household tasks and made the family clothing. To a large extent such families were self-sufficient. In the case of artisans and small merchants the sons as a rule followed the father's trade. If absent members of the family were wage earners, they sent home that portion of their income not required for subsistence. An individual who attempted to keep all his earnings for his own use would be unfilial. Sons, but not daughters, inherited from their fathers, generally receiving an equal share regardless of relative age. The widow and unmarried children were supported by surviving adult sons or by the deceased man's family.

Wealthy families rarely constituted units of production, that is, income was derived from landholdings, professional services, and the like rather than directly from the labor of the male members of the family. Also, much of the household work was done by hired servants rather than by the female members of the family.

Although the individual's social activity was not limited to his nuclear family, or even to relatives, it was within the nuclear family that the closest personal ties were formed and the family was the first recourse in times of trouble or stress. It was the family which provided social services and education. In the case of the poor, this usually consisted of practical education, the parents teaching their children whatever skills and lore they knew. In wealthier homes, the family employed a tutor for the education of its sons or financed their training at a school. Jobs, apprenticeships, and appointments were arranged through family connections. Marriage was a contract between families rather than individuals, and was arranged by family heads. Finally, burial and care for the dependents of the deceased were provided by the family.

The conception of the family as a continuing entity, some of, whose members were deceased, some living, the rest as yet unborn, made vitally important the performance of ancestral rites and duties. It was believed that neglect of these duties almost certainly would bring suffering to the living and unborn members. On the other hand, suitably cared for ancestors were capable of materially aiding their descendants.

The Joint Family

The extended family, of which the joint family was the most important form in China, has always been the ideal family organization in the Confucian system. Although this ideal was open to all segments of the population, it permeated the higher classes much more than the lower classes. The joint family required some surplus wealth for its continued maintenance and the vast majority of the population was never able to accumulate a sufficient surplus. The joint family was often associated with big merchants, landlords, and scholar-officials.

The joint family comprised the patrilineal grandparents, their unmarried children, and their married sons and families, all of whom lived under one roof, typically in separate apartments or wings of a house. Alternatively, they might live in several connected houses within a single compound. The grandparents usually lived in the section occupied by the eldest son and his family. Ideally, the more relatives living together, the more successful the joint family. Nevertheless, it was rare to have more than three generations under one roof.

The head of the joint family was the oldest male of the oldest generation. This was usually the paternal grandfather, or if he was deceased, his oldest surviving brother or son. When a joint family remained together under one roof and functioned as a unit, the relationships described for the nuclear family obtained to a greater or lesser degree. For example, the father-son relationship was extended to the son's paternal uncles, and an uncle was expected to discipline the boy in his father's absence. Such situations might cause strain between father and uncle, and in many cases the uncle would avoid interfering if possible. Relationships existing within the nuclear families were extended in an attenuated form to the wider circle of relatives, but the warmest and closest relationships remained those within a nuclear family. Father and son were more intimately associated than uncle and nephew, and brothers had closer ties than cousins. The range of behavior ultimately depended upon the particular feeling between the individuals involved. In the same way, the joint family head might be a veritable autocrat or a mere figurehead, depending upon the personalities involved.

Theoretically, and to a large degree in fact, loyalty and cohesion within the large family group vis-à-vis outsiders was considerable, no matter what the circumstances. Prestige or shame accruing to one member of the joint family was shared by all. It was inevitable, perhaps, that with a large number of persons inhabiting a single household and sharing a single budget, strains should develop. Nevertheless, the joint family almost always managed to present a united front to the outside world despite any conflicts among individual members. When such cooperation became impossible the family usually divided.

In addition to the relationships that represented extensions of those found in the nuclear family, certain others were characteristic of the joint family system, the most important being the relationship between parents-in-law and a daughter-in-law. A woman had to serve her husband's parents and mourn for them as her husband was expected to do. Because of the pattern of sex segregation, the daughter-in-law had little contact with her father-in-law. In fact, their relationship was almost one of avoidance. Her relationship with her mother-in-law, however, was much more important as she worked at daily household tasks under the mother-in-law's direction. Generally the relationship was not warm. Indeed, it was one of the most strained relationships within the joint family.

A woman saw very little of her husband's older brothers even though they lived under the same roof, the pattern of sex segregation prevailing as in the relationship between a woman and her father-in-law. The husband's oldest brother was, of course, successor to the role of family head on the death of the father. The relationship between a man and his son's wife was very much like that between a man and his younger brother's wife. She could, however, have freer associations with her husband's younger brothers.

A woman's relations with her husband's sisters were informal and unimportant as the sisters remained in the household only until they were married. Usually, however, the relationships were a source of conflict caused by the husband's sisters.

Sisters-in-law, that is, wives of brothers, living and working in the same house under the same mother-in-law, apparently did not become close in their joint unfavorable situation. Instead, a "pecking order" developed in which the older brothers' wives exploited the most recently added sister-in-law to consolidate their own positions in the family. Jealousies frequently arose between the sisters-in-law over differential treatment of their husbands or children by the family head or his wife. Competition for favor and intrahousehold intrigues were sometimes a result. The social ideal of sisters-in-law living in harmony persisted, despite all these conflicts.

Under the joint family system the individual nuclear families lost many of their functions to the joint family. For example, authority rested with the head of the joint family rather than with the senior males in the individual family. Although the latter were responsible for the behavior of their own wives and children, they and their individual families might be disciplined by the head of the joint family.

The family property and budget were also handled by the joint family head. Each of the family members turned over his income to the family head, who allocated it according to need. It should be noted that since the joint family was found more often among the higher classes than the lower classes, income supporting joint families was more usually derived from rents, commercial enterprises, official salaries, and other sources, rather than from individual labor. The joint family functioned, therefore, more frequently as a unit of consumption and less frequently as a unit of production.

The social functions of the joint family were similar to those described for the nuclear family. As the unit was larger and the number of persons involved was greater, the joint family tended to provide even more social contacts and recreation for its individual members. Women in poor families had to work in the fields and trade in the markets, but in wealthy homes, outside errands and business could be attended to by servants. Women in joint families were consequently more secluded and their social contacts were for the most part limited to members of the household.

Larger Kin Groups

There were three groups of kinsmen: relatives through one's father, relatives through one's mother, and relatives by marriage. Certain members from all three groups were considered "mourning relatives" or those for whom one was expected to mourn, the mourning period varying with the distance of the relationship. In life these relatives were expected to assume certain obligations of sympathy and support in case of need. The circle of mourning relatives was a closer unit of kindred than larger groupings such as the subclan or clan and expected a greater degree of solicitude and mutual aid from relatives within the specified degrees.

The clan, *tsu*, occupied a prominent place in Chinese society for centuries. It was a common descent group tracing its ancestry to a first male ancestor who settled in a given locality. In traditional Chinese society, only patrilineal descendants were considered clan members, that is, children belonged to the clan of their father. As marriage within a clan was not permitted, a woman always married outside her father's clan, and her children belonged to her husband's clan.

The families within a clan bore the same surname, but families with the same surname did not necessarily belong to the same clan. There are about 470 surnames in use in China today, but there were many more clans. Nevertheless, until recently, marriage was forbidden between men and women of the same surname.

The clan kept a record of its descent lines by means of genealogies, which were compiled and prepared at some expense by its gentry members. Not all clans had written genealogies, but those that did not boast written genealogies often had long oral traditions that served the same purpose. The genealogies contained not only vital statistics about the ancestors and living members of the clan but also chronicled special achievements of clan members and honors bestowed upon them.

As the fortunes of related families varied, a clan included wealthy and poor families, thereby crosscutting class lines and representing several social strata. Clans achieved their greatest importance in rural areas and small towns. They lost many of their integrative functions in larger cities where there was sharp differentiation of social classes and where other organizations, such as guilds, took over some of the protective functions exercised by the clans in rural areas.

Clan importance also varied from one region to another. Clans were strongest in the south, particularly in Kwangtung and Fukien, where many villages were clan communities, that is, comprised of only one or two dominant clans. In a village consisting of only one clan or one important clan, village organization became identical with clan organization and the major functionaries of the village were also the principal leaders of the clan. The importance of the Fukien and Kwangtung clans is still felt in overseas Chinese communities that have emigrated from these areas. Loyalty to the clan was reflected in funds sent by emigrant members to the clan heads at home. Clans were also important in the rice-growing regions of the Yangtze valley, but had more organizational formality than actual solidarity in southwestern provinces such as Yunnan. They were less prominent and less powerful in the north, but by no means absent. Although not typical, communities with only one clan were reported from northern provinces such as Shantung and Hopeh.

A clan always consisted of a number of lines of descent, known as *fang* (branches or subclans), each line descended from a son of the common clan ancestor. The branches were sometimes graded according to the relative age of the sons from whom they were descended. When a clan had grown large, various administrative duties were handled by the heads of the several branches even though the clan head remained the dominant figure.

As branches of a clan shared certain responsibilities regarding ancestral rites and common property, it was necessary that they should remain fairly evenly balanced. If some branches became larger or wealthier than others, or became extinct, artificial reorganization of the branches was sometimes necessary to distribute the rights and obligations of the group evenly. When this was done, the resulting branches did not correspond to kinship reality.

When a clan became large, some of its branches dispersed or individual families emigrated to a new locality. Relations between the parent clan and its offshoots were not always maintained intact over the centuries. The émigrés may have been later able to trace their connection with the parent clan, or they may have tried to establish a genealogical connection with a stronger group to enhance their own prestige.

If different local groups with the same surname could trace a genealogical connection to a common ancestor, they joined together for rites for this ancestor and held meetings to discuss problems of common interest. This was known as *lien-tsung*, that is, to join in a *tsung* (clan). The clans and subclans, then, were essentially kinship units whose membership or composition may have been, in part, artificial.

As the various groups under discussion were primarily kinship groups, their most conspicuous function was to unite larger numbers of related people in social bonds than the nuclear or joint family could. Clan members, for example, were reminded of the kinship ties uniting them by the use of kinship terminology both for reference to and address of fellow clansmen. Associated with these terms of address were prescribed patterns of behavior, applied in a more attenuated form to clan relatives than to members of the family.

In areas of strong clan development, the clan also had economic, educational, judicial, and political functions. Wealthy members donated land and property to the clan and through investments and rents some clans were able to amass considerable wealth. These resources were used to build and support clan temples, defray the expenses of ancestral rituals, pay for court litigations involving clan members, assist younger members to obtain an education, help orphans and indigent elderly members, and provide burial space for the dead.

Concomitant with this concentration of wealth was a concentration of power. The leaders of the clan and their advisers were drawn from those members who were able through wealth or education to enhance the standing of the clan vis-à-vis outsiders such as other clans or the government. These wealthly or gentry members enjoyed certain rights and privileges—for example, management of ritual land and precedence on ceremonial occasions—not available to lesser members of the clan. The clan and branch heads, like the family heads, had authority over the members of their respective groups. Matters concerning the group at large were referred to the appropriate head and his advisers; cases were heard and punishments meted out in the ancestral hall or clan temple. The clan elders sat in judgment and decided the punishment according to tradition and the rules of conduct set down by the particular clan. Offenses within the clan were handled by the clan. Criminal offenses, such as homicide, were supposedly under the jurisdiction of the government authorities, but in rural areas of strong clan development, far from the seat of the provincial capital, local government authority sometimes found it impossible to interfere even in such cases. Some clans preferred to settle their own disputes and criminal cases and were strong enough in their local area to ignore government authority. Often the local official would merely make a face-saving investigation while the clan usurped the power of the government.

Usually neighboring clans were on good terms since all were exogamous and ties of intermarriage and friendship connected them. Nevertheless, by their very nature as "we" groups, rivalry between clans was inevitable. In some areas this rivalry took the form of competition in education of clan members, or in building better ancestral temples. In other areas the rivalry broke out into interclan feuds which sometimes involved bitter fighting over long periods of time. Large membership provided manpower for these fights. If the cases were eventually brought into court, money was needed to pay litigation fees and, where possible, to bribe the judiciary. Sometimes several clans banded together for mutual benefit, thereby forming a bloc which central government authorities found impregnable.

Factors Affecting Family Structure

Five age groups with prescribed social roles were as a rule distinguished in the patterns of the traditional Chinese family. The first of these, the infant or *ying-erh* period, covered roughly the first four years of life and was a stage of indulgence and freedom for the child. In traditional China children were much desired (unless the family was too poor to support them) and for its first two years the child was subject to no systematic training or discipline. At this early period there was little distinction between the treatment of boys and girls except that the arrival of a son was cause for greater joy.

The next age grade was childhood or *yu-nien*, a term that seems to have referred primarily to the immaturity and inexperience of the person in this category. In the past, during the childhood period the real discipline of Chinese family life was brought to bear upon the child. Here began in earnest the differentiation on the basis of sex that was to persist through life. The boy in this age group, if he belonged to a gentry family, began to attend school or was tutored privately. In either case, the beginning of his formal education marked the advent of a rigorous training. The peasant boy in this age group went to work in the fields or was apprenticed to a craftsman or merchant. In general, nonfamily contacts became important for boys in this age group, whereas girls were more and more confined to the home and had fewer outside contacts.

The next age group in Chinese family structure was youth, known as *ch'ing-nien*. This was a more or less intermediate period covering roughly the time after which a person could no longer be regarded as a child but before his acceptance as an adult. In general marriage took place before the end of this period.

Full-fledged adult status was referred to as *ch'eng-jen*, literally, to become a man. This period was divided into two parts, separated by a point roughly midway between marriage and old age. Sometime during the adult period a man would usually become a family head and perhaps the head of a household.

From about fifty-five on a man was regarded as having reached the respected status of old age, *lao-nien*, and could expect formal deference and veneration from those younger than he. The accumulated wisdom of his years gave him a certain authority and though by this time the duty of supporting the family had passed to his children he remained the venerated head of his family in all other respects.

Although the overwhelming majority of Chinese marriages were monogamous, under the imperial law men were permitted secondary wives or concubines. A concubine, unlike a mistress, had legal rights, but these were inferior to those of the first wife. A concubine's children, on the other hand, had equal legal status with any children of the first wife. It was easier to divorce a concubine, who was socially inferior to the wife. The wife had authority over any concubines, and if she were jealous the relationship could be a strained one. The children of the first wife might in practice have a social advantage over the children of a concubine, especially if the wife produced sons. Legally a man might not depose his wife and place a concubine in her stead, but after the death of his wife a man might raise one of his concubines to the status of a wife. The keeping of concubines was restricted to those men who could afford to purchase and support more than one woman. It was practiced mainly by the gentry, wealthy merchant class, and military and civil officials sent to posts some distance from their homes.

In theory, the reason for concubinage was to insure the all-important continuation of the male line. Thus, if a wife were barren or bore daughters only, she or her husband's family might ask him to take a concubine. Sometimes a sister of the wife might be chosen to fill the position, which meant less adjustment on the part of the women as they were accustomed to living in the same household. A concubine also relieved the pressure of adverse opinion on the wife who produced no sons.

Desire for male descendants was not, however, the sole reason for concubinage, as lack of male descendants was not a necessary requisite. Sexual desire and competitive ostentatious display were certainly factors. Often a man would take a concubine without informing his wife. Although she might be jealous, she had to exercise restraint, as jealousy was one of the legal grounds for divorce. But if the wife had already given birth to sons, she could often effectively block her husband's secondary entanglements; it would also be difficult if not impossible for her husband to divorce her.

The intense desire for male offspring to continue the family line and perform necessary rites for the ancestors might also be fulfilled by adoption. Adoption was not usually favored but if a man could not have a son of his own, it was a way of procuring one. Near relatives were practically under obligation to provide a child in such instances. If no boy was available among his close relatives, a man would look next among his "mourning relatives" and then try the wider circle of clan relatives. In any case, the boy would have to be of the son generation relative to the adopting parents. Adoption of a nonrelative was rare.

If a widow were left childless, her parents-in-law might adopt a son for her to rear. This child would continue the deceased husband's line and become his legal heir, performing the ancestral rites for his "father" and for the widow upon her death. The performance of mourning rites and the right of succession and inheritance were intimately bound together.

If a man had daughters but no sons, he might adopt a husband for one of his daughters. The husband then took his wife's family name and came to live as a member of her family, thereby abandoning his own. Such matrilocal marriages were not highly regarded in most parts of China; it was thought that only a very poor or shiftless person would abandon his ancestors in this manner. Nevertheless, matrilocal marriage was the only solution for the family with no son by either birth or adoption.

Early Attempts at Family Reform

For over two thousand years, except for brief periods of adjustment in times of foreign conquest, the traditional family organization had been basic to all social, economic, and political activity, its structure intact and unchanged from almost the beginning of the imperial period to the 1911 revolution. The first serious challenge to the supremacy of the family came early in the republican period when social reformers, responding to the same forces and influences that were causing restlessness in political and intellectual circles, began a series of attacks on the "evils" of the traditional family system: nepotism, clannishness, authoritarianism, and so on. The political implications of the Confucian theory of the family were felt to be incompatible with democracy: narrow clan and family loyalties, including filial piety, must be superseded by broader national loyalty if a unified nation were to become a reality.

An attempt was made to explain national characteristics and personality traits as consequences of the traditional family system. The reformers pointed out that forbearance, a cardinal Confucian virtue necessary for the maintenance of large undivided family groups, had been overemphasized. As a result, individuals became accustomed to resignation and passive submission to intolerable situations. The combination of filial piety and forbearance was said to lead to the repression or annihilation of individual personality. The repression of personality was in turn decried as the reason why self-expression, originality, creativeness, and the adventurous spirit of exploration and pioneering inventiveness, characteristics which worked fundamental innovations in European civilization, never had a chance to develop among the Chinese.

The joint family system was also accused of fostering laziness and irresponsibility, hindering the development of a capacity for organization among its members and promoting the growth of undesirable features such as nepotism.

In an effort to enlist the support of Chinese women, the reformers actively propagandized for the emancipation of women from the various legal debilities under which they were restrained from divorce, remarriage, choice of mates, and so forth. The movement itself had a strong influence on the attitudes which the Nationalist government later took toward the marriage issue and family reform. Government leaders were alive to the conflict between the traditional family and clan loyalty and the new patriotism for the state that they were trying to inculcate. Many Chinese writers, educators, and statesmen thus became foremost leaders in the fight for the emancipation of women.

The congresses of the Nationalist party repeatedly passed resolutions urging reform in the family system. However, it was not until 1931 that the new Civil Code was promulgated that legally altered the Chinese family system. Although it was strongly influenced by foreign legislation regarding the family, the new code attempted to reconcile essentially Chinese characteristics with modern concepts. Probably the most important break with the past was the complete omission of any reference to ancestral rites, which by the disregard of this fundamental aspect of the traditional family organization implied that the male heir was no longer a vital necessity to the family. According to the code, the family was still patrilineal, patrilocal, patronymic, and patriarchal, but previous powers of the male family head were curtailed.

Another statute in the code required the consent of the parties concerned for a marriage contract. This represented a shift from the idea that marriage was a contract between families to a recognition of the importance of the individual. In principle, men and women were equal with regard to divorce, property rights, inheritance, and even the right to be family head. The old principle of male superiority had lost its legal sanction. The position of children was made more secure in that a father no longer might exercise the right of life or death over them. On attaining majority at the age of twenty, the individual acquired a new legal status, including the right to own property.

The new law did not mention concubinage, but tacitly recognized its existence and the probability that it would not quickly disappear by providing liberally for illegitimate children. As concubines were not recognized as legal wives under the code, their children were now regarded as illegitimate. However, the code made it easy for such children to achieve legal status.

The new legislation, though quite radical in concept and revolutionary in its provisions, had little actual effect on the traditional family system because the laws remained largely on paper. Only in the cities and among the educated strata of the population was there understanding of the new provisions. The number of people who availed themselves of their new rights was relatively insignificant compared to the population as a whole.

Many radical changes in the position of women did, however, occur, some long before the promulgation of the new civil code. The movement to end the custom of binding feet, which had developed from the criticism of social reformers and missionaries, was officially endorsed by the government following the 1911 revolution. A rise in the employment of women was paralleled by an extension of educational opportunities for women and the establishment of public schools for girls. The relaxation of restrictions led to an influx of women in professional work. Although these changes in the status of women were at first confined to the larger towns and cities, the trend toward a more independent status was soon apparent in all parts of the countryside.

Changes under the Communist Regime

The disintegration of the traditional family was considerably accelerated by the Communist effort to create a new social order. Popular agitations together with the stringent enforcement of new legal measures have dealt severe blows to the family organization. The Communists have attacked especially the deeply entrenched Chinese loyalty to the family which they consider detrimental to the establishment of a socialist state. It has been reported that they even attempted to arouse animosity between different members of the family, inciting the young to accuse the old, and the wife her husband. This has had the effect of disrupting the established patterns of patriarchal family relationship and of uprooting the centuries-old Confucian family ethics.

The Marriage Law of 1950

The first major law passed by the Chinese Communist regime was the Marriage Law promulgated on May 1, 1950. It is one of the "fundamental laws" of the People's Republic of China and has been given equal rank with the labor union law and the agrarian reform law.

The marriage law incorporated many reforms, some of which had already existed in the 1931 civil code. In certain instances, however, the new law went further than the civil code. The latter had taken the first step toward recognizing the importance of the individual parties to a marriage agreement by stipulating that their consent was necessary to the contract. The 1950 law goes further in stipulating that marriage should be arranged between the parties concerned and not by their families or a matchmaker. The law bans bigamy, concubinage, child betrothal, interference with remarriage of widows, and exaction of money or gifts as marriage payments.

It defines the duties of husband and wife in terms of equal status, responsibility, and ownership and management of family property. The relations between parents and children are defined in terms of mutual responsibility for care and support. The parents have the duty to rear and educate their children and the children are to support and assist their parents. Provision is made for support of illegitimate children, stepchildren, and children after a divorce.

The equal right of either husband or wife to initiate divorce proceedings was guaranteed. This had been a feature of the 1931 civil code but, because women's social and economic position at the time was still far inferior to men's, very few women had been able to take advantage of the law. The 1950 marriage law, however, by giving women equal rights to employment and to ownership and management of property, has proved much more effective and is profoundly affecting social patterns.

The 1950 marriage law is not revolutionary in western terms, nor is it radically different from the civil code of the Nationalist government. Nevertheless it clearly runs counter to some of the basic Confucian precepts in the old family system and was promoted as a major social reform vital to the destruction of the centuries-old "feudal" system of marriage. Whereas the previous law was never put into effect outside the urban centers, the Communists are apparently making every effort to enforce the new law and have instituted several large-scale propaganda drives to publicize the law throughout the country, including the areas of minority nationalities.

The Communist insistence that family reform is the inevitable and necessary concomitant of agrarian reform is based on the Marxian theory that social organization is predicated upon and determined by economic organization. Consequently, the Communists believe that after agrarian reform and land redistribution, a reform in the family system must follow. They have therefore provided the legal basis for bringing the economic and social aspects of the society into harmony.

To publicize and popularize the marriage law the Communists began using all media. Propaganda in the press included reports to the effect that, all over China, young people were arranging their own marriages on the basis of mutual love, respect, and the desire to build a better homeland. Divorce figures were published to indicate that many people (mostly women) had taken advantage of the new law to free themselves from unhappy marriages arranged by their families. The large numbers of divorces were cited as proof of the evils of the old family system, and it was stated that over half the cases handled by the civil courts had been marriage disputes. Most of these early reports indicating popular support for the new law came from the larger cities.

The whole campaign, however, backfired and caused serious social crises in the country. Toward the end of 1950, through letters to the press, came reports of cases of violations of the law. Some of the violators were cadres who still retained "feudal ideas" about marriage and the status of women. The reports grew in number until it became evident that unsatisfactory conditions were widespread in rural areas. Preliminary investigations indicated that a number of cadres were resisting the new law and refusing to implement it. According to the Communist sources available, the failure of marriage reform was due, not to insistence that the cadres accept it against their will, but rather to refusal of the cadres to support and uphold that portion of the population which wanted to abide by the new law.

A rising number of suicides and murders, mostly of women, reached such an extent that in September 1951 the Government Administration Council (State Council since 1954) issued a directive to all local authorities calling for a general investigation in their respective areas. It was revealed that many women, attempting to take advantage of the divorce law, had found little support from the local cadres and had become the victims of persecution by their offended husbands, parents-in-law, or even their own families.

Communist sources attributed the behavior of the cadres to their lack of understanding of the social significance of the family reform and to their imperfect training in Marxian social theory. Some cadres, convinced that marriage and the family were private concerns and not matters of policy, had been neglecting marriage reform in favor of other reform activities. Others had shelved the law in the belief that the rural areas were not yet ready for such a law and that to advertise it would distract people from their work. Lastly, some of the cadres were themselves opposed to the law and either had not publicized it or ignored it where their own families were concerned. In the summer of 1952, Shih Liang, the woman Minister of Justice, announced that the marriage reform had left the old customs little affected in most parts of the country, and that in only very few counties in China had marriage and family reform been completely successful.

Meanwhile divorce rates had soared. According to government figures there were 186,000 divorces in 1950, 409,000 in 1951, and 396,000 in the first six months of 1952. The marriage law came to be popularly referred to as the divorce law.

Changes in Policy

At the end of 1952 the government, realizing the futility of using force to implement the marriage law and the necessity of patient work and education in its attempt to eradicate the age-old family system, designated March 1953 as Marriage Law Month (probably because Women's Day falls in March) and initiated an extensive propaganda campaign to acquaint every household with the provisions of the new law. Plans were made to set up booths with cartoons and pictures illustrating the law, to show film strips and lantern slides, and to write and publish plays and stories in an all-out effort to popularize the new law. In addition, it was proposed that a family-by-family investigation be conducted to see how well families abided by the provisions of the law. This was amended later to restrict the investigation to the families of government officials and party workers only.

An outline of propaganda issued in February 1953 by the National Committee for the Thorough Implementation of the Marriage Law stated:

> Among the broad masses of the people, the present movement shall be restricted to measures of education and propaganda. No investigation of family relationships and sexual relationships shall be carried out, and no movements for the airing of grievances or the holding of struggle meetings shall be launched. Mistaken and unpermissible are the establishment of "inspection posts" to inquire into family and sexual relationships, the development of "fronts" among husbands and wives, and mothers-in-law and daughters-in-law, the holding of "frank confession" meetings, the convocation of "struggle meetings," and the development of comparisons of families.

If these negative directives can be taken to mean that previously such measures had been undertaken to implement the marriage reform movement, it is not difficult to see how popular resentment against the movement arose. Inquiry into family and sexual matters is usually a difficult matter, and in China, propriety demands extreme reticence on intimate affairs.

The same document states that between seventy and eighty thousand people were killed or committed suicide in a single year in China over marriage difficulties. Whereas earlier accounts attributed all such deaths to conspiracy of "feudal reactionaries," some of the family tragedies may have resulted from the manner in which investigation of the law enforcement was conducted.

Social and Economic Pressures on the Family

The Communist government, like the Nationalist and other governments since the establishment of the Republic, has been endeavoring to shift the loyalty of the Chinese people from kin to state.

The strongest appeal has been to the two groups who were most restricted by the old law: women and young people. The desire to place women on an equal footing has another aspect as well: the Communists hope that new social and economic opportunities for women will release a large source of untapped manpower. One of the advantages cited for the commune system is this hope for the utilization of women in productive labor.

The new supreme value is political reliability, and the Communists encourage accusation by any individual, punishing as unpatriotic anyone who remains silent about political deviation among his friends or even his own family.

The Communist attempt to shift loyalties has involved more drastic methods and more revolutionary ideas than those of their predecessors. While most of the pre-Communist attempts at family reform were compromises of western and Chinese ideas with some effort at reconciliation of the two, the Communists have pitted their ethic squarely against long established values and ideals. Pre-Communist reform movements attempted to strip away the authoritarian features of the traditional family system without seeking to destroy the mutual confidence among family members. The Communists, however, endorse many measures which do in fact seriously undermine family relationships by pitting son against father and wife against husband.

The disintegration of the traditional family system cannot, however, be attributed solely to political and ideological changes. Powerful influences have been at work for several decades to weaken the social and economic bases of the traditional family. In this respect the Communists are merely capitalizing on the trend and attempting to accelerate it. One of the greatest blows to the established order is the growth of a youth-oriented culture. Increasingly, leadership and innovation have had to come from young men attuned to the new ideas and the new methods, while the prestige and authority of the elders dwindled away correspondingly. Since respect for age was an essential bulwark of the old system, this shifting of the locus of prestige has resulted in many upsets of the traditional formulas of deference behavior and the associated authority patterns.

Still more important is the increasing tempo of industrialization and urbanization. With the rise of factory production the economic link between father and son has been weakened. Wages are paid directly to a worker and not to the family head. One potent result of their newly found economic independence is that young members of a family are less inclined to defer to the authority of older members.

Associated with industrialization is the growth of urban centers, which began well before the Sino-Japanese War (1937-45) and has continued steadily since. Improved transportation and communications have made it easier for more people to leave rural homes and look for work in the cities. This shift in population contributes to divided homes and to fragmentation of the larger kin groups, as nuclear families leave the countryside. The crowded urban housing situation also favors small households with adult sons living elsewhere. The establishment of factory dormitories for bachelor workers is one indication of this trend. Increasing job opportunities for women in the cities also make it possible for them to attain economic independence, further enhancing their status within the family group.

Social and economic changes in the rural areas had been slower than in the urban areas in the period prior to the Communist revolution, and the traditional family system had been better preserved. But the drastic changes beginning in 1950 altered the picture completely. There have been three successive stages, the first being the fragmentation of landholdings for redistribution in small plots. This "land reform" had an immediate and serious effect on the larger kin groups, whose possession of land provided the economic base for accumulation of the surplus wealth essential to their existence as organized groups.

The second stage was signaled by the establishment of agricultural cooperatives in which land and draft animals were collectively owned. The individual family head, deprived of his control over the means of production, had also lost the power to transmit family property to his descendants. Another factor contributing to the stability of the family system had been eliminated.

The final blow has been, however, the organization of people's communes. The commune, by providing food for members and paying regular wages directly to each working individual, makes complete economic independence from the family head possible for any adult in the household. The rural women too can work full time in the commune, having been freed from household duties by the establishment of commune messhalls, child care centers, and kindergartens. The significance of the family as an economic unit has been reduced to a minimum along with the authority of parents over adult children and of the husband over his wife. The social functions of the family, another cohesive force in the past, are similarly being reduced as the commune assumes responsibility for the care and education of children and the welfare of the orphaned, the aged, and the incapacitated. The commune system has already effected more fundamental changes in the family than any other legal reform ever attempted.

The progressive fragmentation of the family and kin groups in modern times, culminating under the Communist regime, has stripped away their protective cover over the individual, making him extremely vulnerable to government pressures. In western industrial societies the decline of strong family ties has been compensated for in part by the growth of political rights and the organization of powerful private interest groups such as business, labor, and professional associations which function as an effective check against arbitrariness on the part of the state. Under the Communist dictatorship such countervailing forces are totally absent. The loosening of family ties has thus not set the individual free as reformers in the past had hoped, but regimented him into a larger social organization, the Communist state, from which he has no recourse.

DYNAMICS OF POLITICAL BEHAVIOR

POLITICAL POWER IN CHINA TODAY is entirely in the hands of a single group: the Chinese Communist party. The party, through its estimated ten million tightly disciplined members, controls the government and all groups that could conceivably challenge the party's hegemony. Mass organizations established by the party effectively mobilize and indoctrinate people with common interests such as laborers, women, youth, businessmen, or the intelligentsia while posing as "democratic" and "independent" groups that support the regime. This emphasis on democratic appearances was demonstrated in the election of 1953-54 when the people were given a chance to participate although only Communist-approved candidates were listed.

In all this the party follows closely the pattern set by the Communist party of the Soviet Union. Like its Soviet counterpart, the Chinese Communist party is learning that even modern means of mass control are not enough to completely neutralize latent political opposition within the population as a whole. The sheer size and scope of the Communist agencies of political control are mute evidence that such opposition exists.

Policies of the Regime

The socialist revolution in China gained momentum after the Communists won control of the government for only then could their radical institutional, social, economic, and ideological measures be enforced. Within the framework of Communist doctrine the program of Mao Tse-tung permits great elasticity, however, in the order and timing of policy formulation and implementation in accord with the Stalinist concept of a joint capitalist-socialist revolution. Any retardation or acceleration of the socialist revolution can be justified and it is for the leaders to decide which measures are required by "objective conditions."

Moderation characterized the first year of the Communist regime as time was needed to establish operational control throughout the country. The repair of transportation and communications facilities received top priority. Then, with real authority in the hands of the Communist military commanders of the six administrative regions into which China had been divided, the former government personnel at all levels was either replaced or, where serious practical difficulties would have arisen, induced to remain in office for the time. Concurrently the Communists were busy securing the support of intellectuals whose special abilities would be important to the regime and reassuring those businessmen whose continued activity was essential to prevention of complete economic collapse.

This period of entrenchment-through-moderation ended with the Korean War, which marked the entry of Communist China into world affairs and also served the new regime as a focus for patriotic appeals to the Chinese people. A fierce propaganda campaign against the "imperialist powers," particularly the United States, paralleled violent attacks in China itself against "capitalist" elements of the society. The emphasis in government policy shifted to the social revolution with the promulgation in June 1950 of the agrarian reform law, the preliminary to collectivization.

The redistribution of land carried out under the agrarian reform law was represented as a victory in the "class struggle" and was accompanied by vilification of landlords and wealthy peasants through every medium of propaganda. An estimated ten million people were either executed or forced into camps as a result of this land reform, the Communists' purpose being to eliminate the traditional village leadership. This leadership was taken over by Communist cadres, who promptly began preparing the peasants for the next step, collectivization.

Turning their attention to potential political opposition, the Communists launched early in 1951 a "counterrevolutionary suppression" campaign directed toward all "war criminals, traitors, bureaucratic capitalists, and counterrevolutionaries." Their property was confiscated and they became subject to punishment ranging from three years' imprisonment to death. Former officials, whose critical importance to the regime had by this time ended, were brought to trial in great numbers. The actual trials were secret but public trials were conducted afterward, the purpose being to induce a mass psychosis of hatred against what were called traitors and class enemies. After listening to the accusations of witnesses, the mass of listeners would be asked for judgment and provoked into hysterical exclamations. Public trials were continuous in the cities, and in metropolitan areas like Shanghai and Tientsin tens of thousands of people participated.

Toward the end of 1951 a third campaign, the so-called Three-Anti movement, was initiated, ostensibly to rid the government of three evils—corruption, waste, and "bureaucratic capitalism." Actually the Communist party used the campaign to purge remaining officials of the former regime and to discipline or liquidate certain undesirable party members.

Supplementing the Three-Anti movement was the Five-Anti movement, directed against private enterprise on the basis of five charges—tax evasion, bribery, cheating in government contracts, theft of economic intelligence, and stealing of national property. This movement, aimed at destruction of the independent business class, reached its height in March 1952 but continued until June. A case could be contrived against almost every business firm under one of the five categories and businessmen were tried one after the other at special tribunals set up in the cities.

Through persecution and intimidation, most private firms were brought into close surveillance and control by the government, whose representatives in these firms now assumed a decisive role in determining business transactions; other firms found it so difficult to survive under such pressure that they were forced to accept joint state-private ownership. As the government was already in control of credit, wages, and prices, of the allocation of raw materials, and frequently of the sale of the products, the last vestiges of private direction of business were eliminated.

The social revolution had been furthered in important ways by these campaigns in 1951 and 1952. First, the traditional social order had been greatly weakened by the elimination of most of the former ruling class. Second, the mass hysteria purposely fanned by every kind of propaganda had roused many sections of the population to participation in Communist violence and thus to emotional involvement in the regime's goals.

At the ideological level, a program to reform the thinking of teachers and to train "senior construction cadres" was outlined by Chou En-lai in a five-hour speech in September 1951. The ideology of the "progressive elements" of the working class—that is, Marxism-Leninism as adapted for Chinese conditions by Mao Tse-tung—was impressed on teachers by means of "severe criticism and self-criticism." Similarly other Chinese intellectuals were subjected to the "dialectic struggle" that the Communists have found so useful as a method of mental coercion. At public meetings intellectuals were forced to criticize each other for distorted thinking and for feudalistic and capitalistic backgrounds. This process, which soon divested the participant of any pride or dignity, ended only when he promised to accept the "real truth" of Marxism-Leninism. In fulfillment of this promise he had to write a public confession. Only positive attitudes were permissible in either oral discussion or written statements. Even "the freedom of silence" was taken way.

The reform of the intellectuals was echoed in a general indoctrination of the public carried out through the mass organizations. Political discussion of topics selected by the party was conducted by these organizations in the form of debates, with debating points and conclusions prearranged. Compulsory participation in these "debates," from which all independent argument was excluded, gradually imposed on all members a conformity of thought consistent with party dogma.

A beginning having been made toward assuring an ideological and organizational basis, the Communists turned to the more practical aspects of their economic and political program after 1953. The first goal, industrialization, was formulated in the First Five Year Plan where heavy industry as a means of securing political and military power received great emphasis. Industrialization depended, however, on the complete collectivization of agriculture, and there followed a rapid organization in 1954-56 of a higher type of agricultural producers' cooperative in which all land and means of production were collectively owned. After the tightening of ideological control in the campaign against revisionists and rightists came the Second Five Year Plan in 1958, with special stress on the "big leap forward" in industry. During that year agricultural socialization was carried a big step forward with the establishment of the people's commune—a form of socialist organization that exercises an over-all control of the economic, political, and cultural life of the rural populace. Communist policy has thus moved relentlessly, propelled by a powerful party machinery, toward what the leadership envisages as the realization of the socialist state.

The Chinese Communist Party

The Communist party of China is directed by a small group. In theory the authority of the party rests with its national party congress, which is supposed to elect a Central Committee every five years. The Central Committee has unlimited power to direct the party apparatus. It convenes the party congresses and determines their membership and programs; it elects a Political Bureau (Politburo) which serves as the policymaking body of the entire party and has absolute authority over party members.

The Central Committee functions through a number of *ad hoc* committee organs, the most important of which are: the Administrative Office; the Organization Department, which deals with the party organs and their functions; the Propaganda Department; the United Front Work Department, which controls the "democratic parties" and non-Communist members of government agencies and committees; the Social Affairs Department; the Rural Work Department; and the Marx-Lenin Institute.

Implementation of policy is supervised and controlled by a number of local party agencies. In 1949 a regional party organization was set up in conjunction with each of the regional military administrations. When in 1954 the provinces became administrative units directly under the central government, replacing the regional administration, party organizations were also established in provinces, special municipalities, and autonomous regions and districts.

Subordinate to the party organizations for the larger areas are the city, county, commune, and nationality autonomous county organizations. The basic unit of the party structure, however, is the party branch, representing a specific activity or locality such as a mine, factory, school, cooperative, or an army unit. The branches, formed only on approval of the higher level committee, may have anywhere from three to several hundred members but average about twenty. Their purpose is to carry out propaganda and organizational work among the masses of the people.

Supplementing the branches in function are the party cells, organized according to the party constitution wherever there are three or more party members. Cells have been formed in all branches of the party organization, in all departments of the government, and within the mass organizations. Their primary importance to the party lies in their use as a mechanism by which the party can manipulate government departments and mass organizations.

The method of electing representatives to the party congresses is hierarchical: the members of the party branch congresses elect the members of the county or city congress; these in turn elect the members of the provincial congress; the provincial congress representatives elect the members of the national congress. The 1956 party constitution stipulates that each of these party congresses is to meet once every year, but in the past these meetings were not as frequent. Eleven years elapsed from the party's Seventh National Congress in 1945 to the Eighth National Congress in 1956; and as of October 1959 no new national congress had been held. Many of the provincial congresses, established in 1949, did not meet till 1956.

The party congresses also elect party committees of the same level. Each elected member of the party committee must be approved by the party committee of a superior level. Thus, the provincial committees are subject to the approval of the Central Committee. This system assures that no one whom the higher party committees disapprove is able to attain a leading position on party committees.

Incomplete figures of party membership in various provinces and the number of members elected to provincial party congresses and the Eighth National Congress are given in Table 2.

Membership and Discipline

The growth of the Communist party in China has been spasmodic, sharp increases in membership having been recorded at the time of the Nationalist-Communist collaboration in 1924-27; in the Kiangsi period about 1934; during the last years of the war against Japan; in the period of the Communist triumph in 1949-50; and during the first years of the transition to socialism in 1955-56 (see Table 3). Each period of expansion was followed by reform and a tightening of the ranks, purges, and reorganization, which resulted in the further strengthening and consolidation of the party.

The lack of any substantial increase in party membership during the years 1951 and 1952 coincided with two simultaneous movements: one to change the composition of the membership by making it less rural and the other to tighten party discipline by purging the less desirable elements.

Up to 1949 the strength of the Chinese Communist party had been confined to the mountainous districts and the countryside, and did not extend to large cities. Except at the top level, the major part of the membership was recruited from rural areas and many new members, young men from the villages, were not only uneducated but actually tramps and adventurers. The large percentage of untutored rustics in the party posed a problem for the Communist leaders when they came to power in 1949. The need for trained men became urgent not only because Communist propaganda had constantly proclaimed that the party was a workers' party but also because of the multitudinous political, social, and economic problems arising from the socialist transformation of the state. The leaders, realizing that an overwhelming majority of illiterate peasants impeded the work of the party, decided in the summer of 1950 to absorb one-third of all industrial workers into the party within the space of three to five years and to stop expanding party membership in the newly liberated rural areas prior to the completion of the agrarian reform. The purpose was to turn the Communist party into a party of workers by gradual modification of the membership.

Along with efforts to change the composition of the membership, a movement was launched to purge the party of weak and undesirable members. Increasingly frequent charges of graft, bureaucraticism, waste, commandism, pride, and arrogance had been leveled against party cadres. Much of the corruption stemmed from the tremendous expansion of the party. Leaders themselves felt keenly that a large number of new party members lacked understanding of ideologies or methods; some had little sympathy for workers, peasants, and other laboring masses. To remedy this situation, the party launched a reform movement consisting of compulsory reading and discussion of Marxism-Leninism coupled with public criticism and self-criticism meetings. The reform was carried out most strenuously in the middle echelons of the hierarchy and resulted in a drastic paring of the membership.

To refill the depleted ranks and meet the demand for more cadres for the multiplying government enterprises, the party's Central Committee began a membership campaign, issuing in May 1952 a "Directive to Intensify the Work of Party Expansion." The recruitment of members, conducted by veteran cadres with the help of propagandists and reporters from the party committees, had a second important goal, to correct an uneven regional distribution of the membership that had developed. For instance, of the 5.8 million party members in 1950, 1.2 million were in the army and 3.4 million were concentrated in Northeast, North, and East China, with only 1.2 million in all the other regions of the country. The membership campaign was therefore particularly intensive in the rural areas, factories, mines, and business corporations where party membership had been small.

Most of the recruits selected and trained were those who had distinguished themselves during the land reform and the Five-Anti drive. Nevertheless the recruitment campaign went on slowly. Reports of the campaign were sporadic and incomplete; statistics were given only for a few key cities where new members were accepted mostly from among workers in the business enterprises, including managers, technicians, medical staff, and other employees.

Despite this drive to incorporate urban workers, the membership of the party is still largely rural. Party membership increased greatly in the farming areas following the collectivization of the peasants into agricultural cooperatives. By June 1956, according to a report by the Organization Department of the Central Committee, of the 10,734,000 members in the party about 7,410,000 or 69 percent were drawn from the rural population—5,360,000 poor peasants and 2,050,000 middle peasants. Industrial workers accounted for 1,500,000, or 14 percent of the total membership. Since 1956 a large number of activists, including a sizable portion of industrial workers, have been absorbed into the party ranks, but even then there is still a predominance of rural party members over members from urban areas. The intellectuals constituted about 12 percent of the total membership; 10 percent were women, a ratio that has remained constant in recent years. Among the non-Han minority groups, despite the membership drive, there were only 290,000 party members in September 1956.

The Chinese Communist party has the same system of enforcing discipline as its Soviet model. Attacks against rightist revisionists and leftist deviationists have resulted in the elimination of all potential rivals and opponents to the party leadership. Purges occurred both before and after the assumption of power. The character of the purges, however, was somewhat different from that of the Russian prototype. The power struggle between Communist leaders was probably less complex in China, where the secret police never played as independent and powerful a political role as in Soviet Russia, and where the role of the army was important from the outset. Since the Communist leadership, based from the beginning on a close alliance with the top military echelon, was able to secure its control over the armed forces as well as the party apparatus, the struggle was not so much between organizations as between individuals.

A certain regional factor may have played a role in this factionalism. Most revealing of the type of intraparty struggle carried on in China was perhaps the purge of the Communist leader Kao Kang and his associates in 1955. Kao Kang, who had organized his own Communist group in Yenan before Mao Tse-tung's arrival and later became regional leader of Manchuria, was accused of attempting to build up his own military support in opposition to Mao. This attempt failed, Kao Kang supposedly committed suicide, and his associates were purged.

The Party Congress of 1956

During the eleven years between the party's seventh and eighth national congresses, momentous changes had taken place. In 1945 the party was still an antigovernment organization operating in the countryside and the mountainous regions of Northwest China; in 1956 it was in complete control of the country, its branches extending to many parts of Asia. In 1945 it was mainly a group of hard-fighting peasants; in 1956 it was a privileged group. In these years party membership had increased ninefold from 1.2 million to 10.7 million. Time therefore was ripe for the convening of the Eighth National Congress in September 1956.

More than one thousand delegates attended the national congress in Peking. The agenda had been previously discussed and formulated at a conference of the secretaries of provincial and county party committees, and the revision of the party constitution, a major item of the agenda, had been previously discussed by the Central Committee. Prior to the formal opening of the national congress on September 15, the major resolutions to be adopted were discussed at three meetings of the Seventh Plenum of the Central Committee and at the preparatory conferences which met from August 29 to September 13. Thus everything was prepared beforehand. The formal congress was expected to run smoothly and it did.

The congress was the occasion for the reorganization of the most powerful organs of party machinery. The membership in the new Central Committee was enlarged to 170 (97 full members and 73 alternates), with all but one member of the outgoing Central Committee elected to the new Central Committee. The new Politburo, also considerably enlarged, has seventeen members and six alternates. Within the Politburo was set up a six-member Standing Committee, which is clearly the real depository of supreme power.

The new Politburo, as elected by the congress, is as follows (the asterisks indicate new members):

Full Members

Mao Tse-tung
Liu Shao-ch'i
Chou En-lai
Chu Teh (Marshal)   Standing
Ch'en Yün   Committee
Teng Hsiao-p'ing
Lin Piao (Marshal)
Lin Po-ch'ü
Tung Pi-wu
P'eng Chen
*Lo Jung-huan (Marshal)
*Ch'en I (Marshal)
*Li Fu-ch'un
P'eng Teh-huai (Marshal)
*Liu Po-ch'eng (Marshal)
*Ho Lung (Marshal)
*Li Hsien-nien

Alternate Members

*Ulanfu
Chang Wen-t'ien
*Lu Ting-i
*Ch'en Po-ta
K'ang Sheng
*Po I-po

The role of the military is seen in the fact that of the seventeen full members, seven are army marshals. While ten of the twenty-three members of the Politburo are newly elected, all of them are members of the old guard, not one having a record of less than thirty years of work for the party.

Prior to its adjournment, the Eighth National Congress also adopted a new party constitution to replace that of 1945. It consists of sixty-nine chapters headed by a preamble in which the Chinese Communist party is defined as "the vanguard of the Chinese working class," guided by the principles of Marxism-Leninism.

In the party constitution are enumerated the duties and rights of the members. The duties, ten in number, include the keeping of party and national secrets and precedence of party and national interests above personal interests. The rights, seven in number, include the right to criticize other members or any party organization. Young men and women, eighteen and over, who have had one year of probation and who are sponsored by two party members may be admitted into the party upon approval of the party branch or its superior committee. Members may be excluded from the party for failure to take part in party activities for a period of six months, for not paying dues, or by expulsion. A member of the Central Committee may be expelled, placed under observation, or suspended by the party congress or, in case of emergency, by a two-thirds majority of the Central Committee plenum.

The party constitution deals mainly with the organizational structure and system of the party. It stipulates the organization of central, provincial, and local party congresses and the election of party congresses and committees at all levels; it provides for the election of the Central Control Commission by the Central Committee plenum and the election of regional control commissions by regional committees, the main function of these commissions being to check breaches of party discipline and to impose punishment on the transgressors. The Central Committee is also empowered to appoint a representative organ to supervise party work in provinces, autonomous areas, and special municipalities—a move toward greater centralization of power by the leadership.

Other Political Parties

Of the political parties active in China prior to the Communist seizure of power, several have been permitted by the Communist regime to continue their existence. Of these, only the China Democratic League and the China Kuomintang (Nationalist) Revolutionary Committee have some justification for being separate political entities today. Other minor parties include the China Democratic National Construction Association, the China Association for Promoting Democracy, the China Peasants' and Workers' Democratic party, the China Chih-kung party, the Chiu-san Society, and the Taiwan Democratic Self-Government League.

The China Democratic League was originally a coalition of the middle parties that occupied a precarious position in the conflict between the Nationalists and the Communists. In the negotiation between these two political opponents toward the end of the Sino-Japanese War, the Democratic League attempted to mediate their differences and to bring about a coalition government. After the Communist assumption of power, the Democratic League cooperated with the new regime, later submitting completely to its control. Today the League exists as the main political focal point of non-Communist supporters of the regime. As a reward for their cooperation important members of the League have been given cabinet posts in the State Council and membership in the Standing Committee of the National People's Congress.

The Kuomintang Revolutionary Committee was set up in 1948 in Hong Kong by a number of dissident Nationalist party members. Its most important figures include former high-ranking Nationalist generals, officials, and party leaders. In 1949 the Kuomintang Revolutionary Committee moved to Peking to participate in the Communist government. Leaders of the Committee have been holding high positions in many government organs, including the National Defense Council, but these positions are mostly honorary and advisory.

Of the lesser groups, the China Democratic National Construction Association was founded in Chungking in 1945 by a group of educators, industrialists, and businessmen. Its avowed aim is to consolidate the national capitalist class and to promote its interests. The China Association for Promoting Democracy is a small group of former Nationalist party intellectuals and cultural workers. The China Peasants' and Workers' Democratic party is the successor of the so-called Third party, which was established in 1928 with a program of gradual realization of socialism and land reform. After the execution of its leftist-inclined leader by the Nationalist government, the party was reorganized and later joined the Democratic League. After 1949 it emerged as one of the political parties recognized by the Communist regime. The China Chihkung party, founded by Chinese residents in the United States, functions as a political group to attract overseas Chinese. The Chiu-san Society consists of a small group of intellectuals in cultural, educational, and scientific circles. The Taiwan Democratic Self-Government League was created by the Communists to attract defectors from Taiwan.

These so-called democratic parties are under the over-all control of the United Front Work Department of the Communist party's Central Committee. At first the democratic parties were not permitted to accept any new recruits. A year later they were assigned specific social groups from which recruitment was to be made. The new members are men who do not qualify for Communist party membership but who have expressed their willingness to cooperate with the new regime through the intermediary of these democratic parties. No recruiting is to be done among soldiers, peasants, workers, the police, or members of the Communist foreign service. The parties are to specialize in the following way: the Kuomintang Revolutionary Committee in former members of the Nationalist party or government; the China Democratic League, the intelligentsia; the China Association for Promoting Democracy, middle and primary school teachers; and the Chiu-san Society, college professors and scientists. The China Democratic National Construction Association, which enlists middle and small businessmen, has become a compulsory training organization for former private businessmen. Though still retaining its name, the China Peasants' and Workers' Democratic party has been forced to shift its activities to medical and public health workers. All these parties serve in this way as adjuncts of the Chinese Communist party.

Feelings of discontent and resentment, however, have been latent among some members of these parties. During the Blooming and Contending movement, they seized the opportunity to air their grievances and a few came out openly to criticize the Communist party and government. Alarmed by the vehemence and scope of the criticism, the Communists struck back by launching an antirightist campaign directed toward all the political parties. Several leading members of the Democratic League, the Kuomintang Revolutionary Committee, and the Peasants' and Workers' Democratic party holding high government posts became targets of the attack. They were branded as "rightists," denounced for their bourgeois and landlord background or for their past connections with the "reactionary Kuomintang clique," and accused of plotting against the government. A number of them were subsequently relieved of their government posts although some, after recanting, were readmitted to public office. There is little doubt that the Communist counterattack has inflicted a severe blow on the so-called democratic parties, while the weakening of their political strength will lead further to one-party dictatorship.

Mass Organizations

Besides the official branches of the Communist party and the various other subordinate political parties, there are many mass organizations established by the regime to serve as propagators of Communist doctrine and policy.

The impact of these mass organizations has been cumulative. Through them the Communist regime can carry its political measures into all sections of the population simultaneously. While each organization serves a specific purpose, together they form an integrated machinery for the indoctrination and mobilization of the whole population. The thousands of their branch organizations serve as nuclei not only for the political activity of the masses but also for the discussion of Communist doctrine and policy in continual meetings directed by the party. The constant preoccupation of the participants in these meetings with Communist doctrinal material leaves no time for independent thinking and provides an effective tool for the channeling of thought. Ideologically as well as functionally, the mass organizations constitute the multiple arms of the Communist party.

Operating on the principle of democratic centralism, as in the Communist party itself, each mass organization nominally has elections by the membership, but the candidates are previously designated and the leadership has full control over the organization. A national congress that meets only every four years or so is in theory the ruling body; in practice it is only a sounding board and a transmitter of policy. A central or executive committee, meeting about every half year, is dominated by a standing committee and a secretariat, which are the actual depositories of power. Each of these organizations has its special assignment of policy, but their work is closely integrated. The leadership is strongly permeated with Communist cadres and there is an interlocking directorate at the top level which guarantees uniformity of policy.

Among the mass organizations one of the most important is the All-China Federation of Trade Unions representing, according to the Communists, the "national leadership of all trade unions." Like other popular organizations, it has taken an active part in the major political movements but ostensibly is also concerned with the well-being of the workers. Members in the trade unions have no right to strike but may voice grievances. In addition to providing a program of sports and recreational and cultural activities, which serve purposes of propaganda and indoctrination, the federation has in recent times put its main emphasis on increase of industrial production, labor discipline, promotion of labor heroes, and team competition in production.

Equally important and similar in structure to the labor federation is the All-China Federation of Democratic Youth. As of 1956 it served as the roof organization for four large groups: the New Democratic Youth League of China, the All-China Students' Federation, the National Young Men's Christian Association, and the National Young Women's Christian Association. Of these, the most important is the New Democratic Youth League, which in September 1956 changed its name to the Communist Youth League.

The main purpose of the Communist Youth League is to educate the youths in Communist doctrine and prepare them as future party members and leaders. The power of the organization is vested in the seven original members of the secretariat, who have been the leaders from the beginning. The secretariat, the central committee, and the standing committee have in recent years each been greatly expanded, however, through additional appointments of younger cadres. Members for the Communist Youth League are recruited not only from the traditional groups of students, professionals, and the army but also more recently from industry and agriculture. In fact, the trend to emphasize these groups in the selection of leadership may be noted in all Communist organizations. The program and activities of the Communist Youth League cover the whole range of Communist policy. Members have participated in all the major drives and in ideological reform. By 1956 the League claimed to have nearly 700,000 cells and 20 million members between the ages of fourteen and twenty-five.

Youth under fourteen is organized in the Young Pioneer Corps, which claimed thirty million members. This organization indoctrinates its members in the "five loves": fatherland, people, labor, science, and public property. Significant is the absence of any reference to personal bonds with family or friends.

The All-China Federation of Democratic Women claimed a membership of about eighty million women in 1954. Its over-all aim is equality for women—specifically, equal pay for equal work—and its policy is to place a higher percentage of women in government and political organizations. Since 1952 greater production has been the main emphasis of its program as it has been with other organizations. It has also established nurseries and child-care groups to provide for the children of working mothers.

Another organization of special importance is the Sino-Soviet Friendship Association, which claimed in 1954 a membership of fifty-eight million and over a quarter of a million branches and subbranches. One reason for the large membership in this association is the admission of organizations as blocks as, for example, the entire People's Army of three million. The association, directed by leading members of the Communist party, is the primary agency in China for promoting friendship with Soviet Russia among the people.

Other organizations important in one or more aspects of Chinese life are the All-China Federation of Literary and Art Circles, the Chinese Science and Technology Association, the All-China Federation of Industry and Commerce, and the All-China Athletic Federation (China Olympic Committee).

Agencies of Political Control

In addition to the various government-controlled political parties and mass organizations, whose tentacles reach the people in every walk of life, the Communist regime has set up a multiplicity of public security agencies for the supervision of the people's political activities (see the plate, System of Political Control). Behind these agencies is the all-pervading authority of the Chinese Communist party. Both the United Front Work Department and the Social Affairs Department of the party's Central Committee exert their powers in the regimentation of the people. Communist party cells maintain discipline among party members and supervise the work of the agencies to which they belong. The Communist Youth League, likewise, not only maintains contact with the youth of the nation, but also supervises and molds the political behavior of its members.

Public Security Organs

At the apex of the political control system is the Ministry of Public Security. While ostensibly subordinate to the State Council, in actuality all important decisions affecting its personnel, policy, and even the settlement of important criminal cases are made by the party's Social Affairs Department. In this way, the secret police machinery of the party is effectively meshed with that of the ministry.

The Ministry of Public Security is divided into an administrative office and eight other offices: political security, economic security, police, frontier security, military security, "reform through labor" (that is, the penal system), intelligence, and personnel. The ministry directs and supervises all public security departments at the provincial, municipal, and county levels. It has under its direct

SYSTEM OF POLITICAL CONTROL

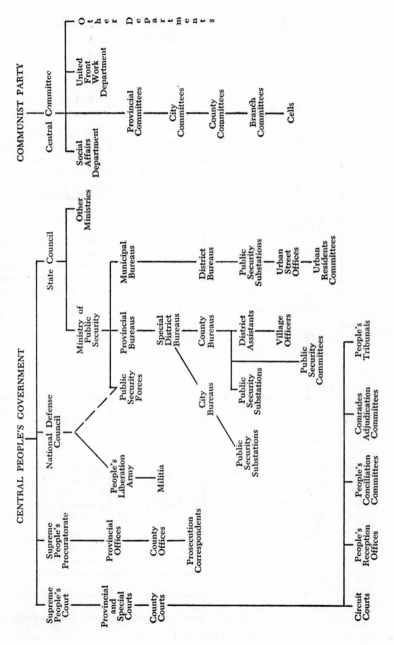

ORGANIZATION CHART OF THE PUBLIC SECURITY SYSTEM

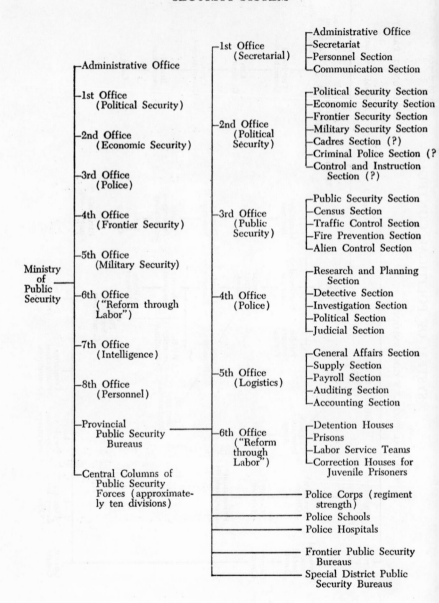

ORGANIZATION CHART OF THE PUBLIC
SECURITY SYSTEM (*Cont'd.*)

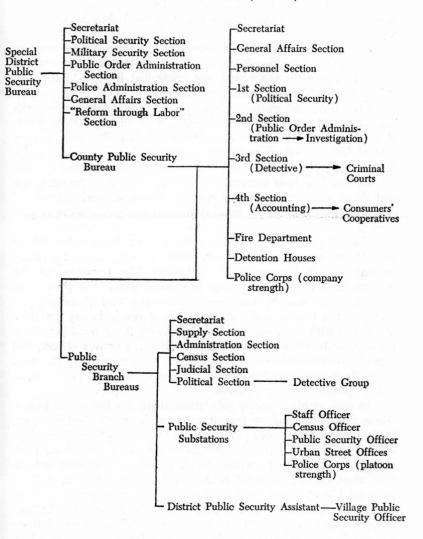

command the "central columns" of the public security forces, in addition to the public security divisions and public security brigades for the provinces, and smaller units for lower levels of administration (see the plate, Organization Chart of the Public Security System).

The public security departments of the autonomous regions, although nominally subordinate to the governments of these regions, are in fact directly supervised and controlled by the Ministry of Public Security of the central government.

The provincial public security bureaus, organized along the lines of the Ministry of Public Security, have among their subdivisions police training schools, police hospitals, as well as census, alien control, fire prevention, and traffic control sections. These are under the control of six main offices. The county public security bureaus are divided into four sections which have control of investigation and detection, registration, houses of detention, and consumers' cooperatives, the latter presumably to serve the public security personnel.

For the purpose of controlling the people down to the lowest level there are, under the county public security bureaus, public security branch bureaus and substations. The functions of the substations include the keeping of general order, the prevention of destructive acts by counterrevolutionaries and criminals, the taking of the census, and the promotion of revolutionary activities in keeping with the observation of law among the general populace. Each substation consists of a staff of officers, a census officer, and a public security officer in charge of the police corps. In the rural areas, there are district public security assistants, and below them, village public security officers.

In each public security substation, there is a household police, whose task is to check on travelers, overnight guests, hotel patrons, births and deaths, unemployment, marriages, and divorces. The ultimate aim is to have dossiers on members of each household, including detailed information on their source of income, education, class category, family background up to three generations, personal history from the age of eight, and friends and relatives inside and outside of China. The household police can visit any home at any time. After the visit a report is submitted in triplicate for distribution to higher levels, thus building up a dossier which will follow the resident wherever he moves.

In addition to regular policing public security forces have functions unique to the Chinese Communist system. The term "census," for example, has a much more comprehensive meaning than it is generally understood to have, and signifies a registration system used by the police to check and to control the movements of individuals. Census officers, who form a very important part of the public security organization, are assigned to police head-quarters at various levels to take care of census registration, statistics, and research, and to submit reports. Others on outside duty take census, map out census districts, form census committees, collect census materials, and investigate the movements of suspicious individuals. They work closely with the public security committees which are formed on every city street. In 1953 the election registers were incorporated into the census records, giving the public security officials further data to determine the political reliability of everyone in the country.

The system of public security committees was officially established by the Ministry of Public Security in June 1952 at the time of the Five-Anti movement and the campaign for the suppression of counterrevolutionaries. Each factory, cooperative, city street, or government department has its own public security committee. In the rural areas there is a public security committee for every village. These committees, each made up of from three to eleven members and headed by a Communist party cadre, are directed and controlled by the basic level governments and public security bureaus.

Officially, the public security committees are in charge of census investigation but in actual practice they perform secret service functions. Working through these committees in the guise of census-taking, the Communist regime is able to exercise direct control over the people. Each household or shop is required to keep a census book giving personal data on the members and their friends and associates, and it is on the basis of these records that the people are classified in the various registration lists under categories such as special, suspicious, ordinary, and reliable.

On December 31, 1954 the Communist government introduced a new and additional system of popular control: urban residents committees and urban street offices. According to the "Organic Regulation of Urban Street Offices," these offices are to be established in districts or cities with a population of 100,000 and over and, if necessary, in districts or cities with a population of 50,000 and over. Manned by three to seven full-time cadres, they are placed under the control of the public security bureaus. The jurisdictional areas of street offices are equivalent to that of the public security stations, and among the various duties of the street offices is the direction of the urban residents committees. The regulations provide for the formation of such committees in every 100 to 600 households. Under the residents committees are "resident cells," each consisting of fifteen to forty households. No committee, however, may control more than seventeen cells.

The urban residents committees operate under the census section of the public security bureau and their functions are: to engage in public welfare work; to report the views of the people to the people's council; to mobilize the inhabitants to respond to government calls and observe laws; to direct mass security work; and to mediate disputes. At the time the organic regulations were promulgated in January 1955, there were already seventy cities in China which had established street offices and residents committees.

The Militia

The militia, or civilian armed forces, of the Chinese Communist government comprises the rural and the urban corps. The rural militia is composed entirely of peasants. The urban militia is further divided into two subgroups: the urban militia corps made up principally of workers and known as the workers' supervisory corps, and the suburban militia corps composed of both workers and peasants. There are also miscellaneous militia units having a variety of designations, such as the military working corps, self-protection corps, and so forth. The militia corps were first organized after the open break with the Nationalists as far back as 1927 when they were known as "red protection corps" in the Communist-occupied regions. The term "militia" was formally used during the time of the Sino-Japanese War in the late 1930's.

Though supposedly organized on the principle of democratic centralism, the militia comes under the direct control of the local Communist party organs. It actually forms a part of the organizational structure of the Communist party committee of the relevant locality and is unconditionally subordinate and responsible to the committee. In localities above the county level, the militia comes under the control and command of the People's Liberation Army. Under these military districts each county forms militia detachments with a detachment leader and a political commissar. Below this are battalion, company, subcompany, and platoon units. The selection of militiamen is made with considerable care to avoid taking in politically unreliable elements.

It is the function of the rural militia to assist the public security bureaus in the maintenance of order, to assist the regular military forces in the suppression of internal elements dangerous to the state, to protect state properties in the form of public works or farm crops, and to enforce the agrarian collectivization program.

The urban militia corps are assigned the task of assisting the public security departments and of collaborating with militia corps in the suburban districts. Their duties are to maintain order in urban areas; to safeguard production and reconstruction work; to protect industrial plants, mining depots, farms, business enterprises, and government offices; and to ensure the safe operation of land and water communication facilities. In addition they are responsible for maintaining order at workers' parades and other mass meetings, and perform guard duty at important meeting places.

The principal functions of the militia corps in suburban districts are to assist in general war mobilization work and in activities pertaining to army enlistment and other wartime contingencies. They are also to maintain order in the rear and take active part in productive activities in their respective localities.

Election in 1953-54

To give itself and its policies a formal constitutional standing based on "popular mandate," the Peking regime decided to hold a nation-wide election. According to the election law published on March 1, 1953, only at the lowest level—which includes the elections of the people's congresses of the villages, towns, and municipal districts in large cities—do the people vote for their representatives. Only in the election of people's congresses above the county level is there a secret ballot. Voters who are illiterate may have others cast votes for them by proxy.

In the 1953-54 election, franchise at the basic level was given to all over the age of eighteen, except in the following categories: members of the landlord class "whose status has not been changed according to law," counterrevolutionaries, "others who have been deprived of political rights according to law," and insane persons. To determine the status of the voters, the people throughout the country were first screened during the taking of the census and then carefully checked again during the registration for the election. The registration sought to separate the landlords and rich peasants and to unearth the counterrevolutionaries.

The candidates were nominated by political factions. According to the election law, the Communist party, the various democratic parties, the various mass organizations, and electors or representatives who were not affiliated with these parties or organizations could nominate candidates for election as deputies either jointly or separately according to electoral districts or electoral units, but the list of candidates had to be published in advance. Under this provision, the nominees were either Communists or Communist choices. Nomination could be made of independents, but in practice it was discouraged and in the preliminary discussions the names of independents who were nominated were stricken off the list of candidates.

Election committees were established according to the law. At the top was the central election committee; under it were the provincial and municipal election committees, then district and county committees down to the village committees. The functions of these election committees were to direct and supervise the election, to deal with information concerning unlawful practices in the election, and to register the elected deputies. It was estimated that the number of members in the election committees would come to two million.

The preparation for the basic level election was the occasion for a tremendous propaganda drive. Throughout the country, meetings and forums were held to study the election law and to discuss the panel of candidates. In many localities mock elections were held to rehearse the election. Actual election started in the summer of 1953 but so huge was the task that it was not completed at the basic level until June 1954.

Altogether, basic-level elections were held in 214,798 electoral units, whose registered voters numbered 323,809,684. Of these, 85.88 percent of the male voters and 84 percent of the female voters cast their votes. These percentages represent a total of 278,000,000 people. They elected a total of 5,665,000 representatives, most of them cadres or ex-cadres, to people's congresses of basic levels.

It was reported that 2.82 percent of the voters were rejected after screening and were disfranchised. On the basis of the number given as registered, this would come to more than 9 million who were not permitted to vote. To this figure must be added approximately another 9 million national minority peoples, who had not been directly registered in 1953. Thus nearly 18 million people did not participate in the 1953-54 election.

Following the basic-level elections, the representatives to the people's congresses then elected deputies (16,807) to the provincial and municipal people's congresses, who in turn elected deputies (1,226) to the First National People's Congress. The geographical representation in the national congress was heavily weighted in favor of the urban areas. Other favored groups were the armed forces, the minority nationalities, and to a less extent, the overseas Chinese. The rural population, on the other hand, had the least voice in the congress (Table 4).

Although Chinese Communist deputies came to only about a third of the total number of deputies to the First National People's Congress, virtually all the leaders of the Communist party as well as "model workers and peasants" and the leading personages of the various mass organizations were elected.

As a whole, the general election held in 1953-54 was nothing more than a staged performance wherein the people of China were manipulated, as in the other major campaigns conducted by the regime, into giving popular endorsement of Communist policies and political behavior. It was obvious that the election was far from a free expression of popular will. At the lowest level, the only place where the election can be called popular, the people were presented with a single panel of names for which they were required to vote in entirety. Through rehearsals and experimental elections, through forums and discussions, through propaganda and the exhortation of the party cadres in charge of the elections, they were told how to vote and for whom. In the voting procedure, the people were assembled and they voted by the raising of hands under the watchful eyes of the cadres.

Popular election is new to the people of China; they have no concept of free election as it is practiced in the western democracies. In the election the trained and indoctrinated voter merely went through the motions he had been taught. Since the election was exclusively Communist-sponsored and conducted, and the candidates hand-picked by the Communists, neither political issues nor personalities were involved. The general election of 1953-54, however, did give the people a sense of participation in the process of government; it also provided the regime with the constitutional basis of popular sanction.

THEORY AND STRUCTURE
OF GOVERNMENT

THE CONCEPT OF COMMON ASSENT to a set of principles for the organization of the state and the conduct of national affairs is by no means unfamiliar to the Chinese; nevertheless, the idea of a written document as the fundamental organic law of the nation dates back only to the last decade of the nineteenth century. Under the influence of the West, a number of constitutions have been drafted during the past fifty years, some earlier ones containing ideas borrowed from the Japanese, French, and British systems. The 1947 constitution of the Nationalist government was largely American in design, but with some of the traditional features of Chinese political thought. On the other hand, the 1954 constitution of the Communist regime is based, with certain modifications, on the Soviet system.

A basic concept of Communist theoreticians is that the state's structure and its system of operation are related to class struggle: one class, or cluster of classes, is to rule; the others are to be subjected to that rule. This constitutes, in Marxist terms, a "joint dictatorship of all the revolutionary classes" working through "democratic centralism." As a principle of political organization, democratic centralism operates in the following way:

> . . . the people's congresses shall be responsible and accountable to the people; the people's government councils shall be responsible and accountable to the people's congresses. Within the people's congresses and within the people's government councils, the minority shall abide by the decisions of the majority; the appointment of the people's governments of each

level shall be ratified by the people's government of the higher level; the people's governments of the lower levels shall obey the people's governments of the higher levels and all local people's governments throughout the country shall obey the Central People's Government (Common Program, Article 15).

In the Communist political structure a distinction is made between "state power" and "state administration." While the National People's Congress is the highest organ of state power, the State Council is the executive organ of the highest state authority. Similarly, on lower levels, the local people's congresses are the organs of government power and the local people's councils are the organs of administrative authority. This parallel system of people's congresses and people's councils, the first being the theoretical source of power and the second having the actual exercise of power, extends to the entire Communist governmental hierarchy.

Constitutional Development in Communist China

The constitutional program of the Chinese Communist party was first proposed in 1940 by Mao Tse-tung in his essay, "On New Democracy." As China was still a "semifeudal and semicolonial" country, he asserted, the Chinese revolution, being of necessity different from that of Russia, should be separated into two stages—new democracy and socialism. The principal task of the party in the first stage was to throw off the yoke of foreign imperialism. This was to be accomplished by the combined and unified forces of the peasantry and the proletariat as represented and led by the Communist party, and the "national bourgeoisie" as represented by the various "democratic parties." This stage would come to an end when China built up its own industry and became independent of foreign capitalism. Industrialized China would then march into the second stage of socialism, the political nature of which, however, was not clearly spelled out.

This program, it would seem, was designed primarily to support the Communist demand for a "coalition government," made at the time of the Sino-Japanese War (1937-45). On April 24, 1945 Mao Tse-tung, in a formal report on coalition government to the Seventh National Congress of the Chinese Communist party, reiterating that China's path to socialism would be Chinese, disavowed any intention of adopting a Russian-type "dictatorship of the proletariat." The Communist aim at that time was to undermine the Nationalist government and to win friends and allies among non-Communist political factions through the advocacy of a united front. They were careful not to alienate potential supporters by any hint that they would adopt a pure dictatorship of the proletariat. Their strategy was to play up the differences between Chinese and Soviet Communism and to emphasize that the first stage of the proposed state, to be based on Mao's "new democracy," would be a coalition of all the "democratic" parties.

After the Chinese Communists came to power in 1949, their real goals gradually became clear. In a speech delivered on July 2, 1949 Mao Tse-tung propounded his ideas on the "people's democratic dictatorship." This was to be a dictatorship of the "people," which Mao defined as being made up of four classes: the proletariat, the peasantry, the petty bourgeoisie, and the national bourgeoisie. During this period state power would be vested in a coalition of these four classes under proletarian leadership. In the people's democratic dictatorship a mixed type of economy would exist and a bitter class struggle would take place to wipe out feudal vestiges and imperialism.

Amplifying his earlier formulations, Mao now defined the new democracy as "democracy for the people and dictatorship for the reactionaries." He made a sharp distinction between the "people" and the "nationals," including among the latter all "reactionaries." In this political system, only the "people" were to have the rights to vote and to voice their opinions while the "reactionaries" were to be suppressed. In uncompromising terms, Mao declared:

> Such state apparatus as the army, the police, and the courts are instruments by which one class oppresses another. As far as the opposing classes are concerned, these are instruments of oppression. They are violent and certainly not "benevolent" things . . . We definitely have no benevolent policies towards the reactionaries or the reactionary deeds of such classes.

While denied various rights, members of the "reactionary classes" nevertheless had duties to the state.

These views of Mao, which represented the crystallization of Communist political philosophy, were incorporated into the Common Program of the Chinese People's Political Consultative Conference, convened by the Communist party on September 21, 1949 in Peking immediately after their conquest of the country. The conference, attended by 662 delegates from Communist and pro-Communist parties, passed the Organic Law of the People's

Republic of China, the Organic Law of the People's Political Consultative Conference, and the Common Program. Although these three documents did not amount to a constitution in the accepted sense of the term, they represented a detailed statement of the theory and structure of the Chinese Communist government. They were not regarded as permanent documents, but rather as temporary guides for the transitional "new democratic" period, a preparatory stage for socialism.

The Organic Law of the People's Republic, which most closely resembled a constitution, set up the central government structure and defined the functions of the various state organs together with their relationships to one another. The Organic Law of the People's Political Consultative Conference outlined the organization, powers, and functions of the Conference, which, pending the convocation of the National People's Congress, was to exercise all the powers and functions of that body as the supreme organ of the state.

The third document, the Common Program of the People's Political Consultative Conference, contained the guiding principles and policies of Communist China during the "new democratic stage" and was the most significant politically. The Common Program consisted of a preamble and seven chapters of sixty articles on general principles, organs of state authority, the military system, economic policies, cultural and educational policies, nationality policies, and foreign policies. It provided for the exercise of state power through a system of people's congresses and people's governments elected by these congresses, and promised the people their civil rights as well as cultural and religious freedom. In accordance with Mao Tse-tung's ideas of people's democratic dictatorship, however, these rights and freedoms were accorded only to certain classes.

Four years later, after having successfully completed the initial stage of political consolidation and economic rehabilitation, the government announced in October 1953 the beginning of a new policy, defined as a "general line of the state during the period of transition to socialism." Politically, the new line was signalized by the announcement of a general election and the drafting of a new constitution. The proposed constitution, which was to comprise all the long-range objectives of the Common Program spelled out in more specific terms, was designed to bring government policy and operations into close correlation with the economic and social developments of the regime.

The Constitution of 1954

Twenty months were to pass before the adoption of the Constitution of the People's Republic of China. Early in 1953 a drafting committee, headed by Mao Tse-tung, was formed which consisted of thirty-two persons, nineteen of whom were Communist party members, mostly from the Central Committee and the Politburo. The presence of these top-ranking Communist officials indicated the importance the Communists attached to the document. Of the non-Communist members of the committee, most followed the Communist line. The final draft of the Constitution, originally written by Mao Tse-tung and other leaders of the Communist party, was adopted by the drafting committee at its meeting on March 23, 1954. An all-out propaganda campaign was then launched to familiarize the people with the contents of the draft constitution. Meanwhile, in September 1954, a general election was held to elect delegates to the First National People's Congress in Peking. One of the delegates' main functions was to adopt the draft constitution; it was passed unanimously by secret ballot on September 20.

The Constitution of the People's Republic of China consists of a preamble and 106 articles in four chapters:

Chapter 1.   General Principles
Chapter 2.   The State Structure
    Section 1. The National People's Congress
    Section 2. The Chairman of the People's Republic of China
    Section 3. The State Council
    Section 4. The Local People's Congresses and Local People's Councils
    Section 5. The Organs of Self-Government of National Autonomous Areas
    Section 6. The People's Courts and the People's Procuratorate
Chapter 3.   Fundamental Rights and Duties of Citizens
Chapter 4.   National Flag, National Emblem, Capital.

While the Constitution contains a few features reminiscent of the political forms of imperial China and the structure of the Nationalist government, its resemblance to Chinese precedents is less significant than its resemblance to the Soviet Constitution of

A COMPARISON BETWEEN THE SOVIET AND CHINESE COMMUNIST CONSTITUTIONS

USSR

Article 1. The Union of Soviet Socialist Republics is a socialist state of workers and peasants.

Article 2. The political foundation of the USSR is the Soviet of Working People's deputies which grew and became strong as a result of the overthrow of the power of the landlords and capitalists and the conquest of the dictatorship of the proletariat.

Article 4. The economic foundation of the USSR is . . . the socialist ownership of the instruments and means of production . . .

Article 5. Socialist property in the USSR exists either in the form of state property (belonging to the whole people) or in the form of cooperative and collective farm property.

Article 6. The land, its mineral wealth, waters, forests, mills, factories, mines, rail, water, and air transport, banks, communication . . . are state property, that is, belong to the whole people.

COMMUNIST CHINA

Article 1. The People's Republic of China is a people's democratic state led by the working class and based on the alliance of workers and peasants.

Article 2. All power in the People's Republic of China belongs to the people. The organs through which the people exercise power are the National People's Congress and the local people's congresses.

Preamble . . . the Chinese people, led by the Communist Party of China, finally achieved their great victory in the people's revolution against imperialism, feudalism, and bureaucrat-capitalism.

Article 5. In the People's Republic of China the ownership of the means of production today mainly takes the following forms: state ownership, that is, ownership by the whole people; cooperative ownership, that is, collective ownership by the working masses; ownership by individual working people; and capitalist ownership.

Article 6. All mineral resources and waters, as well as forests, undeveloped land and other resources which the state owns by law, are the property of the whole people.

Adapted from *North China* (Stanford University, HRAF Subcontractor's Monograph, 1956), Vol. II, pp. 905-7; and Meisel, J. H. and E. S. Kozera, *Material for the Study of the Soviet System* (Ann Arbor: George Wahr, 1950), p. 243; and the *Constitution of the People's Republic of China* (Peking, 1954).

1936. The Chinese Communist Constitution and that of the Soviet Union are generally similar not only in basic principles, but also in style and wording (see the plate, A Comparison between the Soviet and Chinese Communist Constitutions).

There are, however, differences in the government structure. The Chinese Communist Constitution does not provide for constituent republics; in contrast to the bicameral Supreme Soviet of the USSR, the Chinese National People's Congress is unicameral; in the USSR the Council of Ministers, including its chairman or premier, is appointed by the Presidium of the Supreme Soviet, but in Communist China the premier, the head of the State Council, is recommended first by the chairman of the People's Republic and then accepted or rejected by the National People's Congress. The Chinese Communist Constitution therefore gives greater power to the chairman of the People's Republic than that enjoyed by the president of the Presidium of the USSR.

Authority for amending the Constitution rests with the National People's Congress. Constitutional amendments require a two-thirds majority of the entire membership of the National People's Congress, while laws and other bills require a simple majority. The Constitution does not provide other details of the procedure for amendment and in the nearly five years since its adoption there has been no precedent for amending it. It may be observed that the 1954 Constitution, like the Common Program, is only a provisional charter to be superseded later by a fully Communist constitution when China has completed its program of socialization.

Functions and Powers of the State

According to Article 1, Communist China is a people's democratic state led by the working class and based on the alliance of workers and peasants. Article 3 states that China is "a unified, multinational state." The minority nationalities are specifically guaranteed "freedom to use and foster the growth of their spoken and written languages, and to preserve or reform their own customs or ways." These autonomous areas may adopt their own statutes and regulations subject to the approval of the Standing Committee of the National People's Congress, but they are all "inalienable parts of the People's Republic of China."

The first function of the state in the stage of new democracy is held to be the development of industry and betterment of the economy. Another is the elimination of class antagonism, to be achieved primarily by government regulation. The state deprives "feudal landlords" and "bureaucrat-capitalists" of political rights; at the same time it provides them with a way to earn a living, to enable them to reform through work and become citizens who earn their livelihood by their own labor.

Under the Constitution the state has the power to make and enforce laws, to raise revenues by taxes, to own and manage property, to impress citizens for military services. It is also stipulated in the Constitution that the state owns all mineral resources, water courses, forests, wastelands, and other national resources.

The Constitution requires the state to provide the following services for the people: (1) the defense of national sovereignty, territory, and security; (2) the prohibition of discrimination or oppression against any nationality and of acts which undermine the unity between the various nationalities; (3) the maintenance of public order and the suppression and punishment of traitors and counterrevolutionary elements; (4) the protection of the rights of citizens and the protection and regulation of private property rights; (5) the regulation of cooperatives, farmers, handicraftsmen, and capitalists, and the furnishing of help and advice thereto; (6) the promotion of full employment and labor welfare, and the improvement of labor conditions; (7) the operation and management of social insurance, social relief, social welfare, and public health and sanitation programs; (8) the establishment and operation of schools, and the regulation and promotion of educational and cultural activities.

The Constitution was in part designed as a guide for the economic development of China during the period of transition to socialism. It states that the right of capitalists to own means of production and other capital will be protected "according to law," but adds:

> The policy of the state toward capitalist industry and commerce is to use, restrict and transform them. The state makes use of the positive qualities of capitalist industry and commerce which are beneficial to national welfare and the people's livelihood, restricts their negative qualities which are not beneficial to national welfare and the people's livelihood, encourages and guides their transformation into various forms of state-capitalist economy, gradually replacing capitalist ownership with ownership by the whole people. (Article 10.)

Not only does the state forbid capitalists to engage in activities which disrupt the socioeconomic order or undermine the economic plans of the state, but it may, "in the public interest," requisition or nationalize land and other means of production both in cities and in the countryside. It also forbids any person to use his private property to the detriment of public interest. These restrictions on the economic activities of the people, and the power of the state to seize control of land and means of production, provide the government with powerful weapons for pushing through its economic policy.

Rights and Duties of Citizens

The 1954 Constitution contains an elaborate list of the fundamental rights and duties of citizens. These duties are to abide by the Constitution and the law, observe public order, preserve and protect public property, pay taxes, and serve in the armed forces. In addition, citizens have certain moral obligations: they are required to "uphold discipline at work" and to "respect social ethics."

As to rights, the general principle is that citizens of the People's Republic of China are equal before the law. Citizens who have attained the age of eighteen, except those disqualified by mental disease or by law, have the right to vote and to be elected to public office. They are entitled to freedom of speech, freedom of the press, freedom of assembly, freedom of association, freedom of procession, freedom of demonstration. They enjoy, according to the Constitution, freedom of religious belief. The state also "safeguards the freedom of citizens to engage in scientific research, literary and artistic creation, and other cultural pursuits."

Specific provisions are: no discrimination in the exercise of the political right of election; full political, economic, cultural, social, and domestic equality for women; inviolability of person and dwelling; freedom to choose or change residence; privacy of correspondence. Marriage and the family have the protection of the state. Any citizen has the right to make written or oral complaints to a central or local organ of the state against any employee of the state for violation of law or neglect of duty. He is further entitled to compensation if his constitutional rights are infringed by the said state employee. It is stated that "no citizen may be arrested except by decision of a people's court or with the sanction of a people's procuratorate."

The right of asylum is granted any foreign national persecuted for supporting a "just cause," for taking part in the peace movement, or for engaging in scientific activity.

The National People's Congress

The powers of the National People's Congress, as enumerated in Article 27 of the Constitution, are as follows: (1) to amend the Constitution; (2) to enact laws; (3) to supervise the enforcement of the Constitution; (4) to elect the chairman and the vice-chairman of the People's Republic of China (in 1959 two vice-chairmen were elected); (5) to choose the premier of the State Council upon the recommendation of the chairman of the Republic, and the component members of the State Council upon the recommendation of the premier; (6) to choose the vice-chairmen and other members of the National Defense Council upon the recommendation of the chairman of the Republic; (7) to elect the president of the Supreme People's Court; (8) to elect the chief procurator of the Supreme People's Procuratorate; (9) to decide on national economic plans; (10) to examine and approve the state budget and the financial report; (11) to ratify the status and boundaries of provinces, autonomous regions, and municipalities directly under central authority; (12) to decide on general amnesties; (13) to decide on questions of war and peace; and (14) to exercise such other functions and powers as the National People's Congress considers necessary.

The Constitution further provides that the National People's Congress has the power to recall the officials of the Central Government of the People's Republic, including the chairman and vice-chairman of the Republic. In this connection, it is worthy of notice that while it is specifically provided that the State Council, the Supreme People's Court, and the Supreme People's Procuratorate are responsible to the National People's Congress, the chairman of the People's Republic is not. On the other hand, the National People's Congress or its Standing Committee cannot be dissolved, suspended, or prorogued by the chairman of the Republic or the premier of the State Council. This provision makes the People's Congress an organ of state authority as distinguished from a parliament under the cabinet system.

On the whole, the National People's Congress enjoys, in the words of a Communist analyst, "unlimited and illimitable authority." It has all the powers of the British Parliament, in addition to the formal functions of the American electoral college. As regards its power of appointing and recalling the president of the Supreme People's Court and the chief procurator of the Supreme People's

Procuratorate, as well as the corresponding power of its Standing Committee over other constituent members of these two organs, the Chinese Communist legislators drew their inspiration directly from the Soviet Constitution of 1936.

It should be noted, however, that the change of the Soviet Presidium into the Chinese Standing Committee and the provision for a chairman and vice-chairman of the People's Republic of China have made the Chinese version of the Communist government structure so different and distinct from its Soviet prototype that the Chinese structure constitutes a category by itself.

As stipulated in the Constitution, the National People's Congress is composed of deputies elected by (1) provinces; (2) municipalities directly under the central authority; (3) autonomous regions; (4) the armed forces; and (5) Chinese residents abroad. Deputies of the first two categories are elected by the provincial and municipal people's congresses concerned. As for the third category, deputies from a minority nationality administrative unit directly under the Central People's Government are elected by that administrative unit; deputies of a minority nationality in any other area are elected by the provincial or municipal people's congress concerned.

The Constitution provides that the National People's Congress be elected for a term of four years. This must also be the term of the deputies, whose re-election is not defined either by the Constitution or by the Election Law. The term of the National People's Congress may be prolonged if any emergency prevents the holding of elections. Deputies to the congress are subject to the supervision of the units which elect them and these electoral units have the power to recall their deputies at any time, according to the procedure prescribed by law. Each deputy may attend, without the right to vote, the meetings of the people's congress that elected him.

The National People's Congress does not have a speaker, president, or any other permanent officer or officers. At each session it elects a presidium to direct its meetings and a secretary-general to assist in the exercise of its functions. The presidium elects a certain number of its members, usually eight to ten, to preside over the sessions of the congress by turns; it also co-opts a certain number of standing chairmen to convene and preside over the meetings of the presidium itself. The secretariat, created for each session of the congress, is headed by a secretary-general in charge of the administrative affairs of the congress. In the Chinese legislature the presidium of any public assembly is always temporary and should be carefully distinguished from the presidium of the USSR legislature. The number of presidium members varies with each session of the National People's Congress.

Although it has no permanent officers, the National People's Congress has a permanent organization to carry out its functions and powers. This is the Standing Committee, composed of a chairman, vice-chairmen, a secretary-general, and a certain number of members, all elected and subject to recall by the congress.

The Standing Committee, which is responsible to the congress and reports to it, is equivalent to the Presidium of the Supreme Soviet of the Soviet Union. However, unlike the Soviet Presidium, the Standing Committee does not have the power to dissolve the National People's Congress (actually this power is unnecessary as the latter is unicameral), to appoint and remove the higher commands of the armed forces, or to receive the credentials and letters of recall of plenipotentiary representatives of foreign countries.

Of all the powers and functions of the Standing Committee, the enactment of laws or decrees is perhaps the most significant. This and the other powers it exercises to relieve the burden of the national legislature endow it with the nature of a "little congress." Its role in legislation is immensely magnified by the fact that its parent body meets for only a few weeks each year and is actually engaged in legislation probably for only a few days in a year. Subject to necessary changes in schedule, the Standing Committee itself meets twice a month upon the call of its chairman, who presides over the committee meetings and supervises the administrative work of the committee, which is performed by an administrative bureau headed by a secretary-general. Under the secretary-general, there are a number of deputy secretaries-general, appointed by the Standing Committee upon the recommendation of the chairman.

To assist the National People's Congress in the various phases of its work, the Nationalities Committee, the Bills Committee, the Budget Committee, and the Credentials Committee have been set up. None has independent status, all functioning within the duties and powers of the congress, but two—the Nationalities and the Bills committees—are permanent in that they function during adjournments as well as meetings of the congress. During adjournments these two committees are under the supervision of the Standing Committee.

The Budget Committee, which is somewhat similar to the appropriations committee of the United States Congress, is responsible for the examination and review of the budget as well as of final accounts. Judging from its present membership, which consists mostly of secondary leaders of the various political parties and groups, the work of this committee, like that of the Credentials Committee, may be considered technical in nature.

The Nationalities Committee, on the other hand, is more political in character and significance. The political relationship among the various nationalities in China might be said to be midway between the political integration of a nation-state and the association within a multinational federation of the Soviet type. The establishment of the Nationalities Committee represented a compromise between a rigid unicameralism and the creation of a second chamber for the minority nationalities as in the USSR. This is evident from the official functions of the committee which are essentially to examine bills or sections of bills relative to affairs of the various nationalities as handed down by the National People's Congress or its Standing Committee, and to examine and review the organizational charters submitted for approval by the various nationality autonomous areas to the Standing Committee of the National People's Congress.

The Bills Committee, which should more properly be called "Legislation Committee," studies bills or draft decrees submitted to it by the National People's Congress or its Standing Committee and prepares the final drafts. Its present membership includes a number of internationally known jurists, political scientists, and leaders of non-Communist parties. This seems to establish the importance of the committee, which may rectify possible rashness in legislation—a charge commonly leveled against unicameralism. It should be noted that the Bills Committee does not undertake the screening and classification of "legislative proposals," which is the task of the temporary, sessional Legislative Proposals Examination Committee. The Chinese use two terms for bills; namely, *fa-an* and *t'i-an,* translated respectively as "bills" and "legislative proposals." The distinction is that while the *t'i-an* refer to bills ready for action at a sessional meeting of the National People's Congress, the *fa-an* are bills accepted by the National People's Congress for further implementation.

Once a year the Standing Committee calls the National People's Congress into regular session and may call extraordinary sessions whenever it considers such action essential or upon the proposal of one-fifth of the membership of the congress. As mentioned before, the meetings are not presided over by the Standing Committee but by a temporary presidium. The responsible officials of the State Council, the National Defense Council, the Supreme People's Court, and the Supreme People's Procuratorate, if not deputies of the National People's Congress, may, with the approval of the sessional presidium, attend the sessional meetings without the right to vote. This is another similarity to the cabinet system. The meetings are generally open to the public, but the congress has the right to hold secret meetings whenever it deems them necessary.

Nomination of all personnel to be elected by the National People's Congress, including the members of its Standing Committee and the chairman and vice-chairmen of the Republic, is made by the deputies, either individually or in joint motion. Legislative and other proposals may be presented to the congress by the deputies, the chairman or vice-chairmen of the Republic, the presidium, the Standing Committee, the various committees, or the State Council, but not by the National Defense Council, the Supreme People's Court, or the Supreme People's Procuratorate. This is in general conformity with the practice of parliamentary government. Constitutional amendments are passed by the National People's Congress by a vote of at least two-thirds of its entire membership. Sessional rules of procedure are adopted at the beginning of each session.

Prior to attending each session of the congress, deputies are encouraged to make inspection tours of various regions in the country and to report their findings. Whether in or out of session, deputies are expected to assist in the execution of the laws and policies of the state, and for that purpose they may attend the meetings of their electoral people's congresses as observers. Like legislatures of western countries, the National People's Congress is guaranteed against outside interference by the constitutional stipulation that no deputy to the congress may be arrested or placed on trial without the consent of the congress or, when the congress is not in session, of its Standing Committee. The congress may, if conditions warrant it, appoint commissions of inquiry for the investigation of specific questions and charges. All government agencies, public or private organizations, and individual persons are obliged to furnish necessary information when requested, to the investigating committees. Such obligations are enforceable by contempt procedure as in the United States.

The Central People's Government

Prior to the adoption of the 1954 Constitution, state authority in Communist China was vested in the Central People's Government Council, headed by the chairman. At the top of the political structure, it had the supreme power of enacting laws, promulgating decrees, supervising their execution, passing the national budget, and declaring war and making peace. It also had the authority of appointing the leading office holders in all branches of the government, central as well as regional. Directly subordinated to the Central People's Government Council were the Government Administration Council, the People's Revolutionary Military Council, the Supreme People's Court, and the Procuratorate General.

As the chief administrative body, the Government Administration Council corresponded roughly to a cabinet in the government of western countries. It consisted of a premier (*tsung-li*), a number of deputy premiers, a secretary-general, and a number of members, all appointed by the Central People's Government Council. The operating agencies of the Government Administration Council included a Committee on Political and Legal Affairs, a Committee on Financial and Economic Affairs, a Committee on Cultural and Educational Affairs, a People's Supervisory Committee, a number of ministries, bureaus, and commissions, a secretariat, and the People's Bank. The Government Administration Council as a whole was responsible for all its acts and activities to the Central People's Government Council or to its chairman during recess periods.

The People's Revolutionary Military Council was composed of a chairman and an unspecified number of vice-chairmen and members, all appointed by the Central People's Government Council. It was supposed to assume unified control and command over the People's Liberation Army and all other people's armed forces in the whole country; its role, however, seems to have been limited to administrative affairs pertaining to the armed forces.

Under the 1954 Constitution, the National People's Congress took the place of the Central People's Government Council as the highest organ of state authority. As regards the various organs of state administration, the Government Administration Council was replaced by the State Council, the People's Revolutionary Military Council by the National Defense Council, and the Procuratorate General by the Supreme People's Procuratorate. The Supreme People's Court, however, was retained by the Constitution. In addition, the Constitution provides for, as mentioned above, a chairman of the People's Republic to share with the National People's Congress the exercise of state authority (see the plate, Structure of the Central People's Government).

The Chairman of the People's Republic

The functions of the chairman of the People's Republic fall into three categories. First, as the titular head of state he represents the People's Republic of China in its relations with foreign states and receives foreign diplomatic representatives, being empowered by the Standing Committee of the National People's Congress to appoint and recall plenipotentiary representatives to foreign states and to ratify treaties concluded with foreign states. Second, in pursuance of the resolutions of the National People's Congress and its Standing Committee he may promulgate laws and decrees, appoint or remove the premier and other members of the State Council, the vice-chairmen and other members of the National Defense Council, confer medals and titles of honor, proclaim general amnesties and grant pardons, proclaim martial law, proclaim a state of war, and order mobilization. Third and most important, he is vested with certain independent and fully discretionary powers such as the personal supervision and control of the State Council and its premier and command of all the armed forces of the country. These powers are complete in themselves in that they are subject to no other control than the implementary legislation.

The number of vice-chairmen of the People's Republic seems to be flexible. While there was only one vice-chairman in 1954-58, the National People's Congress elected two vice-chairmen in 1959. According to the Constitution, the vice-chairman occupies a peculiar position in the government of Communist China. He assists the chairman in his work and may exercise such functions and powers of the chairman as the latter may entrust to him; these functions and powers may be ceremonial, mandatory, or discretionary. The vice-chairman of the People's Republic succeeds the chairman in case of death or resignation and may act as chairman when the latter is incapacitated by sickness for a prolonged period of time.

The State Council

The State Council, headed by the premier, is the executive organ of the highest state authority. Although the State Council is responsible to the National People's Congress and, when the congress

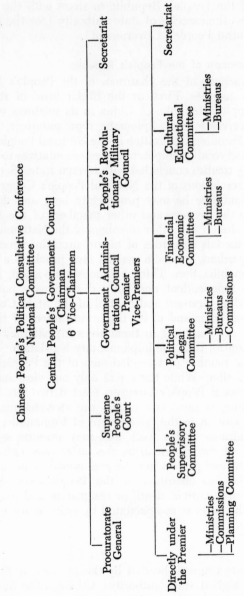

STRUCTURE OF THE CENTRAL PEOPLE'S GOVERNMENT

Central People's Government, 1949-54

Chinese People's Political Consultative Conference
National Committee

Central People's Government Council
Chairman
6 Vice-Chairmen

- Procuratorate General
- People's Supervisory Committee
  - Ministries
  - Commissions
  - Planning Committee
- Directly under the Premier
- Supreme People's Court
- Government Administration Council
  Premier
  Vice-Premiers
  - Political Legal Committee
    - Ministries
    - Bureaus
    - Commissions
  - Financial Economic Committee
    - Ministries
    - Bureaus
  - Cultural Educational Committee
    - Ministries
    - Bureaus
  - Secretariat
- People's Revolutionary Military Council
- Secretariat

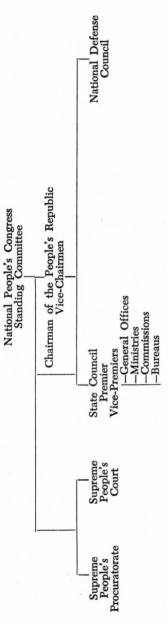

Central People's Government, 1954—

Based on the *Organic Law of the Central People's Government* (Peking, 1949) and the *Constitution of the People's Republic of China* (Peking, 1954).

is not in session, to its Standing Committee, it does not mean that the premier of the State Council should have the confidence or support of a majority of the National People's Congress or its Standing Committee, legislative or parliamentary confidence being not a prerequisite for the premier to remain in office.

Members of the State Council, including the premier, vice-premiers, ministers, commission directors, and the secretary-general, are all elected by and subject to the recall of the National People's Congress. One difference between the premier and the other members of the State Council is in their nomination. As the premier is nominated by the chairman of the People's Republic and as the other members of the State Council are nominated by the premier, the same relationship presumably exists between the chairman of the People's Republic and the premier as between the premier and the other members of the State Council. If the premier supervises and controls the other members of the State Council, which he certainly does, he is supervised and controlled by the chairman of the People's Republic in the same manner and to the same extent.

As of October 1959, the State Council was composed of the following ministries and commissions:

> Ministry of Internal Affairs
> Ministry of Foreign Affairs
> Ministry of National Defense
> Ministry of Public Security
> Ministry of Finance
> Ministry of Food
> Ministry of Commerce
> Ministry of Foreign Trade
> Ministry of Metallurgical Industry
> Ministry of Chemical Industry
> Ministry of Geology
> Ministry of Textile Industry
> Ministry of Light Industry
> Ministry of Civil Engineering
> Ministry of Coal Industry
> Ministry of Petroleum Industry
> First Ministry of Machine Industry
> Second Ministry of Machine Industry
> Ministry of Labor
> Ministry of Railways

Ministry of Communications
Ministry of Post and Telecommunications
Ministry of Agriculture
Ministry of Agricultural Machine Industry
Ministry of Water Conservancy and Electric Power
Ministry of Marine Products
Ministry of Forestry
Ministry of Land Reclamation
Ministry of Culture
Ministry of Education
Ministry of Public Health
Nationalities Affairs Commission
Overseas Chinese Affairs Commission
State Planning Commission
State Economic Commission
Physical Culture and Sports Commission
Foreign Cultural Liaison Commission
State Capital Construction Commission
Science and Technology Commission

The State Council, with the approval of the Standing Committee of the National People's Congress, was empowered to set up, consolidate, or abolish agencies to handle special types of business affairs. There are seventeen such organs, including the State Statistical Bureau, the People's Bank of China, the Chinese Language Reform Committee, the New China News Agency (Hsin-hua Shê), and the Broadcasting Administration Bureau, directly under the supervision of the State Council. In addition, eight general offices have been established since November 1954 to assist the premier in the supervision of the various constituent organs of the State Council. Although the legal position of these offices has not been made clear to the public, it seems that they stand above the ministries with functions similar to those of some of the ministries.

The administrative offices of the State Council constitute its secretariat, which is in the charge of the secretary-general, assisted by a certain number of deputy secretaries-general. Although the secretariat is an administrative office of a nonpolitical nature, the secretary-general is a political officer.

The present State Council, trimmed of its former supervisory committees and ministers without portfolio, is in actuality a "council of people's commissars" of the Soviet pattern. The size of the ministries and commissions and their business nature constitute another likeness between the Chinese State Council and the Soviet Council of the People's Commissars. The Chinese Communists, however, did not adopt the Soviet Union's commissariats but retained the organizational pattern of ministries and commissions of the former Nationalist government.

Although the premier directs the work of the State Council with the assistance of the vice-premiers, the State Council issues orders and decisions mostly through the State Council meetings. There are two kinds of meetings, plenary and administrative, both presided over by the premier. The former are held once a month or whenever called by the premier, and are attended by the premier, the vice-premiers, the several ministers and commission chairmen, and the secretary-general. The latter, attended by the premier, vice-premiers, and the secretary general, are held without a regular schedule. They constitute the "inner cabinet" of the government. Technically these meetings are not merely advisory to the premier for he and the other participants are bound by the decisions made at the meetings. But in view of the fact that the vice-premiers and the several ministers and commission chairmen are controlled through his power of nomination, there is no doubt that the premier has a preponderant voice in the meetings.

The National Defense Council

Under Article 42 of the Constitution, the chairman of the People's Republic of China, who commands the armed forces, is also chairman of the National Defense Council. The vice-chairmen and members of the council are elected by the National People's Congress upon the nomination of the chairman of the People's Republic. They are subject to the recall of the congress.

On November 11, 1954 the chairman of the People's Republic, in pursuance of a resolution of the Standing Committee of the National People's Congress, appointed the following officers of the People's Liberation Army: Chief of General Staff, Director of the General Training Department, Director of the General Political Department, Director of the General Cadres Department, Director of the Armed Forces Supervision Department, Director of the General Rear Service Department, and Director of the Finance Department. Theoretically all these units are under the direct supervision of the chairman of the People's Republic as commander-in-chief of the armed forces.

On February 8, 1955 the Military Officers Service Regulations were promulgated. According to this statute all the higher staff officers are to be appointed by the chairman of the People's Republic in pursuance of the resolution of the Standing Committee of the National People's Congress. As to the line officers, those of the rank of commander or political commissar of a division and above are to be appointed by the State Council, and all others by the Ministry of Defense.

As provided in the Military Officers Service Regulations (and also in the Conscription Law of July 30, 1955), the armed forces of the People's Republic of China consist of the army, navy, air force, and the public security forces. The last mentioned unit is organized and controlled by the Ministry of Public Security. Since the regulations apply to all units of the armed forces, the appointment and removal of the officers of the public security troops are in the hands of the Ministry of National Defense.

Local Government

On the whole the Communist regime has accepted without substantial change the previous pattern of local government divisions. Except for territorial adjustments, most of the provinces, municipalities, and counties remain as they were before 1949. There are, however, two important innovations: the organization of the people's communes on or below the county level; and the establishment of minority nationality areas, consisting of autonomous regions, districts, and counties.

Immediately following their conquest of mainland China, the Communists set up in October 1949 the following six Greater Administrative Regions (*ta-hsing-cheng-ch'ü*): (1) North China Region; (2) Northeast Region; (3) Northwest Region; (4) East China Region; (5) Central-South Region; and (6) Southwest Region. In each of these regions, a Military and Administrative Council was established as the governing and supervisory body of the area. Upon the adoption of the Constitution in September 1954, all Greater Administrative Regions were discontinued, the historical lesson being that the existence of supervisory offices above the highest local government units is destructive of the local government system as well as prejudicial to central authority.

The present local government system is prescribed in the Constitution and the Local Government Law, both passed by the National People's Congress in September 1954. According to this system, local people's congresses at all levels are the organs of government authority in their respective localities, while local people's councils, that is, local people's governments, are the executive organs of local people's congresses at corresponding levels.

People's Congresses

According to the election law of 1953, deputies to the people's congresses of provinces, counties, special municipalities directly under central authority, and other large municipalities divided into districts, are elected by the people's congresses of the next lower level; deputies to the people's congresses of municipalities not divided into districts, municipal districts, villages, nationality villages, and towns are directly elected by the voters. All these deputies are subject to supervision by the units which elect them. The number of deputies to all local people's congresses as provided in the election law (Chapter 2, Articles 9-18) is listed below:

Political Units	Population	Number of Deputies
Villages and towns	Exceptionally small	7-15
	Not over 2,000	15-20
	2,000 or above	20-35
	Exceptionally large	35-50
Counties	Exceptionally small	30-100
	Not over 200,000	100-200
	200,000 or more	200-350
	Exceptionally large	350-450
Provinces	Exceptionally small	50-100
	Not over 20 million	100-400
	20 million or above	400-500
	Exceptionally large	500-600
Municipalities	Exceptionally small	50
	Exceptionally large	800

Since 1958 the majority of villages and towns have become communes but no provision seems to have been made for the number of deputies to the commune congresses.

Under the hierarchical Communist system, only during the elections held every two years and at the lowest level do the people go through the motion of participation in government. Several stages of indirect representation intervene between the election of the Standing Committee by the National People's Congress and the election of the people's congresses of communes and equivalent units by the masses.

The term of office of provincial people's congresses is four years, and that of all other people's congresses two years. As local organs of state authority, the local people's congresses formulate plans and policies of local administration, approve local budgets and financial accounts, and elect and recall local people's councils and presidents of local people's courts, there being no people's courts at the commune level. The sessions of the people's congresses are called by the respective people's councils. The people's congresses of communes and equivalent units meet quarterly; the congresses of all other local units, annually. Extra meetings may be called whenever the people's councils deem them necessary, or when requested by one-fifth of the congress membership.

People's Councils

Members of the local people's councils of different levels, whether they are provincial governors, mayors of cities, county magistrates, district administrators, commune chairmen, or others, are all elected by the respective people's congresses, and have the same term of office as these electoral congresses. The number of delegates to the people's councils is as follows: provinces and special municipalities under direct control of the central government, 25-55; municipalities, 9-25 (for municipalities with an extra-large population, up to 45); counties, 9-21 (for counties with an extra-large population or with an extra-large number of villages and towns, up to 31); districts of a city, 9-21; communes and equivalent units, 3-13.

The people's councils of all local units above the commune level meet monthly, and those of the communes and equivalent units twice a month. The meetings are presided over by the local chief administrators. The president of the local people's court and the chief procurator of the local procuratorate (there being no such agencies at the commune level) may attend the meetings without right to vote.

The people's councils function in three different capacities. First, as the executive organs of the people's congresses, they execute the resolutions of the latter concerning all fields of local administration. Second, as the "presidiums" of the people's congresses, they exercise the powers of the people's congresses when they are not in session, call them into session, and conduct the election of their deputies. Finally, they are the executive agencies for directives and decisions of people's councils of higher levels concerning all fields of administration on these levels.

People's Communes

The basic administrative unit of the country since 1958 has been the people's commune, which may comprise anywhere from one former village to several villages in a county with a population varying from one to several thousand households. The commune assumes the role in the political life of the community formerly exercised by the village government but has in addition jurisdiction over its economic life.

In general the political structure of the commune is identical with that of the village government it replaced: the village people's congress became the commune congress; the village people's council, the commune management committee; and the village council head, the commune chairman. Being an amalgamation of the agricultural cooperatives, the commune also has such economic functions as agricultural production, distribution of incomes, and the support of indigent members. Furthermore, the commune has been given the responsibility of maintaining a rural educational system and the militia, as well as of acting as the agent of the state's trading and banking organs. With complete control of the economic resources of the area, the commune government is able to undertake the building of small-scale industrial establishments and sometimes water conservancy projects, which in the past neither the village government nor the agricultural cooperative was equipped to do.

Nationality Autonomous Areas

There are two types of nationality autonomous areas: former dependencies of China and areas inhabited by minority nationalities in predominantly Han-Chinese populated provinces. As mentioned before, prior to the republican period, these areas were governed by native hereditary tribal chieftains nominally under the jurisdiction of prefectures and counties.

On February 22, 1952 the Government Administration Council passed the "General Program for the Implementation of Autonomy for Nationalities and the Decision and Enforcement Measures Concerning Implementation of Local Nationalities Democratic Coalition Governments." Under the provisions of the General Program,

nationality autonomous regions or districts may be established in areas largely inhabited by minority nationalities. The autonomous regions or districts rank as provinces, counties, villages, or intermediary between provinces and counties. People's congresses are to be elected to serve as their organs of state authority. These congresses would further elect their people's councils. In areas inhabited by two or more nationalities, all nationalities should be represented in the people's council. By 1957 a total of eighty-two nationality autonomous regions (*ch'ü*), districts (*chou*), and counties (*hsien*) had been created. In addition, there are numerous nationality villages where minority nationalities live in small compact communities within a county. But the nationality village remains a regular local unit and not a unit of nationality autonomy.

The governing bodies of the nationality autonomous areas, like all other local governments, may organize local public security forces, manage local finance, and enact local regulations. However, nationality autonomous areas are subject to a tighter control by the central government than provinces and counties. The enactments of their people's congresses must be approved by the Standing Committee of the National People's Congress before they can take effect. The Constitution specifically demands that all higher organs of state administration concerned respect the right of autonomy of the various nationality autonomous areas and assist the various minority nationalities in their political, economic, and cultural development. By this provision the central and provincial governments are given a voice in every aspect of local administration of these autonomous areas.

The Judicial System

Under the Constitution judicial and supervisory powers are concentrated in two government organs: the Supreme People's Court, which is the highest judicial organ with supervisory powers over local and special people's courts; and the Supreme People's Procuratorate, which has supreme supervisory power over all departments of the government, the people at large, and local people's procuratorates at all levels. In addition to these, the State Council as the executive branch of the government has wide powers relative to the maintenance of public order. Under it are the Ministry of Internal Affairs in charge of civil affairs down to the village level and the Ministry of Public Security in charge of the police. The National Defense Council exercises supervisory powers over the armed forces as well as over the people through the public security forces and the militia it controls.

People's Courts

In September 1951 the government adopted the "Provisional Regulations Governing the Organization of People's Courts." These regulations provide for the establishment of a three-level—basic, middle, and high—people's court system. The functions of the people's courts are to try criminal cases, to punish criminals endangering the state, and to settle civil law suits, including disputes between government organs, business enterprises, public organizations, and individuals. Indoctrination of the litigants and the masses concerning observance of the laws of the state is to accompany the performance of these duties.

According to the Provisional Regulations, each people's court was to be guided and controlled by the court next superior to it, at the same time constituting part of the people's government of each level. The judicial conference held in 1953 proposed a reduction of the formal dependence of the courts on the local governments and a greater dependence of lower courts on higher courts; in other words, a greater degree of separation of judicial powers from executive powers at the basic levels.

These views were incorporated into the Organic Law of the People's Courts, promulgated in September 1954. The Organic Law states that "in administering justice, the people's courts are independent, subject only to the Law." It also stipulates, however, that the local courts must report to the local people's congresses, and that their judicial operations are controlled by the courts superior to them.

In addition to sending reports to the higher courts, the local courts must also report to the local Communist party committees and receive comprehensive and effective direction from the committees. This point, however, is significantly omitted in the Organic Law.

Within the people's courts of all levels, judicial committees are to be set up, with members nominated by the courts and appointed by the people's councils. Their functions are to sum up judicial experiences and to discuss important or difficult cases. Thus the executive branch of the government has considerable influence over judicial rulings.

In addition to the regular people's courts, there are three types of special courts: circuit courts, people's reception offices, and people's conciliation committees.

The circuit courts, similar in nature to the people's tribunals to be discussed later, were set up to handle cases arising from the mass campaign, such as land reform, the suppression of counter-revolutionaries, and the Five-Anti campaign against businessmen. As extraordinary courts, they were at work in the villages and cities to handle cases involving irregularities in the election of 1953-54.

The people's reception offices, a new section of the people's court, settle cases of minor importance in an informal manner and the results are collected and presented to the judge for his reference. They relieve, to some extent, the burden of litigation on the judges.

The people's conciliation committees serve two purposes. First, they are set up for the purpose of dealing with criminal elements who resist socialist transformation of agriculture. Second, they attempt to settle petty legal disputes before they reach the courts. The reports on the disputes are furnished to the police and the courts.

In industrial cities comrades adjudication committees have been established to assist the government in disposing of accident and labor discipline cases and to carry out propaganda and education. Members of these committees are supposed to be drawn from among the workers themselves.

People's Tribunals

The people's tribunals were established by the "Regulations Governing the Organization of People's Tribunals" on July 20, 1950. Originally set up for the specific purpose of carrying out agrarian reform, they performed an important function in this program and were retained for the punishment of counterrevolutionaries.

The tribunals were organized with the county as the basic unit, each tribunal to be headed by a committee of judges. One half of the judges, including the presiding and deputy presiding judges, were appointed by the county government; the other half were elected by the people's congress or by public organizations. The people's tribunals had the right to arrest and detain an individual; the right to pass sentence, set terms of imprisonment, confiscate property, and assign labor service; as well as the right to acquit an accused. The death sentence or an imprisonment sentence for more than five years was subject to ratification by the people's government of the relevant province. Lesser sentences were subject to ratification by the people's government of the relevant county. During a trial the use of corporal punishment or torture was strictly forbidden. Observers, that is the public, might speak at a trial upon being given permission by the tribunal, but order had to be maintained.

With the promulgation of the Organic Law of the People's Courts in September 1954, the system of people's tribunals was replaced by the regular court system; it no longer functions independently as an extra-judicial arm of the government.

People's Procuratorates

The people's procuratorate is set up in every court from the highest to the lowest level. Its position is somewhat analogous to that of the prosecuting attorney's office in the United States, but is instituted primarily to safeguard the interests of the party and the state; it also serves as a check on the whole system itself. As such it is undoubtedly the most powerful office in the entire legal system.

In general the Supreme People's Procuratorate exercises procuratorial authority over all departments of the State Council, all local organs of the state, persons working in these organs, and the citizenry in general. Specifically, procurators on all levels have the following duties: to check the decisions, orders, and measures of state organs to ensure their conformity with the law; to inquire into criminal cases and to conduct prosecution; to check the adjudication of the people's courts to ensure their conformity with the law; to check the execution of judgments and reform activities; and to exercise the right to prosecute or join in the prosecution of important civil cases involving the interests of the state and the people. Procuratorates are independent in the exercise of authority and not subject to interference by state organs on the same administrative level.

All procurators work under the unified leadership of the Supreme People's Procuratorate. The latter is responsible to the National People's Congress and reports to it or to its Standing Committee. The Chief Procurator of the Supreme People's Procuratorate attends the meetings of the Judicial Committee of the Supreme People's Court and has the right to request the Standing Committee of the National People's Congress to consider and change any decision of the Supreme People's Court with which he does not agree. Likewise, the procurator at any level has the right to pass on to the court at the next higher level any objection which he may find with the decisions rendered by the court on his level.

As described in the Organic Law, the procurators have the right to send men to attend the meetings of relevant organs and to gain access to their decisions, orders, files, and other documents. The relevant organs, bodies, and personnel are under obligation to supply the necessary information and explanations to the people's procuratorate. All procurators are either elected or appointed by the political bodies of the appropriate administrative level.

Judicial Procedure

Under the so-called three-level, two-trial system established by the "Provisional Regulations Governing the Organization of People's Courts," a single appeal may ordinarily be filed from the verdict of a lower-level court. The county courts are defined as "basic courts of first trial," and the provincial courts are "basic courts of second trial," so that in most cases, a provincial court trial is presumably the final one. In more important cases, the provincial court may conduct the first trial, with the appeal for a second trial going to the Supreme People's Court.

Trial procedure in the people's courts is highly flexible. Without published codes of law upon which to base their decisions, except such legislation as the Marriage Law and the Regulations for the Punishment of Counterrevolutionaries, the judges have to rely on their own common sense as well as on those numerous decrees and orders of the government which apparently have the force of law. Where no provisions have been made, the policy of the Central People's Government is adhered to.

On the county level, the trials are normally conducted first by a one-judge tribunal, but important or difficult cases are tried by tribunals of three judges. On the provincial and national levels, three-man tribunals are the rule.

The jury system, or the "system of people's assessors," is provided for in the Organic Law of the People's Courts adopted in September 1954, and applies in all cases of first instance with the exception of simple civil cases, minor criminal cases, and cases otherwise provided for by law.

The Organic Law reiterates the provisions in the Provisional Regulations, stating that trial must be held in public and that the accused should have the right of counsel, defense, and appeal. The accused may defend his case personally and designate advocates, close relatives, or citizens recommended by a mass organization to defend him. Since in the Communist system a person is practically convicted once he is arraigned, the position of the defending counsel is difficult indeed. He must act both for the accused and for the state. While he must defend the accused, he is first of all a defender of the law of the state. In cases of appeal, the Organic Law has a provision for a collegiate bench of judges. In most cases, however, the judges and prosecutors take a hostile attitude toward anyone wishing to appeal.

Aside from formal trials, the people's courts were often empowered in the past to conduct on-the-spot investigations, on-the-spot trials, and circuit trials, in many cases involving denunciation of the accused by the masses. Mass trials were conducted extensively during the campaign for the suppression of counterrevolutionaries in 1951 and the Five-Anti movement in 1952, the proceedings broadcast by radio in all major cities with moreover a request to listeners to make their accusations by mail or phone.

A typical trial procedure was officially described as follows: The public security bureaus investigated those who were denounced and a preliminary judicial disposal of their cases was made. Cases of local interest were referred to the masses for discussion and on the basis of the "views expressed by the masses" were further reviewed by the government and judicial authorities. Final judgment was passed by the judge advocate's office of the local military control committee.

Through this procedure, the Communists asserted, the people were "educated" and underwent a "revolutionary" awakening. As a result, instances of denunciation against counterrevolutionaries increased rapidly with wives implicating husbands, and sons accusing fathers of crimes against the people and the state. It is obvious that in such cases the court was more an agent of government policy and propaganda than an instrument of justice.

DIFFUSION AND CONTROL
OF INFORMATION

THE CONCRETE MANIFESTATION OF THE COMMUNIST concept of public information, radically different from that of the West, is totalitarian state control over both the public information media themselves and the subject matter disseminated through these media to the people.

Accepting Lenin's dictum that the Communist system rests on a balance of coercion and persuasion, the Chinese Communist regime has methodically placed all means of mass communication under state control, thereby eliminating forces that might tend to counteract or neutralize officially approved propaganda. Absolute control having been assured, the people are fed a monolithic mass of information prescribed by the state in accordance with the dictates of the party leadership.

The use of public information as a powerful instrument for ideological indoctrination and political agitation takes two forms. Negatively, the government restricts the free flow of information to effect a virtual monopoly of all communication media. Positively, the network of public information is extended to every segment of the population to preclude any escape from its omnipresent influence.

Government Propaganda Efforts

Modern media of communication as means for the dissemination of public information and for the expression of public opinion are relatively recent in China. During the imperial period, government gazettes were published for the benefit of officialdom but not until the last years of the nineteenth century did newspapers and magazines gain acceptance as means for the general circulation of news. Contributing to their early growth was the use made of them by reformers and revolutionaries who, amidst the political chaos, economic decay, and social unrest of the time, adopted the new media to advocate social and political changes.

During the early republican period (1912-27), the struggle for power between the northern warlords and the Nationalists was accompanied by the continuing use of the press as an instrument of political propaganda. After the establishment of the Nationalist government in Nanking, a press law governing newspapers, magazines, and other publications was promulgated in 1930. Radio broadcasting stations were set up in major political and commercial centers, and telecommunications facilities were vastly improved.

Throughout the period of Nationalist rule, a concerted effort had been made on the part of the government to regulate the flow of public information by a system of registration for all publications, including newspapers, magazines, and other printed matter. Many of the more influential publications were either directly controlled or subsidized by the government, but on the whole there was enough diversity of opinion and traditional respect for public sentiment to encourage the healthy growth of a free press. In retrospect it may be said that the most significant failure of the Nationalist regime in the field of public information was not so much a lack of effort as the neglect of the rural masses.

On their part, the Communists employed all means of public information, ranging from newspapers and radio broadcasting to billboards and handbills, to win popular support among the peasantry. After their victory in 1949, all mass information media were put under the firm control of the government, opposition views were stamped out, and contacts between Chinese and westerners were restricted to official delegations and a few newspapermen. Consequently the great majority of the population has been isolated physically and psychologically from the rest of the world, particularly the West. With an unrestricted field for operation, government propaganda has become one of the most important means of political control.

Communist Propaganda Campaigns

Political indoctrination and propaganda being their primary concern, Communist publicists, highly adept at manipulating public attitudes, see in every form of popular expression a potential vehicle for political interpretation. The typical propaganda campaign is launched by the announcement of a new state objective in speeches or statements by government leaders or party propagandists. The signal given, all media of communication are mobilized to promote the state's program and the flow of propaganda continues unabated until the objective has been reached. The absolute control and direction of propaganda by the state and the party results in the close correlation observable between campaign and state purposes. If an avowed objective must be temporarily abandoned, as in the case of the "liberation" of Taiwan, the accompanying campaign is held in abeyance, ready however for another violent outburst with the state's next move.

Similarly, propaganda themes, formulated to implement specific goals, are subject to change when policy changes. For example, during World War II, the Communists propagandized Mao Tsetung's doctrine of the new democracy, putting forward the view that there was room in their scheme for all classes, including the capitalists. They shifted only when the party ordered a change from the general line of new democracy to the line of transformation to socialism, at which time propaganda content shifted to an attack on the capitalist class and the necessity of state control of all industries. A similar shift can be seen in the propaganda on agrarian reform. The slogan "Land to the Tillers" had been used with considerable success in the earlier periods of the Communist movement, but was dropped when it became necessary to socialize agriculture. Shifts in propaganda themes became a concerted campaign only after the formal proclamation of a policy shift by the highest authorities.

A study of Communist propaganda materials indicates that government propaganda efforts have been devoted mostly to the following fields: promotion of government-sponsored political campaigns, such as the Aid-Korea Resist-America campaign and the antirightists campaign; publicity on emulation drives for the promotion of industrial and agricultural production; ideological remolding of the people, especially the intellectuals; and dissemination of scientific and technological knowledge as an aid to economic development.

The final success of the Communists in their long struggle with the Nationalists may be attributed in part to their skillful use of the techniques of mass persuasion. These techniques, summarized by the Central Committee of the Chinese Communist party in the form of "Resolutions on Methods of Leadership" and repeatedly referred to in the handbooks for propagandists, are as follows:

(1) First investigate and then propagandize.
(2) Combine general slogans with actual local operations.
(3) Always test the use of slogans in a small locality before applying them nationally.
(4) Make the ideas of the party appear as if they come from the people.
(5) Try to discover the activists or aggressive elements in every mass movement or propaganda campaign and use them to agitate or stimulate the moderate and "backward" elements in the locality.
(6) Educate thoroughly the cadres before sending them out in a propaganda campaign.
(7) Carry out only one propaganda campaign at a given time; support it with secondary or lesser drives.
(8) Carefully review the successes and failures of the campaign after it is completed.

In the actual application of specific propaganda themes in various localities, a considerable degree of latitude is allowed the individual propagandist. Directives from the party's Propaganda Department and its branches stress the importance of adaptation to local conditions. Yet not all is left to individual judgment. Outlines enumerating the items to be propagandized are published by newspapers and in various propaganda handbooks to implement a policy decision made by higher authorities, while detailed outlines are provided for particular drives. Since many cadres work in rural areas remote from supervisors, the use of such outlines ensures a high degree of consistency. Phrases or slogans appear verbatim in press, radio, or propaganda directives throughout the country.

The communalization movement of 1958 may be taken to illustrate the way in which a nationwide propaganda campaign is conducted in China. The first people's commune was formed in April 1958 in Honan province; similar amalgamations of agricultural cooperatives into communes were reported in Heilungkiang and Liaoning. After having studied the experience of these early communes, Mao Tse-tung, on an inspection tour in Shantung on August 9, gave the first official approval of the people's commune as the best form of rural organization. Thereupon, articles on the nature and advantages of the commune system began to appear with great frequency in newspapers and magazines. On August 29 the Central Committee of the party passed a resolution calling for the establishment of communes throughout the country, at the same time enunciating their ideological basis and the principles governing their formation. Immediately afterward the entire countryside seethed with propaganda meetings in which the benefits of the communes were repeatedly discussed and extolled until an apparent majority opinion was reached and a formal petition for the organization of the commune was presented to the county government.

Meanwhile the press and radio discussed the merits of the communes, publicized the ones best organized, and announced the rate of progress in communalization in various localities. Documentary films were made of the bumper harvests gathered by some well-publicized communes. Numerous booklets on the communes were published; one of them, issued by the Chinese Youth Publishing House, had a first edition of 200,000 copies. At the same time, the drive for increasing steel, coal, grains, and cotton production was pushed along with the communalization movement, with the propagandists stressing the amazing increase made by the communes in production and income. By the end of 1958 more than 90 percent of the rural population had joined the communes. Thus, a revolutionary transformation of community life involving about 500 million people was accomplished in less than a year's time.

The commune movement provides a good example of the intimate relation of propaganda to policy implementation. Although force is ever present and has been used to execute government decrees, the fact that most of the revolutionary measures in China have been carried out with relatively minor overt resistance testifies to the effectiveness of Communist techniques of mass persuasion. To convince a large majority of the populace by public exhortation that radical government measures are in their best interest requires a high degree of skill in propagandizing through newspapers, periodicals, radio broadcasts, and films.

Press

The Communist party and government determine the selection and treatment of everything that goes into the press. It is maintained that the newspapers should, among other things, take particular pains to publicize the alliance of workers and peasants, to promote friendly cooperation between different nationalities, and "to consolidate and strengthen incessantly the ideology which places the broad united front of people's democracy under the leadership of the working class."

In order to ensure the strict conformity of newspaper coverage with this basic policy, the Communist authorities have laid down four general rules for all newspapers: no news releases from "imperialist and reactionary" news agencies should be printed; only news releases from the New China News Agency (Hsin-hua Shê) can be used and they must be used in their entirety; prominent space must be reserved for government pronouncements, party declarations, and speeches by government and party leaders; and news releases are to be issued by responsible press officers of the various government agencies, and reporters must not seek to obtain news.

As a result, newspapers demonstrate a considerable degree of uniformity in coverage. Claiming to be free from sensationalism, capitalism, careerism, individualism, idealism, formalism, and bourgeois objectivism, the newspapers are devoted to theories of Marxism-Leninism-Maoism; announcements of economic, social, and political plans; reprints of party and government directives and documents; and instructions for party and government workers on how to organize and improve production and other activities. There are also materials designed to exhort the workers to greater effort; lists of persons who have won special awards; and reports on national movements, industrial construction, the inauguration of new state loans, and the completion of highways, railways, or irrigation projects.

The press is subject to a system of dual control. During the earlier years of the Communist regime it was under the supervision of the Cultural and Educational Committee of the Government Administration Council, which had under its control the Press Administration Bureau and the Publication Administration Bureau. At the same time, the press was also under the supervision of the Propaganda Department of the Central Committee of the Chinese Communist party. The Press Administration Bureau was abolished in August 1952, leaving the press in the hands of the Cultural and Educational Committee. This committee was subsequently abolished in September 1954 with the reorganization of the Government Administration Council into the State Council. At present the press is under the direct supervision of the Ministry of Culture and the party's Propaganda Department. Each provincial and municipal government also has a cultural and educational department modeled after that of the central government. There are no special organs for the press on the county level or below; that function is performed by the party.

The party's elaborate organization for the control of the press is headed by the Propaganda Department of the Central Committee; from the *People's Daily* and other national dailies published by the party, newspapers on the lower levels receive guidance on editorial policy. Under the party's provincial, municipal, or county committee, there is a propaganda section; under the party's district (subdivision of a county) committee, there is a propaganda cadre; on the lowest level, there is always one member of the party cell designated as the "propagandist" (see the Organizational Chart of the Communist Press Control Apparatus).

A powerful instrument for the education and indoctrination of the masses, the press has expanded impressively in recent years. According to government statistics, the annual circulation (in millions) of newspapers and magazines from 1950 to 1955 is as follows:

	Newspapers	Magazines
1950	798	35
1951	......	......
1952	1,609	204
1953	1,672	172
1954	1,711	205
1955	1,954	288

Another set of official figures revealed that for the seven years from 1951 to 1958 the per issue circulation of newspapers increased from 3.4 million to 15 million and that of magazines from 900,000 to 17 million. In 1951 there was one newspaper for every 176 persons; in 1958 there was one for every 40 persons. When it is realized that illiteracy is still widespread among the Chinese populace, the total circulation figures seem surprisingly high, if not deliberately inflated.

Newspapers

Newspapers in China may be divided into four groups: national, regional, local, and minority. Minority newspapers appear in non-Chinese languages such as Mongolian, Uigur, Tibetan, Kazak, Yi, Chuang, and Korean. Regional and local papers differ from the national papers in that they have a wider coverage of local news.

Most of the domestic and foreign news for these papers is

supplied by the New China News Agency, directly under the control of the State Council and the only news agency in Communist China. Besides its main office in Peking, it had in 1957 thirty-seven subbureaus located in all important cities throughout the country as well as twenty-three foreign bureaus mainly in the capitals of Asian and European countries. With such a widespread network, its monopolization of news is complete.

The stringent government control of news results in a drab uniformity of content and presentation in all Communist newspapers. Important news is sometimes withheld from the public until the government decides on an opportune time for its release; for instance, the Khamba rebellion was not mentioned in the Communist press until the news of the Tibetan revolt in Lhasa was known throughout the world. Some of the criticisms directed against the Communist newspapers during the short-lived Blooming and Contending campaign of 1956-57 were the suppression of news and the party control of newspapers. The critics advocated the publication of newspapers by individuals instead of by party or government organizations. The Communist rejoinder was that newspapers are instruments of class struggle which must be held firmly in the hands of the party and the government.

Among the national papers, all published in Peking, the most important is the *Jen-min jih-pao* (People's Daily), the official mouthpiece of the Chinese Communist party. First published in June 1948, it has a circulation of about a million among all segments of China's literate population. It reprints in full the speeches of party and government leaders, government proclamations, official documents, proceedings, laws, and regulations. Its editorials, frequently reproduced in full by other local newspapers and periodicals throughout the country, represent the official "line" of the party and are looked upon by the people as official pronouncements.

The *People's Daily* is generally published in eight pages, following the new format of reading horizontally from left to right. The editorial appears on the left side of the front page, the rest being devoted to important national news and discussion of various problems. The second page also carries national news with occasional feature articles and a part is used for "Letters to the Editors," a column designed to encourage criticism of all aspects of "socialist construction." More national news and feature articles appear on the third and fourth pages; the bottom part of the fourth page is sometimes used for sports. Pages five and six carry

ORGANIZATIONAL CHART OF THE COMMUNIST PRESS CONTROL APPARATUS

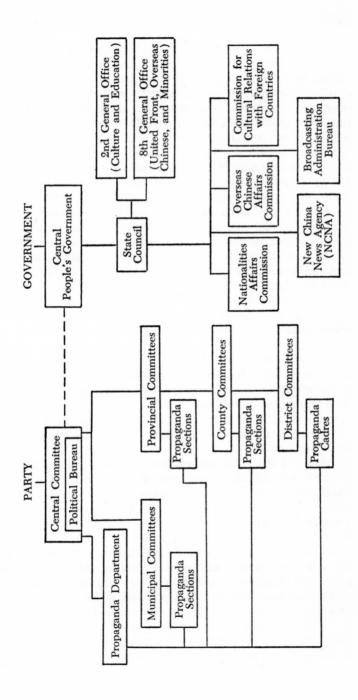

international news, mostly from the Soviet Union and its satellites.. Page seven contains special articles and news of a cultural and educational nature. Page eight often has short articles and poems of the belles-lettres type, as well as occasional reproductions of paintings, sculptures, or photographs of artistic interest. Publication news, public notices, and advertisements appear in the lower half of pages six and eight.

Other important national newspapers are the *Kuang-ming jih-pao* (Kuang-ming Daily) and the *Ta-kung pao* (L'impartial). As an organ of the non-Communist "democratic parties," the *Kuang-ming Daily* specializes in reporting the political and cultural activities of all parties other than the Communist. Addressed primarily to the intellectuals and professionals, it covers topics such as higher education, science, literature and art, legal problems, health, and others. The paper strictly follows the Communist party line and its editor-in-chief and associate editors are all Communist party members except for Ch'u An-p'ing, who served for a brief period from April to June in 1957. A non-Communist, Ch'u was appointed to the chief editorship as a concession to the "democratic parties," but because of his more independent policy in news gathering and editorial writing, he was accused as a rightist and soon relieved of his job. After 1949 the *Ta-kung pao,* formerly one of the most influential privately owned newspapers, lost its position as an "impartial" nonpartisan news organ. At present, it specializes in international problems, commercial and financial affairs, relationships between state and private enterprises, and matters of general economic interest. Its Hong Kong edition is controlled by the Communists.

Most of the provinces and special municipalities have papers of their own, often named after the regions in which they are published. Below these levels are hundreds of local papers, serving rural, urban, and professional groups. These local papers are addressed to readers of a small area or a specific profession and are therefore more direct in approach than either the national or provincial papers. On the whole, the local newspapers, particularly the farm and professional papers, concentrate on the economic, political, and cultural problems of their particular audience or other specific local matters such as health and sanitation measures, higher agricultural and industrial production, and so forth. Their major task is to promote maximum production in factories, mines, and farms within their area of circulation, and to assist in the execution of government, party, and trade union decisions and regulations which apply to these production units. These newspapers also assume responsibility for explaining important government and party decisions to the local populace, with the objective of "improving both the material conditions and cultural standards of the people." The agricultural and industrial newspapers serve the additional function of disseminating technical information.

Another source of information is the wall or blackboard newspaper which appears in factories, schools, government bureaus, army units, and villages. These publications are invariably run by party activists and because they reach a large number of people on the grass-roots level are considered to be "the most popular and powerful means by which the party can contact and influence the broad masses." The rate of literacy being low in villages, factories, and army units, these wall and blackboard newspapers are written in the simplest and most direct form. Thus, in addition to performing the propaganda function, they also provide supplementary reading materials for those undergoing literacy training. Moreover, these handwritten papers deal with matters of immediate personal interest to members of the community and therefore have a greater degree of appeal. The widespread and persistent usage of such inexpensive means of communication has proved highly effective in the political indoctrination of the masses and their importance must not be overlooked.

Periodicals

Like the newspapers, the periodicals are under the exclusive control of the party, government, and party-dominated mass organizations; the subscription and distribution of periodicals are handled by the Ministry of Post and Telecommunications.

As many periodicals are to a large extent merely subsidiaries of the leading newspapers, their contents display an equal degree of uniformity, usually picking up the refrain of the *People's Daily* or other newspapers of national significance. The only variation from the main theme is provided by specialized journals which would carry a series of articles dealing with related topics in their field of specialization.

According to their function and content, the periodicals may be divided into a number of groups, each serving a selected segment of the society. Except for a few comprehensive nationwide publications which cover a wider range of interests, most periodicals deal with one subject only, such as politics, economics, trade unions, science and technology, literature and art, and so forth.

The major emphases in the political periodicals are the study of Marxism-Leninism-Maoism, collaboration between China and the Soviet Union, the history and theories of the Communist party, explanation of party and government policies and directives, and reviews and interpretation of international affairs in strictly Communist terms. Economic periodicals contain articles on the different aspects of the Chinese economy, criticism of the capitalist system, problems related to China's socialist construction, the "advanced economic experience" of the Soviet Union, and the strengthening of the world trade union movement. In these periodicals, purely theoretical articles are fewer in number than what may be called "action" articles, which are published for the purpose of publicizing the government's specific economic projects such as the collectivization of agriculture and the transformation of private enterprises. There are also professional and technical journals published by trade unions, government ministries, and academic societies. The latter have issued specialized journals for the various branches of natural and applied sciences in which a common practice is the translation of articles from Russian scientific journals; since 1956, however, greater attention has been paid to publications in the West. In the periodicals on literature and art, discussion of Soviet theories and representative works take up considerable space. Advocating mass appeal, articles in these periodicals encourage and promote the study of folk music and literature. Popular pictorial materials are found in a number of cartoon serials, the use of which has proved to be extremely effective in indoctrinating the peasants, workers, and children.

For Communist members and activists, the most authoritative interpretation of the latest party line is found in the *Hung-ch'i* (Red Flag), a semimonthly first published in 1958 by the Central Committee of the Chinese Communist party. Its theoretical discussions and factual reports are written by party and government leaders. Another important periodical for party and government workers as well as general readers is the *Hsin-hua pan-yüeh k'an* (New China Semimonthly), published as a monthly from 1949 until January 1956. It contains the texts of important party proceedings, government directives and documents, as well as laws and regulations; it also reprints important newspaper editorials and magazine articles on political, economic, social, and cultural subjects of both national and international interest. Because of its authoritative nature and coverage, the *New China Semimonthly* has a wide circulation among all sections of China's reading public and is an indispensable reference for the study of Communist China.

Among the periodicals published in English and other foreign languages and intended for foreign distribution only, the more important ones are the following:

Scientia Sinica, a monthly published by the Chinese Academy of Sciences for the purpose of exchanging scientific knowledge and experience.

China Pictorial, a semimonthly published in Chinese, Mongolian, Tibetan, Uigur, Korean, English, Russian, French, Japanese, Indonesian, and Spanish, illustrated with pictures and color reproductions of paintings showing "every aspect of life and development in New China."

China Reconstructs, an English monthly published by the China Welfare Institute to publicize through articles and pictures the "economic, social, and cultural progress in China."

Chinese Literature, an English literary monthly published by the Foreign Languages Press, containing articles and translations of both ancient and modern Chinese literary works in all forms— short stories, plays, poems, and folk songs.

Peking Review, a weekly (formerly the *People's China*) published by the Foreign Languages Press, containing news articles on economic, political, cultural, social, and other aspects of present-day China with occasional supplements providing reprints of important government and party documents, particularly in regard to foreign affairs.

Most of these foreign-language periodicals are published in Peking. Their subscription and distribution are handled by roughly seventy agencies throughout the world.

Radio

Chinese Communist radio broadcasting began in September 1945 when the Yenan New China Broadcasting Station was established. Forerunner of the Central People's Broadcasting System, this station was moved to northern Shensi in March 1947 when the Nationalists captured Yenan. The Communists' military successes in late 1947 and 1948 brought additional broadcasting facilities under their control and by the end of 1948 there were sixteen broadcasting stations in Communist-dominated areas. Following their conquest of the country in 1949, the Communists established the Central People's Broadcasting System with the key station in Peking.

The Communist regime fully realizes the importance of radio broadcasting as an instrument of public information and at the very beginning of its rule set up a special organ known as the Broadcasting Administration Bureau under direct central government supervision. It has been responsible for the establishment, improvement, and expansion of the broadcasting network throughout the country.

The restrictive aspect of radio control has been entrusted to the Ministry of Public Security, which laid down the "Provisional Regulations for the Control of Radio Equipment and Supplies" in August 1951 for the purpose of preventing the activities of "counter-revolutionaries and bandits." These regulations require all manufacturers and sales agencies to register with the public security authorities and to submit monthly reports on the types and quantities of radio equipment manufactured and sold. All buyers are required to obtain "confirmatory certificates" from appropriate organizations before making purchases; and various items of equipment can be installed only with permits from competent government authorities. Radio equipment cannot be imported or transported without official permit, and the population is encouraged to report concealment of such equipment, discovery of which results in severe punishment.

The rigidity of these control measures has made it virtually impossible for any person to possess, let alone use, radio equipment capable of receiving broadcasts other than those sent out by the government. In the meantime the Communist regime has methodically built up its own radio broadcasting network. Privately owned facilities have been absorbed into the state broadcasting system by various means. Some of them have been closed down summarily, thereby forcing the owners to transfer all equipment to the government under terms dictated by the latter. Others have been placed under joint state-private operation, with the state assuming complete control. While maximum use is made of existing facilities, new broadcasting stations have also been established at strategic points.

The Broadcasting Administration Bureau distributes receiving sets to different parts of the country and determines the locations of diffusion and monitoring stations. In May 1955, for example, the bureau distributed 6,000 five-tube battery-operated superheterodyne receivers to twenty-one provinces and areas inhabited by the minority nationalities. These sets were issued primarily to monitoring stations of the agricultural, livestock, and fishery cooperatives.

Under Communist administration, radio broadcasting is rigidly channeled into political propaganda, education, or entertainment. Political propaganda includes news and commentaries; education stresses the dissemination of scientific and technological knowledge; and entertainment provides music, literary readings, radio plays, and similar offerings. It should be emphasized here that education and entertainment programs also have their political overtones as they are often arranged with political objectives in mind. The broadcasting station therefore is an instrument of class struggle and the mouthpiece of the party and government; all its programs must necessarily reflect an ideological content based upon the demand of class interest.

According to the latest report, the number of broadcasting stations in mainland China has increased from forty-five in 1949 to ninety-eight in 1959. All provinces, autonomous regions, and a number of large cities now have their own radio stations. The latest, the Tibet Radio Station, started operating on January 1, 1959. One of the characteristics of the Chinese broadcasting project is the development of a wired radio network. Wired radio stations were established in some 1,800 counties and cities and 5,800 people's communes by the end of 1958. A large number of factories, mines, government organizations and schools are supplied with wired radio stations. These stations not only relay radio programs beamed from central and local broadcasting stations but also broadcast their own programs. Listeners are not required to pay fees.

The only radio station of international significance in China is the Central People's Broadcasting Station of Peking, its broadcasts being intended for foreign listeners as well as for the listening public of the entire country. Following the conclusion of a radio agreement between China and the Soviet Union in 1954, Moscow programs in Mandarin can be heard twice a week over the central station. Since 1954 a special program for Taiwan has been broadcast twelve hours a day in both Mandarin and the Amoy dialect. Foreign-language broadcasts, sent out since 1950 under the name "Radio Peking," include daily news and commentaries in English, Japanese, Korean, Vietnamese, Indonesian, Burmese, and Thai. For overseas Chinese listeners, broadcasts are given in Mandarin, Hakka, Cantonese, and Amoy dialects.

As for television, the Peking television station, the first in

China, started experimental telecasting May 1, 1958 and went into full operation on September 2 of the same year. Television stations were established also in Shanghai and Harbin by the end of 1958. At present preparations are under way for television stations in Canton, Tientsin, Mukden, and other cities.

Films

The Chinese motion picture industry began about forty years ago but did not attain much popularity until the 1930's when films of artistic merit and social significance were first produced. Even then, the Chinese film market was dominated by Hollywood products. During the Sino-Japanese War, Chinese movie studios in Shanghai either fell into Japanese hands or moved to Chungking. After the war, Shanghai once more became the film capital of China. Following the Communist victory in 1949, the Central Motion Picture Bureau of the Ministry of Culture was established to direct all film activities, namely, the licensing of new movies, censorship of old films both foreign and domestic, and the export and import of movies. In addition to the establishment of new studios such as the Central Newsreel and Documentary Film Studio, the government also took over the privately owned studios in Shanghai. Up to 1958, Shanghai, Peking, and Ch'ang-ch'un were the only film industry centers in China. During that year, a decision was made to decentralize the film industry. Except for the Central Newsreel and Documentary Film Studio, all film studios were put under the control of the local governments. It is expected that eventually all provinces and autonomous regions will have their own movie industries.

The growth of the Chinese film industry, shown in the following figures, has, though constant, been inadequate in relation to the size of the population:

	Film projection teams	Motion picture theaters
1950	522	641
1951	......	......
1952	1,110	746
1953	2,154	779
1954	2,723	815
1955	3,698	859

In 1958 the total number of projecting teams and theaters was reported to have exceeded ten thousand and the film audience reached 300 million. However, 80 percent of the towns still lacked permanent theaters and the rural population attended an average of less than two shows per year. The government's goal is to set up, within the next ten years, one theater in every town and one projection team in every village. These theaters and projection teams will be financed by the local governments and communes instead of the central government, as has been the case.

The number of films produced in Communist China has not been enough to satisfy the demand of the population. This is demonstrated by the fact that in 1958 about one hundred feature films and several hundred newsreels, documentaries, and scientific films were produced for a population that numbered more than 650 million. To meet this demand, many Soviet and East European films as well as other foreign films had to be imported.

More serious than numerical deficiency is the low quality of many of the films produced, particularly the feature films. This problem was brought up during the Blooming and Contending campaign of 1957. It was reported that 70 percent of the over one hundred features produced between 1953 and the first half of 1957 had lost money, some of them getting back only 10 percent of the cost. Critics attributed this situation to bureaucratic control that stifled the initiative of the producers and directors; uniformity of story content due to the insistence on correct political viewpoints; faulty organization of the film studios resulting in the waste of talents among actors and directors; and insufficient attention to box office requirements.

Since 1957 the government has somewhat relaxed its control over the film industry and the studios are given more freedom in film-making. The Communist authorities, however, have repudiated any suggestion that box office appeal must be the main criterion for motion picture production. To them, the film, being one of the most effective propaganda vehicles, must be put under the firm ideological guidance of the party regardless of its effects upon box office receipts.

Some of the films shown in 1958 are indicative of the general content of the average film produced in China. Many of them are documentary-type films which feature China's scenic landscapes, construction efforts, as well as stories of peasants, industrial workers, and underground party members. However, not all the films are propagandistic. Pictures with themes taken from traditional Chinese operas and stories have enjoyed a good reception, and a number of documentary and children films have won recognition in international film festivals.

Evaluation

There has been a significant growth in the media of mass communication in Communist China. This growth is manifested in the rapid increase in newspaper and periodical circulations as well as in the development of radio and film industries. The high illiteracy rate reduces the effectiveness of printed matter as a vehicle of mass communication and focuses the government's attention upon the expansion of radio networks and film-projection teams. But the large capital investment required in these industries will probably preclude the early realization of the government's goal to cover the entire country with a network of radio stations and movie theaters together with an adequate supply of radios and films. For this reason, although the mass communication media constitute an important means of propaganda in the hands of the government, at present they are used mainly for the purpose of supplementing the more direct method of personal contacts and mass rallies organized by local party cadres. The swift transmission of government propaganda messages through the newspaper and radio broadcasts is an important aid to the cadres, whose function is to translate them into languages readily understood by peasants and workers as well as to arouse their enthusiasm in support of government measures.

There is no doubt that the government considers the mass communication media essentially as instruments of political indoctrination and only secondarily as means of education and entertainment. The question naturally arises as to the effectiveness of the government's propaganda campaigns. The continuous government admonitions for vigilance against counterrevolutionaries, rightists, and revisionists would seem to indicate that its efforts have not been completely successful. Some of the most telling criticisms during the Blooming and Contending campaign, as indicated above, were directed precisely at the strict government control of the mass communication media. The yearning for objective presentation of news as well as for nonpolitical orientation of the entertainment media was manifested in diverse ways. The drop in the attendance of propagandistic movies has compelled the authorities to review the organization of the motion picture industry and pay more attention to enhancing the entertainment value of its products. There is no reason to believe that the government will forego the utilization and control of mass communication media for propaganda purposes, but efforts will be made to disguise its messages in more appealing and less propagandistic forms.

It cannot be denied, however, that Communist propaganda as a whole has attained considerable success in indoctrinating the bulk of the population with its own version of human society and social order. The number of intellectuals in China has been small and the number of those who have had contacts with foreign ideas and peoples is even smaller. The constant reiteration of Communist concepts through government-monopolized channels of information must have its effects upon the formation of public attitudes and opinions. In the domestic sphere, as long as the government is able to increase industrial and agricultural production and to provide the people with expectations of a rising standard of living, they have no choice but to accept, with minimum questioning, the government's point of view. In foreign affairs, the government has played skillfully upon the nationalistic and anticolonial feelings of the Chinese people to elicit support for its policies. Total disillusionment with government propaganda can be expected only if the Communists fail to satisfy the minimum expectations of the people or involve them in a disastrous global war.

FOREIGN RELATIONS

THE YEARS SINCE THE ESTABLISHMENT of the People's Republic in 1949 have been marked by the phenomenal growth of Communist power within China and by the methodical rise of Communist China to its present international position as a major, totally ambitious power hostile to the West. In Communist China the West confronts an antagonist as tenacious and resourceful as the Soviet Union. The Communist leaders in Peking are at once more subtle, more provincial, and more arrogant than the Communist leaders in Moscow.

The international impact of Communist China is based partly upon its military strength, since China, for the first time in a century, commands the mightiest military machine in Asia. Yet western recognition of the strategic implications of China's present program of military modernization, while a useful first step in comprehending Chinese power, is nevertheless inadequate. Realistic discussion of the dimensions of Chinese power must also assess the intangible political and psychological elements which now provide the driving forces in China's international policy. This policy comprises both historical Chinese and contemporary Communist ingredients, and these forces must first be considered before appraising the long-range strategy of the Peking regime and its tactical relations and policies within the Communist bloc and vis-à-vis the non-Communist world. Any summary of the first decade in the evolution of Communist China's foreign relations must be directed toward synthesis, not synopsis, to the end that the general pattern underlying the specific events may be better appreciated.

Communist Foreign Policy

Strands of continuity which are essentially Chinese form an important part of Communist China's foreign policy. The long isolation of the Chinese empire under one sovereign, the Son of Heaven, created a deep and enduring sense of ethnocentrism in traditional China. Through the dynastic centuries, a complex system of tributary relations—centered upon the Chinese imperial court, based upon Chinese political and military power, and buttressed by Chinese cultural pride—served to handle all dealings with non-Chinese states. In the mid-nineteenth century, the sharp impact of the European maritime powers, coinciding with a period of substantial internal strain within the Chinese empire, upset the traditional system and introduced a new, western-imposed system of "treaty relations" to govern Chinese foreign relations. This unique historical heritage did not permit China to adjust easily to the demands of the modern, western state system and to the system of international intercourse which it required.

The legacy left by twenty centuries of Chinese cultural primacy in Asia, combined with memories of a hundred years of Chinese weakness in the face of western and Japanese intrusions after 1840 and augmented by the drives of modern Chinese nationalism in the twentieth century, has now passed to the account of the Chinese Communist party. Peking is again the capital of a unified China under firm, centralized control. The regime in power in Peking, however, is radical and Communist, not conservative and Confucian.

Thus strands of discontinuity are also apparent in the fabric of Peking's policy. China's international influence is now dynamic, endowed with distinctively new characteristics, powered by political and technological forces never found in the imperial past. China is again a major Asian power exerting substantial direct influence upon adjacent areas. And China, through the considered intention of Mao Tse-tung and the other Communist leaders, is now also a major power occupying a key position in a totally new world: the Communist bloc headed by the USSR. To the traditional Chinese view of the world outside China, Mao has added a radical, foreign element: Marxism-Leninism, with its sense of historical prevision, its ambiguous attitude toward "bourgeois" values, and its strategic intentions with respect to international society.

Peking's foreign policy is thus based upon a body of Chinese patterns of thought and behavior, many with deep historical roots, sparked by the *élan* of a revolutionary Communist movement. Each element contributes its share to the compulsive sense of Chinese Communist destiny which is now a fundamental factor in the international politics of Asia. Harnessing the deep-seated latent Chinese distrust of the West and of western "imperialism" and "materialism," Peking has mobilized a formidable national drive focused on a single theme: China resurgent as a strong Communist state. The revival of national pride—of national nerve—is the most intangible and the most dynamic aspect of Peking's foreign policy today.

Strategic Objective

Marxist-Leninist theory, according to the Communists, is not a dogma but a guide to action. Any philosophy worthy of the name seeks to explain the world. The Communists believe that it is the distinctive prerogative of their creed not only to explain but also to change—indeed to improve—the world through positive application of the "objective laws" of Marxist-Leninist theory.

Since 1949 Peking's basic and continuing objective has been to establish and maintain the People's Republic of China as a major world power. The policy framework for the pursuit of this strategic goal—maximum international influence and prestige—has been constructed by a handful of veteran Chinese Communist political leaders. The career of Mao Tse-tung, master and mastermind of the Chinese Communist movement for the past quarter-century, indicates that his pattern of political activity is based upon taking the long, strategic view of current events. For two decades he persisted in the countryside of China without being deflected from his domestic goal: total power in China. That battle won, he is now intent upon winning the next: the building of a strong, industrialized national state possessing modern military and scientific power.

A complex, shrewd, and powerful individual, Mao Tse-tung has been successful in evolving a modern Communist adaptation of an ancient Chinese ability: the capacity of the Chinese to expand their influence in Asia in periods of strong and decisive central government. During the first decade of his rule, he has established Communist China as the most formidable political and military power of Asia. During the years ahead, he plans to establish China as a major world power.

Tactics

The ultimate strategic objective formulated by Mao Tse-tung and his associates has remained constant since 1949. The tactical assumptions of Chinese foreign policy, however, have shifted significantly in accordance with changing conditions. They have varied with the exigencies of China's domestic programs: political consolidation, economic development, industrialization, militarization. Chinese tactics have also reflected differing international conditions: pressure or stimulation from the West, response or resistance in Asia, cordiality or evasion in Moscow, official belligerence or public amnesia in the United States.

The changes in Communist foreign policy tactics during the past ten years also reveal the hardening gap between ultimate intention and immediate possibility. Late in 1949, in a major speech at Peking (before the Asian-Australasian Trade Union Conference, November 16, 1949), Liu Shao-ch'i recited the Communist catechism on foreign relations and posed the People's Republic of China as the model for all revolutionary (i.e., Communist) movements in "colonial and semicolonial areas" in the East. Liu drew a blueprint for Communist-led uprisings in the peripheral countries from Korea through Southeast Asia to India and emphasized that military operations "can, and must, be the main force in the people's liberation struggle" in these areas. Somewhat later, on July 1, 1951, the thirtieth anniversary of the founding of the Communist party of China, Peking focused attention on the international significance of the pattern of political revolution exemplified in the establishment of the People's Republic of China, reiterating the thesis that the "Chinese revolution" must be the model for all "colonial and semicolonial countries."

In contrast to the forthright posture of the early years, marked by belligerence and condescension, Chinese diplomacy of the post-Korean War period became relatively moderate. After mid-1954, Peking began to lay major stress upon the "Five Principles" of peaceful coexistence enunciated jointly, first with India and then with Burma. These principles are: (1) mutual respect for territorial integrity and sovereignty; (2) nonaggression; (3) noninterference in internal affairs; (4) equality and mutual benefit; and (5) peaceful coexistence. Chinese diplomacy at the Asian-African Conference held in Indonesia in the spring of 1955 was discreet and flexible. Chou En-lai, then foreign minister and leader of the Peking delegation at Bandung, made a conscious—and notably successful—effort to align Communist China with the predominant mood of the conference: a deep desire on the part of the nations represented to register their new maturity in international politics and to assert their final independence of western "colonialism." China's tactical diplomacy was marked by consistent efforts to convince its fellow Asian countries that the new China, if treated with due respect, harbored no aggressive tendencies. During 1958-59 Peking's foreign policy posture again hardened significantly in many quarters: toward other major Asian nations (Japan and India); toward deviants within the Communist bloc (Yugoslavia); and particularly toward the United States. Yet no variation in the tactical tone of Chinese Communist foreign policy has been accompanied by substantial subsurface evidence suggesting that Peking has abandoned or revised its long-term strategic objectives in Asia, objectives generated by its national sense of destiny and defined by the political compulsions of the Communist nations.

In its drive for enhanced international status, Communist China has utilized a considerable arsenal of nonmilitary weapons: political, economic, cultural, and intellectual. This drive is supported by a new fabric of distinctively Chinese design: "people's diplomacy." Designed to bypass official governmental relations in cases where such relations are either inconvenient or impossible, "people's diplomacy" aims at the erection of a network of contacts between state-sponsored groups in Communist China and unofficial groups and organizations in non-Communist areas abroad. Through judicious manipulation of this unorthodox type of diplomacy, Peking has not infrequently gained tactical advantages which could not, under present conditions, be attained through official contacts or negotiations. The Communist regime has added a new dimension to China's foreign relations, inviting thousands of individuals and scores of delegations from all parts of the world to visit Peking (still one of the world's most seductive capitals), investing courtesy and expert Chinese service (still unparalleled in Asia) in their care while they are government guests in the People's Republic of China, and re-exporting them as non-Chinese—and often non-Communist—purveyors of the party line.

China in the Communist Bloc

Communist China is not pursuing its present program of "people's diplomacy" in a political vacuum. China operates as an integral part of the Communist bloc, and this intimate alliance with the USSR and the bloc of Moscow-oriented nations constitutes the principal new dimension in the pattern of China's international relations. Peking has diplomatic relations with all twelve governments of the bloc: the Soviet Union, three Communist states in Asia (North Korea, North Vietnam, and the Mongolian People's

Republic), and eight Communist nations in East-Central Europe (Albania, Bulgaria, Czechoslovakia, East Germany, Hungary, Poland, Rumania, and Yugoslavia).

The coalition between the two major Communist nations which dominate the bloc and straddle the interior mass of the Eurasian continent is the most important new factor in world politics since 1949. Neither the shifts in the Kremlin, the turbulent events in East-Central Europe, nor China's recent theoretical and practical investment in people's communes has yet significantly altered the stability of the relations between Peking and Moscow. The alliance remains tolerably durable. Each of the principal partners derives significant advantages from the relation; each is astute enough to be willing to compromise on minor issues in order to assure agreement on the major issues involved in the alliance.

The underlying pattern of relations between China and Russia is complex, for the union embraces two vast, sprawling nations with different historical and cultural backgrounds. It embraces two-fifths of the world's population, scattered across nearly one-fourth of the earth's land area. It embraces the two largest Communist parties in the world, each a product of a distinctive political-psychological environment, each headed by men with only limited experience in the other country. And it embraces issues of doctrine, methodology, radicalism, and faith—issues which are inherent in revolutionary movements deriving their official ethos from Marx, Engels, and Lenin but which may nevertheless be viewed differently by Chinese and by Russian eyes.

From Moscow's standpoint, the present alliance is of major value. Russia has long sought a unified and friendly state to cover its Asian flanks. Mao Tse-tung's victory in China has provided an ally that is not only unified and friendly but also Communist—a development of major immediate importance and of great long-range significance in expanding Communist international influence in a critical theater: Asia. Thus the Soviet leaders view Mao Tse-tung as their principal ally, regard the Sino-Soviet alliance as a cornerstone in their foreign policy, and could—if Russian political or security interests were at stake—take drastic steps to ensure the preservation of Peking's loyalty and cooperation.

Communist China, in turn, is heavily dependent upon the Soviet Union for aid and support for its programs of economic, military, and scientific and technical development. In the economic sphere, the USSR has provided Communist China with the equivalent of about 2.24 billion American dollars in loans since 1950 and has underwritten over two hundred major industrial installations in China: steel mills, smelters, refineries, factories. About three-quarters of Peking's foreign trade is now with the USSR and the other Communist bloc countries. In addition to this economic and technical program, Moscow has also provided major military support for China: both the means—aircraft, high-octane aviation fuel, tanks, artillery, trucks—to modernize the Chinese Communist forces and the skills necessary to utilize these new implements of large-scale slaughter. The Communists had no air force when they gained power in 1949. Ten years later China can boast the largest, most formidable, and most modern air force in the Far East: 1,800 jet fighters and bombers, with trained personnel. And, in the realm of science and technology, Soviet assistance has been indispensable. Chinese scientists have gone to the major research centers in the Soviet Union for advanced training; others are trained in China under Soviet professors and technicians sent specifically for this purpose. By mid-1958 China's first research-type nuclear reactor, provided by the USSR, had been put into operation.

Estimates regarding the future course of relations between the two giants of the Communist bloc must be based upon the pattern of past relations between Peking and Moscow. The first decade of the Sino-Soviet alliance has been marked by three interconnected stages: first, an early period (1949-53) when Stalin was alive; second, a transition period (1953-56); third, a recent period (since 1956) during which Chinese political and psychological stature within the bloc has grown to major dimensions.

Developments in the Sino-Soviet Alliance

The rapid advance of Mao Tse-tung's armies over the mainland of China created a totally new environment for Sino-Russian relations. The basic political and security problems involved in the new phase of contacts were dealt with at an initial meeting in Moscow between Stalin and Mao Tse-tung (December 1949-February 1950). That meeting led to the conclusion of a thirty-year Sino-Soviet Treaty binding the two nations in a military alliance directed ostensibly against Japan but actually against the United States and American military power based in the Far East. Other agreements signed early in 1950 delineated the respective rights of the Russians and the Chinese in Manchuria and Sinkiang, where joint Sino-Soviet companies were established to exploit resources. And initial arrangements were concluded covering Russian financial aid to China (a modest loan—about 300 million American dollars—for the period 1950-54) and the terms of trade between the two countries.

The initial forging of the axis was well begun before the outbreak of the Korean War in mid-1950 and the Chinese intervention in October 1950. The Korean War served to test Sino-Soviet relations. The alliance provided major Soviet assistance for the modernization of the Chinese military machine and furnished an important deterrent (from the Chinese Communist standpoint) to more aggressive action on the part of the United Nations units fighting in the Korean theater. Either intentionally or accidentally, the Peking regime learned the advantages of being linked in a military alliance with a super-power at a time of major conflict. Yet many aspects of the Sino-Soviet situation during the 1950-53 period remain obscure. While the Kremlin did enter into a formal alliance with Peking and did provide major logistical support for the Chinese ground forces in Korea, Stalin nursed a lingering suspicion of his new Asian ally. The initial credit grant to China in 1950 was tiny in relation to China's total investment requirements, and Stalin was never willing to commit the USSR to firm guarantees as to the level of economic and technical aid to China prior to the formal initiation of its First Five Year Plan (January 1953). Politically, Stalin clearly regarded Mao as an inferior and was consistently skeptical of China's intention of gaining a major co-starring role within the bloc.

The death of Stalin (March 1953) had significant repercussions on the Sino-Soviet coalition as well as on Russian foreign policy tactics in other areas. The initial post-Stalin leadership in Moscow in 1953 decided that realism dictated the advisability of starting with a clean slate vis-à-vis Peking and of working toward relations which would leave no doubt as to Mao's status as the principal Soviet ally in Asia. Thus the major problems then complicating Sino-Soviet relations—policy toward the Korean conflict and the level of economic and technical aid to China—were dealt with immediately. An abrupt shift in Communist tactics in the Korean negotiations permitted the armistice agreement signed at Panmunjom (July 1953). Shortly thereafter (September), Peking announced that agreement had been reached in Moscow on Soviet economic support and that the USSR, by the end of 1959, would aid 141 large-scale enterprises in China.

The transitional stage in Sino-Soviet relations initiated after Stalin's death was marked by Russian flexibility in dealings with China and by Chinese consolidation of enhanced status within the bloc. Moscow became decreasingly preoccupied with piecemeal attempts at intrigue in Chinese internal affairs and increasingly concerned with the importance of the axis as an instrument for expanding Communist authority internationally. As evidence of this altered relationship, Moscow manifested a willingness to save Chinese face by eliminating patent sources of embarrassment (the Sino-Soviet joint stock companies and Russian troops garrisoned in Port Arthur). Moscow further mollified Chinese sensibilities by recognizing a steady rise in the hierarchic position of China within the bloc and by paying increased attention to the ideological stature of Mao Tse-tung as an original and "creative" architect of Communist revolution in Asia. And, in practical terms, the Kremlin demonstrated that the Soviet Union, the second strongest industrial nation in the world, was willing to provide more material support to China than had been given during Stalin's lifetime.

In the autumn of 1954 Chinese prestige in the bloc rose with the visit to Peking of a large Russian delegation headed by Khrushchev and Bulganin. The results of the ensuing discussions represented a further advance for the Chinese and a further integration of the alliance. The October 1954 negotiations led to joint Sino-Soviet statements emphasizing the firm alignment of the two governments and to revised economic and financial arrangements (new Russian credits and new Russian assistance to industrial installations in China). Still another increase in the level of Russian loans to China was announced in the spring of 1956 at the time of Mikoyan's trip through Asia.

Growth of Chinese Influence in the Communist Bloc

Recent developments have been marked by China's consolidation of growing political authority within the Communist bloc as a whole. The events of 1956-57 provided a tumultuous backdrop for this third stage in Sino-Soviet relations. Khrushchev's revelations at the Twentieth Congress of the Soviet Communist party (February 1956), focused on drastic treatment of the Stalin myth, had no direct political repercussions within the Chinese leadership at Peking. The initial Chinese statement (April 1956) on the desanctification of Stalin was a relatively detached review of the accomplishments and the shortcomings of the late Soviet dictator, concentrating on theoretical rather than personal issues ("On the

Historical Experience of Proletarian Dictatorship," *People's Daily*, April 5, 1956). With regard to the Chinese situation, Peking affirmed its superiority in comprehending the delicate problem of combining the "general truths of Marxism-Leninism" with "specific conditions in China" and stated that the Chinese party had committed no significant political error since Mao Tse-tung consolidated control more than two decades before.

An even more disturbing crisis arose with the unrest and anti-Soviet nationalistic outbursts in Eastern Europe in late 1956. Moscow's failure to devise a coherent theoretical interpretation of the nature of the post-Stalin Communist world, followed by increasing disunity in the European Communist ranks, presented Peking with a dialectical dilemma. The Chinese leaders reacted with caution to the developments in East-Central Europe centering especially upon Russian relations with Poland, Hungary, and Yugoslavia. Then, ponderously and with premeditated orthodoxy, Peking affirmed the obvious: the unity and stability of the "camp of socialism" must be preserved at all costs. The gravity of the crisis was reflected in a major political statement issued from Peking ("More on the Historical Experience of Proletarian Dictatorship," *People's Daily*, December 29, 1956). The Chinese call for cohesion provided a lengthy exposition, stark but authoritative, of Communist dogma as applied to contemporary world conditions. Chou En-lai flew to Eastern Europe to accent the necessity for all Communists to rally to the banner of Moscow's leadership and to support the unity of the "socialist camp led by the Soviet Union" in the face of alleged threats from the "imperialist bloc of aggression." In Moscow, Chou signed a forthright Sino-Soviet declaration (January 1957) affirming the "full agreement" of the two powers with respect to both Sino-Soviet cooperation and the general international situation.

With the launching of the first earth satellite by the Soviet Union in October 1957, the Communist bloc rushed to claim scientific superiority over the capitalist countries of the world. On his first trip outside China since 1950, Mao Tse-tung journeyed to Moscow to attend the Soviet celebrations of the fortieth anniversary of the Bolshevik revolution and to confer with other leaders of world Communism. Aware of the psychological implications of Sputnik I, Mao stressed the prowess of the Communist system in a speech to the Chinese students at Moscow University on November 18, 1957, saying that the "East Wind" was clearly prevailing over the "West Wind" in the current international competition.

Soviet missile advances, however, did not erase all existing political tensions within the Communist orbit. Since 1949, Communist China has always occupied a special position in the bloc. As its authority has grown, especially since 1953, China has found it increasingly necessary to work out positions and policies to serve two variant sets of political requirements. For domestic reasons, Peking holds a vested interest in the thesis that several "paths to socialism" are possible and permissible, asserting that the general formula for national development worked out by the USSR must be applied by Communist nations in accordance with specific local conditions and that big-nation chauvinism, particularly on the part of the Soviet Union, is both erroneous and dangerous. At the same time, Peking, for international reasons, maintains the position that a unified, integrated, and disciplined socialist camp led by the Soviet Union is as essential for the security of all Communist nations as for the cause of world peace. The political requirements of these two positions led Peking, in the spring of 1958, to launch a propaganda attack against Yugoslavia, accusing Tito of conscienceless revisionism and of straying too far from the confines of Communist orthodoxy. In the early autumn of 1958, the renewed tension over the offshore islands, Quemoy and Matsu, led to a joint communiqué, issued during an emergency meeting between Mao and Khrushchev in Peking on July 31-August 3, expressing strong Russian support for the Chinese Communist position on the Taiwan question.

Intermeshed with this recent crisis diplomacy, a new pattern of bloc activity, focused on a wide variety of practical problems, has gradually emerged. Beginning in 1958, Communist China concluded a new series of trade agreements with Poland, Hungary, Rumania, and other bloc countries. In addition to trade, the agreements covering technical assistance, scientific cooperation, joint exploration of natural resources, and railroad and river transportation have linked the nations of the bloc. In 1957, for example, Sino-Soviet plans were formulated for new hydroelectric development utilizing the waters of the Amur River on the Manchurian-Siberian border. An agreement in December 1957 on scientific cooperation between the Chinese and Soviet academies of sciences was followed by a general Sino-Soviet scientific research protocol covering the period 1958-62. A tripartite Sino-Soviet-North Korean oceanographic survey of the fishery resources of the East China Sea and the Yellow Sea was completed in 1958, and a survey of the geological resources of northern Manchuria was initiated. This increased economic and technical coordination within the bloc has been of substantial assistance to Communist China's Second Five Year Plan, which began in 1958.

These recent developments have supported the sustained though uneven growth of China's position as the second most powerful nation in the Communist world. The balance of Sino-Soviet relations has shifted significantly during the ten years between October 1949, when Stalin first accorded official recognition to the new regime in Peking, and October 1959, when Khrushchev, who had improved and strengthened Sino-Soviet relations after the death of Stalin in 1953, flew to China immediately after his return from the United States to attend the tenth National Day celebrations of the Communist regime. While recognizing Russia's formidable military and industrial capabilities as well as the developed nuclear capacities which buttressed Khrushchev's position, Mao Tsetung, however, had his independent estimates of the Sino-Soviet coalition and of the Communist commonwealth of nations. Although still definitely subordinate to the USSR, Communist China is already a major power in political influence, ideological prestige, and practical autonomy. As Mao Tse-tung is dependent upon the Soviet Union, so is Khrushchev dependent upon Communist China.

China and the USSR: Affinities and Frictions

The Sino-Soviet alliance today is rooted in a reasonably high correspondence of national interests and objectives. As indoctrinated students of Marxism-Leninism, the leaders in Moscow and Peking view the struggle with the non-Communist world as a protracted war. Both training and experience have attuned them to planning in terms of historical trends rather than of current issues, and they believe that time is on their side. Both Moscow and Peking recognize that the total stakes involved in their struggle with the West are impressively high; both feel that Sino-Soviet cooperation is more profitable than Sino-Soviet competition in attaining their long-term objectives.

The development of the coalition during the past decade has had important geopolitical results. It has turned China's face from the sea coast to its continental ramparts and the Mongolian-Russian border. The eastward movement of industrial bases in the Soviet Union has been paralleled by an emergent westward shift in the center of gravity of the economy of Communist China. The tendency of both nations to stimulate industrial production in the deep, protected interior of Asia has been supplemented by the forging of new rail links through Mongolia (opened at the beginning of 1956) and through Sinkiang (scheduled to be completed in 1960).

Already these new bonds have significantly increased mainland China's orientation toward, dependence upon, and vulnerability to the Soviet Union. These bonds will be of major significance in determining the future role of China in world politics and the future position of the Sino-Soviet alliance in the Communist competition with the West to exercise increased power on the international scene. Together, Russia and China exercise direct control over a major segment of the earth's resources: some 850 million people and a growing segment of the world's total economic productivity. Playing reinforcing roles, the two major Communist powers assume that they can maintain political—and, if necessary, military—initiative in the long-term struggle against the non-Communist world.

Strains and frictions as well as strengths have been and are apparent in the Sino-Soviet coalition. The national interests of the Soviet Union are not permanently, or even currently, identical with the national interests of China. The requirements of China's ambitious development programs may in time place a serious burden on the Soviet economic system. Specific military situations —in the Taiwan area, in Korea, in Indochina, and in Tibet—are of more direct concern to Peking than to Moscow, and divergences in estimates, plans, or operations may lead to conflicting policies. Both Russia and China have long had competitive strategic interests in the areas—Manchuria, Mongolia, and Sinkiang—which form the Sino-Mongolian-Russian frontier, the longest land frontier in Eurasia.

And, not least, the alliance must confine treacherous elements of power, prestige, and political prerogatives. The USSR is now incontestably the dominant partner, for it commands clear superiority in the crucial military and scientific sectors. If China should attain a major independent scientific breakthrough, a breakthrough which would enable Peking to initiate autonomous production of thermonuclear weapons, the present balance of power within the bloc could be radically altered. These scientific elements—theoretical and unpredictable initially but of major practical importance ultimately—are as critical within the Communist world as outside. Alteration of the present balance would have significant consequences, for traditional Marxist-Leninist theory provides no explicit definition of the political relations in a situation where two major Communist states possess more or less equal national power.

China in the Non-Western World

A large share of the foreign relations of the People's Republic of China is now centered within the Communist bloc. Yet to limit consideration of China's foreign policy to its Communist context would be to project a distorted image of a nation whose present and future interests are also involved with non-Communist areas particularly in Asia but also, by extension, with all non-Caucasian regions of the world. Russia has only one foot on the continent of Asia. Mao Tse-tung and his Chinese Communist associates stand with both feet planted solidly in Asia.

Contemporary Asia in Flux

The leaders in Peking are aware that Asia today is not the Asia of preceding decades and centuries. The recent attempt of Japan to gain military and political dominance in the Far East had repercussions more widespread, more complex, and more perverse than could have been imagined by those who framed the seductive Japanese slogan, "Asia for the Asians." Of all the powers involved in the turbulent recent history of East Asia, Japan ironically was the most effective contributor, directly, to the rise of Asian nationalism and, indirectly, to the spread of Communist influence in Asia. The military defeats suffered by the white man—at Hong Kong, at Singapore, and in the Philippines—combined with the ideological seeds sown by the Japanese propagandists of the "Greater East Asia Co-prosperity Sphere," have had long-range implications for the western powers in Asia even more significant than the actual Japanese conquests of the World War II period.

Since 1945 Asia has stirred in conscious reaction to a hundred years of western political and economic domination and of Caucasian psychological condescension. Most Asian nations are new nations, inexperienced in handling their own domestic problems, inexperienced in confronting the larger issues of foreign policy. All Asian governments are keenly nationalistic, intent upon running their own affairs independently, free of western interference. Modern nationalist aspirations have combined with ancient memories and indigenous cultural pride to inspirit the present political leaders of non-Communist Asia in their varying quests for modernization, economic development, and status in world affairs.

Surveying the rich human and material resources involved in the contemporary Asian ferment, Peking is intent that no citizen of Asia escape the implications of its dominant vision: the emergence of a strong and integrated China, under Communist leadership, as a major world power. Since 1949, Peking has made a determined effort to establish the fact that the ideological leadership of Asia is again in competent Chinese hands.

The bold image which the new regime holds of itself is buttressed by supporting cornerstones which are both practical and psychological, both Communist and Chinese. In its political propaganda, Peking lays stress upon the fact that China is the first major Asian state to embark upon a general program of radical change aimed at eliminating the backwardness of centuries, at gaining political independence, and at generating economic expansion. Far from attempting to obscure the fact that the transformation of China into an industrialized state on the Soviet pattern is an integral part of a Communist-led revolution, Peking lays special emphasis upon this very imitation.

Beneath the jargon, however, the broader theme echoes and reverberates through the crowded shops and bustling streets of Asia: a constantly reiterated emphasis on China's historic leadership. Peking is confident of China's inherent capacity to expand its influence among its Asian neighbors, many of whom have already in centuries past borne tribute to Peking.

The question of Communist China's relations with its Asian neighbors is, however, multidimensional. Mainland China, with effective mobilized national power for the first time in this century, has assumed a new role which its Asian neighbors cannot ignore. The nations on China's periphery cannot evade the geographical propinquity which may make them targets for China's ambitions, whether by political warfare, armed intimidation, or both. With realism, and perhaps a touch of fatalism, Asia knows that it is the balance in which Communist China's great power potentialities may be weighed.

The events and the political maneuvers of the past few years gain perspective when placed against this strategic background. While Communist China did expand and improve its relations with other Asian states during the 1954-57 period, its achievements in garnering genuine good will may be overemphasized. Each country of Asia has acted upon its own national motives in searching for an adjustment to the reality of the Chinese Communist system; no non-Communist nation of Asia has yet been converted to that system.

The discreet wariness of China's neighbors has been increased by the events of 1958-59: the Chinese suppression of the Tibetan uprising; border disputes between China and India; and the increased Communist pressure upon Laos. The Tibetan debacle and the flight of the Dalai Lama to India in early 1959 had perhaps greater repercussions in the West than in Asia—India excepted—for the issue of China's jurisdiction over Tibet was not disputed. Tensions created by clashes along their disputed border not only alienated the friendly relations between China and India but also caused concerns in neutralistic Asian countries, particularly in Burma and Pakistan, whose boundaries with China are still undelimited and unsettled. The situation in Laos in the autumn of 1959 presented another serious dilemma, for direct Communist inroads there would necessarily involve interference in the domestic affairs of an independent state and thus be contrary to the "Five Principles" of peaceful coexistence which Peking has regularly supported. All these elements have upset China's earlier programs directed toward the stabilization of friendly relations with other Asian governments. Yet the apparent setbacks, like the alleged earlier successes, may easily be exaggerated. The essential power situation in Asia has not altered substantially.

Japan

Modern China's enduring problem in Asia is Japan. China is bitterly cognizant of the past ambitions of Japan's military masters and of the present energies of Japan's sturdy labor force; China has been a reluctant witness to Japan's advance to the highest level of industrial and technological efficiency in Asia. From 1949 until about 1952, Peking's attitude toward Japan combined suspicion and hostility. This attitude was reflected in the 1950 Sino-Soviet Treaty, which explicitly named Japan as a potential enemy and aggressor nation, and in consistent Chinese opposition to the American military position in Japan and to the "illegal" peace treaty concluded between Japan and the United States in 1951.

After 1952 China gradually discarded the former defensive view which appraised Japan principally as its major antagonist in the Far East. Increasingly Peking appeared to regard Japan as a potential complementary power, a non-Soviet source of aid for Chinese industrialization programs. Thus it made a concerted effort to impress its island neighbor with China's resurgent role in Asia. Japanese prisoners of war, held in China since 1945, were repatriated, and Communist China expanded its efforts to establish political and economic ties with influential groups in Japan. Blocked in many practical ways by Tokyo's political alignment with the United States and frustrated by the continuation of Japanese diplomatic relations with Taiwan, Peking reverted in 1958 to a distinctly hostile attitude toward the Japanese government. Accustomed to taking the long view in foreign affairs, Peking relies on the assumption that Japan, while superficially the most westernized nation of Asia, may gradually be weaned from its predominantly western orientation and brought into closer alignment with China, its principal Asian neighbor across the Yellow Sea.

Korea and Indochina

In terms of geographical accessibility, there are two regions— Korea and Indochina—which China can threaten directly and from which it may feel threatened. In both, Communist China has been involved, directly or at one remove, in war against the West. And in both, the conflict must be measured not only in terms of the present expansive tendencies of Communism but also against the long background of assertiveness traditionally characteristic of Chinese power in East Asia. For centuries northern Korea and northern Indochina have been regions of particular Chinese concern, areas where China has never willingly tolerated the presence of any power potentially hostile to its own interests. During the Ch'ing period, Korea and Annam were the most important and intimate tributaries of the Chinese court and sent more missions to Peking than did any other tributary state. Today Peking views these areas as inner strategic zones vital to the national security of China. The agreements terminating active armed conflict in Korea (1953) and in Indochina (1954) reflect the growth of Chinese Communist influence in these borderlands. For the present, Peking has attained the interim goal of creating useful buffer zones. In the long run, China's maximum goal is to ensure the evolution of friendly governments in control of all of Korea and all of Indochina.

Southeast Asia

While Communist China's major security interests rest in the Communist bloc and in East Asia, its involvement with other areas extends throughout the non-western world. Southeast Asia inevitably appears to Chinese eyes as its long-range outer sphere of influence. In the great arc of territories extending from Burma on the west to the Philippines on the east, nearly 200 million people (including nearly 10 million Chinese) inhabit one of the world's richest and least developed areas. Here are rice, rubber, tin, copra, and petroleum. Here are the ingredients of instability: agrarian discontent, political immaturity, economic backwardness, social dislocation, intellectual restlessness. In this region, Peking has established formal diplomatic relations with three new nations (Burma, Cambodia, and Indonesia), while it has failed to gain recognition from the governments more closely aligned with the United States and the SEATO alliance (Thailand and the Philippines). With respect to the overseas Chinese in Southeast Asia, Peking has gradually evolved an assimilationist line, exhorting the Chinese there to respect the local laws and to live in harmony with the peoples of the countries in which they reside.

Areas of Long-Range Competition

Outside the Southeast Asian environment, China has shown itself keenly aware of the fact that the prime issue in international politics now and in the years ahead is the competition between the Communist and non-Communist blocs for the allegiance of the uncommitted, politically volatile millions of people in South Asia and the Middle East, in Africa, and Latin America. A primary competitor in this sphere is of course India, another new nation of post-1945 vintage which has, however, outstripped China in gaining status on its own terms with the West. Since the establishment of diplomatic relations in April 1950, Sino-Indian relations have run an irregular course, exacerbated by continuing tensions arising from Chinese occupation of Tibet (and Sino-Tibetan nationality tensions) and by political and military friction along India's northern frontier, yet alleviated by India's relatively consistent support of Communist China's desire for a recognized position in the United Nations and the other international councils of the world.

Politics and religion have been interwoven in China's policies toward the Moslem world, which stretches halfway around the earth from the Celebes to Casablanca. The Moslem nations, spread as they are across the middle latitudes of Eurasia and Africa, form a strategic zone in world politics. Over three-fifths of the 300 million believers in Islam live in Asia, and most of the remainder are in Africa, where large numbers of negroes have embraced the Moslem faith. With respect to Islam, Peking's argument is shrewd: China is not only a Communist nation but also a country containing over ten million Moslems linked in the Chinese Islamic Association (founded in 1953 with one of its explicit aims "to take an active part in the worldwide movement for peace"). Thus, Peking implies, actions which affect any portion of the Islamic world are of direct as well as indirect concern to China.

Already Communist China has made major political, economic, and propaganda investments in many Moslem areas not only in Asia (Indonesia, Pakistan, Afghanistan) but also, since about 1956, in the Middle East and Africa. Formal diplomatic ties have been established with the United Arab Republic, Iraq, Yemen, and Morocco; trade and cultural contacts have been developed with Lebanon, Jordan, and Saudi Arabia. Peking as a matter of policy has recognized the new governments established in former colonial areas in Africa (Ghana, Tunisia, Morocco, Guinea, Sudan, and the "Provisional Government of the Republic of Algeria"). Nor has Peking's watchful eye ignored the Catholic world of Latin America, for it hopes that the growth of political radicalism, economic distress, and social unrest in these areas may eventually work to Communist advantage. Thus in recent months Peking has regularly directed anti-United States propaganda at Central and South America and the Caribbean—areas still allegedly dominated by "Yankee imperialism"—and has sought the establishment of informal contacts with dissident political groups there wherever possible. The expansion of Chinese contacts with Castro's Cuba and the opening of an official Chinese Communist news agency office in Havana in the summer of 1959 are the most recent, concrete examples of Chinese Communist penetration of the western hemisphere.

In the projection of this global network of contacts, China, while consistently according highest priority to political objectives, has demonstrated a relatively high level of imagination and flexibility. Peking has laid stress upon the "common aspirations and demands" which Communist China shares with the other nations of Asia, Africa, and Latin America: "to oppose colonialism, to oppose imperialist aggression and intervention, to demand peace and oppose war, to press for independent development of the national economy and emergence from backwardness."

If the confusion of concepts inherent in this statement of "common aims" were solely theoretical and uninspired by malice, Peking's verbosity might be amusing. Yet the very correspondence of the idioms emerging from Peking and those from Washington points to acute policy dilemmas for the West. Not all the non-western political leaders concerned will comprehend what the Chinese Communists mean rather than what they say; only a minority will penetrate to the reality which underlies the verbalisms. The resulting confusion is thus practical as well as intellectual, and can only serve to further Communist purposes in the international field.

Communist China and the United States

In its strategic outlook, China is strongly influenced by its Marxist-Leninist image of the western world. It views the United States as the leading "imperialist" power and the major immediate obstacle to the attainment of its foreign policy goals. It believes that the United States, as the fulcrum of the opposing coalition of non-Communist governments, is implacably bent upon blocking the rightful international claims of the People's Republic of China. It sees the United States engaged in an unrelenting attempt to prevent China from expanding its international contacts and from gaining membership in the United Nations. And it estimates that the United States, possessed of naval and air power in the western Pacific and equipped with thermonuclear weapons, looks ultimately to the extermination of China's growing national power.

The United States, moreover, is singularly invulnerable to the varieties of military power which Communist China holds mobilized and available. Though well equipped with combat infantry troops and with the largest indigenous air force in Asia, China is not yet a world military power. It lacks the independent naval and air strength necessary to strike far afield. Nor can mainland China exert significant direct economic pressure on the United States. Despite certain strategic materials (tungsten and antimony, for example) formerly imported by the United States from China, the trade between the two nations was vital to neither. In terms of the total national economy of the United States, the American economic and financial stake in China was minor and—in contrast with British interests and investments—painlessly jettisoned in time of crisis. Also, the amount of direct political pressure which Communist China can bring to bear upon the United States is negligible. American response to the political challenge posed by Peking is more likely to be decided by the vagaries of public opinion in the United States, optimistically intent upon finding simple solutions for complex problems, than by the inherent vigor or intrinsic logic of the political propaganda disseminated by Peking.

Unable to strike directly at American power, Peking's present goal is to attempt to threaten and disrupt the political influence and military position which the United States holds among China's neighbors in the Far East. In this effort, Peking employs policy techniques which are varied, flexible, and mobile. Its political and psychological warfare weapons are well adapted for offensive operations in an Asian environment characterized by uncertainty and unrest. Its policy tools, frequently changing in nature and potency, are aimed primarily at long-range objectives, not at clear-cut, easily recognizable, short-run victories. Its program is cold war diplomacy, adjusted to the realities of a divided Asia, attuned to the tensions of the Asian environment, alert to all opportunities for utilization of its developed national power to extend Communist influence and authority.

The recrudescence of Chinese power in a fragmented and vulnerable Asia has produced a radical strategic imbalance. In the face of this shift, the American reaction—crystallized in the face of Communist aggression in Korea in 1950 and preserved consistently since—has been to act, primarily by military means, as a countervailing force to block further expansion of Chinese influence. Logically coherent, this reaction policy has been based upon specific American security interests in the western Pacific area and upon the general American desire to sustain maximum leverage against the Communist bloc. Given these operational premises, the United States has attempted to inhibit the expansion of Chinese Communist power and prestige both by direct means and by encouraging the development of non-Communist Asian nations in order to diminish China's relative power position in the region.

The incompatibility of United States and Chinese Communist security objectives in Asia is clear. In practical terms, however, Washington has encountered continuous difficulties in defining this general incompatibility in precise geographic terms and in specific and effective military, political, economic, and diplomatic policies. On the premise that the Peking regime is compulsively aggressive, Washington has attempted both to secure a host of isolated positions—military bases, sources of strategic raw materials, trade routes and trading interests—and to bolster uncertain allies and waning western prestige. Yet American policies have not been based upon any conceptual redefinition of the nature of American strategic interests in Asia in the face of the substantial, albeit sometimes elusive, challenge posed by Chinese Communist power.

The Taiwan Dilemma

The most critical and contentious issue involved in the Sino-American competition for influence and authority in Asia is Taiwan. Anchored ninety miles off the coast of Fukien, the island of Taiwan is the present base of Nationalist China, the seat of the refugee government of the Republic of China at Taipei. Peking's foreign policy assumes that Taiwan is indisputably part of China and should logically belong to Communist China. Taipei's foreign policy assumes that the mainland of China is indisputably part of China and should logically belong to Nationalist China. No two goals could be more mutually exclusive, and there is slight prospect of evolving a solution, or even a palliative, which would be either pleasing or persuasive to the Chinese parties directly concerned.

The existence of Taiwan serves to reinforce, not to alter, the long-term strategic outlook of Chinese Communist foreign policy. Both practically and theoretically, Communist China and the United States are in total opposition on the issue of Taiwan. Paradoxically, this opposition is based upon the existence of similar assumptions in both Washington and Peking with respect to the Chinese Nationalist regime. Both view it as a Chinese government on Chinese soil, once removed, possessed of a Chinese leader, a Chinese flag, and Chinese military forces. Neither denies (although Peking regrets) the fact that it is a Chinese government with recognized international status (roughly two-thirds of the Chinese diplomatic establishments outside the Communist bloc are in countries which maintain formal relations with the Republic of China) and a place in the United Nations (in all United Nations forums, the representatives of Taipei rather than those of Peking speak for China). And, finally, neither Peking nor Washington denies that, as a non-Communist Chinese government, Taiwan stands as an existing and operating alternative to the Communist government on the mainland.

The political reality of Taiwan is an unquestioned fact; the political conclusions drawn from that reality are totally at variance. Peking necessarily views Taiwan with distaste and antagonism, while Washington views it with approval. Each government (as well as all Communist and non-Communist Chinese) regards Taiwan as a Chinese domestic issue, with international implications. Most of the rest of non-Communist Asia, as indeed most of the rest of the world, is interested in Taiwan only to the extent that it may give rise to international conflict and regards its continued survival as an American problem.

So far as the United States is concerned, the continued existence of two totally antagonistic Chinese regimes in the Far East has created a corollary policy dilemma. Each Chinese regime refuses to tolerate actions by non-Chinese parties which might, either in fact or in implication, grant approval or acquiescence to the claims of its opponent. The Chinese themselves are thus the most steadfast opponents of any formal international recognition of the present *de facto* situation in Asia. Both Peking and Taipei are in complete accord on one central point: that it is necessary to prevent any third party, particularly the United States, from accepting the reality of two Chinas. Since 1949, American policy with regard to China has thus been confined within limits set by the interests of the Chinese, not by those of the United States. And American policymakers have tacitly accepted the total terms prescribed by each of the two Chinese regimes, Communist and non-Communist, that the United States support it alone.

Prospects

Zealous, ruthless, resilient—Chinese Communism has reshaped the political, social, and economic contours of the most populous nation in the world. The People's Republic of China has already stabilized its position and consolidated its power in the Far East. This eruption of reorganized and revitalized Chinese power has fundamentally altered both the immediate environment of Far Eastern politics and the broader design of world politics.

Mao Tse-tung and the Chinese Communist leaders in Peking possess power, patience, and persistence. Internally, the Chinese Communist elite has, during the past twenty years, demonstrated a far higher level of cohesion, discipline, and stability than the Communist party of the Soviet Union or any other major Communist party. Internationally, the Chinese leadership has shown a shrewd awareness of the fact that there are now far more non-Slavs than Slavs under Communist rule. Peking is dedicated to the establishment of Communist China as a major power on its own terms and is destined to pose a formidable, multipronged challenge to the West throughout Asia and the rest of the world during the years ahead.

BASIC FEATURES OF THE ECONOMY

UNTIL THE END OF THE NINETEENTH CENTURY the Chinese economy was dominated by agricultural production and remained essentially static. The periodic recurrence of natural disasters and the cumulative effect of the rapid population growth in the eighteenth and nineteenth centuries had more than balanced any increases in agricultural production. In addition, there was little incentive for, and considerable cultural resistance against, any economic innovations. The merchant class, moreover, was held in such low esteem that the driving force of entrepreneurship that might have come from this sector was almost wholly missing from the Chinese scene.

The beginnings of modern industrialism were due to continuous contact with foreign investors and the introduction of foreign trade on an increasing scale in the early twentieth century, but the main current of Chinese economic life was only slightly affected by these influences at first. Although a few government leaders were eager to establish some modern industries to increase China's military power, cultural resistance to innovation persisted. A native entrepreneurial class slowly emerged; the rate of capital accumulation, however, remained very low. Most of such savings as were garnered every year could not be efficiently mobilized for lack of technological competence and managerial efficiency. The absence of a protective tariff put many infant native industries at a disadvantage in the face of foreign competition, and both domestic and foreign trade were subject to fluctuations caused by the country's weak international monetary position.

Superimposed on the economic factors was the political instability of the times. The strife of the warlord period, the continual civil war between the Nationalist government and the Communists, and the invasion of China by Japan had either so weakened or so preoccupied the national administration that it failed to exercise leadership in promoting economic progress. The problem of rural overpopulation remained crucial and agitation for a redistribution of income and wealth mounted with the growth of the Communist movement.

Economically, the Sino-Japanese War (1937-1945) stimulated industrial development to a certain extent, especially in areas hitherto unaffected by modern industrialization. Some areas under Japanese occupation were also developed. But the financial and banking structure of Free China and the fiscal administration of the Nationalist government were inadequate to cope with the problems of war finance or to check inflation, and the production bottlenecks which soon emerged in the underdeveloped economy of the hinterland rendered inflation even more acute. Thus although China survived the war as a national state, with increased potential for economic development, a pattern of orderly growth had no opportunity to develop. When the Nationalist government failed to halt inflation and was unable to defeat the Communists by force of arms, the impending economic crisis combined with political tension to create the conditions for a successful revolution by the Communists.

Relatively uninhibited by considerations of existing interests and institutions, the new regime was able to establish certain preliminary conditions for economic development. Ruthless and single-minded, without regard for individual freedom, it accelerated industrial development and made drastic agricultural reforms. Although some policies were designed not so much to promote economic growth as to consolidate the power of the regime, the Communists have succeeded in reactivating the growth process and establishing a high rate of investment through stringent control of consumption and radical institutional change. They have also channeled development in specific directions by socializing production and increasing self-sufficiency to the degree concomitant with economic expansion.

The Communist government's initial economic task, to curb inflation and rehabilitate production, called for monetary and fiscal reforms which it effected by a combination of normal economic methods and political coercion. It was also necessary to rehabilitate the transportation system in order to facilitate the flow of goods and materials; to stimulate industrial production through government assistance to private firms; to adopt at the outset a generally moderate attitude toward private business; and to encourage agricultural production through flood control, irrigation, land reclamation, and other similar measures.

The second task was to tighten economic control: monetary measures aimed at curbing inflation were accompanied by the compulsory amalgamation of commercial banks and their subsequent absorption into the government banking system. A revamping of the tax structure served to sap the financial strength of the remaining capitalists and the expansion of the state sector of the economy increased government revenue from state enterprises. Domestic commerce was promoted through encouragement of large-scale mergers of trading concerns, organization of marketing cooperatives, participation in commerce by government trading agencies, and monopolization of selected areas of trade by the state. Once industrial production had partially recovered, private concerns were swiftly merged into joint state-private concerns or completely absorbed by state industry. A land reform movement which placated the poorer peasants and consolidated the Communist party's political control of rural areas was soon followed by a program of collectivization and later by the establishment of communes. In both cases larger production units made agricultural production more amenable to government direction. Modes of economic control were thus continually sharpened and modified in order to meet the exigencies of the changing economic scene.

The third economic task was, and still is, to increase the rate of investment as against consumption and to concentrate on the development of heavy industry, objectives which can best be achieved by a sharp rise in productivity. Since the immediate prospect of mechanization and advanced technology is limited, such increases must depend upon the intensified use of labor in both industry and agriculture. Communist-controlled labor unions have been used in the continual drives for greater production, and these drives have been supplemented by laws making strikes as well as sabotage offenses against the state. At the same time, it has been necessary to curb consumption since, barring a sudden increase in the national product, investment can be increased only as consumption is restrained. This accounts for the introduction of rationing to conserve domestic supplies and increase the ability to import capital goods, the employment of forced savings to forestall any potential excess of consumption expenditure, and the regulation of individual investment projects so as to determine the rate of growth of the capital goods industry as against the consumer goods industry.

Practically all economic developments during the past years may be viewed in the light of the three foregoing economic tasks, as interpreted by the Communists. Broadly speaking, there have been two periods of development, which overlap one another in some areas. From 1949 to 1952 the Chinese Communists were primarily concerned with the rehabilitation of production and the establishment of certain modes of control. During the period of the First Five Year Plan (1953-57) they maintained and strengthened the machinery and methods of control and experimentally established a rate of economic growth that promised to generate sufficient momentum for further economic expansion. A new phase of development, which began in 1958 with the inauguration of the commune movement and a massive attempt to establish numerous small-scale industrial production units, will test the success of Communist economic policies in the immediate future.

It is estimated that from 1950 to the end of the First Five Year Plan, China's gross national product rose 86 percent on the basis of 1952 prices. The annual rate of increase was 9.3 percent for the entire seven-year period (1950-57) or about 7 percent for 1953-57. This substantial growth was made possible through the full utilization of existing capital resources and the maintenance of a high rate of gross investment approximating 20 percent of the gross national product toward the end of the First Five Year Plan. Along with this rise in national income, industrial output in general and producer goods in particular have increased considerably. The aggregate agricultural output and yield per acre have also gone up although the expansion in the agricultural sector has lagged behind that of industry. The process of socialization is now virtually complete as regards large-scale enterprises, including transportation, banking, industry, and commerce. A number of new industries and new industrial regions have been developed. The volume of China's external trade shows a sizable increase and the degree of self-sufficiency in many items, including capital and producer goods, has risen accordingly. Even if the Communist regime should be overthrown, the structure and character of the Chinese economy would bear the permanent imprint of Communist policy. All this has been accomplished at the expense of the individual, who is now completely under the control of the administrative and party machinery both as consumer and producer.

There is little doubt that the Communists have generated a dynamism in the economic field which may propel the Chinese economy to sustained growth. Their considerable success in this respect, however, should not obscure the fact that much of it was accomplished by ruthless disregard for established values and institutions, and that some apparent economic dangers still exist or have been newly created. Among these are the upsurge in the rate of population growth which may more than offset the benefits of economic expansion; a possible decline in initiative and the spirit of innovation caused by too much hard work and too strict regulation; increasing resistance to the commune movement and the abolition of private ownership which may indirectly stall the expansion of industry; and growing popular impatience with unfulfilled promises for more consumer goods.

The introduction of radical measures designed to bring about continuous expansion after the end of the First Five Year Plan was to some extent a policy of desperation, lest the rate of investment and economic growth falter. There is always the danger of suppressed inflation becoming open inflation should the machinery of monetary control fail to function properly, as well as the danger of internal dissension and corruption, the existence of which is testified to by recurrent purges and rectification campaigns. Thus the fissures and weaknesses in the Chinese economy are no less real than its strengths.

The present state of the Chinese economy bears no comparison with that of the more advanced western countries: in spite of large advances made during the last decade, China is still far behind in gross national product and per capita output. The challenge, therefore, lies in developing the potential rate of growth. That this potential is great was clearly demonstrated in the achievements of the First Five Year Plan.

14

ORGANIZATION AND USE
OF MANPOWER

THE RATE OF CHINESE ECONOMIC DEVELOPMENT depends very largely
on the skill with which the country's vast labor resource can be
utilized to compensate for the scarcity of other components of production. Communist labor policy reflects an acute awareness of
this fact and measures designed to increase production by more
efficient utilization of the labor force are coupled with measures
to control wage levels and consumption as far as possible without
jeopardizing workers' incentive. Such matters as wages, working
conditions, unemployment insurance, welfare provisions, and so
forth have been relegated to the background except insofar as
they serve to stimulate production or support the claim that the
Communists are the friends of the working man.

Output can be increased by employing the unemployed and
underemployed, by reducing the leisure of those already working,
and by raising productivity on the job. The practice of using large
contingents of corvée labor on water conservation and similar labor-
intensive projects was introduced early in the Communist regime
and served to absorb many unemployed. Corvée labor was recruited
largely from among the peasants, but another important addition
to the work force came from the demobilized soldiers and so-called
counterrevolutionaries who were herded into labor camps and
prisons. The more recent commune movement has increased the
number of women working outside the home—since the home in its
traditional form no longer exists—and helped to break down the
barrier that had existed between industrial and agricultural labor.

In addition to increasing the size of the industrial labor force,
greater output can be achieved by demanding more effort on the
part of those already employed and by improving their skills. These

objectives are discernible in the emphasis on labor training, the continual adjustment upward of production quotas, the "proper management" of labor, and the use of labor unions as a channel of political control and a means for obtaining greater participation in production drives by the rank and file. Combined with propaganda to spur the working masses to greater effort has been the threat of punishment for nonfulfillment and "lax labor discipline."

The Growth of the Nonagricultural Labor Force

Prior to the twentieth century, China's industrial labor force was practically negligible. Traditional agricultural methods required enormous amounts of labor during the peak periods at planting and harvest time, permitting only the seasonal pursuit of other occupations. The farmer and his family used their spare time—about two months a year—to make articles for their daily needs and for sale to others in the community. Although for the great majority of farm families the sale of home industry products continued to be confined to the local market, growing demand for certain items encouraged the migration of many better craftsmen to the urban centers where, in their small workshops and retail stores, they could take advantage of foreign as well as national markets. This activity led to the formation of craft guilds in most urban areas and within these guild organizations journeymen learned from masters such trades as silk weaving, furniture making, and dyeing. In 1930 an estimated seven million full-time and seasonal handicraft workers were making articles for the export market alone.

Light industry evolved out of this handicraft tradition and, following the example of foreign factory owners, native industrialists began to employ Chinese laborers in cotton and flour mills, sugar refineries, and cigarette and match factories. The nucleus of China's twentieth-century factory labor force was formed in this manner.

The impressive recent growth of the industrial work force is in sharp contrast to the almost static character of the Chinese labor force of the 1930's. Various interpretations of the term "factory worker" in the statistics cause apparent conflicts, but a conservative report in 1934 of a total 521,175 factory workers is probably closest to the true figure. There was some increase in the number of modern industrial workers during the Sino-Japanese War (1937-45) and the inclusion after the war of about three hundred thousand miners and one hundred thousand factory workers in Manchuria further increased the total.

By the end of March 1950, five months after the establishment of the present Communist regime, there was a total 8,397,243 workers and salaried employees. Of these, 4,721,764 were distributed in the following trades:

Trade or Occupation	Number of Workers
Food	1,062,968
Merchant shipping	700,000
Sales force	627,300
Transportation other than railroads	568,548
Textiles	469,085
Metalware	411,340
Railroads	410,519
Collieries	335,268
Post and telecommunications	104,773
Electric power (Northeast and North China only)	31,963
Total	4,721,764

As the Communist economic program hit its stride the industrial work force expanded rapidly. By the end of 1957 the number of workers registered in trade unions had reportedly reached 16.3 million, a figure which does not necessarily represent the total number eligible for union membership. In addition, official sources reported a total of eight million handicraft workers who had been organized into craft cooperatives to replace the traditional guilds. If members of cooperatives engaged in fishing, salt processing, transportation, and the service trades are added, as well as those members of the cooperatives who spent only part time in agricultural work, the total in these occupations may be estimated at around twenty million. Public functionaries (excluding employees in government-owned factories, the armed forces, and police), professional people (excluding teachers), and other similar groups added another ten million. Thus in 1957 the entire nonagricultural labor force was somewhere around fifty-five million people.

Employment

Recruitment of industrial labor is undertaken directly by the enterprises concerned, frequently through employment exchanges. This method has replaced the former contract system under which each labor contractor received a portion of the worker's wages and was in turn responsible for the welfare of the worker and his family throughout the contract period.

A wave of unemployment arose immediately after the Communist conquest when a great number of factories and stores were compelled to shut down. On May 18, 1950 the Ministry of Labor issued the "General Rules on the Organization of City Labor Employment Offices" and the "Rules of the Registration and Recommendation for Employment of Unemployed Technical Employees and Workers," under which the labor bureaus of the cities were given the responsibility of registering the unemployed under their respective jurisdictions and recommending employment in factories and plants. As there was a general shortage of technicians and skilled labor, their placement caused little difficulty, but the great majority of the unemployed were untrained and unskilled and their assignment to factory jobs without regard to past experience proved extremely inefficient and caused many complaints. The problem of unemployment continued to engross the attention of the Communist regime for several years and regulations were passed forbidding factories and stores to discharge workers without government permission.

A re-employment program was set up to divert actual and surplus farm labor into handicrafts, food processing, afforestation, fishery, road construction, flood prevention, and similar projects; new frontier settlements provided an outlet for the unemployed and relieved population pressure in urban centers and thickly settled farming areas; and jobless intellectuals were re-educated in new techniques for work in such fields as health, commerce, and cooperative management.

Professional and intellectual groups have faced maldistribution of job assignments. Government authorities admitted the arbitrary assignment of college graduates to factories, business enterprises, and government offices, and newspaper reports emphasized the "irrational" employment of badly needed qualified technical personnel, publishing letters of complaint from individuals and institutions.

The employment situation, however, improved with the accelerated economic development of more recent years. By 1958 the efforts to increase agricultural and industrial production had reversed the situation, causing labor shortages in many rural areas, especially during the planting and harvesting seasons. A campaign was undertaken to relieve these shortages through the improvement of tools and technical processes, more efficient organization of the work force, and encouragement of workers to learn more skills.

Training and Scarcity of Skilled Labor

Before 1950 skilled factory workers and miners constituted only a small fraction of the entire labor force because foreign entrepreneurs —who owned more than half the textile industry in China and a large number of factories, mines, and shipping lines—ordinarily engaged foreign engineers and technicians, using Chinese labor largely for unskilled jobs. The scarcity of skilled workers became evident when foreign engineers and technicians, as well as a sizable number of the more skilled Chinese, withdrew from the mainland after the Communist conquest in 1949. The proportion of trained technicians in the iron and steel industry in the spring of 1950, for instance, was only 0.71 percent. East China had the highest percentage, 4.6; and Northeast China, the center of the steel industry, only 0.2 percent.

Workers were trained on the job to fill this tremendous need and the few existing skilled workers were spread among the new industrial centers. For example, about ten thousand skilled workers were moved from Shanghai to Sian, the capital of Shensi and textile center of Northwest China. In the past few years, a total of seventy thousand workers, engineers, technical personnel, and business administrators have left Shanghai for various remote regions. In September 1955 the Shanghai municipal government provided technical training for drivers for service in Sinkiang. Engineers and skilled workers were sent to the automobile and tractor factories, to steel mills and other metallurgical plants, and to oil refineries in the Northwest.

Industrial labor is trained according to two general systems: recruitment training and supplementary training. Recruitment training is intended to teach the basic techniques and skills needed on the production line. Supplementary training is given to improve the worker's efficiency and productivity. In some factories workers are trained by Soviet and East European technicians to handle machinery and tools imported from those countries. The age-old apprenticeship system, however, still prevails in all industries. Apprentices are recruited by management and assigned to technicians for necessary training.

According to the First Five Year Plan, nearly one million workers under the jurisdiction of the following ministries were to be trained:

Ministry	Number of Workers
Heavy Industry	176,800
Fuel Industry	172,000
Machine Building	174,100
Textile Industry	55,400
Light Industry	22,900
Geology	11,800
Building Industry	39,800
Agriculture	21,500
Forestry	33,000
Railways	158,800
Communications	19,800
Post and Telecommunications	19,900
Labor	14,500
Total	920,300

The plan called for the establishment, by the end of 1957, of 140 technical training schools for workers in the various sectors of industry listed above, as compared with 22 such schools in 1952. Moreover, 362,000 skilled workers were to be trained through the technical training classes in the various industrial enterprises, in addition to 43,900 to be trained by the apprenticeship system.

Skilled workers, trained technicians, and college graduates are encouraged to apply for jobs in underdeveloped areas and graduates from schools in Shanghai, Nanking, Foochow, Port Arthur, and Dairen have "volunteered" and been transferred to the Northwest by the hundreds. But work assignments and ultimate destinations are entirely in the hands of government authorities and it is unlikely that many except young adventurous workers with patriotic drive are genuine volunteers. The majority of skilled laborers are undoubtedly forced to go, largely through pressures exerted by party activists. A number of such emigrants have reportedly given up their jobs and returned home, even though this puts them in a highly precarious position since the government will not employ them and few private firms remain.

Another method employed by Communist authorities to increase the work force in frontier areas is to order the release of a certain number of workers by factories in Shanghai for work in Northeast and Northwest China. Some factories have refused, alleging that they cannot achieve their fixed production targets without their full staff. Other factories supply their quotas by selecting the least competent workers. Certain Shanghai factories have trained a minimum of new apprentices, hoping thus to forestall attempts to remove their skilled workers.

Labor Productivity

Official Communist reports claim a 55 percent increase in labor productivity between 1952 and 1957, although uncertainty regarding the manner in which this productivity is measured makes it difficult to determine the true significance of the figure relative to productivity in other countries. There is no question that productivity has been increased during the Communist regime, but the Chinese worker is still far from achieving parity with the skilled worker in more industrialized nations. In the past China's industry has suffered from the extremely low productivity of factory workers and miners, said to be only 6.5 percent of that of their American counterparts. An important contributing factor was the low degree of mechanization; many mines, for example, had no mechanical equipment at all. In addition, low wages and resultant poor health meant low morale, and modern technical training was inaccessible to the illiterate working people who constituted a large percentage of China's labor force. Low individual productivity was aggravated in many instances by poor management.

The Communist government has directed much effort toward the elimination of illiteracy and the increase of production, organizing literacy classes in all industrial plants and factories and supplementing these with mass propaganda campaigns to increase technical competence and promote scientific and technical studies among the workers.

Labor organizations play a key role in implementing production drives, and especially the ubiquitous campaigns known as "labor emulation." Such drives, copied from the Stakhanovite movement in Russia, utilize "model workers" to spur production by surpassing normal production quotas and by engaging in "socialist competition" in "advanced methods of work," the latter phrase being used to cover plain speed-up as well as improved techniques. Model workers are rewarded by extra privileges and emoluments as well as by organized public acclaim. For example, in May 1954 some 250 workers in Shanghai were awarded medals for their achievements at a conference held in their honor. Stakhanovite techniques, introduced into China in the early 1940's in the Communist-controlled Shensi-Kansu-Ningsia border region, had spread by 1950 throughout the country. Three years later about 80 percent of the working population had been forced to participate in drives of this type. Speaking at the Seventh National Labor Congress, Lai Jo-yü (Chairman, Executive Committee of the All-China Federation of Trade Unions) said, "The fundamental method for developing production is to lead the masses to take part in labor emulation . . . an effective way of mobilizing the broad masses to achieve the targets of the state plan."

During the initial phases of a labor emulation drive production generally increases, but accidents also increase as a result of strenuous work. According to an official announcement issued on September 16, 1953, trade unions in state-operated enterprises were guilty of increasing production at the cost of labor safety.

Exhaustion, carelessness, and passive resistance to longer working hours have resulted also in more sick leave. In July 1952 one-fourth of the workers of the Number Six Iron and Steel Works in Shanghai asked for leave because of illness after an intensive labor emulation drive. At a cotton textile factory in Tsingtao, during the first six months of 1952 more than one-half of the women workers who were pregnant suffered miscarriages. Many accounts of industrial accidents were to be found in newspapers in Central-South China during the second half of 1953 and the first half of 1954 when frantic efforts were made to fulfill lagging schedules.

Wages, Working Conditions, Welfare Measures

Wages and hours, housing, insurance, safety, and health and welfare measures are in general the same as or better than before 1949. Following Soviet practice, the Communist regime, while mobilizing, mechanizing, and motivating the work force, is simultaneously trying to hold back the expectations of the workers to prevent dissatisfaction with such material rewards as are available for the present. Relying mainly on social or prestige awards to maintain morale, the Communists stress the "ideology and dignity of the working man" and hope modest gains will, for a time, satisfy the worker who has been inured by decades of experience to long hours, poor food, substandard living conditions, thickly patched clothing, and a hopeless future.

In the pre-Communist period the working day in most private industries varied from 8 to 15 hours; the outstanding exception was the uniform 8-hour day of government-owned or operated industries. At present the 8-hour day has become the nominal standard in large factories throughout the country, the only important variations occurring in local handicraft industries and some joint state-private enterprises. The standard tends to be ignored, however, in the heat of the virtually continuous emulation drives, and complaints are heard that the leadership destroys the enthusiasm of the workers by increasing shifts and working hours at random. Until the introduction of the shorter work day in the construction industry in July 1956, hundreds of workers were reported to have actually walked off the job in North China in protest over mistreatment by management.

Wage levels were low in pre-Communist China although higher for industrial workers than for agricultural and handicraft workers or coolies. Piece rates were prevalent in certain government construction projects and government-owned enterprises, but wages were most commonly paid on a time basis.

During the first years of Communist rule wages were calculated in terms of rice and millet. For example, in Peking in 1949 the privately owned Yung-feng Chemical Works graded the workers according to their skills: in the first group each worker received 5.5 catties (about 6 lbs.) of rice per day; in the second group, 5 catties (about 5.5 lbs.); and in the third group, 4 catties (about 4.4 lbs.). In Tientsin each transportation worker earned almost 15 catties (about 16.5 lbs.) of rice per day. Continuing postwar inflation, however, led to payment of wages on such alternative bases as "commodity-equivalent" units, rice and flour, or cash.

The wage-unit system, or payment according to "commodity-equivalent" units, adopted at the end of 1951, was based on the price of specified commodities. The monetary value of one wage unit, announced daily by the local government, was equal to the sum of the prices in government stores of a list of necessary commodities which in addition to rice, millet, and flour, included vegetable oil, salt, cotton cloth, and coal.

An elaboration of the wage-unit system in 1952 which placed all workers in one of eight different grades according to their relative skills was accompanied by a gradual extension of piece rates to all sectors of the economy. Whereas at the end of 1951 only 43.5 percent of all industrial workers in Northeast China were on piecework, from 1956 until recently piecework was prevalent in all eight grades of workers throughout the country.

Wage rates under piecework were tied to productivity in each enterprise but were changed from time to time to control purchasing power and the danger of inflation. Base rates varied for the same grade of worker according to the industry in which he was employed, all industry having been divided into groups with different base rate scales. In diminishing order of pay scales the groups were: (1) coal mining, the metallurgical industry, mining of nonferrous metals; (2) electric utilities; (3) heavy machine manufacturing, manufacture of arms, and the heavy chemical industry; (4) machine repair and the manufacture of machine parts; (5) cotton textile industry; (6) industries manufacturing paper, rubber products, leather goods, oils, and fats, and the printing industry; (7) food processing and the clothing industry; and (8) match manufacturing and the tobacco industry. Within each industrial group the individual enterprises were again divided into five subgroups, each with its own pay scale. Differentials were also maintained within each enterprise between supervisory, technical, and managerial personnel on the one hand and ordinary workers on the other.

There is also the variation from one region to another. On the whole wages are highest in Northeast and East China, especially around the Shanghai area, and somewhat lower in North and Central-South China; the lowest wage levels are reported in Southwest and Northwest China. Lack of detailed wage statistics makes it difficult to arrive at accurate estimates of the current wage levels in different regions.

The advantages of piece rates were soon apparent. Government enterprises of the Central-South provinces reported that production per man-hour increased following the adoption of piece rates. Job reclassification enabled management to retain those workers who were most essential to uninterrupted and efficient operation. The higher pay scale for certain enterprises had a similar effect in guaranteeing a steady labor supply for industries with the highest priority. Finally, the higher differentials between successive pay grades helped to reduce labor turnover as workers could now increase their income appreciably by moving up within the same enterprise instead of changing employers.

But the piece-rate system also created a higher wage bill. In April 1956 a nationwide wage reform raised the average worker's wage rate approximately 13 percent from that of 1955, making a cumulative wage increase of 40 percent for the 1953-57 period instead of the 33 percent envisaged by the First Five Year Plan.

The higher wage was deemed undesirable for several reasons. First, the increase occurred at a time when there was a concerted drive to increase industrial production and hence industrial employment, resulting in a large increase in total wages. At the same time a rise in piece rates tended to increase wage differentials both between workers receiving an hourly wage and those on piece rates and between industrial and nonindustrial workers. The latter aspect of the problem was dealt with toward the end of 1957 when the Ministry of Labor ordered a sharp reduction in the wage rates of the ordinary industrial worker to bring them closer to the pay of an average peasant in a medium-sized agricultural cooperative. More recently an attempt has been made to narrow as well the industrial wage differentials between grades of workers on the ground that large wage differentials tend to foster the growth of a capitalist mentality if not a capitalist class; that payment for special skills amounts to a return on an investment in training which the state has in most cases made possible; and that skilled labor cannot perform efficiently without the cooperation of the unskilled worker.

Since the disadvantages of the piece-rate system are not new, recent government objections to piecework may be prompted by general policy considerations. The crux of the problem is that the authorities do not wish to see the expected increment in output since 1958 absorbed by consumption. As work quotas cannot be revised upward rapidly enough or on a broad enough basis, abandonment of piece rates may have been the only practical alternative. This is coupled with a general hold-the-line policy on welfare benefits.

In the communes, where the demarcation between agricultural and nonagricultural labor has become rather blurred, the system of payment according to the amount of work done, which was used by the cooperative farms, has been replaced at least temporarily by a combination of the "supply system" and supplementary wage payments. The so-called supply system consists of food rations while the wage payments are essentially a little pocket money. In the Wei-hsing commune in Honan, for instance, the total annual per capita income (including the grain ration) of the peasant amounts to 57.6 yuan (about 23.4 American dollars) or only a little more than 4 yuan a month. But the need for an adequate incentive system may again bring about the restoration of at least a modified form of piece rates.

In considering the compensation of the Chinese worker for long hours of work and strict regimentation, it should be remembered that his income is subject to many deductions such as union fees, "voluntary" contributions, and forced purchases of government bonds. When the Communist government issued the 1950 Victory Bond Series, workers were urged to buy as many units as they could afford. The purchase of even one unit (about 50 to 60 cents in American money) was a big deduction from the worker's small income. After the Chinese Communists entered the Korean War, workers were urged to make voluntary contributions; within three months of 1951, workers in the city of Chungking alone contributed 1.3 million yuan (equivalent to approximately 528,000 American dollars).

The government has reported an increase in workers' bank savings throughout the country, but this does not necessarily indicate surplus spending power for the people. Beginning in 1952 the Chinese Communists instituted compulsory savings of 25 to 30 percent of each worker's income to prevent possible inflation and to accumulate capital for national construction. After deducting compulsory savings and contributions, a worker is not likely to have money for anything other than daily living needs.

The housing situation has become since 1949 increasingly serious for industrial workers in urban centers as well as for workers at the many new factories and mines in previously underdeveloped areas. A construction spurt began in 1952 with the expenditure of 286 million yuan (about 116 million American dollars) for workers' dwellings. Between 1952 and 1956 government housing developments totaled about 795 million square feet. In addition, unions and enterprises aided individual workers in constructing 27 million square feet of housing space in 1956 alone. The resultant housing is cheap and impermanent but far better than anything most industrial workers have ever known.

Under the Labor Insurance Law of 1951 over nine million workers throughout the country were provided by the first half of 1957 with insurance against death, old age, illness, and disability. At first the law applied only to enterprises employing more than one hundred workers, but after its revision in January 1953 insurance was provided for smaller groups as well. Workers' hospitals, sanatoriums, rest homes, and crèches also were established under this law.

Since 1950 most enterprises employing more than three hundred workers have established free medical clinics. Shanghai has become the showcase for labor welfare: the number of sanatoriums and rest homes sponsored by national and local unions there has reached 1,460, with a capacity of over 60,000 beds.

In view of the relatively small number of factories and mines in China before 1950, the industrial accident figures for a representative year (1935) of about three thousand dead and nearly five thousand injured are appalling. The present regime has campaigned for proper safeguards but these are often ignored under the pressure of meeting production quotas. Protective devices have reportedly been installed on dangerous machinery; proper ventilation, temperature reduction, and heat prevention measures have been provided in 93 percent of the shafts of state-owned coal mines and in the majority of nonferrous metal mines. Though absolute figures are not given, it is claimed that accidents in factories and mines have been reduced year after year, the death rate from accidents in 1954 being 16 percent less than that of 1953, and 5 percent less in 1955 than in 1954. During production drives, however, hazards increase sharply. The combined total for thirteen key categories of industrial, capital construction, communications, and transport workers showed an increase of 3 percent in the death rate from accidents in the wake of the speed-up to overfulfill the First Five Year Plan.

So far the major safety efforts have been directed toward educating the worker. In some occupations a "health protection system" has been introduced: a health monitor is appointed in the construction materials industry, for example, to keep a running check on silica poisoning and its prevention. According to government reports, from 1953 to 1956 a total of 290 million yuan (about 118 million American dollars) was expended on factory safety measures.

Labor-Management Relations

Increased production at lower cost is the common goal set by the Communist government for both labor and management. Labor disputes are not allowed to develop into strikes, sabotage, or lockouts that would disrupt production. All labor disputes in state-owned or privately owned enterprises are, in theory, resolved in accordance with the interests of both labor and management.

The first step toward settling a labor dispute is consultation between the trade union and the owner (in the case of any remaining privately owned enterprises) or the management (in the case of state-owned enterprises). If consultation fails the dispute may be brought to a labor bureau for mediation or arbitration. Labor bureaus are established at all levels of local government and each has a permanent committee for arbitration. In June 1950 the Ministry of Labor issued the "Organization and Working Rules of City Labor Dispute Arbitration Committees," directing that each committee be made up of the commissioner or deputy commissioner of the labor bureau and one representative each from the city federation of labor unions, the city bureau in charge of industry and commerce, and the industrial and commercial association. In actual arbitration work, additional members may be appointed temporarily. If the arbitration award is unacceptable to one or both parties, the latter may, within five days after the award is made, request that the case be transferred to a people's court. The resultant collective agreement serves the function, however, of a pledge on the part of both labor and management to fulfill a certain production plan set by the government and must include the following clauses: (1) a procedure for hiring and discharging workers; (2) a procedure for adopting factory and workshop regulations; (3) wages; (4) working time, leaves of absence, and holidays; (5) provisions for women and juvenile workers; and (6) provisions for labor protection (probably referring to factory sanitation and safety) and labor welfare.

The stipulations of the "Outline of Labor Regulations for State-owned Enterprises" issued in July 1954 may have superseded the operations of collective agreements to some extent. The outline provides that the management of each state enterprise should draw up a set of general labor regulations, with the advice of the labor union, to be operative upon the approval of the Ministry of Labor. In a similar manner the management of each local unit is to adopt its own labor regulations, on the basis of the general labor regulations and in consultation with the local labor union, submitting them to the local labor bureau for approval. These regulations provide in detail the duties and obligations of the workers, penalties to insure enforcement, and employment procedures.

Labor's participation in factory management is provided for through an administrative or management committee in each of the state-owned factories in addition to a workers' representative conference.

In privately owned enterprises, on the other hand, the Communist regime had until recently tended to de-emphasize the role of labor in factory management. In the "Directive Concerning the

Establishment of Labor-Capital Consultative Councils" issued in April 1950, compulsory for all private factories and shops employing more than fifty persons, the consultative councils to be set up were expressly prohibited from interfering with factory management or business administration. This policy was adopted in order to make up for the wide shortage of managerial personnel by giving the managers more authority.

After the private sector of the economy gave way to joint state-private enterprises, a national conference of basic-level trade union cadres in the joint enterprises was held in November 1956 to define the new role of labor unions. Out of this conference came the basic decision that labor unions have the right to share in the management of joint enterprises. The task of running such enterprises was to be shared by the administrative or management committee, under the general supervision of the workers' representative conference, and management, which in a joint enterprise would primarily represent the public interest. The workers' representative conference would be composed of representatives of the Communist party, the Communist Youth League, and the state and private shareholders. It would have the right to recommend the removal of any member of the management who "acts against the workers' interests." The decision was considered tentative, however, and further experimentation was planned to find the best way of increasing the labor unions' role in management.

Labor Organizations

The growth of organized labor in China was slowed by the lateness of its industrialization, uneven geographic distribution of industry, foreign control (which generated labor conflict only partly concerned with economic issues) and, perhaps most important of all, the political instability of the country. Labor unions had been subject to political interference well before the Communist period.

Early Labor Movement

Beginning in 1914 legislation on labor conditions and labor-management relations was passed periodically but with little effect on actual practice, being designed as much to give the appearance of keeping pace with other nations by an enlightened labor policy as to improve the position of the workers. The ineffectiveness of the labor legislation was due primarily to the fact that the governments of the early republican period as well as the Nationalist government depended heavily on the support of industrialists and financiers and could not afford to antagonize them. Improved working conditions—for example, the reduction of daily working hours from more than 12 hours to 10 or 8—came largely as the result of strikes or of individual cases of benevolent paternalism on the part of private employers.

China's first labor unions were organized largely under the guidance of the Communist party, which from its founding in 1921 took the initiative in organizing workers' clubs and establishing schools to train prospective labor leaders.

In 1922 the First National Labor Congress convened in Canton, with representatives of some three hundred labor unions in twelve cities reportedly attending. By means of this congress the Communists gained a firm initial control of the labor union movement. With the help of the Communist party, a number of labor unions comprising coal miners, railroad workers, and industrial workers were organized in key cities such as Shanghai, Peking, Hankow, and Canton during the five years from the first congress to the fourth congress held in 1927. At that time, the All-China Federation of Labor, established earlier in 1925, claimed jurisdiction over 2,800,000 organized workers. Shortly afterwards the Communist party was outlawed by the Nationalist government; thereupon both the Communist party and the labor movement it led went underground. The union movement suffered a severe setback and by 1928 there were only 1,901,000 organized workers, or approximately 30 percent less than in 1927. By 1931 union membership had further declined to 364,000.

Under the Nationalist government the great majority of labor unions were craft unions. Up to 1935 a total of 846 labor unions (not all of which survived) had registered with the Ministry of Industry; of these, 751 were craft and 95 were industrial unions. After 1937 and during the war years unions multiplied under government encouragement and at the end of 1942 there were 4,033 registered unions with a total membership of 1,053,000; five years later there were 10,846 with 4,953,000 members.

Development under the Communists

If the Communist figures for labor union membership are taken at their face value, the growth of organized labor since 1949 has been phenomenal:

Year	Total Membership
1949	2,370,000
1950	5,170,000
1951	7,290,000
1952	10,200,000
1953	11,000,000
1954	12,450,000
1955	13,700,000
1956	(*not available*)
1957	16,300,000

In the winter of 1957 labor union members constituted more than 90 percent of the workers in cities such as Shanghai, Peking, and Tientsin, and in provinces such as Liaoning and Kirin; about 80 percent in most other regions; and 70 percent in very remote districts. Federations of labor were organized in all the provinces, special municipalities, and autonomous regions. The number of basic-level union organizations, however, was reduced through amalgamation from some 180,000 in 1954 to 157,000 in 1957.

As much as the spontaneous enthusiasm of the working class claimed by the Communists, this rapid growth of unions reflected the government policy of sending thousands of trade union cadres into factories, mines, and other enterprises to indoctrinate and organize the workers. The great emphasis on the numerical increase of membership has inevitably meant a general lowering of labor organization standards, a fact admitted by the Communists themselves.

Further evidence of the political orientation of union organization is the call of the All-China Federation of Trade Unions in February 1950 for the summary formation of ten to twelve national industrial unions. By October seven of these had been established, and three more had been added by the end of 1952. The latest reliable information (December 1957) listed seventeen national industrial unions, three industrial union preparatory committees, and five working committees.

Structure of Labor Unions

In the Communist state, labor organizations are instruments of the government and the party in helping to carry out the national production plan and enforce control of workers and their families. Serving as schools for Communism and centers of party influence and propaganda, labor unions maintain a close affiliation with the party at all levels. The majority of responsible labor union officers and basic-level labor union committees in China are members of the local Communist party committees or branch committees, and party branch offices or cells have been established in practically all factories, mines, and other industrial establishments as well as in all agencies, farms, institutions, and schools to guide the activities of the unions directly.

The organization of labor unions is regulated by the Trade Union Law of the People's Republic of China, promulgated in June 1950. Only industrial unions (no craft unions) may be organized and all unions are subordinate units of the All-China Federation of Trade Unions: their organization must be approved by this body or by the appropriate industrial or territorial federation of labor and registered with the proper government authorities. All skilled and unskilled workers living wholly or largely on wages, whether or not they are in the service of a permanent employer, are eligible for membership in labor unions, defined as "voluntary popular organizations of the working class."

The All-China Federation of Trade Unions is administered by an Executive Committee elected by the National Labor Congress. This committee further elects the Presidium, which acts in behalf of the Executive Committee when it is not in session, and the Secretariat, entrusted with routine administration.

The National Labor Congress meets once every five years; the national assemblies of the various industrial unions, once every three or four years; and the regional, provincial, and local federations meet at intervals of one to three years.

The working components of labor organizations are the basic-level unions, which may be organized by ten or more workers in a factory, a mine, a shop, a farm, a government department, or a school, or by workers from various places of employment in the same locality. Basic-level union committees may be established in various departments and workshops of a single organization. A model basic-level trade union committee, as outlined in Communist publications, may consist of twelve subcommittees and forty-five work groups. The inclusion of a statistics group in each of the subcommittees indicates the importance placed on collecting data for planning.

This elaborate organizational scheme has led to some ridiculous extremes—for example, ten working committees in the union of a thirty-man factory at Dairen. Another basic-level union in Szechwan had a women workers' committee although the factory in question had only three women workers.

The organizational structure of labor unions above the basic level, clearly set forth in the Charter of the All-China Federation of Trade Unions, is along both territorial and industrial lines in a manner corresponding to the local government. As for methods of financing the labor organizations, the charter lists the following sources of income: (1) registration fees of new members, which amount to 1 percent of the most recent monthly wage of each new member; (2) membership fees, which are 1 percent of the monthly wage of each member; (3) payments by the employers, which are 2 percent of each month's total wages paid to all of their employees; and (4) incomes from cultural, athletic, and other activities organized by the labor unions. All expenditures of the labor unions must be properly budgeted and audited as prescribed in special regulations by the All-China Federation of Trade Unions.

Functions of Labor Unions

According to Communist theory, labor unions are expected to educate and organize the workers to follow government policies and to boost production to the levels set in the numerous drives. They also act as watchdogs on waste and corruption and serve in the joint state-private and privately operated enterprises as a counterpoise to any tendency to place private interests above those of the state. The facilities necessary for the conduct of the union's activities are to be provided by local governments and employers.

Cultural centers and recreation halls are set up by the unions wherever possible to extend the opportunities for utilization of leisure time, which however is spent largely in political studies, criticism meetings, and participation in all kinds of campaigns as well as in literacy classes. Spare-time schools for workers were established by the various labor unions in 1949 and attendance was made compulsory in 1950. Enrollment increased from about a quarter million in 1949 to five million in 1957.

Although major responsibility for technical training rests with management, the various unions have encouraged apprenticeship and tutorship contracts between senior and junior workers to help raise the technical standards of the latter. In 1955 the labor unions operated 44 training schools for union officers with an enrollment of 78,348. Four of these schools were directly under the All-China Federation of Trade Unions. The unions are reported to have established more than fifteen thousand libraries with an aggregate collection of some twenty-nine million volumes, in addition to a number of mobile libraries which serve workers in their shops and dormitories.

To publicize the labor movement, union activities, and other related topics, the unions publish a number of newspapers and periodicals. The *Daily Worker* and the semimonthly *Chinese Worker,* both official organs of the All-China Federation of Trade Unions, have a wide circulation among the workers. Almost every provincial and municipal federation of labor and every national industrial union has one or more periodicals of its own. By the end of 1954 a total of thirteen newspapers were published by the labor unions. As early as 1950, the Workers' Press, operated by the All-China Federation of Trade Unions, claimed to have printed more than 61,212,000 copies of books under 551 titles, all dealing with labor subjects.

Labor Organizations and the Government

Since the functions of labor organizations are closely tied in with those of the government, the operations of the Ministry of Labor and those of the All-China Federation of Trade Unions practically merge, many labor regulations being directly issued by the All-China Federation of Trade Unions. In June 1950 labor unions were requested and authorized to administer the distribution of relief grants. An agreement was entered into by the Ministry of Labor and the All-China Federation of Trade Unions on January 19, 1950 for coordination of their activities.

Union officers often behave like government officials and office holding in unions and government agencies is often interchangeable. In their relations with workers, some labor officials exhibit a tendency toward commandism. "Instead of dealing with the masses in a comradely manner and performing their duties by means of persuasion and education," reported Lai Jo-yü in April 1955, "many union cadres behave as if they were masters and carry out their work by means of coercion. This tendency is the more pronounced toward the so-called backward elements."

But the important role of labor organizations in political indoctrination can be seen in the following example. In the course of organizing the workers in 1949 and 1950, the Communists alleged that "reactionary elements" from the secret societies, as well as Nationalist agents and the remnants of the Nationalist army, had infiltrated the Chinese working class and urged that the masses "clean out such remnants of feudal rule from industry in order to prepare the country for socialization." To initiate a "democratic reform" movement in factory or mine, the union cadres called meetings of criticism and self-criticism, their purpose being to "weld together by ties of sympathy and understanding all who work together." Everyone present was urged to voice complaints and accusations against counterrevolutionaries. Although generally of a minor nature, changes were made after such meetings in factory regulations and working relations, but the major aim of the movement was to purge trade unions of disloyal elements and to indoctrinate the working class. In 1951 socialization of private enterprise became a favorite topic at workers' meetings. The Five-Anti campaign and the Resist-America-Aid-Korea movement were also used for political indoctrination, and particularly the latter campaign was used, as are patriotic appeals of all kinds, to increase production.

Forced Labor

In addition to mobilizing and controlling manpower through the labor unions, the Chinese Communists have established a system of corrective labor that follows the pattern developed in the USSR, even to regulations prepared with the assistance of Soviet legal experts. Landlords, "counterrevolutionary peasants," bureaucratic capitalists, intellectuals, former political functionaries, Nationalist party members, and members of secret societies and religious organizations, especially Catholics and Taoists, were among those forced to undertake corrective labor.

Although information about forced labor in Communist China comes from a variety of sources—laws and regulations; official comments, reports, and editorials; stray references in the Communist press; observations made by visitors; and the accounts of former prisoners (Chinese and foreign) who reach the free world—quantitative data are difficult to get. A 1955 report on forced labor by the Secretary of the United Nations and the International Labor Organization states that in Communist China from 1949 through 1954 there were "twenty to twenty-five millions in regular permanent camps." This is generally considered a reasonable estimate of the number of slave laborers in Communist China. The suggested total of 25 million includes, however, not only persons in regular camps, but also 3 million victims of floods and other disasters committed to forced labor; 1.5 million "slave laborers sent abroad"; and 8 million civilians used as corvée labor. By eliminating these groups, one gets a total of 12.5 million in corrective labor institutions. The victims of the agricultural collectivization campaign, which did not gain momentum until the winter of 1954-55, and the results of the forcible establishment of the communes since 1958 are not included in these figures.

The number of ordinary people who do temporary forced labor (corvée labor) is much larger than the UN report suggests. Careful estimates indicate that during the first seven years of the Chinese People's Republic at least forty million persons served in the corvée for water control, and millions more in work teams on highways, railroads, and other construction projects. In 1956, 1.5 million persons were employed in water control work in the northwestern province of Kansu, and four million were similarly employed in a single Yangtze River province, Anhwei.

Originally the corvée teams consisted mainly of adult males, but by 1956 women were being systematically assigned to heavy work in agricultural collectives and to water-and-soil conservation projects. Millions of women were reported to have been drafted for water conservation corvée in 1958.

Recently the Communist government has begun to require corvée duty of young people, mobilizing adolescents on a gigantic scale for water control and other tasks. During the winter and spring of 1955 about 70 million were assigned the task of collecting manure. The same winter, Communist youth cadres rallied over 66 million people for afforestation work. In March 1956 the Central Committee of the Communist Youth League held a national conference to enlist another 180 million young people and children for the same purpose.

Persons committed to the correctional labor corps come under three categories. Delinquents from thirteen to fourteen years of age are placed in "houses of correction for young prisoners" where they are required "to undertake light labor under conditions favorable to their physical development." The mass of adult prisoners are divided into two major groups: counterrevolutionaries and other major criminals "unfit for labor outside the prison" are made to work under strict supervision in jail; counterrevolutionaries and other criminals "fit for labor outside the prison" are put under the jurisdiction of the corrective labor corps. The task of the reformatory labor corps is to organize prisoners for systematic productive work in agriculture, industry, and reconstruction programs and to impart political education in coordination with productive labor. Lo Jui-ch'ing, Minister of Public Security in charge of the forced labor program, stressed the importance of this last category by calling it "the main type and most appropriate form of organized production by criminal labor."

Reports given by former inmates of prisons and camps generally describe the food as poor, the clothing inadequate, and shelter overcrowded and unsanitary. The 1954 labor reform regulations include certain elements of the "rationalized" policy evolved in the Soviet Union, such as stress on sanitary measures and canteens in which the prisoners may buy "supplementary food." These regulations are somewhat vague with regard to food and shelter, however, and seem to have done little to improve existing conditions. Occasional earlier experiments with the payment of a small wage were discontinued after 1954 but work hours remain from 9 to 10 hours normally and "in seasonal production" up to 12 hours.

The corrective labor force is divided into divisions, regiments, battalions, companies, and platoons. Small units are organized under a system of mutual guarantee and mutual punishment so that no prisoner dares escape for fear of making his fellows suffer, and everyone is induced to watch over his companions.

Discipline is rigid to enforce rules and to speed up production, but labor feats cannot be achieved by compulsion alone: there are incentives. In addition to competitive contests, a number of means are employed to induce "voluntary" speed-up. Prisoners may shorten their sentences if they consistently observe labor discipline and fulfill or exceed the production norms. In prisons and camps, all laborers are required to observe silence during work hours. At the end of the work day, study groups are formed for at least an hour, during which the prisoners are subjected to political and ideological "education" in order to make them "confess their guilt, recognize their criminality, and eliminate their criminal thoughts." This "educational process" is bulwarked by continuing attempts to make convicts furnish "information on counterrevolutionary organizations and activities inside and outside the institution." As a reformatory as well as punitive institution for the hard core of political nonconformists and nonpolitical criminals, convict labor has a significance in the multifaceted system of Communist-controlled labor that makes its abandonment in the foreseeable future very unlikely.

FINANCIAL SYSTEM

ONE OF THE MOST URGENT FINANCIAL PROBLEMS facing the Chinese Communists upon their accession to power in 1949 was the hyperinflation that had paralyzed the nation's economy during the Nationalist period. Fully aware of the part inflation had played in the collapse of their predecessors, the Communists immediately attacked the problem of currency stabilization. Over-all economic and financial stability also demanded simplification of the tax system. The myriad of petty taxes on business and the consumer were therefore reduced to fourteen and immediate efforts were made to equalize nonagricultural and agricultural taxes, the latter having supplied the major revenue of previous governments.

In addition to these measures the new government moved to centralize all types of financial control, to curtail government expenditures through strict economy campaigns, to tap every available source of revenue (supplies confiscated from the Nationalists and "counterrevolutionaries" were either put to use or sold in the open market), to centralize the tax collection system by requiring local governments to deposit all tax receipts in central depositories, and finally to reduce actual cash in circulation. Government departments, for example, were forbidden to keep more than a three day's supply of cash on hand, all excess to be deposited in the People's Bank. The effect of these methods was soon evident: the price level was largely stabilized beginning March 1950.

Currency Reform

Both before and during the Sino-Japanese War the Communists had made use of local currencies in their isolated guerrilla bases as a substitute for the Chinese National Currency (CNC). It was not until the second half of 1943, however, that the Communists prohibited the circulation of CNC in the areas they controlled. By the end of 1944 a system of K'ang-pi ("Resist Japan Currency") was formally established. After the end of the war in 1945 the base of Communist operations was shifted from Shensi and Kansu to Northeast China, and with the advance of the "Liberation Army" banks were set up and notes issued in newly conquered regions. As the previously isolated bases were gradually brought under unified control it became necessary to simplify the currency system. A Financial and Economic Conference of the North China Liberated Areas, held in 1947, led to the consolidation during 1948 of the currencies of the three "Liberated Areas" of North China, East China, and Northwest China. This move was followed by the creation of the Jen-min-pi (JMP) or People's Currency, and by the middle of 1949 issuance of currency other than JMP was terminated in all Communist regions except Northeast China, Inner Mongolia, and Sinkiang. In March 1950 the notes of the Northeast Bank and of the Bank of Inner Mongolia were converted into JMP and the two banks made branches of the People's Bank of China. The replacement by JMP, in September of the same year, of the notes issued by the Sinkiang Provincial Bank completed the establishment of a single currency.

Meanwhile the Gold Yuan, the monetary unit which the Nationalist government had introduced in August 1948 to replace the highly inflated and worthless CNC, had rapidly depreciated. The Communists, therefore, endeavored to set conversion rates from Gold Yuan to JMP that would limit the issue to manageable size. Although it was claimed that official rates of exchange were determined by the relative purchasing powers of the currencies, they were in fact arbitrarily set in each city as it was occupied. The conversion rate of Gold Yuan to JMP rose from 6 Gold Yuan to 1 JMP in January 1949 at Tientsin, to 10 to 1 in February at Peking, 2,500 to 1 in May at Nanking, and 100,000 to 1 in June at Shanghai. Although part of the rise was due to the rapid depreciation in the purchasing power of Gold Yuan, deliberate manipulation by the Communists played an important part.

The prohibition of the use of silver dollars, gold, and foreign currencies as mediums of exchange was an integral part of Communist policy. It was enforced through tight control over intercity movement of these currencies and police raids on the black market, especially the shops of goldsmiths or silversmiths. Foreign currencies had to be surrendered for JMP or a foreign exchange deposit receipt from the Bank of China, valid only if sold within forty days to finance imports. The Communists did not attempt to force the surrender of gold or silver and by arbitrarily low rates actually discouraged conversion to prevent inflationary currency expansion. Any gold or silver not converted to JMP had to be withheld from circulation.

Mere possession of gold and silver is still legal, but a special license must be obtained to wear gold and silver jewelry in excess of maximum limits varying, according to local customs, from one ounce in North China to two ounces in South China.

The first JMP notes were issued in denominations of 1, 5, 10, 20, 50, and 100 yuan, but rising prices caused the introduction of 500-, 1,000-, 5,000- and 10,000-yuan bills in 1949, and 50,000-yuan notes in 1954. It was announced as part of a monetary reform on March 1, 1955, that the new JMP would be exchanged for the old JMP at the rate of 1 to 10,000. Since then, all prices and contractual obligations have been in terms of the new currency. Holders of old JMP were asked to redeem them for new JMP at branches or agencies of the People's Bank. According to official sources 80 percent of the old currency outstanding was converted by April 1, and the remainder by June 10, 1955.

The new JMP are in denominations of 1, 2, 3, 5, and 10 yuan, and 1, 2, 5, 10, 20, and 50 fen (cents). Since December 1957 coins of 1, 2, and 5 fen have also been issued. The notes are printed in four languages: Han (Chinese), Tibetan, Uigur, and Mongolian. To aid the illiterate, bills of different denominations are printed in different colors with pictures of equipment, places, or people on them for easy identification.

The Communists hailed the first JMP as one of the most stable currencies in the world. This was true according to the official explanation, because its stability was insured not by a gold reserve but by the balance of fiscal receipts and expenditures, government control of supplies, and the large cash receipts and payments in government hands. After the monetary reform of 1955 reserves against the new JMP included, it was announced, large amounts of silver, gold, and foreign exchange. Such reserves do not change, however, the essential character of the new JMP as a managed currency. Its value is determined by the amount of commodities it can command in the market and this is controlled by rationing and other means. The total amount of currency issued is kept a top secret; obviously there is no limit other than Communist economic policy. Since 1951 the circulation of JMP has been restricted to Communist China.

On the surface, it may seem that the Communist monetary reform was nothing but an exchange of old JMP for currency of smaller denominations in order to simplify bookkeeping and handling of money. Actually, the issuance of new notes was designed to increase state control in all financial matters. It offered the government an opportunity to take inventory of the cash held by private industrial and commercial enterprises as well as individuals, including the farmers. During the conversion period bank deposits showed a large increase and the sale of the National Economic Construction Bonds was very successful, indicating that pressure had been put on the people and on private enterprises to keep their money in banks or to buy bonds. The limited issuance of 10-yuan notes (new JMP) is additional proof that the determined policy of the Communists has been to contract the amount of money in circulation through forced savings.

The People's Bank remains the only bank of issue in Communist China, but from the latter part of 1955 an increasing number of agricultural producers' cooperatives have issued "vegetable tickets," "cash circulation notes," and "cooperative currency" in denominations of one, two, and even five yuan. These notes first came into being as media of exchange between cooperatives and their members, but they have gained wide acceptance in rural areas as subsidiary currency for all types of transactions. Because of the continued shortage of funds in the rural areas, the government has found it necessary to tolerate the existence of these cooperative notes. As their appearance is in direct contradiction to the government's currency program, it indicates the failure of Communist monetary policy to meet the needs of the rural populace.

The Chinese traditional preference for precious metals and hard currencies has led to a black market in foreign exchange. During 1949, for instance, the exchange rate of the old JMP for the American dollar rose from 2,000 yuan in July to 6,700 yuan in November on the official counter, and from 2,800 yuan to 17,000 yuan on the black market.

At present some black market currency transactions continue between Hong Kong and the mainland, the current value of JMP fluctuating according to conditions on the China mainland. On the eve of the Korean War, the JMP notes were selling at a price approximating the official rate (then at 32,600 old JMP per American dollar, stabilized since 1953 at about 24,600 old JMP or 2.46 new JMP per American dollar). However, just before the issuance of the new JMP in 1955, the quoted value sank to about 63 percent of par though it recovered to approximately 80 percent immediately afterwards.

General Fiscal Policy

The financial policy of the Communist government, formulated in September 1949, called for a national budgetary and accounting system, clear demarcation of the spheres of central and local financial authority, rigid economy, a balanced budget, and the accumulation of funds for state production. Tax policy was to be so formulated as to insure supplies for the revolutionary war, restore and advance production, and meet the needs of national construction. A simplified tax system was to be established and a rational tax burden enforced.

It soon became apparent that an additional objective of fiscal policy was to harass private business as a step toward establishing direct state control and ownership. During the past decade certain aspects of the above program have been de-emphasized and others stressed. Ensuring supplies for the revolutionary war is no longer as important as meeting the needs of national construction. Investment in long-term projects has received increasing emphasis, especially since 1953 when the First Five Year Plan was launched. The orthodox notion of a balanced budget, to which lip service was paid initially because of the popular fear of inflation, has almost completely disappeared from official statements while the concept of a "rational" tax burden is not permitted to take precedence over the financial requirements of rapid industrialization.

Budget

The budgets of Communist China are compiled by the Ministry of Finance from unit budgets submitted by various branches of the central and local governments. The Communists insist that there has been no unbalanced budget since 1949. But for the Chinese fear of inflation due to deficit financing, this claim would be quite unnecessary and it is patently untrue. To take an example, in the budget of 1950 a deficit of 18.7 percent, to be financed partly by bonds and partly by note issuance, was anticipated. In April 1951, official figures showed a 1950 deficit amounting to 16.7 percent of actual expenditures. The smaller deficit, it was announced, would be covered by funds from three sources: subscriptions to bonds, credit from the Soviet Union, and a bank overdraft (that is, creation of new money). In 1953, however, the Ministry of Finance announced that there had been a slight surplus (about 2 percent of total expenditures) for the year 1950. Actually, the 1950 deficits disappeared in the 1953 report only through a different classification of revenues. It is also possible that revenue collected during the early 1952 drive against urban business communities was attributed to previous years and therefore helped to reduce the size of the reported deficits. Such a procedure must have been adopted in reporting a balanced budget for 1951 when the Korean War was at its height. The practice of treating the proceeds of loans and bank overdrafts as a part of regular revenue has been continued to the present day. In addition, the balancing of total revenue and expenditure is frequently accomplished by withdrawals from reserve funds.

These considerations notwithstanding, the large size of the budget and its continuous growth is noteworthy. Before the Sino-Japanese War, the largest state budget was that of 1936 which was approximately equivalent to 600 million American dollars. But the first regular budget of Communist China (1950) was 150 percent more than that of 1936, and the size of the budget has grown continuously until in 1957 it was well over twenty times the prewar peak. Even if one considers the depreciation of the American dollar over this period and the fact that the rate of conversion used is an official rate which may not be very meaningful, it cannot be denied that there has been a tremendous increase in government receipts and expenditures. Although this increase is partly due to the reporting of the central and local government budgets on a consolidated basis, it is mainly due to the increase in governmental activities. The budgets from 1952 to 1959 can be compared in Table 5.

Expenditure Pattern

In the first years of Communist control, military outlay constituted the largest single item of government expenditure, amounting to 41.5 and 42.5 percent of the total in 1950 and 1951 respectively. Since the conclusion of the Korean truce in 1952, the percentage of military expenditure to total outlay has been substantially reduced falling to a low of 11.2 percent in 1959. This statement is, however, somewhat deceptive. Actual military expenditures did not fall, the drop percentagewise being a reflection of the growth of other items of expenditure. Moreover, it is evident that a proportion of the expenditures allotted to economic activities would be more appropriately included under national defense. The percentage devoted to economic construction has risen steadily except for a slight de-cline in 1957. From only 25.5 percent of the 1950 budget this item increased to 61 percent of the total in 1959. But for downward revision in the prices of certain products of heavy industry in 1956, the increase in that and subsequent years would be even larger see Tables 6 and 7). Together with military expenditures, govern-ment administrative expenses have declined steadily in comparison with other items, from 19.3 percent in 1950 to 7.6 percent in 1957. Salaries have remained low and austerity standards continue.

Table 8 shows actual expenditure figures from 1950 to 1957, as given in the yearly fiscal reports of the Communist government.

Sources of Revenue

Several important changes have taken place in the structure of government revenue during the past decade as an examination of the categories of revenue reported in the final accounts will show (see Table 9). These are the unmistakable result of the economic changes that have occurred in China.

First, the relative importance of income from state enterprises increased from 12.5 percent of total receipts in 1950 to over 46 percent in 1957, second only to total tax revenue. This reflects the extent of socialization, which has effectively channeled to the coffers of the state what would otherwise be the profits and depreciation allowances of private business. The contribution of these enterprises to total revenue far exceeds, of course, even these figures as a sizable part of taxes is also paid by them (see Table 10).

Secondly, within the category of taxes, the contribution of agricultural taxation declined sharply from about 29 percent of total revenue in 1950 to a mere 10 percent in 1956. This was mostly a result of the great increase in industrial output and commercial transactions although it also reflected the difficulties encountered in rural tax collection and the substitution of compulsory purchase of farm products in lieu of higher taxation. This had the effect of converting what would have been taxes into profits from state trad-ing enterprises.

Thirdly, the policy concerning changes in the tax system itself during the decade is significant. The prevailing philosophy has been to use multiple taxation as a form of economic control: in addition to ensuring government revenue, multiple taxes have proved the best method of accumulating capital for socialist purposes. There was, however, a certain amount of simplification of the tax structure early in the Communist regime and again in September 1958, both changes motivated by a need to increase efficiency and reduce cost in tax administration.

Urban Taxation

Taxation in Communist China falls into two categories, urban and rural. The former is aimed primarily at industrial and commercial enterprises while the latter applies entirely to the agricultural segment of the economy. Until September 1958, when a consolidated industrial and commercial tax was introduced, urban taxation consisted primarily of the turnover tax, the commodity tax, and the industrial and commercial tax, the last of which included a tax on business volume and a separate tax on business income. Besides these, there exist such additional taxes as customs duties, the salt tax, the stamp tax, the slaughter tax, and the real estate tax. These last taxes affect both the urban and the rural population.

The business tax, instituted shortly after the Communists took power, was a tax on net sales, collected each time a commodity changed hands. In 1953 this was replaced in the case of twenty-two important items by a turnover tax which consolidated several other business taxes including those on gross business receipts, commodity taxes, stamp duties, and business transactions. At the same time the commodity tax was revised to include all commodities not covered by the turnover tax and fifteen new ones as well, the most important of which were foodstuffs.

The industrial and commercial tax combined the business tax and the business income tax, making it possible to eliminate duplication in the registration of industries and commercial enterprises and in the accounts kept by these concerns. Even more important from the standpoint of administration, both taxes could now be collected by a single agency.

The business tax, as revised in 1952, was applicable to any transaction not covered by the turnover or commodities tax. Manufacturers who handled their own distribution were liable to three business taxes: one at the level of production, a second at the wholesale level, and a third at the retail level. Commercial enterprises were subject to two business taxes, at the wholesale and retail levels. The multiple tax applied to transactions within a single firm as well as to sales to an outsider.

Before 1952 all business taxes were payable upon completion of the transaction. After 1952 producers were required to advance the tax due from the wholesaler, and the wholesaler that due from the retailer. This arrangement made it possible to speed up tax collection and simplify its administration. Business taxes from their inception had varied according to the nature of the enterprise. Rates on manufacturing industries were generally higher than those on such services as public utilities, professional services, hotels, and so forth. Rates on those who made their living by commissions were the highest of all. These differentials were kept in the 1952 changes in the tax laws but all rates were revised upward.

In contrast to all other taxes the business income tax has remained virtually the same since 1949. As in Soviet Russia, income taxes are applicable to the profits of business enterprises and interest derived from bank deposits. Wages and salaries are not subject to tax.

Again like the Soviet system, certain individuals and enterprises are given favored treatment under the Chinese income tax laws. A difference is made, for instance, in favor of military or industrial "heroes," and for earnings from industries as against earnings from commercial undertakings (particularly those derived from services, such as commissions). Progressive rates go from 5 to 30 percent and are applied to the entire taxable income rather than by income brackets.

Regulations introduced in August 1956 on the "Payment of Industrial-Commercial Tax during Socialist Transformation of Private Industry and Commerce" were so framed as to make it more attractive for private enterprises to become joint enterprises.

In September 1958 the turnover, commodity, stamp, and part of the industrial and commercial tax were abolished and replaced by a consolidated tax on total sales. This is in effect an extension of the turnover tax and a step toward further tax simplification. With the virtual completion of socialization multiple taxes are no longer necessary to prevent tax evasion by private business or to harass businessmen.

Rural Taxation

Before June 1958 three kinds of agricultural tax were used in various parts of Communist China: proportional taxes formerly used in the "old liberated areas," progressive taxes applicable to those areas where land reform had not yet been completed, and progressive taxes for those areas where land reform had already been completed. Since June 1958 the proportional tax has been placed on a national basis.

Despite evidence that a small portion is remitted in cash, the agricultural taxes are collected primarily in kind and are assessed on the basis of so-called "normal" production. This method of assessment has the double advantage of greatly simplifying tax administration and stabilizing revenue from the agricultural tax. Except for provisions for certain reductions in case of natural disasters, the government is free from the adverse effects upon its revenue of year-to-year fluctuations in agricultural production, leaving that burden to farmers.

The proportional taxation differs from progressive taxation in that a fixed proportion of the "normal" yield to be paid as tax is predetermined for all taxpayers within a certain area. Since June 1958 the rates have ranged between 15.5 and 25 percent for the entire country.

Of several problems related to agricultural taxation the most important are as follows:

(1) Throughout Chinese history the greatest difficulty involved in agricultural taxation has been the lack of reliable statistical information concerning productivity, distribution of land, and rural population. In the last few years the Communist government has probably made some progress in overcoming this difficulty, having been able to obtain many reliable facts not available to previous governments during the nationwide land reform and cadastral survey.

(2) The agricultural tax is applicable to crop yields but not to other sources of agricultural or rural income, which are substantial in some parts of the country. The failure of the tax to cover these rural incomes, probably a concession dictated by administrative difficulties, was not recognized until the end of 1956 when the Ministry of Finance promulgated the "Provisional Regulations Governing Industrial and Commercial Taxes in Rural Areas." This represents an attempt by the government to tap a new source of business tax—the commercial activities engaged in by an increasing number of agricultural producers' cooperatives. So many exceptions are made of various aspects of these transactions, however, that it seems likely the Communist government is wary lest these new tax regulations jeopardize the productive capacity of the cooperatives.

(3) A serious problem confronting the Communist regime arises from collecting the agricultural tax in kind. Collection of the tax in kind protects the government from losses in the real value of its tax receipts at times of inflation and ensures directly

to the government the supply of staple foodstuffs necessary for the maintenance of its army and sometimes for the stabilization of food prices in the domestic market. But the collection-in-kind system also has serious disadvantages. First, the failure to set standards for products accepted as tax payments may result in encouraging taxpayers to meet their tax liabilities with products of inferior quality. As recent reports have indicated, even collective farms are not free from this understandable tendency. Second, the requirement that taxpayers deliver their products at points specified by the government penalizes the taxpayer who happens to live far away from the collection center. Third, the storage and distribution of such agricultural products after they are collected usually involves great cost and additional administrative responsibilities for the government. The use of various commodities rather than a monetary unit as the basis of tax collection necessarily complicates tax accounting and provides fertile ground for graft and corruption.

(4) Another important problem is the failure to allow for costs of production. Under the present system, exemptions and allowances are given only for the labor employed and for crop failures due to natural disasters, but not for other costs. There is, for instance, no allowance for equipment, horses, or other farm animals used in cultivation, for chemical fertilizers, or for special irrigation. Consequently, the use of modern methods to improve agricultural production receives no encouragement from the tax, which actually discriminates against the introduction of such methods. This discrimination, however, is mitigated somewhat by the provision that, once the normal yield is determined, any improvement in production due to investment in irrigation and soil conservation measures, or through better management, will not be penalized by raising the tax base for three or five years respectively.

Other Sources of Revenue

Import duties, a major source of revenue in pre-Communist days, are no longer an important part of government revenue. Most exports are exempt from duties. Special rates are given to imports from the USSR and the Soviet satellites in return for favorable rates from them. The salt tax, formerly another important source of revenue, has also greatly decreased in importance.

Up to 1953 a substantial source of revenue for the government was the special drive. One estimate of proceeds from confiscations during the 1950-51 land reform movement ran as high as the equivalent of 7,860 million American dollars. This figure is probably exaggerated, but it is undeniable that the movement yielded a considerable income to the government. During the Korean War, according to official announcements, the proceeds from the Arms Donation campaign up to May 31, 1952 and from the Resist-America-Aid-Korea campaign up to August 31, 1953 were equivalent to 408 million American dollars. The Three-Anti movement of late 1951 and early 1952 and the Five-Anti movement of 1952 led to confiscation of the property of people found guilty during these campaigns. No reliable information is available as to the exact size of proceeds from these sources but one estimate gives an equivalent of 2,200 million American dollars for the Five-Anti movement alone.

There have not been any widely publicized special drives for funds since 1954. This indicates that the regular sources of revenue are now probably sufficient for the government's needs, partly because the expansion of the socialized sector has enabled the government, from the fiscal point of view, to determine the share it wished to take of the total national product.

Bond issues do not occupy an important place in Chinese Communist government finance. Since it came into power in 1949, only two series of government bonds have been offered: the People's Victory Bonds and the National Economic Construction Bonds.

The People's Victory Bonds were issued in 1950 in commodity units, a device intended to safeguard the interest of bondholders against monetary depreciation at a time when inflation had not been completely curbed. The bonds paid a yearly interest of 5 percent and their sale was directed mainly toward residents in urban areas, particularly the private industrialists and traders. Shanghai contributed a major share of subscribers, followed by Tientsin, Canton, and other large cities. The results of the bond drive were not satisfactory: only 70 percent of the first issue of 100,000 units were sold and a second issue of 100,000 units was never put on the market.

The first National Economic Construction Bond issue, amounting to 600 million yuan (about 244 million American dollars), went on sale in January 1954. The purpose of this bond issue was "the absorption of surplus private savings with a view to speeding up economic construction." Actually one of the chief reasons for issuing the bonds was to re-absorb the funds paid out to holders of Victory Bonds. Issued yearly since 1954 (the total issue was increased to 630 million yuan in 1958) these bonds carry interest of 4 percent per annum and are redeemable in 8 or 10 annual installments. According to official announcement, acceptance of these bonds was very satisfactory and quotas were usually overfulfilled. With the 1958 issue, regular interest payment was abolished and interest is allowed to accumulate until redemption. In 1959 the central government decided to discontinue issuing bonds. Instead, the provincial, regional, and municipal governments were given authority to issue local bonds to finance their own needs for economic development.

National versus Local Revenue

Prior to March 1951 the Communist central government controlled practically all tax revenue. The local governments collected the taxes for the central government, keeping a portion of the proceeds according to their own budgets approved by the Ministry of Finance. This system did not work very well as the local governments were given no incentives to collect all the revenue due the central government. In 1951 sources of revenue were listed separately for local and for central governments. Under this division, provincial governments retained the receipts from the slaughter tax, land title tax, property tax, and profits of state enterprise under the local governments. In addition, the local governments were entitled to 50 percent of the excess amount collected on the agricultural tax as an inducement to surpass the quotas assigned.

This arrangement seemed adequate at the time, but the introduction of the turnover tax in 1953 cut into local revenue. Since the local governments had programs of educational, cultural, and medical activities, they found themselves in a difficult position. Therefore, in spite of the government's aim of "rationalizing" the tax system and eliminating extra taxes, surtaxes have had to be retained. At present the local governments are allowed to levy surtaxes on the agricultural tax, industrial and commercial tax, property tax, and public utility fares. In 1952 the limits set by the central government on the above surtaxes were 10 to 20 percent on the agricultural tax, 10 percent on the industrial and commercial tax, 10 to 15 percent on property taxes, and 5 to 10 percent on telephone, light, and water rates. More leeway has also been given to the local governments in the administration of their revenues and expenditures since 1958.

The Banking System

To the Communists the establishment and proper functioning of a planned economy require that the supply of funds and their direction facilitate rather than inhibit the fulfillment of the production plan. To achieve this objective, funds must be channeled through a central clearing agency that also serves as a point of supervision and control. This is the function of the new banking system. To satisfactorily discharge this function, it was necessary that the existing banking structure be thoroughly revamped and control vested squarely in government hands. These considerations gave direction to the development of Communist China's financial structure during the last decade.

The Banking Structure before 1949

Modern banking in China began with the establishment of foreign banks, among which the British, American, and Japanese were the most influential. The first modern Chinese bank made its appearance in 1896. In 1905 the forerunner of the Bank of China was established and two years later the Bank of Communications. A central banking system did not make its debut, however, until 1928 when the Central Bank of China, established four years earlier by the Nationalist government in Canton, was formally organized as a nationwide central bank with its main office in Shanghai.

During the Nationalist period, the modern Chinese banks were divided into the central government banking group, the local government banking group, and the private banking group. The first group consisted of a nucleus of four major banks—namely, the Central Bank of China, the Bank of China, the Bank of Communications, and the Farmers' Bank of China—together with the Central Trust of China, the Postal Remittances and Savings Bank, and a central reserve bank for cooperatives. These were all partially or fully owned by the government and nominally under its complete control. The local government banking group consisted of provincial, municipal, and county banks, fully or partially owned by the local governments and acting as agents of their treasuries. They also handled general banking business. The private banking group included commercial banks, savings banks, banks promoting specific enterprises, overseas Chinese banks established by Chinese abroad, and semi-banking institutions such as mutual savings associations and trust companies.

The growth of the modern banks did not immediately eliminate traditional native banks although increased competition from the new banks forced many of them to reorganize along modern lines. These institutions had been important in the economic structure of the country from at least the end of the eighteenth century and a large segment of the population continued to rely upon them for their ordinary financial transactions.

There were two groups of native banks: the Shansi banks and the "local banks." The Shansi banks (so called because they were mainly owned and operated by people from Shansi province) dealt principally in the transfer of funds by drafts, for which purpose they maintained a network of branches in important cities throughout the country. The "local banks" specialized in money changing, loans, deposits, and acceptance of commercial bills. They generally operated on a local basis although business connections in important commercial centers were maintained by some of them.

Elimination of the Old Banking Structure

Before 1928 Peking and Shanghai were the two chief banking centers in China. In Peking were the main offices of two government banks, the Bank of China and the Bank of Communications, and a few private modern banks, in addition to the native banks. Shanghai was the headquarters for foreign banks as well as for many of the modern Chinese banks and native banks.

When the Nationalist government was established in Nanking in 1928 the main offices of the Bank of China and the Bank of Communications and those of the major private modern banks were transferred to Shanghai. The head office of the newly established Central Bank of China was also located there. Shanghai thus became the sole banking center of China.

In October 1949 the Communists decided to make Peking again the center of major banking activities. The main office of the People's Bank of China and the Bank of Communications were ordered to return. By the end of 1952 the old banking structure in Shanghai had finally collapsed, effectively preventing any possibility of continuing influence over financial affairs by the established private banks, especially the foreign banks, and accomplishing the government's objective of eliminating Shanghai as the financial center of China. This was in line with its general policy of centralizing all financial controls.

About the same time, following a period of increasingly rigid government control through regulations on their operations, capitalization, and the use of funds, the private modern banks and native banks were completely transformed into joint state-private institutions.

In April 1950, as a result of cash control, government deposits were transferred to the People's Bank. By June 1950, the number of private banks in Shanghai was reduced from 192 to 68, and the total number of private banks in China from 446 to 213. Syndicates in Shanghai and Tientsin under the leadership of the People's Bank were formed to pool capital resources and make joint loans. These syndicates were the forerunners of a series of mergers which ended in the formation in December 1952 of the Joint State-Private Bank which combined nearly ninety major private banks with branches all over the country. Government shares were obtained through direct investment by the People's Bank or confiscation of shares originally owned by "war criminals" and others found guilty during the Three-Anti and Five-Anti movements. Since similar transformations had occurred in all financial centers, private banking came to an end, for all practical purposes, in December 1952. The control over private banking was henceforth exercised by the People's Bank through direction of the policies of the Joint State-Private Bank.

As for foreign banks, they have disappeared completely from the Chinese scene. American banks were taken over by the Communist government at the time of China's participation in the Korean War when all American property in Communist China was frozen and put under government custody. Actually, all foreign banks had been inactive since the Communists came into power, those not directly confiscated having been forced to liquidate their holdings due to loss of profitable lines of business.

Two minor monetary institutions, pawnshops and firms dealing with overseas remittances, were treated in different ways: the former have been liquidated and the latter are being rigidly controlled. Realizing that the firms dealing with overseas remittances had close contact with the senders abroad and the recipients at home, and also that they had long experience in handling this kind of business, the Communists believed it necessary to keep them in operation in order to obtain foreign exchange. Special regulations made these firms agents of the government to handle overseas Chinese remittances.

As for pawnshops, they had been a common source of credit for both the rural and urban population. They served a useful function in that it was simpler for poor people to resort to pawnshops than to banks for short-term loans. In spite of high interest rates charged by the pawnshops, usually exceeding 3 percent per month, the needy turned to them when hard pressed. As the credit network of the People's Bank spread over the country those pawnshops that had survived Communist restrictions on their operations were forced out of business.

Individual moneylenders also suffered a severe setback. Much moneylending on an individual basis was traditionally conducted by landlords and merchants. The disappearance of the landlords and the loss of wealth by the merchant class effectively removed these sources of credit. Moneylending as a profession was forbidden by government policy but the weakness and malpractice of the credit cooperatives in the last several years have led to a limited reappearance of moneylenders. So long as the government fails to satisfy the need of the rural population for easy-to-obtain loans, the practice of moneylending by individuals will continue to some degree.

Present Banking Organizations

Through annexation of different banking units, the People's Bank of China, established on December 1, 1948, has been developed into a huge institution which, for all practical purposes, represents the entire banking system of the country. Administered by a managing director and four assistant managing directors, the People's Bank is divided into eighteen administrative units with the main office located since 1949 in Peking. In addition to branches in provincial capitals and large cities, and subsidiary offices scattered in towns and larger villages, temporary subsidiary offices are set up in rural districts to serve as agencies of the branch offices in supervising auxiliary offices. Mobile banks at street corners collect savings deposits and render ordinary banking services. Postal and telecommunication offices, credit cooperatives, and the credit departments of supply and marketing cooperatives, offices of public organizations, and village cadres are relied upon to render services for the People's Bank. Since December 1950, as a step in implementing currency control, branch offices have been attached to the armed forces. Thus the People's Bank penetrates into every stratum of urban and rural life through its gigantic network of subsidiary offices. The sizable increase in the number of credit cooperatives from 9,831 in December 1953 to 160,500 in December 1955 further expanded the network of the People's Bank.

Besides being the sole bank of issue, the People's Bank of China is the exclusive depository of all government funds, including those of government and cooperative enterprises; it is the sole source of credit for government and cooperative enterprises, as well as the clearing center and supervisory organ of all transactions involving government, cooperative, and certain joint state-private enterprises. It has authority to supervise the operations of a number of specialized agencies, including the Bank of China, the Bank of Communications, the People's Construction Bank, the Joint State-Private Bank, the People's Insurance Company, and the credit cooperatives (see the plate, Banking System in China).

The status of the Bank of China under the Nationalist regime as a special institution for dealing with foreign trade and exchange was maintained after the Communists assumed control; the directors elected by private shareholders were recognized, but the general manager and directors appointed by the Nationalist government were replaced by Communist appointees. The director-general of the People's Bank serves concurrently as the chairman of the board, with the result that the Bank of China has become virtually a subsidiary of the People's Bank.

The Bank of China is charged with the following functions: to attend to matters concerning the control of foreign exchange; to handle exchange, foreign securities, bills of exchange, and other commercial documents payable in foreign currency; to extend credits and accept deposits in connection with foreign trade; to supervise accounts and the clearance of foreign trade transactions conducted through government organizations; and to control overseas remittances.

The head office is in Peking and its twenty-two branches are located at places important to foreign trade or benefiting from overseas remittances. The allegiance of the overseas branches of the Bank of China is divided: those located in countries which have recognized Communist China are now subject to the control of Peking; the others are controlled by the Nationalist government in Taiwan.

As in the case of the Bank of China, the Bank of Communications was allowed to continue operations under its old status as a special institution to foster the development of industries and internal trade. The directors representing private interests were recognized, while the directors representing public interest, the chairman of the board, and the general manager were replaced with appointees of the new government.

The bank's functions were redefined as follows: to handle government appropriations for basic construction as well as screen and approve applications for such construction needs; to organize and lead long-term investment markets; to control public shares

BANKING SYSTEM IN CHINA

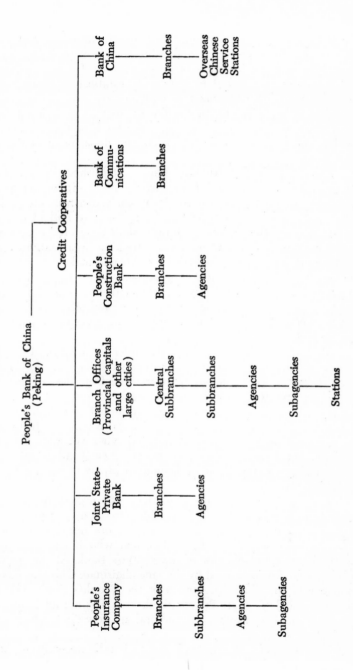

People's Bank of China (Peking)

Credit Cooperatives

People's Insurance Company
— Branches
— Subbranches
— Agencies
— Subagencies

Joint State-Private Bank
— Branches
— Agencies

Branch Offices (Provincial capitals and other large cities)
— Central Subbranches
— Subbranches
— Agencies
— Subagencies
— Stations

People's Construction Bank
— Branches
— Agencies

Bank of Communications
— Branches

Bank of China
— Branches
— Overseas Chinese Service Stations

of enterprises operated by joint state-private interests; and to extend credits to state-owned and joint state-private industries. Of these functions the handling of appropriations for basic construction was later transferred to the newly established People's Construction Bank. The organization of long-term investment markets has been virtually impossible as the number of private capitalists has decreased drastically. Therefore, the Bank of Communications has become in fact an industrial financing department of the People's Bank.

The People's Construction Bank, established by the Communists on October 5, 1954, is entrusted with the following specific functions: to look after the funds of basic construction projects, either provided by appropriations from the state budget or raised by the projects themselves; to supply short-term credits according to the government's credit plan to contracting organizations undertaking work for projects; to settle accounts and make returns in connection with the government's appropriations for the projects; and to supervise the use of funds appropriated or raised, the arrangement for paying contracting organizations, and other matters relating to the financing, cost accounting, and investment policies of the projects.

Although this bank is nominally under the control of the Ministry of Finance, it is in effect another subsidiary of the People's Bank. It receives government appropriations from the People's Bank which are credited to the account of each project, and it draws on the projects in accordance with the government's credit plan. Hence it has no individual discretion over its operations. Its head office is in Peking, and branches are located wherever state industries or basic construction works are found. Nearly all branches use the buildings of the Bank of Communications or of the People's Bank for offices.

The Joint State-Private Bank was established by the Communists in December 1952 from the remaining private banks in Shanghai. A board of twenty-seven directors representing private interests is presided over by a chairman who is concurrently the assistant managing director of the People's Bank. At the operating level a joint staff is headed by the vice-chairman, who also serves as manager of the Shanghai branch of the People's Bank. The head office of the Joint State-Private Bank is in Peking; all branches of the component banks were merged and are now limited to branches in thirteen cities.

The functions of this bank are to handle accounts of private enterprises, to extend short-term credits to private enterprises (subject to the approval of the People's Bank), to handle for the Bank of China overseas Chinese remittances through the branches of component banks still operating in Hong Kong, to handle inland remittances, and to accept savings deposits for the account of the People's Bank.

It is evident that this bank, actually only a department of the People's Bank, was created to deal with private enterprises and will be dissolved when the joint state-private enterprises have been completely nationalized and private commerce eliminated.

On paper, the banking system of Communist China does not differ markedly from the system which existed under the Nationalist government. The latter system, however, never reached the degree of centralization that characterizes the Communist banking system nor succeeded in becoming so all-embracing as the system today. In fact, the very size of the People's Bank of China may prove to be a drawback. When a system is so complex as to encompass all aspects of finance of the state and cooperative sectors of the economy, inefficiencies and errors may be almost inevitable. Available information, however, does not yet indicate just how effectively the banking system in Communist China discharges its functions.

Banking Operations

The emphases of banking operations have shifted in recent years. At the outset, popularization of JMP and promotion of individual deposits were stressed; later, control of cash funds held by public organizations and centralization of credit were emphasized; recently, attention has been focused on coordination of credit with the accelerated program of industrialization and the development of communes, the substitution of bank credit for budget appropriations in providing working capital for industry, and the encouragement of rural savings.

Control of Cash

The currency control instituted in December 1950 stipulates that transactions of all state, cooperative, and certain joint state-private enterprises, as well as government organizations, must be cleared through the People's Bank. It is also authorized to supervise the financial operations of these organizations. Such operations must be in accord with the plan prepared by the authorities.

All public organizations and enterprises must deposit their cash holdings, except small sums as permitted by the authorities, in the local offices or agencies of the People's Bank. All payments, except salaries, wages, and purchases of products in rural areas, must be made by check. All persons engaged in business must deposit the net balance of each day's proceeds into their accounts in the bank and must pay for their purchases with checks. Use of currency is limited to certain transactions with private business and individuals, payrolls, travel expenses, and small sums of petty cash allowed by the bank. All persons in possession of cash exceeding 300 yuan (about 122 American dollars) must deposit their holdings in banks.

Industrial and Commercial Credit

As the Communist banking system has developed, the People's Bank has become the only source of bank credit. Branches of the People's Bank are authorized to extend short-term credits to state enterprises, to production units attached to armed forces, and to cooperatives and private enterprises at places where there is no Joint State-Private Bank. No banking funds, however, are to be used for long-term credit, capital investments being provided by the government in budget appropriations.

In applying for a loan, public enterprises and cooperatives are required to provide the branch office with a budget outlining credit needs and a plan estimating the extent to which the proposed project will increase production, raise labor productivity, and lower production costs. Credits are classified according to their duration and use and borrowers held strictly to the terms stipulated in the contract.

The granting of credit to private enterprises is subject to the same requirements as to plan and budget. Before their socialization, large private industries that were considered beneficial to the national economy, having deposited all their funds in the bank, could obtain a continuing supply of credit under a production and financial plan approved by the bank. Smaller private industrial and commercial enterprises could apply for a fixed amount of credit provided that they had accounts with the bank and disclosed their financial condition to authorities.

The socialization process virtually complete, a new set of interest rates on bank loans was promulgated at the end of October 1957. A uniform rate of 0.6 percent per month was instituted for all borrowers with one exception—credit cooperatives could continue to borrow at the lower rate of 0.51 percent per month. In the case of joint state-private enterprises the rate was 0.6 percent per month for those paying an officially fixed dividend rate to the remaining private stockholders and 0.72 percent per month for all others. The latter rate was also made applicable to loans to private proprietors.

More recently, bank credit has been made the sole source of working capital for industrial enterprises in many areas. Previously funds derived from the state budget accounted for 70 percent of approved working capital. Since no interest was paid on government funds, the effect is a further tightening of business accountability.

Rural Credit

Rural credit is also under tight government control and prior to the commune movement was granted less to help the peasants solve their financial difficulties than to encourage them to join the producers' cooperatives or mutual-aid teams. The Communists reported that in 1953 approximately 72 percent of rural credits went to producers' cooperatives and mutual-aid teams, only 28 percent to individuals. Especially low rates were available to the cooperative farms and to peasants needing loans to finance the formation of cooperatives.

Three forms of rural credit are granted: one- to three-year production loans for machinery, draught animals, irrigation works, small tools, and fertilizers; short-term loans for public trading organizations and cooperatives to cover purchasing, transportation, and marketing expenses; and relief loans with short maturity, mostly for immediate living expenses.

The supply of credit comes from the large number of rural branches of the People's Bank and from credit cooperatives. Branches of the People's Bank, however, do not extend below the district or *ch'ü* level. Consequently the credit cooperatives have been organized on the village level to cope with the needs of individual farms. These cooperatives are of three types. The first, the credit cooperative, is in theory a self-supporting unit, based on the share capital of the members. The second type, the credit department of the marketing and supply cooperative, has no share capital and normally does not do much business. The third type, the mutual-aid group, is generally only a provisional grouping of people for the purpose of mutual financial help. According to Communist sources, there were 153,400 credit units in June 1955 including both credit cooperatives and credit departments of marketing and supply cooperatives, as compared with only 542 in 1950 and 9,800 in December 1953. By 1956 the number of rural credit cooperatives alone had grown to 110,000. The organization of the commune has resulted in many cases in the absorption of the credit cooperatives by the commune, necessitating another reorganization of the rural credit structure.

Up to the present, the bulk of rural credit has been extended by the rural branches of the People's Bank rather than by the credit cooperatives. Agricultural loans extended by the bank totaled four billion yuan (about 1.6 billion American dollars) in 1957 while the corresponding volume for credit cooperatives was only one billion (405 million American dollars). On the other hand, in 1954 alone, of the 470 million yuan (about 191 million American dollars) which the People's Bank received in peasant deposits after the state purchase of grain and cotton, 200 million yuan (about 81 million American dollars) were deposits transferred from credit cooperatives. The credit cooperatives may have served more to absorb rural savings than to extend credit to the peasants.

The total volume of rural credit extended by the bank has increased since 1956 when loans totaling 3.1 billion yuan (about 1.26 billion American dollars) were made, principally to encourage the formation of cooperative farms, as compared with 4 billion for the entire 1950-54 period. To some extent the magnitude of the program of rural credit as indicated by these figures is more apparent than real. Loans have been made in some instances only on paper, with the bulk of the amount taken from the borrower in the form of "voluntary deposits." Other methods of financial juggling involve paper transfer of credits: the banks loan money to the agricultural cooperatives, which deposit it in the credit cooperatives, which in turn place it with the banks. Where actual loans are made, they are often given to agricultural cooperatives without regard to needs. This in turn encourages the cooperatives to become extravagant in their operations, spending money without consulting their own members.

Savings

In order to attract scattered funds held by individuals and to prevent cash balances being kept outside the banks, the People's Bank, in addition to subbranches and agencies, has receiving and paying stations for savings deposits in the residential quarters of each city. Officers of these stations visit residents frequently to collect their savings. By such means most families are forced to open savings accounts with banks. The total volume of savings account balances was 4,023 million yuan (about 1,635 million American dollars) at the end of November 1957, which compares with an outstanding balance of 1,200 million yuan (about 500 million American dollars) of reported rural savings deposits at about the same time.

In rural areas, quotas for increased savings deposits are set for each county which in turn fixes quotas for each village and household. Every year after the compulsory sale to the government monopoly of grain, cotton, and oil-bearing crops, banks and credit cooperatives canvass the rural areas in an effort to induce the peasants to place the proceeds in savings accounts. The higher degree of control under the communes and recent increases in agricultural production should mean greater potential savings in the future.

Until October 1955 a very high interest rate was offered to encourage peasants to deposit voluntarily in banks or credit cooperatives cash received for crops. Interest at 14.4 percent was paid on deposits of under three months and 18 percent after that time. But in spite of these rates, figures for 1954 showed that only in Kiangsi province did deposits reach 30 percent of the purchase proceeds. They were only 5 percent in Honan province and much less in Hunan, Kwangtung, and Kwangsi. Some peasants were afraid to expose their cash receipts; others preferred to hoard commodities.

Many credit cooperatives and banks, in order to achieve their assigned quota of deposits, extort compulsory deposits from the peasants, usually when they apply for agricultural loans. In one village in Hupeh a peasant was compelled to deduct 5 yuan from a 5.5 yuan (about 2.20 American dollars) loan as his deposit with the credit cooperative that granted the loan. In many instances peasants have found that once they deposited funds in the credit cooperatives, withdrawal was almost impossible as their reasons often did not meet with the approval of the cooperatives. Similar malpractice on the part of rural branches of the People's Bank further alienated the peasants, who tended to distrust the banks in the first place because of the complicated procedures required. The provincial authorities found it even more difficult to control the rural branches of the People's Bank than the credit cooperatives, because the branch banks often defied the provincial authorities on the ground that they had independent instructions from the head office. Recent reports indicate a serious lag in the growth of savings deposits during the conflict with Taiwan over the offshore islands in the autumn of 1958 and also as a result of dissatisfaction among the peasants with government measures.

Insurance

Immediately after the Communist occupation, the first move toward control of the insurance field was made when all insurance companies were required to raise capital to meet minimum standards. Most were able to do so and continued in business. In October 1949 the People's Insurance Company of China was formed under the supervision of the People's Bank to handle all kinds of insurance. One by one all state, joint state-private and cooperative enterprises were ordered to carry fire insurance with the People's Insurance Company; passengers on trains, steamships, and airplanes were required to buy accident insurance from the company. Insurance on farm animals and crops was tried but failed. At the beginning of 1951, a little over a year later, 70 percent of the insurance business was reportedly in the hands of the People's Insurance Company, 19 percent with foreign companies, and the remaining 11 percent with private Chinese companies. In November 1951 private insurance companies were absorbed in the newly formed Joint Administration of Insurance Companies. Since that time no mention has been made of either foreign or private Chinese insurance companies.

The People's Insurance Company of China, which has the same standing as any other state enterprise, keeps its funds at the People's Bank and its investments are under the latter's direct supervision.

Policy Trends

It is the policy of the government to channel all available resources into the industrialization program. Consequently there is no pretense that the present tax burden, policy of enforced savings, and curtailment of consumer goods production are in themselves desirable. The government continues to emphasize to the working masses the brighter tomorrow which the sacrifices of today are expected to bring. It claims that tax administration is more nearly uniform and more efficient than under previous regimes, and there is some reason to believe that such claims strike a responsive chord in the population. Many persons, with vivid memories of the chaotic fiscal conditions of the 1940's and the subsequent Communist success in checking inflation in 1949 and 1950, tend to give the present government credit for bringing order out of chaos. The Communists themselves point to a balanced budget as one of their major achievements but this is a dubious claim as the balancing is mostly sham and the dangers of latent inflation are still very real.

Comparison of the tax burden during the republican period and today is difficult since under the Nationalists much tax revenue came from indirect consumption taxes such as customs duties, salt tax, sales tax, and so forth. The large sums which the Communist government at present obtains from state-owned industry have no precedent in previous regimes. In agriculture there seems to be agreement among observers that the actual burden on the peasants has not been reduced. Under the Nationalist government many farmers paid rent as well as taxes, and, although they do not pay rent today, taxes plus "hidden exactions" by the government take about the same proportion of income as rent and taxes took earlier.

It cannot be denied, however, that the fiscal structure has so far met the demands of the government's economic and other programs. The financial basis of the present regime is much sounder today than ten years ago even though in view of rapidly expanding government expenditures, the government's fiscal policy remains vulnerable.

CHINA IS A PREDOMINANTLY AGRICULTURAL COUNTRY with over 75 percent of its population engaged in farming, an officially estimated cultivated area of 280 million acres, and an annual harvest (in 1958) of about 250 million metric tons of principal food crops, including cereals, tubers, and legumes. Agriculture contributed about 60 percent of China's estimated national income for the years 1931 to 1936, and, despite the recent rapid industrial development, was still responsible for about 50 percent of the gross national product in 1957.

Agriculture in China has a threefold task: to deliver an ever increasing supply of food to the growing population, to supply the exports to exchange for imported capital goods needed in the country's industrialization, and to provide raw materials for the country's light manufacturing industry. Clearly, every change in agricultural production and in its organization profoundly affects the level of employment, the rate of capital accumulation and industrialization, the well-being of the population, and the political stability of the regime. The Communist authorities, recognizing this pivotal position of agriculture, have to a significant extent staked their political fortune on their ability to control the peasant population, to socialize agriculture, and simultaneously to raise agricultural output.

Land Utilization and Agricultural Regions

About 60 percent of China's land is above 6,600 feet in altitude and cannot be considered suitable for agriculture. Another 20 percent is relatively unsuitable because of topographic or climatic limitations: it is estimated that there were in 1953 about 250 million acres of wasteland. Only slightly over 4 percent of this area has been reclaimed since that time. In view of China's large population, the relative shortage of farm land means that agricultural yield must be substantially increased and arable land must be used economically. Crop lands occupied 90 percent of the total area of farm land in prewar China and there is still very little animal husbandry in China Proper.

Water and the availability of transport and marketing facilities exert considerable influence on land utilization. A large proportion of the farm land—over one-half of the 280 million acres of cultivated land in 1958—is irrigated, some of it for centuries. North China needs irrigation more than South China and uses, in addition to irrigation ditches, subterranean irrigation by either shallow or deep wells. The main areas for wells are around Peking and along the railway from Peking to Hankow. As the route of a railway is generally determined by the economic development of the land and vice versa, the location of railways in China serves as a guide to industrial crop areas. The planting of improved American-type varieties of cotton in pre-Communist years was, for example, centered along the railway lines in Honan, Hopeh, Shantung, and Shensi; the production of flue-cured tobacco, along the railway lines in Shantung, Honan, and Anhwei. Recent developments in the cotton textile industry under the Communist regime have led to the further expansion of cotton fields in North China and have emphasized most pointedly the importance of irrigation in general although large-scale flood control schemes have tended to draw more public attention, especially abroad.

The country as a whole can be divided into two major regions, the wheat region and the rice region, which in turn can be divided into eight subregions or "areas."

(1) The spring wheat area includes the northern parts of Hopeh, Shansi, Shensi, and Kansu, and the southern parts of the former provinces of Jehol, Chahar, Suiyuan, and Ningsia. The land is generally very rugged; the principal crops include millet, potatoes, and spring wheat.

(2) The winter wheat-millet area comprises a large part of Shansi, Shensi, and Kansu, and corners of Honan and Hopeh. The elevation of the land varies from about 3,280 to 9,840 feet. The best farm lands are found in the Fen and the Wei valleys; the principal crops are winter wheat, millet, cotton, and kaoliang.

(3) The winter wheat-kaoliang area includes the whole of Shantung, a large part of Honan and Hopeh, and the northern parts of Kiangsu and Anhwei. The great plains of North China comprise

four-fifths of this area. The principal crops here are winter wheat, kaoliang, cotton, millet, corn, and soybeans.

(4) The Yangtze rice-wheat area is composed of the land along the Yangtze in Hupeh, Anhwei, and Kiangsu. The principal crop is rice; secondary crops are cotton, winter wheat, and barley. Two-thirds of the area is double cropped.

(5) The rice-tea area includes the hill and mountain lands of southern Anhwei, Chekiang, and Fukien, and the plains around the Tung-t'ing and P'o-yang lakes in Hunan and Kiangsi. Most Chinese tea is produced in the mountainous parts of this area. Rice, rapeseed, corn, wheat, sweet potatoes, and tung trees are also important products. In the vicinity of Hangchow, mulberry trees are grown extensively. Over two-thirds of the cultivated land of the area is double cropped.

(6) The Szechwan rice area comprises the whole of Szechwan province and small parts of Hupeh, Shensi, and Kansu. The elevation varies from 656 to 9,840 feet. Rice is the most important crop of this area, especially on the Ch'eng-tu plain, but tung oil from trees planted in this area is one of the most important export items of China. Over two-thirds of the cultivated land of this area too is double cropped.

(7) The double cropping rice area includes the whole of Kwangtung, the eastern and central parts of Kwangsi and the southern parts of Fukien and Kiangsi. Over three-fourths of the cultivated land is double cropped, the highest percentage of double cropping in any area.

(8) The southwestern rice area includes the whole of Yunnan, a large part of Kweichow, and the western part of Kwangsi. Only 7 percent of the land is cultivated and of the cultivated area 82 percent is irrigated, a higher proportion than in any other area. Rice is the predominant crop. Only a little over one-half of the crop area is double cropped, the lowest percentage in any of the rice areas.

To these eight agricultural areas of China Proper a few more remote areas can be added. One might be called the Inner Mongolian pastoral area, a vast grassland inhabited by nomads; some sections, where irrigation is possible, produce wheat and oats. The Tibetan pastures form a separate area, consisting of meager grazing land and very limited agricultural lands in eastern Tibet, western Szechwan (formerly Sikang), and Tsinghai. In pre-Communist years less than 1 percent of the Sinkiang oasis farming area was under cultivation, producing principally wheat, millet, and corn. The most important agricultural region outside of China Proper is the northeastern soybean-kaoliang area, including the intensively farmed Manchurian plain and the well-forested region of eastern Manchuria. The soybean belt is situated in the northern Manchurian plain, the kaoliang belt in southern Manchuria.

Communist Agricultural Policy

Land scarcity, a large farming population, and equal distribution among the sons in inheritance had over the centuries led to intensive farming of small units, creating in the process the central problem for Chinese agriculture: low farm income as a result of the small size of farms. Prior to the Communist period farms averaged about 3.5 acres per farm household or 0.7 acre for each member of a five-member household. Since a large farm unit is a prerequisite to the employment of more advanced technological methods, including the specialization of different types of land for different purposes, use of farm machinery, deduction of waste, and so forth, any significant increase in agricultural production depended on effecting some form of consolidation of these small farms.

Sociopolitical factors entered here. Communist policy ruled out the development of large private farms and collectivization became the logical goal. But since the Chinese peasants were interested in becoming owner-cultivators and not members of collective farms, a program of immediate collectivization would have encountered considerable resistance. Hence the Communists approached their objective in progressive stages, the first being "agrarian reform."

Land Redistribution

Speaking in 1950, Mao Tse-tung ascribed great importance to land reform as one of the tests for every Chinese and every party in the era of the new democracy. The reform referred to was a program of land redistribution and a great deal of political capital had been gained by the Communists' pose as agrarian reformers. Before the consolidation of the newly "liberated" areas in Central and South China in mid-1950, Communist agrarian policy for these areas was limited to the reduction of rent and interest, while in the old "liberated" areas in North and Northeast China, land redistribution had already been carried out by 1949, if not earlier. By mid-1950, the Communists saw fit to proclaim land redistribution for the whole of China in order to establish the Communist party's monopoly of political and economic power and to serve as a first step toward the gradual nationalization of the rural economy.

Political expediency also explains why the new Agrarian Reform Law adopted by the Government Administration Council on June 28, 1950 significantly modified the earlier agrarian law adopted by the Chinese Communist party in September 1947. For instance, the old law called for the requisition of the surplus rural properties of rich peasants whereas the new law stipulated that land owned by rich peasants and worked by them or their hired laborers was not to be touched. In addition, people engaged in nonagrarian occupations, such as factory workers or professional people, who owned and rented out small parcels of land, were not to be classified as landlords and were allowed to keep and to rent out such parcels of land. The dual purpose of these changes was, of course, to encourage the early restoration of agricultural production and to isolate the landlords as a class.

For the effective execution of the land redistribution policies in Central and South China, where there is a very large rural population, an elaborate official definition of the class status of the rural population groups was adopted by the Government Administration Council on August 4, 1950. When remaining opposition elements in a rural area were subdued, cadres were sent there to organize village peasant meetings, peasant representative conferences, and committees for peasant associations. These meetings and conferences under the leadership of the village people's government then determined through "self-assessment and public discussion" each individual's class status according to the official definition, that is, whether he belonged to the landlord, rich peasant, middle peasant, poor peasant, or farm laborer class.

In the case of landlords, their land, draft animals, farm implements, surplus grain, and surplus houses in the countryside were confiscated. On the other hand, rich peasants were allowed to retain the land cultivated by themselves or by hired labor, small portions of land rented out, as well as their other properties. In the case of middle peasants, who constituted 20 percent of the rural population according to official reports, their land and other properties were also protected. A portion of the confiscated or requisitioned land was divided equally among the poor peasants and farm laborers, who constituted 70 percent of the rural population. The rural lands belonging to ancestral shrines, temples, monasteries, churches, schools, institutions, and other public lands (perhaps 5 percent) were also requisitioned. There were specific provisions for the treatment of special land problems. For instance, land and houses owned by overseas Chinese were handled separately, in accordance with the decisions of the respective provincial people's governments instead of under the 1950 land law.

In general, the Communists adopted a practical attitude, working out different timetables for land reform to fit different areas in China. The tactics in 1950 acknowledged a reliance upon the poor peasants and the farm laborers, and sought the cooperation of the middle peasants and the neutrality of the rich peasants. However, although peasants nominally had a voice in the peasant meetings and conferences, the Communist party guided and controlled the direction and execution of this agrarian reform through party directives and by providing party cadres to initiate and supervise the reforms. To mobilize peasants and encourage them to reveal their grievances, to help convene the peasants' representative conferences, and to set up short-term training classes for the active elements, land reform teams were organized in large numbers.

Land redistribution continued on a massive scale for more than three years from 1949 to 1952, usually accompanied by violence and bloodshed. Toward the end of 1952, the movement was reported to have been practically completed throughout China. According to official reports, about 300 million peasants, or between 60 and 70 percent of the rural population, had received some 110 million acres, or roughly 45 percent of the total land under cultivation at that time. The amount of land acquired by peasants through land redistribution varied from 0.15 to 0.45 of an acre per capita in different localities.

The land redistribution program was meant to extend and consolidate Communist power at the village level in several ways. The transfer of ownership of rural properties to the poor peasants and farm laborers aimed not only to elevate their economic status, but also to influence them to replace the old system of social values with an entirely new pattern of living. The land reform struggle had created large numbers of "active elements" among the peasants. In East China alone in 1951, more than 300,000 young peasants reportedly joined the New Democratic Youth League (Communist Youth League since September 1956). Membership in peasant associations in East, Central-South, Southwest, and Northwest China totaled more than 88 million, of whom about 30 percent were women.

Finally, the Chinese Communists asserted that land reform would release a part of the productive forces which were not fully and efficiently used under the old system, and that increased productivity in rural areas would provide a basis for improving living standards. However, the result of equal redistribution of farm holdings among the large numbers of poor peasants was that the size of the average farm became even smaller than before.

Forms of Progressive Collectivization

The Agrarian Reform Law of 1950 in effect preserved the institution of private ownership of land while confiscating the landlords' holdings. But the Communists never desired permanent peasant ownership. The fate of the rich farmers, in the end, would be that of the kulaks of Soviet Russia: restriction and extinction.

In December 1951 the Central Committee of the Communist party issued a "Decision on Mutual Aid and Cooperation in Agricultural Production." A revised decision was promulgated on February 15, 1953. These decisions laid down in detail the methods for the promotion of mutual-aid organizations and producers' cooperatives. So along with progress in industrialization, the Communist policy was to make collectivization of agriculture the major task of national construction in the rural areas.

The path of collectivization was marked by several distinct stages from mutual-aid teams through agricultural producers' cooperatives to collective farms, and finally communes. Mutual-aid organizations constituted the first and lowest form of collectivization and were in most cases organized on either a seasonal or temporary basis for limited sharing of manpower, draft animals, and agricultural tools, but there were also long-term mutual-aid teams involving permanent arrangements for unrestricted sharing of these assets. The peasants accepted this form of cooperation readily as some degree of mutual help had always existed in the countryside.

Beginning in 1954 the transformation of mutual-aid teams into agricultural producers' cooperatives was pursued with increasing vigor, and by 1956 it was complete. In contrast to the mutual-aid arrangements, the producers' cooperatives represented the pooling of land, as well as implements, draft animals, and labor. The land was considered the peasants' investment in the cooperatives. This semisocialist organization differed from the Russian collective farm in that there was remuneration for land as well as for labor. The land itself remained in private ownership but entered the cooperative as a share. However, there was a rule that remuneration for labor should always be higher than that for land although the gap should not be so wide as to arouse discontent among the peasants.

Moreover, when the yield of the land increased, the remuneration for labor was to be further increased.

According to the State Statistical Bureau, the number of pro- ducers' cooperatives taking part in the autumn harvest rose from 19 in 1950 to 3,644 in 1952, 15,068 in 1953, 114,366 in 1954, and 633,200 in 1955. By June 1956 this number was further raised to 992,000; in terms of total farm households, 91.7 percent were said to have been organized into cooperatives.

Despite the claim that output increased where the farmers became progressively more organized, the multiplication of these semisocialist organizations did not appear to have proceeded as smoothly as expected. In addition to discontent and dissatisfaction on the part of some peasants, the financial and accounting work in the cooperatives failed to keep up with their rapid development. A sample survey of the motives which induced farmers to join the cooperatives revealed that 40 percent did so spontaneously. These turned out to be Communist party and New Democratic Youth League members, village cadres, heads of former mutual-aid teams, and farmers in financial trouble. The remaining 60 percent were reported to have joined hesitantly, some out of fear that refusal would result in their being regarded as "backward elements."

The next step was the advance from semisocialist cooperatives to collective farms, described in an article in the *People's Daily* of January 1, 1954 as follows: "The present agricultural producers' cooperatives are an appropriate form of organization to lead the peasants toward the higher and fully developed socialist form of agricultural producers' cooperatives, namely the collective farms." Two types of collective farms were distinguished: a higher type of producers' cooperatives, differing from the former ones in that the members theoretically owned the land in common instead of "investing" their individual holdings; and the state farm in which land became the property of the state. By the summer of 1958 more than 95 percent of all the peasant households were said to be in collective farms.

The first state farm was established in 1951 by the central gov- ernment in what was then Sungkiang province in Northeast China. It consisted of some sixty peasant families, with administrative authority vested in a general farm members' meeting which deter- mined production plans, standards of labor, and rates of remunera- tion. The actual operation of the farm was in the hands of a control committee elected by the meeting. The revised 1953 decision on mutual aid and cooperation in agriculture called for the establishment of more mechanized or semimechanized state farms, and a greater number of experimental state farms, the latter being nonmechanized farms operated under the supervision of local authorities.

In April 1953 it was reported that only 0.3 percent of all land under cultivation in the country was worked by state farms, including the few large mechanized farms and the more numerous small nonmechanized farms. To facilitate their operation, machinery received from abroad was used to set up new state farms. A February 1955 report, for instance, stated that 98 tractors, 100 harvester combines, 128 tractor plows, and 120 tractor-drawn grain planters had arrived from the Soviet Union at the new 80,000-acre Friendship State Farm in Heilungkiang. By June there were 110 mechanized and semimechanized state farms, 2,300 provincial and local state farms, 89 state ranches, 19 aquatic enterprises, and 101 tractor stations. The new land program of 1956 called for a tenfold increase in the acreage of state farms in the coming twelve years to a total of over 22 million acres.

Regionally, most of the state farms set up in 1955 were located in Northeast China. Heilungkiang, for instance, had 32 mechanized state farms. In the northwest four state farms were established in Sinkiang in 1955, with some 76,000 acres. Many of those planned for 1956 and 1957 involved the reclamation of wasteland in Heilungkiang and the Sinkiang Uigur Autonomous Region on the frontiers.

The final stage of the collectivization movement has been the amalgamation of the cooperative and collective farms into communes, which are more comprehensive than the collective farms. The communes are not organized for purposes of agricultural production alone, but have other economic as well as broader political and social functions. Started in the summer of 1958, they numbered 26,500 toward the end of 1958 and averaged 5,000 farm households each. In most cases communal ownership of all the land and other assets has been established although state ownership has been substituted in some cases.

A fact that should not escape notice is the gathering momentum of collectivization. There were good economic reasons for caution in the formation of cooperative farms inasmuch as rural underemployment might become outright unemployment and the population movement to urban centers would present serious problems unless it could be matched by industrial growth. There were equally important political considerations. A directive published for domestic circulation in the spring of 1955, while calling for the consolidation of existing cooperatives, actually ordered that the creation of new producers' cooperatives be slowed. The *People's Daily* of March 3, 1955 warned against forcible measures that interfered too much with the economic life of the peasantry, explaining that economic measures should be combined with political education of the peasants so that they would accomplish their tasks in the cooperatives voluntarily.

There were, however, considerable differences of opinion in party councils on the question of how fast the peasants could or should be pushed. After much deliberation the government finally decided in October 1955 on a renewed acceleration in the formation of agricultural producers' cooperatives. The new drive, completed by 1956, was followed by one and a half years of consolidation during which cooperatives were converted into collective farms. That the gradual approach to collectivization has given way to a more rapid course is symptomatic of the urgent need to increase agricultural output. The government's effectiveness in channeling agricultural production through the public sector of the economy has also been increased through progressive collectivization, culminating in the commune system, which, by simultaneously directing farm labor to nonagricultural uses, also has averted large-scale rural unemployment.

According to party functionaries, the cooperative movement was far more important than the land reform program and the cadres were urged to function more effectively in overcoming peasant resistance as the pace increased. At the same time, a drive for party membership was carried on in rural districts. The emphasis on building party leadership in rural areas has since been reasserted in connection with the propagation of the communes. But there have evidently been many instances of shortcomings and blunders in carrying out the collectivization program. Lack of sufficient technical competence and unfamiliarity with local conditions and practices have often hampered the planning and direction of farming operations, while the actual working of the system has in many places undoubtedly lowered peasant morale, nor has production invariably come up to expectations.

Agricultural Loan System

The institutional changes represented by the initial redistribution of land and the formation of collective farms and communes put the local branches of the Communist party in a position of control over the rural population. The effect on the distribution of the farmers' output, including income derived from nonagricultural activities, has been reinforced by the financial control of the government-sponsored rural credit cooperatives, the People's Bank, and the taxation and compulsory purchase policies of the government.

In the pre-Communist period, short-term loans were acquired mostly from individual lenders at usurious rates rather than from lending institutions. Since 1949 private moneylenders have gradually disappeared in the countryside, and the monetary and credit policy of the state in rural districts has become increasingly important. During the first years of the Communist regime, with all energies concentrated on land redistribution, rural monetary and credit organization was rather neglected. By the end of 1953 this need began to be filled by cooperative finance assisted by state finance or, in the absence of cooperative finance, by state finance alone.

Loan policies in earlier years can be found in the instructions issued by the Government Administration Council in July 1953 and the People's Bank in the spring of 1954. The bulk of the loans was reserved for state-owned farms and other organized farming. However, loans were also granted to individual farmers to keep them from dealing with private moneylenders and to induce them to join the producers' cooperatives. In other words, credit policies have been closely tied up with the organization of credit cooperatives and producers' cooperatives. The operations of the now defunct Agricultural Bank of China after 1955 were similarly motivated, and they probably contributed to the fresh surge of such cooperatives. For instance, long-term, low-interest loans were extended to poor peasants to enable them to join agricultural cooperatives, since all members were required to contribute to the cost of fertilizer, seed, fodder, draft animals, farm tools, carts, and other means of production. Loans were also used effectively to influence the direction of agricultural production. At one time, for instance, loans were made in certain areas only to those who changed their production from food crops to industrial crops; or they might be earmarked for water conservation, fisheries, or logging.

With progressive collectivization and the establishment of more direct control by local Communist officials over the production and investment policies of the expanded farm units, the function of the rural credit institutions has shifted its emphasis to the collection of rural savings on a semicompulsory basis. This of course is in furtherance of the policy of regulating the volume of consumption. An indication of this trend is found in the growth of rural savings deposits from an annual rate of 153 million yuan in 1953 to 800 million yuan in 1955 (about 63 and 325 million American dollars respectively). An even greater rate of increase has been reported since the formation of the communes.

Taxation and Compulsory Purchase

The Chinese Communists have charged that under the Nationalists the major portion of the tax burden fell upon the peasant. They point out that in 1949 the agricultural tax in kind provided the principal source of government revenue, but that since 1950 it has been gradually replaced by industrial and commercial taxes, with the result that the agricultural tax which in 1950 constituted 29.63 percent of the total revenue has progressively declined to only 10.17 percent in 1956. But even if their figures are correct, it should be remembered that tax grain has been priced throughout these years below the market price and as a consequence income from grain taxation is grossly understated. Furthermore, agriculture has been an important source of revenue through its substantial contribution to the profits of the state trading enterprises, derived mainly from transactions with the rural population. Profits for the state monopoly on the sale of agricultural products represent smaller receipts for the farmers and therefore constitute a hidden tax. The government also collects substantial levies in the form of various "contributions" and "offerings" made by the rural populace. The total per capita burden of taxes and "contributions" on the peasants during 1950 to 1952 was estimated at about 52 percent of their income. In other words, the amount (averaging 40 percent) the peasants previously turned over to the landlords was turned over to the state under the Communists. In 1956 about 25 percent of the net output of agriculture was channeled to the government through a combination of taxes and compulsory purchases. The burden on the farmer does not appear lighter than it was before 1949.

The marketing and distribution of rural products have also undergone radical changes since 1949, particularly in the extension of state trade and price-fixing by the state trading companies and their nationwide network of branches, which worked in close collaboration with the supply and marketing cooperatives that had a purchase network of 183,182 units and a staff of nearly one million at the end of 1955. In 1952 the cooperatives handled between 60 and 70 percent of the total quantity of agricultural products bought by the state, although only 10 percent of the nation's total retail trade was transacted by the cooperatives. In spite of the expansion of direct purchases by specialized government-controlled companies, the cooperatives still played a dominant role in the purchase of certain crops until supplanted by the communes.

The cooperatives were organized to supply members with consumer and producer goods "at prices lower or at least not higher than the market prices," and at the same time to buy members' products "at reasonable prices." The cooperatives also actively participated in the relief campaigns in response to government orders. The aim of these cooperatives was to restore and develop production, and "to coordinate, through every specific business activity, the interests of individual peasants with the interests of the state as a whole." By 1954 trade in essential commodities produced in the rural areas had been gradually taken over by the state, with the state determining the rations for different categories of population, fixing official purchasing and retail prices, and handling the trade through a network of government marketing centers. In the cities, ration books had been issued to individuals by November 1955.

To close the inflationary gap between effective demand and supply of agricultural commodities and to facilitate the progress of socialization, planned purchase and planned supply were introduced. As early as January 1, 1951 large-scale government purchases of cotton and cotton cloth were made through the cooperatives. Toward the end of 1953 food grains were put under the planned purchase and supply system, followed by edible oils and other commodities.

To assure the government an adequate supply of the goods in question, the method of advance purchase was adopted, beginning with cotton in 1951. Later, by the directive of March 23, 1954, the All-China Federation of Supply and Marketing Cooperatives began purchasing grain, cotton, peanuts, tea, jute, ramie, hemp, silk cocoons, raw silk, and wool through advance contracts. This system guarantees the peasants an opportunity to buy many necessities which would otherwise not be easily available to them and it has encouraged them to organize themselves more extensively. It has also given rise to the practice of the so-called "link contracts" by which the supply and marketing cooperatives guarantee to supply principal producer and consumer goods to the mutual-aid teams and the agricultural producers' cooperatives, which in turn give the supply and marketing cooperatives priority in buying their farm produce and the products of their subsidiary enterprises.

All sales of agricultural products after the collection of taxes in kind have been rigorously controlled since the end of 1953 at which time it was apparently believed that any further increase in taxation would encounter diminishing returns. One result of this strict control is that China which for fifty years had been on balance a net importer of foodstuffs has had a net export balance of these commodities since 1951. Reports for the year 1953-54 claim that government purchases of all food crops were 77 percent higher than in previous years and that food was sold through state agencies to 100 million city dwellers and an equal number of villagers. The villagers who bought foodstuffs from the state included three categories of farmers: those who grew industrial crops (said to be about fifty million); those in areas devastated by natural calamities ("several tens of million"); and the "needy farmers who had sold the state too much foodstuffs, and thus from abundant farming households had become needy farming households."

In early 1955, for a combination of reasons, food was in short supply in many parts of the mainland. Not only did agricultural production in 1954 fail to meet the planned goal, but there was faulty administration in the state monopoly which buys and sells agricultural products. As a way out of this crisis, the State Council on March 3, 1955 introduced a new system, fixing for a three-year period the amount of food each village was to produce, the amount it must sell the state, and the amount it could buy from the state. According to the ruling of the State Council, only in cases of serious calamities would the figures for planned purchase of grain be reduced; on the other hand, peasants in bumper harvest areas would be required to increase the amount of grain sold to the state. The three sets of figures for the whole country were determined by the central government, which distributed the figures to the provinces. The latter assigned them to the counties, which in turn notified the villages. The village authorities then transmitted the figures to every household so that, according to a *People's Daily* editorial (March 9, 1955), "all households could know for sure where they stood, arrange properly the household affairs for the whole year, and then throw themselves actively into the spring plowing and production movement."

Agricultural Production

Food and Industrial Crops

A major test of the success or failure of Communist China's agri-cultural program must be sought in the production figures. Accord-ing to official statistics, the total production of food crops—including rice, wheat, millet, proso millet, corn, kaoliang, barley, oats, buck-wheat, soybeans, broad beans, green beans, field peas, and Irish and sweet potatoes—has registered an uninterrupted increase since 1949 (see Table 11). Production of food crops, which had suffered a substantial reduction during the war years (1937-45), picked up rapidly following the cessation of the war. After 1952 the upward trend was, however, slowed down and a new upsurge did not occur until 1958. The increase in production up to 1958 in comparison with prewar output was due principally to the extension of double cropping, a larger planted acreage, and better irrigation and flood control. This increase was especially noticeable in the rice crop. Of a total 373 million acres in crops in 1955 about 72 million acres were devoted to rice as compared with an estimated prewar annual average of 49.5 million acres. Wheat, on the other hand, failed to register a comparable increase in production. The planted acreage in 1955 was about 66 million acres and nearly 20 percent larger than the prewar average, but this increase in acreage was more than off-set by a decline in output per acre.

To a large extent the same factors were responsible for the very large increase in output in 1958 although the intensive application of fertilizers, deep plowing, close planting, and various other tech-nological improvements should also be given due credit. The com-mune movement has had the advantage not only of making the farm unit much larger, but also of increasing the cheap labor supply available so that farming is even more intensive than formerly. It is worth noting that one-quarter of the increase in total output in 1958 consisted of potatoes and other tubers instead of the prin-cipal cereals which are the staple diet of the population.

Of the industrial crops, cotton, the principal textile fiber, pro-vides the raw material for the country's textile industry which has been expanded vigorously in order to achieve self-sufficiency, while oilseeds are important not only as the source of the domestic supply of edible oils, but also as a principal export item.

The average for 1931-37 in China Proper was 9.4 million acres in cotton, producing some 809,500 metric tons of lint. The highest production figure for prewar years, slightly over one million tons, was recorded in 1936. Under the Communist regime, cotton production rose from 445,000 tons in 1949 to 1,305,000 tons in 1952. After a sharp decline in the following two years, it has made significant gains since 1955 and reached 1.64 million tons in 1957 and 2.1 million tons in 1958. The 1959 target has been set at 2.3 million tons. Fluctuations in output are partly the result of weather conditions, but also reflect the changing price ratios between cotton and grain.

Aside from soybeans, rapeseed and peanuts are the principal sources of edible oils in China. Estimated production in 1958 was 1,384,000 metric tons of rapeseed and six million tons of peanuts. Large quantities of the latter are diverted to the export market.

The following are 1956 production figures for the other industrial crops: hemp and jute, 257,800 metric tons; tobacco, 399,000 tons; and sugar cane, 8,654,000 tons. With the possible exception of flue-cured tobacco and tea, the production of most industrial crops now compares favorably with prewar levels.

Livestock and Fisheries

Food crops, textile fibers, tea, and tobacco, along with vegetables and fruits, constituted about 80.5 percent of China's prewar total agricultural production; livestock and fisheries about 7.1 percent. The small size of the farms was responsible for the insignificance of animal husbandry outside Inner Mongolia, Manchuria, and parts of Northwest China. This, and the fact that beef cattle are uncommon, is reflected in the character of the Chinese diet, which is largely vegetarian.

The livestock population in 1958 was officially reported to be: "large animals" (including cattle, horses, camels, donkeys, and mules), 85,060,000 head (38,400,0000 in 1937, excluding mules and donkeys outside China Proper); sheep and goats, 108,860,000 (29,800,000 in 1937); and pigs, 180,000,000 (65,600,000 in 1937). These figures represent substantial increases in livestock production over previous years although earlier figures may be underestimates.

The annual production of fisheries in prewar years was estimated at 1.4 million metric tons, one-third of which represented fresh-water catches. Output was reported in 1949 at only 448,000 tons or about one-third of the prewar level, but has increased rapidly since 1952. In 1956, production jumped to 2.6 million tons.

Forestry Products

Timber in commercial quantities was produced in three areas in prewar years: Fukien, Manchuria, and Hunan. The same areas continue to supply the country's present needs. Production in 1956 was about 19 million cubic meters. The estimated output for 1957 reached 24 million cubic meters. Large-scale afforestation programs are being carried on, both to develop timberlands and to establish shelter belts. Some 111 million acres are reported to have been afforested in 1949-59.

Recovery and Expansion

As seen from the preceding account, the pace of recovery in agricultural production during 1949-52 was rapid. On the other hand, the slowdown of the upward trend in 1953-57 was equally significant.

Contributing factors to the achievement of the early years, according to official pronouncements, were the systematic execution of a nationwide land reform, the organization of peasants into mutual-aid teams and cooperatives, state loan and price policies, water conservation works, improvement of farm technique, and the patriotic emulation drive for increased production. It may be commented that the last item can be effective only for a short period. As for the net effect on production of the first two items, which represent institutional changes within the rural economy, the Communist contention that they are major reasons for the increase is not convincing. Nor could the state loan policy have been an important factor in recovery, the old farm credit system having been seriously disrupted and the new state credit system not yet well organized by 1952.

As far as recovery was concerned, the restoration of peace and order was unquestionably the most important factor. A succession of favorable harvests in 1950-52 added to the farmer's incentive. Improvements in transportation and distribution facilities as well as better irrigation and flood control measures contributed substantially to the expansion of the area under cultivation. Finally, the introduction of improved seeds in large areas, as in the case of cotton in 1952 when for the first time improved seeds were used in 51 percent of the area planted, also played a significant role in speeding the rate of recovery.

Millions of peasants have participated in the rehabilitation of existing dikes and the building of new ones since 1949. The low production level of 1949 was a result not only of the devastation and dislocation of civil war but also of floods, which during the high-water period affected more than 15 million acres of farm land. As a result of flood control work facilitated by favorable weather conditions, the figure for flooded farm land was reduced to 9 million acres in 1950, 3 million acres in 1951, and 2.4 million acres in 1952. To harness the Huai River, the first large-scale, multiple-purpose river basin development project, affecting a population of approximately 60 million, was initiated in 1950; since then a number of reservoirs, flood detention basins, and drainage ditches have been built. Other flood control measures include works on the Yung-ting River near Tientsin, the Liao River in Manchuria, and the Han River near Hankow. Preliminary steps have been taken on a comprehensive plan for the control of the Yellow River and the Yangtze.

Important also is the intensive building of many small irrigation projects all over the country. Irrigation work completed in the period from 1950 to 1954 included 8,400,000 ponds and ditches and 900,000 wells. The area under one form of irrigation or another toward the end of 1958 was approximating 160 million acres.

The increase in agricultural production has not been without setbacks. Production fell short of the planned targets for both 1953 and 1954. For one thing, 1954 witnessed one of the worst floods in the present century along the Yangtze and Han rivers. It affected some 26 million acres of farm land, mostly rice fields, or more than 10 percent of the total cultivated land. As a result, rice production in 1954 was below the 1953 level despite increased production in Szechwan province. The total grain output remained high, however, owing largely to a considerable increase in wheat production in North and Northeast China, as well as an increase in maize and millet crops in Inner Mongolia and Northwest China. The tremendous flood damage may be attributed partly to the magnitude of the flood and partly to the mismanagement of relief work on the part of the local authorities.

Serious floods and typhoons, as well as drought, again affected agricultural production in 1956. Crops fell short of government goals although the authorities had introduced improved seeds in larger areas, applied more chemical fertilizer, and distributed more new farm tools than ever before. Apparently, the recovery period having ended, further expansion of agricultural production must now rely on the application of more capital to land development, supplemented by better water utilization, more land reclamation, continued technical improvements, and a fundamental change in the size of the farm. The measures now employed by the Communist authorities, spurred on by the commune movement since 1958, apparently confirm this analysis.

Plans and Prospects

As a whole, Communist reorganization of China's agrarian structure has had mixed effects upon the rural economy. The improvement of farming techniques and the changes in the methods of credit, marketing, and purchase of farm products may have increased productivity in some areas, but until 1958 the expansion of agricultural production was not as substantial as the Communists had anticipated. Even though the state had streamlined the mechanism of extracting food from the rural population and gross agricultural production in 1957 had increased by 24.7 percent over the corresponding figure for 1952 (the target in the First Five Year Plan was for a 23.3 percent increase) actual performance in agriculture still lagged behind progress in industry. While the actual rate of agricultural development would be sufficiently impressive under normal conditions, it does not measure up to, and was in effect a drag upon, the rate of development in the industrial sector of the economy and in the general economic development of the country as a whole.

The preliminary targets of the Second Five Year Plan as announced in 1956 included a 35 percent increase in the total value of agricultural output over the figures originally planned for 1957 (grain, 181.59 million tons; soybeans, 11.22 million tons; cotton, 1.64 million tons). The production of food crops in 1962 was to be raised to 250 million tons and that of soybeans to 12.5 million tons while the target for cotton production was set at 2.4 million tons. A twelve-year program to increase crop yields was also prepared in 1956, projecting double the 1955 grain output by 1967. As reports of the 1958 crops indicate, the agricultural targets have been attained in great part well ahead of schedule, primarily as the result of an increase in unit area yields.

Setbacks in agricultural production in 1953 and 1954 were attributed by the authorities to natural calamities. Flood and drought control may improve in time, but unfavorable weather conditions cannot be entirely discounted. To increase production, therefore, there must be increased use of fertilizers, improved seeds, and more efficient farm implements and methods. But the outstanding problem of Chinese agriculture has always been the size of the farm.

"Without any change in technology whatsoever," wrote an American observer in 1948, "production and wealth per capita could be increased from 60 to 240 percent if, by some magic, the average size of all Chinese farms could be raised to thirteen acres."

From a purely economic view, the Communist answer—the commune—seems to have been effective, as evidenced by the increase in agricultural production. The addition to commune operations of a number of nonagricultural activities has had a further advantage of averting the unemployment and underemployment that would have followed the formation of large private farms, which in any case were precluded by Communist theory.

The degree of success of the commune system cannot as yet be fully assessed. Much depends on the absence of serious natural calamities which would, by causing a sudden drop in output, destroy what confidence there is among the peasants in their commune. Perhaps even more depends on such factors as the peasants' willingness to forego private ownership of land and traditional family life, their share of increases in farm output, the availability of consumer goods, and the taxation and purchase policies of the government. Reports have begun to appear less than a year after the formation of communes of modifications in several of the harsher aspects of commune life. The nature of the relaxations—abandonment in many communes of compulsory communal eating, some decentralization of control, even the reappearance of a few private plots for spare-time cultivation—indicates a return to features of the collective farm but may be a tactical move to allow more time for political indoctrination. Whatever the social or political considerations, the Communist agricultural goal remains to increase the unit yield to such a degree that acreage under crops can be reduced to one-third the present area and the farm economy radically changed.

INDUSTRY

THE COMMUNIST DETERMINATION TO INDUSTRIALIZE CHINA, reflected in the two five-year plans (1953-57 and 1958-62) and the accelerated program since 1958, is motivated by both ideological and economic factors. Ideologically, the gains made by Communism may be further consolidated through the growth of an industrial working force. The basic economic problem of rural overpopulation and the resultant low level of per capita income cannot be resolved short of the development of alternative opportunities of employment in industry and other nonagricultural pursuits. The growth of national prestige and power—usually justified under the more appealing watchword of national defense—cannot be realized without a large national industry. Since the last factor carries, in the minds of the Communists, a note of urgency, rapid industrialization is considered a political necessity. Further justification of a program of forced industrialization is cited in the weak economic position of the country relative to other modern nations. Chinese industrial development has on the whole lagged so far behind that considerable sacrifice and exertion will be required to provide the base for sustained growth.

The Communist regime must of course work with the means at its disposal, and the nature of the industrial heritage cannot but affect the content, emphasis, and method of its planning. This limiting effect of the past makes itself felt in the balance of individual industries, their geographical distribution, the over-all rate of development, and the need for foreign assistance, to mention only a few of the important factors. The way in which the Communist authorities have proceeded with their industrialization program—given the initial circumstances—is important to their whole effort to consolidate political control of China, as well as for its probable psychological effect on other Asian countries with similar aspirations.

Resources

Although investigation and geological surveys are still being conducted on a large scale and no exact figures have been released, the general picture of China's mineral resources is fairly clear (see plates, Distribution of Metallic Minerals; Distribution of Nonmetallic Minerals). On the whole, China has sufficient mineral resources for a substantial development of modern industries but is not as well endowed as other leading powers. Coal is by far the most important, being comparatively abundant and well balanced for large-scale industrialization. The iron supply is moderate but sufficient to meet the country's industrial needs for many years. Supplies of tungsten and antimony are relatively large, while those of tin, copper, and mercury are moderate. Other metallic ores, such as lead, zinc, and so on are widely distributed geographically, but only small reserves have been found. Sulphur is rather limited in supply, as are manganese, chromite, and fluorspar. Recent discoveries of petroleum and bauxite are significant and with adequate equipment production can be increased to supply domestic needs. So far as is now known, however, China's petroleum resources cannot compare with those of the Middle East, the United States, or the USSR.

Although there is gold in North Manchuria, Sinkiang, Tibet, and western Szechwan (formerly Sikang) China is poor in precious metals. Some rich deposits of phosphate and nitrate have been found in East and Southwest China but not elsewhere; potash is in limited supply.

Generally speaking, distribution falls into two major regional divisions: coal, iron, and petroleum in the North, Northeast, and Northwest (the Southwest may be becoming more important in oil production); the nonferrous metals and ferroalloys in the South and Southwest. The loess regions of Shansi and Shensi (possessing almost 70 percent of all the coal in the country) and Manchuria are natural sites for heavy industries. The lower Yangtze valley, with its convenient water transport and proximity to the metalliferous belt of South China, is most promising for a variety of industrial developments. The Manchurian basin with 70 percent of China's iron ore, together with some good coking coal fields

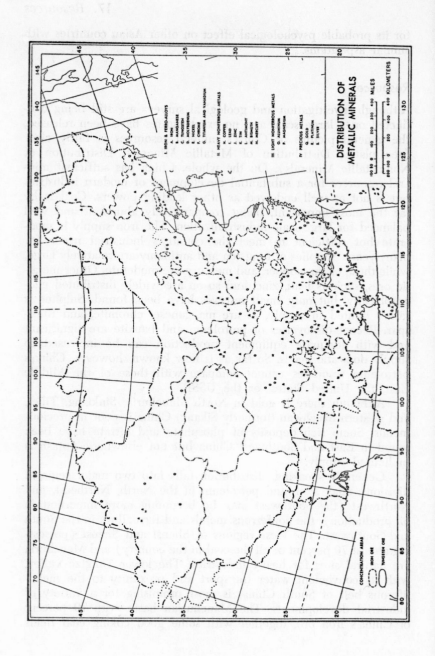

DISTRIBUTION OF
METALLIC MINERALS

I. IRON & FERRO-ALLOYS
A. IRON
B. MANGANESE
C. TUNGSTEN
D. MOLYBDENUM
E. NICKEL
F. CHROMIUM
G. TITANIUM AND VANADIUM

II. HEAVY NONFERROUS METALS
H. COPPER
I. LEAD
J. ZINC
K. TIN
L. ANTIMONY
M. BISMUTH
N. MERCURY

III. LIGHT NONFERROUS METALS
O. ALUMINUM
P. MAGNESIUM

IV. PRECIOUS METALS
Q. GOLD
R. PLATINUM
S. SILVER

MILES
500 100 0   100   200   300   400   500
0 100 200   300   400
KILOMETERS

CONCENTRATION AREAS

IRON ORE

TUNGSTEN ORE

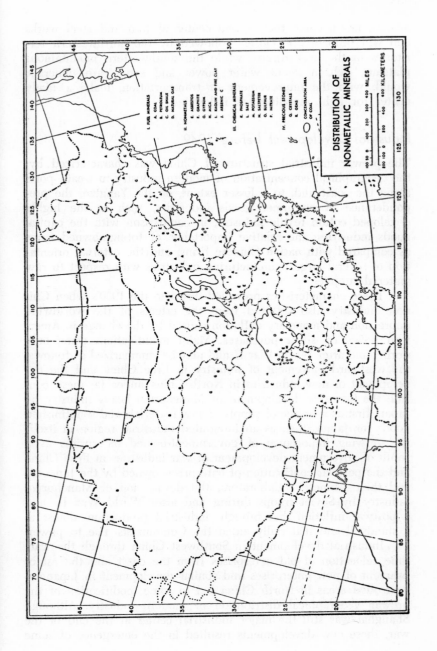

DISTRIBUTION OF NONMETALLIC MINERALS

I. FUEL MINERALS
A. COAL
B. PETROLEUM
C. OIL SHALE
D. NATURAL GAS

II. NONMETALS
E. ASBESTOS
F. GRAPHITE
G. GYPSUM
H. MICA
I. KAOLIN AND FIRE CLAY
J. ARSENIC C

III. CHEMICAL MINERALS
K. PHOSPHATE
L. SALT
M. POTASSIUM
N. SALTPETER
O. SULPHUR
P. NITRATE

IV. PRECIOUS STONES
Q. CRYSTALS
R. GEMS

○ CONCENTRATION AREA OF COAL

MILES
100 50 0   100   200   300   400
800 100 0   200   400   600 KILOMETERS

nearby, has become the leading center of iron and steel works and will probably be closely followed by the northwestern territories in the near future; while the southwestern mountainous plateaus, rich in latent water power and some rare minerals, would, with the improvement of transportation, make a likely center for light metallurgical industries.

Industrial Development before 1949

The prewar industrial structure of China was characterized by: the geographical concentration of modern industry in treaty ports along the coast and, to a lesser extent, on the Yangtze; the preponderance of consumer goods industries, such as the highly developed cotton textile industry, in comparison with the capital goods industries; the relative importance of foreign-owned firms as compared with native Chinese firms; and the external orientation of several large manufacturing industries with respect to raw material supplies.

These characteristics prevailed down to the 1930's when Chinese industry also suffered from the effects of the worldwide depression and monetary deflation caused by the change in American policy on silver purchases. Major modifications came only during and after World War II and may be summarized as follows: the westward movement of industry in Free China and the development of new industries in North China under Japanese control; the intensive development of Manchurian heavy industry by Japan, first as a source of supply of raw materials and semifinished goods for Japan, then as an integrated industrial region in itself; the growing importance of government-owned enterprises as a result of government development of war industries in Free China and the postwar confiscation of enterprises owned by the Japanese and their Chinese collaborators; the devastation of Manchurian industry by Soviet troops during and after Warld War II; and a postwar inflation that brought industrial production almost to a standstill and materially aided the Communists' rise to power.

Industrial development in Southwest China through the wartime relocation of old enterprises from the coast and the establishment of new enterprises and similar development in Japanese-controlled areas in North China led to some modification of the prewar geographical distribution of modern industry. Although Shanghai was still the major industrial center at the end of the war, these new developments resulted in the emergence of some minor industrial bases elsewhere which have since proved of material benefit to Communist planning. There was, for example, the growth of a nucleus iron and steel industry in Chungking, the beginning of a metallurgical and machinery industry in T'ai-yüan, and the development of the Tientsin, T'ang-shan, and Shih-ching-shan industrial triangle in North China.

The most important modification of the geographical distribution of Chinese industry was undoubtedly the development of Manchuria, particularly the Dairen, An-shan, Fou-hsin, Fu-shun, Mukden, and Harbin areas, as a huge industrial complex of the metallurgical, machinery, chemical, petroleum, and coal industries by the Japanese. The devastating effects on Manchurian industry of Soviet removals at the end of the war resulted in a loss estimated at 2 billion American dollars. It did not, however, diminish the potential importance of Manchuria. Consequently, the rehabilitation of Manchurian industry became the first order of business in Communist planning.

A final factor in shaping the course of industrial development under the Communist regime was the growth of the state sector of the economy under the Nationalist government. It had controlled not only all the important heavy industries in China Proper and Manchuria but also large sections of the consumer goods industries, notably the cotton textile mills in which Japanese interests had been predominant. With the establishment of the Communist regime, these enterprises passed automatically into the hands of the new authorities.

Industrial Development under the Communists

When the Communists assumed control in 1949, industrial production had fallen to a deplorably low level due to wartime destruction (see Tables 12 and 13 for a statistical summary of industrial conditions at this time) and the immediate task was one of rehabilitation.

In addition to taking over the industrial enterprises formerly controlled by the Nationalist government, the Communists seized many factories belonging to former Nationalist officials, "counter-revolutionaries," or those found guilty in the Three-Anti and Five-Anti campaigns. Many of these establishments were reorganized as joint state-private enterprises.

Upon the outbreak of the Korean War, American assets in Communist China, including industrial firms owned and operated by Americans, were frozen and put under government custody. The Communist authorities did not confiscate outright properties belonging to citizens of other nations, but through Communist-agitated labor disputes and government-imposed restrictions, many foreign-owned firms were forced out of business and finally purchased by the government at nominal cost.

Thus in various ways the Communist government acquired interests in many industries. The heavy investments of the Communist government in various sectors of the economy, the movement to form joint state-private enterprises, and the establishment of cooperatives put more firms and factories under government control and furthered socialization of the economy. The contribution of various economic sectors to the total value of industrial output for the years 1949-57 is given in Table 14. According to these figures, 98.7 percent of the value of industrial output was under socialist control by the end of 1956.

The Immediate Postwar Period

Industrial production in mainland China during 1949 had dropped to 56 percent of its pre-1949 peak. The decline in the output of producer goods from the previous peak was 70 percent, while the decline in the production of consumer goods was 30 percent. The much sharper drop of production in the heavy industries reflected the marked contraction in Manchuria's industrial capacity while the general decline of industrial output was the result of hyperinflation, disruption due to the civil war, evacuation of the productive facilities of some firms to Hong Kong and Taiwan, and the shortage of power and raw materials in Shanghai following the Nationalist blockade of the port.

It took the Chinese Communists some time to bring the economy back to normal. Through drastic fiscal and monetary measures, inflation was brought under control by the end of 1950. Transportation was improved through restoration of old railroads and construction of new ones. Supply of raw materials was increased by more efficient means of resource distribution and the removal of some factories along the coast to the sources of raw materials in the interior. Heavy investments were made each year by the government in new equipment and factories. Labor productivity was increased through rationalization and work contests. Although industrial production would have risen somewhat in any case upon the restoration of peace and order, the substantial increase in output on the mainland since 1949 must be attributed to various measures taken by the Communist government.

By the end of 1952, gross industrial production had reached about 250 percent of the 1949 value, surpassing the pre-1949 peak in most key products. Using the Communist figures for the pre-1949 peak, only the production of pig iron was short of its peak level by 1952. The output of a selected number of commodities from 1949 to 1952 is given in Table 15.

The failure of pig iron production to rise as rapidly as other commodities was due to the destruction of blast furnaces in Manchuria by Soviet troops, as well as to changed market relationships. During the Japanese occupation at least one-half of Manchuria's pig iron production had been exported to Japan. With changed trading conditions, this market was lost and current output was governed by the rate of domestic steel production which, although it increased rapidly between 1949 and 1952, was still quite low.

The expansion in steel production (both crude and rolled steel), despite Soviet removals of equipment in 1945, was due to the fact that even at its peak the Japanese iron and steel industry in Manchuria had operated at only about 60 percent of capacity. With reasonable maintenance of plants and replacement of dismantled equipment, and by increasing worker productivity through various devices, it was possible to achieve the 1952 output with limited investment.

Light industries such as cotton textiles, flour milling, and tobacco received due attention from the Communist authorities during this period of rehabilitation and reconstruction. Before the Communist take-over, in spite of the relative importance of these industries, a large portion of the domestic consumption was met by imports. Owing to the Communist insistence on self-sufficiency, considerable progress was made in these fields. Output increased at a rapid pace and by 1953 imports had been reduced to negligible proportions.

The First Five Year Plan

With the restoration of industrial and agricultural production to the pre-1949 level, a more ambitious program was launched. The guiding principles for the First Five Year Plan, begun in 1953, were as follows: the rate of growth of producer goods and defense industries must exceed that of consumer goods; the development of the producer goods industries must be such as to allow "reproduction on an extended scale"; agricultural development must be such as to ensure an adequate supply of grain and industrial raw materials, and to provide a surplus with which to finance industrialization; the rate of growth of labor productivity must be greater than the rise in wages in order to ensure accumulation of capital; and new industrial centers must be established close to raw material supplies.

The new plan was designed primarily to foster the development of heavy industry. But it also aimed to alter the location of industry by establishing new centers mainly in the North, Northwest, and Southwest, and by transferring light industry away from the coastal cities. Shanghai and Tientsin would still be the most important centers of light industry, and Manchuria of heavy industry, but there would be other important industrial centers.

The purpose of the plan was clearly expressed in the allocation of planned investment. Of the 42.74 billion yuan (about 17 billion American dollars) earmarked for the creation of fixed assets, 58 percent was allocated to the various industrial ministries; 19.2 percent to transport and communications; and only 7.6 percent to agriculture, forestry, and water conservation, leaving the remaining 15 percent to trade, banking, warehousing, urban utilities, and cultural, educational, and health activities. Within the industrial sector, the allocation of investment funds was as follows: machinery industry, 26 percent; fuels, 25.5 percent; other "heavy industries," 24.4 percent; geological survey and the construction industry, 3.4 percent; textiles and other "light industries," 20.7 percent. In all, according to official statistics, 88.8 percent of the planned industrial investments for 1953-57 was devoted to industries producing means of production, and only 11.2 percent to industries producing consumer goods.

This plan for industrial development called for 2,994 new industrial capital construction projects to be built, 694 major or "above-norm" projects and 2,300 smaller projects. Included in the major projects were the 156 (later increased to 179 and then changed to 166) pivotal works undertaken with Soviet supervision and assistance. Some 455 major industrial projects were scheduled for completion during the five-year period. In the nonindustrial fields, the plan envisaged 220 major or above-norm projects in transportation and communications; 252 in agriculture, forestry, and water conservation; 180 in public utilities; 156 in cultural, educational, and public health activities; and 160 in other fields. The plan included 1,600 major and 6,000 smaller construction projects in all fields; of these, 1,271 major projects and most minor ones were to be completed in the five-year period.

The plan also called for an annual increase of 14.7 percent in industrial output, which amounted to an increase in total value of industrial output of 98.3 percent over a five-year period. By 1957 modern industry was to account for 36 percent of the aggregate value of industrial and agricultural output, compared to 26.7 percent in 1952. The rise in producer goods was set at 17.8 percent annually, while that of consumer goods was not expected to exceed 12.4 percent.

According to an official report in April 1959, government investment in capital construction in the "economic and cultural" sector during the five-year period actually totaled 49.3 billion yuan (about 20.7 billion American dollars) or 15.3 percent above the planned figure. The percentage distribution by major categories was: industry, 56 percent; transport and communications, 18.7 percent; agriculture, forestry, and water conservation, 8.2 percent; and all others, 17.1 percent. Thus there was a slight downward revision of the relative share of state investments in industry, transportation, and communications, and an increase in agriculture and the remaining areas. Because of the increase in the total amount invested, however, there was no decline in the absolute volume invested in the first two categories. On the other hand, since investments in agriculture were said to have risen only after the completion of collectivization and therefore probably took the place of private investments that might otherwise have been made but were not included in the original plan, the increase in total agricultural investment was perhaps more apparent than real. Finally, within the industrial sector, 87 percent of the investment was devoted to heavy industry and 13 percent to light industry, a slight revision in favor of the latter as compared with the original plan.

The number of "above-norm" industrial projects was increased from the original 694 to 921, but only 428 had been completed by the end of 1957 although 109 others were said to be partially in operation. Construction was begun during 1953-57 on 135 of the 166 projects scheduled to be built with Soviet aid and 68 of these were reported to be in full or partial operation by the end of 1957. Furthermore, 64 of a total of 68 projects to be built with aid from the East European countries were begun during this period and 27 had been completed by the end of 1957.

The increase in industrial production was officially given as

19.2 percent a year, with a 141 percent rise in total value for the five-year period—both in excess of the planned figures. The annual increase in the output of producer goods was 26 percent while that of consumer goods was 13.5 percent, the excess over and above the planned rates being substantially larger in the first case. The output of a number of commodities for the years 1952-57 and the corresponding planned figures for 1957 are presented in Table 16. The same 1959 report cited above also indicates that of the forty-six major products listed in the First Five Year Plan, the output targets for twenty-seven commodities were attained a year ahead of time while the goals were reached in six others by 1957. It may therefore be inferred that the goals were not reached in the remaining thirteen cases; the failure was probably severest in the production of nonferrous metals, alloy steels, the more complex machinery items, and certain chemical products.

It should be noted at this point that statistical reports on the degree of plan fulfillment cannot be used by themselves to give a correct evaluation of either the efficiency of planning or the effectiveness of its implementation. While overfulfillment may indicate efficient performance, it may also reflect poor judgment in the original plan. Similarly, underfulfillment may be a result of overoptimism in planning rather than of poor execution.

The question may also be raised as to the accuracy and truthfulness of official Communist reports on the progress of the First Five Year Plan and on the expansion of individual industries. Economists in the West who have specialized in Chinese development seem to agree that the real issue is not so much the truthfulness of the published figures, which are not seriously disputed, but rather the questionable methodology used in some cases to arrive at these figures. Furthermore, the figures do not disclose the total state of Chinese industrial development.

The Communist authorities have admitted that it might require half a century of continuous effort before China can be made a major industrial country comparable to the United States or the Soviet Union. Whether China can ever achieve such a high stage of industrialization is open to question, but no one can deny that at present industrial production is still very backward in China. This is particularly true when comparison is made on a per capita basis with an industrialized Asian country like Japan even though China's relative position has improved remarkably in recent years (see Table 17). Within the over-all problem of rapid industrialization, specific puzzles have plagued the Chinese

Communist planners. Lags have developed in particular industries, such as heavy machinery, alloy steels, synthetic chemicals, and others. If the burden of heavy investment is to be reduced, existing industrial facilities in Manchuria and the coastal regions must be exploited more fully at the expense of the development of the new centers of industry.

The increasing demand for consumer goods has again raised the question whether some shift in emphasis in the allocation of investments may not after all be desirable, and toward the end of the First Five Year Plan one detected some serious questioning even among the Communists themselves. This is closely connected with the need to increase the supply of industrial products to farmers whose cooperation in the production of food, raw materials, and agricultural exports is indispensable to the industrialization program. Already the effect of agricultural shortages has been felt during 1956 and 1957. Finally, the reported figures of plan fulfillment fail to show the true cost in lower quality, frequent industrial accidents, and the exhaustion of workers.

The "Great Leap Forward"

Although some preliminary targets were announced in 1956 for the Second Five Year Plan, including a 100 percent increase in the gross industrial output and substantial advances for coal, power, steel, and others, these earlier estimates were replaced in 1958 by the slogan the "great leap forward." In effect, with the end of the First Five Year Plan in 1957, the Chinese economy entered a new phase of development, although the path forward is not as clearly defined as the Communists seem to believe.

There would appear to be several reasons why the Communist planners may have decided that to sustain the kind of growth that had been attained under the First Five Year Plan was either impossible or unwise. The success of the first plan was based to a considerable degree on utilizing and bringing into full production the plant and resources which, because of political upheaval, were virtually idle when the Communists took over. But by 1957 very little slack remained in the productive plant and further increase in the national product would depend on the creation of major new production units requiring large sums of investment capital. Moreover, in spite of the tremendous growth of production in the years between 1952 and 1957, there were still serious gaps in such areas as machine production, chemical fertilizers, and specialized metallurgical products. Modern technology has made it very costly to build and equip plants for this type of basic industry and such costs are multiplied where industries are located in new geographical areas. Yet it is important to the government to industrialize these areas in order to ease the pressure of an expanding population and for reasons of military and political strategy.

Undoubtedly another consideration was that no major source of investment funds other than the savings of the broad masses was available. Since, however, the level of per capita consumption was already very low, another severe curtailment of consumption such as had occurred in 1956 (when investment was stepped up abruptly at the expense of consumer goods) might prove politically impossible without a further tightening of the reins of political control. Political considerations also pointed to the fact that the greatest pressure for consumer goods came from the urban centers where the ranks of the industrial work force were being continually swollen by a stream of migrating peasants. But housing was already a major problem and supplying food to an increased city population would add to the already existing strain on agricultural production and the transportation system. Any attempt to alleviate these shortages and bottlenecks would have meant a major shift of economic resources to the consumer goods industries and, even had the planning authorities desired this, would have been almost impossible until the gaps in capital goods industries had been filled.

What was needed, therefore, was a way to continue along the path of economic growth without large sums of investment capital, and without aggravating the already dangerously marginal situation in regard to consumption. The logical solution would be to reduce the amount of capital needed per unit of industrial output and to bring new resources into play, chiefly the one resource in which China is richest, manpower. If at the same time some of the problems arising from the tendency of the population to concentrate in urban centers with its consequent burden on the transportation system could be mitigated by spreading the centers of production over a wider geographical area the situation would be further alleviated.

These considerations constitute the economic *raison d'être* of the two major developments since the end of the First Five Year Plan; namely, the establishment of many small-scale, locally financed and directed industrial enterprises that produce both consumer and producer goods; and the consolidation of the collective farms into communes that do not engage exclusively in farming. The advantages to the Chinese economy of small-scale, rural industries are obvious: the low initial capital outlay; the relatively short period needed for construction; the proximity to the market and to the source of supplies; and the spread of knowledge of new productive techniques and skills among the rural population. The communes, for their part, constitute an entirely new development in collectivization.

In economic terms a commune enables the authorities to organize available manpower with maximum mobility and flexibility, and, theoretically at least, fully adaptable to the purposes of those who direct it. Workers can be employed at any place and on any job for an average of twelve working hours each day, or as long as the last man-hour yields, in the opinion of the administrators, more than it costs. The only limitations are what is physically possible and politically safe. The unit cost of such labor can be ascertained fairly easily inasmuch as the rigorous use of a ration system, which calls for a little more than one pound of food a day per person, supplemented by very nominal wages, enables the planners to think of real wages in terms of a determinable subsistence fund. Thus the aggregate volume of consumption can be regulated far more accurately than before and the risk of inflation lessened.

Reports from official Communist sources at first indicated that, apart from increases in agricultural production noted earlier, a "giant leap forward" was actually made in 1958, with increases over 1957 as high as 131 percent in pig iron and 107 percent in crude steel (see Table 18). Although more recent reports have drastically lowered the earlier estimates, it is probable that substantial increases have occurred. The over-all increase in industrial production was said to be about 60 percent. As more and more information becomes available, some of the spectacular increases have become more explicable and have correspondingly lost some of their luster. For instance, the quality of some of the steel produced is said to be inferior and the coal production figures may be for unwashed coal, that is, including rocks and other alien matter. Allowing for these and other qualifications, however, the increase in industrial output probably would still be very impressive, and one cannot dismiss as sheer propaganda the Communist assertion that another "leap forward" would be made in 1959 and possibly in succeeding years.

Apparently the commune movement and the development of

many small-scale local industries were largely responsible for the advances in 1958. The massive scale of operations dwarfed previous statistics and is impressive even considering China's great size. For instance, 73 million women in 24 provinces were reported to be working on water conservation projects at one time; 60 million persons were said to be engaged in the extraction and transportation of ores and in iron smelting; some 520,000 small local industrial plants were added in 1958 over and above some 3 million industrial units organized by the collective farms (later communes) in the first half of the year alone. These units included large numbers of iron smelting furnaces, small blast furnaces, power stations, cement kilns, and coal pits. The annual capacity of the projected blast furnaces is said to be 20 million tons or about five times that of the country's largest iron and steel complex at An-shan in Manchuria. Further examples could be given but they all point to two significant features—the massive scale of the movement and its concentration on a few objectives at a time. In fact, the process of expansion envisaged by the Communist high command is apparently that of "selective breakthroughs" followed by a continual adjustment in the related sectors. Thus production targets selected for the attention of the communes and the local small industries have shifted during the past fifteen months from food grains to iron and steel and then to the machinery required by the decentralized local metallurgical plants and the chemical fertilizers needed by the farms. It is entirely possible that certain consumer goods will receive full attention in the next round.

Prospects

In spite of the Communist regime's initial claims, recent disclosures indicate that the "great leap forward" was by no means an unqualified success. The local production of steel in the "backyard furnaces," at one time so prominently featured in Communist propaganda, has proved a failure, and the expansion of small industries has been accompanied by many problems in organization and also in quality of product. The question remains whether with continued efforts China can be made a major industrial power in a short time. No definite answer can be given here but certain points deserve consideration.

In the first place, the industrialization of a nation depends upon the availability of natural resources. China has only a moderate reserve of petroleum and copper. Though China is relatively rich in coal and iron, its iron ore deposits are of comparatively low quality and most of its coal deposits are not of the coking variety. On the other hand, since vast areas of China have not been explored for mineral deposits, it is difficult to predict what the country's industrial potential is. Short of radical technological innovations, at least a part of the success of the industrialization program will depend on the findings of the geological surveys which are being conducted by Chinese scientists and prospectors under Communist supervision.

Another major difficulty is the need for capital. To start a program of industrialization, a tremendous amount of initial investment has to be made in capital goods. As most of these capital goods have to be imported, in the absence of substantial foreign loans or aid, they have to be paid for by whatever exports China can produce, principally agricultural products. This poses the problem of how much agricultural surplus can be set aside for this purpose. With the ever increasing population and the already highly intensive cultivation of land, the prospect is not too promising unless, without provoking serious popular resistance, the economic benefits expected of collectivization and the commune movement can actually be realized on a long-term basis and the newly built local industry, designed partly to serve the needs of agricultural production, can be accelerated.

China is also handicapped by the lack of power and transport facilities which are prerequisite to any program of industrialization. The huge overhead expenditure required to build railroads and power stations will continue to constitute a drain on the available capital for many years to come.

The strain of forced industrialization is already reflected in the rationing and compulsory sales of agricultural products since 1953 and in the increasing severity of political controls. When heavy investments are made in producer goods, resources must be diverted from the consumer market. It is still too early to tell with any degree of assurance whether Communist China can pass successfully this crucial stage of industrialization.

DOMESTIC AND FOREIGN TRADE

THE GENERAL PURPOSE OF ALL TRADE, within national borders as well as between countries, is to improve the distribution of resources and take advantage of special skills and lower costs. Under the Communist system the purely economic functions of supply and demand are modified by considerations based on Communist theory and practice such as the strict control of national resources, the requirements of centralized planning, the drive for self-sufficiency, and relations with Communist and non-Communist countries. Within the country, the trade pattern is determined by the planned allocation of goods for both political and economic reasons, the control of distributive agencies, and in general the promotion of a socialized economy.

Domestic Trade Pattern

The inadequacy of the Chinese land transportation system has over the years dictated a domestic trade pattern in which the bulk of the country's commerce is local, most often dependent on human or animal transportation, and large-scale movement of goods between regions is confined largely to the rivers, particularly in central and southern China where canals and navigable rivers are more numerous than in the north. Trade between regions consists largely of essential commodities such as rice, cotton and cotton cloth, salt, and coal; specialty and luxury items such as silk, tea, herbs, chinaware, furs, and hides; handicraft products of high quality; and manufactured goods. In contrast, local trade is composed largely of foodstuffs, vegetables, poultry products, livestock, fish, and general handicraft products. Much of this type of trade is carried on as a subsidiary occupation to agriculture, many peasants engaging in a modest trade in locally produced items during the slack season to add to their incomes. Women carry on handicraft activities such as weaving and basketmaking, selling their products locally. The marketing pattern, therefore, is that of a large number of self-contained units dependent on outside trade only for those commodities not produced locally, such as salt, tea, chinaware, and the like. Such a pattern aggravates the severity of regional famines as an inadequate transportation system prevents the importation of surplus grains to compensate for local shortages.

In the traditional commercial structure of China there were three types of trade outlets: the periodic market, the peddler, and the urban shop. In their modified forms they are still basic today. For the vast majority of the rural population and a large part of the urban population as well, the periodic market, found in all towns, is the most common place for buying and selling. At these markets, which generally follow a set schedule of three- or five-day intervals, foodstuffs make up a major portion of the commodities offered for sale although other items used in daily life are also important. A periodic market usually draws upon the surrounding area to the distance of a day's journey on foot for its supplies and its patrons as distinguished from daily markets held near sizable urban centers or from the seasonal and annual fairs held in well-known locations. The former are convenient outlets for urban-rural exchange, while the latter, because they are held at greater intervals of time than the periodic markets, draw their patrons from wider areas. These seasonal fairs, with entertainment as well as commercial facilities, fulfill both social and economic functions.

Another form of urban-rural exchange is carried on by the peddlers, most of whom obtain wares in the city to sell along set routes in the rural countryside. Because everything must be personally transported, peddlers generally deal in light commodities not readily obtainable in rural areas, such as needles and threads, toilet articles, candies, and sweets.

The small street-side stalls, a variant of the urban store, differ in the amount of capital invested and the variety of items offered for sale but are almost without exception specialty shops dealing in one line of commodities. In larger urban areas shops of the same type tend to congregate in the same area, often on the same street, giving rise to the practice of calling streets by such names as Silk Street, Tea Street, Medicine Street, and so forth. A great number of the shops are family enterprises under the effective control of the head of the family. Larger business establishments may be partnerships but even these are organized like a family: the manager of the store acts as the head, with clerks, shopmen, and apprentices living on the premises under the manager's absolute authority.

Marketing Practices

Traditional marketing methods and business practices were irregular and wasteful. Personal relations were important and practices that would never be condoned in dealing with an old customer were resorted to without scruple in the case of strangers. By western standards, packaging, transportation, and storage methods were all inadequate and the quality and grade of various commodities differed from store to store. In recent years, however, standard weights and measures have been gradually adopted although Chinese units like the catty and picul have not been uniformly replaced by the metric system. The institution of the middleman, once important in the transfer of goods from wholesaler to retailer, has been virtually eliminated with the taking over of wholesale channels by the government.

In today's transactions, barter is the exception. In the frontier regions of northwestern China, wholesale trade is carried out largely by an exchange of cloth and tea for wool, fur, and hides, and in certain rural areas, notably in Yunnan, handicraft products are exchanged directly for rice. These exceptions aside, however, money serves as the medium of most exchanges. For a large part of retail trade, especially with the peddler or at the markets, there are no set prices, bargaining being the normal practice. Within recent decades, however, set prices have met increasing acceptance.

Much of modern business practice grew out of experience in foreign trade. The establishment of foreign business concerns in the concession territories encouraged a comparable growth of modern Chinese shops and business concerns in or near the concessions. Large stores organized as stock companies began to replace firms owned by families and partnerships in centers of foreign influence such as Shanghai, Tientsin, and Canton. Specialty shops faced a new type of competition, the department stores, which accounted for a larger portion of the retail trade than their numbers would indicate. In these port cities a new class of merchants emerged whose wealth and prestige was a direct result of their dealings with foreign business interests. These modern business groups and institutions, though their appearance was significant, did not replace traditional commercial outlets; on the contrary, throughout most of the country, especially in the interior areas, traditional forms prevailed.

The basic pattern of domestic trade continues under the Communists in spite of the drive to socialize channels of wholesale and retail trade. Local trade still predominates and transportation is still a major problem despite improvements made in rail and highway transportation. Except in the wholesaling of essential commodities the government's insistence on "rational business practices" has only partially transformed old marketing and exchange practices. For the time being sheer practical difficulties make it mandatory that the old ways and the millions of petty retailers survive a little longer, although improved channels of urban-rural exchange will have to be developed as soon as possible.

State Trading Agencies

During the last ten years a number of state trading companies have been established for dealing in commodities such as food grains, fodder, cotton and textiles, vegetables, animal products, food products, general merchandise, salt, coal and building materials, tea, minerals, hog bristles, oils and fats, industrial equipment, silk, petroleum, metals and machinery, chemical industrial materials, communications and electrical equipment, medicine, and "special trade" or consumption items not covered in any other category. The six most important companies, all established early in 1950, are the China Grain Company, the China Cotton and Textile Company, the China Coal and Building Material Company, the China Salt Company, the China General Merchandise Company, and the China Native Products Company. With main offices in Peking under the control of the Ministry of Commerce, these six companies have together established more than ten thousand branch offices and retail stores in cities and towns throughout China. Some companies, such as the China General Merchandise Company and the China Native Products Company, have set up branches in rural areas. The state companies and their branches deal mainly in wholesale trade while retail trade is handled by state retail stores, cooperatives, and private merchants.

Cooperatives

There are two types of domestic trade cooperative: the consumers' cooperative and the supply and marketing cooperative. The consumers' cooperative serves as a retail outlet to supplement the state retail stores. A supply and marketing cooperative is formed on a "voluntary basis" by the members, who hold shares; it is, however, under the direct supervision of its parent body, the All-China Federation of Supply and Marketing Cooperatives. It supplies members with farm implements, fertilizer, and daily necessities, and markets their agricultural produce and the products of the local industries. Despite the largely rural character of the supply and marketing cooperatives, as of 1956 only 80,000 of the 178,000 cooperatives were in rural villages.

Cooperatives are considered by the Chinese Communists the basic form of nonprivate commercial organization. They cut across all aspects of domestic trade: urban and rural, wholesale and retail, supply and marketing. It is safe to say that cooperatives, even though of doubtful popularity among the peasants, will remain an integral part of the commercial network of China for some time to come.

Trade Fairs

The Communists have expanded the scope of the trade fair, both to stimulate domestic trade and to compensate for the loss of international markets in Chinese specialty items such as silk and handicraft products. These fairs, held in various large cities since 1951, are an outgrowth of the traditional annual fairs and markets and like them feature entertainment as well as commodity exchange. That these fairs occupy a significant position in domestic trade may be seen from the official total sales figure of 3.39 billion yuan (equivalent to about 1.38 billion American dollars) as early as 1952. Some of the more prominent fairs are the East China Fair at Shanghai, the Central South Commodity Fair at Wu-han, the South China Commodity Fair at Canton, and the North China Autumn Commodity Fair at Tientsin. Most of the trading concerns represented at these fairs are state-owned.

Control of Trade

In addition to establishing the state trading organizations on the wholesale and retail levels, the Communist government regulates domestic trade by control of supply and demand and by control over merchants and merchant organizations. These might be termed respectively the material and social aspects of trade control.

The material aspect covers unified and compulsory buying and allocation, rationing, and price control. Since modern industrial production implies large-scale operations by a relatively small number of enterprises, socialization of these enterprises automatically secures government control over the disposal of the products. In agriculture, however, the large number of producers presents a far more difficult problem. The difficulty has not disappeared altogether even with the complete socialization of agriculture. As long as products not available on the official market can be sold profitably, there are always people who will produce them, regardless of the over-all government plan.

Between 1953 and 1956 a system of market control was developed for agricultural products and scrap metals, dividing controlled commodities into two groups. Grain, cotton, edible oils, and oil seeds constituted the first group to be placed under the system of compulsory government purchase. After tax payments in kind, peasants producing these commodities are required to sell at fixed prices their entire output except what they are permitted to keep for their own use. Various incentive schemes supplement compulsion in this arrangement. Once the government purchases have been completed, the peasants may sell the stock left them for their own use. Prior to August 1957 these sales could be made on officially supervised markets; since then sales have been permitted only to purchasing agents designated by the government.

The second group of commodities is composed of such diverse products as cured tobacco, hemp, jute and ramie, sugar cane and sugar, silk cocoons, tea, live hogs, wool, cow hide, paper produced by handicraft, wood oil, scrap copper, lead and tin, major types of timber, medicinal herbs, apples, oranges, and marine products. The government determines the proportion of these commodities it desires to purchase and, once the purchase quotas have been fulfilled, the rest may be sold by the producer. Here again sales could be made freely on the officially supervised markets before August 1957, but thereafter the same restriction as on the first group has applied.

The obvious purpose of this program of compulsory purchase is to assure the government control over supply, a prerequisite to effective allocation whether within the various regions of China or for export. It is also useful for the enforcement of price ceilings in the case of an excess of demand over supply.

In the summer of 1956, partly to placate the small trader who had become virtually unemployed and partly to promote healthier trade, a third group of commodities known as "minor native products" was listed. These commodities were to be sold freely, presumably at uncontrolled prices.

A rather revealing comment on this development is afforded by the fact that once a free market was established, commodities of all kinds, including those in the first two groups, began to appear on it. Accordingly, stricter controls were introduced and in August 1957 the second group of commodities was broadened to include additional products ranging from steel scraps to watermelon seeds. The scope of the free market was drastically limited to such items as poultry, fresh eggs, fruits not included in the other two categories, and similar perishables.

Difficulties have also plagued the Communist authorities in allocating the products of industry. Industrial products under the control of the Ministry of Commerce are divided into two categories according to whether regional supplies are to be centrally allocated or not. In the case of commodities subject to central allocation the regional quotas may not be disturbed without official sanction. Yet in 1957 there were said to be buyers from other regions congregated in a few large urban centers to purchase goods in this category without either the prior knowledge or approval of the central authorities. Some of the buyers were agents sent by the socialized trading agencies in an effort to circumvent the rigidity of the central plan.

As a part of the program of direct allocation certain consumer goods are subject to rationing. The rationing of grain, first introduced in November 1953, is by far the most important.

In order to facilitate rationing in cities, industrial and mining districts, and rural areas where the supply of grain is deficient, state grain markets have been set up throughout the whole country. These take the place of the former private wholesale and retail grain outlets. The system of state markets is based on regulations issued in August 1955 according to which the size of the individual ration is determined by a person's occupation and the degree of energy needed in his particular work. Age and regional eating habits are also taken into consideration. For the greater part of China, where rice is the staple diet, the monthly per capita ration is stipulated in nine categories, ranging from workers engaged in extra heavy work to ordinary citizens and children. For the typical urban resident and child over ten years of age the permissible monthly ration is from 22 to 26 catties, the exact amount within a maximum average of 25 catties a month to be determined by the local authorities. The caloric value of the rationed staple food is generally insufficient although to some extent deficiencies can be made up by the consumption of unrationed foods. However, in a country where the staple food forms upwards of 75 percent of the regular diet, marked deficiencies in the staple diet mean a state of relative malnutrition for the population as a whole.

Aside from grain, rationed commodities include cotton cloth, edible oils, and more recently pork. Some form of rationing of cotton cloth and edible oils was introduced as early as 1950, but there are indications that rationing has not always been stringently enforced. The average per capita ration of cotton cloth for the period between September 1957 and August 1958, disregarding regional differences, was fixed at only 17.5–19.7 feet. The per capita goal for 1959 has been fixed at 26.2 feet. Pork rationing, announced in November 1956, caused expressions of popular discontent but was made necessary by a decline in hog production from a peak of 101.7 million in 1954 to about 85 million by the middle of 1956.

One of the most effective means of manipulating the domestic flow of commodities, however, has been price control. By setting maximum and minimum prices for different commodities at different stages of production and sale, the government has accomplished at least three of its economic aims. First, it has made a maximum profit from the purchase of grain and other commodities at low official prices. Second, by raising the price of supplies to private concerns and lowering the prices of their products, the government has made these businesses unprofitable and forced them to accept state participation or disband altogether. Third, the maintenance of a comparatively high price level on consumer goods has prevented an excessive gap between demand and supply. Certain price increases were ordered during 1957 as a result of the pressure of demand. At the same time, the Communist regime has played up for propaganda purposes every price reduction, attempting to convince the populace that the government is doing something concrete about lowering prices and raising the standard of living.

The administration of price control was originally vested in the Ministry of Commerce. During the period of active "socialist transformation" of private commercial firms the responsibility was in effect shared by the ministry and the supply and marketing cooperatives for the urban and rural areas respectively. During and after the "big push" in capital investment in 1956 many prices rose without official sanction. In response to this development price increases were ordered for the purchase and resale of certain of the principal agricultural products, as well as for the public sale of some industrial products. The criticism remained, however, that the central government's price control had been too rigid and unresponsive to local conditions. The result was the establishment of a national price control commission in July 1957 and the subsequent organization of price control committees for individual provinces, municipalities, and counties. Since this reorganization, the national commission determines the prices of commodities in the first two categories of the unified purchase and allocation scheme although local authorities are given some discretion in permitting variations in those primary markets where production is not concentrated. On the other hand, the prices of "minor native products" (goods in the third category) are under the control of the local authorities, subject to an annual review by the national commission. In the case of industrial products, including products of the handicraft industry, the prices of all major products, as well as of all products on the major markets, are to be fixed by the central government, leaving the minor products on minor markets to the local authorities.

There has been little information regarding stability of prices since 1957, but it appears that they are more flexible and regional price differentials larger than before. This price flexibility may interfere with the requirement of the plan that state enterprises fulfill profit quotas while at the same time producing specific physical quantities of a given commodity. Here the dilemma between central planning in physical terms and even partial freedom in price formation becomes manifest.

Another important part of the Communist program began in 1953 with a drive against the traditional merchant organizations and chambers of commerce, the first step of which was to convene an assembly of manufacturers and merchants in Peking. Out of this assembly came the All-China Federation of Industry and Commerce, organized like all mass organizations in China on provincial, municipal, and county levels.

Socialization of Private Commerce

Full socialization of a private enterprise is generally preceded by three stages of "state capitalism." In the lowest manifestation a private merchant is designated an agent of the state for the sale of commodities on a commission basis. Next he purchases controlled commodities from state stocks for resale at retail prices fixed by the state. In the final stage, joint state-private ownership, the state invests a part of the capital and retains a large measure of control.

The case of the Yung-an (Wing On) Company of Shanghai may be taken as an example of the steps by which a privately owned company is transformed into a joint state-private operation. A family-owned firm, Yung-an was the only one of four leading Shanghai department stores to remain in business after 1949. For the next six years government regulations and harassment were such that the company consistently lost money. At one point in 1954 income was insufficient to pay the wages of its employees and the company was kept in business only through using the profits from other interests of the owners. In March 1955, the owners of Yung-an finally submitted a petition to the government asking that it be made an agent of the government trading companies. The allotment of sixty-two commodities which the government permitted it to sell improved its financial situation. Nevertheless, continuing difficulties forced Yung-an to become a joint state-private concern in early 1956. Under this new arrangement the former manager is retained in his position, but the first assistant manager, representing the interest of the state, has the real power. This is indicated by the fact that at a company meeting held in July 1956 the executives representing the private interests asked to have eighteen of their members given responsibilities commensurate with their positions.

There are many exceptions to this three-stage process and a number of private firms have been made joint enterprises or taken over by the state directly without going through the lower transformations. In both wholesale and retail trade the government began by taking control of agencies dealing with essential commodities. This policy led to the establishment of state companies in the wholesale distribution of grain, cotton, salt, coal, and so forth, eliminating wholesale merchants in these commodities and transferring forcibly their capital to industry in the name of government guidance and relief. Retail outlets in grain, cotton, and edible oils have been taken over also by the state and placed under the respective state-owned companies. Until 1956, however, the majority of the outlets dealing in the less essential commodities were still in some phase of state capitalism.

Under the First Five Year Plan, private and joint retail trade was to be reduced from 66 percent of the total in 1953 to 45 percent by 1957. For wholesale and retail trade combined the goal for 1957 was: state-owned, 55 percent; state-capitalist, 24 percent; private, less than 21 percent.

These goals were sharply upgraded in the latter part of 1955 when the government intensified the process of socialization all the way down the line, including industry, trade, and handicrafts. A message addressed to industrial and commercial circles asking for the acceptance of socialist transformation reported that more than 50 percent of the private retail merchants had become agents of state-capitalist trade by that time. The percentage varied in different localities. By early 1956 in no less than six major cities— Peking, Shanghai, Tientsin, Canton, Wu-han, and Mukden—all commercial activity was being conducted by either joint enterprises or state-owned organizations.

The complaint that personnel of former private businesses are not given jobs for which they are suited is not uncommon in China today. A symposium held in Canton in August 1956 revealed that a group of wholesale merchants skilled in dyeing materials was assigned work in theaters after the "socialist transformation" of their business. The Communists claim that joint enterprises are nevertheless actually more profitable. In the case of Yung-an, it was reported in the summer of 1956 that for the first time in eight years the company distributed dividends.

Nevertheless, the accelerated program of socialization of commerce ran into obstacles. Apparently the Communists underestimated the intrinsic difficulties of transforming domestic trade, especially retail trade, at such a precipitous rate. The first sign that all was not well came when the official annual yield of 1 to 6 percent to private capital in joint state-private enterprises was replaced by a minimum return of 5 percent, with the stipulation that all higher rates would remain in force. Then in the summer and fall of 1956 a series of official pronouncements indicated broad policy changes in the program as a whole. The plight of small traders in competition with the large state companies was recognized and the initiative and experience of the small trader deemed worthy of preservation. Each state-owned or joint enterprise was assigned the task of supplying commodities to a specified number of small traders. In effect the state organizations were to act as wholesalers with most of the retail trade remaining in private hands. Retail concerns were to have greater freedom of choice in the goods that they sold and the consumer was promised more variety in such items as towels, stockings, toiletries, and enamelware. Government profits in the future were to come from manufacturing enterprises rather than those engaged in distribution. Finally, the need of more decentralized buying and selling of nonessential commodities was recognized, as well as price levels that would encourage the manufacture of high quality goods.

To encourage competitive distribution of nonessential items, free markets were permitted to open in many provinces. These free markets are practically indistinguishable from the periodic markets so common in the pre-Communist days: foodstuffs and local products form the bulk of the commodities offered for sale and direct transactions are conducted at their natural price levels.

Foreign Economic Relations

Foreign trade throughout the twentieth century was vital to China's economic well-being. It played a major role in breaking down the old closed economy, generating an impulse toward modernization and, in general, bringing about social and political change. But the characteristics of China's foreign trade and the unfavorable balance of payments pointed to China's unsatisfactory economic position vis-à-vis the rest of the world and underscored the fact that economic and industrial development would be a slow and painful process under the best of circumstances.

China's pattern of trade up to World War II was essentially that of an underdeveloped country: exports consisted chiefly of agricultural goods and raw materials; capital and consumer goods were imported. Two important departures from this generalization, however, should be mentioned. Frequent political disturbances and recurring natural calamities made necessary sizable imports of cotton and basic foodstuffs, especially rice and flour. On the other hand, with the gradual growth of light industry, particularly cotton textiles, yarns and other partly manufactured goods entered the export trade. Generally speaking, however, China's imports consisted of cotton goods, liquid oils and fuel, machinery and vehicles, chemicals, foodstuffs, and miscellaneous consumer goods. China's main exports included animal products, wax and oils (especially tung oil), cotton and yarn, egg products, bristles, silk, tea, coal, and metal ores.

Except for a brief period following the opening of the treaty ports in 1840, China's foreign trade was characterized by a persistent deficit. For the two decades preceding World War II, the average annual trade deficit was about 130 million American dollars. China produced little gold or silver but rather imported precious metals and, lacking sizable investments abroad, it was in no position to perform commercial and financial services in payment for the excess of imports. Although there was some inflow of capital, the gap in the trade balance was bridged primarily through the expenditures of foreign governments, loans, and emigrant remittances. Quite obviously these sources of foreign exchange were unstable in view of the changing international political and economic situation.

The earliest investments by foreigners in China were made mostly by merchants to facilitate commercial operations in the treaty ports. By the turn of the century the economic rivalry of the great powers led to many politically motivated investments, among which the most important were loans for railway construction. Such loans, on occasion forced upon China by foreign governments, were implemented chiefly through private business channels. Investment in transportation and communications constituted approximately one-third of all foreign investments in China up to 1931. Geographically, foreign investments—mostly British and Japanese—were concentrated in Shanghai and Manchuria. Shanghai, the scene of the first foreign investments, received an increasing percentage during the 1930's. Similarly, foreign investments in Manchuria had been substantial even before the Japanese occupation. After 1931, and especially after Pearl Harbor, Japan bent every effort to build up Manchuria as an important industrial complex and to monopolize its foreign trade.

Loans made to China during World War II and in the postwar period up to 1949, including grants from such agencies as UNRRA, far exceeded the total volume of all previous foreign loans. Thus for example, between 1938 and 1944 China received loans amounting to the equivalent of nearly 1.5 billion American dollars. Made primarily to stabilize China's faltering economy, these loans served also in some degree to bolster political morale. Military lend-lease from the United States amounted to over 600 million dollars by April 1945.

Foreign Trade under the Communists

The Communist government took over in China at a time when the economic policy of the Nationalist government had already turned toward increased economic planning and control. Although many of the controls imposed by the Nationalist regime in its last years were dictated by the emergency demands of the war and the chaotic postwar situation, the importance of linking foreign trade to industrial reconstruction and economic development was recognized.

In March 1949, shortly after the Communist conquest of North China, the Foreign Trade Control Office for the North China Region was established for the purpose of licensing exports and imports. A month later the Bank of China in Tientsin officially opened a foreign exchange department to handle overseas transactions. Once the Communists had consolidated their power on the mainland these beginnings were expanded to a nationwide framework for the control of all foreign trade.

At first the Communists followed a policy of promoting exports while limiting imports in order to gain an exchange surplus abroad. Foreign trade showed a favorable balance in 1950, an important factor being the return of Manchuria, which had frequently had a favorable balance of trade in the prewar period. Restrictions on imports of nonessential consumer goods such as plastics, cigarettes, and nylon stockings also served to build up an export balance.

In March 1950 the United States announced that any strategic materials destined for Communist China would require export licenses and during the Korean War imposed a ban on the shipment of petroleum and gasoline, later extending it to all commodities. Measures were also taken by the United States to control dollar assets held by Communist China as well as foreign exchange and other funds deposited in American banks.

In May 1951 the United Nations General Assembly approved an embargo on the export of strategic materials to Communist China and in October of that year the United States passed the so-called Battle Act, denying aid to any country that engaged in trading in strategic goods with the Soviet bloc. Japan, Britain, the Netherlands, Portugal, and several other countries followed this action with their own bans against trade with China. These countries later constituted the Paris CHINCOM, a coordinating control agency for dealing with the China trade prohibitions.

The embargo was not immediately felt. Chinese trade with the free world remained on about the same level from 1950 to 1951, while great increases were registered in trade with the Soviet bloc. The impact of western trade controls apparently began to be felt in the second half of 1951. From 1952 to 1954, trade with non-

Communist countries continued at about 75 percent of the volume of 1950 (which was equivalent to 886 million American dollars), while trade with the Soviet bloc expanded continuously.

The volume of Communist China's external trade has continued to increase in spite of the United Nations embargo. Vital commodities from non-Communist countries have been obtained through the device of re-export through neutral countries, and the build-up of trade with the Soviet bloc compensated for other losses. Nevertheless the embargo has affected Communist China's foreign trade in two ways: the restriction in the number of countries with which it can trade openly has weakened Communist China's bargaining position; and the embargo, plus the Nationalist blockade of the southern ports, has forced Communist China to depend more on the northern ports or costlier overland routes. This fact is graphically illustrated by the decline in importance of Hong Kong as a port of entry for Chinese imports. During the critical period of 1950-53, the percentage of imports from Hong Kong to the total volume of imports fell from 67 percent to 11 percent.

Since 1956 there has been a general tendency to relax the embargo against Communist China, particularly among those nations that are finding it difficult to sell their products in the non-Communist world. Indonesia, for example, has totally rejected the embargo. In May 1957 British trade with China was placed on the same footing as its trade with the Soviet Union and other Communist bloc countries. Industrial machinery, automobiles, precision instruments, and certain chemicals formerly on the prohibited list are now sold to Communist China. West Germany, Japan, Canada, and France, already inclined to revise their trade policies toward China, have followed the example set by Great Britain. So far the United States has made no substantial changes in its policy.

By mid-1957 Communist China claimed to have trade relations with sixty-eight countries, twenty-one of which had signed trade agreements with it, and by the end of 1958 the number of trading partners had reportedly increased to ninety-four. The majority of these trade agreements are bilateral barter pacts, generally renewable on a yearly basis.

Trade Administration

The highest administrative organ for foreign trade is the Ministry of Foreign Trade, established in 1952 after the reorganization of the Ministry of Trade into two ministries, Commerce and Foreign Trade. In January 1953 the various regional foreign trade control offices were amalgamated into a system of customs administration subordinate to the Ministry of Foreign Trade. All import and export firms, state or privately operated, were required to register with the Customs Office and apply for a license. Even barter trade is subject to such approval. The Ministry of Foreign Trade is vested with full authority to set prices of exports and imports. To implement a resolution passed at the International Economic Conference in Moscow, the Chinese Committee for the Promotion of Foreign Trade was organized in Peking in 1952 to negotiate trade agreements with official or private trade representatives of other countries.

Under the Ministry of Foreign Trade the following state trading companies have been established: China Foodstuffs Export Company, China Native Products Export Company, China Sundry Export Company, China Import-Export Company, China Silk Company, China Tea Company, China Minerals Company, China Grain, Fats and Oils Export Company, China Animal By-Products Export Company, China Metals Import Company, China Machinery Import Company, China Transportation Equipment Import Company, and China Technical Import Company (the last dealing mainly with the exchange of technical assistance). Of these the three companies dealing in silk, tea, and minerals are active in domestic trade as well. All are authorized to establish branches in the major cities or ports. The China Import-Export Company, for instance, has branches in Mukden, Tientsin, Tsingtao, Shanghai, and Canton, and an overseas branch in East Berlin (established in May 1952) in addition to agents in Hong Kong and Macao.

Government Control of Private Organizations

In July 1950 private exporters and importers were ordered by the government to form three types of organization: trade research units to study problems connected with foreign trade; special committees in each branch of trade to work out a common business program under state supervision; and joint state-private organizations to unify the handling of exports and make collective purchases for importers. In Canton, for example, there were exporting teams for ginger, firewood, fresh eggs, and so on. Similar trade teams extend to every kind of trade activity, subject to the supervision and control of the Customs Office. The private sector was required to follow the lead of the state-operated sector, working as agents for state companies and participating directly in foreign trade only by special permission.

With the gradual expansion of state-operated firms, control over private import and export has become progressively more rigid. It was reported that in 1950 the private firms contributed about 56 percent of the total value of foreign trade; but by 1952 the figure had declined to 37 percent; and by 1953 approximately 92 percent of all foreign trade was in the hands of state trading concerns. Today the government controls every aspect of foreign trade.

Changes in the Trade Pattern

Through the persistent efforts of the government, changes in China's foreign trade pattern are discernible in (1) the commodities traded, (2) the increasing importance of barter trade, and (3) trade partners.

Trade Composition

Export items of the pre-World War II era such as silk and silk products, tea, egg products, soybeans, tung oil, bristles, handicraft products, coal, and metallic ores still figure largely in foreign trade, but increasing domestic consumption of such items as coal has cut down the amount available for export, and the widespread use of synthetics has rendered the world market less dependent upon such natural products as tung oil and silk. Grain, which used to be imported, is now being exported by Communist China, but grain exports amount to only about 2 percent of total production.

In recent years China has shipped some consumer goods and other manufactures to Southeast Asian countries. Such exports will undoubtedly increase as industrialization progresses. A report in late 1957 showed that 31.5 percent of total exports in that year consisted of industrial and mineral products in contrast to 17.9 percent in 1952. The importance of processed agricultural products and by-products as export items had also increased at the expense of non-processed products.

In contrast to the relatively unchanged composition of exports within the last two decades, imports have undergone a decided change since 1949. Manufactured consumer goods as well as agricultural products such as flour, sugar, and tobacco have steadily declined in relation to total imports. Capital goods and raw materials, on the other hand, have risen tremendously. In 1951 industrial machinery, transportation and communications equipment, and a few major raw materials made up 78 percent of all imports. By 1954 these items had risen to more than 88 percent of total imports. It is estimated that machines alone constituted 60 percent of all imports in 1956. This emphasis on capital goods and raw materials is the natural result of a policy of accelerated industrialization.

Barter Trade

Another significant change in China's foreign trade is the rise in importance of the barter system. Before the United Nations embargo was imposed, a National Conference on Foreign Trade at Peking in January 1951 decided that in order to curtail the drain of foreign exchange, trade with capitalist countries was to be conducted by barter. Subsequently barter has become the principal form of foreign trade with all countries.

Barter trade is carried on in four ways: direct barter, clearing, compensation, and back-to-back barter. Direct barter is characterized by import preceding export, back-to-back barter by the synchronization of export and import, clearing by purchase on account, and compensation by sale on credit.

Three restrictions are imposed on barter trade: the imported goods must correspond in commodity classifications to those exported; the value of import and export should be equal, any discrepancy to be cleared with the Bank of China; and finally, a barter agreement must adhere strictly to the time limit set for it.

The Communist authorities have done their best to make barter trade successful. It has a number of advantages, among which are restricting imports, husbanding capital and foreign exchange reserves, protecting against losses due to confiscation of shipments en route, and balancing trade by binding import nations to take an equivalent amount of exports. But barter also has certain disadvantages: goods exported are in exchange for a corresponding category of imports to the exclusion of all other types of commodities, and the possibilities of multilateral trade are minimized. An attempt has been made to promote multilateral trade as much as possible within the framework of bilateral arrangement. In 1954, for example, rice was imported from Burma while at the same time it was exported to Ceylon. Such arrangements, however, are often dictated more by political than by economic considerations.

Reliance on barter agreements has generally minimized the problem of trade deficits with Soviet bloc countries. As for trade relations with countries with which Communist China does not have barter agreements, a deficit with a particular country or currency area can usually be met by drawing on surplus balances elsewhere. The existence of a number of free foreign exchange markets in the world, among them Hong Kong, provides ample opportunity for such operations. In addition, Communist China is believed to have substantial sterling reserves to cover short-term trade deficits.

Trade Partners

The third significant change in Communist China's foreign trade is the switch in trade partners. Excluding Hong Kong (which occupies a unique position vis-à-vis China in that it serves mainly as a transshipping point for both imports and exports), the major trade partners of China before World War II were the United States, Japan, and Great Britain in that order. Since 1949, and especially since the United Nations embargo in 1951, trade with these countries has dwindled as trade with the Soviet bloc expanded by leaps and bounds.

Trade relations between China and the United States, once of paramount importance for China, have become almost nonexistent since 1951. Before the outbreak of the Korean War, the United States was still an important source of trade although trade between the two countries was much less than before World War II. But with the imposition of the embargo, American exports to China practically ceased and American imports from China were drastically reduced. For the period 1952-56 United States trade with China was estimated at no more than 0.14 percent of China's total trade in contrast to 15.76 percent in 1927-30.

For many years China was the principal market for Japanese industrial goods and the principal supplier of raw materials for Japanese industry, but after World War II Japan relied more and more on the United States, and following the United Nations embargo, Japanese trade with mainland China was reduced from 27.17 percent in 1927-30 to 2.02 percent in the 1952-56 period. In recent years a number of unofficial pacts, mostly barter agreements, have been concluded between Japanese business interests and Communist Chinese trade delegations and there has been some trade revival interspersed with occasional setbacks mostly due to political differences.

Trade with Great Britain, which accounted for 11.7 percent of China's total imports in 1936, declined to 6 percent in 1950.

For the entire 1952-56 period Britain's share was an estimated 1.28 percent in spite of the conclusion of barter arrangements and repeated British pressure on the United States to ease the restriction on shipments to China.

In contrast to the declining trade with western countries Communist China's trade with the Soviet bloc has risen sharply from 26 percent in 1950 to 61 percent in 1951, to 70 percent in 1953, and to 81 percent in 1954 and 1955. A leveling off since 1955 (75 percent in 1956) may reflect Communist China's recent efforts to promote non-Communist trade, especially with the Afro-Asian countries.

Trade with the Soviet Union alone accounted for approximately 23 percent of China's total foreign trade in 1950 and about half since 1951 (48 percent in 1951, 52 percent in 1952, 56 percent in 1953, and about 50 percent after 1954). In 1956 Sino-Soviet trade reached the magnitude of 6 billion rubles according to official Soviet statistics. Czechoslovakia, Poland, and East Germany have also carried on a sizable trade with Communist China. The Soviet bloc sent industrial and farm machinery, tools and equipment for oil and mining industries, chemicals, rolled metals, rails and other transportation equipment in exchange for Chinese agricultural and animal products, handicraft articles, and mineral ores.

Trade relations with other Communist countries in Asia have followed a different pattern, with China acting as the supplier of consumer and capital goods in exchange for raw materials. China has also provided various forms of economic aid to North Korea, North Vietnam, and Outer Mongolia.

Within the limitations of its ability to allocate surplus commodities for export, Communist China has sought to promote trade with non-Communist countries. Trade on a limited scale has been carried on with a number of western European countries and feelers have been extended to Chile and Uruguay. In the last few years China has initiated trade relations with Egypt and other Middle Eastern countries; expanded trade with Ceylon, Indonesia, Malaya, and Cambodia; sent industrial equipment and consumer goods to Burma in exchange for Burmese rice, and in turn shipped Chinese rice to Ceylon for Ceylonese rubber. Indonesia has offered China rubber, copra, hemp, and other agricultural products for manufactured goods, building materials, and machinery. Pakistan has exchanged hemp and jute for rice and coal. Chinese products are actively competing with western and Japanese manufactures in these markets while Chinese agricultural exports compete with the agricultural exports of the Southeast Asian countries. Most of these dealings are in the form of barter, and the volume of trade, though still modest, has been increasing despite the fact that the Chinese have frequently been accused of dumping and other acts of economic warfare.

Size and Balance of Foreign Trade

Using 1950 as the base year, Communist China's total foreign trade rose to 195 in 1953, 204 in 1954, and 265 in 1955 according to official Communist reports. Assuming that the official index numbers represent a value series at either current prices or at 1950 prices it is possible to derive the computed figures in JMP for the period 1953-56 as well as for 1950 (see Table 19).

Unfortunately, there is no way to determine definitely the value of these figures in terms of foreign exchange receipts and payments. An estimate may be attempted on the basis of the information that the total volume of trade between Communist China and the Soviet Union in 1956 amounted to approximately 6 billion rubles while trade between Communist China and the other Soviet satellites in the same year came to about 2.91 billion rubles. As 75 percent of its total trade was conducted with the bloc, the size of Communist China's foreign trade in 1956 may be estimated at 11.88 billion rubles. This would give us an implicit conversion rate of 0.914 JMP per ruble or a cross rate of 3.656 JMP per American dollar. At the latter rate the value of the 1956 trade turnover would be equivalent to 2.97 billion dollars. This is a much lower figure than several previous estimates.

Nontrade Transactions

Since Communist China's trade balance was unfavorable during most of the 1953-56 period, mention should be made of the principal balancing items, particularly remittances from overseas and foreign loans.

Before World War II remittances from overseas Chinese averaged 100 million American dollars a year and were a major factor in balancing China's trade deficit. After the war, as a result of both war damages in some of the Southeast Asian countries with large Chinese communities and the unstable economic situation in China, remittances fell off. The Chinese Communists have striven to increase the volume of overseas remittances but the exact amount of foreign exchange received by Communist China from this source has not been made public. One Japanese estimate puts the figure for the first half of 1954 at 170 million American dollars, which, however, seems too high to most informed observers. It is likely that overseas remittances have grown since then, and if the figure even appoaches the prewar average, it constitutes a significant factor in balancing Communist China's trade deficits with the non-Communist world.

So far as it has been possible to determine, direct foreign capital investment in Communist China has not been very significant. Government policies have all but liquidated any trace of the former British and American investments in the country, and nothing comparable has taken their place.

Soon after the establishment of the Communist government, several Sino-Soviet joint companies were organized in the fields of civil aviation and petroleum, in the nonferrous metal industry in Sinkiang, and in shipbuilding at Dairen. They have since been returned to complete Chinese control and the Soviet investments treated as loans. The Chinese Ch'ang-ch'un Railway, which was once a special case of Sino-Soviet joint operation, was also returned to complete Chinese control in 1952. The total volume of Soviet loans to Communist China for economic purposes has been estimated at the equivalent of two billion American dollars since 1949 while military aid has been put at slightly over one billion dollars.

Soviet financial support of its nationals in China constitutes another source of foreign exchange for China. This form of revenue is comparable to the money which tourism contributes to countries like Switzerland and Italy, except that it does not occupy nearly so important a place in relation to the total foreign exchange revenue of Communist China. Estimates of the number of Russian personnel in China range widely from fifteen to ninety thousand, and the scale of their expenditures has not been revealed.

More important than their mere numbers is the role played by the Soviet advisers in the industrial development of Communist China. Much of the technical know-how that has gone into China's industrialization program has come from these advisers. In 1956 alone eleven agreements were signed and 165 delegations involving 2,004 persons were exchanged between China and Russia. The flow will unquestionably continue in the foreseeable future.

An additional word should be said about the sizable exports of narcotics that are reported to have been made by Communist China. The volume of this trade has been estimated at more than 50 million American dollars a year. It is also believed that the government derives some foreign exchange from the export of Chinese labor to the Soviet Union and other satellite countries.

PUBLIC HEALTH AND WELFARE

HIGHLY DESIRABLE IN ANY SOCIETY, GOOD HEALTH and welfare practices have become essential in China to the success of the industrialization program. Every available human resource is required if the goals set by the Communist regime are to be reached. A study of government pronouncements and reports leads to the belief that considerable progress has been made in these fields, a clear recognition by the Communists of the political significance of high health standards and a modern system of public welfare.

The political motivation of much current health and welfare activity is readily apparent, for example in the preferential distribution of benefits to certain sectors of the population. Along with opportunities for employment, adequate food, and other necessities for survival and well-being, health and welfare benefits are an instrument of state control over the individual.

In the field of environmental sanitation, especially in the large cities, the regime boasts of its successes but these have been achieved not so much by raising the standard of living as by intensive regimentation of the masses. It is clear, however, that strong state pressure, relentless propaganda, and careful supervision are having a profound effect on traditional attitudes.

Traditionally, the functions of public welfare were undertaken largely by the basic units of production: the family and its extension, the clan. Locally and regionally, welfare activities were led and directed by gentry members, with or without government assistance. The participation of the state was minimal and in proportion to the prosperity of the economy, so that the effectiveness of state participation was in inverse ratio to the need for such participation. Indeed, the state through crushing taxation and bureaucratic inefficiency in the maintenance of flood control projects was often itself the cause of economic distress. Only during the last half century has the Chinese government directed any substantial effort toward public welfare.

After establishment of the Chinese Republic in 1912, welfare activity was aided by the contributions of outside agencies, principally United States philanthropic organizations, the International Red Cross, some religious organizations, and overseas Chinese communities. But the relief and welfare machinery of the state was not developed to the point of efficiency expected in a modern nation. Government aid was in general sporadic and poorly administered.

Under the Communists, some measures, such as labor insurance, are administered by an efficient central agency; others, like famine relief, have been left in the hands of local cadres, with the government appealing to agricultural cooperatives and similar organizations to engage in self-help. In general, the relief work organized by the Communist government has been greater in scope and effectiveness than the programs under previous regimes. Strict control over transportation and food prices has enabled the government to assure an adequate supply of grains at normal prices in famine stricken areas.

Public Welfare

A curious mixture of humanitarian idealism and power politics is present in the Communist attitude toward public welfare, health, and the treatment of social problems, and this becomes understandable if it is acknowledged that the state is interested in the individual only when there is a promise of return in terms of labor and loyalty to the regime. In China nonemergency welfare programs are set up with three groups in mind: soldiers, children, and workers.

Army Welfare

In granting preferential treatment to military dependents and disabled or demobilized servicemen the guiding policy has been to organize them into mutual-aid and cooperative organizations. The government also has stabilized subsidies for dependents, periodically allocating money and grain for this purpose. The allocations are relatively generous, in all cases higher than those for local paupers. Funds have been provided for the recuperation and education of disabled veterans, and families of revolutionary martyrs (soldiers killed in action during the Communist revolution) and army dependents have found long-term jobs or been organized into industrial production units. To those who cannot work, the municipal and district governments have extended subsidies and direct material aid.

Communist sources claim that this so-called "comforting" campaign has resulted in the employment of more than 80 percent of China's disabled veterans and the dependents of revolutionary martyrs. Incomplete data in the *People's Daily* showed as high as 60 percent had been accepted into groups such as agricultural producers' cooperatives.

Their assimilation into the country's economic life has not been as successful as the figures indicate, however, and newspaper accounts from a number of areas tell of urgent problems caused by poor organization and inadequate housing arrangements. In addition there have been complaints about the carelessness of civil affairs departments in spending the enormous sums of aid money, complaints that range from arbitrary disbursements to embezzlement and misappropriation.

Government pensions and aid are only a minor part of the care for the disabled and dependents in any case; the greater part of the welfare work for these persons is provided by the population through direct contributions and through specific agencies where administration of the program is in the hands of the superintending party agent.

Worker's Welfare

Because of his importance to the new regime, the industrial worker has been provided, at least on paper, with by far the most elaborate program of welfare aids and services. Special laws covering protection of his job, his income, and his family's health, including allowances for sickness and injury that are generous by Chinese standards, were promulgated in 1951 and extended in 1953.

The government also classifies the "workers' cultural palaces" under welfare activities and agencies, although these are primarily recreational centers. There are hundreds of them in the principal cities, and workers' clubs are found in every big factory and mine. Some famous resorts, like the West Lake in Hangchow, have been converted to vacation resorts for workers.

In return for these benefits, the state expects absolute submission from the workers. The trade unions being party-controlled, there is no room for genuine bargaining, and continued employment and survival depend upon conformity. Moreover, such welfare benefits as paid vacations at rest resorts are reserved for the so-called "labor heroes," who become eligible by virtue of their high production. Workers' welfare measures, therefore, are among the many devices by which the state enforces labor discipline and encourages productivity.

Child Welfare

"All for the children" is a popular slogan in mainland China, but is also an apt description of Communist welfare thinking. The future of the Communist regime, it is felt, depends upon today's children, and because their mothers are drafted for work in the communes and in industrial enterprises, the regime must provide crèches and nurseries to take care of the children.

The claim is made that in 1949, the first year of the Communist government, some 18,900 nurseries of various types were established throughout the country, enabling the mothers of 579,000 children to take an active part in national construction. According to Communist sources, provisions for child care, by relieving working mothers of anxiety, have increased their productive efficiency by an average of one-third, and in many cases have doubled it.

Since 1949 crèches and nurseries have steadily increased in number and, with the establishment of village communes and the increasing demand for the labor of women, have become permanent features of the Chinese countryside. As these institutions are generally supported by commune funds, the burden of child care and training has been shifted in great measure from the individual family to the commune as a whole.

In the cities, factory nurseries have multiplied and been improved. Their operation is undertaken jointly by the local people's government, the women's department of the local trade unions, the child welfare department of the women's federations, and the respective factories. Model nurseries have been established in such cities as Peking, Tientsin, Nanking, and Shanghai, where accommodations, food, medical, and sanitary facilities are much better than those in smaller cities and rural towns. Crèches have been organized also according to the streets or lanes of the mothers' residences; others are attached to primary schools, enabling mothers who teach to nurse their babies at intervals. Public nurseries and crèches require payment only for the children's food; private ones require payment of tuition as well.

Communist sources insist that children in nurseries and crèches receive better care than those at home. Rapid increase in the numbers of these institutions has resulted in a shortage of personnel, however, and most of the nurseries are understaffed, in spite of efforts by women's federations and others to train new child welfare personnel in short-term classes. The majority of the children are in the nurseries from 8 A.M. to 5 P.M., and some party cadre children are kept from 8 A.M. to 7 P.M. The result is that children spend most of their waking day in nurseries, and little time with their parents, and are more a product of institutions than of home rearing.

The child care program as well as the welfare activities in behalf of workers and disabled soldiers are continuing programs of a nonemergency nature. There are special programs for public welfare when emergencies arise.

Famine Relief

Famine has been one of China's most serious and most ancient problems, and it has not yet been solved. According to a study made from historical records, it was found that between 108 B.C. and 1911 A.D., there were 1,828 famines, or one almost every year. Potential or actual famine is so much a part of cultural expectation that official figures include a factor for famine in the normal death rate.

The famine areas are, generally speaking, those regions most susceptible to drought and floods. The Yangtze and Yellow rivers and their tributaries account for most floods, while drought conditions are prevalent in the semiarid regions of North and Northwest China. Although these areas are often referred to as the "famine zone," practically every province has at one time or another been subject to famine.

China under the Communist regime has not ceased to be a "land of famine." The 1949 flood was minor in comparison to many in the past, but besides the flood the nation suffered from drought, frosts, tornadoes, hailstorms, insect pests, and cattle plagues. According to Communist reports, more than 120 million mu (over 20 million acres) of arable land were inundated or otherwise affected by natural disasters, and approximately forty million people suffered in varying degrees. The spring and summer of 1951 carried all the signs of a major drought and some 125 million mu (about 21 million acres) of cultivated land were threatened by drought but a crop failure was prevented through concerted efforts of the people and government.

To meet these and similar emergencies the Communist regime has adopted a five-part "self-help" relief program:

Preventive action. Local governments are instructed to be on the alert for impending disasters such as floods or insect invasions in order to organize the peasants immediately to help avert their effects. For example, the Minister of Internal Affairs reported that during the 1954 floods the soldiers at Wu-ch'ang formed a "human wall" with their bodies to plug breaches in the dike.

Disaster area control. In an inundated area, peasants are to move to safety in an orderly manner—rather than flee in all directions as in the past—and keep themselves available nearby for such work projects as digging canals and building dams when the flood subsides.

Secondary occupations. The mainstay of the relief-by-production campaign has been the development of secondary occupations among the peasants of areas susceptible to floods and drought. Capital accumulated either by pooling of the peasants' own resources or from government loans has been used to establish local industries such as spinning, weaving cloth and mats, fishing, and the gathering of medicinal herbs.

Direct relief and resettlement. The regime also grants in some cases direct relief in the form of cash, kind, or loans—the latter comprising the largest part. The administration of relief loans is, however, a complicated and slow procedure. Moreover, the amount of direct relief is so small in proportion to the need that it has on the whole been ineffective.

Resettlement as a partial solution of economic dislocation was tried but proved expensive and impractical. During the 1949 flood the government extended substantial assistance toward the resettlement in the Northeast of distressed peasants from North China, but because the long journey had to be made by primitive means of transportation, migrants suffered more than if they had merely fled from the flood in the traditional manner.

Outside assistance. The "save-a-bowl-of-rice" drives initiated by the government among army units, government organizations, schools, factories, other public institutions, and the general public to help flood victims were regarded as "outside assistance" to the welfare program.

Social Problems

Although theoretically Marxism attributes all social problems to the poverty of the masses, the Chinese Communists have realized that in order to establish a new social order with a new ethic and a new morality they must eliminate the sources of social and cultural disorganization.

A case in point was the drive against prostitution, which represented an attempt to eliminate not only nonproductive women but also the social and moral deterioration that accompany prostitution. Prostitutes, traditionally regarded as the victims of poverty, have been subjected to "reform-through-labor" in order to make them productive laborers. This coercive rehabilitation program has in many cases, however, merely driven the prostitutes "underground."

A similar drive was launched against beggars. Professional beggars used to organize themselves into guilds, divide cities into zones, and assign a certain number of beggars to each area. In spite of periodic attempts by the police to curb their activity, the guilds were never wiped out. The Communists have subjected most beggars to reform-through-labor and have then sent them where their labor is needed.

In traditional China, there was no problem of juvenile delinquency in the modern sense of the term. From the age of six or earlier, children were expected to abide by rigid standards of behavior and were carefully supervised and disciplined by their parents, other grownups, and even older siblings. When a child was sent to school, it became the right and duty of the teacher to discipline him. Corporal punishment was considered necessary for bringing children up properly. Children were taught to respect and obey their elders and to cooperate with their associates and with society in general. These sanctions worked well because the withdrawal of parental support and approval meant the denial of basic social and personal needs important to every individual.

The increasing social disruption of the last fifty years has profoundly affected the attitudes of the young to family and society. One manifestation of this phenomenon is the organization of gangs in large urban centers. Their leaders are often vagabonds, thieves, and other vagrants whose very existence represents a challenge to the Communist state theory. So far, the government has attained only partially its aim of isolating and controlling the members of these gangs. Those who are caught are sent to "New Men's Villages" where they are taught skills and heavily indoctrinated in Communist ideology. It appears that this method is on the whole successful; most of the "graduates" of such training prove themselves to be industrious workers in the village environment. It seems unlikely that crime rates will soar under the new regime.

Health

Soon after its accession, the Communist government scheduled a national health conference in Peking to assess the available medical facilities and to plan a program for extending health services to the entire nation. In her report on the conference, Li Te-ch'üan, Minister of Public Health, summed up the results in three guiding principles for the state's health work: priority for workers, farmers, and soldiers; emphasis on preventive measures; and the combined use of modern and old-style medicine and medical practitioners. The objective of the program is seen to be the most expedient adaptation of current resources to the needs of the population and to the expansion of health services in the future.

Traditional Medicine

Traditional methods in China grew in part out of practical experience, in part out of research, and in part out of deductions from philosophical and metaphysical systems. Among the achievements of early medical practitioners, whose role was wholly professional and quite comparable to western doctors of medicine, were the use of anesthesia as early as the Han period (206 B.C.-220 A.D.), the discovery of inoculation (not vaccination) against smallpox as early as the Sung period (960-1279 A.D.), and the use of cauterization to clean wounds. Acupuncture (piercing the skin with a needle, often heated and therefore aseptic) was practiced with considerable skill by traditional physicians, and the practice of taking the pulse was developed into a highly sophisticated medical art very early in China.

Ancient Chinese medical treatises seriously investigated the relation of parts of the human body and their functions. The anatomy of the body was not very well known, however, and the Confucian injunction (in the *Classic of Filial Piety*) that "one should not destroy or mutilate the body, hair, and skin one receives from one's parents," being taken literally, effectively ended experimental studies of anatomy until the Sung period. A brief relaxation of imperial restrictions at this time made possible some elementary investigations.

Contributions of Chinese herbal knowledge to medical science have been widely recognized. The Chinese pharmacopoeia contains many medicinal herbs like ginseng *(jen-shen)*, dextra camphor *(chang-nao)*, lovage *(tang-kuei)*, and ephedra *(ma-huang)*, as well as substances like iodine, sulphur, mercury, and others, some of which produce excellent results with specific diseases. Large segments of the population still believe firmly in the efficacy of herbal medicine. Even today, western surgical methods for serious illness are combined with traditional internal medicine for less serious disorders.

Faced with an acute shortage of medical personnel, the government is currently reviving and encouraging the use of traditional herb medicine. The herbal physicians are being given a rudimentary training in advanced medical practices and techniques to increase their effectiveness in preventing and treating many common diseases, with the hope that these physicians will at least partially fill the personnel gap until more doctors and nurses with modern training are available. It has become fashionable to criticize in print those who deride traditional medicine and its practitioners. Attempts have also been made to study the problems of unifying western and Chinese medical sciences, especially herb medicine, and to popularize its use.

Many modern hospitals now admit some traditional physicians, and it is claimed that they work well with western-trained doctors. To prove the effectiveness of traditional herb medicine, the Ministry of Public Health announced that an ancient prescription for bacillary dysentery was used on thirty-two patients afflicted by the disease, and all were cured in three to eight days. (It should be pointed out that the numbers involved make the result insignificant statistically.) The prescription in question is found in the *Treatise on Fevers (Shang-han lun)*, and it was administered in the Shanghai Number Two People's Hospital, staffed entirely by traditional physicians.

The Incidence of Disease

The most widespread diseases in China are not the diseases most feared. Tuberculosis is perhaps the most common of all, and yet the means by which it is spread, the way to prevent infection, and even the existence or nature of the disease is unknown to many people. Because of this ignorance, tuberculosis accounts for 10 to 15 percent of the entire death rate. It is very prevalent among students. In 1946, prior to the Communist period, 60 percent of Chinese applicants for admission to the United States for advanced study were rejected because of active tuberculosis. In 1956 tuberculosis among students was still one of the gravest problems facing the current regime in its effort to increase the number of teachers and technicians available. It has been estimated that every year a total of 240,000 persons (out of a total population of 650 million) die of tuberculosis. It is evident that an effective attack on this disease requires a large number of cooperating agencies and a whole new set of attitudes toward food practice and hygiene. It constitutes the single most important public health problem in the country today.

Trachoma, a highly contagious type of conjunctivitis which results in granular inflammation under the eyelid, is as common as tuberculosis, but much more easily prevented. A majority of the Chinese do not consider it a disease, make no attempt to treat it, and ignore the most simple means of preventing its occurrence: good sanitary habits. It is possible that with the current emphasis on public hygiene, the toll of blindness from this cause may decrease.

Smallpox ranks third among the widespread diseases in spite of efforts to extend the ancient knowledge of inoculation for its prevention. Together with measles, diphtheria, scarlet fever, and whooping cough, it is responsible for 8 to 12 percent of all deaths each year.

Diseases associated with childbirth rank fourth in this listing; again, lack of cleanliness, resulting in infant death and childbed fever, is responsible for this high incidence. Death of infants in tetanic convulsions eight, nine, or ten days after birth is so common in China that the disease is called the "nine-day disease." Its cause lies in the custom practiced by most rural and some urban people of employing local midwives who, ignorant of the necessity for cleanliness in obstetric practice, dress the umbilical cord of the newborn child with dirty rags and unsterilized herb medicines. Tetanus toxin is hence inoculated into the navel of the newborn child, and within eight or nine days enough toxin is generated to cause death. About 6 to 8 percent of the total death rate is attributable to practices associated with parturition.

Malaria and pneumonia are responsible for 2 to 5 percent of the total death rate, as are venereal diseases. In the past syphilis and gonorrhea were widespread because every town and city had a number of prostitutes, especially such large cities as Shanghai, Tientsin, and Hankow. The vigorous campaigns of the Communists to eliminate prostitution may have, however, reduced the number of such diseases.

Some chronic diseases are regional in occurrence. For example, though malaria can be found in every part of China, it is especially prevalent in the rice region extending south from the Yangtze valley, and in western Yunnan where it spread along the Burma Road during the Sino-Japanese War. Typhus is widespread in the colders areas of the country, partly due to the fact that people in rural areas rarely bathe during the winter, giving body lice a good chance to multiply. The thick mud walls of houses along the Fukien and Chekiang coasts shelter large numbers of rats, which are the secondary carriers of typhus lice. Relapsing fever, transmitted by the bites of ticks and lice, is found principally in the north, while leprosy is most common in the south, in Kwangtung and on Hainan Island. Goiter is common in Kwangsi, Kweichow, and Yunnan, where the diet is deficient in iodine, due to its lack in the rock salt used in these provinces. Taken all together, this group of diseases accounts for about 3 to 5 percent of the total death rate.

The diseases feared most of all are those that arise without warning, spread like wildfire, and almost invariably leave a trail of dead and crippled. Cholera, scarlet fever, typhoid and bubonic plague, for example, generally occur in the form of epidemics. Because preventive techniques and adequate medication are lacking, these highly contagious diseases spread quickly and cause many deaths.

In addition to the above, there is another group of afflictions that makes up about one-fourth of the total death rate from disease: these are the fecal-borne diseases that are spread through human waste. The seriousness of this group of diseases is underlined by the intimate association of conditions for their spread with the specific practices of the cultivation of certain crops, mainly rice. These diseases may be conveniently divided into two groups: those caused by intestinal worms, principally hookworm, and those caused by flukes of various types, which may lodge in the human liver, lungs, or blood. The practices of using night soil from the fertilizer bed to aid plant growth and of working in the fields either barefoot or with loose straw sandals mean that the farmers can hardly escape contact with the larval forms of the hookworm parasite. Fluke diseases take various forms, several depending primarily on contact with snails at some intermediate stage of the development of the parasite. Others are transmitted through the consumption of raw fish or raw water chestnuts and through the bare feet and hands of the farmers as they pull rice plants from the larvae-laden, fecal-fertilized culture beds.

It is apparent that an attack on parasitic diseases such as these is a major public health project for the authorities.

Special Health Services

The health of women and children is given special attention in Communist writings and in the 1954 Constitution. The training of midwives, the re-education of "old-style" midwives, the establishment of maternity stations and health centers for women and children, and the prevention of various children's diseases have been particularly publicized in public health work in the country as a whole. Separate departments for child and maternal health have been set up at all levels of the public health service. Several major child and maternal health institutes have been established in such industrial centers as Shanghai and Tientsin. A Central Maternal and Child Health Institute has been set up in Peking. The main efforts are directed against the high infant mortality rate which was reduced from 20 per 1,000 in the pre-1949 period to 7.03 per 1,000 in 1957.

In rural areas, experimental county health centers have been established to specialize in health problems of a local nature. Most industrial centers and large municipalities have organized industrial hygiene divisions in their respective health departments. The Ministry of Public Health, in cooperation with the All-China Federation of Trade Unions and other ministries concerned with industry, has established a Health Service Department which gives free care to all eligible industrial workers and their dependents.

To prevent the spread of epidemics, the Ministry of Public Health organized medical work in the flood-ravaged regions in the years 1949, 1952, 1953, and 1954. During and immediately after the floods, anti-epidemic corps were organized and sent to the seriously flooded areas. As emergency measures, anti-plague teams were formed or transferred from one region to another wherever the need was acute. In all these areas, disease was checked before it could reach epidemic proportions. The success of the anti-plague campaign was due in part to the government health service and in part to the campaign to exterminate rats. It is reported that in 1950 alone, 14,500,000 rats were killed.

When plague broke out in 1949 in Luichow Peninsula in Kwangtung, the anti-plague team was successful in swiftly bringing it under control. Not only was an epidemic prevented, but treatment with a combination of sulfa drugs and streptomycin succeeded in curing 97 percent of the 200-odd cases of bubonic plague.

Serious outbreaks of this sort provide the regime with an opportunity to introduce western medicine, as an emergency measure, and thus prove its effectiveness over diseases which traditional medicine has been powerless to resist. Swift and effective action in the face of real crisis has done more to spread new attitudes toward modern medicine than any amount of propagandizing, and the regime is alert to this fact. As a consequence, little difficulty has been met in administering vaccinations for smallpox or injections for cholera, plague, typhoid, and other diseases on a mass scale. Anti-epidemic corps are also following up on favorable attitudes toward cure of the most dreaded and chronic diseases like malaria, kala azar (a highly contagious malarial-type fever), schistosomiasis (intestinal disease), typhus, and relapsing fever. Work on an experimental basis is thus possible, for example, against tuberculosis and venereal disease, and plans are being made to extend this work as more trained personnel and facilities become available.

All of the above special services are supported by an allegedly improved system of hospital care. It has been claimed that the total number of hospitals and sanitariums as well as health stations, clinics, and industrial health units has increased considerably in recent years.

Working conditions in factories and mines are reported to have been improved through strengthened safety and health measures. A close examination of newspaper editorials, however, reveals repeated charges that the hospitals serve party members and government officials first, workers and soldiers second, the "people" last; officials use their position to obtain drugs which they sell on the black market. Moreover, the facilities of the various hospitals fall far short of even minimum standards; they range from those with superb and modern equipment, supplies, and personnel, especially those supported by western interests before 1949, to some which can hardly be called poor outpatient clinics. There are also indications that the tremendous need for doctors leads to a highly accelerated and spotty medical education.

Private hospitals are organized and controlled in the same

way as other private enterprises: by installation of party members on governing boards and by incorporation of the hospital staff into the government-led labor unions. Physicians do not practice privately but are consolidated into "united dispensaries"; several doctors are grouped into one unit and, when the occasion warrants it, are sent wherever they are needed. Nevertheless, the status of the few western-trained doctors is very high indeed. Even traditional physicians, or the best of them, are accorded almost the same respect they formerly enjoyed; those who acquire some knowledge of western medicine can consolidate their new high status with considerable security and prestige.

Health Campaigns

In order to integrate health work with the mass propaganda drive in 1952 involving the so-called "bacteriological warfare" of the United States, the Chinese Communists launched the Patriotic Health Drive. Started during the Korean conflict, it has proved so successful that it has become an annual event. The purpose of the movement was, and is, to solicit and obtain free labor, in the name of patriotism, for the cleaning of cities and rural areas and for the general improvement of environmental hygiene as part of the national health program.

Thousands of students, teachers, and medical and health workers spearhead these annual drives which are aimed specifically at removing refuse from streets, dredging ditches, digging new wells and improving others, reconstructing public comfort stations, eliminating flies, rats, mosquitoes, and so forth. It is claimed that as a result of the drives, epidemics have been prevented, the health of the people is protected, and the production of the nation is maintained without serious losses due to illness; the masses also receive valuable health information.

To the individual Chinese, the Patriotic Health Drive, which became the anti-four pests (flies, mosquitoes, rats, and grain-eating sparrows) movement of 1958, is one more in a long list of drives and campaigns into which his labor is commandeered by exhortations appealing to his patriotism and enthusiasm for a new China. Exhortations are evidently necessary, for unless continual pressure is brought on the individual citizen the many drives and campaigns may cause him to be apathetic in the face of so many things to be done all at once. Reports indicate that municipalities do better, on the whole, than rural areas in most of the campaigns. It is in the urban centers, where day-to-day living is more highly organized and under almost continual direct control, that mass programs can be most effectively activated. Peking was largely cleared of flies, mosquitoes, rats, and dogs; ditches were dug, and other important measures taken to prevent the spread of disease; but according to one report, only twelve miles southwest of Peking, in the village of Ch'ang-hsin-tien, the streets remained dirty, melon rinds were everywhere, and flies and mosquitoes multiplied as prolifically as ever.

Moreover, the level of a nation's health cannot be determined merely by the elimination of disease-carrying agents. It rests more generally on the well-being of the population—in short, on its standard of living. It is on the success of the Communist regime in producing food and distributing it, in providing adequate housing, and in producing consumers' goods, that standards of public health will ultimately depend. Evidence of concern at the inadequate food supply is indicated by the yearly push to conserve grain and improve transportation, while cutting down consumption through appeals to patriotic sentiments.

Nutrition and Diet

In general, it may be said that the Chinese diet is sufficient in calories to sustain heavy manual labor, but the amount of protein is inadequate. Wheat-eating northerners get more proteins than do rice-eating southerners, a fact which may account in part for the difference in stature, northerners tending toward somewhat greater height than southerners.

There are other food factors either lacking altogether or present in an insufficient quantity in the Chinese diet. Calcium is one of these. The leafy vegetables, comprising only 5.2 percent of the entire diet, are the only source of calcium so important in the formation of strong teeth and bones. Rickets is therefore quite common, especially in Central and South China. In some backward areas, custom precludes any food other than thin rice gruel for the newly nursing mother. In consequence, the infant begins life seriously deficient in calcium requirements. The average Chinese diet also lacks sufficient iron, and sufficient variety and quantity of vitamins for protection against common diseases.

The Chinese drink hot tea instead of fresh water because of the widespread realization that sickness may result from the careless use of impure water. Milk was, and generally is, distrusted for much the same reason; since demand for it is low, facilities for preparing milk for consumption, such as pasteurization, are inadequate, and the price is high. A minority of well-to-do people have adopted its use in the last few decades. Soybean milk is often drunk in place of cow's milk.

Although animal foods—meat, eggs, and the like—are highly preferred the majority of the population cannot afford them except for special occasions, generally the dozen or so annual holidays. Such foods are conspicuously absent in the mess halls in the communes. For those who can afford them, pork, poultry, and in some regions fish are popular. Except for the Moslems, there is, however, a disinclination toward the eating of beef, probably a long-standing prejudice against killing animals essential for plowing and hauling.

Transportation difficulties impede the flow of essential materials like salt, sugar, and oil to the average household. Often, salt has been critically short just at the time when autumn pickling of vegetables was to begin, and the supply of edible oil has been seriously deficient even when used thriftily. Vegetables, though not rationed like pork and other food stuffs, are not adequately distributed because of transportation difficulties, and there is evidence of vegetable shortages on the open market in urban areas with the government giving preferential treatment to industrial workers, government offices, the army, hospitals, and schools. The bumper harvest in 1958 eased the grain supply situation, but transportation shortages still plagued the distribution of foodstuffs in the urban areas.

Sanitation

Fresh water is available in many areas, but is often distributed by the simplest methods. Wells are dug wherever no convenient sources of water are found in streams, ponds, or lakes. Running water is not found in rural farmhouses, but, because water is generally nearby, this does not usually impose undue hardship on peasant families. Modern water systems are widespread in the cities; since a household supply of running water in towns, however, is expensive, only wealthy people can afford it. In some places, community taps form another source of water, from which residents nearby may obtain fresh water at little cost.

Except for liquid waste, which is easily disposed of through the sewer system in the cities, the two systems of water supply and waste are quite independent. The nature of the water source (wells, ponds, lakes, or others) often isolates it from waste disposal of any kind except near the largest rivers, and the extensive use of night soil in agriculture generally results in the removal of that portion of waste from the cities.

Where sanitation measures are most urgent—for example in clearing public areas of garbage and other refuse or in eliminating the breeding places of rats, flies, and mosquitoes—the public's help is enlisted as part of the Communist health campaigns.

Although the average Chinese may occasionally resent the regimentation that goes with the government's health and welfare programs, the relative success of these programs in improving the country's standards in these fields is increasingly apparent.

EDUCATION

IN TRADITIONAL CHINA, THE THEMES OF CONFUCIAN thought bound together state and family, public life and private life, education and the process of acculturation into one harmonious whole. The fact of being educated exercised such an overwhelming influence on attitudes toward learning and the status of the intelligentsia that these have persisted essentially unchanged even to the present.

It is difficult to assess fully the extent and depth of penetration of the prestige of education throughout the whole of Chinese society. Entry into the ranks of the scholars was for a long time the only path that led to political influence, high status, and wealth, irrespective of the changing fortunes of dynasties. It was an achievement devoutly desired for every young man, no matter what the social and economic position of his parents. It was an important source of the continuity of the ideological basis of state rule for two millenia.

The Chinese educational system, however, has been undergoing a radical transformation from about the beginning of the twentieth century. New concepts of the nature and function of education led to a fundamental reorganization of the educational structure, to be greatly accelerated by the Communist regime. The most notable of the changes made during the last ten years have been the rapid extension of educational facilities for the common people, the introduction of basic language and curricular reforms, and stress on manual labor as an essential part of the learning process. The utilization of the educational system to satisfy the needs of the state has never been so extensive as under the present Communist regime.

The phenomenal growth in educational facilities in recent years (see Table 20) reflects the paucity of educational opportunities prior to the Communist revolution and the energetic measures adopted by the present government to correct this deficiency. Such speed, however, has given rise to numerous problems, of which the most pressing are the lack of teachers, the inadequacy of physical facilities, and the confusion resulting from the drastic reorientation of educational aims and methods. Serious concern has been voiced by Chinese educators regarding the quality of middle school and university graduates. A crucial task for the Communist leaders today, therefore, is how to provide a nation of 650 million people with a modern education adequate for the demands of an atomic and space age—an education that in many basic features has departed significantly from education in the traditional period.

Features of Traditional Education

Prior to the twentieth century, the far-flung Chinese empire was administered by a huge bureaucracy recruited from the educated segment of the population. For the majority, education was practically the sole avenue to power and prestige. Through its control of the civil service examination, the central government was able to influence decisively the educational content, which throughout the imperial period was based upon Confucian philosophy and was essentially humanistic in orientation. The Confucian scholars, in particular, carried the burden of learning, kept alive the knowledge of the ancients, and aimed to apply their wisdom in the management of the empire. Education and scholarship were central concerns of the official class, and scholars won a place in the political hierarchy.

Examination and Bureaucracy

Learning was a central element in Confucian thought along with a sense of historical continuity and a duty to cultivate through education the essentially good nature of man. Thus, in traditional China, learning became the basis of moral propriety and was reinforced by official recognition of the merit of ancient knowledge, particularly of the Confucian classics. There were differential rewards for the several levels of scholarly attainment from *hsiu-ts'ai* (cultivated talent), the first degree, to *chü-jen* (elevated man) and *chin-shih* (advanced scholar). Recipients of these degrees were all highly respected by society and often awarded official positions. The *chin-shih*, who attained the highest degree by passing all the different levels of examinations, in particular received high official emoluments or became members of the highest literary institution, the Han-lin Academy.

Those who failed in the examinations at least shared the feeling of having bettered their nature through instruction. Some, who had no land to manage, became teachers for other aspiring students. They established the private schools which served as the traditional equivalent of elementary and secondary schools. Even though they usually received a low salary (supplemented by food), they were highly respected by pupils and parents.

Thus, on the basis of their importance to the empire and partly because of their exalted place in history, the scholars of traditional China held a pre-eminent position. The esteem in which scholars were held affected the class structure of China throughout the entire imperial period up to the twentieth century. It also influenced to such a degree the subjects studied by the educated elite and the intellectual environment in which they were nurtured that, in time, the prestige and the orthodoxy of the traditional scholars interfered strongly with the ability of the social order to renew and to adjust itself to the changing conditions of the modern world.

In a large measure, this lack of resiliency was due to the almost perfect adaptation of education to the moral purposes and goals toward which traditional learning was oriented. The moral concepts were all contained in the Confucian classics, which were studied, memorized, and then expounded at the civil service examinations. Such studies were designed to provide talented, incorruptible, and filially pious officials for the imperial government. Whoever might rule, it was always the scholars who would be called upon to administer the government. They alone possessed the necessary mastery of the written language and essential administrative techniques to insure continuation of the social and economic order.

With the establishment of a bureaucracy of scholars and the concurrent need for education of a very special sort, control over the educational process, a characteristic of Chinese education which remains unchanged to this day, was given its initial impetus. Under state control, the examination system degenerated into the compilation of highly stylized and artificial essays, proficiency in which determined capability for public office. Instead of providing the state with "competent and learned" civil servants, it produced men, who, although well versed in the classics, had very little comprehension of the social and political problems of the state. They were also expected to be subservient to the reigning power.

The Beginning of Modern Education

Throughout the imperial period, contact with the West was not, on the whole, very extensive. Aspects of western learning had always been admired; Jesuit missionaries like Matteo Ricci and Johannes Adam Schall impressed Chinese scholars in the seventeenth century with their knowledge of science, especially astronomy. In each case, contact with the culture of the West followed the same pattern as contact with any other alien culture impinging on China in the course of its history: assimilation and absorption into the vast complex of traditional learning and belief. It is not surprising that after the opening of coastal ports to western influence in the mid-nineteenth century, the trend was toward "western learning in application and Chinese learning in substance." In spite of the pressure exerted by students returning from study abroad and the programs for reform of educational structure and practice advanced by men like Yung Wing (the first Chinese scholar to have graduated from an American college), the conservative Chinese scholars were able to preserve the system which gave them their jealously guarded grip on power, wealth, and prestige. It was only after the defeat of China in the war of 1894-95 with Japan, which had been considered a second-rate oriental power by the Chinese, that the tide for educational reform began to turn.

The events of the next few years before the Revolution of 1911 are evidence of a desperate effort to salvage the imperial educational system. Government edicts of 1901 and 1905 abolished examinations for civil service; many more modern-type schools were planned for the prefectures and districts, and western science was to be introduced into the curriculum. Normal schools were established along with what would appear to be a modern school system. Many students went abroad to study, first principally in Japan, later in Europe and America, and the returning scholars began to play an increasingly important role in the government.

In the republican period (1912-49), especially after the establishment of the Nationalist government in 1927, the school system was modeled mainly after American prototypes. Compulsory education in the lower grades was introduced; the Confucian classics were no longer required subjects in the curriculum; and "practical" courses such as the natural sciences and technology were stressed.

Meanwhile, efforts were made to reduce illiteracy which had been estimated as high as 75 to 80 percent of the population. Different kinds of schools for adults were set up in the cities and rural areas and the mass education movement, initiated by Yen Yang-ch'u, an American-trained educator, attracted wide attention among educated leaders. The eventual failure to eradicate illiteracy was due not so much to the inherent weakness of the movement as to political instability, the lack of adequate funds, and the chronic shortage of trained teachers and administrative personnel.

In spite of these difficulties, educational progress during the Nationalist period was substantial. The major effort was to increase the number of children in elementary schools as rapidly as possible. Between 1912 and 1932 the number of school-age children receiving an elementary education remained fairly constant at about 20 percent, but between 1932 and 1944, the number rose to about 75 percent; at the same time, the number of adults attending literacy classes increased slowly but steadily.

The middle schools (corresponding to American high schools and divided into junior and senior middle schools) had a single over-all administration for all normal, vocational, and academic courses. Such a program was difficult for many counties to support, and eventually many schools became either normal or vocational schools. In 1938 regulations were drawn up to govern the distribution of normal, vocational, and academic middle schools on the basis of population, financial condition, cultural level, and communication facilities. The courses in the academic middle schools, standardized during 1932-34, were designed mainly as preparation for higher education, with emphasis either on the sciences or the humanities, although most of the courses contained what would be considered "practical" materials as compared with traditional curriculums.

Institutions of higher learning exhibited similar growing pains. In 1929, laws governing the organization of universities and technical colleges provided for standardized courses of study, uniform requirements for entrance and for the various degrees, and a minimum requirement for funds. In accordance with these legislative measures, the system of higher education was reorganized and consolidated. Independent colleges were integrated into universities, and new schools were established on the basis of need and location. Graduate studies were fostered at the institutions of higher learning, and research work in the humanities and social and natural sciences was carried on at the Academia Sinica, the nation's highest institute for advanced learning. The Sino-Japanese War (1937-45) took its toll among universities, driving them inland with inadequate equipment and supplies, but also forcing them into contact with areas hitherto ignored. After 1946, under the stimulus of an ambitious government program of student subsidies, enrollment increased in the newly re-established universities and colleges by 100 percent in private institutions and by 400 percent in public institutions.

Thus a half century after the discarding of traditional learning, a modern educational system had grown up in China. During these years, western influence had been predominant in shaping the structure and content of Chinese education. But the goal of a literate and informed citizenry, a prerequisite for the growth of a democratic nation, was far from being realized. The Nationalists admitted in 1946 that 46.9 percent of the population was still illiterate. The groundwork had been laid, however, for the education of a populace attuned to the requirements of the modern world.

Developments under the Communist Regime

To dovetail education and national needs, the Communists have been utilizing the same technique of strict control over the educational process practiced both in traditional China and during the Nationalist period. The Nationalists, for instance, had established an elaborate and highly complex system of supervision over the school system and monitored curriculums to ensure adherence to the Three People's Principles of Sun Yat-sen. This system of state control has virtually assured the Communists minimum opposition to their educational policy.

Communist Policy in Education

Mao Tse-tung stated in his essay "On New Democracy" that "a given culture is the ideological reflection of the politics and economy of a given society." In molding a culture for the new China, Mao believed that education would be a decisive force if it contained scientific substance, and if it were oriented toward the masses and adapted to suit China's nationalistic aspirations. This policy for education was incorporated into the Common Program of 1949 which states that the purpose of education is "the raising of the cultural level of the people, the training of personnel for national construction work, the eradicating of feudal, compradore, and fascist ideology, and the developing of the ideology of service to the people" (Article 41). To apply this basic policy to education, it is further specified that "universal education shall be carried out, secondary and higher education shall be strengthened, technical education shall be stressed, the education of workers during their spare time and that of cadres at their posts shall be strengthened, and revolutionary political education shall be accorded to both young and old-type intellectuals" (Article 47).

These pronouncements became the guiding principles for the Communist regime in its effort to revamp the educational system of China. The Constitution of 1954 reiterates the principles already adopted. Article 94 of the Constitution says that "citizens of the People's Republic of China have the right to education. To guarantee enjoyment of this right, the state establishes and gradually extends the various types of schools and other cultural and educational institutions. The state pays special attention to the physical and mental development of young people."

Attention must be given to the gradual shift of emphasis from 1949 to the present in the Communist basic policy for education. In the beginning, the central theme was to bring to reality a "new democracy" in education. By this the Communists meant that the *petit bourgeois* and national capitalist classes would still be tolerated and placed on a level with the proletariat. Soon afterward it became apparent that the Communists would make a constant effort to control the educational system and to root out every trace of thought and practice in education that did not help develop socialism.

This rigid Communist policy was opposed by the intellectuals at the time of general relaxation of government control during the 1956-57 Blooming and Contending campaign, whose original purpose was to free scientific and artistic endeavors from the stultifying orthodoxy imposed upon them by rigid Communist theoreticians and administrators. The more liberal atmosphere following this major concession to the intellectuals was utilized by a great number of teachers to criticize the shortcomings of the existing educational structure. The most telling criticisms were directed against the uncritical application of the Soviet system to Chinese educational needs, the overspecialization of technical courses, the heavy schedules carried by the students and teachers, and the concentration of authority in the hands of the party organization within the schools and universities.

In the educational field, one unforeseen consequence of this and the other campaigns that followed was the public questioning of the ability and qualification of the non-professionally trained party cadres to administer academic work and direct the course of education. The Communist reaction to this challenge was swift and decisive and critics were accused of plotting to usurp party control of education. The government decreed that all educators should participate for varying periods of time in manual labor to adjust themselves to Communist ideology and to get as close as possible to the laboring masses. Political indoctrination was further emphasized in all educational institutions, followed by a drastic reorganization of school curriculums and a new policy toward the educational development of "cultured and socialist-minded workers."

One of the most important tenets in the present Chinese educational policy is embodied in the slogan: "Work diligently and conduct schools frugally." In practical terms this means the establishment of spare-time schools on all levels as well as the introduction of part-time study and part-time work in all regular schools and universities. Such a system would unite education with production, theory with practice, and mental labor with physical labor, thus realizing the objective of training a new generation of cultured and socialist-minded workers. The government further directed that the public schools must have a well-defined work program and, in general, should not try to be financially self-supporting; the private schools, on the other hand, should try to support themselves through productive work.

To understand the Communist educational policy correctly, one should also consider it in conjunction with the present government plan to increase industrial production and to keep abreast with the rest of the world in scientific and technological development. To realize these goals, the acute demand for more skilled workers, technicians, and scientists will increase from year to year. Obviously the only solution to the financing of an ever expanding education system with limited funds is to utilize as much as possible private resources and to shift part of the financial burden to the schools themselves. The result has been an astonishing mushrooming of private schools run by the communes, industrial enterprises, and other urban groups, and the inauguration of work-study programs as a part of the school curriculum.

Educational Reorganization

The changes the Communists brought to the schools in the early years of their conquest were imposed unsystematically and arbitrarily. Even after the establishment of the People's Republic, the measures designed to revise the educational system and school organization remained haphazard. In the field of education the main activity of the Communist administration appeared to be the seizure of private schools, especially those sponsored by religious groups and foreign missions.

The first systematic reorganization was occasioned by the issuing of a directive, "Decisions Concerning the Reform of the Educational System," on October 1, 1951 by the Government Administration Council. The main features of the reform were the regrouping of departments in large universities and specialization in the colleges to achieve a balance of higher educational facilities; the introduction of a five-year and one-level primary school system to replace the previous six-year and two-level system so that children of poor peasants could receive a complete basic education within a shorter period of time; the expansion of special educational facilities such as adult classes, spare-time schools, and vocational schools to provide opportunities for party cadres, soldiers, peasants, and industrial workers who had been denied formal education. By September 1952 the major reorganization of schools had been completed. Since then the only important change in education has been the restoration in 1954 of the old six-year and two-level primary school system because of the inadequate preparation of the new system for a child's basic education (see the plate, Chinese Educational System).

Administration of the School System

Under the State Council, the Ministry of Education controls and administers the nation's educational system. Prior to 1958 education at higher and secondary levels of technical and administrative personnel to be used in the national reconstruction program was administered by the Ministry of Higher Education; while teacher training schools, regular middle and primary schools, and adult education schools were supervised by the Ministry of Education. Since 1958 the functions of both ministries have been combined under a single Ministry of Education (see the plate, Communist Government Control of Education).

One significant development in the control of education by the Communist government is the role played by the party. Although the party has no place in the official chain of command, its branches on all levels are actually the authorities for the inter-

CHINESE EDUCATIONAL SYSTEM

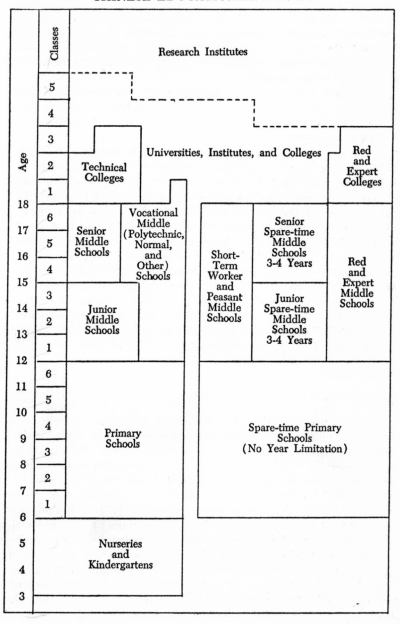

pretation of official policy and make the final decisions on how a school should be run. Evidence shows that some schools refer all important problems to the local party secretary before taking any action. Close-range party supervision, together with the assignment of well-trained veteran cadres to key positions on the administrative staff of the school, ensures the Communists' control over the entire school system from the kindergartens to the institutions of higher learning.

Kindergartens

The kindergartens have a definite place in the reorganized educational system. In most regions, the development of kindergartens has followed the basic Communist policy and is tied in with child welfare programs. The communalization of rural China in 1958 further spurred the establishment of kindergartens as a means of relieving mothers from the care of children so that they could engage in productive labor. The total enrollment in kindergartens for that year was reported to be thirty million. It is reasonable to assume that the lack of qualified teachers and facilities in the villages would place the majority of these institutions in the category of child care centers rather than adequately staffed kindergartens. The local authorities, however, have started short-term training courses for kindergarten personnel which should remedy this situation gradually.

Primary Schools

The development of primary schools received prompter attention than the kindergartens in the Communist educational scheme. The policy has been to strengthen the primary schools in cities and important villages and to encourage the villagers in outlying districts to establish their own primary schools under local government supervision. To consolidate party control over these numerous schools scattered over the country, the government in Peking ordered the assignment of experienced political cadres to supervise the educational agencies in county governments. In addition, primary school principals and other administrators were indoctrinated in Marxian theories and Peking's educational policies.

The tremendous growth of primary education in the last few years is attributable to government encouragement for the establishment of schools by industrial enterprises, urban organizations, handicraft cooperatives, and communes. These schools are called people-sponsored schools as distinct from public or state

COMMUNIST GOVERNMENT CONTROL OF EDUCATION

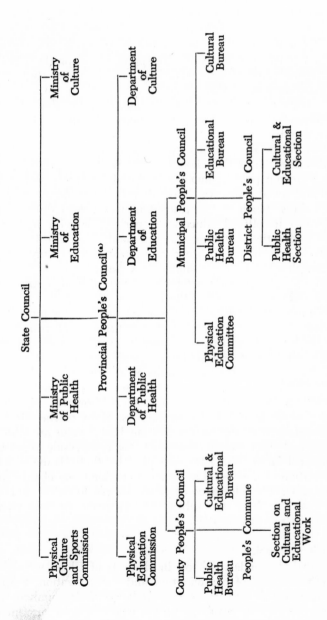

State Council

| Physical Culture and Sports Commission | Ministry of Public Health | Ministry of Education | Ministry of Culture |

Provincial People's Council(a)

| Physical Education Commission | Department of Public Health | Department of Education | Department of Culture |

County People's Council

| Public Health Bureau | Cultural & Educational Bureau |

People's Commune

Section on Cultural and Educational Work

Municipal People's Council

| Physical Education Committee | Public Health Bureau | Educational Bureau | Cultural Bureau |

District People's Council

| Public Health Section | Cultural & Educational Section |

(a) Also special municipality people's councils.

schools. Many are haphazard in nature, the teaching staff being drawn from primary or middle school graduates and supervised by a committee from the sponsoring organizations. Operating expenses are defrayed partly by the sponsors and partly by incomes from school farms and workshops as well as student fees. The consolidation of these schools, especially in teacher training and curriculum, will be an important task for the educational authorities if the over-all level in primary education is to be raised in the country.

One of the most difficult problems facing the authorities was the dissatisfaction of the school teachers with their present position. They were not paid as much as industrial workers and their political and social status was lower than the often untutored government cadres. Much of this discontent was voiced during lengthy discussions in official educational periodicals with hundreds of letters and articles arguing the pros and cons of this issue. Attempts were made to create the impression that many dedicated teachers thoroughly indoctrinated in Communism would willingly forego a higher remuneration for the honor of being entrusted with the responsibility of "being the people's teacher."

Some of the controversies were settled by the June 16, 1956 decision of the State Council to increase salaries of primary school teachers by 32.8 percent and give an over-all salary increase of 28.72 percent to other teachers and staff personnel. It was promised that with further development of the national economy, salaries would be proportionately raised. The average salary of teachers in people-sponsored schools is, however, substantially below that of the public school teachers. Many teachers in people-sponsored schools are on a part-time basis; some are also intellectuals and office workers sent out to the countryside to participate in physical labor. The latter are paid by their "home office" for the duration of their rural assignments without any change in their salary scale. The reluctance of young people to enter the teaching profession has been the subject of discussion by educators and officials as recently as 1959.

Secondary Schools
In 1950 the secondary schools in all parts of China went through the initial stages of consolidation and reorganization. Suspension and merging of private schools reduced their numbers greatly during the ensuing years, but on the whole student enrollment did

not show any appreciable decrease. In fact, as a result of the construction of additional facilities, and the drive to register students from proletarian families, the total number of secondary schools, especially agricultural schools and vocational schools of secondary level, has greatly increased.

It should be noted, however, that more than half of the middle schools and practically all of the agricultural and vocational schools are people-sponsored schools. Their curriculums usually consist of political indoctrination, Chinese language and literature, mathematics, agricultural techniques, and/or other vocational courses. Occasionally, when teachers are available, courses such as biology, chemistry, and physics are added to the curriculum.

The aim of secondary education is to teach the students to cultivate nationalism (but not at the expense of internationalism), respect labor, and realize their duties and responsibilities to their country. For the fulfillment of these objectives, a system of rotating indoctrination was inaugurated for the secondary school principals and other administrators under the supervision of the educational commissioner of the provincial government. By September 1954 about 75 percent of all teachers and administrators had been trained under the new policy. In some areas, particularly in North China, the Ministry of Education periodically dispatched inspectors to observe the schools and educational agencies at secondary and other levels. Recommendations based on these inspection tours are usually referred back to the schools for action.

To make political indoctrination interesting to the students, the Ministry of Education instructed that it should be related to the important events of the day. Formal lectures were held to a minimum and no textbook for the course was issued on the ground that events in the country had moved so rapidly that textbooks would become outdated in a relatively short time. Instead, the students were asked to study theoretical treatises of current interest such as Mao Tse-tung's speech, "On the Correct Handling of Contradictions among the People," and related documents and editorials from the *People's Daily*. The teachers were enjoined to discover the students' attitudes on all important current topics, such as the leadership of the party in education, collectivization, planned purchase and sale of grains, Sino-Soviet relations, and the students' plans after graduation. In classroom discussions, different points of view were debated among the students under the proper guidance of the teacher until all students were indoctrinated in the official line. Such classroom procedure was claimed to have been favorably received by students as being more interesting and, therefore, more effective in the inculcation of political ideas.

A new development in secondary education since 1958 has been the experimental amalgamation of factories and schools. Students in these schools work in the factories for a varying number of hours each day to learn technical skills, while workers are sent to study in the schools to improve their education. In some cases, the managers of the factories act as vice-principals of the schools and the school principals become assistant managers of the factories. In the rural areas, secondary education is oriented strongly toward the training of farm workers who will be able to apply the newest scientific technique to agriculture and to manage the manifold activities of a commune.

In general, secondary education in new China is designed to provide the state with a vast pool of skilled workers and technicians to keep up with the accelerating tempo of its industrialization program. Science and mathematics are being stressed while the humanities are relegated to a secondary position. More students are attending middle schools but the quality of the teaching varies greatly.

Normal Schools

Colleges and secondary schools for teacher training have equal standing with general schools on the same level. In their curriculums, the teacher training schools stress certain aspects which are not emphasized in general educational institutions. The urgent need for trained teachers at schools of different levels was recognized by government authorities who estimated that according to the planned expansion of schools from 1950-57, China would need one million new teachers. Of these, 200,000 would be for spare-time schools for peasants and workers, 130,000 for regular middle schools, 10,000 for colleges, and the remainder for kindergartens.

Measures adopted to expedite the training of teachers included the consolidation of courses and the setting up of special short-term courses for primary school teachers. Those who had left the profession were "induced" to return. Some high school graduates were hired after a period of apprenticeship to serve as instructors in the same school. To improve their qualifications, these and other teachers were encouraged to use their spare time to take refresher courses in evening and Sunday classes especially organized for them. Teachers in outlying districts learned through correspondence courses as well as reference materials brought to them by mobile libraries and formed correspondence clubs for the exchange of teaching experiences, thus helping one another to improve teaching techniques. Associations were formed for the discussion of particular subjects taught in school. These stop-gap measures were not, however, enough to meet the teacher shortage, which has become a continuing crisis in the Chinese educational scene.

Political training is stressed in all the teachers' colleges. The curriculums designed by the Ministry of Education specify that 33.8 percent of the total credit hours for a teacher in training must be devoted to the history of the Communist revolution, Marxian and Leninist theories, psychology, the theory of education, the study of teaching methods, and physical education. Like other colleges in China today, students in teachers' colleges are participating with faculty members in revising teaching plans, syllabuses, and textbooks for their own training.

Institutions of Higher Learning

Since 1958 the control of institutions of higher learning, which formerly was exercised by the Ministry of Higher Education, has been centralized under the Ministry of Education. However, the various central government ministries in charge of different industries have also been given the responsibility to "supervise and coordinate" the programs for advanced technical schools, and local government personnel are appointed for these schools to maintain close supervision. Since 1958 local governments, mainly provincial, have been given more and more authority in the field of higher education.

Immediately after the "liberation," the main effort of the government was directed toward the administrative reorganization of the higher educational institutions. Out of the 227 schools of higher education in 1950, 65 were universities, 92 specialized colleges, and 70 specialized schools. Through the process of "consolidation and integration," this number was reduced to 182 by the end of 1953. Most institutions became centers of one specialty, such as agriculture, medicine, engineering, mining, foreign languages (especially Russian), teacher training, or physical education. In Peking, for example, Tsinghua University, which absorbed the natural science departments of the former Yenching University, an American missions-supported institution, became in fact a vast polytechnic university; only Peking University together with the newly established Chinese People's University are today universities for general studies. However, the trend toward integration and reduction has been reversed, and by 1958 there were more than a thousand institutions of higher learning with an enrollment of 600,000 to 700,000. Among them, sixty are supervised by the various ministries of the central government; more than four hundred are supervised by the provinces, municipalities, and autonomous regions; about sixty are operated by factories and mines; and the rest are under the jurisdiction of local governments. It may be assumed that only institutions belonging to the first two categories are adequately staffed and equipped.

Among the difficulties experienced during the reorganization process were the thought reform of university professors and the transfer of certain departments from one university to another, which disrupted the administrations of both institutions. The realization grew slowly that something was wrong with higher education when standards became progressively lower along with morale, and in 1953 three important conferences were held by the Ministry of Higher Education. In these conferences numerous complaints were heard, of which the most significant were the disappearance of the distinctly Chinese universities, the haphazard and arbitrary reshuffling of the schools, and the lack of enthusiasm among professors. The conclusion of the conferences was that the essence of the Soviet system, "planned study in the Marxist spirit," should be maintained, but the external form of the system should be modified or abandoned.

The departmental divisions and curriculums of the leading institutions were reorganized with the assistance of Soviet advisers, the basic principle being to copy the "advanced" experience of the Soviet Union. The study of Russian, started in the middle schools, has become a required subject in most colleges and universities. Whenever available, translations of Russian materials are used as textbooks and reference works, and Russian instructors are known to be present in some of the important centers of learning.

In recent years, as a result of the public criticism of the many shortcomings in higher education and the subsequent student unrest which disturbed the operation of the educational machinery, the government has decided that political education must be further strengthened in the classrooms and that students and professors must henceforth participate in manual labor as a means of acquiring a proletarian viewpoint. To eliminate some of the more obvious grievances, party cadres were enjoined to maintain more friendly contacts with nonmembers on the university staff and to eliminate any overbearing attitude. Waste and inefficiency in the administration were exposed and corrected. Teaching plans, textbooks, and student schedules were re-examined. It was demanded that courses such as history, literature, and philosophy be directed more to the contemporary period, while courses in science and technology be geared to the needs of the state and incorporate the newest advancements made by other countries. Many educational institutions have organized a number of industrial enterprises under the spur of the "leap forward" movement. For example, Tsinghua University, the foremost polytechnic institute in China, had established fifty-five factories and workshops, three designing companies, and five construction companies by 1958. Its Department of Hydraulic Engineering undertook the designing and construction of forty dams capable of irrigating a million acres of land. Many universities have revised the teaching schedule in such a way that the students are now required to work from three to four months on farms or in factories, and have about a month of vacation during the school year. The Communist authorities asserted that this plan will not only improve the moral outlook and physical stamina of the students but also facilitate the union of book knowledge with practical training.

While emphasizing the merits of manual labor, the Communists have not neglected the necessity of keeping abreast with the world in the field of science. On September 20, 1958 the Chinese University of Sciences and Technology was inaugurated in Peking with an initial class of 1,600 students. It admits students of exceptional academic ability and high political consciousness. The faculty is drawn from the research members of the Chinese Academy of Sciences with Kuo Mo-jo, the President of the Academy, as chancellor. The university, at present, has thirteen departments concentrating on the most advanced branches of the physical sciences and technology such as nuclear physics, electronic computation, automation, geophysics, and others. The students will be given the most rigorous training and will participate, in their third and fourth years, in research work conducted by the Academy of Sciences.

An important adjunct to higher education in China is the government program of sending students abroad for special training. The USSR is receiving the greatest number of students. According to a 1959 report, from 1951 to 1958 China had sent 6,561 students for study in the Soviet Union, of whom 1,064 had already returned. The East European countries, especially East Germany and Czechoslovakia, are also receiving a fair number of Chinese students. Others are studying in India and Egypt. No statistics are available of the total number of students studying abroad, but it may be assumed that it is below the peak of the pre-Communist period when thousands of students went to Japan, Europe, and the United States for training. The Communist program emphasizes the systematic sending of postgraduate students abroad for study in the disciplines most needed in China. It is probable that the number of undergraduates being sent abroad will dwindle as years go by and the exchange of professors and specialists will be stepped up.

Higher education in China is subsidized entirely by the state and the students are expected to go wherever they are needed after graduation. Throughout the years in college, students are told to consider salary as secondary in importance and refusal to accept government assignment as akin to political desertion. College graduates who request assignment to the toughest jobs and the remotest areas are publicly commended. However, many problems have been created by the government's "planned distribution." From the beginning of 1950 to the end of 1952, the central government had assigned 74,000 graduates of higher institutions to various parts of the country, and a 1957 report stated that over 300,000 graduates had been assigned in the last few years. But to place so many graduates where each would make use of what he has studied is by no means a simple undertaking, and there were, and are, undoubtedly many misassignments which result in dissatisfaction and complaints.

To place job assignment on a more systematic and equitable basis, the State Council issued in 1957 a decree on the assignment of college and technical school graduates. While offering the students guarantees in job opportunities after graduation, the government decree permits only very limited freedom to the graduates. It is intended primarily to effect a more efficient utilization of educated manpower through better coordination between the universities and the employing agencies, and to enforce the political conformity of the students through the state's monopoly of the most desirable jobs. During 1958 the demand for qualified personnel was so great that there was a shortage at all levels and in all localities. The problem facing the government now is not where to find jobs for the graduates but where to place them so that they will do the most good. The complaint that "graduation means unemployment," frequently heard during pre-Communist days, has disappeared together with the freedom of individual choice of employment.

Special Education

To give political and technical training to peasants, workers, and party activists is one of the basic aims of Communist education. A broad program for this purpose as outlined at the All-China Conference on Education for Peasants and Workers in September 1950 stressed the following objectives: elimination of illiteracy; education of the cadres among the peasants and workers to provide proper leadership for the masses; and tailoring of this kind of education to local conditions which vary from place to place.

No clear line of demarcation can be drawn between the educational institutions for peasants and workers and those for party and government cadres. The development of this type of education under the Communists could be traced back to Mao Tse-tung's Peasant Movement Institute in Hunan in the early days of the Chinese Communist movement. Later, when the Communists established a stronghold in southern Kiangsi province, cadre schools were established to train political and military personnel. These institutions were succeeded by the College of the War of Resistance and by the Northern Shensi Institute in Yenan in the 1930's and early 1940's. As the Communist army occupied North China after World War II, the North China University and the North China People's Revolutionary University were established for cadre training. After 1949 the Chinese People's University emerged in Peking, with 30 percent of its curriculum devoted to political education and 70 percent to the specific fields in which the cadre students specialized.

A 1950 Communist survey asserted that about 765,000 workers and over 25 million peasants were enrolled in night schools, winter schools, and other classes during their spare time. In the same program, the much publicized "accelerated course" invented by Ch'i Chien-hua, a cultural cadre attached to the armed forces, to teach the Chinese written language was first tried and pronounced successful.

A more recent report claimed that from January to August 1958 a total of 90 million illiterates had been taught to read as compared to the total of 27,970,000 that emerged from illiteracy from 1949 to 1957. Among the more than two thousand counties and municipalities in China, 67.2 percent had been essentially successful in wiping out illiteracy. An important aid to this literacy program was the promulgation in 1957 of a set of Latin letters for the spelling of Chinese characters. It was reported that, in experiments conducted in Shantung, illiterate peasants were able to learn the alphabet in a few days, which aided enormously their ability to recognize and pronounce complicated Chinese characters. One of the problems facing the rural educators is how to prevent the new literates from slipping back to illiteracy. The lack of adequate reading materials and opportunities for further education is said to be the most serious obstacle toward the consolidation of the gains accrued from the whirlwind campaign to wipe out illiteracy in the countryside.

The development of spare-time schools for peasants and workers is one of the most impressive gains in the Chinese educational scene. In 1958, according to Communist claims, 60 million people enrolled in all types of spare-time schools were distributed as follows: 20 million students in 340,000 "red and expert" schools and colleges; 610,000 students in more than 5,000 night colleges and correspondence schools; 1.5 million students in some 30,000 spare-time technical middle schools; 4 million students in 90,000 newly established spare-time middle schools; 31 million students in 680,000 newly established spare-time primary schools; and about 800,000 at various types of spare-time technical and remedial classes.

Most worthy of attention among these spare-time schools are the "red and expert" schools and colleges developed in the rural areas in response to the state's needs for expanding educational facilities. Formerly, the rapid expansion of public middle schools and colleges had enabled a large percentage of primary school and middle school students to continue schooling after graduation, but during 1957 the rate of absorption fell off considerably. Confronted with the situation that many graduates of primary and middle schools were faced with the prospect of discontinuing further formal education, the government decided on two important measures: a campaign to persuade educated youth to participate in agricultural pursuits and a call for the establishment of schools by the masses. The government realized that its long-range program for the increase of agricultural production was dependent upon the training of a vast number of educated youths willing to work on the farms; therefore, facilities had to be provided for them to continue their education. The communalization movement of 1958 enabled the rural cadres to pool the resources of many villages for the establishment of a complete system of regular and part-time schools, including the spare-time "red and expert" schools and colleges. The availability of primary and middle school graduates in the communes also provided teachers as well as students for the various types of rural educational institutions.

Flexibility is the keyword in the operation of these "red and expert" schools and colleges. The schools admit students with a primary education or its equivalent, and the colleges admit those with a middle school education or its equivalent. There is no age limit except that most of those fortunate enough to have gone through primary or middle schools belong to the younger generation. School hours are geared to the requirement of the farm; the students may study and work every other day, or work in the morning and study in the afternoon; classes may be held more often in the slack farming periods and suspended during the busy seasons. Political courses are required and generally taught by local party secretaries. Academic courses such as Chinese language, mathematics, and sciences are given by teachers from the regular schools or by those who have some training in these subjects. The most important part of the curriculum consists of technical courses such as the growing of agricultural crops, the rearing of farm animals, the making of chemical fertilizers, and the surveying and building of water conservation projects—all taught by peasant experts and specialists.

Usually the communes set aside tracts of farmland where students and teachers can work together and experiment with the latest agricultural methods propagated by the government or conduct their own experiments in accordance with the needs and conditions of their own localities. The results of their experiments are applied quickly to the rest of the commune lands. The students also participate in the renovation and invention of farm tools and machinery and in setting up rural workshops and factories. The academic courses are closely related to the technical courses; for example, biology teachers will plan a program of agricultural experimentation for the students who will also work with peasant experts in the field to gain practical knowledge of plant life; mathematics teachers will emphasize the principles of farm accounting and field surveying. The labor expended on school farms by teachers and students is paid for by the commune and the produce is used to defray part of the school expenses. Thus, without any need for state support, the "red and expert" schools and colleges, while satisfying the thirst for education among the rural youths and adults, also serve as centers for the advancement of agricultural science in the rural districts.

The urban counterpart of rural "red and expert" schools and colleges are the spare-time schools run by factories. Since modern factories cannot be operated efficiently with uneducated workers, the government has always been concerned with wiping out illiteracy among factory laborers and training them for more skilled work. Factory schools are, therefore, an important component in the Communist educational system. The new trend in this field, however, is to make each modern factory an educational institution in addition to being an industrial enterprise. Many factories in China are now adopting the 6-2 or 4-4 system in which workers may work six hours and study two hours a day, or work and study four hours each day. Workers with large families who cannot afford to lose the two or four hours' pay per day are urged to study in the night schools. The curriculum of these schools is geared to the nature of the enterprise. The Ch'ang-ch'un Automobile Factory in Manchuria, for instance, is now operating a number of schools ranging from the primary school level to the technical school level. Their curriculums, aside from the academic courses, provide training in automotive mechanics as well as in engineering and designing. This factory also has plans for the establishment of an automobile engineering institute. Since modern factories are usually staffed by many engineers, technicians, and skilled workers, the problem of providing an adequate faculty for their schools is much less acute than that of the rural schools. The Communist authorities have stated that turning the factories into schools will not interfere with the fulfillment of production targets; on the contrary, as the workers become better educated and trained, a rapid increase in per capita productivity will result in the future.

The government's program for the improvement of the educational level of the minority nationalities requires the establishment of schools and colleges in the minority regions, in addition to the enrollment by minority students in regular and special schools in Peking and other cities adjacent to the minority regions. Government statistics claimed that for the minorities throughout China, the number of primary schools increased from 9,103 with 943,285 students in 1951 to 23,890 with 3,150,000 students in 1957; in the corresponding period, the number of middle schools increased from 117 with 45,628 students to 363 with 267,000 students. The number of primary students in the Thai Nationality Autonomous District in Yunnan registered a thirty-six fold increase from 1951 to 1957. Tibet, which did not have any primary school prior to the "liberation," had seventy-eight primary schools and one middle school in 1958. There were, in 1957, ten higher educational institutions in the minority regions of Inner Mongolia, Sinkiang, and Yen-pien Korean Autonomous District in Manchuria. The number of minority students attending colleges throughout China was reported to be 14,159. According to the population ratio, the number of Korean, Mongolian, and Manchu college students was higher than that of the Chinese students.

There are now eight academies of nationalities located in Peking and in seven provinces where large numbers of minority peoples are found. The total enrollment of these academies was 12,430 in 1957. The students are trained for political, economic, and cultural work among their own peoples after graduation. Some of them have become leading cadres.

To provide textbooks and reading materials for the minority peoples, publishing houses and printing presses were set up in various areas. From 1950 to 1956 more than five thousand books were published in the Korean, Mongolian, Tibetan, Uigur, and Kazak languages.

There are, however, still many problems besetting the educational development of the minorities. Uneven progress in the different regions reflects the different rate of economic development. The most retarded areas are in the mountainous districts of the southwest where some of the most primitive cultures in China are to be found. The uncritical application of Chinese experience in the minority areas is also a major drawback and one that could only be corrected if the use of Chinese teachers and textbooks, and the employment of Chinese as the language of instruction among the nonliterate peoples were to be replaced by trained minority teachers using textbooks written in their own languages and specifically related to their own cultural context.

Educational Trends

In appraising current developments and future trends, two significant features of the Communist educational system should be noted: the extent of specialization in the school system and the centralization of control over the educational content. In the reorganization of the schools, the emphasis has been placed on thorough specialization, especially in the technical institutions, while the movement to combine schools with factories would seem to indicate that the trend toward technical training would continue. The rigid state control over education, which begins with the indoctrination of the teachers, also extends to the compilation and publication of textbooks. In content, the social sciences taught in schools are oriented toward Soviet-type socialism, and Soviet technique in science and engineering has provided "advanced experience" for Chinese students. To meet current needs, translated Russian texts on scientific subjects have been used in schools, but the wholesale adoption of Russian materials has resulted in course content unrelated to Chinese conditions and difficult to absorb by the students. The recent movement to encourage collective efforts by the faculty and students to compile teaching plans, syllabuses, and textbooks stresses the fact that Chinese experience should also be incorporated in classroom teaching.

Teacher shortages, as has been noted, will continue to hamper the development of education and the improvement of standards. Lack of educational equipment cannot be solved by improvisations and, until sufficient classrooms have been built, classes cannot be properly conducted. Above all, the lack of well-trained educational administrators will be the greatest obstacle to educational progress, already handicapped by the multiple system of government control.

Also of serious concern to educational authorities are poor health and conditions of overwork among both students and teachers. To meet these problems, emphasis has been laid on physical education and lessening of pressure on students and teachers alike. With the inauguration of part-time work and part-time study programs in all school levels in 1958, the demand on the physical stamina of the students and teachers is again increasing and the improvement of their health becomes even more urgent. Physical education schools for the training of teachers and coaches are part of the educational system under the jurisdiction of the Ministry of Education. Within schools and colleges the students are expected to participate in the "labor and national defense" program, under which all adults and youths over thirteen years of age, except those who are weak and infirm, are encouraged to pass the minimum standards set by the commission. These include short-distance and middle-distance running, high jump or broad jump, grenade throwing or target shooting, weightlifting, body lifting, rope and pole climbing. Different requirements are set according to age and sex. This program, which has the objective of training all able-bodied men and women for the arduous task of national construction and defense, has now been extended from schools and armed forces to factories and farms.

Partly to help the students build up their physical stamina and more importantly to change their attitude toward learning, a movement for manual labor by students and teachers has been launched. The Communist leadership firmly believes that the traditional disdain for manual labor among the intellectuals is an arrogant manifestation of class distinction unacceptable in the new Communist society, in which there shall be no distinction between mental and manual labor. Consequently, one of their educational tenets is that education should not be separated from productive work.

Beginning with the kindergarten, the Communists teach students to respect the "fruits of labor," to care for school property, and to aid their parents by doing chores at home. Grade-school children are taught manual work, partly as physical exercise and partly as a means to cultivate respect for labor. Older students are urged to prepare themselves for work on the farm or in the factory. Such a preparation, the Communists say, is the most glorious assignment which can be offered new China's youth. Students in advanced schools are reminded of their duty to accept government assignments regardless of the working conditions involved.

The culmination of this trend is the institution of a part-time study and part-time work educational system, mentioned above. By combining farm or factory labor with school work, party leaders hope to gradually remove the psychological barrier between mental and manual workers. There is no doubt that this measure will accelerate the training of technicians for the industrialization drive, besides contributing to the economic growth of the country. However, in view of the complexity of modern sciences and technology, whether or not the removal of exceptional students from the classrooms to the workshops and farms for half of their school year will retard the development of their talents is still a moot point. Furthermore, the time devoted to manual labor is often taken at the expense of subjects like the fine arts and humanities which are important to the development of personality but unproductive in the eyes of many Communist cadres.

In summary, it should be noted that although the Communists have launched a thorough reorganization of the Chinese educational system, their work is far from accomplished. The attitude of so many people involved in the system of education cannot be quickly changed; hence the renewed effort on the part of the government to root out "bourgeois" and anti-Communist thought among teachers and students. The number of students has greatly increased since 1949 as a result of "accelerated schooling," but quantity has been achieved at the expense of quality. As pointed out previously, part of this has been due to the lack of qualified teaching personnel and administrators. Although the national budget for education is now seven times the pre-Communist figure, it is still inadequate to meet the needs for the rapid expansion of educational facilities in recent years.

SCIENCE AND TECHNOLOGY

No PREVIOUS GOVERNMENT OF CHINA has been as deeply committed to the development of science and technology as the present Communist regime. Without modern scientific and technological knowledge the rapid expansion of industrial production—cornerstone of Communist economic policy—becomes impossible. Preoccupation with science as a practical instrument for improving the material well-being of the nation is stressed again and again in the pronouncements of Communist leaders.

Although Chinese science and technology has a long history, the introduction of modern scientific concepts and research methods occurred only late in the nineteenth century when the need to modernize for defense against foreign aggression prompted government leaders to erect modern arsenals and shipyards. At the same time the traditional educational system was scrapped in favor of western-type schools in which natural sciences formed an integral part of the curriculum.

After the overthrow of the monarchy in 1911 Confucian orthodoxy rapidly declined among the rising generation of Chinese intellectuals and during the following years liberals such as Hu Shih and Fu Ssu-nien and Marxists such as Ch'en Tu-hsiu and Li Ta-chao called for the replacement of religious superstitions with modern scientific knowledge. In the course of time scientific research gained recognition in the universities, and professional scientific organizations were established in such fields as geology, chemistry, physics, and biology. Further impetus was given to scientific development with the founding of the Academia Sinica and the Peiping Research Institute in 1928 and 1929 respectively.

In spite of this beginning, scientific research continued to be handicapped by financial difficulties and general political instability. Government funds allocated to the research bodies were limited and there were no private foundations or large-scale industrial enterprises to promote scientific work. Few universities possessed laboratories and research facilities adequate for advanced graduate training. Practically all of today's outstanding older scientists found it necessary to complete their education abroad. The Sino-Japanese War (1937-45) forced the universities to migrate into the interior with the resultant loss of laboratory equipment and valuable collections of scientific books and specimens. Wartime and postwar inflation reduced the scientific community to penury and compelled it to carry on under the most adverse conditions.

Nevertheless, in the few decades preceding the Communist victory, Chinese scientists had laid the foundation for the development of the natural sciences. They had trained a new generation of college students in the fundamentals of scientific research, introduced the latest scientific discoveries from abroad, studied and classified China's fauna and flora, explored its geological structure, recorded its meteorological phenomena, and unearthed its archaeological past.

Those decades of preparation placed Chinese science on the threshold of a new era of rapid development that would have proceeded under any political regime, assuming a period of peace and relative prosperity. Thus the Communist government inherited from modern China a substantial scientific legacy together with the responsibility for providing the conditions necessary to scientific advancement.

Development under Communism

Under the Communists the emphasis has been mainly on science as a practical means of forwarding the industrialization program and promoting the other objectives of the regime. The heavy damage sustained by the Chinese economy during the Sino-Japanese War and the resumption of the civil war afterward made it imperative that the small number of scientists and engineers available in the country should be put to work to rehabilitate the nation's industry and agriculture. The trade embargo maintained by the western countries against China made it necessary to devise ways and means to produce embargoed items or to find substitutes. With the inauguration of the First Five Year Plan in 1953, the fulfillment of economic goals depended to a large extent upon the success of the scientists in solving technical problems in industrial production. Furthermore, during the more than twenty years of armed struggle with the Nationalist government, the Communists were completely cut off much of the time from contact with the outside world and had thus developed an intensely pragmatic viewpoint. The average Communist probably considered any scientific research that did not produce immediate results in terms of production as bourgeois squandering of the people's wealth. Even though the party leadership has been aware of the importance of a better balance between theoretical and practical research, the insistence on the unity of theory and practice among the Communist rank and file may well have discouraged the more speculative types of scientific investigation.

The conclusion must not be drawn, however, that Chinese scientists object to the practical aims of the government. There have been dissensions as to the wisdom of the state's plans for scientific development, but no objection seems to have been voiced to the assumption that it is the responsibility of Chinese scientists to help build a strong and prosperous China.

Among both scientists and government leaders there is a determination to catch up with the western powers as quickly as possible in order to ensure the progress of the nation and enable it to play an enhanced role in international affairs. This feeling is reflected in Chou En-lai's *Report on the Question of Intellectuals* (delivered on January 14, 1956):

> We are constantly saying that our science and culture are backward, but we seldom stop to consider just where our backwardness lies. Comrades! I want to speak more particularly here about science, not only because science is a decisive factor in our national defense, economy, and culture, but also because during the last twenty or thirty years world science has made particularly great and rapid progress, leaving us far behind in scientific development.

After enumerating the latest advancements in science and technology, Chou continued:

> We must catch up with this advanced level of world science. And, bearing in mind that while we are forging ahead others are also advancing rapidly, we must give our best to this task. Only by mastering the most advanced sciences can we ensure ourselves of an impregnable national defense, a powerful and up-to-date economy, and adequate means to join the Soviet Union and the other People's Democracies in defeating the imperialist powers, either in peaceful competition or in any aggressive war which the enemy may unleash.

Another indication of this nationalist feeling is the admonition to shake off a sense of inferiority and a blind worship of western scientific achievement as an outgrowth of China's past semicolonial status. The noted geologist, Li Ssu-kuang, in an address delivered at the All-China Natural Science Workers' Conference in August 1950, argued that Chinese scientists in the past had neglected to develop in their own country really independent and creative academic organs or associations and instead had turned Chinese scientific organizations into satellites of foreign, especially American and British, academic circles. Many of them published their important writings in foreign journals. Among Chinese scientists, consequently, there has grown "a decadent psychological outlook," as though the Chinese were unfit for independent academic work and China was destined to remain backward in scientific achievements.

This indictment of Chinese scientists, although partly justified, is not the whole truth. The circulation of scientific journals in China was extremely limited and the market for serious scientific writings practically nonexistent. Many scientists had to have their findings published abroad in order to gain recognition, besides which they subscribed to the view that science knew no national boundaries and that recognition abroad would help to build a reservoir of scientific prestige for China. Nevertheless, a certain sense of national inferiority did exist. With the establishment of a strong Communist regime and the emergence of China as a world power, the reaction against past subservience, real or imaginary, to foreign science was manifested in the demand for the development of Chinese science on an equal footing with the West. At present, continued dependence upon Soviet scientific assistance, although necessary, is probably looked upon as an affront to national pride.

To reiterate, the motives for the government's promotion of the sciences are: the rapid transformation to a socialist economy; an awareness that, in the age of atomic power and space flight, national security and prestige are dependent upon the country's ability to keep abreast with western scientific developments; and an emotional urge to place China at an equal level with the world's most advanced scientific powers.

There is, however, still a wide gap between the government's aspirations and the present state of scientific development in China. The measures with which the Communist leaders have chosen to close this gap are related to their social, economic, and political policies.

Political Control

The most important aspect of political control is the enforcement of ideological conformity on scientists. The majority of the older scientists in China today were trained abroad. When the Communist party came into power in 1949, it appealed to the patriotic sentiments of the scientists to collaborate in building a new China. It promised to encourage scientific discoveries and inventions, and the dissemination of scientific knowledge. Intense efforts were made to organize the scientists and induce those abroad to return to their homeland. Those scientists who responded to the government's call in all probability felt themselves morally obliged to contribute their talents to national reconstruction. Very few of them could be called Marxists, still fewer Communists. It is doubtful if any were willing to subscribe to the view that science could be divided into Marxist and bourgeois varieties.

The Communists, for their part, needed scientists to serve industry, agriculture, and national defense, but they distrusted the intellectuals' predilection for independent thinking. For this reason, scientists, like all other intellectuals, were forced to submit to a series of measures for "thought reform" and to publicly declare their commitment to Communist ideology. On June 20, 1950 Kuo Mo-jo, president of the newly reorganized Chinese Academy of Sciences, declared that a basic task of the academy was to strengthen political study by those members engaged in research in order that they might grasp Marxist-Leninist viewpoints and methods.

Such admonitions do not appear to have been very effective and many scientists continue to consider themselves above politics. The Communist position has been that the task of the scientist is not only to explain the world but to remake it. Since only Marxist-Leninist theory contains the "truth" and can serve as a guide for remodeling the world, no scientist can fulfill his basic responsibilities without knowing and following this "truth." Official doctrine holds that though science itself is apolitical, the scientist as a member of society cannot dissociate himself from its political and economic character. Whereas in the past science has been the tool of a reactionary ruling class, now, under the new democracy,

Chinese science for the first time in history is serving the people and must be guided toward the socialist goal. By subscribing to the world view of the proletariat and reforming his own thought processes the scientist can increase his effectiveness in the struggle for a new society. Thus the authorities continue to urge that men of science serve the people and the country by transforming their bourgeois outlook, as expressed in liberalism and individualism, into one thoroughly permeated by Marxism.

This line of thinking, despite continued lip service to the universality of science, led to repercussions in the fields of genetics, psychology, and linguistics following the Soviet purge of so-called "idealistic" or "bourgeois" tendencies in the natural sciences. As early as February 1949, the Michurin Society was founded in China and when the first annual meeting was held in Peking a year later the membership had increased from thirty to over three thousand. Branches were then established all over the country. A cardinal objective was the eradication of the "reactionary" theories held by western-trained Chinese geneticists. In the universities, only Lysenko's theory was taught. After the death of Stalin and the subsequent downgrading of Lysenko in Russia, Chinese geneticists were again permitted to question the validity of Michurinism. From the discussions at the joint forum on genetics held by the Chinese Academy of Sciences and the Ministry of Higher Education in 1956, it was apparent that most of the older scientists had remained unconvinced by Lysenko's ideas. The upshot of the forum was an official truce between the two schools. Michurinism is still enjoying great popularity among the younger generation. During the "leap forward" year of 1958, newspapers printed accounts of young labor heroes who had succeeded in producing new plants by following the methods of the Michurin school. But administrative interference with scientists who held to the orthodox line of investigation seems to have lessened. The importance of genetics to modern agriculture and animal husbandry is probably one of the reasons why the government is willing to adopt a hands-off policy.

It is against the background of what Chou En-lai called the "very crude treatment of scientists and scientific problems" by the party cadres that one can understand the enthusiasm with which the intellectuals greeted the Blooming and Contending campaign of 1956. The campaign brought out into the open some deeply felt grievances among the scientists, as among other intellectuals. It was pointed out, for instance, that in previous years there had been a lack of controversy in Chinese scholarship not because the intellectuals lacked initiative and resourcefulness but, fearing party criticism if their opinions were found to be anti-Marxist, were reluctant to state their opinions. The scientists went on to advocate that they should learn both from socialist and capitalist countries for, in science as in trade, it would be injurious to one's own interest to always rely on a single "company." These remarks revealed some of the most pernicious aspects of party control of science in China, for in every institution of higher learning and research organization, the party cell has had the decisive voice not only in administrative matters but also in research and teaching programs. Since most of the party cadres were ignorant of the concepts and methods of science, they accepted uncritically every Soviet import as the epitome of scientific progress and freely castigated as harboring remnants of bourgeois ideas those who dared to dissent.

To the credit of Chinese scientists many of them have held tenaciously to their concept of scientific truth despite these harassments. The experience of the American-trained botanist, Pao Wen-k'uei, is highly instructive. In 1951 he began the artificial induction of polyploidy by colchicine and succeeded in producing four strains of wheat and three strains of rice, but in 1953 he was forced to discontinue this "reactionary" and "Morganistic" experiment. Attempts to use ultraviolet ray and X-ray to induce mutations were also obstructed by the authorities of the Szechwan Institute of Agricultural Science. In spite of his protests that such interference violated the spirit of the Constitution which guarantees the freedom of scientific research, Pao was notified to stop all research in polyploids. Although he had succeeded in crossbreeding polyploid wheat, the sowing was stopped and the seeds which had been sown and sprouted were dug out by workers under the personal supervision of the party cadres. In November 1954, in the Szechwan Provincial Conference on Technology, Pao submitted a report on the use of colchicine, but it was rejected on the grounds that the use of colchicine for the induction of polyploidy was divorced from reality and from politics, and that it contradicted Lysenko's theory which held that the use of X-ray and colchicine in plant breeding was contrary to "progressive" science. Pao, however, was unwilling to allow seeds from previous experiments to become a total loss. In May 1956 he reported the whole case to the Chinese Academy of Sciences and the Ministry of Agriculture. A month later he was instructed by the Ministry to resume his experiments. This incident, revealing as it does the arrogant ignorance of party cadres toward scientific experiment and development, is not an isolated case.

Besides administrative interference and the uncritical application of Russian experience, other complaints of Chinese scientists are lack of freedom for research, neglect of theoretical in favor of practical projects, favoritism to politically reliable students, indiscriminate classification of scientific information as state secrets, excessive demands on their time by political activities, and lack of mutual confidence and respect between scientists and party cadres.

Because of the concern of the party leadership for the progress of science a number of ameliorative measures have been offered. In addition to calling for open discussion of scientific theories, the government has promised: greater emphasis on theoretical research, though also stressing the importance of ideological indoctrination of the scientists and government planning of scientific development; improved placing of scientists wherever they can employ their talents most advantageously; improvement in the system of promotion, academic degrees and titles, and rewards for inventions and discoveries; assurance that the intellectuals will have at least five-sixths of the working day (or forty hours a week) available for their work; improvement in the supply of reference books, materials, equipment, or suitable assistants; improvement in the living conditions such as housing; greater confidence in and respect for intellectuals by party cadres; reasonable definition of state secrets; and admittance of a greater number of intellectuals into the party ranks.

Government Organization and Planning

The numerous government organizations and agencies responsible for the development of science and technology, many of which occupy an important position in the government hierarchy indicate how thoroughly science is controlled by the state. Aside from various industrial ministries, which generally have their own research institutes and laboratories, the following government organs under the direct jurisdiction of the State Council are all concerned with science and technology to a greater or lesser degree: State Statistical Bureau, State Bureau of Weights and Measures, State Bureau of Survey and Cartography, Central Weather Bureau,

Ministry of Geology, Ministry of Education, Ministry of Culture, Bureau of Foreign Experts, Chinese Academy of Agricultural Science, and Chinese Academy of Medicine. The two most important organizations, however, are the National Science and Technology Commission and the Chinese Academy of Sciences.

The National Science and Technology Commission was first set up as the National Science Planning Commission in March 1956 to direct the formulation of a twelve-year plan for the development of sciences. In May 1957 it was made into a permanent agency with Vice-Premier Nieh Jung-chen as director and several important government leaders and intellectuals as vice-directors. The offical functions of the commission are to: draw up and supervise the execution of long-range scientific research plans and important individual projects; coordinate the work of various research institutions such as that of the Academy of Sciences, the higher institutions of education, and the ministries and industrial enterprises; solve problems concerning the material conditions of scientific research, such as the supply of books and instruments; manage funds allocated to important research projects; and make over-all plans for the training, placement, and utilization of experts as well as their repatriation from capitalist countries. In other words, the commission has primary responsibility for the direction and planning of the scientific efforts of the entire country.

The Chinese Academy of Sciences was organized to include government research institutes and one private research institute taken over from the Nationalist regime. These included eleven institutes under the former Academia Sinica, ten institutes under the former Peiping Research Institute, the Chinese Institute of Geography under the former Ministry of Education, and the private Ching-sheng Institute of Biological Survey. Through a process of reorganization, thirteen research institutes, one astronomical observatory, one engineering laboratory, and three preparatory committees were formed. The steady expansion of the Academy of Sciences in the last few years is shown by the following figures:

	1952	1957
Research institutes	31	68
Total personnel	5,239	17,336
Research personnel	1,292	5,506
Research and technical personnel of higher ranks	317	746

Assistant research		
personnel	314	755
Graduate students	661	4,005
Books		2,500,000
Periodicals		1,700,000

The academy also has branch academies in various provinces, autonomous regions, and municipalities. Up to November 1958, there were fourteen branch academies located throughout the country. Twelve more branch academies were in the preparatory stage. Each branch academy has a number of research institutes; for example, the Lan-chou Branch Academy has under its jurisdiction fifteen such institutes.

The Academy of Sciences is the leading center for scientific research in the nation and has the responsibility of assisting research work in the institutions of higher education, industrial enterprises, and local research institutions. Its specific research functions include the following: large-scale basic research; research in new scientific and technological fields; interdisciplinary scientific research; study of key problems in national construction that require sustained efforts over a long period of time; systematic collection and compilation of source materials, as well as theoretical study in the fields of philosophy and social sciences.

Research work in the academy is carried out under the direction of four academic departments: physics, mathematics, and chemistry; biology and earth sciences; technological sciences; and philosophy and social sciences. Each department is composed of a director, vice-directors, and a varying number of members. The departments decide on the general research plans, advise the academy of the latest developments in various scientific fields, examine the work of the research personnel, organize scientific conferences, recommend the awarding of science prizes, oversee the studies of graduate students and staff, and supervise the publication of scientific writings.

In conjunction with the academic departments, the Committee on Translation and Publication and the Science Publishing Press make decisions on translation and publication programs. From 1952 to 1957 the Academy of Sciences published 1,106 books totaling more than four million volumes, and 95 journals totaling twelve million copies. Besides highly specialized studies, a number of journals publish articles and translations of general scientific interest and theoretical import as well as reports of latest developments.

One of the more important functions of the Committee on Translation and Publication is the standardization of scientific terms, most of which come from foreign sources. Chinese scientists in general welcome proposals for the alphabetization of the Chinese language because it would simplify the use of western scientific terms and eliminate the need to translate or transliterate these terms into Chinese characters. The introduction of many newly coined terms as a result of the rapid progress of world science has strained the Chinese language to the utmost.

The Academy of Sciences is also an important center of postgraduate training. The latest regulations governing the admission and training of graduate students by the academy were promulgated in 1955. Candidates for admission must have either a college degree or recommendations from scientific institutions, colleges, universities, or government organs. The period of matriculation is four years. Besides the thesis, academic courses include dialectical materialism, one or two basic courses, a specialized course pertaining to the candidate's thesis, the Russian language, and one other foreign language. All students are given government subsidies except those who draw salaries while on leave from employment. On graduation, the students are given the academic degree of *Fu Po-shih* or the Associate Doctoral degree equivalent to the Russian *Kandidate*.

The Committee on Combined Surveys is responsible for large-scale scientific expeditions. During 1953-57 the following projects were undertaken: an investigation of the soil conditions along the middle and lower courses of the Yellow River and of the Yangtze River valley in order to draw up long-range water and soil conservation and land utilization plans; investigation of the natural resources of the Amur River valley in cooperation with Soviet scientists; an investigation of the natural resources of the frontier regions of Sinkiang, Tsinghai, Kansu, Inner Mongolia, and Yunnan; and a survey of Chinese coastal and inland aquatic resources. An ambitious project to exploit the natural resources of Chinese desert regions is now in progress. For this undertaking an 800-member scientific team, composed of research workers in soil chemistry, water conservation, agronomy, botany, forestry, and animal husbandry was formed by the academy in cooperation with forty central and local government institutions, universities, and colleges.

As focal points for research and laboratory work, six comprehensive experimental stations were set up in various desert areas to start grass planting, afforestation, and water conservation projects. Subjects to be studied include the phenomena connected with the formation of deserts and the shifting of sand dunes, the use of sandy land for farming, the ecology of desert vegetation, the tapping of underground water resources and artificial rain-making, and the use of solar and wind energy and other techniques in transforming the deserts.

The Liaison Bureau is responsible for contacting and cooperating with scientific groups outside of the academy. It is the agency through which the academy establishes contacts with foreign scientific institutions, especially its Soviet counterpart. Beginning in 1956 the Soviet Academy of Sciences and the Chinese Academy of Sciences started a program of student exchange, a similar program of book and periodical exchange having been in force for a number of years. In 1957 an agreement for scientific cooperation was concluded between the two academies. On January 18, 1958 in a separate protocol of the new Sino-Soviet Economic-Technical Agreement signed in Moscow, the two academies agreed to enlarge their programs of cooperation. Prior to October 1955 the Chinese Academy of Sciences had been given the task of coordinating the research programs of various universities, industrial enterprises, and government ministries. The latter were required to invite members of the academy to participate in conferences having to do with scientific research, report to the academy their research plans and progress, and cooperate with it in popularizing new techniques and discoveries. The academy was made responsible for rendering technical aid to the ministries, coordinating its research program with the needs of the ministries, reporting on the latest scientific advances in the country and abroad, convening nationwide scientific conferences.

To coordinate scientific research more closely with economic development during the First Five Year Plan, the academy announced in September 1955 a proposal to draft a fifteen-year program covering the three five-year plan periods from 1953 to 1967. This long-range program will include the following objectives: research on important scientific problems such as the exploitation and utilization of China's natural resources, regional geology, and the use of rare elements; development of various branches of science and technology, such as oceanography, inorganic chemistry, and electronics; training of scientific personnel and establishment of new research facilities; organization of important scientific expeditions; and editing and compilation of important scientific publications and source materials.

In 1956 the academy plan was incorporated into the national twelve-year plan (1956-67) for the development of science under the direction of the National Science Planning Commission. To draft the program, more than two hundred scientists gathered in Peking in December 1955. A list of important tasks in the development of the national economy was drawn up, supplemented by another list of several hundred research problems necessary to the completion of these tasks. On the basis of these problems, a General Plan for Natural Sciences was agreed upon. Individual research units were then directed to make their own plans to conform with the tasks set forth in the General Plan. It was reported that over a score of first-rank scientists were sent from the Soviet Union to assist in the planning.

Personnel and Research Facilities

The successful implementation of this plan is dependent upon two very important factors: an adequate supply of scientific personnel and the availability of research facilities. Of the two, the problem of personnel is probably of greater import to the planners. In 1949 and 1950, the Academy of Sciences undertook a survey of available scientific experts and came up with a list of 865 names, among whom 171 were still living abroad. While this list is by no means complete, it indicates the paucity of scientific talent in a population of over 600 million. An official estimate in 1956 showed 100,000 intellectuals engaged in scientific research, education, engineering and technology, public health, cultural work, the arts, and similar occupations. Assuming that half were scientific personnel, China may have in the neighborhood of 50,000 scientists of all types, many of whom are still young and only recently trained. The same estimate gave 31,000 engineers. Even allowing for increases in the last few years, it is clear that in spite of progress, the shortage of scientific and technical manpower remains a cause of official concern.

Construction of physical plant for research purposes has gone ahead steadily and in November 1957 the Science Planning Commission introduced proposals for improving research facilities such as libraries, the availability of documentary materials, and scientific equipment of various types.

Existing libraries fall into three categories: those under the control of the Ministry of Culture, including all provincial and municipal public libraries; those under the control of the Ministry of Education, including all school, college, and university libraries; and those under the control of the Academy of Sciences. There are also libraries belonging to various government ministries, industrial enterprises, labor unions, communes, and other organizations. According to a 1956 estimate there were about 30 million volumes in the public libraries and 37 million volumes in 212 libraries of the institutions of higher learning. The Academy of Sciences had in 1957 a collection of 2.5 million volumes. However, there were a number of serious shortcomings in the management of these libraries such as inefficiency in cataloguing and shelving, duplication and uneven distribution of books, lack of library space and trained librarians, and unsystematic and therefore uneconomical purchase of foreign scientific publications and periodicals. In purchasing foreign periodicals, some libraries refused to order publications originating in capitalist countries, while others subscribed to every title listed in foreign catalogues regardless of its content. In 1956 and 1957, the government spent 1.8 million and 1.5 million pounds sterling respectively for the purchase of non-Communist periodicals.

In order to make the best use of existing library resources for scientific research, the Science Planning Commission proposed the establishment of a system of central libraries and the compilation of national catalogues. The functions of the central libraries are to serve as centers of information for scientific research, collect books and periodicals of a greater variety and value, compile union catalogues and bulletins of new books, serve as centers of international exchange, perform microfilm service, and plan and carry out programs of librarian training.

Two nationwide central libraries will be located in Peking and Shanghai and will be formed from those libraries having the best resources in each of the two cities. The National Peking Library will be the guidance center for library service in the country. Regional central libraries will be established in a number of strategically located cities as the need arises. Each central library will be administered by a committee composed of responsible personnel from the component libraries.

One serious handicap scientists faced was the inaccessibility of pertinent documents and statistics from government and industrial sources. This was due to the strict and often unreasonable definition of state secrets on the one hand, and the lack of systematic classification and preservation of such documents on the other. It was proposed that the State Bureau of Archives be responsible for the establishment of a standardized system of classification, preservation, and utilization of documentary materials in all government offices and industrial enterprises, and that the definition of secret materials be liberalized and a wider circle of research personnel permitted access to them.

The acute shortage of scientific apparatus was recognized by the Science Planning Commission. Besides recommending that domestic production be stepped up, it proposed that industrial enterprises engage in repair work which they had hitherto been reluctant to do. Research institutes and universities were urged to set up their own factories and workshops for the production and repairing of scientific apparatus and instruments. This recommendation was enthusiastically carried out during 1958. The procedure for the importation of foreign-made apparatus was simplified and the commercial distribution of needed articles facilitated.

The Science Planning Commission also proposed that within five years 1,600 to 2,000 types of commonly used reagents be produced in the country in adequate quantity to satisfy ordinary domestic requirement. Machinery for importing and distributing reagents commercially was also to be improved. It is significant that by 1958 reagents and other laboratory chemicals were on China's export list.

As an incentive to scientific discovery, the State Council approved the awarding of prizes by the Chinese Academy of Sciences. Three first prizes, five second prizes, and twenty-six third prizes for accomplishments in the natural sciences were awarded in 1956. The first prize carried a monetary award of 10,000 yuan (4,000 American dollars), the second prize 5,000 yuan (2,000 American dollars), and the third prize 2,000 yuan (800 American dollars). The prizes were to be awarded every two years, but in 1957, the period for awards was extended to every four years.

Popular Dissemination of Science

One of the most cherished aims of the party in power is the complete remolding of the people according to the Communist ideological image. The new socialist man is a person who interprets social changes according to the tenets of historical materialism and explains the natural world in terms of modern scientific theories.

The widest dissemination of scientific ideas is, therefore, a political as well as an educational task. With their skill in promoting mass participation, the Communists have succeeded in infusing into the minds of the people some elementary scientific knowledge of their natural environment to aid in their campaigns to eradicate diseases and promote production.

As early as November 1, 1949 the Bureau for the Dissemination of Sciences was established within the Ministry of Culture. In meetings held with the various educational, scientific, and mass organizations, the participants equated the dissemination of scientific knowledge with the spread of dialectical materialism. It was said that such knowledge would enable the people to better shoulder the task of national construction through an improved understanding of production techniques and the laws of nature. Since workers, peasants, and soldiers constitute the bulk of the population, most propaganda efforts were to be directed toward them. All methods of dissemination—publications, lectures, exhibits, slides, and movies—were to be used in such a way that the contents could be easily assimilated by the masses and the information have a direct bearing on their daily life.

To carry on the work of dissemination more effectively over a long period of time, the All-China Science and Technology Dissemination Association was established with headquarters in Peking. A national committee of fifty members, including the best-known names in Chinese scientific and educational circles, were elected to coordinate activities on a nationwide basis. In March 1957 the Association had 27 branch associations and 983 subbranches with a total membership of 180,000,000. In 1956 alone, it sponsored 200,000 lectures, 3,000 exhibits, 11,000 showings of science films, and 3,000 booklets and pieces of propaganda. A Science Dissemination Press was established and its journals, *Popular Science* and *Science Pictorial*, were widely circulated. A planetarium and a Museum of Ancient Astronomical Instruments were built in Peking. In 1958 the All-China Science and Technology Dissemination Association and the Federation of All-China Natural Science Associations were amalgamated to form the Chinese Science and Technology Association. The new organization was intended to speed the technological and cultural revolution among the Chinese people.

The dissemination of scientific and technological knowledge is not conceived as a one-way transmission of ideas and techniques from the better educated to the masses. The Communists have contended, time and again, that the intellectuals must also learn from the masses, and that the pragmatic experience of the people in such fields as traditional medicine, agriculture, and animal husbandry contain scientific truths which the intellectuals are urged to study without prejudice. They are encouraged to analyze these popular experiences in the light of modern scientific theories and to systematize or refine them in order to enhance their usefulness. Peasants and workers who have invented new techniques or machines are given nationwide publicity, and sometimes invited to be members of natural science associations and to lecture in the universities. Exhibits of improved tools and technical processes are held on county, provincial, and national levels. There is no doubt that the prestige accorded peasants and workers who have been responsible for innovations has tended to encourage them and to make them more receptive to new ideas and techniques in their daily life.

Evaluation

The Communist government of China has devoted a considerable part of its efforts to the development of science and the dissemination of scientific information. It realizes the importance of science in industrialization and the modernization of the armed forces. The backwardness of Chinese science and the rapid progress of world science generate a sense of urgency to which the Communist planners have responded with the determination to use every means to catch up with the rest of the world in the most important branches of science within the shortest possible period of time. Consequently, the scientific manpower and national resources are to be harnessed for the fulfillment of the planned objectives of the state. The party leadership has realized that ideological dogmas exert a baneful influence on the sciences and now advocates free discussion of scientific theories; however, it also stresses that scientists, as members of society, must follow the party line in all other activities.

In promoting the development of sciences in China, the totalitarian nature of the Communist government makes it possible to draw up a coordinated long-range plan. It can relate its educational program to its scientific plans in a way that is impossible in a democratic society. It has been generous in allocating funds for the establishment of research institutes and the purchase of books and equipment. The scientists have been deprived, however, of freedom to pursue research according to individual interests and are required to devote a part of their time to political activities. Soviet assistance has been an important factor in the present progress of Chinese science, but the uncritical application of Soviet experience has had a detrimental effect in some fields. Communist leaders are now stressing the importance of learning from all countries, including the capitalist nations. For this reason, they have been promoting extensive foreign contacts as well as publishing translations and digests of foreign scientific writings. Dissemination of scientific knowledge is also conducted on a popular level through all types of communication media. The Communist effort to orient the minds of the people toward a scientific explanation of the world may prove to be one of their most significant measures in the transformation of the Chinese society and culture.

ART AND INTELLECTUAL EXPRESSION

THE MEASURE AND SYMBOL OF THE GREATNESS of Chinese civilization for more than two thousand years have been China's artistic and intellectual achievements, particularly in philosophy, poetry, and painting. The Chinese people are proud of their cultural heritage and of its original and innately Chinese character. Foreign influences that reached the brilliant and all-embracing world of the Chinese intellectuals stimulated but never dominated their philosophical thought or literary and artistic creations.

In imperial China, and to a lesser degree in modern China, intellectual and artistic expression was the child of learning; and learning, whether formal or speculative, so set the intelligentsia apart from the masses that its possession formed the basis of a more or less distinct class. The Chinese intellectuals, almost exclusively from the gentry, wrote for the readers and critics of their own class. The common man, illiterate and indigent, had little time or opportunity to enjoy the amenities and refinements of life. Popular artistic traditions thrived then as now, however, and the vigor and primitive beauty of folk ballads, tales, and dramatic presentations provided a stimulus to Chinese literature.

Cultural indebtedness to the outside world was insignificant when compared with the gifts China bestowed upon its neighbors. Chinese intellectual thought, literature, and art were dominant influences in Korea, Japan, Annam, and surrounding areas in Southeast Asia. Europeans in the eighteenth century were fascinated by Chinese porcelain, embroidery, and landscape gardening as well as the moral concepts of Confucius and other Chinese philosophers. But today the situation has been reversed, and China draws much of its artistic and literary inspiration from the West and Russia. Democratic idealism and dialectic materialism, both imported from abroad, compete for the mind of

China's intellectual in the realm of political thought as traditional concepts become less and less valid for him in the modern world. This latter tendency has been especially marked during the last forty years as Chinese intellectuals turned to the West for guidance in artistic expression as well as intellectual thought, and the Communist elite today hail their Soviet predecessors as models and sources of inspiration.

The Communist regime emphasizes the political awareness and social functions of writers and intellectuals in opposition to the theory of art for art's sake. Service to the socialist cause, advocated by Mao Tse-tung in his 1942 "Talks at the Yenan Forum on Art and Literature," becomes the prime concern of art and literature and any work that deviates from or is opposed to socialism, particularly Marxism-Leninism, is to be decried. The current policy is to channel all intellectual and artistic efforts to the popularization of party ideology, to foster the growth of a proletarian art and literature, and before this can be achieved to encourage writers and artists who profess working-class sympathies and are willing to learn from working-class experiences. With persistent indoctrination for conformity, the Communists have been building up in China a monolithic system of intellectual thought, in which literature and the arts under the banner of socialist realism will help fulfill the needs of the state.

The Fine Arts

The austere simplicity and harmonious design of the linear style perfected in classic Chinese art reflected deeply rooted religious, philosophical, and social ideas. Taoism, Confucianism, and Buddhism, as well as early animism, contributed to the character of Chinese art, whose essence was a striving for harmony between man and nature as conceived by China's great philosophers. The experimentation in method and perfection of art forms in the imperial era were pursued primarily by the scholar-gentry, who had the leisure for developing the prerequisite techniques and sensibilities. Art forms associated with religious observances or folk traditions, imitative of great Chinese art but more utilitarian in nature, were used by artists of lower social levels and were less highly valued. Chinese jade, porcelain, and embroidery, though prized by westerners, belonged to this classification and were not ranked as pure art by the Chinese themselves.

Traditional Art

Their artistic tradition included significant development in painting, sculpture, architecture, music, and dance, but to the Chinese the highest and purest form of art was calligraphy. Every scholar received rigid training in calligraphy, beginning in childhood soon after he learned to read and write. The mastery of the symmetry, balance, and vigor of brush stroke that went into elegant penmanship was an accomplishment greatly desired in the scholarly world as well as a basic requirement for success in the literary examinations. The abolition of the examination system, however, and the introduction into the school curriculum of many modern subjects resulted in the neglect of calligraphy in children's education. The growing use of western-style pens and pencils has all but eliminated the time-honored study of calligraphy.

A direct outgrowth of calligraphy in its requirement for a mastery of brush strokes was painting in the native Chinese tradition. Ancient Chinese paintings, most often on paper or silk but also on walls, lacquer wares, and other surfaces, portrayed historical figures and religious scenes. With the exception of portraits of donors, early Buddhist frescoes and banner paintings were influenced by mural traditions from India and other foreign regions. Figural Buddhist painting became a Chinese art only after it had accommodated itself to the technique and format of scholarly painting.

The primary theme of painting after the T'ang era was landscape, known in China as *shan-shui* or "mountain and water" painting. A true painting of this genre presupposed acceptance of a Chinese philosophy of nature and man's place in it. Although closely based on the actual appearance of nature, Chinese landscape painting represented a highly intellectual effort to grasp the inner reality of nature and the meaning of the universe. Perhaps as a consequence of traditional painting's affinity with the written language and calligraphy, a vast number of type forms evolved, pictorial abstractions by which the general characteristics and permanent aspects of nature could be represented. By thus universalizing natural phenomena and dispensing with the need for pursuing its exact representation, as in western artistic tradition, the Chinese painters were left free to explore the inner spiritual forces of nature with which man was intimately involved.

Due to the special objective of traditional painting, Chinese painters had little interest in the technical problems of perspective, light, and color. An educated person who could use the brush competently and who learned the type forms was able to turn out an acceptable and pleasing picture. But it was the philosophic meaning or the extent to which the painter succeeded in using these conventionalized types to penetrate the objective forms and reveal the inner harmony of nature and man that distinguished a good painting from a mediocre one. In spite of significant western influences, several traditional schools of Chinese painting have continued to exist to the present.

Sculpture was never accepted as a major art and even in its great periods was the product not of known artists but of anonymous artisans in the service of religion. Ancient Chinese sculpture was mainly a tomb art, a by-product of ancestor worship and the belief in a spirit existence after life. It consisted largely of small objects and figures representing the worldly possessions necessary to the happiness and protection of the deceased.

With the arrival of Buddhism, sculpture came into full light, reaching its culmination in the famous Buddhist cliff chapels at Yün-kang (in Shansi), Lung-men (in Honan), and Tun-huang (in Kansu), where whole caves were chiseled out into thousands of Buddhist statues and often adorned with paintings. But gradually sculpture lost its spiritual impulse and deteriorated once again into an essentially decorative art.

The principal feature of traditional Chinese architecture, both secular and religious, was a massive roof with upcurving edges, resting upon a post-and-lintel system of beams supported by short columns. Buildings were usually one-storied and unimpressive in height, additions being made horizontally on a symmetrical plan. In the residences of the wealthy and noble, side-buildings, court-yards, and pavilions were often built around the main structure, the whole encircled by high walls and forming a symmetrical arrangement. The roof of a palace, temple, or pagoda, considerably greater in elevation than other types of buildings, and generally remarkable for its beauty and grandeur, was covered with brilliantly colored tiles and decorated by dragons, phoenixes, and other ornamental animals fixed to the crest, eaves, and corner ends. The great weight of the roof rested entirely upon multiple columns, usually of wood, with the areas between filled in with nonstructural brick walls, windows, doors, or various decorative features.

From the deep recesses of ancient history, music came down to posterity as a form of ritual observance, as an educational agent, and as a religious force capable of regulating the universe. In the classical period, the influence of music on men's feelings, moods, passions, and humors was held to be of utmost importance. Music education was essential to an aristocrat, and musicians were a part of any noble household. Music also contributed to the popular theater with its orchestra of stringed instruments, flutes, drums, bells, and clappers as an accompaniment to singing and dancing.

Like music, Chinese dancing had its origin in religious rites. These ecstatic dances had a natural significance and were performed to the magic of the shaman or by the shaman himself. In the feudal period, dances were performed at court functions or ceremonials, the dancers carrying plumes and flutes, or shields and hatchets, during civil or military performances. The dances took place to the singing of poetry, the pattern of the poetic lines being intimately related to the music and the dance movements. The palace dances of the later period were rather elaborate, and groups of boy and girl dancers in gorgeous costumes presented a lavish spectacle during court entertainments. As a whole the Chinese seem to have shown little interest in the dance except as a form of theatrical presentation.

Folk Art

There is no strict line of demarcation between formal art and folk art in China. Foreign dancing of folk origin was performed at court festivities while the best specimens of Buddhist painting and sculpture were done by anonymous artists from among the people. Chinese folk art, like folk art in other countries, exhibited a close relation to the daily life of the common people, reflecting their customs and beliefs just as the formal art of calligraphy and painting reflected the personality and outlook of the intellectuals. Although the creation of a work of folk art was often extemporaneous, the form was generally recognizable in a tradition developed over a long period of time, just as in the more formal arts.

Chinese folk art is mainly the product of local artisans specializing in objects of daily use such as ceramic vessels, textiles, bamboo articles, toys, dolls, lanterns, and so forth. It also serves decorative purposes for peasant households. In rural areas in northern China, cut-out pictures from red tissue paper are pasted on the white translucent paper windows of peasant huts as a year-round decoration. In their traditional form, the New Year pictures, now chiefly reproduced by various graphic mediums, show the general character of folk painting. The origin of the New Year pictures is believed to have been in the "door gods," representing deities who since ancient times had been placed on doors to deter the entry of malevolent spirits into the house. The earliest known New Year pictures represented two famous generals of the seventh century. Later, the subjects of the New Year pictures were extended to portraits of heroes of legend and history and to various designs of symbolic objects. The pictures also included illustrations from popular tales and plays, while old subjects, like the door gods, continued to be popular. As a whole, since folk art generally follows traditional forms rather than the inspiration of individual artists, little distinction can be made between works of the past and present.

Contemporary Art

A revolutionary change has been effected in Chinese art by the Communists; even long before assuming power they began advocating a cultural line patterned on the Soviet model and proclaimed socialist realism as the only acceptable approach to literature and the arts. At the same time a policy was formulated for creating a new national style based upon a selective scrutiny of the Chinese art tradition.

The Central Academy of Fine Arts was founded in Peking early in the Communist regime to train artists of the working class. These artists were directed to such fields as public sanitation, education, and national construction for their themes or encouraged to participate through their art in campaigns against landlords, counterrevolutionaries, and other capitalist elements. The traditional landscape painting was abandoned for realistic scenes of socialist construction such as railroad trestles, bridges, and dams. The result is a socialist art in which people and their activities are consciously idealized to promote "the new man and his new life." Workers and peasants are uniformly portrayed as heroic, happy, intensely energetic, strong in character, and so completely dedicated to the building of the socialist state that so-called works of art often bear a close resemblance to magazine advertisements or billboard posters.

To ensure his working-class point of view, the trained artist is periodically sent to the countryside or to factories, mines, and construction projects for familiarization with the life and working conditions of peasants and workers. Workers themselves are urged to participate in spare-time art activities. Their oil paintings, watercolors, sketches, papercuts, and cartoons are regularly exhibited at factories and mines alongside production records and other announcements.

The Communist influence is also apparent in modern Chinese sculpture, which consists largely of close replicas in clay of Soviet models, and in architecture, where nationwide economy drives have dictated drab, barracks-type buildings. An unplanned consequence of the indoctrination of the people to this unaesthetic, functional architecture has been the criticism of recent government experiments in expensive, multicolored, tiled buildings of stately, modified-traditional style.

Another important emphasis in Communist art policy has been the encouragement of folk art. Popular entertainments such as local operas, shadow plays, puppets, storytelling, ballad singing, drum playing, dancing, and acrobatics have been promoted and patronized by the new regime.

The Communist government is especially interested in encouraging the development of traditional theatrical forms. The Peking opera, with songs and dialogues in the Mandarin dialect, has dominated the stage from the nineteenth century to this day. Regional operas, which are generally cruder in form, take on local characteristics and dialectal peculiarities. Today the most important local theatrical works are the Canton opera, the Shao-hsing (in Chekiang) opera, and the K'un (K'un-shan, a district near Soochow) opera. One of the K'un operas, *Fifteen Strings of Cash*, has recently been revived in a revised version and acclaimed by Communist critics.

The dance, which formerly was subordinate to the theater, has become an independent art form. Folk dancing emphasizes the cultural heritage of the peasant class and provides a splendid opportunity for group participation and mass attendance. The Yang-ko (harvest song) dance, originally a very old harvest fertility dance in North China, was taken over and popularized by the Communists shortly after the Sino-Japanese War. The simple steps became known all over China and were associated with liberation, unification, peace, and the national spirit. Dancing troupes from regional and ethnic groups have been organized and given opportunities to perform in the big cities and occasionally abroad. Ballet dancing is being developed with the assistance of Russian experts. Dance festivals, in which competitions are staged and prizes awarded, are held each year and attended by thousands of people.

Popular music, directly promoted by the new regime, includes songs extolling the new system, political activities, and production methods; songs about the daily life of the farmers, industrial workers, or soldiers; and background music for films, plays, musical comedies, and so on. The movie and phonograph industries have opened a new field for musicians in popular songs and light music. The Communist regime has also been encouraging the growth of both traditional Chinese and classical western music. Visiting tours by famous Soviet and East European performers are reported to be enthusiastically received by Chinese audiences. While very few Chinese musicians are making concert tours, traditional itinerant musicians still enjoy popular support among the masses.

The folk tradition in Chinese art has been revived and is reproduced in New Year pictures and papercuts for windows. The new folk artists, however, have introduced modern propaganda scenes with peasant workers standing beside sheaves of grain, scythes, and plows, as well as new themes and objects such as tractors, mutual-aid teams, and rural cooperatives. Although the familiar designs of flowers, birds, insects, animals, and human figures have been retained, they are given a new interpretation representing objects and values in a socialist society.

By far the largest output of art creation under the Communist regime has been illustrative art: posters, cartoons, woodcuts, and picture storybooks. Their enormous production serves a vast number of illiterate or barely literate persons. The woodcut, an ancient Chinese art that grew from block printing, is the most frequently employed medium of book illustration, being decorative and often of high artistic quality. Small serial cartoon books for both children and adults present in an easily understandable form educational and propaganda programs such as health and sanitation, care of livestock, new farming methods, and so on. In addition, many traditional tales are brought up to date and made into picture books to point up politically useful morals or to illustrate various Communist virtues.

Like all professional groups, Chinese artists today have been organized into various government-sponsored associations under the over-all direction of the All-China Federation of Literary and Art Circles. In the field of art, the member organizations include the Association of Chinese Artists, Association of Chinese Dramatic Workers, Association of Chinese Musicians, Association for the Study of Chinese Folk Literature and Art, Association for the

Study of Chinese Choreography, and many others. All these are directed by artists who won national fame in pre-Communist days and who have identified themselves with the art activities of the new regime.

The status of Chinese artists and artisans as a whole has been raised under the Communist regime. For the purpose of political propaganda and education, the government needs the service of artists to popularize through art forms socialist ideas among the people and provides for their training in a number of government schools, such as the above-mentioned Central Academy of Fine Arts, the Central Dance Corps, and the Central Experimental Opera Institute, which also gives instruction in ballet. Some theater troupes are supported by the central government and others by provincial governments. Leading troupes with famous actors have taken part in command performances before government officials during national celebrations and for the entertainment of foreign dignitaries. The acclaim won by Chinese theater troupes abroad has given the performing artists new prestige at home. Women are taking an equal and active part in the theater. The star system has been gradually abolished and the difference in wages between the bit player and the principal actor is not as disparate as it used to be.

Literature

Until the end of the imperial period, two separate literary traditions existed side by side in China, the most apparent distinction between them being their use of the literary language or the vernacular. Works in the literary language were produced by and for the scholar officials, the educated members of the gentry, and the enlightened elements of the merchant class; vernacular literature, consisting mainly of novels and plays, was never highly regarded as a serious literary form. In general, the literary language was considerably more stylized than the vernacular and the two came to have extensive differences in vocabulary.

Besides the Confucian classics, which set the standard in literary style, literature proper comprised poetry and prose of various forms. Literature as such was the substance of the scholars' education and the basis of the civil service examinations through which educated persons acquired gentry status and official rank. Thus the circumstances of the scholar-officials' life encouraged their concentration on the production of literature.

464

Literate and Vernacular Traditions

Traditionally the Confucian ideal of a moralistic literature, embodied in all prose writings including history and philosophy, was opposed by the aesthetic view, which emphasized the importance of style and form. An elegant prose style, which employed parallel grammatical constructions having antithetical meanings and which observed strict rules of euphony based on the four tones, flourished briefly in the fifth and sixth centuries A.D., when Confucianism was in eclipse. The style of the Confucian classics, however, was revived and reasserted during the ninth century and used in most prose writings until modern times.

Regular Chinese poetry, called *shih*, is characterized by an even number of lines in a poem and a definite number of words, from four to seven, in each line. While the earliest Chinese poems in the *Book of Poetry*, one of the Confucian classics, were originally written to music and sung to musical accompaniment, later poets composed poems according to the rules of euphony based on the four tones. The use of a tonal pattern, a parallel structure, and a strict rhyming scheme, characteristic of modern-style poetry—in contradistinction to old style poetry with its less strict metrical requirement—was introduced in the T'ang period, during which Chinese poetry reached the height of its development in the works of Li Po, Tu Fu, and many other famous poets. But in lesser hands, this style of poetry became increasingly artificial and formalized, and poets had to draw their inspiration from folk poetic forms like the *tz'u* and *ch'ü*, both of which have popular song tunes employing a more colloquial language. The *tz'u* was developed to its fullest by the Sung poets and the *ch'ü* became popular as a kind of aria used in dramatic compositions of the Yüan period.

The growth of drama with its colloquial songs and dialogues marked an important step in the development of Chinese vernacular literature. From a variety of theatrical acts such as farces, *ch'ü* songs, instrumental music, dancing, and acrobats, a type of musical drama with alternating sung and spoken parts, developed in the thirteenth century. Although the dialogues were generally of an inferior quality, the poetic excellence of the Yüan drama was recognized. Dramatic writing since the Yüan period had degenerated into mere literary compositions, more suitable for the study than for the stage, until the rise of the Peking theater in the nineteenth century. The features of the Peking theater are operatic singing with orchestral accompaniment, elaborate make-up and costuming, and a language of gestures and posturing resembling the dance.

Chinese fiction stemmed mainly from the oral tradition of the professional storytellers. The storytelling tradition was undoubtedly very ancient, although the tales did not appear in the published form until the twelfth or thirteenth century. Eventually, these crude tales attracted the attention of writers with literary talents, who rewrote them, retaining much of the colloquial language and folk flavor of the original. This was the background of some of the great Chinese novels of the fourteenth century. Instead of an over-all plot, each novel is constructed around a series of action-filled episodes, reflecting the storyteller's need to hold his audience in suspense.

Major types of traditional Chinese fiction include the historical novel; the supernatural novel; the family novel; the realistic social novel; the romantic novel of love and beauty; the legal-case novel centered on an upright magistrate; and the novel of adventure, featuring bandit-heroes in their struggle against the evil forces of officialdom. In the latter half of the nineteenth century, as the attention of the novelists was increasingly focused on the corruption and chaotic conditions of the bureaucracy, many of them wrote bitter satirical novels to attack the government and to expose the social evils of the time. Together with other forces and ideas, the growing realization of the usefulness of literature as a vehicle of social criticism led to the literary revolution of the late 1910's.

Literary Revolution and the New Literature

Important literary efforts in the older, stylized form came to an end after the literary revolution when proponents of a new written style using the vernacular overcame the last of the traditionalists. This literary movement had been motivated primarily by the desire to inject new vigor into Chinese literature and to dispel the lethargy among Chinese writers who were creating very little of interest.

The literary language, which was based on the ancient classics, was considered inadequate for the expression of modern ideas, especially democratic and scientific thought. Hu Shih, Ch'en Tu-hsiu, and other leading scholars first advocated in 1917 the use of the vocabulary and syntax of the spoken language in order to simplify education and increase the size of the reading public. The student movement on May 4, 1919 provided another rallying point in the attempt to modernize Chinese education and learning. Within a few years vernacular literature was widely in use and taught in the schools. The literary revolution thus resulted in a re-evaluation of Chinese letters and an important change in the form, style, and theme of literary writings aimed at a larger group of readers.

The rejection of traditional literature was accompanied by a predilection for foreign literature which came to have a tremendous impact on China's new writers. A vast assortment of western works began to appear in Chinese translation. The new poetry bore imprints of western romanticism and symbolism, and the new drama presented realistic scenes of contemporary life and people with a social message in the manner of modern western playwrights. Chinese critics now accepted the novel and the short story as important literary forms which were cultivated by the best talents under the influence of French, Russian, and American writers.

Chief among the writers of the new literature from 1917 to 1949 were Lu Hsün, Mao Tun, and Kuo Mo-jo. Lu Hsün, the most influential literary figure of modern China, was strong in his conviction that the traditional Chinese society was rotten to the core and had to be drastically changed through revolutionary means. Because of his pre-eminent position, his name has been evoked by Communist propagandists as the symbol of the socialist literature advocated by the People's Government. Mao Tun was a faithful chronicler of his period. Like Lu Hsün and other leftist writers, he regarded literature as a means of social reform and depicted in his novels the reality of class strife. Kuo Mo-jo was the most vociferous spokesman of the anger and rebellion that characterized the intellectuals of the pre-Communist period. It is interesting to note that Kuo Mo-jo, whose unrestrained emotion is unusual among Chinese poets, should eventually have become one of the advocates of the Communist policy of suppressing individual freedom in writing.

Even before the Communist domination, the new literature was essentially a realistic literature with a definite social message. Although western influence was generally prevalent, the largest single body of foreign literature to profoundly affect the thoughts and sentiments of Chinese writers was the Russian, particularly after the late 1920's. This was attested by the emergence of the so-called proletariat literature movement and the organization of the Federation of Left-Wing Writers under Lu Hsün's leadership.

The Nationalist government had made some attempts to counteract these leftist tendencies and activities by advocating a nationalist literature of its own, but its voice was drowned amidst a rising wave of revolutionary outcries. The Sino-Japanese War (1937-45) actually helped to undermine the political control the Nationalists had imposed on all literary publications. In consequence, immediately after the war, the stage was set for a Communist domination of the literary world even before its military conquest of the country.

Communist Literary Policy and Measures of Control

In spite of the fact that many Chinese writers had long been leftists disillusioned with the Nationalist regime, they were apparently unprepared for the sudden strict enforcement of the Communist policy after 1949. The Nationalist censorship had been almost ineffectual compared with the total control of literature exercised by the new regime. Writers soon awoke to the fact that their novels, stories, plays, and film scenarios were not at all what the new leaders wanted, for they had continued to write of their individual reactions to war and social injustices and were inexperienced in presenting the collective Communist viewpoint.

Literature and art, Chinese writers soon learned, are created for and must serve the masses, reflecting the ideals and responding to the political demands of the working class. The writers were therefore urged to substitute "working-class ideology" for their "petty bourgeois intellectualism."

The First National Conference of Writers and Artists, held in Peking in 1949, was attended by a large majority of well-known writers and artists, and paved the way for the organization of the All-China Federation of Literary and Art Circles. Kuo Mo-jo was elected chairman of the federation and Mao Tun and Chou Yang (Communist party spokesman on literary matters) were elected vice-chairmen. Subsidiary organizations of writers and artists were set up at the same time, membership being requisite for professional status. One of these organizations, the All-China Association of Literary Workers (renamed in 1953 the Association of Chinese Writers) was headed by Mao Tun who, together with Kuo Mo-jo, has been instrumental in the implementation of Communist cultural policies since 1949. Chou Yang, however, has been the chief architect of Communist literary and art policies.

In the few years after the first national conference, regional conferences of writers and artists were held, local groups were organized, and literary periodicals and publishing houses were established under party supervision. The government having thus insured its control through both organization and publication, pressure was exerted to put the official line into practice. Writers and students of literature were required to go to the rural areas and factories, and to participate in government-sponsored campaigns such as the land reform and Aid-Korea-Resist-America movement. Many "volunteered" to go to the battle front in North Korea to comfort the soldiers and to glorify their heroism in the war. But in spite of these efforts, the writers were exhorted to still greater endeavors. The literary organizations and periodicals were found to have been ineffectual in their criticisms and negligent in directing the creative efforts of the writers. Plans were announced for a nationwide study movement to re-educate the writers, to set literary and art works in the proper direction, and to effect a closer supervision of literary organizations.

In the early years of the Communist regime, an important institution for the indoctrination of writers was the Central Literary Institute, established in Peking for the training of young writers from the working class. The intensive two-year courses in the institute consisted of a thorough grounding in Communist thought as well as of practice writing in factories and rural areas. Some established writers suspected of ideological uncertainties were also among the "research students" at the institute.

To secure control of the art and literary circles and to rid them of members maintaining attitudes deemed contrary to party interests, a number of campaigns have been waged in the last few years. The anti-rightist drive in literature was centered upon Hu Shih, the spokesman of the new literature movement since its beginning in 1917. For his contribution to the movement, Hu Shih has been known in the West as "the father of the Chinese Renaissance" and recognized as a champion of democracy and liberalism in opposition to totalitarianism. His prestige and influence on Chinese thought has made him the target of the Communist onslaught.

In the past years the continuous and extensive campaign to wipe out "Hu Shihism" was directed not only against Hu Shih's literary criticism but also his language reform program and philosophical ideas. In volume after volume of collective criticism of Hu Shih, his former colleagues and students as well as others of some literary renown have contributed scathing articles, belittling Hu Shih's role in the new literature movement, pointing out errors in his studies of Chinese literature, ridiculing his empirical methods and idealistic thought and, most important of all, accusing him of collaborating with the "Kuomintang reactionaries and American imperialists." It is apparent that these concerted attacks were planned and directed by the party's hierarchy to expunge the so-called "bourgeois" intellectual spirit of the republican period, of which Hu Shih has been the symbol.

An offshoot of the anti-Hu Shih campaign was the controversy over a famous eighteenth-century novel, the *Dream of the Red Chamber*. In a critical study of the novel published in 1952, Yü P'ing-po, an eminent scholar, interpreted the novel as an auto-biographical account of the author Ts'ao Hsüeh-ch'in—a view first advanced by Hu Shih and generally accepted by modern critics. Yü P'ing-po also stressed the quiet resignation with which the various characters accepted their fate. For this study he was accused of following the "bourgeois idealism" of Hu Shih because, according to Communist interpretation, the novel was supposed to have portended the dawn of a new era in the hero's resistance to the "feudalistic morals" of his family. This attack was promptly taken up by the leading party organs and augmented into a nation-wide offensive against the bourgeois tendency among Chinese writers.

Shortly after the *Dream of the Red Chamber* controversy, a split in the party's literary ranks provoked a series of campaigns against the so-called revisionists. While a number of party writers had been previously subjected to purges, a more recent case involving Hu Feng, a veteran Communist critic and a close friend and favorite disciple of Lu Hsün, may be cited as an example. Hu Feng had considerable prestige in party literary circles and was a serious rival to Chou Yang. Irascible and outspoken by nature, Hu Feng had never been able to submit to party authority and further incurred its displeasure by attacking the rigidity of the party's control of literature, which, he asserted, had caused much of the formalism, dogmatism, and generalization in present-day Chinese literature. It seems hardly likely that Hu Feng would have made such an attempt to discredit the party leadership in literature had he not been hopeful of a favorable reaction from most of the writers. But contrary to expectation, Hu Feng found himself the object of an intensive criticism campaign accusing him of the worst possible ideological crimes, including Hu Shihism. He was deprived of his party post, and he and his friends were labeled "revolutionary pretenders."

Chou Yang's position as the literary boss of Communist China was further strengthened during the 1957 campaign against other leading Communist critics and writers such as Ting Ling, the novelist; Ai Ch'ing, the poet; Wu Tsu-kuang, the dramatist; and Feng Hsüeh-feng, formerly editor of the *Literary Gazette*. Among them, Ting Ling especially had been a leading figure in the Communist literary society, her novel *The Sun Shines over the Sangkan River* having been awarded the Stalin prize in art and literature in 1951. Both she and Feng Hsüeh-feng had been party members for about twenty to thirty years and had a national reputation. At the time of the Blooming and Contending campaign, when there was some freedom in literary and artistic expression, they had voiced misgivings about the party supervision of literary publications and criticized the quality of contemporary literature and its failure to reveal faithfully the true aspects of life. For these deviations from the party line, they were dubbed revisionists and reactionaries. Ting Ling, in particular, was assailed for the anti-party utterances and behavior of the characters in her stories and accused of having abused the trust and confidence the party had placed in her by building up a "kingdom" of her own in the literary world. Revisionism, it was asserted, is an expression of capitalist thought inside the working class; it camouflages its opposition to socialist literature and the party's leadership by holding aloft the signboard of Marxism and by putting up a false front of antidogmatism and antiformalism.

The party's policy of keeping the literary scene in perpetual ferment with "revolutionary struggles" against both right and left results in the dovetailing of one major criticism campaign after another. Such attacks are significant in revealing the Communist intolerance of all intellectual thought which does not meet political requirements, and of any opposition to party bossism in the factional struggle for power and leadership.

These campaigns to impose on the writers the rigid party ideology have impaired the quality of the literary output in the ten years since the organization of the All-China Federation of Literary and Art Circles. Not only was there a conspicuous paucity of works by established writers, many of whom failed to produce anything comparable to their previous writings, but also a general apathy and inertness in literary activities, except those sponsored by party organizations. The writers had lost their initiative and resourcefulness, and although many followed dutifully the party directive to live among and learn from the working class, such experiences did not seem to inspire or enrich their writings. They found the emphasis on ideology little inducement for creative work and felt diffident in having to "peep right and left before each step" for fear that any false move, although taken unwittingly, might lead to trouble with the authorities. The orthodox Communist explanation, however, is that the writers and artists have not yet been able to divest themselves of the bourgeois burden they have been carrying since their early childhood. The writers are therefore urged to spend longer periods and labor more closely with the peasants and workers to benefit from their new experiences.

Having failed to spur the literary activities of the old writers, the Communists have been attempting to train new writers and artists of working-class origin by organizing cultural groups and developing cultural activities in the farms and industrial plants under the leadership of the party's local propaganda organs. These efforts are correlated with the movement to wipe out illiteracy and to establish vocational and technical schools for peasants and factory workers. Facilities for cultural stations, clubs, reading rooms, and broadcasting centers in the rural areas have been expanded and their numbers increased. Opportunities are provided for the publication of the works of the fledgling proletarian writers and artists in local papers and magazines. The Communists have asserted that there would be in the future thousands of such cultural groups and millions of workers and peasants engaged in art and creative writing.

Following the current "leap forward" campaign in the economic field, a similar cultural movement has been initiated to create and propagate the mass line in poetry. Under the slogan that "wherever there is work, there is poetry," and in the belief that poetry both inspires and increases production, peasants and industrial workers have been encouraged to compose poems and exhibit them. The result is that the walls and doors of peasant huts and factory plants are covered with poems and drawings of the untutored artists, and poetry contests are held frequently, big sheets of the most popular poems (and drawings too) being hoisted on a stage in the center of the village.

Chinese literary theory during the last ten years has been Soviet-oriented. In order to learn from the advanced experience of the Soviet writers, a large number of works, from Gorky to Mayakovsky, have been translated. The book market as well as the literary periodicals have been flooded with these translations, regarded as models by the Communist writers. Soviet criticism, particularly socialist realism, has been adopted as the standard for Chinese authors. They have been urged to create, as embodiments of Communist ideals, heroes and heroines in the guise of actual people of the working class, and to describe these new characters in their fight with old ideas and institutions, as well as their new relationships in a socialist society.

More recently, Communist critics have advanced a new theory that literature should be an amalgamation of revolutionary realism and revolutionary romanticism. This seems to be a modification of the Soviet dictum. The official endorsement of romanticism alongside realism as an ingredient of socialist literature is certainly a departure from the orthodox Communist literary creed.

The new literary theory was attributed to Mao Tse-tung by Chou Yang in an article published in August 1958. Mao's idea of the union of revolutionary romanticism with revolutionary realism was praised as a "scientific generalization of the total experience of literary history" and a correct approach to the problems and particular needs of the times, which could best be expressed in the spirit of revolutionary romanticism. Since its first appearance, the slogan has been greeted by a wave of enthusiasm in literary periodicals and gatherings. As Kuo Mo-jo states, the idea of merging revolutionary romanticism with revolutionary realism supplements the concept of socialist realism and should be regarded as the basic and permanent principle of literature and art.

Romanticism and realism, according to this interpretation, are interdependent and inseparable. Realism embraces the spirit of romanticism, just as romanticism embraces the substance of realism. In representation, the substance of art and literature may be realistic, but in the process of creation it may be transformed into the romantic through the catalytic action of the author's mind. In the new literature, however, both romanticism and realism should be geared to revolutionary—that is, Communist—ideas and efforts. Revolutionary romanticism is therefore the kind of romanticism that expresses in literature the people's highest ideals, their heroism and optimism, their keen imagination and creativeness; whereas revolutionary realism aims to depict the life and struggles of the working people without, however, exposing the seamy side of life in a socialist regime.

Ch'ü Yüan (famous fourth century B.C. poet) among the ancients and Lu Hsün among the moderns have been cited as examples of the successful merging of revolutionary romanticism with revolutionary realism. Ch'ü Yüan is extolled for his patriotism and his struggle against the corrupt political factions in the court; even though his poems of imaginary trips to the land of myth and legend are essentially romantic, they are interpreted as symbolic of a search for ideal values and persons to save his native land, to aid the suffering people, and to effect the unification of the country. Behind the icy surface of Lu Hsün's nonchalant and satirical depictions of life is said to be a depth of intense warm feeling like flameless white heat that burns without being combustive.

The interpretation of Mao Tse-tung's literary writings as illustrative of achievements in this direction is even more far-fetched. According to Communist critics, the *Nineteen Poems of Mao Tse-tung* (published in 1958) represent the culmination of this new spirit in literature. His technique of enlivening realistic themes with romantic fantasy and revolutionary spirit is considered a model for all writers. No other works by contemporary writers have been cited as outstanding examples of the new theory.

These trends indicate that although actual achievements in literature and art in Communist China have been unimpressive, tremendous efforts have been made to develop them in accordance with the ideological and propaganda requirements of the regime. Writers have been subject to a barrage of exhortations to work and produce under the party leadership, which is inflexible and all-powerful. They have been told to develop a national style from the great cultural heritage of China, to learn from the progressive writings of the rest of the world, and especially to benefit from the experiences of the people and the literary thoughts of Marx and Lenin. That all cultural efforts must be subservient to political ideology and necessity seems to be the inexorable guiding principle of Communist policy on art and literature.

Intellectual Expression

The changes that are being made in the artistic, literary, and intellectual life of the country by the Communists will, if successful, remold virtually the entire pattern of Chinese life. The new China is to live, breathe, and have its being in Marxism-Leninism as taught by Mao Tse-tung. But China's traditions are still not wholly dead, and for the present, Chinese Communism is as much the product of Chinese conditions as of Soviet dialectics. As might be expected, some of the policies and actions of the present regime are an extension of trends and patterns evident in the development of Chinese thought, a review of which is essential to an understanding of the intellectual climate in China today.

The Confucian Tradition

Of the so-called "hundred schools" of ancient Chinese thought, the major ones are Confucianism, Taoism, Mohism, and Legalism. Confucianism and early Taoism had approximately contemporaneous beginnings in the fifth century B.C., but the former was to remain more important in Chinese intellectual history. Whereas Confucianism stressed family solidarity, friendship, social relations, and imperial allegiance, Taoism was profoundly metaphysical and in an age of positive challenge and war, called men to contemplation, inaction, and hermit-like withdrawal. Mohism offered the principles of universal love and utilitarianism, equating the good chiefly with social order, peace, prosperity, and divine favor. Legalism, on the other hand, advocated the absolute authority of the sovereign and state power; in this system, the individual disappeared in the corporate state, and the administration was urged to be harsh in securing its aims.

After a period of contention among the hundred schools, Confucianism gradually won ascendancy with its more humane tenets. Legalism fell into disrepute although every Chinese dynasty had recourse to some of its statutory harshness. Taoism became popularized as a religion and acquired a conglomeration of gods and superstitions which long discredited it among most educated men. Mohism disappeared in the substitution of Confucian virtues for its own. With all its rivals in a state of decline, Confucianism, which had the advantage of better suiting the whole context of Chinese life, became the state doctrine of the Chinese people and helped establish the continuity of Chinese intellectual traditions.

A system of thought monopolized by the gentry class, Confucianism was accepted both officially and unofficially as a national ideology and constituted a monolithic philosophy for China. The Confucian ethic contained the concept of filial piety, principles of moral cultivation, and rules for detailed applications of the virtues to human relationships and problems. Confucian politics envisaged a feudal hierarchy whose guiding principle was to be personal loyalty, applied socially and politically. In some respects, Confucianism never lost its feudal coloring. Gradually, however, a new emphasis appeared in the Confucian political concept. This principle was based on the idea of Heaven as the

Supreme Ruler and the emperor as Heaven's deputy on earth, and by extension of the solitary character of the emperor, the concept of "one-man" authority and responsibility. From this new exegesis, the justification of the unitary state followed easily; Confucianism became the instrument of at least minimal centralism, and was occasionally used to justify absolute authoritarianism.

The question of the right of rebellion in Chinese philosophic history is popularly misunderstood. In theory, something like it existed; in practice, the Chinese were empirical. No rebellion was moral until it succeeded, and the mandate of Heaven which the emperor (or dynasty) received could be withdrawn only when the use of swords and political skill had succeeded in driving him from power. When an attempt failed, although the surviving ruler was as licentious and ineffectual in administration as any in history, no philosopher would doubt in public the validity of his mandate or the viciousness of the defeated rebels. It follows that popular descriptions of Confucian "democracy through the right to rebel" did not necessarily apply to actual Chinese conditions under the emperor.

Paradoxically, Confucianism, which was variegated and flexible in its philosophy, was also the center of a monolithic thought system. The key to its functioning was the special position and character of the scholar class, whose formation marked more than a simple social-intellectual phenomenon, suggesting in addition the expanding Confucian orientation of all China in one of the great epochal developments of the country. Orthodoxy came to mean the particular Confucian configuration held by a majority of the scholar-gentry and sanctioned by the court. The vested interests of the institutionalized gentry class most often favored conservative attitudes toward philosophical change. This was especially true of those scholars chosen for the bureaucracy, whose security often rested with the stability of the status quo. The adoption of the system by the imperial power and the final crystallization of a monopoly class of thinkers tended to lead the natural drift of institutionalized philosophy to ossification.

The Chinese mind found satisfaction in traditions that conformed to the culture with which it was familiar. Confucianism survived because it fitted Chinese society; China remained substantially Confucian because Confucianism responded to the familiar and adequate patterns. This state of affairs, however, was modified and conditioned by the continual existence of rival or complementary systems which, while never dominant, were often widespread and able to introduce occasional new ideas into the Confucian framework. Thus there was, in spite of this monolithic thought system, an atmosphere of toleration, in which the heterodox Confucian and even the non-Confucian could live and work together with the dominant Confucian group.

Chinese Thought in Transition

In the general divergence and confusion which accompanied the gradual sloughing off of Confucianism, the scholar class of modern China began to find itself self-consciously adrift, and a growing number of its members appeared to realize that they and their society were slipping into an intellectual void. By 1900 the search for a new rationale was well under way and gained momentum with the introduction of western ideas. Those which first and always most strongly appealed to the imagination of the Chinese were scientific thought with its empirical method and universal phenomenal inquiry, and democratic ideals embodied in some form of popular representative government. Chinese interest in science followed curiosity about the technological advancement and material well-being of the West; and democracy was initially in accord with the theories of a rising faction of scholars who wished a more positive role for their class in national policy.

But the fact that western thought came to China in the train of overwhelming power and that it was expressed among them by persons who generally had little understanding or sympathy for Chinese traditions combined to influence the Chinese reaction to it. Basic responses to western ideas in the first years of the impact were of three main types: conservative resistance, compromising synthesis, and total westernization. But whatever attitude its individual members might take, the Chinese intelligentsia as a whole retained a legacy of resentment which has been used by the Communists to shape their present attitude toward the West.

In this transitional period, the major lines of intellectual development—conservative traditionalism, empirical utilitarianism and liberalism, nationalism, and Marxism-Leninism—were represented in the universities which came to be the strongholds of the new intelligentsia of twentieth-century China. The most influential of them, the National Peking University, was the center of exploratory study and dissemination of western ideas. Besides providing the broadest possible scope for academic discussions, the universities also encouraged active student-faculty interest in political, social, and intellectual life outside the campus itself. In times of national crisis, students participated in political movements such as that of May 4, 1919. Student lecturers toured the countryside and cities, addressing the common people to stimulate national spirit, to seek nationwide support against foreign aggression and internal disunity, and thus to establish for the academic profession a reputation of leadership in national affairs.

The students' activities, more than a reassertion of the traditional scholar's interest in politics, underlined the change that the impact of western ideas and political realities had made on Chinese intellectuals. No longer committed to a single ideology nor identified with bureaucracy, the students and scholars emerged as a devoted nationalist group of reformists, agitators, and leaders of a society in flux. Far more influential than any other type of leaders in modern China, the new intelligentsia was interested not so much in preserving the continuity of their influence and their culture as in finding some standard for a new China along the general lines of nationalism.

During the first three decades of the twentieth century, the new Chinese intellectuals were captivated by the western liberal ideal in one or another of its outward manifestations. Their major attention, as has been mentioned, was centered on scientific method and democratic process, the study of which they hoped would enable them to rival the West and preserve their nation's independence. In fact, the new technology and modern democracy came to have nearly exclusive validity for the new intelligentsia. One after another the remaining Confucian defenders of the old school were discredited not only by the obsolescence of their theory but also by the bad company of political reactionaries, imperial "restorationists," and later Japanese collaborationists.

The success of the student-scholar group was emphasized by the status and prestige they enjoyed in the nation, which as a whole looked more often to them for ideas than to any others. In rural areas the old traditions of ancestor worship and Confucian virtues survived, but even there the new scholars could receive the general veneration formerly shown the Confucian scholars. Their influence was felt most, and their activities were most fruitful, in cities and treaty ports. So when the Nationalists assumed control of the country in the late 1920's, they lost no time in enlisting the new intellectuals for their cause.

The response of scholars to the bulk of official thought, however, was restrained. Anxiously patriotic, they were able to accept the anti-imperialist orientation of the Nationalist party, and a considerable number of them, heeding the call of duty to serve their country, turned from academic to government work. In the decade from 1927 to 1937, there was a substantial movement of scholars into administration. But these men were more interested in national service than in party philosophy, and in the course of time the spirit of cooperation with the Nationalist party waned among the new intellectuals. Politics and corruption disillusioned some, the Japanese occupation overtook others, but the strict demand and erratic extension of orthodoxy by the party leaders alienated most of them. In the end the attempt of the Nationalist government to control intellectual and artistic expression led to a general resentment among the intellectuals, some of whom, either in exasperation or through conviction, turned to Marxism-Leninism as their new creed.

Ideological Remolding under Communism

While Marxism-Leninism has no roots in the Chinese soil, the modifications made upon it by the Chinese Communist party have at least some bases in tradition: the use of the peasantry as a revolutionary group, a monolithic thought system, an educated elite group, and a close interrelation of literature, philosophy, politics, social structure, and economic system. Typically Chinese, this effort at justification by tradition was common to other reform and revolutionary systems of thought in the past, whether their advocates were liberal, moderate, or nationalist thinkers.

The appeal to the past helped, in a limited way, to introduce Marxism to China. The new intelligentsia was oriented to the doctrine itself through familiar patterns of thought and through appeals to national pride. Liu Shao-ch'i, leading party theoretician, cites Confucius, Mencius, and later thinkers to support various special aspects of the Peking regime's program. Beyond tradition, however, there is much in the doctrine of the party, at least theoretically, to appeal to the intellectuals.

Chinese Communism itself was the child of the new intellectual movement. The intelligentsia, from about 1900 to 1940, tended to be apologetic concerning their cultural traditions. To them, Marxism, although foreign in origin, offered a new national purposiveness, an assurance that their country could, through their efforts, become a real power. Originally, scholars probably responded to Marxism from a fundamental dissatisfaction with other foreign ideas and actions, particularly the exploitation of China by the colonial powers. As Communism became a political creed and the policy of an organized party, it also became the chief opponent of those very groups which the new intelligentsia viewed as reactionary or imperialistic.

In its purely philosophical aspects, the development of Chinese Communism is only an ancillary development of Communism in general and of Stalin's adaptations of Marxism-Leninism in particular. It is a part of a European philosophical movement, and party ideologues accept this fact. Chinese conditions necessitate some apparent variations in the Soviet dogma. These, however, have been largely limited to matters of revolutionary technique and tempo and to the practical application of Communism in the conduct of the revolution. Mao Tse-tung has seen fit to adjust the application of Communist theory to a Chinese setting, but in the main the ideas of Mao are only a tactical divergence from orthodox Communism.

For political, economic, and social control, the key standard urged in Mao's thought is service. Service to the people, service to the goals of revolution, and service to the party and government all demand the compliance and full support of the intellectuals through collective effort. Mao has called upon all teachers, scientists, engineers, technicians, doctors, writers, artists, and other men of culture to serve the people, saying that only those who have distinguished themselves in their service to the people will be esteemed by government and society. With the combined force of party doctrine, national pride, quasi-humanistic sympathy, and real police power, the command to serve under party control and direction gives the Peking regime a philosopher's stone with which to turn adversaries into traitors and criticism into heresy.

Beyond this fact it remained true that the success of the Communist dogma among educated men was in large part what the party leaders made it. In China as elsewhere, the winning of support among intellectuals netted the Communist party good dividends in prestige, reduced vitality in the opposition, and a freer hand once power was achieved. Winning support before victory and retaining it afterwards, however, are quite different problems. For the Chinese Communist party, the preconquest policy of ingratiating non-Communist scholars was a rule not from the canon but from the tactical handbook, whereas mobilizing them and regimenting them later were orthodox necessities. Popular mass movements, the organization of all occupational groups under party supervision, and techniques such as brainwashing in particular have made possible Communist control of the intelligentsia.

The Chinese Communist party behaved toward the intelligentsia as the problems of the time and its own program required. Generally speaking, from 1949 to 1951, the years of consolidation, the party was conciliatory and tolerant of other than Marxist-Leninist-Maoist thought. By 1952, having achieved relative security and anxious to begin using intellectuals to full advantage, it undertook the program of brainwashing, euphemistically called "ideological remolding." From 1953 to the present, apparently having successfully applied its psychological pressures to the bulk of scholars in China, it continued brainwashing at a relaxed pace, at the same time fitting the "reformed" into its operation.

Basically, the selection of the intellectuals to be "re-educated" by the Chinese Communist party depended on the purpose to which the particular individual was to be put. While government administrators were drawn mainly from veteran party organizers, activists, and agents, it was those members of the intellectual group intended for the higher level of technical service and educational work who needed brainwashing. Scholars whose work could not be immediately directed to the state's use were less intensively reformed. But all were held strictly accountable for orthodoxy and loyalty to the regime.

The official government program of intellectual remolding began in September 1951, with required training courses and study groups. The advisers and directors of the program were well-known Communist theorists. The scope and significance of what followed can hardly be overestimated. In a country whose highest cultural achievements had been carried on traditionally by scholars and whose people by habit venerated learning, brainwashing signified the end of an epoch. It signified the intent of the regime to replace the old culture with a new one, to suppress any possible intellectual deviation, and to limit the scholar's professional outlook and contacts to such an extent that they would be safe for the regime's ideology. It meant the wiping out of the principles of previous academic experience and their replacement with ideas which, if not new in theory, were very much so in their application to the intelligentsia.

In addition to controlling the intellectuals through the application of intense psychological pressure, the Communist regime has also made considerable effort to stimulate voluntary enthusiasm and support from the intelligentsia. It has held frequent propaganda meetings, rallies, and forums for popular reforms, all designed to appeal to the civic-minded among the intellectuals. It has encouraged international cultural exchange by sending missions to Soviet Russia, Japan, India, and other Asian and European countries, and by entertaining in return foreign cultural delegations. It has awarded art, drama, and literature prizes for outstanding achievements and service to the people.

The nature and direction of the intelligentsia in China is in the process of a radical change under government supervision. In traditional society, literacy in any degree admitted one to the controlling group, the scholar-gentry. In Communist society, an effort is made to spread literacy universally so that knowledge of the written language no longer constitutes intellectual supremacy. The new political elite is not intelligentsia in the sense that the old gentry was but rather a special section of the intelligentsia oriented first to real politics, next to economic-political canon, and only thirdly to scholarship as such.

In imperial times, though scholars were not rulers themselves, at least they were tools of those rulers who accepted the doctrines evolved and interpreted by them. Under Communism, scholars have the same political role as tools, but the doctrine is not their making and is imposed upon them by the new party elite. Formerly, the scholar-gentry, recruited under authoritarian governmental direction, set the cultural-moral pattern of China; now the political elite controls the state and possesses the means and power to impose its ideology, through enforced indoctrination, on the entire intelligentsia. In this stifling atmosphere, independent thought is impossible, independent research is difficult at best, and the potentials for progress and intellectual achievements are severely limited.

In the interests of substantiating the official philosophy of history—dialectical and inevitable progression through class struggle to the classless society—the Communist regime is sponsoring a vast project of historical rewriting and reinterpretation through a special research institute. The staff, largely brainwashed but thoroughly competent historians, are allowed to plot the course of their work, but only through the uniform outlook of required doctrine. Historical personalities and events are used to support the official philosophy. To interpret them, scholars must neglect or rationalize any data which do not conform to the preconception.

As a result, the intellectual atmosphere is so regulated that both the party and the historical profession breed the same ideas in the minds of the readers.

What is happening to history is true of the social sciences in general. The past is being radically and continually re-evaluated by the standards of the present. Men, movements, and causes which conduced to the development of modern conditions or in any way, however vague, affected the masses of their times are adjudged good. Any variants, obstacles, or conservative reactions are adjudged evil. Even the economic interests and classifications of past times are likened to the contemporary in conformity with dogmatic interpretation.

There is also a radical redirection of cultural attitudes both inwardly and outwardly. In some matters, especially in patriotic sentiments and loyalty to the state, the Communists have simply appealed to, confirmed, strengthened, and universalized those attitudes which had already developed before their rise to power. In others, notably matters of cultural pride, they have posed as restorers of self-confidence lost through the intellectual impact of the West. In general, however, they have bent all attitudes toward their own new world view and interpretation of history.

While it is true that the Communist regime is trying to de-emphasize the scholars as a class, they also treat them as a functional group with national prestige. Ideological indoctrination should probably not have been so necessary otherwise. In terms of outward cultural attitudes, it has been important to the Communist government to secure the support of the educated for state projects, foreign policy, and for acceptance among them of the Communist world view. The monolithic ideology itself and government control of all formal means of intellectual organization and expression have made the task a relatively simple one, and there is no doubting the Communist success in mobilizing a large number of the intellectuals to serve their cause.

This ideological certainty and political assurance led the Communist leaders to relax, though only for a short interim, their control over intellectual and artistic expression. In May 1956 Mao Tse-tung first set forth the new policy of encouraging "a hundred flowers to bloom and a hundred schools of thought to contend," the latter being a reference to the philosophical activities of the early classical period. Instead of relying on administrative orders to exercise the party leadership, the so-called Blooming and Contending movement, which did not gain momentum until early

1957, aimed to promote free discussion and free emulation to foster the development of science and art, and to encourage open debate so that "materialist thinking could overcome idealist thinking."

The new movement was enthusiastically hailed and taken advantage of by China's intellectuals, writers, and artists. Many of them were quick to air their grievances; some seized this opportunity to ask for elbow room in writing, teaching, and research; while still others demanded more freedom in creative work and thought. The mass of demands for freedom from party control avalanched and the repercussions so alarmed the Communist rulers that the movement was stifled before it could develop. It was immediately followed by a series of anti-rightist campaigns, in which a number of well-known intellectuals in the government, universities, and literary and art circles were disgraced and punished. The reinstallation of tight intellectual control in mid-1957 after only a few months of relaxation clearly indicates that the newly promised freedom of thought and expression is merely part of a technical maneuver that can be easily changed as soon as it fails to satisfy the requirements of the regime's over-all policy.

VALUES AND PATTERNS OF LIVING

THE PRINCIPAL REASON FOR THE STABILITY and longevity of the old order in China was its social homogeneity. The uniformity of attitudes and values fostered by the imperial government proved a remarkably binding and durable cement for the traditional order. Old China was primarily a way of life and system of values and the state was organized on this premise. An alien resident who accepted the Chinese way of life was considered a Chinese, whereas a Chinese who did not abide by the traditional system of values was regarded a "barbarian." As a result regional variations in basic social values were practically nonexistent.

In the new China conformity is being enforced by the Communist regime with a determination and resourcefulness unmatched by the imperial governments. The introduction by the Communists of radical new concepts and values was preceded, however, by almost a century of gradual but profound change in basic Chinese attitudes. Too rigid in its institutions and outlook, the old social and political order proved inadequate in the face of problems and pressures of a modern world. The Chinese people, growing critical of the older attitudes, turned increasingly to the modern ways of life as being more compatible with changing conditions, and finally repudiated the old order completely by overthrowing the last imperial dynasty in 1911.

The Communists have combined coercive power and the systematic exploitation of individual and group dissatisfaction with the old order to inculcate a new set of basic social values. Appealing particularly to women and youth, whose modern independent status is an important symbol of the new society, the regime paints the old order as feudal and oppressive, the new one as enlightened and progressive. An example of this approach is the *Three-Character*

Classic for Women, a literacy primer that takes its form from the three-character rhymed verses used in old China for teaching the young. One verse translates:

> Cooperative agriculture has organization,
>   and women are not left out,
> In the old society we were badly mistreated,
>   but the new society teaches friendship and love.

Another approach is the skillful association of elements from the new order with elements from the old that retain a strong emotional appeal for the Chinese people. For example, the people are taught to engage in class struggle and in the campaign against deviation even when it involves attacking their family and friends. This idea of struggle as a guiding principle of personal behavior is utterly contrary to the old ideal of harmony in personal relationship, an ideal that meant in practice a comfortable adjustment to one's natural and human environments. Yet in urging all to struggle, the Communists insist that the ultimate goal is *ta-t'ung,* the traditional utopia of a harmonious social order—in Marxist language, the worldwide classless Communist society.

Basic Social Values

In discussing the basic values of a society in transition such as that of contemporary China, it must be borne in mind that the power of the old and the appeal of the new vary not so much according to regions as to social groups. Among the more westernized population in big cities like Shanghai the old values were being challenged at a time when the peasantry and rural gentry, despite many discontents and tensions, continued to hold fast to them. Intellectuals and members of the new industrial and commercial groups were the first to discard traditional attitudes and adopt western values, a process that was slower among other groups. These variations affect Communist tactics to the extent that different types of persuasion are used with different groups. But the final goal is the universal adoption of the attitudes and behavior that Communist leadership considers conducive to socialist transformation.

Good and Bad

In the dominant philosophy of old China, derived from Confucius and Mencius, man was considered inherently good and capable of socially harmful behavior only if he lacked guidance or was placed in adverse circumstances. For example, if the ruler of the state failed to provide for the basic physical needs of the people, the latter would be forced to rebel. Or, if those in authority failed to provide instruction, particularly in setting an example in conduct, their subordinates would have no guideposts to the good and would fall into evil ways.

Bad conduct was not, as in the West, a violation of the laws of God but deviation from the age-old norms of acceptable social behavior. Specifically, behavior was categorized as "bad" if it went against such prescribed norms as filial piety to parents, duty to older brothers, loyal and submissive devotion to superiors, good faith among friends and associates, propriety or accepted procedures in human relations, and righteousness in one's dealing with others.

The laws of imperial China provided punishments for violations of some of these norms, the most serious crimes being those against filial piety. Yet the ideal in the application of law was not blind justice but punishment administered with due regard for "human feelings" and for the specific circumstances surrounding the crime. This attitude stemmed from the high value traditionally attached to moderation and restraint from excess, even in the enforcement of law. The criteria for judging behavior as good or bad were therefore neither religious nor legalistic, but the prevailing norms in the community, the customary practices endorsed by tradition and ratified by community consensus.

From the traditional viewpoint goodness could be cultivated through practice, study, and contemplation. The path to goodness was open to all and those who attained a high order of goodness should be a moral elite, a group of models for others. This moral elite was also, in Confucian theory, the group that should hold and exercise political power and enjoy the rewards of status and wealth, a notion that sanctioned the long political dominance of the scholar-official.

The Chinese Communists have set up new standards of good and bad, the purpose being, in the words of their leading theoretician, Liu Shao-ch'i, "to reform mankind into the completely selfless citizenry of a Communist society." The Communist moral code consciously and unconsciously makes use of traditional moral ideas: some have been taken over with little change and others have been modified to fit Communist patterns and concepts.

The virtues associated with the traditional family system,

however, have largely been discarded as family functions are taken over by the modern conjugal family on the one hand and by state and party organizations on the other. These traditional virtues are castigated as feudal and backward relics of what the leadership calls "the squalid old society of China."

The Marxist dogma that the individual is molded by his class and, indirectly, by the historical stage of the society into which he is born has a good deal in common with the Confucian view of the prime importance of environment in character formation. Thus the Communist effort to create a new society, whether in traditional or Marxist terms, envisages a favorable environment for the development of individual goodness. But the "goodness" expected is different: the highest expression of Communist morality is seen as the sacrifice of the individual, even to the extent of giving one's own life, for the sake of the party, the working class, and the nation. This precept is close to the traditional virtue of absolute loyalty to superiors.

Some of the personal qualities of a model party worker are also linked in many ways to the Confucian tradition. The good Communist is "able to love others and hate others," that is, he never injures his comrades for his own benefit but vigorously fights the enemies of the revolution. Toward his comrades his attitude is one of "genuineness and sympathy." He "does nothing to others that he would not have done to himself." He "grieves before all the rest of the world grieves and is happy only after all the rest of the world is happy" (a Confucian adaptation of the Buddhist ideal of the bodhisattva-savior). He "has no individual apprehensions or private desires to obscure and pervert his investigation of things and his understanding of true principles"—a restatement of the Neo-Confucian view of purity of mind as necessary for true knowledge.

To attain these and other "good" qualities the Communist, like his Confucian ancestor, is to pattern his character after approved models and to subject himself to intensive self-cultivation. In traditional China, the models of character and behavior found in the classics and histories were to be studied and followed by individuals who sought to improve themselves. Selected heroes from the past and highly productive workers of the present are now recommended as models and presented in fiction, textbooks, and newspapers for emulation by the young and old; model farmers and soldiers are feted and publicized, and their pictures and idealized biographies appear in all propaganda media.

The long list of qualities condemned by the Communists includes liberalism, formalism, bureaucratism, and opportunism. To rid oneself of these vices, the following formula, here used by a Communist writer against the vice of individualism, is typical:

> The methods transmitted by the ancients for raising oneself out of the vulgar and entering sagehood, becoming a Buddha or a Taoist spirit, all required one to go through a long period of discipline. If we want to shed the earthly form of individualism and acquire a spiritual form of collectivism, we must cultivate and discipline ourselves over and over . . . we should continually ask ourselves this question: "Am I or am I not still guilty of individualism?" If we have a thought, utter a sentence, walk a step, or do a thing, we should then ask ourselves, "Is this individualism or not?" And then we should listen for the response of others: "This is—or is not—individualism."

The notion of group criticism and group pressure is the universal Communist device for fostering approved behavior and eliminating the actions or attitudes considered undesirable by the authorities. Members of party organizations, professions, government bureaus, and all other groups meet continually for criticism and self-criticism, and these confessions and criticisms are published in the media of mass communication. The study meetings, popularly called "struggle meetings," are characterized by an atmosphere of tension and fear. Confessions of deviation or defection are made by individuals or exposed and analyzed by the group; criticisms are leveled at individuals and promises of reform are exacted. This has proved to be a device of deadly effectiveness for making individuals conform to the new Communist standards of both thought and behavior.

Work and Leisure

In traditional China, except for a small group of idle rich, all people were expected to carry a maximum load of work. There were neither Sundays nor regular hours of work, and officials and administrators maintained a routine of early rising and midnight conferences. In the country, farmers and their families worked hard during the seasons of planting and harvesting. Everyone was in the fields before sunrise and worked as long as there was enough light.

The long hours of toil, however, were relieved by moments of relaxation and recreation such as group singing and the exchange of greetings and gossip in the fields. Often, after their day's work was done, neighbors, relatives, and friends would gather to talk over events in the city or in their own villages. All village occurrences were common knowledge and the conversation for the most part centered on affairs close to village life such as the rice crop, buying and selling, the care of farm animals, and so forth. Storytelling was popular, ranging from tales of heroes and historical figures to local legends, fairy tales, and ghost stories. Elder members would relate their own experiences or memories of some exciting bygone events.

Leisure was a part of the work routine and not entirely separated from work as in the West. Leisure patterns of the scholar-gentry centered around self-cultivation, writing of poems and prose, and the exploration of nature's beauty. Friendship and tea drinking were also closely allied in this traditional pattern. A leisurely tempo and sociable atmosphere were essential elements in the enjoyment of life in traditional China.

During the transitional period, a gradual change in the ways of life and concept of labor was apparent. The Nationalist government proclaimed the eight-hour work day and the six-day week for government offices and business enterprises. Factories also changed the life pattern of the urban worker in large industrial centers. Nevertheless, the pattern remained much the same in rural districts among the farming population, and small businessmen continued more or less at their own pace.

The accession of the Communist regime, however, disrupted the rhythm and routine of life for all groups. The "enjoyment of labor" has replaced the enjoyment of leisure. The masses are urged to adopt new habits of work and play.

Professedly working for the improvement of their standard of living, the government has extended its influence over the people. If the lot of the Chinese peasants and workers has never been easy, current production schedules certainly have not made it any easier. Slogans such as "support the rural people" and "labor created the world" have facilitated the establishment of Communist-directed mass organizations at the village level. Party-controlled trade unions for the workers and communes for the peasants have stimulated individual competition in production with medals and titles of "model worker" as rewards. Driven by such incentives, the present-day worker attends meetings, participates in discussions, and submits to criticism sessions.

Thus the concepts of labor and leisure have changed; the

emphasis has shifted and the tempo has quickened. Everyone, including young people and women, is engaged in the party-directed activities of "self-cultivation" and "national reconstruction." Work has been divorced from leisure. Under the present system even recreation is usually a community affair, directed and supervised by the activists. Leisure as a form of desultory, purposeless relaxation is devalued, yielding place to group participation and active sports that develop competitive spirit. Leisure as a mark of high status has virtually disappeared.

Authority and the Individual

A father's relation to his sons was the model for the exercise of authority in traditional China. Ideally a father was stern and aloof, seeing to it that his children were well cared for and given proper instruction. A son was to submit unquestioningly to his father's will at all times, showing his loyalty and devotion by anticipating his parents' wishes, providing for their comfort in old age, and arranging at their death a proper funeral and burial, followed by periodic sacrificial offerings.

In the political sphere local magistrates of the traditional bureaucracy were often referred to as "parents of the people." To reciprocate the care and concern of those in authority the people were to provide material support through taxes and labor; they were to obey the custom and the laws laid down for them and the heaviest punishments were decreed for those guilty of unfilial behavior in the family or rebellion and treason against the state, the family's political counterpart.

These were the patterns of authority to which the individual was subject. His personality was formed within the family; his status in society was determined by his family's status. Through the complex relations of the family, his life and character were circumscribed by the role assigned him. Freedom of choice and freedom to develop individuality were thus rigidly limited. It has been suggested that, while individualism has been emphasized in the West, in China the central theme has been individuation.

In exchange for his submission to authority and discipline in every phase of his personal life, the individual was given the basic necessities of life and was backed by the family's influence in obtaining jobs, choosing a bride, and so on. Nepotism was sanctioned by society, and family members benefited when one of them rose to wealth and power.

The only social relationship that an individual could enjoy

with less family interference was friendship, which was often cherished throughout life. Many Chinese poets have dealt with this theme, and popular fiction and drama have treated it with vividness and force. Friendship has overtones of the elder-brother and younger-brother relationship, which between mutually selected individuals with virtual equality between them was a refuge from the father-dominated rigid hierarchy of the family.

The two patterns, paternal domination and fraternal association, were reflected in political life. Established governmental authority was of the paternal type; everyone was subject to the will of the emperor who was the patriarch of the "nation-family." But dissident movements were organized on the basis of the brotherly friendship pattern: the organization of bandit gangs, the leadership of rebel armies, and the members of secret societies were all bound together by ties of friendship and brotherhood.

Today the Communists are developing a new image of the individual and a new relationship between authority and the individual. To fit him for membership in the Communist society, they stress loyalty to the state rather than to the family, at the same time bitterly denouncing the tyrannies of the old system. In Communist literature this new type of individual, freed from traditional family and so-called feudal relationships, is claimed to have boundless opportunities for self-development.

"Comradeship," the brother-friend type of relationship, built on an age-old Chinese ideal, is strongly emphasized in party and mass organizations. The Communist leadership which was itself bound together by comradeship during the long years of suppression, is continually romanticized and extolled in literary writings. This pattern of human relationships, attractive to those who suffered most under the old family system, is used to encourage cooperation between individuals in a common task. In the textbooks it is fostered by moral tales—a pail of water is too heavy for Little Brother and too heavy for Big Brother but is easily carried by the two; a lone tree is easily shaken by the wind but many trees standing together can withstand a heavy storm.

Nevertheless, the brotherhood-friendship pattern among top Communist leadership has subtly shifted, and Mao Tse-tung and the party have begun to exercise paternal authority over subordinates and over the people as a whole. Mao has taken on many of the attributes of the supreme patriarchal emperors of old; his paternal guidance is praised in these lines from a song published officially:

> The great leader is like a father
> Mao Tse-tung educates us . . .

Another praises his paternal care for the people:

> In his loving care for the people
> He surpasses that of their own parents.

As Mao takes on more and more the attributes of the father, the party and the state take over both the functions and the emotional focus once supplied by the family. A labor heroine is described as a "good daughter of the party." A song says:

> Our great fatherland—
> We should pay it the same filial reverence
> We would show to our mothers.

These quotations suggest the reorientation of loyalties away from the family, but the terms and images used are those of the family system itself—a typical example of the Communist use of the symbols of the old order to destroy the order itself.

The functions of the traditional extended family are divided among the party, the state, and the new conjugal family. The individual, not the family, now chooses his mate; and the state, not the family, sanctions the match through marriage registration. Commune-operated kindergartens take over, for many parents, the care of children, who are taught to rely on themselves rather than on family members and relatives. The family's function as an administrative unit for mutual surveillance and responsibility has been eliminated and each citizen is responsible to the state. Family connections are no longer a means of getting jobs, which are now dispensed to individuals by state and party organizations. In this way the Communists undermine the last vestiges of the old family, including nepotism.

Nevertheless, the individual is still urged to work in a disciplined and cooperative way for the larger social group. Official prescriptions for individual behavior recall the formulas for good conduct by members of the traditional family. The people are expected to engage in labor and productive activities and to place the common good above personal benefit. They are asked to be helpful and submit willingly to the discipline of group life. They must always be ready to learn and to accept criticism for self-improvement.

It would appear, then, that the Communist government seeks

to adapt earlier patterns of individual-group relationships to its own purposes. On the one hand it encourages the pattern of co-operation associated with the old image of brotherhood and friend-ship; on the other hand it increasingly subjects each individual to a type of authority that is reminiscent of the old all-powerful head of the family. For certain types of work, such as team projects carried on by party cadres, equal cooperation is considered an ideal norm, but for the masses of the population submission to absolute paternalistic authority and the subordination of the in-dividual to the group is the ordained pattern.

Face

In traditional China "face" meant one's accumulated moral and social prestige in the eyes of the community. One's prestige was solidified by adherence to the ethical norms in all human dealings. It could be increased through important contacts and by acts of conspicuous generosity, but only within the role which society assigned to the individual. To "get above oneself" in a play for pres-tige was actually "to lose face." The widespread use of go-betweens in business, marriages, and political negotiations was a device for insuring that, in the event of failure, neither principal would lose face. Consideration for the face of others was highly regarded and, in actual behavior, care for one's own and others' face, particularly the family's, was conducive to the surface harmony of Chinese social relations.

Modern Chinese critics have argued that this harmony was too dearly bought and that individual concern for face, intensified by community pressure, stifled individual initiative and turned creative people into timid conformists who sacrificed all for the preservation of superficial prestige in the community. This, they insist, worked against China's successful adjustment to the modern world.

The Communists have encouraged this kind of criticism in seeking to release individual energies for the purposes of the Com-munist state and have made a frontal attack on the notion of face. In a speech in 1937, Mao Tse-tung severely criticized such atti-tudes and behavior as, for example, failure to start an argument with a person even when he is wrong; the overlooking of differences for the sake of peace and cordiality when dealing with an old friend, colleague, or subordinate; and unwillingness to make any clear decision in order to preserve harmony and unity.

The Communists single out for public recognition individuals who have ruthlessly battered their way toward one of the Communist goals with utter disregard for face, their own or others'. Liu Shao-ch'i, for instance, denounced as wrong any idea of trying to avoid intraparty struggle, or of refraining from criticizing others' mistakes so as to escape criticism of one's own. Obviously the frequent criticism and self-criticism in group meetings are destroying the old feeling for face. Indeed the leadership may regard these sessions as one of the principal devices for the complete elimination of this traditional attitude.

Life in the Villages

In traditional China life in the village was characterized by meagerness and poverty. During recent decades life in rural areas became increasingly difficult as factory-made goods destroyed village handicrafts, wars and ineffectual governments brought disruption and oppression, and overpopulation lowered the standard of living. Such manifold pressures created tensions that replaced the formerly harmonious village life fostered by a delicate balance of human and economic factors. Despite the isolation of most villages, ideas and ideals from the West have slowly undermined the authority of the older mores and customary laws. But peasant life everywhere suffers a tremendous inertia, remaining highly resistant to all the forces of change. Thus, before the Communist period, many of the sweeping changes that were transforming city life were not reflected in the countryside.

The Traditional Pattern

From time immemorial the rhythm of village life and its annual cycle of farming activities were well established. In regions south of the Yangtze the farmer's life was dominated by the need for intense toil through the year if his tiny plot of land were to support him and his family, and rice cultivation set the rhythm. In the early spring, after the New Year, the farmer raised his rice plants in nursery beds near the farmhouse. Then he prepared his fields by plowing and removing, in some areas, his winter crop stubble. Fertilizer was spread carefully over the ground and water was admitted; when the water reached a certain depth, the ground was carefully harrowed. The field was then ready for transplanting the young rice from the nursery beds. This very difficult chore, done while crouching in water, completed the spring routine. Except for repeated cultivating and weeding, the farmer had an easier life during the ripening of the grain. As the grain matured, the fields dried and at last it was harvest time. The harvesting and threshing, using primitive implements, again required all available hands. The harvest in, the farmer had to ready his fields for the winter crops. In some parts of the country these were winter wheat and rape; in others two or three rice crops were produced during a single agricultural year.

In North China the farming cycle was governed by the need to conserve water and by the demands of the principal crops: wheat, millet, and kaoliang. In early spring, the northern farmer began his year-long effort to conserve the moisture that had accumulated in the soil during the autumn and winter rains. About half of the fields were then in winter fallow awaiting spring planting and fertilizing from the household pit; the rest were planted in winter wheat, which was brought to maturity by careful hoeing and by hand irrigation with well water—a backbreaking operation in which the farmer was helped by his whole family.

In April or May came the time to plant millet, kaoliang, or cotton in the fallowed fields, which had to be well irrigated to ensure the germination of seeds. Then came the harvest of the wheat, and once again the farmer's whole family and often his neighbors were called upon to help. All harvesting, threshing, and winnowing were done by hand with the greatest care to preserve every grain and the stalks and straw as well. Following this, the winter wheat land was planted in soybeans and corn. The farmer and his family could then relax a little, but not for long, for autumn brought the harvest of the summer crops, the fall plowing, and once again the planting of winter wheat.

Autumn was also the time, before the abolishment of tenancy by the Communists, to bring to the landlord a portion of his share of the crop. If the weather had been favorable and the landlord and the tax collector were not unduly rapacious, the farmer might retain enough grain to see his family through to the next harvest. If things had gone badly, a grim winter season lay ahead. Winter was the time for repairing farm buildings and implements, weaving, spinning, and doing other household chores. With the approach of another year the farmer might look forward to some festivity and respite from work.

The New Year holiday, comprising the first fifteen days of

the year, was the main period of festivity, a leisurely and happy occasion for the villagers to visit friends and relatives, enjoy the best food, and wear the best clothes. The New Year was followed by the spring festival, called *ch'ing-ming*, the Chinese equivalent of Easter, during which family ties between the living and dead were renewed as the living members resorted to the family or clan cemetery, made food offerings to the dead, swept the grave-yards, and then enjoyed their feast. All relatives made special efforts to join in this annual manifestation of family solidarity, and the outing made the occasion a pleasant relief from winter and indoor work. On the fifth day of the fifth lunar month the Dragon Boat Festival was celebrated, a very popular occasion in the south, where dragon boat races were held on rivers and lakes. On the fifteenth day of the seventh lunar month occurred the Feast of Souls, a festival for the souls of one's ancestors as well as a com-munity salute to the dead. The Mid-Autumn Festival on the fifteenth night of the eighth lunar month was a moon festival, and the ceremonies in the honor of the moon carried out at moon-rise on this autumn night included many symbols of fertility and longevity. Sacrifices were made to the Old Man in the Moon as the one who arranged all marriages on earth. In some areas people enjoyed boating; in others it was a popular time, as was the Double Ninth Festival (ninth day of the ninth lunar month), to make pilgrimages to nearby mountains.

In addition to these annual festivals, the farmer's life of toil was relieved by ceremonial family events. For a family with re-sources, a wedding meant a great feast with ample wine; even poor families often went heavily into debt to arrange a festive marriage ceremony. Practical jokes were played on the bridegroom, tradi-tional songs were sung, and the guests, particularly the men, thoroughly enjoyed themselves. The birth of a male child was often celebrated, as were betrothals and other milestones of family and individual life.

Besides these occasions for relaxation, special events added interest and variety to the routine of village life. Itinerant dra-matic troupes performed occasionally on makeshift stages and professional storytellers appeared frequently on the village streets and in the teahouses to spin their yarns to an impromptu audience. Pilgrimages to famous mountains or shrines were undertaken by wealthier farmers during the slack agricultural season. Perhaps the most universal diversion was, as in all other communities, gossip and desultory conversation. The topics discussed ranged from rumors about national affairs and market prices to local rights and wrongs.

Despite his grim struggle for survival, the average villager tended to be cheerful, self-respecting, and possessed of a robust sense of humor. He went through life with a continual concern for his own standing and prestige among his fellows, and with a determination and faith that, despite all difficulties, the fortunes of his family would steadily improve.

Changes under Communism
It is useful to note that these "styles of living," although simple and austere compared to western standards, provided multiple social satisfactions to a large proportion of the rural populace. This was true even during the period of change prior to 1949. Data on Communist efforts to alter the Chinese way of life, however, are particularly meager; statistics, declarations, and news releases give few realistic details of life in the villages—now the people's communes—under Communist domination, and most refugees have come from the cities. Certain gaps in our knowledge, therefore, can only be filled in by inferences from previous knowledge of these areas.

The farmer's annual routine remains basically the same in spite of communalization. The most striking changes in the farmer's life are the new work schedules, the rigid discipline imposed by local authorities, and the daily barrage of political advice and exhortation to which he is subject. He no longer cultivates his land in the manner of his ancestors with the assistance of his family, his clan, and his neighbors; no longer sets himself periods of work and rest. The Communist leadership is determined that the peasant shall be transformed in three ways: he must be made to produce more; he must become a politically conscious, active supporter of the Communist regime; and his basic attitudes and values must be radically changed, especially with regard to the ownership of land.

The visible and active instrument of this transformation in the villages is the party cadre who acts as the eyes, ears, and voice of central authority. Since the beginning of the Communist regime, the cadre has been called upon to organize production and to participate in all types of farm activities. In the past the village cadre was usually an outsider, but recently the party has been recruiting youths from specific localities and training them as native leaders. At the time of the land reform movement the cadre was the instrument for land redistribution, bringing into the countryside the first major change decreed by the central government. The cadre organized the peasants' association in the village and manipulated its meetings and elections; later he coordinated the mutual-aid teams for the sharing of labor and equipment, a practice that struck at the familial organization of farm labor. More recently the cadre has been the instrument for the concerted attempt to build, promote, and direct the communes in rural areas.

The cadre carries on the drive to destroy traditional mores among the rural populace and helps to enforce the new marriage law by discouraging or preventing arranged marriages. Sometimes with the help of radio, films, and mobile theatrical units, issues of the day are publicized and dramatized: the need for the farmer to sacrifice, to sell surplus grain to the state, to send his sons to the army, to contribute labor to community projects, to buy bonds, and so forth. The cadre establishes winter schools in which the peasants are given intensive political indoctrination, practical training, and instruction in reading and writing.

The villager's way of life has been greatly altered by the intervention of the government in all social, economic, and political activities. The pressure to conform, at least outwardly, is formidable. Self-chosen activities are few and far between, most leisure time being taken by attendance at public meetings or entertainments with clear ideological messages presented by traveling theatrical groups. The slack winter season may now find him at school or in a community work project directed by the local cadre.

Today the New Year festival is still characterized by some traditional activities, modified to promote government aims. The peasant may buy New Year pictures to decorate his house, but they will probably be portraits of Mao Tse-tung and Communist model workers rather than the heroes and deities of former days. He may decorate his gate with paired New Year mottoes, but they will no longer carry the old wishes for long life, happiness, and wealth, but rather exhortations to conform to Communist standards. The government may allow some additional food for the season but gambling is forbidden and social life is no longer restricted to family and friends. The peasants have been urged to organize their own dramatic troupes and to attend "cultural lectures" and mobile movies arranged by the cadre. The exchange of visits with relatives in nearby towns has now its Communist counterpart: interchange of visits between urban and rural workers' groups and other mass organizations to observe one another's progress in socialist reconstruction.

Urban Patterns of Living

In the traditional period, urban life, although different in patterns of work and activities, was closely akin to village life. Town and city dwellers kept their ties with their native villages and returned there whenever possible; many looked upon commercial activity in the town only as a means to acquire enough wealth to buy farm land and return to the village. Most of the town population was made up of artisans and laborers, plus a small number of land-lords, retired officials, county functionaries, and established merchant families. The county seats were the centers for tax collection and administration of the surrounding farm villages; they also served as market towns where the peasant might sell his crops and purchase the manufactured goods he could not produce.

The life of the average small town artisan was as meager as that of his relatives in the village. Long hours, hard work, low pay, and few holidays were the lot of the majority. Proprietors of many shops required their employees to live on the premises, which often were crowded, poorly lighted, and poorly ventilated. The diet of the town dweller, like that of the farmer, consisted mostly of cereals, vegetables, and some condiments; meat and fruit were to be had on holidays only. On these occasions, towns-people usually tried to return to their villages, but if this was impossible would enjoy such delicacies as they could afford and stroll the streets, perhaps visiting friends and attending fairs and theaters.

While life in the towns was slow to change, life in the treaty ports and big cities had greatly altered under the impact of modern innovations and institutions such as schools, newspapers, motion pictures, and radio, all of which made the people more aware of the outside world. In Shanghai and other cities, major industries built large dormitories for workers, and labor unions and clubs became new centers of social activity. Yet the living conditions grew worse as workers moved into urban centers where crowding reached unbelievable proportions. Workers in the newer industries were somewhat better off than those in the traditional trades, but the number of holidays was reduced without, in many cases, the introduction of a shorter week. The festivals of the agricultural year continued to determine the holidays although national holidays were increasingly observed in the big cities.

Contemporary Changes

In the towns and cities, as in the countryside, the greatest change in the patterns of living has been brought about through a network of new associations by which the Communist regime envelops and controls the individual. Industrial workers, artisans, and merchants are all organized by the party and strenuously indoctrinated by the cadres. In long and frequent meetings, the urban worker is under intense pressure to manifest "correct attitudes," to show himself free of all feudal and bourgeois taint, and to demonstrate his complete commitment to Communist goals. Through these and other channels he is under continual pressure to step up his efficiency and productivity.

City and town dwellers are organized into street and ward units, through which they are given further directives on the management of their lives. The townsman, more than the peasant, is open to an around-the-clock propaganda barrage. From the first call to early morning calisthenics, the radio plays in every street until late at night. There is pressure to join sports groups and study groups with their ideological purposes. Major Communist holidays such as the International Labor Day on May 1 and the National Day on October 1 are celebrated in the cities with great parades and endless speeches. Privacy or the chance to be at ease with family or friends is rare.

The New Year's holiday in the towns has some of its old gaiety although subject to the same restrictions imposed on the peasant. A recent Communist press account of festivities in Peking suggests the way in which the old and the new are currently blended. Firecrackers, in the traditional pattern, were set off on New Year's Eve. On New Year's Day people crowded the streets and made mass visits to the holiday fair in the southwestern part of the city. Kites, balloons, and dolls were available for children, and some were given model airplanes bearing the slogan, "We must liberate Taiwan." Theaters and cinemas were crowded, and continuous and varied shows were performed in the workers' "palaces of culture." Further innovations symbolic of the new order included a Soviet skating exhibition, chess tournaments, finals of the municipal soccer tournament, and entertainments by workers' dramatic troupes.

Beggars and prostitutes have been taken off the city streets, sanitation has been improved, and a campaign against rats and flies has been partially successful. Building has apparently proceeded rapidly although most improvements in housing probably benefit only the industrial workers, who constitute the favored class. Since the party is anxious to recruit from among his class, the urban worker has an opportunity to rise in life through party work and as a member of the new industrial force, he may feel some sense of identification with the most rapidly expanding sector of the Chinese economy. This identification and the opportunities offered by the party have probably affected the goals of the urban worker. Thus he may be less interested than he once was in returning to a plot of land in the country where economic opportunities are increasingly restricted.

The urban elite are the functionaries of the government and party. The pattern of their private lives is little known, but if the old Chinese bureaucratic elite acted in a leisurely and cultivated manner, the badge of the new is a full brief case and an air of practical and energetic activity. Their incomes permit a life somewhat easier than that of the rest of the urban population, but they are constantly under discipline, watched by their colleagues, and obliged to meet work quotas and submit to continuous indoctrination. Party and government workers, for instance, are urged to use the New Year holiday to plan their work for the year to come.

The bulk of the bourgeois class may have survived, but its activities have been increasingly restricted by government controls and the growth of government producing and marketing facilities. They are a tough and tenacious group, but their old comfortable life is gradually disappearing and, as a class, they are scheduled for extinction.

The growing cities now appear to be replacing the country as the goal of the ambitious. It is likely that, as urbanization and industrialization proceed, the cities rather than the farm villages will determine the mores and the patterns of living for the society as a whole.

NATIONAL ATTITUDES

A PEOPLE'S ATTITUDES AND SENTIMENTS toward their society and government are not of course shared equally by everyone in the population. The intensity and depth of feeling in any given individual and the spread throughout the population of a given attitude or set of attitudes will vary according to age, occupation, sex, ethnic affiliation, and many other factors. The following description, therefore, of necessity represents the thinking of an "ideal-typical" Chinese rather than any one individual. This "ideal-typical" Chinese would be a composite individual, his sentiments regarding his society and culture derived from the tenor of the mass media and his response to governmental control over every aspect of living, from popular reaction. Some of these attitudes, like those toward China's cultural heritage, derive their strength from deep-rooted traditional values. Others, like those toward science and progress, represent a careful manipulation by the state of desires which lie uppermost in the minds of a significant portion of the Chinese people concerning China's place in the family of nations.

Nationalism and Ethnocentrism

Underlying many attitudes, and lending support and foundation to them, is the fundamental belief of the Chinese in the greatness of their nation and culture. In the past, the Chinese took it for granted that their cultural level was the highest in the world. The confrontation with the West, however, has torn great patches out of the fabric of this belief. But the feeling remains that Chinese culture represents one of the high points in world culture, and that given favorable conditions for its growth, this superiority can be demonstrated in concrete terms.

Formerly, with little knowledge of comparable cultures, there seemed to be tangible reasons for the Chinese belief in their greatness. China had been one of the first integrated and continuous societies to emerge from the dawn of history. There were periods, of course, when Chinese culture showed signs of stagnation or even deterioration, but these were always followed by periods of rejuvenation. Chiefly because of this continuity and also because of the repeated reassertion of national vigor, China accumulated a heritage of tremendous scope, richness, and complexity, much of it being of high intellectual quality.

The basic content of this heritage is shared by a very large number of people spread over a vast territory. It is remarkable, therefore, that the general features of the culture were undiluted by any other culture. The Chinese who left China to live abroad continued to be Chinese in a cultural sense, and for centuries Chinese culture overshadowed both the aboriginal cultures of the border regions and the cultures of its immediate neighbors. While China's cultural frontiers were widely extended, its national boundaries were ill-defined, fluctuating, often imperceptibly, with the expansion and contraction of Chinese domination over the border tribes. International relations were characterized by tributary relationships with lesser powers rather than by treaty relationships concluded on the basis of equality. The natural result of these circumstances was a strong ethnocentrism in which China was regarded as the center of the civilized world and the peoples of foreign lands the object of condescension.

The sense of national unity was derived mainly from the continuity of historical tradition and the homogeneity of Chinese culture. Patriotism was expressed in terms of personal loyalty to the imperial house instead of to the state in the abstract. The orthodox political theories, founded on paternalism, extolled government by a benevolent sovereign. Throughout the centuries, in spite of numerous dynastic changes, the theoretical foundation and political structure of the state had undergone remarkably little change. However, as China experienced repeated humiliations at the hands of western powers in the late nineteenth century, there arose serious doubts regarding the validity of these traditional attitudes.

Reaction to Western Influences

The first manifestation of the changes in attitude that would result from contact with the West was a reassessment of the basis of

Chinese cultural pride. The apparent superiority of the western powers in certain respects had forced the Chinese to a critical analysis of their cultural and political values and institutions. The consensus of the majority of informed Chinese was that, although traditional Chinese institutions had been relevant and valuable in the China of the past, major adjustments were called for if China were to meet the modern western challenge.

In general, two distinct schools of thought arose: one asserted that a new Chinese culture must be developed to combine the desirable elements of both traditional culture and western culture, particularly its science and technology; the other demanding nothing short of a revolutionary change, advocated repudiation of all the old traditions, especially Confucian doctrines and practices, as incompatible with the growth of science and democracy. Such a view called for the introduction of new ideas, new principles, and new methods—in short, a new culture.

This demand for a new culture and a new way of life was a direct reaction to the inherent weaknesses of Chinese society. For a people that had for centuries believed in their cultural superiority, the sudden realization of their backwardness was a painful awakening. The resultant cultural dislocation had the most profound effect upon the attitudes and reactions of the Chinese people who, in a desperate search for rejuvenation, became susceptible to all forms of ideology, including the Marxist, that held any promise of political stability, economic development, social progress, and, above all, fulfillment of nationalist aspirations.

The educated, who were the most articulate and influential section of the Chinese population, were the first to be aware of the need for a new form of government. Although there was a profound desire for the introduction of western democracy, the politically active members of the Chinese intelligentsia recognized as the first imperative the unification under a highly centralized government of the divergent elements of the society. The intellectuals and political leaders further reasoned that political unification and national sovereignty depended on the elimination of all forms of foreign imperialism. Imperialism having been declared the mortal enemy of China, nationalism became the strongest single rallying force for all political parties and progress toward nationalist goals the gauge of political success.

Because of their focus of interest, the new intellectuals favored state control over many individual activities. State leadership in all kinds of collective programs such as the nationalization of industries, education, and social welfare as well as radical government measures for the improvement of agriculture and rural life received their enthusiastic support as consonant with their belief that only a strong and efficient state could lead China to prosperity. The Communists capitalized on these sentiments and practically rode to power on the wave of nationalism that swept the land.

Since 1949 this attitude has been skillfully promoted among the masses as well largely by means of various campaigns initiated by the students and government workers for the enlightenment of the general populace. For the first time the common people have acquired definite ideas about the country, their place in it, and its position in the family of nations. This political awareness has been followed by the many economic and social responsibilities imposed upon them by the present regime. Rural community organization has also been tightened. There is no doubt that through these programs the people have been brought into closer contact with the government. Feeling the influence of the state in their everyday lives, they inevitably develop a consciousness of their part in the larger environment. Their attitudes toward such involvement vary according to how their personal interests have been affected.

Attitudes toward Foreign Powers

To the Chinese, discrimination or prejudice based on racial differences alone had always been untenable. Their experiences with western powers in the nineteenth and early twentieth centuries, however, created a resentment toward particular foreign countries that gradually developed into race consciousness. In their contacts with colonialists and traders, the Chinese became aware that Europeans and Americans in general considered themselves superior not only technologically and culturally, but also racially. This assumption seemed to be borne out by the contradiction between western ideals and western behavior toward the Chinese: the white men used a different moral standard when dealing with the Chinese, treating them as members of an inferior race. An increasingly desperate desire to rid their country of foreign influences did in fact predispose the Chinese leaders to radical measures for their elimination.

Since coming to power, the Communists have skillfully used every opportunity to keep this sentiment alive. The latent antagonism of the Chinese toward foreign powers has not only helped the Communists to stir up antiwestern feelings but also provided a pretext for both international adventures and domestic repression. The Communists were able to justify the military adventure in Korea largely on this basis; and the belief of many intensely nationalist Chinese that only under Communist rule is China capable of throwing off the "imperialist yoke" and that for this purpose no sacrifice is too great testifies to the acceptance in the domestic area of the official Communist rationalization. British and French power being already on the wane, the United States is the logical focus of the most intensified anti-imperialist campaigns. It is doubtful if the Communists have completely negated the good will created by many American missionaries, philanthropic organizations, and private citizens, but it is certain that the Communists will continue to present the United States as the enemy of the Chinese people as long as the latter is determined to check further Communist aggression and expansion in Asia. As for the other western powers, especially Great Britain and France, there still seems to be considerable popular resentment against them because of their historical role in reducing China to a semicolony, but the government attitude toward them has varied, depending upon the nature of specific issues at hand.

On the other hand, there is an incessant profession of good will between the governments of China and the Soviet Union although, broadly speaking, the record of neither tsarist nor Soviet Russia in China would be likely to recommend the Russians to the Chinese. The Communist regime in Peking has found it difficult to convince the Chinese people of Russia's good intentions, especially in the face of fresh memories of the postwar Soviet dismantling of Manchurian factories, Soviet seizure of control of the Ch'ang-ch'un Railway, Soviet dominance in Sinkiang, and, from a truly Chinese point of view, the detachment from China of Outer Mongolia. Inasmuch as the nationalist aspirations of the Chinese people have been directed toward the expulsion of all forms of foreign influence, the distinction between foreign influence and the avowed dependence upon the Soviet Older Brother may be difficult to maintain.

Attitudes toward the Regime

Under the Communist system, attitudes and reactions of the people are molded by the state as far as its persuasive and coercive forces permit. The system being totalitarian, the state possesses absolute power over the dispensation of reward and punishment for individuals and groups according to their response to the state-approved ideology. By condemning traditional Chinese patterns of thought, political philosophy, economic structure, and social institutions as feudal, backward, and reactionary, the Communists hope to give the pseudo-scientific and dogmatic system of Marxism-Leninism-Maoism a cloak of respectability and legitimacy. All efforts in thought reform or ideological education are therefore aimed at the remolding of the people's attitudes and reactions. In so doing, the Communists naturally emphasize the accomplishments of the regime, which in some cases are concrete gains from a strictly nationalist point of view. The claim to big-power status, for example, has obviously had the effect of winning some of the educated and urban segments of the society to the state on the basis of its professed anti-imperialism. Industrial development and certain gains in public welfare likewise have inspired some elements of the population with a sense of progress.

The Chinese people have a long experience of making the best of unpleasant situations, but passivity and acquiescence need not be equated with content and enthusiasm. Nor is the generally passive acceptance of Communist rule in its initial stage a necessary indication of stability of the regime. Although the old order has been discredited and on the whole discarded, the present phase of Communist domination is still transitional in that a new order has not yet been firmly established. Furthermore, the Chinese poeple's desire for modernization or westernization did not begin with the introduction of Communist ideology, nor is it completely materialistic in orientation. Even if many Chinese have been impressed or even dazzled by the positive aspects of Communist rule, it seems probable that eventually they will decide that the price exacted from them, in terms of personal liberty and dignity, is too high.

Any generalization for the Chinese people as a whole runs a risk of oversimplification. To a degree this can be corrected by focusing on attitudes and reactions of several large groupings in the population, where certain generalities are perhaps possible. Older people, for example, are generally more conservative, less willing to adapt to change, and less likely to show enthusiasm for the Communist program. Wealthy people, with more to lose under Communist rule, are generally more dissatisfied with the regime than the others. These patterns of attitudes tend to cut across the occupational lines drawn in the groupings below.

508

Peasants

The Chinese Communists as well as the Russians exploited peasant aspirations, knowing full well that peasant interests were fundamentally at variance with Communist aims. According to the Communists, conservatism, narrow-mindedness, backwardness, and a traditional reverence for private ownership constituted common—and intolerable—characteristics of all peasants. Peasants were, furthermore, too often profoundly conservative defenders of a static social structure, respecting patriarchal authority and the traditional family system. Only after losing all patience as a result of suffering would peasants rebel against the leading forces in society. Although they made use of this rebellious spirit, the Communists had to destroy the peasant tradition for political as well as for economic reasons.

The rich landowners of China, who ranked with government bureaucrats in social status and whose interests were identified with those of traditional society, are all but nonexistent in China today. The Chinese peasant class consists chiefly of poor peasants and "middle peasants," now herded in the communes. These people have had little opportunity to identify themselves with the state or its destiny. In fact, their mode of living tends to confine their interest to their own villages or communes, or else to the limited area defined by the dialect they speak.

The Communist regime has made persistent efforts to "educate" the peasants. The fact that peasants have learned a few political terms as a result of propaganda does not, however, mean that they have become politically articulate, nor will forced collectivization raise their social awareness. Some regard the Communist effort as unwelcome interference, though the younger generation usually shows a more favorable response and indeed has spearheaded many rural programs.

During the land reform, the idea of being given land of his own with its promise of an improvement in his standard of living generated enthusiasm in the landless peasant, and his gain through the process of land redistribution must have given him some satisfaction. Subsequent grain taxes have remained heavy, however, and the drive to collectivize has caused much resistance. In the end the peasant becomes utterly confused and disillusioned for the commune has not only taken away the long-cherished land itself but also deprived him of the means of independent living. The fact that peasant immigrants have been arriving in sufficient numbers in many large urban centers to create serious problems for the authorities indicates that life in the rural communities does not offer them enough incentive.

The Chinese peasantry being extremely conservative in outlook and highly property-conscious, the program of collectivization has had to be implemented primarily through coercive means and the terror of the land reform period is still fresh in the minds of the peasantry. But even if the majority of peasants have resigned themselves to the fate of being no more than state laborers in the communes, their reaction to the regime's policy and treatment cannot but be conditioned by the state of economic well-being in which they find themselves. In this respect, the Communist regime has openly admitted that the peasants, as the largest single social group, have not fared nearly as well as other groups in the society, and that a contradiction exists between the agricultural and industrial sectors of the national economy. The state's avowed emphasis on industrialization quite naturally creates in the peasants a feeling that they have been exploited more ruthlessly than any other social group for an economic program that so far has failed to bring them any tangible benefits.

Moreover, after ten years of concentrated propaganda promising a glorious and prosperous tomorrow, the Communist regime has not been able to satisfy the basic needs of the people. Unless the peasants derive what they consider an appropriate portion of the fruits of the so-called national reconstruction, their attitude toward the regime will probably change from disillusionment to bitterness. Even passive resistance and noncooperation on the part of the peasants could have the effect of wrecking the economy, with far-reaching political and social repercussions.

Industrial Workers

In appraising the attitude of the laboring masses toward the Communist regime grounds for genuine dissatisfaction must be balanced against factors that favor the workers. To the Chinese working man the most important contribution of the Communists is the enhancement of his status. He is constantly being reminded of his importance in the gigantic plans for economic construction. He derives a measure of pride in his country when a steel plant is erected or when a bridge or new factory is opened, even though he may not readily believe, as he has been told, that the workers are the "masters of the new China." The elevation of picked individuals to the honorable status of "model worker" is a device to popularize the concept of devotion among those who best serve the interests of the state. The status of ordinary labor is further enhanced by the practice of requiring white-collar workers and professional people to participate in manual work.

The popularity of the regime among the workers can also be related to their higher material status. There is little question that workers have benefited from the job security, better housing, more comprehensive medical care, and increased opportunities for cultural and recreational activities provided by the state. Sanitariums, rest homes, workers' dormitories, and athletic teams have appeared in profusion. Although inadequacies in essential areas such as housing still remain, the workers are less likely to complain about shortcomings if they feel that the government is making a real attempt to overcome them.

On the liability side the workers are disillusioned by such equally apparent effects of Communist labor policy as the lack of substantial wage increases (although some relief was effected in the spring of 1957); the persistence of a low standard of living; the incessant demands for greater production; a harsher work schedule; the loss of leisure time due to meetings, rallies, and political classes; and the failure to achieve a visionary welfare program which the Communists themselves admit cannot be realized until the worker has made even greater sacrifices. Despite frequent Communist promises, no substantial alleviation of consumer shortages has or can be undertaken while the country is committed to an accelerated program of capital construction. The recent abolition of the piece-work system has actually resulted in a loss of take-home pay for a considerable number of workers in spite of the "leap forward" in production. Thus the worker's attitude toward the government and its policy must depend on how much he believes in a glorious tomorrow and how well he can put up with the physical hardships of today. In addition, the worker's attitude may also be influenced by the rise of a new managerial class which is being fostered by the government and which, for whatever reasons, receives better treatment than do those who work on the production line.

There may have been some difficulties over the use of foreign advisers and technicians. They had been employed in many factories in pre-Communist days and many workers had become accustomed to accepting the general excellence of foreign technology. But the privileged treatment accorded such technicians or advisers has always made them objects of resentment among Chinese workers. The Communist government, therefore, runs the risk

of demoralizing its own working force by according similar privileges to Soviet technicians in Chinese factories. Latent dissatisfaction may still exist even though the Russians have tried very
hard to fit into the Chinese pattern of life and make themselves
inconspicuous on the job.

Despite government exhortation, there is little evidence that
the worker has abandoned his hope of greater personal advancement in the material sense. Although here again the promotion of
the young and ambitious to serve in the huge government machinery may satisfy some of the workers, the lack of a substantial
rise in their standard of living will lead many others to feel that
their hopes cannot be realized under the present regime.

Handicraft workers and artisans, who constituted the bulk of
the former working class, have been reduced in number. Many
of them have gone to the factories. The remainder, who still constitute a considerable portion of the labor force, do not enjoy the
same esteem granted industrial workers and as a result are more
dissatisfied than the miners, steel workers, and others whom the
regime is attempting to build up as the backbone of the new
industrial labor force.

Students and Intellectuals

Of all the groups in China, the intellectuals are probably the most
varied in their attitudes. Without the social or economic focus of
a class, their attitudes do not show any distinctive group characteristics. There are those whose strong convictions make them
active leaders of social and political movements in defiance of
authoritarian rule; there are others whose education and experience
make them more flexible under pressure. Hence no dependable
generalizations on the attitudes of the Chinese intellectuals as a
group can be made.

There are, however, a few deductions that would be valid for
many Chinese intellectuals. The great majority are exceedingly
patriotic, for example, and it is therefore conceivable that to some
at least the Communist emphasis on loyalty to the state rather than
the traditional loyalty to the family must have a great appeal.
There is reason to believe that most of them who accepted or
sympathized with Communism in 1949 did so because the Communist program offered some hope of restoring China to a position
of dignity and power. After ten years of Communist rule, some
of the intellectuals are probably elated by the independence with
which China has been conducting its foreign affairs, and by the

feeling that China, at long last, has become a unified nation of importance. But on the negative side there are the restrictions on intellectual freedom imposed by the Communists. Furthermore, the Communist policy of gradually substituting newly trained and well-indoctrinated intellectuals for those with liberal or conservative backgrounds must have created a sense of insecurity among many older scholars.

For those intellectuals who aspire to high government positions, the road to success lies in cooperating with the Communist regime. But their tenure in office is precarious and, as recent events have shown, any open criticism of the party and government by these intellectuals has led to violent personal attacks on them by the government press and in party-sponsored meetings, resulting eventually in their dismissal, if not more severe punishment. Other intellectuals have modified their personal ambitions and attempted through teaching and technical service to make their training useful to the country. The Communist policy of finding a place for intellectuals in the national reconstruction program is undoubtedly welcomed by this group. However, the government's failure to place college graduates and other trained personnel where they are most needed has caused dissatisfaction and open criticism in the press. The government on its part has complained of "improper attitudes" toward such assignments of those graduates who expect soft, well-paid jobs because they are educated men and not production workers.

Since the early days of the Chinese Communist movement, the Communists have had the enthusiastic support of many students. In early 1957, however, reports began to come out of mainland China indicating widespread dissatisfaction and even riots among middle-school and university students. Student discontent can be attributed to the stifling academic atmosphere that has prevailed since the Communist assumption of power and also to the rigid regimentation to which the students have been subjected. Under the present education system, the students find no opportunity for self-expression, and government control over both academic and extracurricular activities has given rise to genuine resentment.

Judging by the importance of the intellectuals' role in Chinese society, the attitude of this group toward the Communist regime is a matter of significance. Upon the indoctrinated intellectuals the Communist regime relies for leadership in many government organizations, but there is every sign that the Communist ideology is becoming increasingly inadequate to satisfy the intellectual needs of the educated. Restlessness of the mind will lead to doubt and eventually to a search for remedies.

Businessmen and Industrialists

Few capitalists are left in Communist China today, but manufacturers and small businessmen, who made up a sizable segment of China's urban population, continue to exist and function under careful control of the state. In general, merchants and industrialists, who had been forced to operate under government restrictions even in pre-Communist days, are cool-headed and not easily swayed by high-sounding slogans. There have been few occasions when symbols of the state could evoke sentiment among the merchants and small manufacturers, except perhaps at a time when foreign goods flooded the Chinese market and caused dislocation in the economy.

Under the current regime, businessmen and industrialists as a group fare badly (possibly not much better than rich landowners), and the general mood in industrial and commercial circles is most probably unfavorable toward the government. The Communists have made it clear that small businessmen and manufacturers are only tolerated in the transitional stage of socialist transformation and that there will be no room for private enterprise in a socialist society. The current policy calls for full incorporation of private interests into the state by the end of the Second Five Year Plan in 1963. Meanwhile these people have to carry a large share of the tax burden and face the stiff competition of the state enterprises. There is evidence that the remaining businessmen and manufacturers, accustomed as they are to state interference, are finding the controls imposed by the government increasingly strict, making it ever more difficult to manipulate or elude restrictive measures. This general mood of discontent is particularly observable among merchants and private industrialists in large manufacturing centers of prewar days like Tientsin and Shanghai, which have been allocated the largest portions of government bonds.

Under present circumstances most businessmen and manufacturers have been forced to abandon or at least restrain their ambition of making profits and accumulating wealth. Some of them have changed their career in sheer exasperation. Only the more adaptable have escaped the wave of purges by cooperating with the regime and continuing their business. As a conciliatory gesture to win business support, the government has also appointed a number of erstwhile influential financiers and industrialists to serve in the bureaucracy; if nothing else, it provides this group of persons one temporary alternative to lost hopes.

An additional and aggravating factor has been the control over foreign trade. International traders, particularly those in the East China area, had their business virtually cut out from under them when the government took over all phases of foreign trade. Their role has been reduced to that of conducting limited export transactions supervised by the government, and there is little hope that they may be allowed to import western manufactured goods, at least not for private interests.

Women

Chinese women who have assumed more active roles in society are generally expected to have a degree of political consciousness similar to that of men of equal education and comparable environment. In many cases women prove to be even more loyal to the regime than men as a result of unprecedented government efforts to show women that they too can achieve social and political recognition by a strong show of national spirit.

Under the Communists, the role of women in society has been further broadened. Women are encouraged to participate in political activities and to work in industry. They are provided with facilities for child care and adult education. Thus freed from "feminine drudgery" they can reap additional welfare benefits by joining the labor force. If the increase in the number of women workers in factories could be taken as an indication of the women's own free choice, then women could indeed be said to favor the current regime. But this may not be a true index as it appears that many women are still reluctant to work in factories, those who do being propelled by financial necessity or state pressure rather than by an abstract desire to support the government's industrialization program.

Housewives of well-to-do families in larger cities may contrive to live in leisure, but those of more modest means have to work outside the home. Although many are resigned to their new role, especially if the work is not heavy or manual in character, and "labor heroines" are found in all industries, the regime finds it necessary to continue indoctrination of women to "respect and enjoy labor" and to take pride in political activity. The age-group differential in particular asserts itself in the reactions of women to the new regime: older women who had enjoyed respect and authority within the extended family are likely to dread the Communist effort to reduce it to conjugal types; younger women are apt to feel favorably disposed toward this aspect of the state's activities.

Minority Nationalities

The concept of China as a multinational state has great propaganda value for the regime in dealing with the minority nationalities, for whose protection it professes to have instituted a policy embodying their "free and equal" status with the dominant Han-Chinese population. It is clear from the government's own statements, however, that while it claims to protect the minority cultures, it is also intent upon eventually Sinicizing and communizing them. The fact that neither the minority people themselves nor the Han-Chinese cadres who worked among them shared wholeheartedly in the Communist programs was confirmed in a government report of 1952 that charged both the minority nationalities and the Han-Chinese with certain "improper" attitudes. The former were found to be hostile to some of the changes the government was trying to bring about; the latter were unwilling to delegate real authority to minority representatives and were also lacking in respect for the religious beliefs, customs, and traditions of the minority groups.

This resistance to change among the minority peoples continues to the present, but many of the key religious and educational institutions of the minority cultures have been thoroughly infiltrated by well-trained minority nationality cadres working under express orders from the central government. This Communist technique will undoubtedly make the minority groups more closely dependent on Peking. However, the resistance and inertia of these groups is high, as in Tibet and Sinkiang, and it is to be expected that some time will yet be required to bring these peoples into the Communist fold.

Other Groups

In addition to the groups already discussed, there are some others which, although minor in numerical strength, are of importance because their attitudes have some bearing on the tensions in Chinese society.

It is evident that all Communist party members and all government bureaucrats do not necessarily have the same attitudes, despite the fact that they are regimented by a well-controlled machinery.

As a whole, high-ranking Communist officials exhibit intense feelings of loyalty and dedication to the Communist cause. They work to strengthen the machinery that brought them to power, thereby making certain they will not be deposed. Granted that the behind-the-scenes struggle for personal power in a soviet-type system is most difficult for the outsider to discern until it breaks out into the open, there have been few signs of antagonism among the leaders. Although a few high-ranking Communist officials have been purged from the party, a purge as violent as that which took place in Russia in the 1930's cannot at present be predicted for China. Overshadowed by the unique personal prestige of Mao Tse-tung and the cohesive power of his personal leadership, the high-ranking Communist leaders have yet to offer evidence of power-seeking at the risk of disrupting party harmony and hegemony. This, of course, does not preclude the development of discord among party leaders.

The personnel in lower party echelons is subject to tremendous pressures from all sides. Even the most devoted party workers are expected to prove their loyalty to Communism. The fact that the party relies on close surveillance and an atmosphere of fear to keep members in line indicates the existence of some dissatisfaction and dissidence within the party ranks. Among new members there are possibly some opportunists who joined the party because they saw a chance for personal advancement. These people are apt to be less faithful to the party than those who joined it before it came to power. On the other hand, veteran party members may be provoked to discontent by the rise of new cadres to positions equal to or higher than their own. Generally speaking, cadres assigned to rural areas are less enthusiastic about the regime than those in urban areas who live in more comfortable circumstances and who have more frequent opportunities for promotion.

Former Nationalist officials and middle-class elements had their darkest days during the Three-Anti and Five-Anti campaigns, when almost all lived under the imminent threat of violence or death. After these intensive campaigns had subsided, a few of them still remained among the government bureaucracy. There is no doubt that these former Nationalist officials, some newly converted to Communism, will be reminded of the continual necessity of proving their loyalty to the regime. A sense of insecurity affects this group more than it does other segments of the Chinese population.

24. *Attitudes toward the Regime*

Traditionally resistant to government control, members of secret societies, composed mainly of peasantry and local tradesmen, had generally antigovernment and antiforeign characteristics. Some of them may have upheld a standard of loyalty to the individual above loyalty to the family or state; others may have condoned banditry and defied all forms of established order. For these reasons, the secret societies have been treated with utter ruthlessness by the Communist regime and this source of resistance is not likely to last much longer if the Communists succeed in further consolidating their political gains.

On the whole, however, the reaction of the Chinese people to Communist policies is one of acquiescence. They are pleased to find themselves members of a nation which, for the first time in over a century, can demand and expect international recognition of its power and importance in world affairs. They have been constantly reminded that their country can meet and exceed the requirements for modernization and industrialization in the foreseeable future. They are told, and some are willing to believe, that they have a mission in the new world: to help other Asian countries to "throw off the colonial yoke" and to join the "free and united democratic nations" of the Communist bloc. By fanning the fire of anti-imperialism and by using saturation in its propaganda tactics, the Communist regime has succeeded, at least partially, in satisfying the nationalist aspirations of the population. But there is a price to pay for these gains and no doubt many people, aside from the devoted party and government workers, hold at least some serious though secret reservations about the new regime.

TABLES

Table 1. RESULTS OF THE 1953 CENSUS

By direct registration	574,205,940
Estimates for border regions and other areas where no elections took place	8,397,477
Taiwan(a)	7,591,298
Overseas Chinese and students abroad(b)	11,743,320
Total	601,938,035

(a) The population of Taiwan, according to the census taken by the Nationalist government in October 1950, was 7,647,703, excluding troops. The more recent estimate made in mid-1957 raises the total figure to more than 10 million.

(b) Other sources indicate that the total number of overseas Chinese may be well over 14 million. There are almost 11 million in Southeast Asia: Thailand, 3.5 million; Indonesia, 2.5 million; Malaya, 1.9 million; South Vietnam, 1 million; Singapore, 960,000; Burma, 300,000; Philippines, 300,000; North Vietnam, 200,000; Sarawak, 150,000. (*Newsweek*, January 30, 1956.) Recent estimates give 3 million Chinese in Hong Kong and more than 300,000 in Macao. According to the 1950 census, there were about 118,000 Chinese in the United States.

Source: *Jen-min shou-t'se* (People's Handbook), 1955, p. 251.

Table 2. **PARTY MEMBERSHIP IN PROVINCES AND REPRESENTATIVES IN PARTY CONGRESSES**

Province	Population (in millions)	Party Membership	Ratio to Population	Number of Provincial Congress Members	Number of National Congress Members
Anhwei	30.3				
Chekiang	22.9	190,000	120	849	
Tsinghai	1.7				
Fukien	13.1				
Honan	44.2	509,000	87	979	53
Hopeh	36.0			634	70
Heilungkiang	11.9				
Hunan	33.2	280,000	118	596	31
Hupeh	27.8				
Inner Mongolia	6.1	152,000	40	399	21
Kansu	12.9	216,000	61	703	17
Kiangsi	16.8	250,000	67	499	23
Kiangsu	41.2				
Kirin	11.2	196,000	57	690	
Kwangsi	19.5				
Kwangtung	34.7			41	28
Kweichow	15.0	139,000	108	400	
Liaoning	18.5	400,000	46	623	
Shansi	14.3				
Shantung	48.8	1,120,000	40	975	
Shensi	15.9	200,000		470	24
Sinkiang	4.8	68,000	71	561	
Szechwan	62.3			715	53
Yunnan	17.5	182,000	70	744	
Shanghai(a)	6.9	150,000	41	700	37
Tientsin(a)	2.7				
Central Government		40,000		601	

(a) Special municipalities.

Source: *China News Analysis,* No. 144 (August 17, 1956), p. 6.

Table 3. GROWTH OF THE CHINESE COMMUNIST PARTY

Year	Membership
1921	50
1924-27	59,000
1927	10,000
1934	300,000
1937	40,000
1945	1,210,000
1950	5,800,000
1953	6,000,000
1954	6,500,000
1956	10,734,000

Source: *Shih-shih shou-t'se* (Current Events Handbook), No. 16 (figures for 1921 to 1950); *People's Daily*, February 18, 1954 (1953 and 1954 figures); and the New China News Agency, September 13, 1956 (1956 figures).

Table 4. REPRESENTATION IN THE NATIONAL PEOPLE'S CONGRESS

Group	Population (in millions)	Number of Deputies	Ratio
Urban residents—workers	30	300	100,000
Members of the armed forces	6	60	100,000
Minority nationalities	35	150	235,000
Overseas Chinese	12	30	400,000
Rural inhabitants—farmers	550	680	800,000

Source: Adapted from *Jen-min shou-t'se* (People's Handbook), 1955, pp. 18-22, 32-33.

Table 5. BUDGETS OF COMMUNIST CHINA, 1952-59

(in millions)

	1952			1953		
	New JMP Yuan(a)	American Dollars(b)	Percent	New JMP Yuan	American Dollars	Percent
Revenues						
Taxes	9,175.8	4,120	57.8	11,469.6	4,685	49.1
Industrial and commercial				(8,746.9)	(3,573)	(37.5)
Agricultural				(2,566.2)	(1,048)	(11.0)
Other				(156.5)	(64)	(0.6)
Income from state enterprises	3,697.0	1,660	23.3	6,998.0	2,859	30.0
Credit and insurance income	444.3	200	2.8	1,027.4	420	4.4
Other revenues	2,568.3	1,153	16.1	3,855.1	1,575	16.5
Subtotal	15,885.4	7,133	100.0	23,350.1	9,539	100.0
Balance from last year	....			....		
Total	15,885.4	7,133	100.0	23,350.1	9,539	100.0
Expenditures						
Economic construction	5,806.1	2,607	36.6	10,352.8	4,229	44.3
Social, cultural, and educational	2,018.5	906	12.7	3,480.8	1,421	14.9
National defense	4,437.9	1,993	27.9	5,225.4	2,134	22.4
Administration	2,370.4	1,019	14.3	2,378.0	971	10.2
Other expenditures	1,252.5(c)	608(c)	8.5(c)	364.5	149	1.6
Subtotal	15,885.4	7,133	100.0	21,801.5	8,904	93.4
Reserve or carry-over	....			1,548.4	634	6.6
Total	15,885.4	7,133	100.0	23,349.9	9,538	100.0

(a) The monetary reform of March 1955 made the new Jen-min-pi (People's Currency) the legal tender. The conversion rate is 1 new JMP to 10,000 old JMP. For the sake of convenience, the figures for earlier years are also expressed in new JMP.

(b) The following monthly average exchange rates in new JMP yuan per American dollar are used for conversion: 1950, 3.26; 1951, 2.25; 1952, 2.23; 1953 to 1956, 2.46; 1957-59, 2.343.

(c) Includes a statistical discrepancy of 568,400,000 new JMP yuan.

Table 5. (continued)

	1954			1955		
	New JMP Yuan	American Dollars	Percent	New JMP Yuan	American Dollars	Percent
Revenues						
Taxes	13,559.7	5,501	49.4	13,780.6	5,602	44.2
Industrial and commercial	10,445.5	4,237	38.0	10,000.0	4,065	32.1
Agricultural	3,114.2	1,264	11.4	2,800.0	1,138	9.0
Other				980.6	399	3.1
Income from state enterprises	8,334.2	3,380	30.3	11,115.8	4,519	35.7
Credit and insurance income				3,153.4	1,281	10.1
Other revenues	1,294.3	525	4.7	(d)	(d)	(d)
Subtotal	23,188.2	9,406	84.4	28,049.8	11,402	90.0
Balance from last year	4,282.7	1,738	15.6	3,142.7	1,278	10.0
Total	27,470.9	11,144	100.0	31,192.5	12,680	100.0
Expenditures						
Economic construction	11,322.7	4,593	41.2	14,188.8	5,768	45.5
Social, cultural, and educational	3,669.2	1,489	13.4	3,850.7	1,565	12.4
National defense	5,267.0	2,137	19.2	7,193.2	2,924	23.1
Administration	4,686.9	1,901	17.0	2,241.6	911	7.2
Other expenditures				1,245.2	506	4.0
Subtotal	24,945.8	10,120	90.8	28,719.5	11,674	92.2
Reserve or carry-over	2,525.1	1,024	9.2	2,473.0	1,006	7.8
Total	27,470.9	11,144	100.0	31,192.5	12,680	100.0

(d) Included in "Credit and insurance income."

Table 5. (continued)

	1956			1957		
	New JMP Yuan	American Dollars	Percent	New JMP Yuan	American Dollars	Percent
Revenues						
Taxes	13,980.0	5,683	45.5	14,570	6,206.8	49.7
Industrial and commercial	(9,970.0)	(4,053)	(32.5)	(10,500)	(4,473.0)	(35.8)
Agricultural	(3,020.0)	(1,228)	(9.8)	(2,990)	(1,273.7)	(10.2)
Other	(990.0)	(402)	(3.2)	(1,080)	(460.1)	(3.7)
Income from state enterprises	14,328.1	5,824	46.6	13,669	5,823.0	46.7
Credit and insurance income	742.0	302	2.4	623	265.4	2.1
Other revenues	681.0	277	2.2	430	183.2	1.5
Subtotal	29,731.1	12,086	96.7	29,292	12,478.4	100.0
Balance from last year	1,011.0	411	3.3	....	....	....
Total	30,742.1	12,497	100.0	29,292	12,478.4	100.0
Expenditures						
Economic construction	16,055.2	6,526	52.2	13,683	5,829.0	46.7
Social, cultural, and educational	3,916.0	1,592	12.7	4,835	2,059.7	16.5
National defense	6,141.4	2,497	20.0	5,523	2,352.8	18.9
Administration	2,410.9	980	7.8	2,445	1,041.6	8.3
Other expenditures	1,428.5	581	4.7	2,212	942.3	7.6
Subtotal	29,952.0	12,176	97.4	28,698	12,225.3	98.0
Reserve or carry-over	790.8	321	2.6	594	253.0	2.0
Total	30,742.8	12,497	100.0	29,292	12,478.4	100.0

Table 5. (continued)

	1958			1959 (preliminary)		
	New JMP Yuan	American Dollars	Percent	New JMP Yuan	American Dollars	Percent
Revenues						
Taxes	16,497	7,027.7	49.9	......	......	......
Industrial and commercial	12,390	5,278.1	37.5	......	......	......
Agricultural	2,997	1,276.7	9.1	......	......	......
Other	1,110	472.9	3.4	......	......	......
Income from state enterprises	15,716	6,695.0	47.5	......	......	......
Credit and insurance income	630	268.4	1.9	......	......	......
Other revenues	220	93.7	0.7	......	......	......
Subtotal	33,063	14,084.8	100.0	......	......	......
Balance from last year	......	......	......	......	......	......
Total	33,063	14,084.8	100.0	52,000	(22,152.0)	100.0
Expenditures						
Economic construction	17,548	7,475.4	53.1	31,720	(13,512.7)	61.0
Social, cultural, and educational	4,896	2,085.7	14.8	5,720	2,436.7	11.0
National defense	5,000	2,130.0	15.1	5,824	2,481.0	11.2
Administration	2,000	852.0	6.0	......	......	......
Other expenditures	2,528	1,076.9	7.6	......	......	......
Subtotal	31,972	13,620.1	96.7	......	......	......
Reserve or carry-over	1,091	464.8	3.3	......	......	......
Total	33,063	14,084.8	100.0	52,000	(22,152.0)	100.0

Source: Adapted from Wu, Yuan-li, An *Economic Survey of Communist China*, pp. 97-99; and official Chinese Communist budget reports.

Table 6. **ECONOMIC CONSTRUCTION, 1950-58**
(in millions)

	New JMP Yuan	American Dollars(a)	Percent of Total Government Expenditures
1950 *(actual)*	1,736	538	25.5
1951 *(actual)*	3,511	1,545	29.5
1952 *(budget)*	5,806	2,607	36.6
1952 *(actual)*	7,307	3,288	44.8
1953 *(budget)*	10,353	4,229	44.3
1953 *(actual)*	8,602	3,495	33.5
1954 *(budget)*	11,323	4,593	41.2
1954 *(actual)*	12,358	5,023	40.2
1955 *(budget)*	14,189	5,768	45.5
1955 *(actual)*	13,762	5,594	45.3
1956 *(budget)*	16,055	6,526	52.2
1956 *(actual)*	15,915	6,779.8	52.1
1957 *(budget)*	13,683	5,829.0	46.7
1957 *(actual)*	14,861	6,330.8	48.4
1958 *(budget)*	17,548	7,475.4	53.1

(a) For conversion rates, see footnote (b) to Table 5.

Source: Same as for Table 5.

Table 7. **BUDGETED ECONOMIC CONSTRUCTION EXPENDITURES BY CATEGORIES, 1953-58**

(in percentage of total)

	1953	1954	1955
Industrial enterprises under state budget	46.1	47.8	45.0
Heavy industry	.....	(37.5)	(40.3)
Light industry	.....	(10.3)	(4.7)
Agriculture, forestry, and water conservation	11.4	10.6	9.3
Railways, communications, post and telecommunications	14.3	15.6	15.1
Trade and banking	4.3	11.3	20.1
Others	23.9	14.7	10.5
Total	100.0	100.0	100.0

	1956	1957	1958
Industrial enterprises under state budget	53.2	59.4	52.3
Heavy industry	(47.1)	.....	.....
Light industry	(6.1)	.....	.....
Agriculture, forestry, and water conservation	13.6	14.9	16.8
Railways, communications, post and telecommunications	18.0	16.2	14.5
Trade and banking	5.4	1.9	1.6
Others	9.8	7.6	14.9
Total	100.0	100.0	100.0

Source: Adapted from Wu, Yuan-li, *An Economic Survey of Communist China*, p. 252; and official Chinese Communist reports.

Table 8. **ACTUAL GOVERNMENT EXPENDITURES OF COMMUNIST CHINA, 1950-57**

(in millions)

	1950			1951		
	New JMP Yuan	*American Dollars(a)*	*Percent*	*New JMP Yuan*	*American Dollars*	*Percent*
Economic construction	1,735.6	538	25.5	3,511.0	1,545	29.5
Social, cultural, and educational	755.2	234	11.1	1,343.6	591	11.3
National defense	2,827.4	876	41.5	5,060.8	2,227	42.5
Administration	1,313.2	407	19.3	1,745.6	768	14.7
Other expenditures	176.8	55	2.6	241.4	106	2.0
Subtotal	6,808.2	2,110	100.0	11,902.4	5,237	100.0
Reserve or carry-over	....	....	....	....		....
Total	6,808.2	2,110	100.0	11,902.4	5,237	100.0

	1952			1953		
	New JMP Yuan	*American Dollars*	*Percent*	*New JMP Yuan*	*American Dollars*	*Percent*
Economic construction	7,307.0	3,288	44.8	....	....	....
Social, cultural, and educational	2,233.3	1,005	13.7	....	....	....
National defense	4,277.7	1,925	26.2	....	....	....
Administration	1,933.7	870	11.9	....	....	....
Other expenditures	570.2	257	3.4	....	....	....
Subtotal	16,321.9	7,345	100.0	21,388.3	8,694	80.3
Reserve or carry-over	....	....		4,282.7	1,741	19.7
Total	16,321.9	7,345	100.0	25,671.0	10,435	100.0

(a) For conversion rates, see footnote (b) to Table 5.

Table 8. (continued)

	1954			1955		
	New JMP Yuan	American Dollars	Percent	New JMP Yuan	American Dollars	Percent
Economic construction	12,358.2	5,023	40.2	13,762.1	5,594	45.3
Social, cultural, and educational	3,460.5	1,407	11.3	3,189.3	1,296	10.5
National defense	5,813.5	2,363	18.9	6,499.9	2,642	21.4
Administration	2,162.1	879	7.0	2,154.1	876	7.1
Other expenditures	838.1	340	2.8	3,741.6	1,521	12.3
Subtotal	24,632.4	10,012	80.2	29,347.0	11,929	96.6
Reserve or carry-over	6,113.4	2,485	19.8	1,011.0	412	3.4
Total	30,745.8	12,497	100.0	30,358.0	12,341	100.0

	1956			1957		
	New JMP Yuan	American Dollars	Percent	New JMP Yuan	American Dollars	Percent
Economic construction	15,915	6,779.8	52.1	14,861	6,330.8	48.4
Social, cultural, and educational	4,596	1,957.9	15.0	4,739	2,018.8	15.4
National defense	6,116	2,605.4	20.0	5,509	2,346.8	17.9
Administration	2,660	1,133.2	8.7	2,322	989.2	7.6
Other expenditures	1,287	548.3	4.2	3,118(a)	1,328.3	10.2
Subtotal	30,574	13,024.5	100.0	30,549	13,013.9	99.5
Reserve or carry-over	......	......	......	153	65.2	0.5
Total	30,574	13,024.5	100.0	30,702	13,079.1	100.0

(a) Also included in "Other expenditures" are foreign loan repayment, 1,293 million; repayment of overdraft and credit funds allotted to the banks, 1,553 million; and rotating funds allotted to local authorities, 73 million.

Source: Same as for Table 5.

Table 9. **REALIZED GOVERNMENT REVENUE OF COMMUNIST CHINA, 1950-57**

(in millions)

	1950			1951		
	New JMP Yuan	American Dollars(a)	Percent	New JMP Yuan	American Dollars	Percent
Taxes	4,898.6	1,518	70.5	8,113.3	3,570	57.1
Industrial and commercial	(2,987.8)	(926)	(43.0)	(5,847.8)	(2,573)	(41.2)
Agricultural	(1,910.5)	(592)	(27.5)	(2,169.9)	(955)	(15.3)
Other	0.3	neg.	neg.	95.6	42	0.6
Income from state enterprises	869.4	270	12.5	3,053.5	1,343	21.5
Credit and insurance income	327.4	102	4.7	567.8	250	4.0
Other revenues	848.6	263	12.3	2,474.0	1,088	17.4
Subtotal	6,944.0	2,153	100.0	14,208.6	6,251	100.0
Balance from last year	......	......	......	......	......	......
Total	6,944.0	2,153	100.0	14,208.6	6,251	100.0

(a) For conversion rates, see footnote (b) to Table 5.

	1952			1953		
	New JMP Yuan	American Dollars	Percent	New JMP Yuan	American Dollars	Percent
Taxes	9,621.8	4,330	50.8	......	......	......
Industrial and commercial	(6,898.3)	(3,104)	(36.4)	......	......	......
Agricultural	(2,560.2)	(1,152)	(13.5)	......	......	......
Other	163.3	74	0.9	......	......	......
Income from state enterprises	4,657.9	2,096	24.6	......	......	......
Credit and insurance income	251.0	113	1.3	......	......	......
Other revenues	4,397.1	1,979	23.3	......	......	......
Subtotal	18,927.8	8,518	100.0	21,547.7	8,759	83.9
Balance from last year	......	......	......	4,123.3	1,676	16.1
Total	18,927.8	8,518	100.0	25,671.0	10,435	100.0

Table 9. (continued)

	1954			1955		
	New JMP Yuan	American Dollars	Percent	New JMP Yuan	American Dollars	Percent
Taxes	13,218.1	5,373	43.1	12,745.4	5,181	42.0
Industrial and commercial	(8,971.5	(3,647	(29.2	(8,725.5	(3,547	(28.4
Agricultural	3,277.5	1,332	10.7	3,054.3	1,242	10.1
Other	969.1	394	3.2	965.6	392	3.5
Income from state enterprises	9,961.5	4,049	32.4	11,194.0	4,550	36.8
Credit and insurance income	3,057.2	1,243	9.9	2,360.8	960	7.8
Other revenues	......(b)	......(b)	......(b)	903.1	367	3.0
Subtotal	26,236.8	10,665	85.4	27,203.3	11,058	89.6
Balance from last year	4,509.0	1,832	14.6	3,154.7	1,242	10.4
Total	30,745.8	12,497	100.0	30,358.0	12,300	100.0

(b) Included in "Credit and insurance income."

	1956			1957		
	New JMP Yuan	American Dollars	Percent	New JMP Yuan	American Dollars	Percent
Taxes	14,088.3	6,001.6	46.1	15,439	6,577.0	50.3
Industrial and commercial	(10,098.4	(4,301.9	(33.0	......	......	......
Agricultural	2,965.4	1,263.3	9.7	......	......	......
Other	1,024.5	436.4	3.4	......	......	......
Income from state enterprises	13,426.4	5,719.6	43.9	14,221	6,058.1	46.3
Credit and insurance income	723.9	308.4	2.4	673	286.7	2.2
Other revenues	1,324.5(c)	564.2	4.3	369	157.2	1.2
Subtotal	29,563.1	12,593.9	96.7	30,702	13,079.0	100.0
Balance from last year	1,011.0	430.7	3.3	......	......	......
Total	30,574.1	13,024.6	100.0	30,702	13,079.0	100.0

(c) Included in "Other revenues" are 504.8 million from central and local governments, deposits from the banks made in 1954, and bank overdraft of 180.3 million.

Source: Adapted from Wu, Yuan-li, *An Economic Survey of Communist China*, pp. 27-99.

534

Table 10. SOURCES OF GOVERNMENT RECEIPTS, 1953 AND 1957
(in percentage of the total annual receipts)

	1953	1957
Government enterprises, supply and marketing cooperatives and handicraft cooperatives	65.4	79.2
Joint state-private industrial and trade enterprises	1.2	7.2
Cooperative and individual farms	13.4	11.2
Private industries and trade	16.9	1.1
Other[a]	3.1	1.3

(a) Including fees, bond purchases by urban residents, etc.

Source: *Jen-min shou-t'se* (People's Handbook), 1958, p. 218.

Table 11. GRAIN PRODUCTION IN COMMUNIST CHINA
(in million metric tons)

Year	Total Grain[a]	Rice	Wheat
1949	113.18	48.64	13.81
1950	131.40	....	....
1951	143.40	....	....
1952	163.91	68.42	18.12
1953	166.83	71.27	18.28
1954	169.51	70.85	23.33
1955	184.00	77.93	22.87
1956	184.25	....	....
1957	192.81	....	23.60
1958 (preliminary)	250.00	....	....
1959 (plan)	275.00	....	....
Prewar average	140.00	50.00	22.00

(a) Including soybeans with the exception of 1958 and 1959.

Source: Communique of the State Statistical Bureau of China on the Development of the National Economy and the Results of the Implementation of the State Plan for 1954, Peking, September 21, 1955; Communique on the Fulfillment of the National Economic Plan for 1955, Peking, January 14, 1956; and New China News Agency, August 26, 1959.

Table 12. EMPLOYMENT, MOTIVE POWER, AND NUMBER OF MANUFACTURING CONCERNS IN CHINA PROPER, 1947

City	Number of Factories	Total Employment	Motive Power Horse-power	Motive Power Kilovolt-ampere
Shanghai	7,738	406,371	325,268.2	73,063.8
Nanking	888	12,010	18,077.5	4.0
Tientsin	1,211	65,734	110,476.9	9,624.0
Peiping (Peking)	272	9,974	13,256.9	24,509.0
Hankow	459	23,863	10,167.0	4,527.0
Ch'ang-sha and Heng-yang	216	10,289	4,040.5	39.3
Nan-ch'ang and Chiu-chiang (Kiukiang)	161	7,192	4,059.0	636.0
Chungking	661	36,940	11,709.5	3,545.0
K'un-ming	66	7,543	5,298.5	....
Kuei-yang	83	5,597	1,311.1	94.4
Canton	473	30,016	10,022.1	476.0
Swatow	121	5,942	266.0	5.0
Sian	69	7,090	3,655.0	506.0
Lan-chou	39	3,212	1,974.2	28.0
Fu-chou (Foochow)	176	3,698	3,291.0	....
Tsingtao	185	31,518	34,403.0	14,000.0

Source: Adapted from National Economic Commission, *Industrial Survey of Principal Cities: Preliminary Report*, Peiping, 1948.

Table 13. **EMPLOYMENT, MOTIVE POWER, AND NUMBER OF FIRMS IN CHINA BY INDUSTRIES, 1947**[a]

Industry	Employment	Motive Power		Number of Factories
		Horse-power	Kilovolt-ampere	
Textiles	337,734	329,213.5	36,408.5	3,773
Food processing	108,297	74,661.0	14,547.3	1,379
Chemicals	78,905	80,423.3	9,841.5	1,553
Apparel	51,981	9,482.4	20.0	1,783
Paper and printing	38,569	56,624.3	2,489.0	1,669
Machinery	36,392	20,670.5	161.5	1,505
Metallurgical	28,747	65,781.8	12,252.2	494
Metal products	21,893	26,744.4	61,041.0	682
Electrical equipment	16,213	7,093.6	42.8	303
Clay and stone	15,731	117,676.3	24,965.0	152
Transportation equipment	12,380	4,845.5	255.0	269
Woodworking	4,497	4,693.5	60.0	156
Miscellaneous	20,311	30,362.3	127.5	360
Total	771,650	828,272.4	162,211.3	14,078

(a) In addition to the cities listed in Table 12, these data also include Taiwan and the Manchurian cities under Nationalist control at that time. If the Manchurian factories were excluded, the predominance of the light manufacturing industries would be even more marked.

Source: Adapted from National Economic Commission, *Industrial Survey of Principal Cities: Preliminary Report,* Peiping, 1948.

Table 14. CONTRIBUTION OF VARIOUS ECONOMIC SECTORS TO TOTAL VALUE OF INDUSTRIAL OUTPUT, 1949-57[a]

(percent of total)

Year	State	Joint Enterprise	Cooperatives	Private[b]
1949	26.3	1.6	0.4	71.7
1951	45.0	3.0	2.0	50.0
1952	41.5	4.0	3.2	51.3
1953	43.1	4.5	3.8	48.6
1954	47.1	9.8	4.7	38.4
1955	51.3	13.1	6.3	29.3
1956	54.5	27.1	17.1	1.3
1957 (plan)	61.3	22.1	4.4	12.2

(a) No statistics available for 1950.
(b) Including private handicraft enterprises.

Source: *Jen-min shou-t'se* (People's Handbook), 1957, p. 428; and *ibid.*, 1958, p. 456.

Table 15. **PRODUCTION OF SELECTED COMMODITIES IN MAINLAND CHINA, 1949-52**

Product	Units in	Peak	1949	1950	1951	1952
Pig iron	1,000 metric tons	1,900	244	961	1,399	1,880(b)
Crude steel	1,000 metric tons	920	158	605	894	1,350
Rolled steel	1,000 metric tons	500(a)	90(a)	251	432	738
Coal	1,000 metric tons	63,000	31,535	41,596	51,680	63,530(b)
Crude oil	1,000 metric tons	330(a)	125(a)	201	304	436
Cement	1,000 metric tons	2,280	657	1,400	2,473	2,860
Paper	1,000 metric tons	163	108	139	238	370(b)
Flour	1,000 metric tons	2,450(a)	1,911(a)	1,360	1,940	2,990
Sugar	1,000 metric tons	410(a)	164(a)			451
Cotton yarn	1,000 bales	2,400	1,728	2,383	2,206	3,618
Cotton cloth	1,000 bolts	41,000(a)	29,930(a)			111,630
Cigarettes	1,000,000 sticks	82,000(a)	47,000(a)			132,500
Electric power	1,000,000 kilowatt hours	6,000	4,320	4,579	6,030	7,260

(a) Estimates made by W. W. Rostow.

(b) The output figures including production by handicraft methods were, for 1952: pig iron, 1,930,000 tons; coal, 66,490 tons; and paper, 540,000 tons (New China News Agency, April 13, 1959).

Source: Adapted from Chao, I-nung, "1955 Industrial Construction and Production of Communist China," *Tsu-kuo* (China Weekly), January 16, 1956, p. 19; Shabad, T., "Communist China's Production Statistics," *Far Eastern Survey*, 1955, p. 106 ff.; Rostow, W. W., *The Prospects for Communist China*, p. 239; Wu, Yuan-li, *An Economic Survey of Communist China*, p. 260; and official Chinese Communist reports.

Table 16. PRODUCTION OF SELECTED COMMODITIES IN MAINLAND CHINA, 1952-57

Product	Units in	1952	1953	1954	1955	1956	1957 (plan)	1957 (actual)
Pig iron	1,000 metric tons	1,880(a)	2,261	3,074	3,686	4,777	4,674	5,940
Crude steel	1,000 metric tons	1,350	1,768	2,210	2,686	4,465	4,120	5,350
Rolled steel	1,000 metric tons	738	989	1,160	1,575	3,921	3,047	4,478
Coal	1,000 metric tons	63,530(b)	69,245	83,094	92,750	105,922	112,985	130,000
Crude oil	1,000 metric tons	436	627	797	959	1,163	2,012	1,460
Electric power	1,000,000 kilowatt-hours	7,260	9,140	10,970	12,560	16,590	15,900	19,300
Cement	1,000 metric tons	2,860	3,861	4,591	....	6,393	6,000	6,860
Paper	1,000 metric tons	270	427	556	....	746	655	1,220(c)
Flour	1,000 metric tons	2,990	3,438	3,748	....	....	4,670	....
Sugar	1,000 metric tons	451	....	....	518	....	686	864
Cotton yarn	1,000 bales	3,618	4,088	4,578	3,970	5,246	5,000	4,650
Cotton cloth	1,000 bolts	111,630	127,263	143,818	....	....	163,721	.........(d)

(a) 1,930,000 tons if steel produced by native furnaces is included.

(b) 66,490,000 tons if coal produced by native pits is included.

(c) Including hand-made paper. This is believed to have been excluded in the data for the earlier years. The figure for 1952, including hand-made paper, was reported at 540,000 tons.

(d) Reported to be 5.05 billion meters, including home-spun cloth. The corresponding figure for 1952 was 3.83 billion meters.

Source: Same as for Table 15.

Table 17. COMMUNIST CHINA, JAPAN, AND INDIA: COMPARISON OF SELECTED INDUSTRIAL AND MINERAL PRODUCTION, 1957

Total Production

Item	Unit in	Mainland China	Japan	India(c)
Electricity	1,000,000 K.W.H.	19,300	73,582(b)	10,810
Pig iron	Metric tons	5,940,000	6,815,457	....
Coal	1,000 metric tons	130,000	51,732	43,717
Cement	Metric tons	6,860,000	15,176,298	5,629,200
Soda ash	Metric tons	506,000	394,786	....
Sulphuric acid	Metric tons	632,000	6,291,710	....
Crude steel	Metric tons	5,350,000	12,570,166	1,723,200(d)
Cotton yarn	1,000 pounds	1,860,000	1,139,948	1,769,853

Per Capita Production(a)

Item	Unit	Mainland China Production	Japan Production	Japan Index, China=100	India Production	India Index, China=100
Electricity	Kilowatt hours	30.4	809.5	2,662.8	27.5	90.5
Pig iron	Kilograms	9.4	75.0	797.9	....	....
Coal	Kilograms	205.0	569.1	277.6	111.4	54.3
Cement	Kilograms	10.8	167.0	1,546.3	14.3	132.4
Soda ash	Kilograms	0.8	4.3	537.5	....	....
Sulphuric acid	Kilograms	1.0	69.2	6,920.0	....	....
Crude steel	Kilograms	8.4	138.3	1,646.4	4.4	52.4
Cotton yarn	Pounds	2.9	12.5	431.0	4.5	155.2

(a) The population data used are: China, 634,271,000, projected at 102.1 percent of the 1956 population; Japan, 90,900,000; and India, 392,440,000.

(b) Fiscal year (April-March).

(c) Annual rate based on the production of January-November.

(d) Annual rate based on the production of January-October.

Source: New China News Agency, April 13, 1959; Japan, Ministry of Finance, Quarterly Bulletin of Financial Statistics, Second and Third Quarters, 1958 Fiscal Year (Tokyo, October 1958), pp. 92-3; the United Nations, Economic Survey of Asia and the Far East, 1957, pp. 198, 221-2.

Table 18. **PRODUCTION OF SELECTED COMMODITIES IN MAINLAND CHINA, 1958**

Product	Thousand Metric Tons unless Otherwise Noted	Increase over 1957 in Percent
Pig iron	13,690	131
Crude steel	11,080	107
Coal	270,000	108
Crude oil	2,260	55
Electric power[a]	27,500	42
Cement	9,300	36
Paper	1,630	34
Sugar	900	4
Cotton yarn[b]	6,100	31
Cotton cloth[c]	5,700	13

(a) Million kilowatt-hours.
(b) Thousand bales.
(c) Million meters.

Source: New China News Agency, April 14, 1959.

Table 19. **ESTIMATES OF COMMUNIST CHINA'S FOREIGN TRADE, 1950 AND 1953-57**
(in million JMP)

	Total	Exports	Imports
1950	4,158	2,120	2,038
1953	8,112	3,488	4,624
1954	8,487	4,074	4,413
1955	11,024	4,961	6,063
1956	10,865	5,568	5,297

Source: Adapted from Mah, Feng-hwa, "The First Five-Year Plan and Its International Aspects," in Remer, C. F. (ed.), *Three Essays on the International Economics of Communist China*, 1959; and official Chinese Communist reports.

542

Table 20. **GROWTH IN EDUCATIONAL FACILITIES, 1949-58**

	1949	1958(b)
Primary Education		
Schools	346,700	950,000
Students	24,390,000	92,000,000
Secondary Education		
Schools	5,216	118,000
Students	1,270,000	15,000,000
Higher Education		
Schools	227(a)	1,400
Students	117,133	790,000

(a) 1950 figure, including also schools in Taiwan and political party and army schools on the mainland.

(b) The 1958 figures are taken from the *People's Daily*, November 1, 1958. In a report to the 1959 session of the National People's Congress the Minister of Education, Yang Hsiu-feng, gave the following enrollment figures: primary schools (in 1958), 86 million; ordinary secondary schools, 8.52 million; vocational secondary schools, 1.47 million; agricultural and other professional secondary schools (organized in 1958), 2 million; and higher educational institutions, 0.6 million. No figures were given, however, for the number of schools or higher educational institutions.

A SELECTED BIBLIOGRAPHY

A SELECTED BIBLIOGRAPHY

Chapter 1.   THE CULTURE AND THE SOCIETY

BODDE, DERK. *China's Cultural Tradition: What and Whither?* ("Source Problems in World Civilization.") New York: Rinehart, 1957.

CHI, CH'AO-TING. *Key Economic Areas in Chinese History, As Revealed by the Development of Public Works for Water-Control.* London: Allen & Unwin, 1936.
> *Analysis of the role of water-control development in shaping Chinese history, based mainly on records in provincial gazetteers.*

CHIANG, MONLIN. *Tides from the West.* New Haven: Yale University Press, 1947. (Reprinted in 1957 by the China Culture Publishing Foundation, Taipei.)
> *Autobiography illustrating the cultural and educational changes that took place in China as a result of the western impact.*

EBERHARD, WOLFRAM. "The Formation of Chinese Civilization According to Socio-anthropological Analysis," *Sociologus*, VII (1957), 97-112.

FAIRBANK, JOHN KING (ed.). *Chinese Thought and Institutions.* With contributions by Tung-tsu Ch'ü and others. ("Comparative Studies of Cultures and Civilizations.") Chicago: University of Chicago Press, 1957.
> *Essays centered around Confucianism as the main factor in the cohesion of Chinese life and institutions.*

GRANET, MARCEL. *Chinese Civilization.* (Translated from the French by Kathleen E. Innes and Mabel R. Brailsford.) New York: Knopf, 1930. (Reprinted in 1958 by Meridian Books, New York.)
> *A penetrating study of the development of early Chinese civilization.*

KUO, PING-CHIA. *China: New Age and New Outlook.* New York: Knopf, 1956.

LATTIMORE, OWEN. *Inner Asian Frontiers of China.* New York: American Geographical Society, 1940.

> *An analysis of the interaction between the Chinese cycles of power and the cycles of power of the non-Chinese peoples on the northern frontier.*

MACNAIR, HARLEY F. (ed.). *China.* Berkeley and Los Angeles: University of California Press, 1946.

> *A useful introduction to Chinese culture, arranged topically and written by well-qualified writers, with emphasis on the humanities, politics, and economics.*

ROSTOW, W. W. *A Comparison of Russian and Chinese Societies under Communism.* Cambridge: Center for International Studies, Massachusetts Institute of Technology, 1955.

> *A brief survey.*

WITTFOGEL, KARL A. "Chinese Society: An Historical Survey," *Journal of Asian Studies,* XVI, No. 3 (May 1957), 343-64.

> *Based on his chapter on the character of Chinese society written for* A General Handbook on China, *cited in "Editor's Note."*

————. *Oriental Despotism: A Comparative Study of Total Power.* New Haven: Yale University Press, 1956.

> *Within the framework of a comparative analysis of hydraulic society, this study discusses Chinese society, with full documentation, in accordance with the ideas developed in the text.*

ZEN, SOPHIA H. CHEN (HENG-CHE CHEN) (ed.). *Symposium on Chinese Culture.* Shanghai: China Institute of Pacific Relations, 1931.

> *A collection of essays by Chinese scholars on various aspects of the culture, useful for presenting Chinese views on different subjects during the transitional period.*

Chapter 2.   HISTORICAL SETTING

BISSON, T. A. *Japan in China.* New York: Macmillan, 1938.

> *One of the best accounts of the social, economic, and political developments leading to the Sino-Japanese War in 1937.*

CHENG, TE-K'UN. *Archaeology in China.* Vol. I, "Prehistoric China." Cambridge: Heffer & Sons, 1959.

> *Well illustrated with maps, text-figures, and plates.*

CHOW, TSE-TSUNG. *Intellectual Revolution in Modern China: The May Fourth Movement.* Cambridge: Harvard East Asian Studies, 1959.

A Selected Bibliography

CREEL, HERRLEE G. *The Birth of China: A Survey of the Formative Period of Chinese Civilization.* London: Jonathan Cape, 1936.
> *Important study of the development of Chinese civilization of the Shang and Chou dynasties from 1400 to 600 B.C.*

FITZGERALD, C. P. *China: A Short Cultural History.* (rev. ed.) New York: Praeger, 1953.
> *One of the best books on the subject, giving a good coverage of Chinese civilization; scholarly and easy to read.*

————. *Flood Tide in China.* London: Cresset Press, 1958.

————. *Revolution in China.* London: Cresset Press, 1952.

GOODRICH, LUTHER CARRINGTON. *A Short History of the Chinese People.* (3rd ed.) New York: Harper, 1959.
> *Emphasis more on the cultural development of the Chinese than on political and military events. Especially good are the short accounts of the scientific and technological achievements of the Chinese.*

GROUSSET, RENE. *The Rise and Splendour of the Chinese Empire.* (Translated from the French by Anthony Watson-Gandy and Terence Gordon.) Berkeley: University of California Press, 1953.
> *General historical reference with useful analyses of philosophical and political trends and developments. Should be used with caution as some of the conclusions are outdated and some analyses incomplete. Not documented.*

KIERMAN, FRANK A., JR. *The Chinese Communists in the Light of Chinese History.* Cambridge: Center for International Studies, Massachusetts Institute of Technology, 1954.
> *Shows how the Chinese Communist movement is a development of China's past.*

LATOURETTE, KENNETH SCOTT. *The Chinese: Their History and Culture.* (3rd ed., rev.; two vols. in one.) New York: Macmillan, 1946.
> *Standard book on the subject. First volume deals with history; second volume with culture, divided according to topics.*

————. *A History of Modern China.* Harmondsworth, Middlesex: Penguin Books, 1954.
> *A short sketch of the history of China from the decline of the Ch'ing dynasty to the advent of the Chinese Communists.*

LI, CHI. *The Beginnings of Chinese Civilization.* Seattle: University of Washington Press, 1957.
> *Three lectures illustrated with finds at An-yang.*

LI, CHIEN-NUNG. *The Political History of China, 1840-1928.* (Translated from the Chinese and edited by Ssu-yü Teng and Jeremy Ingalls.) Princeton: Van Nostrand, 1956.
> *Good summary of the chaotic years before the fall of the Ch'ing dynasty and after the establishment of the republic.*

LIU, F. F. *A Military History of Modern China, 1924-1949.* Princeton: Princeton University Press, 1956.

548

> Written by a former officer of the Nationalist Army, it tells of the influence of the Whampoa Military Academy, the war against Japan, and the civil war against the Communists.

LIU, JAMES T. C. *Reform in Sung China: Wang An-shih (1021-1086) and His New Policies*. Cambridge: Harvard University Press, 1959.

MACNAIR, HARLEY FARNSWORTH (ed.). *Modern Chinese History: Selected Readings*. Shanghai: Commercial Press, 1923.

> The history of China from the middle of the nineteenth century to recent times as told in the words of those who were the principals in the drama.

TANG, PETER S. H. *Communist China Today: Domestic and Foreign Policies*. New York: Praeger, 1957.

> Useful, comprehensive survey.

WALEY, ARTHUR. *The Opium War through Chinese Eyes*. London: Allen and Unwin, 1958.

WILHELM, RICHARD. *A Short History of Chinese Civilization*. (Translated from the German by Joan Joshua.) New York: The Viking Press, 1929.

> Still a classic. Contains an excellent treatment of Chinese cultural development.

WITTFOGEL, K. A. "The Historical Position of Communist China: Doctrine and Reality," *Review of Politics*, XVI (October 1954), 463-73.

WRIGHT, MARY C. *The Last Stand of Chinese Conservatism: The T'ung-chih Restoration, 1862-1874*. Stanford: Stanford University Press, 1957.

YANG, LIEN-SHENG. *Topics in Chinese History*. Cambridge: Harvard University Press, 1950.

Chapter 3.   GEOGRAPHY AND POPULATION

Geography

BUXTON, L. H. DUDLEY. *China, the Land and the People: A Human Geography*. Oxford: Clarendon Press, 1929.

> Basic work, somewhat outdated.

CHANG, CHI-YUN. *The Natural Resources of China*. New York: Sino-International Economic Research Center, 1945.

> Selected bibliography.

CRESSEY, GEORGE B. *China's Geographic Foundations*. New York: McGraw-Hill, 1934.

A Selected Bibliography

Standard work on the geography of China, with extensive bibliography.

————. *Land of the 500 Million: A Geography of China.* New York: McGraw-Hill, 1955.

The earlier work brought up to date, including information on Communist China; also a good bibliography.

GINSBURG, NORTON S. "China's Changing Political Geography," *Geographical Review,* XLII (1952), 102-17.

LEE, J. S. (SSU-KUANG LI). *The Geology of China.* London: T. Murby, 1939.

Comprehensive in treatment.

LINDNER, KENNETH R. "Military Geography of China," *Military Review,* XXXIII, No. 4 (July 1953), 42-56.

Includes maps.

ROXBY, PERCY M. "The Major Regions of China," *Geography,* XXIII (1938), 9-14.

SHABAD, THEODORE. *China's Changing Map: A Geography of the Chinese People's Republic.* New York: Praeger, 1956.

The latest general work on the geography of China, including facts and figures from Chinese Communist sources.

Cities and Communications

CHAO, YUNG-SEEN. *Railways in Communist China.* Hong Kong: Union Research Institute, 1955.

Discusses the repair of old railways and construction of new lines by the Chinese Communists, the policy and administration of railways, and the establishment of special railway courts.

LOCHOW, E. J. VON. *China's National Railways: Historical Survey and Post-War Planning.* Peking: National Peking University Press, 1948.

Informative and scholarly survey on railways in pre-Communist China.

MURPHEY, RHOADS. *Shanghai: Key to Modern China.* Cambridge: Harvard University Press, 1953.

Discusses geographical, economic, and political factors in the growth of Shanghai with emphasis on the particular dependence of Shanghai on water transportation.

SUN, E-TU ZEN. "The Pattern of Railway Development in China," *Far Eastern Quarterly,* XIV, No. 2 (February 1955), 179-99.

TREWARTHA, GLENN T. "Chinese Cities: Origins and Functions," *Annals of the Association of American Geographers,* XLII (March 1952), 69-93.

WIENS, HEROLD J. "Riverine and Coastal Junks in China's Commerce," *Economic Geography,* XXXI (1955), 248-64.

CHEN, TA. *Population in Modern China.* Chicago: University of Chicago Press, 1946.
    Good source for the age structure of the population of China.
"China: Analysis of Population Census," *Keesing's Contemporary Archives,* X (1955-56), 13999D.
HO, PING-TI. *Studies on the Population of China, 1368-1953.* Cambridge: Harvard University Press, 1959.
KEYES, FENTON. "Urbanism and Population Distribution in China," *American Journal of Sociology,* LVI (May 1951), 519-27.
MA, YIN-CHU. "A New Theory of Population," *Current Background,* No. 469.
ORLEANS, LEO A. "The 1953 Chinese Census in Perspective," *Journal of Asiatic Studies,* XVI, No. 4 (August 1957), 565-73.
    Discusses how the Chinese Communists obtained their statistics and evaluates the degree of accuracy.
————. "The Recent Growth of China's Urban Population," *Geographical Review,* XLIX (January 1959), 43-57.
SHABAD, THEODORE. "The Population of China's Cities," *Geographical Review,* XLIX (January 1959), 32-42.
STEINER, H. ARTHUR. "Chinese Communist Urban Policy," *American Political Science Review,* XLIV (March 1950), 47-63.
THOMPSON, WARREN S. *Population and Peace in the Pacific.* Chicago: University of Chicago Press, 1946.
————. *Population and Progress in the Far East.* Chicago: University of Chicago Press, 1959.
    Completely revised version of earlier work, cited above.

Chapter 4. ETHNIC MINORITIES

General

BUXTON, L. H. DUDLEY. *The Peoples of Asia.* New York: Knopf, 1925.
DE FRANCIS, JOHN. "National and Minority Policies," *Annals of the American Academy of Political and Social Science,* CCLXXVII (September 1951), 146-55.
GJESSING, GUTORM. "Chinese Anthropology and New China's Policy toward Her Minorities," *Acta Sociologica* (Copenhagen), II, Fasc. 1 (1956), 45-66.

A Selected Bibliography

Li, Chi. *The Formation of the Chinese People.* Cambridge: Harvard University Press, 1928.
> *An anthropological inquiry. Good on the southward migrations of the Chinese people; traces the move of some of the major groups.*

Policies towards Nationalities in the People's Republic of China. Peking: Foreign Languages Press, 1953.

Wang, Shu-tang. *China, Land of Many Nationalities: A Sketch.* Peking: Foreign Languages Press, 1955.
> *Illustrated.*

Wiens, Herold J. *China's March towards the Tropics.* Hamden, Connecticut: The Shoestring Press, 1954.
> *A discussion of the southward penetration of Chinese culture and political control in relation to the non-Han peoples of South China, with special emphasis on historical and cultural geography.*

Mongolia and Manchuria

Ahnert, E. E. "Manchuria as a Region of Pioneer Settlement." Pages 313-29 in *Pioneer Settlement.* (Cooperative Studies, AGS, Special Publications, No. 14.) New York: American Geographical Society, 1932.

Carruthers, Douglas. *Unknown Mongolia: Record of Travels and Exploration in Northwest Mongolia and Dzungaria.* 2 vols. Philadelphia: Lippincott, 1914.
> *Has good accounts of the Mongol tribes.*

Chang, Yin-t'ang. *The Economic Development and Prospects of Inner Mongolia (Chahar, Suiyuan and Ningsia).* Shanghai: Commercial Press, 1933.
> *Detailed source on the economic geography of the region, the degree of industrial development, and population policies of the government.*

Haslund-Christensen, Henning. *Mongolian Journey.* London: Routledge & K. Paul, 1949.
> *Excellent account of Mongolia and the Mongols in the last decade.*

Kler, Joseph. "Birth, Infancy and Childhood among the Ordos Mongols," *Primitive Man,* XI (1938), 58-66.

————. "Hunting Customs of the Ordos Mongols," *Primitive Man,* XIV (1941), 38-48.

Lattimore, Owen. "Chinese Colonization in Inner Mongolia: Its History and Present Development." Pages 288-312 in *Pioneer Settlement.* (Cooperative Studies, AGS, Special Publications, No. 14.) New York: American Geographical Society, 1932.

————. *Manchuria: Cradle of Conflict.* New York: Macmillan, 1935.
Mostly concerned with Chinese-Manchu relations; little information on native tribes.

————. *The Mongols of Manchuria: Their Tribal Divisions, Geographical Distribution, Historical Relations with Manchus and Chinese, and Present Political Problems.* New York: John Day, 1934.
An excellent study of the recent history of the various Mongol groups in Manchuria and Inner Mongolia.

MONTELL, GOSTA. "The Torguts of Etsin-Gol," *Journal of the Royal Anthropological Institute of Great Britain and Ireland,* LXX (1940), 77-92.
On the Torgut Mongols in Inner Mongolia.

Shirokogoroff, S. M. *Social Organization of the Manchus.* (Royal Asiatic Society, North China Branch, Extra Vol. III.) Shanghai: Royal Asiatic Society, 1924.
Though thirty years old, it is still a definitive study of the Manchu clan organization.

VREELAND, HERBERT H. *Mongol Community and Kinship Structure.* New Haven: Human Relations Area Files, 1954.

YOUNG, C. WALTER. "Chinese Immigration and Colonization in Manchuria." Pages 330-60 in *Pioneer Settlement.* (Cooperative Studies, AGS, Special Publications, No. 14.) New York: American Geographical Society, 1932.

West and Northwest China

BELL, CHARLES A. *The People of Tibet.* Oxford: Clarendon Press, 1928.
————. *The Religion of Tibet.* Oxford: Clarendon Press, 1931.

EKVALL, ROBERT B. *Cultural Relations on the Kansu-Tibetan Border.* Chicago: University of Chicago Press, 1939.

LATTIMORE, OWEN. *Pivot of Asia.* Boston: Little, Brown, 1950.
Good background for the political and racial frictions in Sinkiang.

LI, TIEH-TSENG. *Tibet: Today and Yesterday.* New York: Bookman Associates, 1959.

"Local Nationalism in Sinkiang: Enlarged Session of CCP Sinkiang Uighur Autonomous Region Committee and Other Reports," *Current Background,* No. 512.

MACDONALD, DAVID. *The Land of the Lama.* London: Seeley, Service, 1929.
Valuable for the description of Tibetan religious life and its relationship to the rest of the culture.

MASON, ISAAC. "The Mohammadans of China," *Journal of the North China Branch of the Royal Asiatic Society,* LX (1929), 42-78.

A Selected Bibliography

MOFFAT, ABBOT LOW. "The Salar Muhammadans," *Geographical Journal,* CLXXXV (1935), 525-30.

MOSTAERT, A. *The Mongols of Kansu and Their Language. (Bulletin of the Catholic University of Peking, No. 8.)* Peking: Catholic University, 1931.

NORINS, MARTIN R. *Gateway to Asia: Sinkiang, Frontier of the Chinese Far West.* New York: John Day, 1944.
  Has some chapters on the racial question in Sinkiang.

SCHRAM, L. M. J. *The Monguors of the Kansu-Tibetan Frontier: Their Origin, History, and Social Organization.* Philadelphia: American Philosophical Society, 1954.

————. *The Monguors of the Kansu-Tibetan Frontier: Their Religious Life.* Philadelphia: American Philosophical Society, 1957.

SHEN, TSUNG-LIEN, and SHEN-CHI LIU. *Tibet and Tibetans.* Stanford: Stanford University Press, 1953.

SHIH, CHENG-SHIH. "Sinkiang under the Rule of the Chinese Communists," *Tsu-kuo* (China Weekly), XI, No. 12 (September 19, 1955). (English translation in supplement to Union Research Service.)

"Sinkiang-Uighur Autonomous Region," *Current Background,* No. 365.

STUBEL, HANS. *The Mewu Fantzu: A Tibetan Tribe of Kansu.* (Translated from the German by Frieda Schutze.) New Haven: HRAF Press, 1958.

WHITING, ALLEN S., and SHIH-TS'AI SHENG. *Sinkiang: Pawn or Pivot?* East Lansing: Michigan State University Press, 1958.

South and Southwest China

BEAUCLAIR, INEZ DE. "The Keh Lao of Kweichow and Their History According to the Chinese Records," *Studia Serica,* V (1946), 44 pp.

CHANG, CHI-JEN. *The Minority Groups of Yunnan and Chinese Political Expansion into Southeast Asia.* Ann Arbor: University Microfilms, 1956.

CHEN, HAN-SENG. *Frontier Land Systems in Southernmost China: A Comparative Study of Agrarian Problems and Social Organizations among the Pai Yi People of Yunnan and the Kamba People of Sikang.* New York: Institute of Pacific Relations, 1949.

CHENG, TE-K'UN, and CHAO-T'AO LIANG. *An Introduction to the South-Western Peoples of China.* Chengtu: Museum, West China Union University, 1945.

CLARKE, SAMUEL R. *Among the Tribes in South-West China.* London: China Inland Mission, 1911.
  On the Miao, Chungchia, and Lolo tribes.

CREDNER, WILHELM. *Cultural and Geographical Observations Made in the Tali Region.* (Translated from the German by Major Erik Seidenfaden.) Bangkok: The Siam Society, 1935.
  With special regard to the Nan-chao problem.

554

EMBREE, JOHN F., and WILLIAM L. THOMAS. *Ethnic Groups in Northern Southeast Asia.* New Haven: Yale University Press, 1950.
> *Useful for the identification of tribal names.*

FITZGERALD, CHARLES P. *The Tower of Five Glories: A Study of the Minchia of Ta Li, Yunnan.* London: Cresset Press, 1941.

GOULLART, PETER. *Forgotten Kingdom.* London: John Murray, 1955.
> *On the Moso.*

GRAHAM, D. C. "The Customs of the Ch'uan Miao," *Journal of the West China Border Research Society,* IX (1937), 13-70.

————. *Songs and Stories of the Ch'uan Miao.* Washington: Smithsonian Institution, 1954.
> *Twenty stories on the relation of the Miao with the Lolo.*

HUDSPETH, WILLIAM H. *Stone Gateway and the Flowery Miao.* London: Cargate Press, 1937.

LIN, YUEH-HWA. "The Miao-Man Peoples of Kweichow," *Harvard Journal of Asiatic Studies,* V, Nos. 3 and 4 (January 1941), 261-345.

MICKEY, MARGARET PORTIA. *The Cowrie Shell Miao of Kweichow.* (Papers of the Peabody Museum of American Archaeology and Ethnology, Harvard University, XXXII, No. 1.) Cambridge: The Museum, 1947.

MONINGER, M. M. "The Hainanese Miao," *Journal of the North China Branch of the Royal Asiatic Society,* LII (1921), 40-50.

ODAKA, KUNIO. *Economic Organization of the Li Tribes of Hainan Island.* (Translated from the Japanese by Mikiso Hane.) New Haven: Southeast Asia Studies, Yale University, 1950.

POLLARD, S. *In Unknown China.* Philadelphia: Lippincott, 1921.
> *Based on personal observations during a prolonged stay among the Lolo aborigines in Szechwan.*

"The Proposed Kwangsi Chuang Autonomous Region," *Current Background,* No. 451.

ROCK, JOSEPH F. *The Ancient Na-khi Kingdom of Southwest China.* 2 vols. Cambridge: Harvard University Press, 1947.
> *On the distribution of the Moso in northeast Yunnan. Mostly translations from Chinese texts.*

STEVENSON, P. H. "Notes on the Human Geography of the Chinese-Tibetan Borderland," *Geographical Review,* XXII, No. 4 (1932), 599-616.
> *On the stratification of tribes in the Ta Liang-shan region of southwest Szechwan. Discusses the Lolo, Hsifan, and Jarung.*

STUBEL, H. "The Yao of the Province of Kwangtung," *Monumenta Serica,* III (1938), 345-84.
> *Good on the economy of the Yao tribes and their use of slash-and-burn agriculture.*

WARD, F. K. "Yunnan and the Tai Peoples," *Journal of the Royal Central Asian Society,* XXIX (1937), 624-37.

A Selected Bibliography

Chapter 5. LANGUAGES

CHAO, YUAN-REN. *Mandarin Primer.* Cambridge: Harvard University Press, 1948.
> *An excellent introductory chapter on the Chinese language.*

DE FRANCIS, JOHN. *Nationalism and Language Reform in China.* Princeton: Princeton University Press, 1950.
> *On movements for developing a phonetic script during the past fifty years as an integral part of the Chinese nationalist movement, prior to the Communist period.*

FORREST, R. A. D. *The Chinese Languages.* London: Faber and Faber, 1949.
> *General survey, including languages of the non-Chinese minorities.*

HSIA, TAO-TAI. *China's Language Reforms.* New Haven: Institute of Far Eastern Languages, Yale University, 1956.

KARLGREN, BERNHARD. *The Chinese Language: An Essay on Its Nature and History.* New York: Ronald Press, 1949.
> *Good general work.*

LI, CHI (Miss). *Studies in Chinese Communist Terminology.* Berkeley: East Asia Studies, Institute of International Studies, University of California, 1956 to 1957. (Mimeographed.)
> *In four sections: I. Preliminary Study of Selected Terms. II. General Trends of Chinese Linguistic Changes under Communist Rule. III. Part 1. Literary and Colloquial Terms in New Usage. Part 2. Terms Topped by Minerals. IV. Part 1. The Communist Term "the Common Language" and Related Terms. Part 2. Dialectal Terms in Common Usage. Part 3. Literary and Colloquial Terms in New Usage.*

MILLS, HARRIET C. "Language Reform in China: Some Recent Developments," *Far Eastern Quarterly,* XV, No. 4 (August 1956), 517-40.

Reform of the Chinese Written Language. Peking: Foreign Languages Press, 1958.
> *Contains official documents and reports by Communist leaders on language reform.*

SWADESH, MORRIS. "Nationalism and Language Reform in China," *Science and Society,* XVI (Summer 1952), 273-80.

TUNG, TUNG-HO. *Languages of China.* Taipei: China Culture Publishing Foundation, 1953.
> *Useful summaries by a specialist.*

ALEXEIEV, DAVID M. *The Chinese Gods of Wealth.* Hertford, England: The China Society, 1928.
> *On a popular cult.*

BLOFELD, JOHN EASTERN CALTHORPE. *The Jewel in the Lotus: An Outline of Present-Day Buddhism in China.* London: Sidgwick and Jackson, 1948.

BOYLE, SAMUEL E. *The Church in Red China Leans to One Side.* Hong Kong: Empire Printing, 1950.
> *Report on how Christians in China are being forced by the Communists to sever their ties with the world churches.*

BROWN, WILLIAM A. "The Protestant Rural Movement in China, 1920-1937." Pages 173-202 in Harvard University, Committee on Regional Studies, East Asia Program, *Papers on China,* IX. Cambridge: Harvard University Press, August 1955.

CHAN, WING-TSIT. *Religious Trends in Modern China.* New York: Columbia University Press, 1953.
> *One of the best books on pre-Communist, modern Chinese religious developments. Based on notes made by the author during his travels in China just before the Communist triumph.*

DAY, CLARENCE BURTON. *Chinese Peasant Cults.* Shanghai: Kelly and Walsh, 1940.
> *A study of Chinese paper gods.*

DE GROOT, J. J. M. *The Religious System of China: Its Ancient Forms, Evolutions, History and Present Aspect.* 6 vols. Leiden: E. J. Brill, 1892 to 1912.
> *One of the largest and most comprehensive works on traditional Chinese religions, based on a scholarly study of Chinese texts and upon observations largely in the vicinity of Amoy.*

EDWARDS, E. D. "Religion in Modern China," *Pacific Affairs,* XXVIII, No. 1 (March 1955), 79-82.

FERRIS, HELEN. *The Christian Church in Communist China, to 1952.* Lackland Air Force Base, Texas: Air Force Personnel and Training Research Center, 1956.

HUGHES, E. R., and K. HUGHES. *Religion in China.* New York: Hutchinson's University Library, 1950.
> *A good short summary largely devoted to Confucianism, Buddhism, and Taoism.*

JONES, FRANCIS P. "The Christian Church in Communist China," *Far Eastern Survey,* XXIV, No. 12 (December 1955), 184-88.

LATOURETTE, KENNETH SCOTT. *A History of Christian Missions in China.* New York: Macmillan, 1929.
> *Authoritative work on the subject.*

A Selected Bibliography

PALMER, GRETTA. *God's Underground in Asia.* New York: Appleton-Century-Crofts, 1953.
> *On Communist persecution of Christianity.*
REICHELT, KARL. *Truth and Tradition in Chinese Buddhism: A Study of Chinese Mahayana Buddhism.* Shanghai: Commercial Press, 1934.
> *Summarizes Buddhist literature, religious ideas, monastic life, and ordination of monks.*
SHRYOCK, JOHN K. *The Origin and Development of the State Cult of Confucius.* New York: Appleton-Century, 1932.
> *History of the rise and influence of Confucianism.*
SIH, PAUL K. T. (KUANG-CH'IEN HSUEH). *Chinese Culture and Christianity.* Taipei: China Culture Publishing Foundation, 1957.
United States Joint Publications Research Service. *Religion in Communist China.* New York, April 19, 1958.
> *Reports are based on Chinese Communist publications issued in 1956.*
VARG, PAUL A. *Missionaries, Chinese, and Diplomats: The American Protestant Missionary Movement in China, 1890-1952.* Princeton: Princeton University Press, 1958.
WELCH, HOLMES. *The Parting of the Way: Lao Tzu and the Taoist Movement.* London: Methuen, 1958.
WRIGHT, ARTHUR F. *Buddhism in Chinese History.* Stanford: Stanford University Press, 1959.
YANG, I-FAN. *Buddhism in China.* Hong Kong: Union Press, 1956.
————. *Islam in China.* Hong Kong: Union Press, 1957.
YANG, Y. C. *China's Religious Heritage.* New York: Abingdon-Cokesbury Press, 1943.
> *On Confucianism, Buddhism, Taoism, and Christianity.*

Chapter 7. SOCIAL ORGANIZATION

BARNETT, A. DOAK. "Social Controls in Communist China," *Far Eastern Survey,* XXII (April 22, 1953), 45-48.
BURGESS, J. S. *The Guilds of Peking.* New York: Columbia University Press, 1928.
> *Based on a study made with S. D. Gamble in 1921 and after.*
CHANG, CHUNG-LI. *The Chinese Gentry: Studies on Their Role in Nineteenth-Century Chinese Society.* Seattle: University of Washington Press, 1955.
> *A scholarly and informative work on the place and influence of*

558

the gentry class, their leadership in government and society, and their economic standing and mobility.

CHEN, THEODORE HSI-EN. "The Marxist Remolding of Chinese Society," *American Journal of Sociology,* LVIII (January 1953), 340-46.

FEI, HSIAO-TUNG. *China's Gentry: Essays in Rural-Urban Relations.* (Rev. and ed. by M. P. Redfield.) Chicago: University of Chicago Press, 1953.

> Contains six life histories of Chinese gentry families; an attack on the gentry class by a leftist sociologist according to the Marxian interpretation of Chinese society.

FRIED, MORTON H. *Fabric of Chinese Society: A Study of the Social Life of a Chinese County Seat.* New York: Praeger, 1953.

> An examination of the culture of Ch'u-hsien, near Nanking. Discusses all classes of society with sharp distinction between town and countryside. Written at a time of political chaos in China (the Nationalist Communist civil war and the Communist triumph, 1945-49), the work gives a picture of China in transitional times, and the author dwells on the exploitation of the peasantry as conducive to revolution.

HAN, SUSAN (SU-SHAN HAN). *The Concept of the Proletariat in Chinese Communism.* Chicago: Library, Department of Photographic Reproduction, University of Chicago, 1955. (Microfilm of typescript.)

HO, PING-TI. "Aspects of Social Mobility in China, 1368-1911," *Comparative Studies in Society and History,* I, No. 4 (June 1959), 330-59.

LAMSON, HERBERT DAY. *Social Pathology in China.* Shanghai: Commercial Press, 1934.

> Facts and figures on various aspects of Chinese society as it was taking shape after the establishment of the Nationalist government in 1928.

LEVY, MARION J., JR., and KUO-HENG SHIH. *The Rise of the Modern Chinese Business Class.* New York: Institute of Pacific Relations, 1949.

> Book is divided into two parts: I. The Social Background of the Modern Business Development in China, by Levy; II. The Early Development of the Chinese Business Class, by Shih.

MORSE, HOSEA B. *The Gilds of China: With an Account of the Gild Merchant or Co-Hong of Canton.* (2nd ed.) London: Longmans, Green, 1932.

PULLEYBLANK, E. G. "The Origins and Nature of Chattel Slavery in China," *Journal of the Economic and Social History of the Orient,* I (1958), 185-220.

SUN, E-TU ZEN, and JOHN DE FRANCIS. *Chinese Social History: Translations of Selected Studies.* Washington: American Council of Learned Societies, 1956.

CHEN, EDWARD KING-TUNG. "Communist China's War on the Family," *Southwestern Social Science Quarterly*, XXXIII (September 1952), 148-55.

CHEN, WEN-HUI C. (Mrs. THEODORE H. E. CHEN). *The Family Revolution in Communist China*. Lackland Air Base, Texas: Air Force Personnel and Training Research Center, 1955.
> *Contains documentation from Chinese Communist sources on the effects of the new marriage law.*

CHIU, VERMIER Y. "Marriage Laws of the Ch'ing Dynasty, the Republic of China, and Communist China," *Contemporary China*, II (1956-57, pub. 1958), 64-72.

FENG, HAN-YI (HAN-CHI FENG). *The Chinese Kinship System*. Cambridge: Harvard University Press, 1948. (Reprint from *Harvard Journal of Asiatic Studies*, II (1937), 141-275.)
> *First-rate and highly technical linguistic and structural study of Chinese kinship terminology and historical changes in the functions of the terms and the system as a whole.*

FREEDMAN, MAURICE. *Lineage Organization in Southeastern China*. (London School of Economics, Monographs on Social Anthropology, 18.) London: University of London, Athlone Press, 1958.

FRIED, MORTON H. *Kin and Non-Kin in Chinese Society: An Analysis of Extra-Kin Relationships in Chinese Society*. Ann Arbor: University Microfilms, 1951.
> *With diagrams and illustrations; special reference to a selected community, Ch'u-hsien.*

GAMBLE, SIDNEY. *How Chinese Families Live in Peiping*. New York: Funk & Wagnalls, 1933.
> *Study of the income, expenditure, and standards of living of 283 families in pre-Communist period.*

HSU, FRANCIS L. K. "The Myth of the Chinese Family Size," *American Journal of Sociology*, XLVIII, No. 5 (March 1943), 555-62.
> *The article surveys the problem of family size in China and cites statistics to show that the size of Chinese families is actually small; also points out the connection between large families and the veneration of ancestors.*

————. *Under the Ancestors' Shadow: Chinese Culture and Personality*. New York: Columbia University Press, 1948.
> *A community study of a village in Yunnan. The author stresses the influence of ancestor worship on family life and devotes considerable attention to religion.*

560

Hu, Hsien-chin. *The Common Descent Group in China and Its Functions.* (Viking Fund Publications in Anthropology, No. 10.) New York: Viking Fund, 1948.

> *A definitive work in English on the Chinese clan. The first half of the book analyzes the organization, regional variation, and leadership of the clan system. Ancestor veneration, genealogies, judiciary powers, and common property of the clans are discussed; also an examination of inter-clan relations is included. The second half consists of appendices (Chinese text material in translation) illustrative of the theoretical points made in the first half of the book.*

Lang, Olga. *Chinese Family and Society.* New Haven: Yale University Press, 1946.

> *In this work, the Chinese family in traditional and republican China is viewed in its socio-historical context. The author makes use of social surveys, statistics, questionnaires, interviews, census figures, etc., in order to draw a broad picture of Chinese family structure and economy in the course of China's history, with special attention to the 1930's. This study has the usual limitations of an all-inclusive work (i.e., broad conclusions based on spotty data) but deals with or touches upon all the basic aspects of family structure and function. It contains a mine of information indispensable as a reference on this subject.*

Lee, Rose Hum. "Research on the Chinese Family," *American Journal of Sociology,* XLIV (May 1949), 497-504.

Lee, Shu-ching. "China's Traditional Family: Its Characteristics and Disintegration," *American Sociological Review,* XVIII (June 1953), 272-80.

Levy, Marion J., Jr. *The Family Revolution in Modern China.* Cambridge: Harvard University Press, 1949.

> *A sociological analysis of family structure in "traditional" and "transitional" China with special reference to the role and impact of industrialization on the family system. Contains excellent material on roles and interpersonal relationships within the family and age groups. The bulk of the book is devoted to theoretical formulations.*

Lin, Yueh-hwa. *The Golden Wing: A Sociological Study of Chinese Familism.* London: K. Paul, Trench, Trubner, 1948.

> *Account of the varying fortunes of two families in Fukien. The author writes of his native village and presumably his own relatives. The book is written in the form of a novel and gives a highly readable, though limited, view of some aspects of village and town life in Fukien, particularly family relations.*

Lindbeck, J. M. H. "Communist Policy and the Chinese Family," *Far Eastern Survey,* XX (July 25, 1951), 137-41.

LIU, HUI-CHEN WANG. *The Traditional Chinese Clan Rule.* Locust Valley, New York: J. J. Augustin, 1959.
> *Monograph of the Association for Asian Studies.*

"Marriage in Communist China," *Current Background,* No. 136.
> *Translation of articles on changes in the marriage institution under the impact of the new marriage law.*

YANG, C. K. *The Chinese Family in the Communist Revolution.* Cambridge: Massachusetts Institute of Technology, Technology Press, 1959.

Chapter 9. DYNAMICS OF POLITICAL BEHAVIOR

Communism: History and Ideology

BRANDT, CONRAD, and BENJAMIN SCHWARTZ, and JOHN K. FAIRBANK. *A Documentary History of Chinese Communism.* Cambridge: Harvard University Press, 1952.
> *Translations of the texts of resolutions, circulars, manifestoes, speeches and selected writings of Chinese Communist leaders from 1918 to 1950. The materials deal with propaganda, ideology, party affairs, rectification and remolding of ideas, etc. Arranged chronologically, each section is preceded by a short introduction.*

CHEN, PO-TA. *Mao Tse-tung on the Chinese Revolution.* Peking: Foreign Languages Press, 1953.
> *Published to commemorate the thirtieth anniversary of the founding of the Chinese Communist party, this article underscores the claim that the Chinese revolution was a "classic type" revolution for pre-industrial "colonial and semicolonial countries," just as the Russian October revolution of 1917 was a "classic type" revolution for industrialized "imperialist" countries.*

————. *Stalin and the Chinese Revolution.* Peking: Foreign Languages Press, 1953. (Also published in *China Weekly Review,* CXVI, No. 8, January 21, 1950, 123-26.)
> *Article written by a well-known Communist writer on the occasion of Stalin's seventieth birthday; stresses the importance attached by the Chinese Communist party to the Stalin-Mao approach.*

CHEN, THEODORE HSI-EN. *Chinese Communism and the Proletarian-Socialist Revolution*. Los Angeles: University of Southern California Press, 1955.

"Constitution of the Communist Party of China—1956," *Current Background*, No. 417.

> *Also contains text of the 1945 party constitution and the report by Teng Hsiao-p'ing on the revision of the party constitution.*

Documents of the National Conference of the Communist Party of China, March 1955. Peking: Foreign Languages Press, 1955.

> *Contains the resolution on the draft of the First Five Year Plan for developing the national economy, the resolution on the anti-party bloc of Kao Kang and Jao Shu-shih, and the resolution on the establishment of central and local control committees of the party.*

HU, CHIAO-MU. *Thirty Years of the Communist Party of China: An Outline History*. Peking: Foreign Languages Press, 1951.

> *The first official outline history of the Chinese Communist party prepared by the vice-director of the Propaganda Department of the party's Central Committee and at one time director of the Press Administration. The history is of interest in summarizing the official Chinese Communist line, as of 1951, on domestic and international problems during the past three decades and in paying tribute to the consistently "correct" guidance of Mao Tse-tung.*

ISAACS, HAROLD R. *The Tragedy of the Chinese Revolution*. Stanford: Stanford University Press, 1951.

> *History of the Chinese Communists by a Trotskyite.*

LIU, SHAO-CHI. *How To Be a Good Communist*. Peking: Foreign Languages Press, 1951.

————. *On Inner Party Struggle*. Peking: Foreign Languages Press, 1951.

> *The bulk of this lecture is devoted to three deviations: mechanical and excessive inner party struggle, unprincipled disputes, and struggles with the party. The last part is on "how to conduct inner party struggle."*

————. *The Political Report of the Central Committee of the Communist Party of China to the Eighth National Congress of the Party*. Peking: Foreign Languages Press, 1956.

> *Delivered on September 15, 1956.*

LU, TING-I. "The World Significance of the Chinese Revolution," *People's China*, IV, No. 1 (July 1, 1951), 9-12.

MAO, TSE-TUNG. *On the Correct Handling of Contradictions among the People.* Peking: Foreign Languages Press, 1957.

> *This is the text of a speech made on February 27, 1957 at eleventh session (enlarged) of the Supreme State Conference.*

A Selected Bibliography

————. *Selected Works.* New York: International Publishers, 1954-56. *Official versions of Mao's most important works. Only four volumes have been published, containing speeches, reports, and writings up to 1945: Vol. I, period of the First Revolutionary Civil War, 1926-36; Vols. II, III, IV, period of the war of resistance against Japanese aggression, 1937-38, 1939-41, 1941-45.*

Mao's China: Party Reform Documents, 1942-44. (Translated and with an introduction by Boyd Compton.) Seattle: University of Washington Press, 1952. *Speeches by Mao Tse-tung, Liu Shao-ch'i, Ch'en Yün; resolutions of the Central Committee of the Chinese Communist party; and propaganda guides.*

PALMER, NORMAN D., and SHAO-CHUAN LENG. "Organization of the Chinese Communist Party," *Current History,* XXIII (July 1952), 13-19.

PENG, CHEN. "The Victory of Marxism-Leninism in China," *"People's China,* IV, No. 1 (July 1, 1951), 3-8.

ROSTOW, W. W. (ed.). *Essays on Communism in Asia.* Cambridge: Center for International Studies, Massachusetts Institute of Technology, 1955. *In three parts: Communism in China, Communism in Free Asia, and a comparative study.*

ROY, M. N. *Revolution and Counter-Revolution in China.* Calcutta: Renaissance Publishers, 1946. *Useful account of the early years of the Chinese Communist movement by an Indian Communist who was on the scene as a participant of the events he discusses.*

SCHWARTZ, BENJAMIN. *China and the Soviet Theory of "People's Democracy."* Cambridge: Center for International Studies, Massachusetts Institute of Technology, 1954. *On the difference between a "people's republic" and a "people's democracy."*

————. *Chinese Communism and the Rise of Mao.* Cambridge: Harvard University Press, 1951. *On the Wu-han and Kiangsi period. Story of Mao's triumph over his rivals.*

————. "Marx and Lenin in China," *Far Eastern Survey,* XVIII (July 27, 1949), 174-78.

SNOW, EDGAR. *Red Star over China.* New York: Random House, 1944. *On the "Long March" of the Chinese Communists.*

STEINER, H. ARTHUR. "Ideology and Politics in Communist China," *Annals of the American Academy of Political and Social Science,* CCCXXI (January 1959), 29-39.

564

————. "The People's Democratic Dictatorship in China," *Western Political Quarterly*, III (March 1950), 38-51.

————. "The Rise of the Chinese Communist Party," *Annals of the American Academy of Political and Social Science*, CCLXXVII (September 1951), 56-66.

TANG, PETER S. H. "Power Struggle in the Chinese Communist Party: The Kao-Jao Purge," *Problems of Communism*, IV, No. 6 (November-December 1956), 18-25.

TAYLOR, GEORGE E. "The Hegemony of the Chinese Communists, 1945-50," *Annals of the American Academy of Political and Social Science*, CCLXXVII (September 1951), 13-21.

TENG, HSIAO-PING. *Report on the Rectification Campaign*. Peking: Foreign Languages Press, 1957.
> *Delivered at the third plenary session (enlarged) of the Eighth Central Committee of the Communist party of China on September 23, 1957.*

WALKER, RICHARD L. *China under Communism: The First Five Years*. New Haven: Yale University Press, 1955.
> *Good for the study of the methods of control exercised by the Communists over the people.*

WAN, YAH-KANG. *The Rise of Communism in China (1920-50)*. Hong Kong: China Educational Supplies, 1952.

WILBUR, C. MARTIN, and JULIE LIEN-YING HOW (eds.). *Documents on Communism, Nationalism, and Soviet Advisers in China, 1918-27*. New York: Columbia University Press, 1956.
> *English translation of papers seized in the raid on the Soviet Embassy in Peking in 1927. In six parts as follows: an introduction to "a brief history of the Chinese Communist party"; organization policies of the party, 1920-26; consolidation of the revolutionary base in Kwangtung, 1921-25; frictions and reconciliations; policies on mass movements; and relations with Feng Yu-hsiang and others.*

WITTFOGEL, KARL A. "The Influence of Leninism-Stalinism in China," *Annals of the American Academy of Political and Social Science*, CCLXXVII (September 1951), 22-34.

Other Parties

CHANG, CARSUN (CHUN-MAI CHANG). *The Third Force in China*. New York: Bookman Associates, 1952.
> *On the events from 1945 to 1949.*

CHEN, REN-BING. "New China's United Front," *China Monthly Review*, CXXI, No. 4 (October 1951), 165-70.

COLE, ALLAN B. "The United Front in New China," *Annals of the American Academy of Political and Social Science*, CCLXXVII (September 1951), 35-45.

A Selected Bibliography

Political Control and Mass Organizations

CHAO, KUO-CHUN. *The Mass Organizations in Communist China.* Cambridge: Center for International Studies, Massachusetts Institute of Technology, 1953.

A study of the organization and leadership of the All-China Federation of Democratic Women, the New Democratic Youth League, the All-China Federation of Trade Unions, and other mass organizations.

GOURLAY, WALTER E. *The Chinese Communist Cadre: Key to Political Control.* Cambridge: Russian Research Center, Harvard University, 1952.

A short but careful study of the cadre system in Communist China, with discussions of its ideological basis, the techniques and systems of training, and the leading personalities directing the recruitment and training of cadres.

TING, LI. *Militia of Communist China.* Hong Kong: Union Research Institute, 1954.

Elections

CHAO, KUO-CHUN. *Basic Level Elections and the Draft Constitution of Communist China.* Cambridge: Center for International Studies, Massachusetts Institute of Technology, 1954.

Review of the mechanics of election according to the draft of the constitution.

The Electoral Law of the People's Republic of China. Peking: Foreign Languages Press, 1953.

Text of the law adopted by the Central People's Government Council on February 11, 1953. Also contains "An Explanation on the Electoral Law" by Teng Hsiao-p'ing, in which the fine points of the law are clarified.

Chapter 10. THEORY AND STRUCTURE OF GOVERNMENT

Pre-Communist

CHEN, CHIH-MAI. *Chinese Government.* 3 vols. Chungking: Commercial Press, 1944.

Structure of the Nationalist government of China.

CHIEN, TUAN-SHENG. *The Government and Politics of China.* Cambridge: Harvard University Press, 1950.

An extensive discussion of the political forces and the government structure during the republican and Nationalist period.

Constitution of the Republic of China. Nanking: Ministry of Information, 1947.

This is the constitution adopted by the National Assembly at Nanking on December 25, 1946 and promulgated on January 1, 1947. It went into effect on December 25, 1947 and is still today the constitution of the Republic of China in Taiwan.

LINEBARGER, PAUL. *Government in Republican China.* New York: McGraw-Hill, 1938.

On the Nationalist government.

————. *The Political Doctrines of Sun Yat-sen: An Exposition of the San Min Chu I.* Baltimore: Johns Hopkins University Press, 1937.

PAN, WEI-TUNG. *The Chinese Constitution: A Study of Forty Years of Constitutional Making in China.* Washington, D. C.: The Catholic University of America Press, 1946.

Good historical summary of the various attempts at constitution writing in China.

SUN, YAT-SEN. *San Min Chu I: The Three Principles of the People.* (Translated from the Chinese by Frank W. Price; edited by L. T. Chen.) Shanghai: Commercial Press, 1927.

Guide book for the Nationalists.

TSAO, WEN-YEN. *The Constitutional Structure of Modern China.* Melbourne: Melbourne University Press, 1947.

WANG, KAN-YU. *The Local Government of China.* Chungking: China Institute of Pacific Relations, 1945.

Communist

CHAO, KUO-CHUN. "The National Constitution of Communist China," *Far Eastern Survey,* XXIII, No. 10 (October 1954), 145-51.

CHENG, CHU-YUAN. *The People's Communes.* Hong Kong: Union Press, 1959.

CHIEN, TUAN-SHENG. "How the People's Government Works," *China Reconstructs,* I, No. 4 (July-August 1952), 8-12.

The Common Program and Other Documents of the First Plenary Session of the Chinese People's Political Consultative Conference. Peking: Foreign Languages Press, 1950.

Documents of the First Session of the First National People's Congress of the People's Republic of China. Peking: Foreign Languages Press, 1955.

Includes an address by Mao Tse-tung, a report on the draft of the constitution by Liu Shao-ch'i, a report on the work of the government by Chou En-lai, the text of the constitution, and texts of organic laws.

A Selected Bibliography

HARAHAN, GENE Z. "The People's Revolutionary Military Council in Communist China," *Far Eastern Survey*, XXIII, No. 5 (May 1954), 77-78.

LINEBARGER, PAUL M. A., et al. *Far Eastern Governments and Politics: China and Japan.* New York: Van Nostrand, 1954.
> Brings up to date his earlier work on the Chinese government.

LIU, SHAO-CHI. *Report on the Draft Constitution of the People's Republic of China* and *Constitution of the People's Republic of China.* Peking: Foreign Languages Press, 1954.
> Provides insight into Chinese Communist conceptions of constitutional government. English translation of the constitution varies slightly in wording from Constitution of the People's Republic of China, apparently an official version, also issued by the Foreign Languages Press in 1954.

People's Communes in China. Peking: Foreign Languages Press, 1958.
> A collection of editorials and articles on the people's commune movement, recently published by the People's Daily and the Red Flag. The resolution on the establishment of people's communes in the rural areas adopted by the Central Committee of the Chinese Communist party is also included.

STEINER, H. ARTHUR. "Constitutionalism in Communist China," *American Political Science Review*, XLIX (March 1955), 1-12.

————. "New Regional Governments in China," *Far Eastern Survey*, XIX, No. 5 (May 31, 1950), 112-16.

SUDARIKOV, N. G. "The Creation and Consolidation of the Local Organs of Power in the Chinese People's Republic," *Soviet Press Translations*, VII (February 15, 1952), 99-110.

————. "The Development and Consolidation of the Organs of State Power in the Chinese People's Republic," *Soviet Press Translations*, VI (November 1, 1951), 571-86.

THOMAS, S. B. *Government and Administration in Communist China.* (Rev. ed.) New York: International Secretariat, Institute of Pacific Relations, 1955.
> Originally published in 1953 and revised to include the political events of 1953 and 1954. Excellent study of all phases of Chinese Communist politics with discussions of the treatment of minority nationalities, regional governments, and the elections and the National People's Congress of 1954.

WEI, HENRY. *State and Government in Communist China: Their Ideological Basis and Statutory Pattern to the Spring of 1953.* Lackland Air Force Base, Texas: Air Force Personnel and Training Research Center, 1955.
> Discusses the Chinese Communist government from 1949 to 1953.

Chapter 11. DIFFUSION AND CONTROL OF INFORMATION

BRITTON, ROSWELL S. *The Chinese Periodical Press, 1800-1912.* Shanghai: Kelly & Walsh, 1933.
> *Good for historical background.*

CHEN, THEODORE H. E. "Education and Propaganda in Communist China," *Annals of the American Academy of Political and Social Science,* CCLXXVII (September 1951), 135-45.

CHEN, WEN-HUI (Mrs. THEODORE H. E. CHEN). *Chinese Communist Anti-Americanism and the Resist America and Aid Korea Campaign.* Lackland Air Force Base, Texas: Air Force Personnel and Training Research Center, 1955.
> *On the nationwide propaganda campaign against the United States at the time of the Korean War.*

Culture and Education in New China. Peking: Foreign Languages Press, 1950.
> *Articles on "The Press in New China," "The Chinese People's Broadcasting System," "The Chinese Film Industry," "Publication Works in New China," and related topics.*

EVANS, F. BOWEN (ed.). *Worldwide Communist Propaganda Activities.* New York: Macmillan, 1955.
> *Describes the theme and techniques.*

HOUN, F. W., and YUAN-LI WU. "Chinese Communist Publication Policy and Thought Control," *Pacific Spectator,* X (Summer 1956), 282-91.

LIN, YUTANG. *A History of the Press and Public Opinion in China.* Chicago: University of Chicago Press, 1936.
> *Good survey of past history.*

YU, FREDERICK T. C. "How the Chinese Reds Transfer Mass Grievances into Power," *Journalism Quarterly,* XXX (Summer 1953), 354-64.

————. *The Propaganda Machine in Communist China, with Special Reference to Ideology, Policy, and Regulations as of 1952.* Lackland Air Force Base, Texas: Air Force Personnel and Training Research Center, 1955.
> *On mechanics and themes of Chinese Communist propaganda.*

————. *The Strategy and Tactics of Chinese Communist Propaganda, as of 1952.* Lackland Air Force Base, Texas: Air Force Personnel and Training Research Center, 1955.
> *Study of the techniques used.*

A Selected Bibliography

Chapter 12. FOREIGN RELATIONS

BARNETT, A. DOAK. "Red China's Impact on Asia," *Atlantic*, CCIV, No. 6 (December 1959), 48-53.

————. "The United States and Communist China." Pages 105-71 in *The American Assembly: The United States and the Far East.* (Report on the Tenth American Assembly, November 1956.) New York: Columbia University Press, 1956.

BELOFF, MAX. *Soviet Policy in the Far East, 1944-51.* London: Oxford University Press, 1953.

BOORMAN, HOWARD L., and ALEXANDER ECKSTEIN, PHILIP E. MOSLEY, and BENJAMIN SCHWARTZ. *Moscow-Peking Axis: Strengths and Strains.* New York: Council on Foreign Relations, Harper & Brothers, 1957.
> Important study on Sino-Soviet relations.

BRANDT, CONRAD. *Stalin's Failure in China, 1924-1927.* Cambridge: Harvard University Press, 1958.

CHAO, CHIN-YUNG. *A Brief History of Chinese Foreign Relations.* Taipei: China Cultural Service, [1954].

CHEN, YIN-CHING (comp.). *Treaties and Agreements between the Republic of China and Other Powers, 1929-1954.* Washington, D. C.: Sino-American Public Service, 1957.
> Contains certain international documents affecting the interests of the Republic of China.

CHENG, TIEN-FANG. *A History of Sino-Russian Relations.* Washington, D. C.: Public Affairs Press, 1957.

CHRISTOPHER, JAMES WILLIAM. *Conflict in the Far East: American Diplomacy in China from 1928 to 1933.* Leiden: E. J. Brill, 1950.

"Communist China's Foreign Policy: Symposium," *Current History*, XXXIII (December 1957), 321-57.

DAI, SHEN-YU. *Peking, Moscow and the Communist Parties of Colonial Asia.* Cambridge: Center for International Studies, Massachusetts Institute of Technology, 1954.

DULLES, FOSTER RHEA. *China and America: The Story of Their Relations since 1784.* Princeton: Princeton University Press, 1946.

FAIRBANK, JOHN KING. *Trade and Diplomacy on the China Coast: The Opening of the Treaty Ports, 1842-1854.* Cambridge: Harvard University Press, 1953.

————. *The United States and China.* (Rev. ed.) Cambridge: Harvard University Press, 1958.

FAIRBANK, JOHN KING, and SSU-YU TENG. "On the Ch'ing Tributary System," *Harvard Journal of Asiatic Studies*, VI, No. 2 (June 1941), 135-246.

570

    A comprehensive survey, supplemented by extensive bibliographical references to sources.

HARRIS, RICHARD. "China in the Twentieth Century—Nationalism and Revolution," *History Today,* IV, No. 4 (April 1954), 227-35.

HINTON, HAROLD C. *China's Relations with Burma and Vietnam: A Brief Survey.* New York: International Secretariat, Institute of Pacific Relations, 1958.

KAHIN, GEORGE MCTURNAN. *The Asian-African Conference, Bandung, Indonesia, April 1955.* Ithaca: Cornell University Press, 1955.

LENG, SHAO-CHUAN. *Japan and Communist China.* Kyoto: Doshisha University Press, 1958.
    Distributed by the Institute of Pacific Relations.

LEVI, WERNER. *Modern China's Foreign Policy.* Minneapolis: University of Minnesota Press, 1953.
    Especially useful for the extensive bibliographical citations contained in the notes on pages 357-89.

LINDBECK, JOHN M. H. *Communist China and American Far Eastern Policy.* Washington, D. C.: Department of State, 1955. (Reprinted from the Department of State *Bulletin* of November 7, 1955.)

LINDSAY, MICHAEL. *China and the Cold War: A Study in International Politics.* Melbourne: Melbourne University Press, 1955.

MCLANE, CHARLES B. *Soviet Policy and the Chinese Communists, 1931-1946.* New York: Columbia University Press, 1958.

MORSE, HOSEA BALLOU. *International Relations of the Chinese Empire.* 3 vols. London: Longmans, Green, 1910-18.
    One of the best works on the international relations of China prior to the revolution of 1911. Has background history going back to the first contacts of the Chinese with Europeans by sea in the sixteenth century; main body of the work covers the period from 1834 to 1912.

NORTH, ROBERT C. *Moscow and Chinese Communists.* Stanford: Stanford University Press, 1953.
    On political and ideological ties.

PAVLOVSKY, MICHEL. *Chinese-Russian Relations.* New York: Philosophical Press, 1949.
    Essays on early as well as modern relations.

STEINER, H. ARTHUR. "Mainsprings of Chinese Communist Foreign Policy," *American Journal of International Law,* XLIV (January 1950), 69-99.
    Excellent study of the basic underlying concepts of Communist China's foreign policy.

————. *The International Position of Communist China: Political and Ideological Directions of Foreign Policy.* New York: Institute of Pacific Relations, 1958.

TUNG, LIN. *China and Some Phases of International Law.* London: Oxford University Press, 1940.

A Selected Bibliography

A treatise on some legal aspects of China's relations with foreign peoples.

United States. Department of State. *The Sino-Soviet Economic Offensive in the Less Developed Countries.* (Department of State Publication, 6632.) Washington, D. C., May 1958.

————. *United States Relations with China with Special Reference to the Period 1944-1949.* (White Paper on China, with an introduction by Dean Acheson.) Washington, D. C., 1949.

With appendices containing documents from the files of the State Department.

VEVIER, CHARLES. *The United States and China, 1906-1913: A Study of Finance and Diplomacy.* New Brunswick: Rutgers University Press, 1955.

Based on a re-evaluation of the Straight papers and records of the State Department.

WALKER, RICHARD L. *The Continuing Struggle: Communist China and the Free World.* New York: Athene Press, 1958.

Expansion and revision of the author's "Communist China: Power and Prospects" which appeared as a special issue of the New Leader *on October 20, 1958.*

WEI, HENRY. *China and Soviet Russia.* Princeton: Van Nostrand, 1956.

Account of interactions of Chinese and Soviet Policies since 1917, which culminated in the rise of the Chinese Communists.

————. *Mao Tse-tung's "Lean-to-One-Side" Policy.* Lackland Air Force Base, Texas: Air Force Personnel and Training Research Center, 1955.

On the background and ideology of one of Communist China's cardinal points of foreign policy.

WHITING, A. S. *Contradiction in the Moscow-Peking Axis.* Santa Monica, California: Rand Corporation, 1957.

————. "Foreign Policy of Communist China." Pages 264-94 in Roy Macridis (ed.), *Foreign Policy in World Affairs.* New York: Prentice-Hall, 1958.

————. *Soviet Policies in China, 1917-24.* New York: Columbia University Press, 1954.

Scholarly account of the first Soviet contacts with the Nationalists.

————. "The United States and Taiwan." Pages 173-201 in *The American Assembly: The United States and the Far East.* (Report on the Tenth American Assembly, November 1956.) New York: Columbia University Press, 1956.

WILLOUGHBY, W. W. *Foreign Rights and Interests in China.* (Rev. ed.) 2 vols. Baltimore: Johns Hopkins Press, 1927.

General study on extraterritoriality in pre-Nationalist China.

WU, AITCHEN K. *China and the Soviet Union.* New York: John Day, 1950.

Historical review.

Chapter 13. BASIC FEATURES OF THE ECONOMY

BARNETT, A. DOAK. *Communist Economic Strategy: The Rise of Mainland China.* Washington, D. C.: National Planning Association, 1959.

CHAO, KUO-CHUN. *Economic Planning and Organization in Mainland China: A Documentary Study (1949-1957).* Cambridge: Harvard University Press, 1959.

> *First volume of a work in progress.*

ECKSTEIN, ALEXANDER. *Conditions and Prospects for Economic Growth in Communist China.* Cambridge: Center for International Studies, Massachusetts Institute of Technology, 1954.

GANGULI, B. N. *Economic Development in China.* London: Oxford University Press, 1955.

> *Short general survey.*

HOLLISTER, WILLIAM WALLACE. *China's Gross National Product and Social Accounts, 1950-57.* Glencoe: Free Press, 1958.

HSIA, RONALD. *Economic Planning in Communist China.* New York: International Secretariat, Institute of Pacific Relations, 1955.

KIRBY, E. STUART (ed.). *Contemporary China: Economic and Social Studies, Documents, Bibliography, Chronology.* 2 vols. Hong Kong: University of Hong Kong Press, 1956 (Vol. I). London: Oxford University Press, 1958 (Vol. II).

> *Objective survey of economic conditions in Communist China. Chinese sources cited.*

————. "Economic Planning and Policy in Communist China," *International Affairs,* XXXIV (April 1958), 174-83.

————. *Introduction to the Economic History of China.* London: Allen and Unwin, 1954.

> *Review of the schools of thought and the bibliography on the economic and social history of China. Good as an introductory study.*

LI, CHOH-MING. *Economic Development of Communist China.* Berkeley: University of California Press, 1959.

> *An appraisal of the first five years of Communist China's industrialization and economy.*

LI, FU-CHUN. *Report on the First Five-Year Plan for Development of the National Economy of the People's Republic of China in 1953-1957.* Peking: Foreign Languages Press, 1955.

> *Delivered on July 5 and 6, 1955 at the second session of the First National People's Congress.*

New China's Economic Achievements, 1949-52. Peking: Foreign Languages Press, 1952.

> *Compilation by the China Committee for the Promotion of International Trade of speeches by Mao Tse-tung, Liu Shao-*

*ch'i, Ch'en Yün, Po I-po, Li Fu-chun, Lai Jo-yü, and others on
the budget, finance, taxation, land reform, water conservation,
commerce, foreign trade, labor, and agricultural production.*
Rostow, W. W. *The Prospects for Communist China.* New York: John
Wiley, 1954.
Wu, Yuan-li. *An Economic Survey of Communist China.* New York:
Bookman Associates, 1956.
*Comprehensive survey on all aspects of economic development
in Communist China, giving plans, statistics, and conditions,
all documented with materials from Chinese Communist sources.
Perhaps the best single-volume work on the subject.*

Chapter 14. ORGANIZATION AND USE OF MANPOWER

Chen, Ta. "Basic Problems of the Chinese Working Classes," *American
Journal of Sociology,* LIII (November 1947), 184-91.
————. *The Labor Movement in China.* Honolulu: Institute of Pacific
Relations, 1927.
*Paper read at the Second General Session of the Institute of
Pacific Relations, July 15-29, 1927.*
Epstein, Israel. *Notes on Labor Problems in Nationalist China.* New
York: Institute of Pacific Relations, 1949.
*Concise study of Chinese labor problems in wartime and post-
war China.*
Labor Insurance Regulations of the People's Republic of China. Peking:
Foreign Languages Press, 1953.
*Promulgated as amended by the Government Administration
Council, January 2, 1953.*
Lai, Jo-yu. *The General Conditions of China's Labor Movement.* Peking:
Workers' Press, 1952.
*Speech made on May 1, 1952 by the secretary-general of the
All-China Federation of Trade Unions.*
Lamb, Jefferson D. H., and Tung-hai Lin. *The Labour Movement and
Labour Legislation in China.* Shanghai: China United Press, 1933.
Historical background.
Ma, Chao-chun. *History of the Labor Movement in China.* (Translated
from the Chinese by Peter Min Chi Liang.) Taipei: China Cultural
Service, 1955.
Ong, Shao-er. "Forced Labor in China Today," *World Affairs Inter-
preter,* XXIV (April 1953), 80-86.

SHIH, KUO-HENG. *China Enters the Machine Age.* (With a supplementary chapter by Ju-k'ang T'ien; edited and translated from the Chinese by Hsiao-tung Fei and Francis L. K. Hsu.) Cambridge: Harvard University Press, 1944.
> *Good on the problems of labor in Chinese wartime industry.*

STEINER, H. ARTHUR. "Trade Unions in Mao's China," *Problems of Communism,* V, No. 2 (March-April 1956), 27-33.

Trade Unions in People's China. Peking: Foreign Languages Press, 1956.

Trade Union Law of the People's Republic of China. Peking: Foreign Languages Press, 1951.
> *Among the relevant documents appended are the provisional rules of procedure for settling labor disputes and the organization of labor-capital consultative councils.*

United States. Bureau of the Census. *The Population and Manpower of China.* Washington, D. C., 1958.
> *An annotated bibliography.*

WAGNER, AUGUSTA. *Labor Legislation in China.* Peking: Yenching University, 1938.

WALES, NYM. *The Chinese Labor Movement.* New York: John Day, 1945.
> *Pro-Communist in treatment.*

WITTFOGEL, KARL A. "Forced Labor in Communist China," *Far Eastern Economic Review,* XXI (September 13, 1956), 327-31.

Chapter 15. FINANCIAL SYSTEM

BOLDYREV, B. "Finances, Money and Credits in the Economic Construction of the Chinese People's Republic," *Soviet Press Translations,* VII (January 15, 1952), 35-47.

CHANG, KAI-NGAU (CHIA-AO CHANG). *The Inflationary Spiral: The Experience in China, 1939-1950.* Cambridge: Technology Press, Massachusetts Institute of Technology, 1958.

CHENG, CHU-YUAN. *Monetary Affairs of Communist China.* Hong Kong: Union Research Institute, 1955.
> *Study of the problems confronting the Chinese Communists, documented by materials from the Communist press.*

HSIA, RONALD. *Price Control in Communist China.* New York: International Secretariat, Institute of Pacific Relations, 1953.

HSIAO, CHI-JUNG. *Revenue and Disbursement of Communist China.* Hong Kong: Union Research Institute, 1954.
> *Analysis of the revenue of Communist China showing inconsistencies, critical problems, and future prospects.*

HSIN, YING. *The Price Problems of Communist China.* Hong Kong: Union Research Institute, 1954.

KANN, E. "The Great Inflation in China (1946-49)," *Far Eastern Economic Review,* XVIII (May 12 to June 9, 1955), 592-95; 621-23; 653-56; 689-90.
> *Parts I-IV are on the 1946-49 period and Part V on inflation in Communist China.*

REMER, CHARLES F. *Foreign Investments in China.* New York: Macmillan, 1933.
> *On investments and economic conditions in the pre-Communist period.*

TAMAGNA, F. M. *Banking and Financial Control in China.* New York: Institute of Pacific Relations, 1942.
> *One of the best general surveys on the financial conditions of China during the 1930's.*

Chapter 16.   AGRICULTURE

Agrarian Reform Law of the People's Republic of China and Other Relevant Documents. (4th ed.) Peking: Foreign Languages Press, 1953.
> *In addition to the text of the law which was passed in June 1950, this book also contains "Decisions Concerning the Differentiation of Class Status in the Countryside," "Regulations on the Organization of Peasants' Associations," and a report by Liu Shao-ch'i on the Agrarian Reform Law.*

BARNETT, A. DOAK. "China's Road to Collectivization," *Journal of Farm Economics,* XXXV (May 1953), 188-202.

BUCK, JOHN LOSSING. *Chinese Farm Economy: A Study of 2866 Farms in Seventeen Localities and Seven Provinces in China.* Chicago: University of Chicago Press, 1930.
> *Standard work; the first detailed study of the Chinese land system and farm economy, using modern statistical methods.*

————. *Land Utilization in China: A Study of 16,786 Farms in 168 Localities, and 38,256 Farms in Twenty-two Provinces in China, 1929-1933.* Chicago: University of Chicago Press, 1937. (Reprinted in 1956 by the Council on Economic and Cultural Affairs, New York.)
> *The statistics on land tenure refute Communist claims of the large percentage of tenancy and show that the bulk of the farmers possessed some land in pre-Communist China.*

576

————. *Some Basic Agricultural Problems of China.* New York: International Secretariat, Institute of Pacific Relations, 1947.

CHANG, C. M. "Mao's Stratagem of Land Reform," *Foreign Affairs,* XXIX (July 1951), 550-63.

CHAO, KUO-CHUN. *Agrarian Policies of Mainland China: A Documentary Study (1949-1956).* Cambridge: Harvard University Press, 1957.

————. *Agricultural Development and Problems in China Today.* New York: Institute of Pacific Affairs, 1958.
> *Survey of Chinese Communist agrarian policies.*

CHEN, HAN-SENG. *The Story of Chinese Cooperatives.* New York: Institute of Pacific Relations, 1947.
> *Cooperative movement prior to the Communist period.*

CHEN, PO-TA. *A Study of Land Rent in Pre-Liberation China.* Peking: Foreign Languages Press, 1958.

CHOU, PEI-KANG. *Agriculture and Industrialization.* Cambridge: Harvard University Press, 1949.

GAMBLE, SIDNEY D. *Ting Hsien: A North China Rural Community.* New York: International Secretariat, Institute of Pacific Relations, 1954.
> *Study of an experimental farming community in North China, location of the mass education movement.*

HO, FRANKLIN L. "Land Problem of China," *Annals of the American Academy of Political and Social Science,* CCLXXVI (July 1951), 6-11.

————. *Rural Economic Reconstruction in China.* New York: Institute of Pacific Relations, 1936.

KOVALYOV, E. "The Agrarian Policy of the Chinese Communist Party," *Soviet Press Translations,* VI (April 1, 1951), 163-72.

MAO, TSE-TUNG. *The Question of Agricultural Co-operation.* Peking: Foreign Languages Press, 1956.

Mutual Aid and Cooperation in China's Agricultural Production. Peking: Foreign Languages Press, 1953.
> *Decisions on mutual aid and cooperation in agricultural production; basic tasks and policies in rural areas.*

ONG, SHAO-ER. *Agrarian Reform in Communist China to 1952.* Lackland Air Force Base, Texas: Air Force Personnel and Training Research Center, 1955.
> *Survey of the methods and policy of the land reform of the Communists.*

————. *Chinese Farm Economy under Agrarian Reform.* Lackland Air Force Base, Texas: Air Force Personnel and Training Research Center, 1955.
> *Study of conditions by a trained agriculturist.*

SHEN, TSUNG-HAN. *Agricultural Resources of China.* Ithaca: Cornell University Press, 1951.

Discusses water resources, land utilization, main crops, live-stock, fishery, etc. Lacks definite statistics.

SUN, HO-SHENG. *Cooperative Farming Systems and Their Application in China.* Ann Arbor: University Microfilms, 1954.
Abstracted in Dissertation Abstracts, No. 16 (April 1956), 613-14.

THOMAS, S. B. "Communist China's Agrarian Policy, 1954-1956," *Pacific Affairs*, XXIX (June 1956), 141-60.

TUNG, TA-LIN. *Agricultural Co-operation in China.* Peking: Foreign Languages Press, 1958.

WU, YUAN-LI. *The Land Program of the Chinese Communist Party: An Interpretation.* San Francisco: Committee for Free Asia, 1952.

Chapter 17. INDUSTRY

CHENG, TSU-YUAN (CHU-YUAN CHENG). *Anshan Steel Factory in Communist China.* Hong Kong: Union Research Institute, 1956.
Study of a major steel mill in Manchuria.

FONG, H. D. (HSIEN-T'ING FANG). *China's Industrialization: A Statistical Survey.* Shanghai: China Institute of Pacific Relations, 1931.

HSIA, RONALD. "China's Industrial Growth, 1953-1957," *Annals of the American Academy of Political and Social Science*, CCCXXI (January 1959), 71-81.

————. *The Role of Labor-Intensive Investment Projects in China's Capital Formation.* Cambridge: Center for International Studies, Massachusetts Institute of Technology, 1954. (Mimeographed.)
Analysis of the relationship between construction projects and capital formation in Communist China from 1949 to 1953.

LIEU, D. K. (TA-CHUN LIU). *The Growth and Industrialization of Shanghai.* Shanghai: China Institute of Pacific Relations, 1936.
Good detailed study of industries in Shanghai prior to the outbreak of the Sino-Japanese War.

SHABAD, THEODORE. "Communist China's Production Statistics," *Far Eastern Survey*, XXIV (July 1955), 102-08.

WANG, FOH-SHEN. *China's Industrial Production, 1931-1946.* Nanking: Institute of Social Sciences, Academia Sinica, 1948.

WU, CHING-CHAO. *Industrial Planning in China.* Chungking: China Institute of Pacific Relations, 1945.

WU, YUAN-LI. "China's Industry in Peace and War," *Current History*, XXXV, No. 208 (December 1958), 327-35.

Wu, Yuan-li, and Robert C. North. "China and India: Two Paths to Industrialization," *Problems of Communism*, IV, No. 3 (May-June 1955), 13-19.

Yeh, Kung-chia. *Electric Power Development in Mainland China: Prewar and Postwar*. Santa Monica, California: Rand Corporation, 1956.

Chapter 18. DOMESTIC AND FOREIGN TRADE

Chen, Han-seng. "The Future of China's Foreign Trade," *China Monthly Review*, CXXIII, No. 7 (July 1952), 15-19.

Cheng, Cho-yuan (Chu-yuan Cheng). *The China Mainland Market under Communist Control*. Hong Kong: Union Research Institute, 1956.

Cheng, Yu-kuei. *Foreign Trade and Industrial Development of China: An Historical and Integrated Analysis through 1948*. Washington, D. C.: University Press of Washington, D. C., 1956.

Hsia, Ronald. "Private Enterprise in Communist China," *Pacific Affairs*, XXVI (December 1953), 329-35.

Hsin, Ying. *The Foreign Trade of Communist China*. Hong Kong: Union Research Institute, 1954.

>   *Chapters on the changing phases of foreign trade, government organizations, relations between official and private trade, barter trade, restrictions, and prospects.*

Miyashita, Tadao. *Development of Trade between Japan and Communist China: Its Present Problems and Its Future*. Tokyo: Japan Institute of Pacific Relations, 1958.

>   *Paper prepared for the Thirteenth Conference of the Institute of Pacific Relations, Lahore, February 1958.*

Remer, C. F. *The Foreign Trade of China*. Shanghai: Commercial Press, 1926.

>   *Historical discussions of China's foreign trade in the nineteenth and twentieth centuries.*

Remer, C. F. (ed.). *Three Essays on the International Economics of Communist China*. Ann Arbor: Center for Japanese Studies, University of Michigan, 1959.

United States Joint Publications Research Service. *Domestic Trade in Communist China*. New York, December 6, 1957.

>   *Reports based on Chinese newspapers and periodicals.*

Chapter 19. PUBLIC HEALTH AND WELFARE

GAMBLE, SIDNEY D. *Peking: A Social Survey.* New York: Doran, 1921.
   Discusses some of the charitable organizations.
HUME, EDWARD H. *The Chinese Way in Medicine.* Baltimore: Johns
   Hopkins Press, 1940.
————. *Doctors East, Doctors West: An American Physician's Life
   in China.* New York: W. W. Norton, 1946.
"Labor and Public Health Conditions in Communist China," *Current
   Background,* No. 405.
SCOTT, JAMES C. *Health and Agriculture in China: A Fundamental Ap-
   proach to Some of the Problems of World Hunger.* London: Faber
   and Faber, 1952.
   On public health and rural conditions.
TSU, YU-YUE (YU-YU CHU). *The Spirit of Chinese Philanthropy.* New
   York: Columbia University, 1912.
   On the tradition of charity and mutual aid in China.
TUNG, FANG-MING. "The National Red Cross Society of China," *People's
   China,* No. 16 (1952), 27-28.
WINFIELD, GERALD F. *China: The Land and the People.* New York:
   William Sloane, 1948.
   Good on the problems of health and agriculture.
WONG, K. CHIMIN, and LIEN-TEH WU. *History of Chinese Medicine.*
   Tientsin: The Tientsin Press, 1932.
   *Except for the first part on traditional Chinese medicine, the
   bulk of the work is on modern medical practice in China.*

Chapter 20. EDUCATION

CHAO, CHUNG, and I-FAN YANG. *Students in Mainland China.* Hong Kong:
   Union Research Institute, 1956.
   *Documented with press items in a survey of students under
   Communist rule.*
CHEN, THEODORE HSI-EN. "New Schools for China," *Current History,*
   XXII (June 1952), 328-33.
CHI, TUNG-WEI. *Education for the Proletariat in Communist China.* Hong
   Kong: Union Research Institute, 1954.
   *General discussion of Communist policy of using education as
   a means of political indoctrination.*

CHIANG, MON-LIN. *A Study in Chinese Principles of Education.* Shanghai: Commercial Press, 1924.
> *Education in the traditional period and the first years of the republic.*

CHIANG, WEN-HAN. *The Chinese Student Movement.* New York: King's Crown Press, 1948.
> *On periodic student agitations from the May 4th, 1919 movement on, through the strikes and demonstrations in the 1930's, to the activities in the postwar period. Discusses also the ideological background.*

CHUNG, SHIN. *Higher Education in Communist China.* Hong Kong: Union Research Institute, 1953.
> *On colleges, universities, and technical schools in Communist China.*

"Education in Communist China," *World Today,* VIII (June 1952), 257-68.

FREYN, HUBERT. *Chinese Education in the War.* Shanghai: Kelly & Walsh, 1940.
> *On the migration of colleges and students from the coastal regions to the interior in the first years of the Sino-Japanese War.*

GREGG, ALICE H. *China and Educational Autonomy.* Syracuse: Syracuse University Press, 1946.

HSIAO, THEODORE F. *The History of Modern Education in China.* Shanghai: Commercial Press, 1935.
> *On the introduction of western systems of education in China.*

KIANG, WEN-HAN. *The Chinese Student Movement.* New York: King's Crown Press, 1948.

KUO, PING-WEN. *The Chinese System of Public Education.* New York: Teachers College, Columbia University, 1915.
> *Good historical discussion.*

LI, TA. "Concerning the Thought Rehabilitation of University Professors," *Soviet Press Translations,* VII (February 1, 1952), 86-89.

LINDSAY, MICHAEL, *et al. Notes on Educational Problems in Communist China, 1941-47.* New York: Institute of Pacific Relations, 1950.
> *Personal account of the educational system of the Chinese Communists in the Shensi-Kansu-Ningsia border region. The supplement on the developments in the years 1948 and 1949 is by Marion Menzies, William Paget, and S. B. Thomas of the International Secretariat of the Institute of Pacific Relations.*

LU, TING-I. *Education Must Be Combined with Productive Labour.* Peking: Foreign Languages Press, 1958.

LUTZ, JESSIE GREGORY. *The Role of the Christian Colleges in Modern China before 1928.* Ann Arbor: University Microfilms, 1955.
> *Abstracted in Dissertation Abstracts, No. 16 (February 1956), 327-28.*

PEAKE, CYRUS H. *Nationalism and Education in Modern China.* New York: Columbia University Press, 1932.
   Partly on the educational changes since 1860 and partly a summary of the Nationalist program of education.
"Progress of Education in China," *Far Eastern Economic Review,* XVIII (February 3, 1955), 149-55.
WANG, CHARLES K. S. *The Control of Teachers in Communist China: A Socio-political Study.* Lackland Air Force Base, Texas: Air Force Personnel and Training Research Center, 1955.
   Based on materials gathered from the Communist press.
YEN, JAMES Y. C. *The Mass Education Movement in China.* Shanghai: Commercial Press, 1925.
   On the system of teaching people to read "Basic Chinese" of a thousand words by a well-known promoter of mass education.

Chapter 21.   SCIENCE AND TECHNOLOGY

BERNAL, J. D. "Science and Technology in China," *Universities Quarterly,* XI (November 1956), 64-75.
CHAN, WING-TSIT. "Neo-Confucianism and Chinese Scientific Thought," *Philosophy East and West,* VI (1957), 309-32.
CHANG, ALFRED ZEE. "Scientists in Communist China," *Science,* CXIX (June 1954), 784-89.
CHU, COCHING. "Surveying the Heilunkiang Basin," *Peking Review,* I (April 8, 1958), 12-14.
FAIRBANK, JOHN KING. "The Influence of Modern Western Science and Technology on Japan and China," *Explorations in Entrepreneurial History,* VII (April 1955), 189-204.
HSIEH, CHIAO-MIN. "The Status of Geography in Communist China," *Geographical Review,* XLIX (October 1959).
   An excellent account of the influence of Marxian ideology upon the study of geography.
IKLE, FRED C. *The Growth of China's Scientific and Technical Manpower.* Santa Monica, California: Rand Corporation, 1957.
NEEDHAM, JOSEPH. *Science and Civilization in China.* (3 volumes published out of 7 projected volumes.) Cambridge: Cambridge University Press, 1954, 1956, 1959.
   Vol. 1, "Introductory Orientations," gives the bibliographical, historical, and geographical introduction to Chinese science,

and also an outline of the scope of the work. Vol. 2, "History of Scientific Thought," describes the Confucian milieu, the rise of the organic naturalism of the Taoist school, the scientific philosophy of the Mohists and Logicians, the quantitative materialism of the Legalists, the effect of Buddhist thought, and the Neo-Confucianist climax of Chinese naturalism. Vol. 3, "Mathematics and the Sciences of the Heavens and the Earth," discusses mathematics, astronomy, meteorology, geography and cartography, geology, seismology and mineralogy.

United States Library of Congress. Science Division. *Chinese Scientific and Technical Publications in the Collections of the Library of Congress.* Washington, D. C., 1955.

WILSON, J. TUZO. *One Chinese Moon.* New York: Hill and Wang, 1959.

————. "Red China's Hidden Capital of Science," *Saturday Review of Literature,* XLI, No. 45 (November 8, 1958), 47-56.

Chapter 22. ART AND INTELLECTUAL EXPRESSION

Art

ALEXANDER, MARY CHARLOTTE. *A Handbook on Chinese Art Symbols.* Austin, Texas: Press of Von Boeckmann-Jones, 1958.

BURLING, JUDITH, and ARTHUR HART BURLING. *Chinese Art.* New York: Studio Publications, 1953.

CHIANG, YEE. *Chinese Calligraphy: An Introduction to Its Aesthetic and Technique.* (2d ed.) London: Methuen, 1954.

> Explains construction, technique, strokes, and composition; chapters on abstract beauty and relation between calligraphy and other arts are particularly interesting.

Folk Arts of New China. Peking: Foreign Languages Press, 1954.

> Contains articles and illustrations on the dance, music, drama, shadow plays, puppets, papercuts, etc.

LEVIS, HAZEDEL JOHN. *Foundations of Chinese Musical Art.* Peiping: Henri Vetch, 1936.

> A thorough study of fundamental historical aspects.

MAO, TSE-TUNG. *Talks at the Yenan Forum on Art and Literature.* Peking: Foreign Languages Press, 1956. (Published in 1950 as *Art and Literature* by International Publishers, New York.)

> An important pronouncement made in 1942 during the Yenan period on the direction of Chinese Communist art and literature. Widely used as an over-all directive in Communist China.

ROWLEY, GEORGE. *Principles of Chinese Painting*. Princeton: Princeton University Press, 1952.

SICKMAN, LAWRENCE, and ALEXANDER SOPER. *The Art and Architecture of China*. Harmondsworth, Middlesex: Penguin Books, 1956.
With 190 plates; a popular work.

SILCOCK, ARNOLD. *Introduction to Chinese Art and History*. London: Faber and Faber, 1936.
One of the best summaries for the layman.

SIREN, OSVALD. *Chinese Painting: Leading Masters and Principles*. 7 vols. New York: Ronald Press, 1956-58.
A definitive work tracing and interpreting Chinese painting from earliest times to the end of the eighteenth century. The volumes are as follows: I, Early Chinese Painting; II, The Sung Period; III, Plates; IV, The Yüan and Early Ming Masters; V, The Later Ming and Leading Ch'ing Masters; VI, Plates; VII, Annotated Lists of the Works of Chinese Painters of the Yüan, Ming, and Ch'ing Periods.

—————. *Gardens of China*. New York: Ronald Press, 1949.
A valuable history of Chinese landscape design and its relation to art and civilization; interpretation of underlying aesthetics and analysis of fundamental characteristics.

Songs of New China. Peking: Foreign Languages Press, 1953.
A collection of Communist folk songs and marching songs, with piano accompaniment. Chinese and English texts.

SULLIVAN, MICHAEL. "The Traditional Trend in Contemporary Chinese Art," *Oriental Art*, II (Winter 1949-50), 105-10.

SZE, MAI-MAI. *The Tao of Painting: A Study of the Ritual Disposition of Chinese Painting*. 2 vols. New York: Pantheon Books, 1956.
The first volume is an essay on the "tao" or way of Chinese painting and the second volume a translation of the Mustard Seed Garden Manual of Painting *(1679-1701) with 400 examples of brushwork.*

VINCENT, IRENE V. *The Sacred Oasis: Caves of the Thousand Buddhas, Tun Huang*. Chicago: University of Chicago Press, 1953.
Description of the Tun-huang grottoes and frescoes, some showing traces of Indian, Persian, and Greco-Roman influences.

WALEY, ARTHUR. *An Introduction to the Study of Chinese Painting*. London: E. Benn, 1923. (Reprinted in 1958 by Grove Press, New York.)

WILLETTS, WILLIAM. *Chinese Art*. 2 vols. Harmondsworth, Middlesex: Penguin Books, 1958.

Literature

ARLINGTON, L. C. *The Chinese Drama from the Earliest Times until Today*. Shanghai: Kelly & Walsh, 1930.

584

> The book traces the origin of Chinese drama and describes the accompanying music and instruments.

BISHOP, JOHN LYMAN. *The Colloquial Short Story in China: A Study of the San-yen Collection*. Cambridge: Harvard-Yenching Institute, 1956.

> A study of the development, and structural, stylistic, and thematic aspects of Chinese short stories. The last chapter contains translations of four examples.

BOROWITZ, ALBERT. *Fiction in Communist China, 1949-53*. Cambridge: Center for International Studies, Massachusetts Institute of Technology, 1954.

> On the use of fiction for propaganda and for the program of collectivization.

CHAN, SHAU WING. "Literature in Communist China," *Problems of Communism*, VII, No. 1 (1958), 44-51.

CHAO, CHUNG. *The Communist Program for Literature and Art in China*. Hong Kong: Union Research Institute, 1955.

> Survey of Chinese Communist policies toward writers and how they are organized and treated. Documented with items from the Chinese Communist press.

CHOU, YANG. *A Great Debate on the Literary Front*. Peking: Foreign Languages Press, 1958.

————. *China's New Literature and Art: Essays and Addresses*. Peking: Foreign Languages Press, 1954.

CHU, SU-CHEN. *Fifteen Strings of Cash: A Kunchu Opera*. (Translated from the Chinese by Hsien-yi Yang and Gladys Yang.) Peking: Foreign Languages Press, 1957.

> Original libretto by Su-chen Chu; revised by Chuan-ying Chou and other members of the Chekiang Kunchu Opera Company; final version by Sze Chen.

FENG, YUAN-CHUN. *A Short History of Classical Chinese Literature*. Peking: Foreign Languages Press, 1958.

GILES, HERBERT ALLEN. *A History of Chinese Literature*. London: W. Heinemann, 1901. (Reprinted in 1958 by Grove Press, New York.)

> Written toward the end of the nineteenth century; outdated.

GOLDMAN, MERLE. "Hu Feng's Conflict with the Communist Literary Authorities," *Papers on China*, XI (1957), 149-91.

GRIEDER, JEROME B. "The Communist Critique of Hung Lou Meng," *Papers on China*, X (1956), 142-68.

HIGHTOWER, JAMES ROBERT. *Topics in Chinese Literature: Outline and Bibliographies*. Cambridge: Harvard-Yenching Institute, 1950.

> Useful for a discussion of various genres of Chinese literature and titles of selected Chinese literary pieces that have been translated.

HU, SHIH. *The Chinese Renaissance*. (Haskell Lectures on Comparative Religion.) Chicago: University of Chicago Press, 1934.

HUANG, SUNG-KANG. *Lu Hsun and the New Culture Movement of Modern China.* Amsterdam: Djambatan, 1957.

LI, TIEN-YI. "Continuity and Change in Modern Chinese Literature," *Annals of the American Academy of Political and Social Science,* CCCXXI (January 1959), 90-99.

LU, HSUN. *Selected Works of Lu Hsun.* (3 vols.) Peking: Foreign Languages Press, 1956-1959.

> *Additional volumes to be published.*

LU, TING-I. "*Let Flowers of Many Kinds Bloom, Diverse Schools of Thought Contend!*" Peking: Foreign Languages Press, 1957.

> *Speech, May 26, 1956, on policies toward art, literature and science.*

MAO, TSE-TUNG. *Nineteen Poems.* (With notes by Chen-fu Chou and an appreciation by Kehchia Tsang; translated by Andrew Boyd and Gladys Yang.) Peking: Foreign Languages Press, 1958.

MAO, TUN. *Spring Silkworms and Other Stories.* Peking: Foreign Languages Press, 1956.

SCHULTZ, WILLIAM R. "Kuo Mo-jo and the Romantic Aesthetics: 1918-1925," *Journal of Oriental Literature,* VI, No. 2 (1955), 49-81.

SCHYNS, J. *1500 Modern Chinese Novels and Plays.* Peiping: Catholic University Press, 1948.

> *Synopses of modern Chinese fiction and drama, including an article on modern Chinese fiction by Hsueh-lin Su, and short biographies of Chinese writers by Yen-sheng Chao.*

SCOTT, ADOLPH CLARENCE. *The Classical Theatre of China.* London: Allen and Unwin, 1957.

> *Good on the technical aspects of the Peking theater, such as instruments, costumes, make-up, props, gestures, etc.*

YANG, I-FAN. *The Case of Hu Feng.* Hong Kong: Union Research Institute, 1956.

Philosophy and Thought

BRIERE, O. *Fifty Years of Chinese Philosophy (1898-1950).* (Translated from the French with additional annotation and bibliography by Lawrence G. Thompson.) London: Allen and Unwin, 1956.

> *Despite the title most of the philosophic trends discussed are from the 1920's and after; Chinese Communist thought is not well covered.*

CHAN, WING-TSIT. "Basic Chinese Philosophical Concepts," *Philosophy East and West,* II (July 1952), 166-70.

————. *An Outline and an Annotated Bibliography of Chinese Philosophy.* (Rev. ed.) New Haven: Far Eastern Publications, Yale University, 1959.

CHANG, CARSUN (CHUN-MAI CHANG). *The Development of Neo-Confucian Thought.* New York: Bookman Associates, 1957.

586

Review of Neo-Confucian philosophy from the beginning to the end of the Sung and beginning of the Yüan periods.

CHEN, THEODORE HSI-EN. "The Thought Reform of Intellectuals," *Annals of the American Academy of Political and Social Science,* CCCXXI (January 1959), 82-89.

CHOU, EN-LAI. *Report on the Question of the Intellectuals.* Peking: Foreign Languages Press, 1956.

CREEL, HERRLEE G. *Chinese Thought from Confucius to Mao Tse-tung.* Chicago: University of Chicago Press, 1953.
> On various schools of philosophy in pre-modern China; little on Communist thought.

FUNG, YU-LAN. *A History of Chinese Philosophy.* 2 vols. (Translated from the Chinese by Derk Bodde.) Princeton: Princeton University Press, 1952-53.
> A broad and inclusive survey of Chinese philosophy with detailed discussion and analysis of each school.

LEVENSON, JOSEPH RICHMOND. *Confucian China and Its Modern Fate: The Problem of Intellectual Continuity.* Berkeley: University of California Press, 1958.

LIFTON, ROBERT J. "Chinese Communist Thought Reform." Pages 219-312 in *Conference on Group Processes.* Princeton, 1957.

————. "Thought Reform of Chinese Intellectuals: A Psychiatric Evaluation," *Journal of Asian Studies,* XVI, No. 1 (November 1956), 75-88.

LIN, MOUSHENG. *Men and Ideas: An Informal History of Chinese Political Thought.* New York: John Day, 1942.
> A popular study of the lives, ideas, and influences of some key figures in Chinese intellectual history.

LIU, WU-CHI. *A Short History of Confucian Philosophy.* Harmondsworth, Middlesex: Penguin Books, 1955.

NIVISON, DAVID S., and ARTHUR F. WRIGHT (eds.). *Confucianism in Action.* Stanford: Stanford University Press, 1959.

WILHELM, RICHARD. *Confucius and Confucianism.* (Translated from the German by George H. Danton and Annina P. Danton.) New York: Harcourt, Brace, 1931.
> Contains a short biography of Confucius and his works; evaluates sources and documents.

WRIGHT, ARTHUR F. (ed.). *Studies in Chinese Thought.* ("Comparative Studies in Cultures and Civilizations.") Chicago: University of Chicago Press, 1953.
> Contains nine articles on philosophy, art, language and problems of translation.

A Selected Bibliography

Chapter 23.   VALUES AND PATTERNS OF LIVING

Values

CHENG, TIEN-HSI. *China Moulded by Confucius: The Chinese Way in Western Light.* London: Stevens & Sons, 1946.

HSU, FRANCIS L. K. *Americans and Chinese: Two Ways of Life.* New York: H. Schuman, 1953.

> *A popular sociological study of the values of the two peoples.*

————. *Religion, Science and Human Crisis.* London: Routledge, 1952.

HU, HSIEN-CHIN. "The Chinese Concept of 'Face'," *American Anthropologist,* XLVI (1944), 45-64.

LIN, YUTANG. *My Country and My People* (2d ed.). New York: John Day, 1939.

> *Observations on the Chinese as a people by an astute Chinese writer. Part 1 on Chinese character; Part 2 on Chinese mind; and Part 3 on the ideals of life.*

NIVISON, DAVID S. "Communist Ethics and Chinese Tradition," *Journal of Asian Studies,* XVI, No. 1 (November 1956), 51-74.

> *An analysis of certain aspects of Communist thought in the last two decades and of the ways in which the Peking regime may relate its ideology to the great corpus of traditional Chinese thought.*

WRIGHT, ARTHUR F. "The Chinese Monolith: Past and Present," *Problems of Communism,* IV, No. 4 (July-August 1955), 1-8.

> *On the popular Chinese attitude toward authority, past and present.*

————. "Struggle versus Harmony: Symbols of Competing Values in Modern China," *World Politics,* VI (October 1953), 31-44.

Patterns of Life

BURKHARDT, Col. VALENTINE RODOLPHE. *Chinese Creeds and Customs.* 2 vols. Hong Kong: South China Morning Post, 1954-1955.

> *On popular beliefs, ceremonies, and festivities.*

CROOK, DAVID, and ISABEL CROOK. *Revolution in a Chinese Village.* London: Routledge, 1959.

> *Economic, political, and social changes from the landlord regime during the Nationalist period to the land reform movement of the Communists.*

EBERHARD, WOLFRAM. *Chinese Festivals.* New York: H. Schuman, 1952.

FEI, HSIAO-TUNG. *Peasant Life in China: A Field Study of Country Life in the Yangtze Valley.* London: Routledge, 1939.

588

KULP, D. H. *Country Life in South China: The Sociology of Familism.*
New York: Teachers College, Columbia University, 1925.
    *The first volume, "Phenix Village, Kwantung, China," is an
    on-the-scene account by a trained sociologist.*
LEONG, Y. K., and L. K. TAO. *Village and Town Life in China.* London:
Allen and Unwin, 1915.
    *A sketch of rural-urban life in the last years of the empire and
    the first years of the republic.*
THOMPSON, DOUGLAS W. *Rise and Build: Chinese Pattern for Village
Life.* London: Edinburgh House Press, 1949.
    *A description by a British observer sympathetic to the Com-
    munists. Written before the massive land reform program was
    carried out.*
TUN, LI-CHEN. *Annual Customs and Festivals in Peking.* (Translated
from the Chinese by Derk Bodde.) Peking: H. Vetch, 1936.
YANG, C. K. *A Chinese Village and Early Communist Transition.* Cam-
bridge: Technology Press, Massachusetts Institute of Technology,
·1959.
YANG, MARTIN. *A Chinese Village.* New York: Columbia University
Press, 1945.
    *Describes life in the village of T'ai-tou in Shantung, home of
    the author.*

Chapter 24.   NATIONAL ATTITUDES

AN, TZU-WEN. "Struggle for the Eradication of the Passive Attitude and
Unhealthy Conditions in Party Organizations," *Current Background,*
No. 231.
    *Article by a deputy director of the Department of Organiza-
    tion of the Central Committee of the CCP; attacks the lack
    of development of the process of criticism and self-criticism and
    the failure of the leadership to understand the peasants.*
CHIU, SIN-MING. *Some Basic Conceptions and Rules of Conduct of
Chinese Communism.* Lackland Air Force Base, Texas: Air Force
Personnel and Training Research Center, 1955.
    *On the conceptual and operational code of the Chinese Com-
    munist leaders; based on Communist publications.*
CLARK, GERALD. *Impatient China—Red China Today.* New York: David
McKay, 1959.
KIERMAN, FRANK. *The Chinese Intelligentsia and the Communists.* Cam-
bridge: Center for International Studies, Massachusetts Institute
of Technology, 1954.

A Selected Bibliography

WANG, CHARLES K. A. *Reactions in Communist China: An Analysis of Letters to Newspaper Editors.* Lackland Air Force Base, Texas: Air Force Personnel and Training Research Center, 1955.

WRIGHT, ARTHUR F., and HELLMUT WILHELM, and BENJAMIN SCHWARTZ. "Chinese Reactions to Imported Ideas: A Symposium," *Journal of the History of Ideas,* XII, No. 1 (January 1951), 31-74.
> Covers the period from late Ch'ing to the Chinese Communist regime.

GENERAL REFERENCE WORKS

Bibliographies

Bibliography of Asian Studies. Published annually at Ann Arbor by the Association for Asian Studies (formerly *Far Eastern Bibliography* before 1957).
> Lists of books and important articles in western languages, including Russian.

CHAO, KUO-CHUN. *Selected Works in English for a Topical Study of Modern China, 1840-1952.* Cambridge: Regional Studies Program on East Asia, Harvard University, 1952.

————. *Source Materials from Communist China.* 3 vols. Cambridge: Russian Research Center, Harvard University, 1953.
> Divided into three parts: (1) agrarian policy; (2) aspects of economic planning; and (3) fiscal, monetary, and international policies of the Chinese Communist government. Contains titles and brief summaries of 193 laws, decrees, reports and discussions, as well as recent western articles on these subjects.

CORDIER, HENRI. *Bibliotheca Sinica: Dictionnaire Bibliographique des Ouvrages Relatifs à l'Empire Chinois.* (2d ed.) 4 vols. Paris: E. Guilmoto, 1904-08. (*Supplement.* 1 vol. Paris: P. Geuthner, 1924.)
> Although outdated, it is still a good compendium on sinological studies of pre-republican China.

DAVIDSON, M. *A List of Published Translations from Chinese into English, French, and German.* 2 pts. Ann Arbor: American Council of Learned Societies, 1952-57.

FAIRBANK, JOHN KING, and MASATAKA BANNO. *Japanese Studies of Modern China: A Bibliographical Guide to Historical and Social-Science Research on the 19th and 20th Centuries.* Rutland, Vermont: C. E. Tuttle, 1955.
> A wide range of Japanese works on pre-Communist China; published by the Harvard-Yenching Institute.

FAIRBANK, JOHN KING, and KWANG-CHING LIU. *Modern China: A Bibliographical Guide to Chinese Works, 1898-1937.* Cambridge: Harvard University Press, 1950.
> *Largely works in the Chinese-Japanese Library of the Harvard-Yenching Institute at Harvard University. Works and documents in Chinese.*

GOODRICH, L. C., and H. C. FENN. *A Syllabus of the History of Chinese Civilization and Culture.* (6th ed.) New York: China Society of America, 1958.
> *Contains lists of basic works.*

SHIRATO, ICHIRO, and C. MARTIN WILBUR. *Japanese Sources on the History of the Chinese Communist Movement.* New York: Columbia University, 1953.
> *An annotated bibliography of materials in the East Asiatic Library of Columbia University and the Division of Orientalia, Library of Congress.*

SUN, E-TU ZEN, and JOHN DE FRANCIS. *Bibliography on Chinese Social History: A Selected and Critical List of Chinese Periodical Sources.* New Haven: Institute of Far Eastern Languages, Yale University, 1952.
> *Good for recent Chinese economic and sociological studies.*

THOMAS, S. B. *Recent Books on China, 1945-51.* New York: Institute of Pacific Relations, 1951.
> *A list of recent popular books on China.*

WILBUR, C. MARTIN. *Chinese Sources on the History of the Chinese Communist Movement.* New York: East Asian Institute, Columbia University, 1950. (Mimeographed.)

WU, EUGENE. *Leaders of Twentieth-Century China: An Annotated Bibliography of Selected Chinese Biographical Works in the Hoover Library.* Stanford: Stanford University Press, 1956.

YUAN, TUNG-LI. *China in Western Literature.* New Haven: Far Eastern Publications, Yale University, 1959.
> *Designed as a continuation of Cordier's Bibliotheca Sinica with entries arranged according to subject categories.*

————. *Economic and Social Development of Modern China: A Bibliographical Guide.* New Haven: Human Relations Area Files, 1956.
> *Essential titles of monographs and pamphlets published in English, French, and German from 1900 through 1955.*

Serials and Collections

China News Analysis. Weekly newsletter published privately in Hong Kong.

Soviet Press Translations. Published biweekly by the Far Eastern Institute of the University of Washington from October 31, 1946 to March 15, 1953.

Contains Soviet writings on China and speeches and articles by Chinese Communist leaders in the Soviet press. After 1951, direct translations from the Chinese Communist press were added.

STEINER, H. ARTHUR (ed.). *Chinese Communism in Action.* 3 pts. Los Angeles: University of California, 1953.

Based on translations by the United States Consulate-General in Hong Kong.

United States. Consulate-General (Hong Kong). *Current Background.*

Translations of important Chinese Communist documents and statements. Each issue is usually devoted to one or more selected topics and includes translations of relevant laws and decrees, treaties and agreements, speeches, resolutions, reports, magazine articles, newspaper editorials, as well as a chronology of events, lists of government personnel, structure of government departments, directories of government and semi-government mass organizations. All significant events and developments in Communist China are given full coverage. A typical issue will also have an analytic introduction and research articles by consulate staff members, giving the background and statistics of the topics presented. This series, begun in September 1950, is an indispensable source of information for any research on Communist China.

————. Consulate-General (Hong Kong). *Extracts from China Mainland Magazines.* Published weekly.

Translations of significant articles from China mainland periodicals.

————. Consulate-General (Hong Kong). *Survey of China Mainland Press.* Published daily from Monday through Friday.

Translations of important articles in Chinese Communist newspapers as well as the releases of the New China News Agency. Useful for day-by-day study of events in Communist China.

Handbooks

CRESSEY, EARL H. *Understanding China: A Handbook of Background Information on Changing China.* New York: Nelson, 1957.

A Guide to New China. (2d ed.) Peking: Foreign Languages Press, 1952.

Mainly political in focus but valuable also for lists of universities and colleges in Peking, Radio Peking's program for overseas listeners, foreign-language periodicals published in Peking, embassies and legations, national holidays, memorial days, and other data.

Handbook on People's China. Peking: Foreign Languages Press, 1957.

Semiofficial English-language publication from Communist China, organized in eleven sections: geography; history; con-

stitution and government; administrative divisions and national regional autonomy; political parties; Chinese People's Political Consultative Conference; economy and finance; science, education, and the press; people's organizations; miscellaneous; and chronicle of events.

Jen-min shou-ts'e (People's Handbook). Published annually in Peking by Ta-kung-pao shê.

Semiofficial Chinese-language handbook of Communist China, appearing annually since 1950 with the exception of 1954. Valuable for the documents and statistics, the data and the lists of government offices, officials, and official and semiofficial institutions.

ROWE, DAVID NELSON, and WILLMOORE KENDALL (eds.). *China: An Area Manual.* 2 vols. Chevy Chase, Maryland: Operations Research Office, Johns Hopkins University, 1955.

Working paper prepared specially for ORO on Chinese geographical, historical, military, cultural, and political background. First volume contains section on military organization of Communist China, with biographical sketches of over a hundred Chinese Communist leaders.

Shih-shih shou-t'se (Current Events Handbook). Published semimonthly in Peking by the Hsin-hua shu-tien.

Useful for current information.

INDEX

600

system, 410-412; higher education, 425-429; in autonomous areas, 93; in Republican period, 413 ff.; language reform, 106; language teaching, 425, 426; libraries, 450; Ministry of, 423; postgraduate, 447; programs for study abroad, 427; reorganization of 1951, 416 ff.; research incentives, 451; school system described, 418-428; scientific, 427, 444-451; secondary schools, 422; teachers' salaries, 422; teacher training 424 ff.; technical training schools, 289; trends and prospects, 433-436; under Nationalists, 30; under 1954 constitution, 416; western influences on, 413 ff.

Egypt, 389

Elections: general, of 1954, 203-205, 210; in mass organizations, 194; local government, 228 ff.; to party congresses, 186

Emigration, 63

Emperor: Confucian theory of, 3, 22, 116, 140; role in Chinese society, 6, 22, 140, 157, 474

Emperors: Ch'ien-lung, 23; Hsia, 12; Hsüan-tung, 28; Hung-wu, 21; K'ang-hsi, 23; Kao-tsu, 16; Manchu, 22-23; Ming, 21 ff.; Mongol, 21 ff.; Sung, 19; T'ai-tsung, 18; Wu-ti, 16; Ying Cheng, 15; Yung-lo, 22

Employment, 286-288. See also Industrialization, Labor force, Manpower

Epidemic control, 403, 405. See also Public health

Episcopal Church, 137. See also Protestantism, Religion

Ethnic groups: autonomous areas, 48-50; classification, 62-67; relations with Han-Chinese, 85-87; under Communism, 63, 87-93. See also Languages, Minority nationalities

Europe, 25, 26 ff., 256-262, 264, 265, 266

Examination system, imperial, 2, 24, 115, 116, 141, 144, 411

Exports, 381-385, 388, 390

Expropriation, 188, 233, 304, 317

Extraterritoriality, 4, 25-27, 381

"Face," 493, 494

Factionalism, political, 189

Factories. See Economy, Chinese; Industrialization

Family: ancestral cult, 111, 112; Communist attack on, 131, 174, 180, 492; folk religions and, 114, 115; Hsiao, 3; Mongol, 75; moral values of, 158, 163, 165, 171; Tibetan, 78; Uigur, 76; Yi culture, 82, 83. See also Kinship patterns, Marriage

Family system: basis of social structure, 157-163; Communist influence, 174-176; Confucianism and, 157-165, 171, 474; disintegration, 178-180; family reform, 171-174; in communes, 179, 180, 230 ff., 431

Famine relief, 33, 397

Farming. See Agriculture

Federation of Left Wing Writers, 466

Fei River Battle, 17

Fellowship of Reconciliation, 135

Feng-chien, feudal authority pattern, 13

Feng Hsüeh-feng, editor, 470

Ferghana, 16

Feudalism, 13, 15, 16

Films, 252-254

Financial and Economic Conference of 1947, 308

Financial system: Bank of China, 324, 383; Bank of Communications, 324; banking, 319-333 (plate, 325); bond issues, 318; budget, 311-319; commercial credit, 328 ff.; currency reform, 307-310; foreign exchange, 388; inflation control, 32, 307; Ministry of, 311, 316, 326; People's Bank of China, 1959, 225; rural credit, 329, 330, 343

Fine arts, 456-463. See also Artistic expression, Literature, Poetry

Fiscal policy, 311-319